D0722381

NATIONAL UNIVERSITY LIBRARY

Psychotherapy

A BASIC TEXT

CLASSICAL PSYCHOANALYSIS AND ITS APPLICATIONS

A Series of Books
Edited by Robert Langs, M.D.

050758

Psychotherapy

A BASIC TEXT

Robert Langs, M.D.

NEW YORK   Jason Aronson   LONDON

Copyright © 1982 by Jason Aronson, Inc.

10 9 8 7 6 5 4 3 2

All rights reserved. Printed in the United States of America.
No part of this book may be used or reproduced in any manner
whatsoever without written permission from *Jason Aronson, Inc.*
except in the case of brief quotations in reviews for inclusion
in a magazine, newspaper or broadcast.

Library of Congress Cataloging in Publication Data

Langs, Robert J.
  Psychotherapy: a basic text.

  Bibliography: p. 752.
  Includes index.
  1. Psychotherapy. I. Title. [DNLM: 1. Psychoanalytic
    therapy. WM 460.6 L285P]
RC480.L358   616.89′17   81-17663
ISBN 0-87668-466-5   AACR2

Manufactured in the United States of America.

050758

Psychotherapy

A BASIC TEXT

Robert Langs, M.D.

NEW YORK   Jason Aronson   LONDON

Copyright © 1982 by Jason Aronson, Inc.

10 9 8 7 6 5 4 3 2

All rights reserved. Printed in the United States of America.
No part of this book may be used or reproduced in any manner
whatsoever without written permission from *Jason Aronson, Inc.*
except in the case of brief quotations in reviews for inclusion
in a magazine, newspaper or broadcast.

Library of Congress Cataloging in Publication Data

Langs, Robert J.
  Psychotherapy: a basic text.

  Bibliography: p. 752.
  Includes index.
  1. Psychotherapy. I. Title. [DNLM: 1. Psychoanalytic
    therapy. WM 460.6 L285P]
RC480.L358   616.89′17   81-17663
ISBN 0-87668-466-5   AACR2

Manufactured in the United States of America.

To Joan,
for the basic text of life and living

Contents

Part II   The Listening-Formulating-Validating Process

**Part III The Ground Rules and Boundaries of
           Psychotherapy**

Part VI Perspectives

Preface

This volume is an effort at definition, synthesis, and innovation. It is a work that required the negotiation of a difficult course set between a number of opposing requisites. The effort has been made to be comprehensive and yet highly selective; to be concise and yet thorough; to offer a foundation in clinical excerpts and yet not to inundate the volume with clinical material; to define the most important technical principles and the most established therapeutic techniques, and yet to include critical nuances and important new ideas; and finally, to be as definitive as possible in the statement of basic technical precepts and at the same time leave room for individual clinical judgment, styles of working, and all of the essential and ill-defined sensitivities that contribute to sound therapeutic work.

It proved necessary to be selective and to restrict most discussions to basic essentials. The reader who is interested in expanding his or her understanding in any of the areas of technique delineated in this volume will find the four technique books—*The Listening Process* (1978), *The Therapeutic Environment* (1979), *Interactions: The Realm of Transference and Countertransference* (1980), and *Resistances and Interventions: The Nature of Therapeutic Work* (1981)—of considerable help. Further, since the present book is clinically founded and essentially empirical, there has been little opportunity to trace the foundations of the present work in the writings of earlier analysts. This has been done in considerable detail, however, in the technique series and in *The Therapeutic Interaction* (1976) in particular.

The present volume is an amalgam in which the basic tenets of psychotherapy, hard-won and clinically validated, form the core structure. To this has been added many new clinical observations and concepts that elaborate upon earlier fundamentals. Most of these insights have unfolded rather naturally upon the completion of the study of the four basic dimensions of the psychotherapeutic experience: listening, ground rules, interaction-relationship, and resistances and interventions. Psychotherapy is a basic technique that must be understood step-by-step. It lends itself to full comprehension only when the entire circle of study has been completed (and at that point, it is well to carry out a second run-through).

Thus, even though I had given some consideration to all of the dimensions of the therapeutic experience from the outset, it was only after *Resistances and Interventions: The Nature of Therapeutic Work* (1981) was completed that the ground was prepared for a fresh look at the listening process, ground rules and boundaries of the therapeutic relationship, and the therapeutic interaction itself. The present work therefore integrates a number of new findings in each of these areas.

Specifically, the reader will find an extended discussion of the listening process in the second part of this volume. This section provides an integrated presentation of the many principles developed in *The Listening Process* (1978). However, it also includes a number of critical refinements that have only recently fallen into place. The most notable of these involves a thorough delineation of listening in the object relationship sphere and an extremely careful definition of the listening process as it applies to the unconscious implications of the therapist's interventions. There is also the development of a clear distinction between the generally accepted psychoanalytic method for determining latent contents, and a newly established conception of the nature of the patient's unconscious expressions. The classical therapist tends to concentrate on direct inferences and the hidden implications of a specific but seemingly important derivative element; however, this fresh approach emphasizes the use in unconscious communication of *scattered* derivative *images* reflected in associations that involve distinctly different communicative vehicles. It therefore takes as its model of optimal communication allusions to rather different incidents and themes, each of which contains an important derivative image that ultimately requires synthesis by the therapist.

This distinction proves especially critical as a determinant of the techniques used by the therapist. In particular, the therapist is advised to apply *silence* as the most important means of facilitating derivative expression, and not to mistakenly turn to questions, clarifications, and confrontations for such purposes (these latter tend to interfere with, rather than enhance, unconscious communication).

In respect to the ground rules and boundaries of the psychotherapeutic relationship and experience, the most important new contribution in this book is the clear definition of two types of basic therapeutic experiences founded on two clases of therapeutic contracts—secure and deviant. In the first, the ideal ground rules and boundaries are clearly established and maintained, and in the second, the therapeutic arrangements and rules involve one or more basic alterations in the optimal tenets of therapy and often a relatively loose approach to the remaining propositions. The present volume offers a careful study of the clinical correlates and implications of the secure and deviant therapeutic contracts. It traces the positive and threatening aspects of each type of frame, and it deals extensively with the implications of the responses of the patient and therapist to the question of whether they adhere to or modify the fundamental and ideal therapeutic agreement. Two modes of therapeutic unfolding and work are identified on this basis, and the distinctive techniques used in each mode are defined.

The delineation of the therapeutic contract is shown to be fundamental to the basic modes of cure, communication, and relatedness that develop between the patient and therapist. It is in this latter area, defined in terms of maturational modes of relatedness (autism, symbiosis, parasiticism, and commensalism) that many additional new clinical concepts have been forged. The factors that determine the mode of relatedness between the two participants in treatment and the implications of this dimension for the therapeutic experience and for the nature of therapeutic work are clarified from many vantage points.

The text is clinically founded on recorded excerpts from supervisory sessions. All such material has been suitably disguised and faithfully condensed. I am deeply grateful to all of those who have worked with me in supervision, and especially to those whose specific efforts are reflected in this volume. In addition, as is true for many years now, I remain deeply grateful to Dr. Jason Aronson for his support of my work. Sheila Gardner typed and retyped the manuscript with a tireless devotion with which I am now familiar, and for which I am endlessly grateful. Neil Litt lent his superb editorial skills to the manuscript and helped to trim and shape it with great care. And Melinda Wirkus supervised the production of the volume with enormous sensibility and proficiency. Any work of this kind draws upon the support and skills of many other persons, all of whom have my deepest appreciation.

In concluding the preface to my first technique books, I wrote of the necessity to crystallize a set of technical precepts in terms of present understanding and of the need to do so with all humility. I was aware then, as I am now, that my own clinical understanding continues to enlarge from week to week. Most of the time the differences are small, although eventually they become measurable and sometimes even significant. It is clear to me now that these changes are a sign of a viable therapeutic technique and of a healthy clinical theory. Without change, there is stultification and decay. The present volume, then, is offered as a fresh crystallization at a moment when it seems necessary to offer a new set of integrated concepts and principles. The hope is that these will serve us as statements of the best insights and techniques available and yet provide a foundation for future revision and enhancement.

In this context, it is well to stress that my approach to psycho-analytic psychotherapy has been forged largely through the attention paid to one major and overridingly important sphere of listening to the patient's communications—the *derivative* functions of the patients behaviors and associations. This stands in contrast to prior techniques which tended to disregard issues of listening and to operate entirely on the level of manifest contents and/or isolated (Type One derivative) latent contents. Often, no specific clinical methodology was in evidence. In contrast, every precept and insight offered in this volume has been repeatedly, clinically validated through attention to the patient's Type Two derivative expressions—indirect, encoded forms of confirmation whose fresh meanings have a distinct bearing on the spiraling communicative interaction.

This realization helps to account for much of what is new in the book and for ways in which it departs from generally accepted clinical practice. It also asks the reader that he or she test out and confirm the tenets developed in these pages through a similar means of validation. Patients—and therapists—express much that is misleading and deceptive on a conscious and manifest content level; their unconscious derivative communications are virtually always free of such qualities and are quite insightful, perceptive, and valid. They prove to be a highly reliable guide for the development of sound techniques.

Unencumbered listening on a derivative level, containing highly incisive unconscious perceptions of ourselves (and often our failings) as therapists, is a difficult accomplishment. Our natural proclivity, partly cognitive and partly defensive, is to listen and formulate in terms of direct and surface contents and to think solely in terms of dynamics and genetics—and these almost exclusively in regard to the patient. It asks a great deal of a therapist to do otherwise; yet to do so is to be well rewarded. This is, after all, what our patients ask of us, although they do so, once again, almost entirely on the derivative level.

To dare to expose the unconscious struggles of a patient is dangerous enough and yet, when well done, not only curative but also a sign of inordinate courage and therapeutic devotion. To dare to expose comparable struggles within ourselves as therapists is bound to be as vital for cure and yet likely to be met with even more anxiety. Yet this too our patients ask of us, as we require it of ourselves in having chosen the profession of psychotherapist. If this book makes such endeavors more tolerable and insightful, as I hope it does, it will have been well worth the effort.

Part I
Emotional Disturbance and the Process of Cure

Chapter 1

Introduction

Psychotherapy is a relationship and interaction between an individual with an emotionally founded problem who is seeking help (a designated patient) and an expert who is capable of assisting him or her in effecting its resolution (a designated therapist). The nature of this therapeutic relationship, and of the transactions between the two participants, is structured and shaped by the implicit and explicit attitudes and interventions of the therapist and secondarily by the patient. The treatment is designed to offer the patient the best possible means of relief or cure.

Insight-oriented, or psychoanalytic, psychotherapy is a treatment modality of cure through hold, understanding, and inevitable unconscious identification. It unfolds under a particular set of conditions and in terms of a set of ground rules and boundaries that help to shape the nature of the therapeutic process. Each participant is afforded a role and a set of functions in keeping with a number of specific requisites. The patient's primary responsibility is to accept the conditions of treatment and to engage in free association. The therapist's role is to provide unbiased, evenly hovering attention to the patient's communications, to maintain an ideal therapeutic environment, and to use an interpretive approach. This type of therapy is the effort to create a set of conditions within which the patient may express, and the therapist may interpret, the underlying or unconscious factors that form the basis for an emotional disturbance whatever its surface manifestations.

Psychotherapy exists in may forms. This book is based on and extends the classical psychoanalytic understanding of the process and techniques of insight-oriented therapy. Technical precepts and clinical understanding are offered in outline form as definitive statements, with clinical illustrations to validate the therapeutic principles. Although they have been condensed, they offer an opportunity for study, evaluation, formulation, and confirmation. It is hoped that these illustrations will engage the reader in an attempt at active mastery of the technique of psychoanalytic psychotherapy, so that the basic concepts presented in this volume will have immediate clinical meaning and utility.

The main purpose of this book, however, is to present a synthesis of basic techniques. Thus, many of the important psychoanalytic papers and books that form the foundation for the present crystalization are not cited. It is also not feasible to present extended clinical documentation of controversial technical precepts.

The technique of psychoanalytic psychotherapy embodies a sense of order, organization, and feasibility, but it also embodies the inevitable complexities and difficulties that confront the therapist in his or her daily labors. This book provides a framework of definitive principles within which a therapist may be highly creative and deeply sensitive.

Chapter 2

The Manifestations of Emotional Disturbance

The specific type of therapeutic relationship that should, in principle, offer the patient the greatest potential for the cure of his or her emotional disturbance, the dimensions of the setting that must be created for this work, and the techniques that are used, cannot be defined until one has a conception of the patient whom the therapist will be treating and the emotional disturbance from which he or she is suffering. Some sense of the patient's positive capabilities and the intact functioning on which the therapist will rely in working with the patient are also necessary.

The Dimensions of an Emotional Disturbance

Emotional disturbance is used throughout this volume to allude to all emotionally founded, psychologically based difficulties, whether expressed primarily through somatic, psychological, or characterological means. The adoption of a fresh term to cover all forms of emotional illness creates a relatively unbiased position from which to identify and trace out the sources of these disturbances as they exist within the patient, within those to whom he or she relates, and in the conditions of his or her immediate and past life.

Neurosis (with a capital *N*) is used to refer to those emotional disturbances that have structuralized and become relatively fixed to the point where the illness persists even in the absence of the conditions and relationships that helped to create it. *Neurosis* (with a little *n*), *psychosis*, and other clinical syndromes are used more narrowly than in their usual definitions. All of these distrubances are based on highly complex processes and structures, intrapsychic and interpersonal, and may be understood from a number of separate but interrelated vantage points.

THE PATIENT'S BASIC LEVEL OF FUNCTIONING AND ADAPTATION

Patients enter therapy with a set of ego capacities that constitute their armamentarium for adaptation. These abilities develop from innate and constitutional factors that mature and unfold in the context of the individual's early object relationships and developmental thrusts. They involve a variety of executive and synthesizing functions, and are under the influence of a host of inner and outer pressures.

The patient's basic mode of adaptation lends itself to categorization in terms of specific ego functions, and may in addition form the basis for a broad diagnostic classification. In this regard, the patient's capacity for logical thinking and his or her ability to test and relate to reality can be used to identify two fundamental types of emotional disturbance: the psychoses and the neuroses.

THE PSYCHOSES

The psychotic mode of (mal)adaptation involves distinct impairments in reality testing, relatedness to reality, and in the use of logical, reality-oriented, directly adaptive modes of action and thought (i.e., those that are dominated by the secondary processes). Psychotic patients may show hallucinatory phenomena (false sensory experiences) or delusions (false beliefs). Their thinking and behaviors may be disharmonious with consensually validated reality. Their perceptions may be grossly distorted, and their inner fantasies may account for their responses to others far more than the external actualities of the situation. These patients often show difficulties in handling and modulating their emotions, and have problems in impulse control and in the postponing of need satisfactions. Their object relationships tend to be primitive and unstable.

The thought disorder in these patients may be seen as loose, circumstantial, unrealistic thinking that is dominated by the patient's internal needs and impulses, and that shows some disregard for the actualities that confront the patient. Other ego functions, such as those used in processing, synthesizing, and integrating incoming stimuli, the capacity to modulate emotions and to maintain anxiety at a signal level, and perceptive and executive functions, may also be impaired.

Manifestations of instinctual drives—the id—tend to be primitive and poorly managed. Expressions of conscience also tend to be archaic and severe. There may be concomitant characterological and symptomatic disturbances that derive in part from the basic disturbances in the patient's ego functioning.

To illustrate briefly, the following is an excerpt from a therapy session:

> Patient: Sometimes I feel like a robot. I'm part of a group, but then things become confusing. I get angry with my husband when he disciplines me like a little girl. He's very sensitive, but he's also closed-minded. I noticed a rash on my arm, but he wouldn't let me go to the doctor. The voice in my head just told me he doesn't like you (*referring to the therapist*). I can't make up my mind what to do about school.

This sequence of relatively unrelated thoughts suggests some difficulty in integrated thinking. There is also the presence of an hallucination. In typical fashion for psychosis, this patient fluctuates in respect to the extent to which her thinking is appropriate to external reality and the degree to which it is dominated by her inner, primitive, and distorting, fantasy life (i.e., by the primary processes).

Among the psychoses, there are those that are organic, chemical, schizophrenic, manic-depressive, paranoid, and involutional or depressive.

The Neuroses

The neuroses, narrowly defined, occur in patients who experience some type of symptomatic or characterological difficulty in the context of good contact and relatedness with reality, and in the presence of essentially logical, goal-oriented adaptive ego capacities such as thinking, executive functions, perception, and the like.

Although there may be selected impairments in one or several ego functions, the total functioning of these individuals is in keeping with the actualities of their environment and relationships. In general, their emotional disturbance is relatively encapsulated and does not pervade the basic personality to the point of major dysfunction.

The neuroses include symptomatic disorders in relatively intact patients, which take the form of obsessions and/or compulsions, phobias, disturbances in affect (such as anxiety and depression), and selected disorders and inhibitions of sexual, aggressive, and daily functioning. These symptomatic difficulties are usually ego dystonic, in that the patient suffers with them and wishes to be relieved of his or her suffering.

This brief excerpt is from a first psychotherapy session:

> Patient: I've been feeling depressed. I have difficulty in sleeping. I have been lonely since I divorced my husband, and I can't seem to get going. I have a job, but I do not find it especially satisfying. I am hesitant to look for new work because I am past 55 and people are reluctant to hire me. I have a full relationship with a man I am seeing, but I seem to have difficulty in extricating myself from him.

The patient describes a symptomatic sense of depression and a tendency to remain too long in job situations and relationships that cause her suffering. This last may reflect a masochistic disorder—a need to suffer inappropriately—although the clinical material does not permit a definitive answer in this regard, since there may be some appropriate reasons for the patient's seeming immobilization. In any case, the patient's thinking is logical and apparently in keeping with the realities with which she is surrounded, and there is no evidence of gross impairment in her basic ego functions. Her emotional disturbance is therefore to be viewed as neurotic, and may well be a combination of symptomatic and characterololgical difficulty.

Psychoses and neuroses are on a continuum. Some therapists have identified a group of borderline patients who fall on the middle of this continuum, although others believe that such patients are actually either ambulatory psychotic patients or severely disturbed neurotics. These patients do, however, tend to show momentary disturbances in reality testing, thinking, and other major ego functions, with a concomitant capacity to recover spontaneously and relatively quickly from these dysfunctions. Many perversions appear in these patients.

DISORDERS OF PERSONALITY AND CHARACTER STRUCTURE

Character and personality may be seen as interrelated terms. The former has been defined as reflecting the ego's habitual modes of adjusting to the id, superego, and external world, and as constituting the individual's enduring mode of relating and adapting to others. Personality is a broader term that touches upon all of the attributes of an individual, including his or her values and ideals, sensitivities, interests, and attitudes, synthesized into a general mode of being and relating. The terms personality disorder and characterological disturbance overlap and may be used interchangeably.

Characterological disturbances constitute a broad diagnostic category that includes enduring maladaptive responses, attitudes and modes of being as reflected in daily life and relationships with others. The disturbance is usually not acutely symptomatic, but is reflected in relatively stable attitudes and modes of functioning that are problematic and prove disruptive for either the patient (ego dystonic characterological disorders) or others (ego syntonic characterological disorders), or both.

Characterological disturbances may occur in individuals whose basic mode of functioning is either psychotic or neurotic. Thus a psychotic paranoid character will show gross disturbances in perceptions of reality and in thinking, and will be delusional. In contrast, a neurotic paranoid character will be consistently wary and suspicious, although always with a strong basis in reality stimuli, so that neither a clear-cut break in contact with surroundings nor a definitive thinking disturbance is manifested.

Characterological types tend to be identified in terms of symptomatic trends. They have been classified as paranoid, anxious, hysterical, psychopathic, obsessive, narcissistic, perverse, and schizoid, to name a representative sampling. Each of these reflects a basic mode of being and relating with a particular constellation of features. For example, the obsessive character tends to be ruminative and uncertain, while the hysterical character is overemotional, flighty, and tends to sexualize relationships.

The patient described above as psychotic and schizophrenic tended to become involved sexually with men other than her husband, to experience blatant sexual fantasies, and to be flighty and labile. Her basic character structure was seen as hysterical, and she was therefore viewed as having a psychotic hysterical character disorder. In contrast, the patient described as depressed and neurotic tended to be ruminative, overly neat, distant from her affects (making use of isolation) and overorganized. Characterologically, she was diagnosed as having a neurotic obsessive character disorder, since these traits were so exaggerated that they interfered with her functioning and with her relationships with others. Both patients were concerned with their characterological pathology, so both suffered from ego dystonic personality disorders.

THE PATIENT'S CAPACITY FOR OBJECT RELATEDNESS

The capacity for mature object relatedness entails the ability of a person to interact meaningfully and realistically with others, to effect the gratification of personal needs in such interactions, and to maintain as well a reasonable consideration of the needs of others. The mode, manner, and level of object relatedness that a patient has with others may fluctuate as he or she relates to different persons, and from interlude to interlude. It is possible, however, to characterize this aspect of human functioning along certain lines that tend to be relatively consistent and characteristic for each individual.

THE MATURATIONAL SPHERE

The main axis of the maturational sphere extends from autism, a form of relative unrelatedness, to the commensal mode of relatedness, which is characterized by virtually equal satisfaction for both members of a relationship dyad. Developmentally, the transition begins with a symbiotic mode of relatedness in which the infant's needs are overridingly central (the symbiotic receiver) and the mother's needs are secondary, although also satisfied to a lesser extent (the symbiotic donor).

There are two distinctive ways in which the symbiotic mode of relatedness may be structured: (1) as a period of healthy transition directed toward eventual separation, individuation, relative autonomy, and a capacity for commensal relatedness (the healthy symbiosis); or (2) as a means of maintaining a skewed mode of need-satisfying contact that is static and antithetical to growth, and that is designed for pathological satisfactions and to maintain a sense of fusion or merger between the symbiotic receiver and symbiotic donor (the pathological symbiosis). In this latter type of symbiosis, the balance of satisfaction may be reversed to the point where the maternal or other supposed caring figure (such as a therapist) becomes the symbiotic recipient, and the child (or patient) becomes the symbiotic donor.

The other major pathological maturational mode of relatedness may be termed the parasitic mode. It entails interactions designed for the destruction of one or both of the participants far more than for any type of nurturing or caring response and gratification (see Bion 1977, Mahler 1979, and Searles 1979).

Primitive and Mature Modes of Relatedness

A primitive relationship is self-serving, relatively narcissistic, and tends to disregard the needs of others—the objects. It may involve responses to aspects or parts of the other person (the object as a part object), rather than a consideration of the other individual in totality. There tends to be a blurring of self-object boundaries, sometimes with a confusion between the self and other. These relationships tend to be highly ambivalent (i.e., characterized by extremes of love and hate), and often are orally incorporative and devouring. Relatively primitive modes of perception of, and relatedness to, reality, and some degree of thought disorder and other forms of ego dysfunction are also present.

In contrast, a relatively mature mode of relatedness involves the consideration of one's own needs as well as the needs of others, is based on sound reality-testing and intact ego functions, and tends to consider the entire individual and the full context of the relationship (i.e., to involve nonnarcissistic responses to whole objects). This mode of relatedness is characterized by a capacity for delay and sacrifice, when necessary. There is a balance between the influence of inner fantasies and the actualities of the other person (see Kernberg 1976).

INTERNAL AND EXTERNAL OBJECT RELATIONSHIPS

There is an interplay between the actual or realistic external object relationship and the representation intrapsychically of these relationships in terms of self- and object-representations, introjects, and fantasy formations (i.e., internal object relationships). Valid conscious and unconscious perceptions and introjects, and intrapsychically founded distortions, combine in the development of an internal representational world. Similarly, an actual relationship will be experienced in terms of consensually validated implications and, in addition, will be influenced by the inner state of the individual. In this regard, object relationships may be quite realistic or fantasy-dominated.

In the clinical situation, the therapist takes into account influences on the patient from both external and internal objects, and considers as well the unconscious fantasies, memories, and perceptions that play a role in both spheres. Judgments are made of the extent to which an object relationship appears to be realistic, appropriate, and in keeping with the actualities of the situation; or unrealistic, inappropriate, and discordant with these actualities.

THE BASIC NATURE OF THE RELATIONSHIP

Object relationships may be classified as primarily dependent, seductive, hostile, etcetera. It is through this classification that the main instinctual drive satisfactions, defenses, and other purposes of the relationship are defined. Mixtures, of course, may exist. The relationship link may be mainly those of love (L), hate (H), or knowledge (K)—or their opposites (Bion 1962).

THE COMMUNICATIVE RELATIONSHIP

Finally, object relationships may be defined in terms of the nature of the communicative interchanges between the subject and object. Relationships may be communicatively meaningful or essentially devoid of meaning. They may be designed for understanding or as a way of destroying such a possibility. Some object relationships are created for action-discharge, pathological satisfactions and defense, projective identification, and riddance, while others are designed for containing, metabolizing, mastery, and genuine insight.

The communicative qualities of an object relationship can be determined by identifying the adaption-evoking stimuli to which each of the dyadic members is responding. It must be determined first whether these stimuli have been responded to or ignored. Responsive communication may be restricted to surface expressions whose meanings reside almost entirely in the manifest contents of the relevant messages. A different type of communicative interaction is seen when responsive messages have meaning and function on a latent level in terms of derivative processes and contents (see Part II).

A patient's manner and mode of relating embraces the totality of his or her internal and interpersonal functioning. Among the most important aspects of object relationships are the nature of the basic tie (the maturational sphere), the presence or absence of self-object differentiation, the degree of maturity, the extent to which the relationships are realistic or fantasy-dominated, and the nature of the communicative tie.

NARCISSISM AND THE EXPERIENCE OF THE SELF

The patient's experience of, and relationship with, himself or herself includes the capacity to maintain an integrated sense of self; an adequate level of self-esteem, and a set of sound, consistent, and realistic values; the extent to which the patient utilizes others as extensions of the self (i.e., as so-called self-objects); the degree to which others have been idealized and viewed as omnipotent and then incorporated into the self; and the extent to which there is an overidealized or grandiose image of the self that is maintained internally and projected onto others. Disturbances in self-esteem are reflected in a variety of symptoms, such as a sense of emptiness, a selfish use of others, problems in empathy, work inhibitions, and perverse sexual activities. However, the underlying basis of such symptomotology may be ascertained only through an analysis of the implication of the patient's associations and behaviors within the therapeutic situation. Other indications of a narcissistic disorder involve a subjective sense of impairment with respect to self-definition, self-concept, self-worth, self-esteem, and self-continuity, as well as the highly selfish use of others as a means of gratifying needs for aggrandizement, self-value, reassurance, and the like (see Kernberg 1975 and Kohut 1971, 1977).

SYMPTOMS OF ACUTE AND CHRONIC EMOTIONAL DISTURBANCES

A patient's disturbance may include any of a wide range of emotional or psychological symptoms. They include disturbances in affect such as anxiety, depression, boredom, and anger, and specific symptom complexes such as obsessive and/or compulsive symptoms, inhibitions, phobias, and hysterical symptoms—lability of affect, inappropriate seductiveness, and infantilism. These symptoms may be quite acute or chronic, the latter seen as suspiciousness, hypochondriasis, chronic anxiety, etcetera. Some symptoms involve basic disorders of thinking and breaks with reality, seen as delusions and hallucinations. However, these are not always associated with a basically psychotic mode of adaptation; they may occur as highly isolated and momentary breaks with reality that quickly give way to reality testing and reintegration. These latter symptoms would be termed borderline neurotic delusions and hallucinations.

Symptoms may appear as inhibitions, such as those seen in sexual and work situations. They may involve other types of sexual disturbances and include perverse sexual practices and gross perversions. They may entail problems in impulse control and in managing sexual and aggressive impulses. In all, any disturbance of mood, of smooth emotional and mental functioning, or of mature sexual and nonsexual relatedness, can be included in the emotional disturbances that are termed psychological symptoms. They may occur in either psychotic or neurotic individuals.

EMOTIONALLY FOUNDED PHYSICAL SYMPTOMS

Psychologically based emotional disturbances may be reflected in physical or somatic symptoms. One group of such disorders has been characterized as psychosomatic, as a way of indicating a relatively consistent correlation between a constellation of emotional difficulties (fantasies and perceptions) and a particular somatic symptom, which serves in part as a symbolic representation of these emotional factors. This category includes such diseases as asthma, peptic ulcer, ulcerative colitis, and rheumatoid arthritis.

In addition, there is as a rule some measure of emotional contribution to all somatic illness. The presence of real or fantasied object loss or separation is among the most common precipitants of physical illness. Other psychodynamic factors and depression difficulties also play a frequent role.

Concluding Comments

In the initial session and throughout therapy, the therapist will attend to these interconnected areas, searching for the presence of difficulty and dysfunction. Positive capabilities and smooth functioning must be noted as well, but the therapist is concerned mainly with identifying signs of emotional disturbance. These may be termed indicators or therapeutic contexts, active signs of emotionally founded disorders that the therapist hopes to help the patient to resolve. Virtually every psychotherapeutic session contains some type of therapeutic context. It follows, then, that it is this immediate and dynamically active expression of emotional disturbance with which the therapist hopes to deal (interpretively and otherwise).

There are many means through which a therapist and patient can attempt to deal with therapeutic contexts. The physical environment and the persons to whom the patient is relating might be manipulated or changed. Medication might be used, or efforts to logically convince the patient that the symptoms are unrealistic or unnecessary. Attempts might be made to decondition or set up an abreaction. However, the efforts of psychoanalytic psychotherapy are different from all of these pursuits in important ways. First, the hidden or unconscious basis for the patient's emotional disturbance must be understood. Factors must be identified of which the patient—and sometimes others, including the therapist—are unaware. Then, on the basis of a full conceptualization and understanding of both overt and covert elements, the therapist endeavors to help the patient to modify his difficulty.

When the main basis for the emotional disturbance lies within the patient, the primary tool is to offer insight into the unconscious dimension of the difficulty. The patient is shown that his or her response to reality is inappropriate to the situation and based on distorting intrapsychic fantasies and memories. These images are made concrete for the patient in the hope that therapist and patient will be able to understand these previously unrecognized sources of maladaptive response and, in the future, react more appropriately and without symptoms.

On the other hand, when it is discovered that the behavior of others, including the therapist, is contributing significantly to the emotional disturbance, the approach must be somewhat different.

Although such therapeutic work is also founded on the realization of previously unrecognized and unconscious factors, the emphasis here must be on enabling the patient to understand the outside sources of the emotional disturbance. Efforts must be made to rectify the therapist's contribution to the patient's emotional disorder. In the absence of corrective measures the emotional disturbance will continue despite all other endeavors. Thus, both rectification of pathological external contributions to the patient's emotional disturbance and interpretation of the unconscious factors as they exist within the patient and others are vital to the therapeutic effort.

Chapter 3

The Development and Structure
of Emotional Disturbances

Although the manifestations of emotional disturbances have been identified, a series of important questions still remain unanswered: How do these dysfunctions come about? What are their developmental vicissitudes? How are they sustained? What is their underlying structure and function? Answers to these critical questions provide the therapist with the vantage point from which to decide on the definitive therapeutic approach for the resolution of these disorders.

Developmental Factors

OBJECT RELATEDNESS

Emotional disturbances arise out of an interaction between an individual's psychophysiological endowment and the persons and settings that constitute his or her environmental matrix. These difficulties may begin in utero or arise at any point in the development of the neonate, from newborn status through the months and years into adulthood and senescence.

In general, the earlier and more traumatic the significant disturbance, the more severe the pathology. Similarly, the more adaptive and flexible the individual's endowment, the greater the capacity to tolerate environmental disturbances. The more stable and secure the holding and containing capacities of the mother, and the greater her capability to respond to the specific needs and distresses of her child, the greater the likelihood that the child will be able to adequately cope with and adapt to acute crises and ongoing developmental tasks.

The development of the infant and his or her growth into childhood, adolescence, and adulthood may be examined from many viewpoints. For one, there is the nature of the object relationship with the maternal figure. Some analysts postulate that this relationship is autistic initially, in that there is no functional representation of the outside world in general, and of the mother in particular, within the infant's mind (see Mahler 1979). Other analysts point to the actual intense symbiosis that exists between the two from the outset. They view autism mainly as a defense or regression directed against threats posed by maternal failings, fears for survival, and by other sources of anxiety (see Balint 1968).

It may be postulated in respect to object relatedness that the creation of global and largely ill-defined object- and self-representations take place in the early months of life. The mode of relatedness is highly general and diffuse, and is limited by and in keeping with the initial capacities of the newborn and young infant. An awareness of part objects and a blurring of the boundaries between self and other begins to develop. There is a gradual transition from an overriding dependence upon the mother, in which the young child is by and large the symbiotic recipient, to a relative dependence that leaves room for independent functioning. This includes the capacity to become the symbiotic donor, and eventually to develop commensal (mutually satisfying) relationships. The development of a sound identity, a clear sense of self, and an awareness of the separateness between the self and others are all factors in the process of individuation and movement toward relatively autonomous functioning.

The potential for pathological developments in this sphere may arise either because of the endowment of the child or disturbances in the mother. In the former instance, there are defects in the ego functions necessary for object relating and in managing the separation anxieties inherent to growth and development. There may be problems in mastering basic fears of annihilation, inhibiting separation from the mother and leading to innate difficulties in maintaining the distinction between self and others. There may be inherent impairments in defining inner and outer reality, and in establishing the boundaries between the self and others. Maternal difficulties that may disturb the infant's movement toward mature object relatedness may derive from pathological, parasitic, symbiotic, and narcissistic needs in the mother, which interfere with the child's development of a separate identity. There may be failures in holding and in containing the projective identifications of the child. The mother may have difficulty in maintaining a separate image of herself as distinct from her child, and also may communicate a variety of disruptive unconscious fantasies and anxieties related to the dangers of separateness, relative autonomy, and their achievement. In addition to the interplay between processes within the mother and those within the child, the child's experience of maternal difficulties is always mediated in terms of his or her own mode of experiencing, capacities for conscious and unconscious perceptions, and conscious and unconscious fantasy formations.

Psychopathology derived from early disturbances in object relatedness involves several factors: (1) actual failings in the capacities of infant and mother, (2) specific deficits in the mother in meeting the needs of her particular child, (3) specific failures in the child to accept the seemingly adequate ministrations of the mother, (4) aspects of the conscious and unconscious communications that transpire between the two, and (5) the strong influence of the child's own inner mental life on whatever is experienced. In some situations correction of the developmental defect or of the maternal failure may prove sufficiently ameliorative. In other circumstances, however, the resultant dysfunctions and the presence of established or structured introjects and unconscious fantasy-perception constellations have so distorted the patient's mode of relatedness (and contributed as well to other symptoms) that a full resolution of these problems requires some type of effort capable of modifying these relatively fixed internal residuals. As the child grows older and becomes more and more structured, this last necessity becomes increasingly critical.

PSYCHIC STRUCTURE

Another means of tracing out the development of the individual can be described in terms of the relative structuralization of the psychic apparatus into the *id* (the source of the instinctual drives and their representations), the *ego* (the realm of the individual's capabilities and functioning, including behavioral and psychic defenses, sensory and motoric capacities, synthesizing abilities, and ability to test out reality), and *superego* (an amalgam of ideals, self-concerns, prohibitions, values, etcetera). There is the familiar unfolding that may be described in terms of psychosexual stages—oral, anal, phallic, Oedipal, and post-Oedipal—as well as the broader conceptualization offered by Erikson (1950), which takes into account not only psychic structuralization but social development as well. Each phase has a characteristic constellation of instinctual drive needs, danger situations, defenses, and superego manifestations. It is possible to offer a timetable for both ego and superego development, as well as one related to the instinctual drives.

In general, the oral phase is characterized by strong incorporative needs; global and primitive instinctual drives; the presence of ego nucleii and global functions, some of which eventuate into superego capacities; and a relative lack of distinction between the functioning in each of these psychic spheres. The anal stage, in which anal incorporation and explusion is central to the instinctual drives, includes the extensive development of ego functions and the growing presence of superego precursors; primitive qualities are still in evidence.

In the oral phase, separation anxieties, the dread of annihilation, and fears of the actual loss of the maternal object predominate. In the anal phase, there is some dawning awareness of bodily anxieties and the fear of the loss of love and favor from the maternal object. Each of these sources of anxiety and danger mobilize defensive operations in the ego. In this regard, the oral phase defenses tend to be primitive, with an emphasis on denial, primal or global (automatic) repression, splitting, primitive projection and introjection, as well as primitive forms of projective and introjective identification. In the anal phase, there is a growing development of specific defenses such as repression, isolation, and undoing, which, develop subsequently in even more definitive fashion.

Throughout, the infant's instinctual drive expressions, developing ego, and unfolding superego functions become elaborated in the context of a deep conscious and unconscious interaction with the maternal person and other important caring and influential figures. Together they should provide a safe environment for the child's general maturation and development. In addition, these individuals communicate consciously and unconsciously in ways that shape the utilization of certain kinds of defenses, create a preference for selected types of instinctual drive expressions, and generate pressures toward a particular type of superego formation. All of this involves a constellation of actualities, communicated consciously and unconsciously, and introjected and processed within the infant in terms of the infant's own internal state and needs—healthy and pathological—and in terms of the infant's sound and burgeoning ego and superego capacities.

The phallic and Oedipal phases follow. The distinction between id, ego, and superego increases. The maturation of functioning in each of these spheres develops to a point of relative autonomy, consistency, persistency, and therefore relative structuralization. Anxiety, which is global initially, becomes more specific, and may eventually be restricted to signal responses by the ego. At this level, anxiety is derived mainly from the additional sources of castration fears, general body anxieties, further expressions of fear of the loss of the love of the parental figure, and eventually from intrapsychic conflict.

Thus the nature of the conflictual danger situations that provide the soil for emotional disturbance gradually develop. At first there is a predominance of situations in which the disruptive conflicts are primarily between the infant and the actual maternal figure (e.g., interpersonal conflict), although the issues are always experienced in terms of the inner state of the infant and on an unconscious as well as a conscious level. Later pathology-promoting situations tend to involve important additional internal conflicts between the maturing structures of the child's mind and within the mental systems themselves. Although actual conflicts continue to contribute to Neurosis formation, intrapsychic conflict becomes an increasingly major source of anxiety, danger, the use of pathological defenses, and symptom formation. Still, whether the conflict is with an external object or an internal one, whether it is with reality and others or essentially within the individual, there is a constant influence on the entire constellation that derives from both the actual parental (or other) figures and the inner mental life of the child. Even with structuralization, every intrapsychic conflict involves some interplay with the actual relationships of the child, while earlier, every actual conflict with the parental figure is influenced by the intrapsychic life of the infant.

A basic model for the development of an emotional disturbance, or Neurosis, includes the following factors during the phase
of infancy and early childhood: (1) an unresolved conflict between
the maternal figure and the infant; (2) the experience of some type
of danger situation, often involving fears of separation, loss, and
annihilation; (3) the relative failure of the infant to master the
conflict and danger because of either innate dysfunctions or because
of the overwhelming nature of the disturbing expressions from the
environment or mother; and (4) the mobilization of efforts at
adaptation and defense that result in a compromise formation
reflecting some degree of failure at adaptation with resultant symptom formation. If the defensive and adaptive resources of the infant
are sufficient to master the anxieties and dangers with which he or
she is confronted, there will be no notable evidence of emotional
disturbance. It is only when these efforts at adaptation fail that
symptom formation takes place.

In these early years, symptoms may be of the psychotic type, in
that they involve impairments in the ego's capacity for reality
testing and the use of inner fantasies (i.e., the development of
hallucinations and delusions) as substitutes for painful realities.
These may include autistic withdrawal and a breakdown in object
relatedness, and selected or massive areas of disturbed ego functioning. The underlying basis for these dysfunctions must be understood in terms of the infant's capacities, the maternal inputs, and
the mediating factor of the internal mental world of the child.

In general, in the absence of a psychotic syndrome, many of the
emotional disturbances seen in infants and young children involve
emotional difficulties that may be modified through environmental
manipulation and alterations in the attitude of the parental figures.
However, some measure of structuralization with fixed maladaptive
patterns does take place quite early in life. Thus it is possible to
find well-formed Neuroses in the young child as well. Under these
conditions, environmental manipulation proves to be less effective
than when it is applied to an emotional disturbance. It is often
necessary to engage the child in some type of active therapeutic
intervention.

As the infant matures and establishes sound contact with reality
and strong object relationships, there is a tendency toward the
development of neurotic symptoms in the narrow sense, disturbances that are based primarily on intrapsychic conflicts. The key to

the emotional disturbance lies within the mobilization of instinctual drive expressions that are forbidden by the superego, and that create an internal conflict and a sense of anxiety or depression, against which the ego acts defensively. Defenses such as repression, isolation, and neurotic forms of projection and introjection are brought into play. When these defenses fail and there is a return of the repressed instinctual drive expressions, symptoms emerge as either a continuation of the anxiety related to the original conflict or as a symbolic representation of the total unconscious fantasy-perception constellation with which the ego is struggling. Thus, in later years, Neuroses arise from unresolved intrapsychic conflicts, and from unconscious fantasy-perception constellations that involve both valid and distorted structured introjects, as well as valid and distorting unconscious fantasy-memory elements. The ego synthesizes these elements into some type of unconscious fantasy-memory constellation, which constitutes the unconscious basis for the neurotic symptom. The role played by both unconscious perception-introjects and unconscious fantasy-memory constellations is critical. The structuralization of these elements and of related unconscious conflicts may lead to relatively persistent symptomatic and characterological disturbances that may continue into adulthood.

The interplay between internal psychic constellations and reality and object relatedness continues throughout life. At all times the individual's inner mental world is part of an open system under influence from internal drive constellations and outside factors. Thus id, ego, and superego development always unfolds in terms of both internal and external factors.

The intrapsychic shift is from relatively primitive, global, heavily instinctualized formations into those that are more modified, specific, definitive, and mature. There may be disturbances in any one of the psychic macrostructures, though their interrelatedness tends to create situations in which pathology in one sphere will coexist with problems in the other spheres. There is also a relatively healthy or normal line of maturational development that includes the sound expression of instinctual drives, both aggressive and sexual, flexible and reasonable superego formations (developed in part through introjections and identifications with the parents, development of resilient and adaptive defenses. When the instinctual drives are overintense or inappropriate, the superego relatively harsh and primitive or too demanding, and the defenses of the ego inadequate for its task in dealing with the id, superego, and reality (including others), maladaptation ensures and symptom formation or characterological disturbance takes place.

Unconscious communication, unconscious introjection and projection, unconscious fantasies and memories, and unconscious contents and processes of all kinds are all important factors in the development of emotional disturbances and Neurosis formation. Much of the contribution of the maternal figure to the emotional state of the child is imparted through unconscious expression, and much of the fantasy-memory-perception constellations that account for early and later (structuralized) Neuroses operate outside of the awareness of both the mother and the child.

In this regard, it should be recognized that it is mainly through encoded or derivative communication and the use of manifest messages that contain hidden (disguised or latent) intentions and meaning that the mother exerts much of her influence on the healthy development and pathology of the child. Similarly, the inner fantasy formations that exist in disguised or derivative form within the individual (i.e., unconscious fantasy-perception constellations) form the internal basis for emotional disturbances and Neuroses. It follows, then, that whenever a patient communicates the meanings or implications of his or her emotional illness to a therapist, the patient will do so with the same type of language: encoded or derivative communications that embody realizations and images outside of his or her direct awareness. This capacity of the human mind to express itself meaningfully through derivatives stands high among its achievements. Such expressions tend to follow the laws of the primary processes—condensation, displacement, symbolization, and considerations of representability—and they may show a relative disrgard for reality, although they often involve sound but encoded, valid perceptions. As such, their influence can be understood only through proper decoding within an appropriate context.

Summary

Emotional disturbances are dysfunctions within the individual that are based on some type of psychological disturbance. They derive from two interrelated sources: (1) maternal (environmental) failures and other external pathological influences, and (2) intra-psychic malfunctions and unresolved conflicts.

Emotional disturbances are based on, and expressed through, unconscious processes that derive from unconscious perception-introjects and unconscious fantasy-projections. They are founded largely upon unconscious communicative processes, and their maintenance relies mainly upon effects taking place outside of the awareness of the individual. In those situations where the environmental disturbance is significant, there is always an additional unconscious and intrapsychic component. Similarly, in situations where intrapsychic conflict and unconscious fantasy-perception constellations account for the major portion of symptom formation, actual environmental realities continue to play a supplemental role.

Emotional disturbances have complex structures, and include disturbances in the area of object relatedness, narcissism, psychic structure, and communication. Neurosis formation tends to impair the relative autonomy of the individual, to cause psychic pain, and to interfere with maturation, growth and development, and individuation.

Chapter 4

A Model of the
Therapeutic Process

Given the complexities of Neurosis formation and the multiplicity of factors that contribute to and sustain Neurotic symptoms and characterological disturbances, it should not be surprising that a plethora of therapeutic techniques are currently offered to provide relief from the emotional suffering involved. It should be understood, however, that in actual practice, the development of insight-oriented psychotherapy derives from two interrelated and interacting sources: (1) a growing understanding of the nature and function of emotional disturbances and Neuroses (the present line of thought); and (2) empirical observations in the actual clinical situation through which validated constructive techniques can be developed (the approach that will be used in the balance of this volume).

There has been a gap in the understanding of emotional disturbances and Neuroses and the development of psychoanalytic psychotherapeutic techniques. The ultimate test of any therapeutic model lies in its use with patients. It entails the offer of interventions based on a sound listening-formulating process, which then obtains indirect (derivative) validation. There then follows some measure of conscious working through of the unique insights afforded the patient in this way, and with it, improved adaptation, symptom resolution, and growth. Thus a validated set of psychotherapeutic principles must be formulated through a careful analysis of the actual effects of the particular therapeutic setting and approach. A relationship and set of conditions must be designed to provide the patient with an optimal opportunity for the meaningful expression of emotional disturbance in terms of its surface manifestations and unconscious basis. It must also create the atmosphere within which the patient's Neurosis can be most effectively modified in a manner that is lasting and provides the patient with adaptive resources with which to deal with future conflicts and emotional problems.

The Therapeutic Relationship

The core or background (holding) relationship requires a number of basic attributes in order to offer an optimal opportunity for insight therapy for the patient:

1. The establishment of a growth-promoting or healthy symbiosis. The patient requires a *healthy therapeutic symbiosis* (Searles 1979). This is a basic mode of relatedness designed as much as possible to help the patient to generate insight and understanding, growth and individuation, relative autonomy, and a capacity for the adaptive resolution of inner and outer conflicts. The study of Neuroses (Chapter 3) suggests that a healthy symbiosis with the therapist will entail a relationship with specific attributes that are in some sense both phase specific to the patient's state of development and therapy specific, in that the proper functioning of a psychotherapist will be in important respects different from the proper functioning of a parental figure or friend. Thus, while the mode of relatedness should bear some resemblance to the sound maternal role, it must also entail certain distinctions, since the therapist is not entirely a parental figure.

Some of the specific dimensions of a therapeutic symbiosis may be anticipated on the basis of our understanding of emotional disturbances. Others will emerge only through the empirical studies described later in this book.

2. A sense of safety and trust. The therapist must relate to the patient in a manner that implicitly encourages the patient's trust and affords the patient a realistic sense of true safety. This implies that the therapist will respond to the patient in a manner that permits free communication without retribution and, further, that the relationship will be geared primarily to the therapeutic needs of the patient. This requires the renunciation by the therapist of inappropriate needs and of misuses of the patient that would immediately disturb the patient's sense of security. The therapist must have a sense of appropriate boundaries in the context of his or her reasonable concern for the patient, and the therapist must respond to the patient's communications and behaviors in a manner that is consistently helpful. The therapist's honesty, integrity, and trustworthiness will be a constant issue.

3. The therapist's capacity to hold and contain the patient, his or her communications, and his or her interactional pressures and efforts at role and image evocation. The therapist must offer a holding environment to the patient, a basic relationship that provides the latter with a sense of security, respect, and as noted above, trust and safety. The therapist must also be capable of containing and metabolizing toward understanding all of the patient's efforts at interactional projection (projective identification) and role and image evocation. The therapist must accept and ultimately interpret introjected aspects of the patient's psychopathology, doing so without inappropriate behavioral responses (acting out). Similarly, he or she must respond interpretively to efforts by the patient to actualize a pathological mode of relatedness or to repeat in some way past pathological interactions, and must also avoid the development of symbioses that gratify the pathological needs and Neurosis of both participants to treatment. The therapist must be able to appropriately frustrate and interpret the patient's wishes to activate and gratify specific unconscious fantasy-memory-introjection-perception constellations through which past pathogenic relationships are recreated and the patient's present Neurotic adjustment is justified. Such measures are essential to the creation of a healthy therapeutic symbiosis and to open communication, which fosters the full analysis and resolution of the patient's emotional disturbance.

4. The nonreinforcement of the patient's emotional disturbance or Neurosis. The therapist must create a set of conditions and a mode of relatedness that as much as possible does not consciously or unconsciously support the patient's Neurotic maladaptation, and does not in any significant way constitute the type of pathological symbiosis that provided the core mode of relatedness upon which the patient's Neurosis first developed. Similarly, the therapist should not behave in a manner that is consonant with the patient's *pathological* unconscious fantasies, memories, and introjects. The therapist should not consciously or unconsciously gratify the patient's Neurotic needs, pathological instinctual drive wishes, or in any way support the patient's pathological defenses or inappropriate superego requisites.

Unconscious interactions that support or pathologically gratify aspects of the patient's Neurotic adjustment tend to undermine or contradict the implications of the therapist's verbal-affective interventions—the interpretive work. Similarly, pathological symbioses tend to belie the therapist's conscious intention to work interpretively with the patient toward insight and autonomy. The goal, therefore, is to establish a therapeutic attitude and approach that reflects essentially nonneurotic functioning in the therapist and does not in any significant way support the patient's own Neurotic adjustment. In this way the important differentiation in the level of functioning and mode of adaptation between the patient and therapist is established (Loewald 1960). This distinction forms a basis for growth-promoting, unconscious, introjective identifications by the patient with the well functioning therapist, and provides a background relationship, constituted as a healthy therapeutic symbiosis that inherently supports interpretive efforts of the therapist that aim to develop specific cognitive insights in the patient.

The attributes of the therapeutic relationship described to this point involve the establishment of a set of boundaries, basic attitudes, and conditions for a potentially curative therapeutic relationship. These function in a manner that hold the patient in a secure fashion and implies the quest for insight, growth, and individuation. Simultaneously, they permit the patient to undergo the therapeutic regression necessary for the specific expression of the manifestations and underlying basis of the emotional disturbance. They enable the patient to communicate the derivatives of the unconscious fantasies and perceptions, present and past, that have caused and perpetuate the emotional illness. These may be termed the holding or framework-management functions of the therapist.

There is a second basic attribute that characterizes the efforts of the therapist—the interpretive function. A healthy therapeutic symbiosis involves both the development of a secure holding relationship and an interpretive approach by the therapist. These two fundamental attributes of the therapist are the foundation of insight-oriented psychotherapy.

5. The development of an interpretive relationship. The therapist's interpretive approach is both phase specific and therapy specific for the patient. It provides a highly distinctive dimension to the therapeutic relationship. On an unconscious level every patient who enters a therapeutic experience wishes to have a sound core relationship with the therapist and hopes to experience a basically interpretive approach. On a conscious level, however, many patients not only wish, but also actually insist, that the treatment experience be constituted quite differently. However, there is considerable evidence that ego-enhancing, positive, introjective identifications by the patient with the therapist can take place only when the latter is engaged in maintaining and securing a sound background relationship and framework of treatment. True insight into the unconscious basis and actualities of the patient's emotional disturbance can occur only in this context, and through the correct and validated interpretations of the therapist.

Noninterpretative reponses by the therapist (other than managements of the ground rules) tend to blur the distinctions between the patient and the therapist, and between the therapist and pathogenic figures outside of treatment. In general, they constitute failures on the part of the therapist to function in keeping with the patient's therapeutic needs. Most, if not all, noninterpretive or noninsight-directed interventions reflect failings and aspects of pathology in the therapist, and thus support the patient's Neurotic adjustment.

6. The creation of an understanding rather than pathologically gratifying mode of relatedness. The therapist creates conditions for the patient's expression of his or her emotional disturbance in terms of meaningful *derivative* (i.e., disguised or encoded) communications through which the therapist can respond with appropriate framework-management interventions and interpretations. Direct pathological needs are given up in favor of an understanding of the truth, with its consequent adaptive changes.

Patients enter treatment seeking relief. Understanding, especially insight into unconscious factors in the patient's emotional suffering, is but one means of obtaining such relief. It involves delay and a capacity to accept the offer of tools of adaptation rather than some immediate sense of remedy. As a rule, the participants to treatment must make a basic choice between direct and immediate nonunderstanding satisfactions, which set aside meaningful communicative relatedness, or the pursuit of painful derivative expressions based on capacites for delay and detour, which provide ultimate gratifications through sound insight and constructive introjective identifications. The former approach is characteristic of a pathological autism, parasitism, or therapeutic symbiosis, while the latter is an aspect of a healthy therapeutic symbiosis. Thus neither the patient nor the therapist, nor both, may wish for, or engage in, a search for symptom alleviation on the basis of insightful understanding.

The therapeutic situation must be constantly monitored: The patient may wish for directly pathological satisfactions, and be entirely uninterested in expressing meaningful derivatives and in relating to the therapist in a manner geared toward ultimate insight into the Neurosis; the patient may wish instead to destroy or preclude such understanding, and may go so far as to refuse to accept conditions of treatment under which such understanding might develop. Similarly, the therapist may create a basic setting or respond with interventions that are in no way designed for the insightful understanding of the truth of the patient's Neurosis; the therapist may look toward the satisfaction of his or her own pathological needs, toward the pathological gratification of the patient, and toward the establishment of untruths or lie-barrier systems designed defensively to seal off the truth of the patient's Neurosis and, secondarily, of the emotional disturbances within the therapist.

Final Perspectives

The model presented here consists of factors that are strongly interrelated and that have been defined, for the moment, in relatively broad terms. It remains for the rest of this volume to empirically determine the specific attitudes, interventions, setting, and other behaviors of the therapist that would meet these difficult requirements.

It seems likely that the establishment of a healthy therapeutic symbiosis would provide the patient with a strong, broad-based means of implicit ego support and a special opportunity for the expression and understanding of the Neurosis. Specific conflict resolution and structural modifications could then take place based on the therapist's definitive interpretations, an articulation of insights into the specific unconscious fantasy-perception constellations that account for the patient's symptoms and characterological difficulties. The therapeutic modality would be both ego-enhancing and capable of producing the specific resolution of unconscious conflicts. It would help the patient to insightfully modify the pathological components of id and superego, as well as the use of pathological defenses. It would also enable the patient to resolve the psychopathology inherent to his or her mode of relatedness to others to the point where he or she would become capable of mutually gratifying, commensal interactions. In addition, the pathology of the patient's self-system and ego ideal would find appropriate insightful modification.

The therapist must create a relationship with specific features that are inherently and implicitly supportive and that permit a full expression of the patient's Neurosis on a derivative level. Further, once there has been meaningful expression, the therapist must prove capable of offering the necessary interpretive responses.

The creation of this kind of setting, an openness to this type of pathological derivative communication, and a capability for the use of sound framework management and interpretative responses, requires a great deal of the therapist. He or she must possess a large measure of self-understanding, a capacity for renunciation, an ability to manage his or her own inner mental world and conflicts, and a dedication to the patient through which to operate in terms of the latter's therapeutic needs to the greatest extent humanly possible. This is a task filled with both cognitive and emotional challenge, and fraught with difficulties of such proportions that one must expect that many therapists could be easily moved in other directions.

Part II

The Listening-
Formulating-
Validating Process

Chapter 5

Neurosis and Listening

No two patients are entirely alike. No two sessions are identical. This sense of uniqueness promises fresh stimulation for the therapist with each therapeutic experience, but it also creates difficulties for the therapist, since each hour must be approached with some degree of systematization, even as an open, creative, and empathic attitude is maintained. The listening process—the intaking (listening and experiencing)-formulating-validating process—is critical. A sample session illustrates the clinical experience of listening in the context of an understanding of the nature of emotional disturbances.

A Representative Session

A young adult woman patient is being seen by a male psychiatrist in psychotherapy. The therapist accepted this woman into treatment on the basis of a self-referral after she had taken an adult education course with him. The patient is a professional woman who teaches on the graduate level.

Patient: I was really shaken last session. I kept thinking about those memories from my childhood. There's this guy, Armand, who is in a class I teach. He asked me to have lunch with him. I fantasized having sexual relations with him. But then he goes and asks two other women along with us and talks to them. He turns his sexuality on for any woman, not just me. One of the gals is real smart. She's writing a book about going crazy in the 1980s. That ends my fantasy about

35

Armand. I'm so naive with men, I can't handle them. I keep thinking about when I was a child and how I had no one to play with. I was nasty. I would pinch and bite and I drove everyone away. My father would take me into bed a lot. I have been thinking of how I first came to see you in therapy. Your comment about how it all came about disturbed me.

How does the therapist sort out this material? This is but a small segment from the beginning of an hour. The material before the therapist in an entire session is far more complicated and confusing. Even this small fragment introduces a variety of matters: the patient is shaken; she's thinking of her childhood; she's becoming involved with and having sexual fantasies about one of her students who seems interested in many women simultaneously; one gal is writing a book about going crazy; the patient is naive about men; she was nasty as a child; her father took her into his bed.

Where is this patient's emotional disturbance? What in this material would help to understand its meanings and sources? Do these associations contain encoded communications of importance in understanding the emotional problems of this patient, who entered therapy because of anxiety and depression and a tendency to develop relationships with men that hurt her and failed?

Answers to these important questions require an understanding of the structure of emotional disturbances and Neuroses.

The Structure of an Emotional Disturbance

Disturbances arise from an internal or external stimulus—the adaptation-evoking context, or the adaptive context for short. The most critical precipitants for emotional disturbances in patients in psychotherapy involve the interventions of the therapist. The term intervention context is therefore also used here to refer to emotionally meaningful stimuli that initiate sequences with symptoms as one of their end products.

An adaptive context that leads ultimately to symptom formation constitutes a trauma or danger situation. The major source of danger may be mainly internal. In this case, the adaptation-evoking stimulus leads to evoked instinctual drives that are forbidden by the superego. The ego then responds to the intrapsychic conflict between the id and the superego (between the evoked instinctual wish and an internal forbidding response) with anxiety or some other disturbing affect such as depression, shame, etcetera. The unconscious conflict finds psychic representation, and the signal of disturbing affect is followed by efforts at adaptation on the part of the ego, much of it through the use of defensive formations.

When the ego's defenses fail and a maladaptive compromise is effected, symptoms occur. The symptoms themselves represent all aspects of the conflict: the instinctual drive wish, the superego response, and the ego's defensive formations. This constellation has been termed an unconscious fantasy. A pathological unconscious fantasy is one that pertains to an emotional disturbance. Thus an emotional disturbance may be based on a pathological unconscious fantasy or unconscious-fantasy-memory constellation. In all such instances, however, there is a prior adaptation-evoking context that derives from external reality and the patient's object relationships. Thus every instance of primarily internal danger stems in part from some type of external circumstance, itself often of an evocative or dangerous nature. A similar interplay between external reality and intrapsychic response applies when the danger arises primarily from outside the psyche.

The danger situation may arise primarily from external reality and from some aspect of an object relationship. In this type of situation, the external transactions may themselves realistically signal danger and prompt responsive fear and emotional disturbance. Most of the time, however, there is an intrapsychic contribution to the patient's experience of danger, through which the external realities are to some extent regressively evaluated and experienced in terms of distortions that lead to intrapsychic conflict and anxiety. External dangers evoke instinctual drive wishes within the patient that may be forbidden by the superego. These arousals lead to the type of sequence described above for primarily internal dangers. It is not uncommon for a patient to project aspects of his or her own intrapsychic response to an initial danger situation onto an external object, thereby heightening the patient's sense of danger and both fear and anxiety.

In this second sequence, unconscious perception and introjection play an important role. A validly perceived dangerous introject will prompt an emotional disturbance on its own. Additional intrapsychic responses from the structural elements of the mind add intermixtures of fantasies, anxiety, and other disturbing affects to the patient's response. Reacting to the realistic and internal dangers, the ego then responds with defenses and other efforts at adaptation. As noted, it is when these measures fail that symptoms arise. In regard to external dangers and pathological introjects, it is when the ego's efforts to master the influence of these disturbing stimuli prove to be inadequate that the patient experiences an emotional disturbance.

In this model, both actual and imagined sources of danger, those that are realistic and external, as well as those that are unrealistic and intrapsychic, are taken into account as sources of emotional disturbance. Threats to the patient's self-concept, self-system, and identity are related to ways in which these basic dangers are experienced. They consistently involve the mobilization of instinctual drive wishes and superego-ego ideal reactions, as well as defensive and other adaptive reactions by the ego. Clinically, it is always essential to identify these underlying factors in the presence of an emotional disturbance characterized by dysfunctions in the self-experience and sense of identity.

The distinction between the surface manifestations of an emotional disturbance and its underlying structure is critical. The surface manifestations of these emotional disorders are *indicators* or *therapeutic contexts,* and include all actualities that have a potential for disturbing the patient—e.g., an error by the therapist or a deviation from the ideal therapeutic hold.

Indicators, or therapeutic contexts, include the manifestations of the patient's emotional disturbance or Neurosis that require a therapeutic response. They are the immediate expressions of the patient's emotional illness as they arise in a particular session. In general, they call for one of two responses from the therapist: (1) Rectification and interpretation when the cause of the patient's emotional disturbance is an external danger situation to which the therapist has significantly contributed. (Under these conditions, the response must include both the cessation of this contribution to the patient's suffering and an interpretation of the nature of the symptom—in this instance, with considerable stress on valid unconscious perceptions and introjects of the errant therapist.) Or (2) when the danger is primarily internal and without significant actual contribution from the therapist, interpretation alone will suffice.

When dealing with indicators or therapeutic contexts, the interpretation involves the dynamics and genetics that form the underlying structure of a symptom. This entails a tracing out of the basic sequence of transactions, interpersonal and intrapsychic, that led to the emotional disturbance. This may involve unconscious perception-introjects as well as unconscious fantasy-memories. The dynamic components involve all known dimensions of interpersonal and intrapsychic experience. The genetic element is the specific personal history of the patient as it pertains to the immediate intrapsychic and interpersonal sources of the emotional difficulty.

An immediate emotional disturbance within the patient may arise mainly through actual perceived dangers derived from the therapeutic interventions or internal dangers stimulated by the therapist's nontraumatic efforts. Each of these two basic sequences will evoke conscious and unconscious memory responses within the patient that touch upon a wide variety of genetic factors. In turn, these earlier experiences and the patient's responses to them have contributed to the vulnerabilities that render the ego's adaptive efforts inadequate and lead thereby to symptom formation. Thus, as noted, interpretation must take into account both genetic and currently dynamic factors. It must also take as its point of departure the adaptation-evoking stimuli constituted by the therapist's interventions. These efforts, valid and erroneous, prove most significant in setting off sequences that lead to emotional disturbance in the patient, and to their structuralization in Neurosis formation.

Entirely separate consideration must be afforded to ways in which patients (and therapists) *communicate* about their emotional disturbances. An emotional disturbance may be expressed through a manifest symptom, or it may be mentioned directly or alluded to indirectly through some type of representation or encoded (derivative) expression. Thus indicators or therapeutic contexts—the patient's target illness and its interactive sources—may be reflected in the patient's manifest associations or latent to them.

The situation is more complicated when it comes to the underlying basis for an emotional disturbance. At times, the sources of this type of dysfunction may be reflected in a patient's manifest associations. Some of the factors in the disturbance may also be identified consciously and manifestly by the patient and alluded to directly. Under these conditions, however, the emotional disturbance is almost always in keeping with the traumatic qualities of the reality situation—it is not Neurotic, it is primarily a painful response to real danger, and often an essentially adaptive reaction.

In most actual situations, however, the patient, even when faced with a realistic danger, responds at least in part through encoded messages. Since the most significant sources of external danger for a patient arise from the erroneous interventions of the therapist, the strong, usually unconscious, motives that would prompt the patient (i.e., his or her ego) to make use of encoded expressions (derivatives) when attempting to let the therapist know something about his or her frightening unconscious perceptions and introjects can be readily understood. At the same time, the ego's efforts at encoding serve defensive and adaptive functions in sparing the patient the full impact and realization of the dangers with which he or she is confronted. This sense of anxiety and the other disturbing affects prompt defensive encoding, which if successful, may lead to a diminution of the patient's sense of internal disturbance. As noted, it is mainly when these defenses are unsuccessful that a noticeable emotional disturbance takes place.

The undisguised perception or fantasy, external or internal, to which an individual (an ego) responds with unconscious efforts at encoding is best termed a raw message. The term is derived from Freud's (1900) *Interpretation of Dreams,* where he describes the latent dream thoughts that are subjected to disguise (encoding) through the primary process mechanisms of condensation, displacement, symbolization, and concern for matters of representability. For Freud the raw, latent dream thought was usually an unconscious fantasy or memory. Here Freud's basic understanding is supplemented by the realization that there may be either an unconscious fantasy-memory or an unconscious perception latent to a manifest dream or free association. The term *raw message* has been coined to leave room for both dangerous (needing to be disguised) perceptions and fantasies.

When the raw message involves the patient's unconscious perceptions and introjects, encoded interpersonal realizations and their dynamics are present. When the raw message involves an intrapsychic conflict and unconscious fantasy-memory constellation, encoded expressions of instinctual drives, superego manifestations, and the defensive and other adaptive and maladaptive responses of the ego are present.

All emotional disturbances with Neurotic implications are based unconsciously upon perceptions and fantasies outside of the awareness of the patient. These raw messages are without exception subjected to encoding, and expressed manifestly (in disguised form) in the patient's free associations. Manifest associative elements that contain encoded messages are called *derivatives*.

The key point here may be the recognition that critical unconscious perceptions and intrapsychic fantasy-memories—the dynamic and genetic basis for Neurosis and emotional disturbance—are expressed by the patient through derivatives. *Derivative communication is therefore the hallmark of Neuroses.* It reflects the remarkable capacity of the human mind to express itself simultaneously and meaningfully on two levels when under emotional stress; i.e., when confronted by disturbing adaptation-evoking contexts responding in a seemingly logical and reality-oriented fashion, while at the same time conveying a wide range of displaced and encoded perceptions and reactions (some of which are quite logical, while others are not).

When therapists formulate dynamics and genetics as they pertain to an emotional disturbance, they are usually expressing themselves in terms of raw messages. On the other hand, when patients express themselves regarding the underlying basis of an emotional disturbance, they are usually doing so in terms of encoded messages. Because of this, the material from patients must always be subjected to decoding before dynamic and genetic statements can be developed with any measure of accuracy and validity.

Furthermore, it is this very process of encoding raw messages and subjecting them to distortion that leads to the formation of symptoms. Thus it is because the ego does not become directly aware of an external danger or an internal conflict, and because the ego instead automatically encodes the issues involved, that a Neurotic response takes place. This follows largely because such encoding almost always involves displacement, so that the ego's reaction to a given situation is inappropriate for the meanings of that situation, but instead (when symptomatic) derives from another situation whose meaning has been displaced onto the present set of conditions.

When patients express themselves regarding the underlying factors of an emotional disturbance, they do so through encoded messages. Neuroses involve internal and external danger situations and perception-fantasy constellations that are outside of the patients' awareness. Nonetheless, these factors are dynamically active and involve pertinent genetics. Since their influence does not take place manifestly and consciously, it occurs instead latently and unconsciously, and through encoded communications. There is therefore no conceivable way the unconscious basis for a Neurosis can be conveyed directly and manifestly by the patient.

These are important clues to the elements that must be developed for the listening process of insight psychotherapy. Indicators, therapeutic contexts, and signs of emotional disturbance must be identified. Adaptation-evoking stimuli that prompt Neurotic emotional difficulties must be recognized. Both of these elements may be found either manifestly represented or conveyed through encoded expressions. Finally, the means of identifying derivatives, the encoded messages that reveal the dynamics and genetics of the patient's emotional disturbance, must be developed. This material is termed the *derivative complex*.

Psychotherapy is constituted as a relationship between the patient and therapist, and unfolds as an interaction between the two. Among the potential stimuli for emotional disturbance and encoded communication by patients, those that eminate from the therapist are by far the most significant. With few exceptions the derivative communications from patients that illuminate their Neuroses are prompted by the silences and active interventions of the therapist. As a rule traumatic adaptation-evoking stimuli created by relationships outside of treatment are linked up by the patient to adaptive contexts within therapy. As a result the important encoded communications expressed by the patient find their greatest meaning in light of the efforts of the therapist. Since unconscious communication is so vital in this regard, the therapist's own unconscious messages to the patient have the greatest influence on the patient's unconscious communications to the therapist.

In this light, decoding efforts that involve stimuli from the therapist must be distinguished from those pertaining to the patient's outside relationships and from those that treat the patient's associations as derivatives of isolated intrapsychic contents. The latter two efforts are divorced from the therapist's interventions and the ongoing therapeutic interaction. The formulations arrived at in this first way are termed Type One derivative formulations. Manifest associations from the patient that are used for this type of noninteractional decoding are called Type One derivatives.

In contrast, any formulation that is organized around an intervention of the therapist is termed a Type Two derivative formulation. Those manifest associations from the patient that are decoded in this fashion are called Type Two derivatives. Studies have shown that interpretations couched in terms of Type Two derivatives are the only kind to obtain indirect or Type Two derivative validation (i.e., true psychoanalytic confirmation). Thus it is only through the development of Type Two derivative formulations—an understanding of dynamics and genetics in light of activated intervention or adaptive contexts—that a therapist can arrive at a correct and confirmed appreciation of the implications of the patient's material.

Clinical Application

The vignette presented at the beginning of this chapter provides a clinical introduction to the basic components of the listening process. In principle the first effort must be directed to identifying adaptation-evoking stimuli and their representations in the patient's material. In this way stimulus is separated from response, adaptive context from (reactive) derivative complex.

Proper decoding can only take place in light of a full understanding of the nature of the therapist's interventions. Since both conscious and unconscious raw perceptions and raw fantasies are subjected automatically to an encoding process when they prompt anxiety, the critical task is to distinguish those expressions from the patient that involve relatively valid perceptions of the therapist from those that involve primarily distorted perceptions and reactions based on pathological intrapsychic fantasies and memories. The same dynamic *contents* can serve *functionally* one moment mainly as an expression of a valid unconscious perception and introject of the therapist based on the unconscious implications of a particular intervention and, at another moment, as a reflection of an unconscious fantasy-memory of the patient generated as a response to rather different stimulus from the therapist.

THE ADAPTIVE CONTEXTS

The pursuit of representations of adaptive contexts begins with a search for direct expressions. In the vignette presented at the beginning of this chapter, there are two: the conditions of the patient's self-referral (alluded to in terms of thoughts by the patient about how she first came to see the therapist) and the therapist's specific intervention in the previous hour regarding this issue (referred to directly in the patient's associations). In this respect the therapist had, based on the material of the previous session, suggested that something was disturbing the patient regarding the conditions under which she came into treatment, though he had not specified the nature of the patient's disquietude.

The balance of the material from this session may be scanned in light of these two interrelated adaptive contexts for derivative or encoded representations of implications of either of these efforts at intervention. For the sake of simplicity, the main adaptive context for this hour is defined here as the therapist's acceptance of the patient after a prior contact with her as her teacher. Adaptive contexts related to the ground rules of therapy prove to be among the most powerful adaptive contexts with which patients must and do deal (see Part III).

FORMULATING THE IMPLICATIONS OF THE ADAPTIVE CONTEXT

Identification of the adaptive context and its best representation must be followed by the formulation of its important implications. This is tantamount to identifying its manifest and encoded messages. The therapist must rely on his or her own understanding of the meanings and functions of a particular intervention, and on the patient's material (manifest and latent), which is often replete with unconscious perceptions and introjects.

In this session, the patient manifestly describes having had lunch with one of her students. She fantasizes having sexual relations with him, but finds him interested not only in herself, but in other women. There is then an allusion to going crazy and ending her fantasy about the student, Armand. Next, there is a shift to the patient's childhood, her nasty qualities, and how she drove everyone away. Finally, there is a reference to her father taking her into bed, and the allusions to the conditions under which the patient came into treatment. In what ways does this material help the therapist to characterize the implications of the adaptive context?

The patient introduces themes of having lunch with a student and of fantasizing having sexual relations with him. There is, then, an allusion to a contact between a professor and a student outside of the classroom. There is also the image of sexual intercourse. The first element may be seen to represent the adaptive context itself, and to do so in encoded form: there has in actuality been a shift in the meeting place between the patient and therapist from the classroom to his office. The patient represents this change by mentioning that she agreed to have lunch with her own student. The manifest element may therefore be seen to represent symbolically a different, latent element that involves the therapist. It is useful to note that in addition to representing this adaptive context verbally, the patient also expresses it in her behavior. To the extent that this involves a pathological introject or fantasy related to the therapist, the behavior should be seen as a form of interactional acting out.

Evaluation of this adaptive context would readily lead to the conclusion that, first, the therapist has indeed inappropriately altered a boundary between himself and the patient. Ideally, their relationship should have been confined to the classroom and should have precluded therapeutic contact because of the lack of relative anonymity involved (see Chapter 24). Second, the decision to see in therapy a student with whom the therapist has had prior contact appears indeed to have clear unconscious seductive qualities. The patient has strong reason to question the therapist's motives for accepting her into treatment. She also has reason to be concerned that a therapist who is unable to maintain clear boundaries, and to clearly identify the nature of the transactions between himself and another individual, might well have a similar uncertainty in regard to whether the relationship would continue on a nonsexual course or shift to sexual contact. These kinds of confusing, uncertain, and mixed messages from a therapist often create a strong sense of mistrust, and deprive the patient of a feeling of certainty about reality. This is experienced typically as efforts by the therapist to drive the patient crazy (Searles 1959)—a perception that is represented later in this hour.

In addition to the patient's valid perceptions of the therapist as someone who has violated necessary interpersonal boundaries and behaved in a seductive manner, the very nature of this self-referral may also stimulate responsive wishes within the patient to further modify the boundaries between herself and the therapist, and to become engaged in some type of manifest or latent sexual contact. There may therefore be a mixture of reality and fantasy, nontransference and transference. As is true in all such situations, however, the elements that involve justified readings of the unconscious messages from the therapist must be identified and interpreted first. Only then can the patient's own unconscious contributions be clearly stated and analyzed.

It appears that this patient has experienced the acceptance of her self-referral under the conditions noted as a danger situation. This danger has both interpersonal and intrapsychic qualities. It may be postulated that the patient feels in jeopardy because of her uncertainties regarding the therapist, including doubts as to whether he will respond to her with interpretations or with sexual behaviors, and because of other concerns that extend from there.

There is, in addition, an internal danger situation. The patient's own instinctual drives have been aroused, and there are specific wishes to have sexual relations with the therapist. There are signs that these wishes are condemned by her superego and seen as dangerous (i.e., as involving a poor object choice, as crazy in some way, and genetically, as related to seductive intimacy with her father). There is therefore a need to renounce this fantasy-wish. The patient expresses this renunciation by giving up her fantasy about Armand. She also holds up this model of rectification to the therapist as a way, it seems likely, of suggesting that he too should correct the situation between himself and the patient.

The raw (unconscious) perception of the therapist (the critical *image* derivative) is that he has broken appropriate relationship boundaries and has been seductive with the patient. The manifest and encoded representations of these images involve the patient's having lunch with a student of her own, and her having fantasies of sexual relations with him. These raw messages have been encoded into manifest contents (derivatives) through the operation of *primary process mechanisms*. Displacement is used, through which the situation with the therapist is represented by a different situation, that between the patient and her student. The evidence for displacement lies in the realization that in both situations there is the common tie of an involvement beyond the classroom between a teacher and a student. There is evidence for condensation, in that the therapist not only accepted the patient under the conditions described, but also made use of an office within his home. The use of symbolic representation is also quite clear: the therapist's decision to see a patient who was his former student is represented manifestly by the patient having lunch with a student of her own. The lunch representation suggests perceived orally greedy and devouring qualities to the therapist's decision, although there may be an additional coloring from the patient's own unconscious fantasy-memory constellations.

The patient's fantasy of having sexual relations with her student represents her unconscious perception of something seductive in the therapist's acceptance of her into treatment. Here implicit seductiveness is represented by an image of explicit sexual relations. A manifest fantasy serves to represent an unconscious (latent) perception.

In general, patients tend to encode raw sexual fantasies and perceptions through desexualized and deinstinctualized representations. Here, at this level, a behavior that is not overtly sexual is represented in directly sexual terms. This suggests that in addition to valid unconscious perceptiveness, there is a contribution from the patient's own fantasy-memory constellations. However, all alterations in the ideal therapeutic environment are experienced by patients as having powerful sexual vectors (see Part III). In terms of listening, then, these two derivative elements involve symbolic representations of underlying raw images (i.e., an unconscious perception has been portrayed in some different or disguised form and language other than its raw elements).

There are also considerations of representability: The patient is talking about an experience with a student of her own. She has a need to maintain a logical sequence of thoughts, ideas, and fantasies regarding this relationship. She succeeds in doing so in her manifest associations. She has therefore met the necessity of communicating in a logical and rational, secondary process form to the therapist. She has nonetheless simultaneously expressed herself in terms of encoded messages that represent a series of raw unconscious perceptions and unconscious fantasies in a disguised form. The manifest allusion to how the student turns his sexuality on to any woman, not just the patient, has clear derivative meaning, because the therapist had accepted two other students in the patient's class into treatment with him. The raw message, then, is, "You (the therapist) have been seductive not only with me but with two other students." This raw perception is then displaced onto the patient's own situation with her student and the other two women. The encoded message also conveys the patient's unconscious reading of the implications of the therapist's acceptance of all of them into treatment after having worked with them as a teacher. The vehicle for this encoded message is the patient's allusion to her own student, Armand, and how he turned his sexuality onto several different women at one time.

The allusion to how the patient was nasty and would pinch and bite as a child may well contain in encoded form the hostile, attacking, and alienating qualities of the therapist's decision to accept the patient into treatment under these conditions. It may also convey a reaction to this particular adaptive context, and indicate that the stimulus has mobilized aggressive feelings and fantasies within the patient, including the wish to drive the therapist away.

The allusion to how the patient's father would take her into bed is of course the critical genetic link in this sequence. What then is the raw message? Is it that the patient wishes to go to bed with the therapist as she had wished to do with her father? Or instead, is it that through the nature of the conditions under which he accepted the patient for therapy, the therapist has in actuality, on some level, taken the patient into bed (symbolically) in a manner comparable to the behavior of her father? The first formulation is couched in terms of transference, while the second involves non-transference. The first implies projection and distortion by the patient, while the second implies perception and nondistortion. This particular association must be evaluated in terms of its communicative qualities to reach a decision as to which formulation is most applicable.

The manifest element of the patient's father taking her into bed is best understood as a displaced symbolic representation of the therapist's taking the patient into treatment after having worked with her as a student. In addition, more clearly than the earlier elements, the influence of condensation is present in that the therapist has also taken the patient into his house. Here the father's bed is used manifestly in part to represent the therapist's home-office. The clear parallels between the acceptance of a patient into a home-office after having worked with her as a student and a father who takes his daughter into bed with himself must be acknowledged. In both situations, there is a loss of appropriate interpersonal boundaries and a strong sense of seductiveness. The patient's representations of the therapist's deviations have strong qualities of actual physical seductiveness, and studies show that this is indeed how patients experience such deviations. However, it must also be suspected that the patient's own latent sexual wishes and fantasies also have been aroused by these conditions.

As happens so often, it must be concluded that this material has strong *transversal* qualities, in that it traverses transference and nontransference, perception and fantasy, and condenses them all into a single expression. The patient appears to have encoded these messages because she views the therapist as dangerous, and because of the reaction of her own superego to her own aroused instinctual drive wishes. The ego has brought into play the primary process mechanisms and defenses that enable the patient to encode a series of raw, but unconscious, perceptions and fantasies into a logical and different manifest message, containing a multitude of hidden and encoded messages.

In psychotherapy the therapist actually begins listening with a series of encoded manifest messages. Although the patient's manifest associations have other functions, their role as the carrier of the patient's disguised, raw and threatening perceptions and fantasies is extremely important.

A symptom or Neurosis is itself an encoded message. If the encoding is understood as being reflected in the patient's manifest associations, the therapist is immediately in a position to understand the unconscious meanings of the symptoms. On this basis, valid interpretations are generated that provide insightful symptom alleviation for the patient. Insight into psychotherapy is the means by which the therapist listens to these surface and encoded messages and strips them of their disguise in order to arrive at the raw perceptions and fantasies that underly these communications and, simultaneously, the patient's emotional disturbance.

Summary

An emotional disturbance arises in the presence of an adaptation-evoking stimulus with dangerous and frustrating qualities. The danger may be primarily interpersonal or intrapsychic. In the former situation, the object is threatening in some way; while in the latter, the threat arises mainly from instinctual drive derivatives with secondary threats to the sense of self and identity. In response to the threat, the ego mobilizes its defenses and adaptive resources.

When these are successful, there will be no emotional disturbance. When these are inadequate or fail, there will be a symptomatic response.

A symptom is a dysfunctional encoded message. Through the operation of the ego's defenses, it contains representations of the nature of the danger situation, the mobilized instinctual drives, the superego reaction, and the implications and nature of the ego's defenses—all in disguised form. A single manifest disturbance therefore contains a multiplicity of latent meanings in encoded form. Dynamically and genetically, a symptom is a compromise formation that involves both interpersonal and intrapsychic dynamics, operating in resonance with genetic antecedents.

These intrapsychic and interpersonal transactions are represented and worked over in the patient's associations. Unconscious communication and dynamic-genetic transactions are two separate though intimately related problems. This distinction, and the fundamental necessity of understanding communication before dynamics and genetics, seems implicit to Freud's monumental study of the interpretation of dreams (1900), which served as the critical gateway to his study of the nature of Neuroses. Dynamics and genetics are conveyed largely through encoded expressions. It is therefore necessary for a therapist to develop and master a comprehensive listening process before he or she can identify the true dynamic and genetic implications of a patient's material.

In situations of conflict and danger, patients resort to the use of encoded messages. When a reaction to a danger situation leads to a symptomatic response, it is the underlying and encoded raw messages that reveal the meaning and functions of the symptom.

Raw messages may take the form of an unconscious perception or fantasy-memory. Manifest expression of the raw message is dangerous and a source of interpersonal or intrapsychic anxieties. The message is thus automatically and unconsciously encoded through the use of displacement, condensation, symbolic (and disguised) representation, and considerations of representability. The resultant manifest message may take the form of a behavior, a thought, a fantasy, a free association, or a symptom—physical or emotional. However, all such manifest messages must be decoded in order to understand their underlying meanings and functions, and the raw messages on which they are based.

The most critical raw and unconscious messages for Neuroses

are developed in terms of specific images (perceptions or fantasies). As a result, the most meaningful aspects of the patient's material are *image derivatives,* i.e., manifest representations of underlying raw images. Of far lesser importance are nonimage derivatives; these tend to be highly intellectualized, quite defensive, and functionally meaningless.

Since encoded raw messages in the form of perceptions and fantasies are the basis of emotional disturbance, the interpretation of the patient's encoded communications as they reveal underlying raw messages is the main means through which the patient is afforded insight into the unconscious basis of his or her emotional illness. Such interpretations must be carried out in terms of the adaptation-evoking stimulus that has shaped and prompted the need to encode raw messages and that has, in addition, produced dynamic-genetic responses, which involve conflict and interpersonal and inner disturbance. Such raw messages clarify the basis for a patient's maladaptive responses to adaptation-evoking contexts. The most critical adaptation-evoking stimuli for encoded messages that are related to emotional disturbances in patients are derived from the silences and interventions of the therapist, including his or her management of the ground rules and boundaries of the therapeutic relationship.

Before a therapist can unambiguously interpret the underlying meanings of the patient's encoded messages, a sound and healthy therapeutic symbiosis with the patient must be established. The basic conditions of the therapeutic relationship must be secure before successful interpretive work can take place. The therapeutic environment serves as an extremely powerful adaptation-evoking stimulus. Interventions that involve the ground rules and boundaries of the therapeutic relationship take precedence over those that pertain to the patient's encoded messages as they relate to other types of intervention from the therapist. Rectification of deviant conditions to the basic therapeutic relationship is necessary before the therapist's own communications to the patient will be experienced mainly in terms of their manifest properties and intentions.

Thus the therapist's management of the ground rules and framework of the relationship with the patient contains within it a rich and critical variety of manifest and encoded messages to the patient. Such messages must be consonant with the therapist's verbal interventions for the latter to have their intended effects.

Chapter 6

The Means of Listening

A therapist is usually faced with communications from a patient that are remarkably complex, not only on the surface but also in respect to their multileveled deeper implications. A means of categorizing and organizing these impressions is required as a sound basis for ultimate active intervention or as justification for silences. After considerable clinical research, two basic schema for listening-formulating, which appear to include virtually every important level of meaning and function at which a patient expresses and that a therapist will need, have been generated. The first of these schema is specifically geared to the practicalities of intervening and is called the listening-intervening schema. The second is an organized means by which the therapist is able to observe the most important areas of meaning in the patient's material, considerations that are then funneled into the schema for listening-intervening. This second schema is termed the six-part observational schema.

The Schema for Listening-Intervening

The listening-formulating process consists of three basic components that are specifically required for a sound intervention. They are developed as a cognitive-affective formulation, a silent hypothesis that is not offered to the patient, though it is geared to eventual intervention if necessary. The three components are:

1. *The identification of all activated adaptation-evoking contexts.* These critical stimuli virtually always involve the silences and interventions of the therapist. Both the manifest and latent mean-

ings and functions of each adaptive context must be determined. The clearest representation of each precipitant in the material from the patient must be identified. (In a relatively resistance-free situation, the patient will represent adaptive contexts manifestly and in passing.)

2. *Recognition of the indicators or therapeutic contexts.* Indicators often take the form of expressions of emotional disturbances or resistances in the patient. They reflect internal needs within the patient for an intervention by the therapist. Ideally, they emerge in the patient's manifest associations. However, indicators may also involve signs of difficulty for the therapist when errors in therapeutic technique cause disruptions of the therapeutic experience. In the latter case, they usually appear in the patient's material in disguised form. The therapist must evaluate the *nature* and *weight* of the indicators in each particular session, and thereby develop some sense of the extent to which the patient is experiencing a therapeutic need for an active intervention.

3. *A formulation of the derivative complex,* which contains the patient's adaptive and maladaptive reactions to the adaptation-evoking stimuli. These responses, filled with dynamic and genetic implications, will take place on an unconscious and encoded level in situations in which emotional disturbance is involved. The goal in listening is to understand the nature of the patient's unconscious responses in terms of both perceptions and fantasies, and their dynamic and genetic meanings. These factors form the underlying (unconscious) basis of the patient's emotional disturbance, and can be interpreted in the light of activated intervention contexts (Type Two derivative formulations).

Efforts at integrating these components into a silent hypothesis and actual intervention to the patient must meet the requirements of the validating process that is described in Chapter 12. Encoded or indirect (Type Two derivative) confirmation from the patient is essential to this process, as is the patient's conscious working over of an offered intervention. The approach to listening and intervening is, therefore, founded on a validating clinical methodology that serves as a guide to both the therapist's creative and displined contributions to the work with the patient.

The Observational Schema

Six other interrelated spheres of listening that a therapist will utilize from time to time in each session are listed below. The therapist will be guided in part by direct observations of himself or herself and the patient, and in part by the representations in the patient's associations. These areas of listening tend to involve both cognitive and noncognitive qualities, though all of the therapist's impressions must eventually be given cognitive assignment and funneled into the schema for listening-intervening. They appear to be the best and most comprehensive means of identifying the most pertinent aspects of the patient's material at a given juncture. They are:

1. *The nature and status of, and presence of impingements upon, the ground rules and boundaries of the therapeutic relationship and setting.* The rules of relatedness and interaction in psychotherapy are the single most critical determinant of the mode of relatedness between the patient and therapist, and of the nature and implications of the other dimensions of the treatment experience that are outlined here. Involved too are the basic hold and containment of the patient, and secondarily the therapist, the qualities of the core or background relationship established between the two members of the therapeutic dyad, and the actual mode of cure. Listening in this sphere is therefore a first-order therapeutic task. Because of its critical importance, this realm of listening is the sole subject of Part III.

2. *The actual and fantasied mode of object relatedness between the patient and therapist.* It is important for the therapist to identify the many aspects of object relatedness as they pertain to his or her interpersonal relationship with the patient. The actual mode of relatedness, as well as the mode sought for and fantasied by each participant, must be formulated. These efforts are reflected in the patient's associations and behaviors, and in the behaviors and interventions of the therapist. They involve monitoring the state of the core or background mode of relatedness, as well as the ongoing foreground maturational mode of relatedness sought for and effected on both sides. Mode of relatedness is determined in large measure by the responses of the patient and therapist to the ground rules of treatment, and by a variety of intrapsychic and interperson-

al factors. In turn, it influences the implications of all the other transactions between the patient and therapist, including the mode of cure and the dynamic meanings of the patient's associations and the therapist's interventions. This particular level of understanding is presented in Chapter 13 and reconsidered in Chapter 32.

3. *The mode of cure sought for and effected by each participant to treatment.* The main polarity of this continuum involves (a) cure through true understanding and insight in terms of the patient's activated responses to intervention contexts as they pertain to his or her Neurosis, and (b) cure or relief achieved through action-discharge and pathological modes of defense, lie-barrier systems, and drive satisfactions. This important polarity applies not so much to the patient's stated wishes and intentions as it does to his or her unconscious expressions and efforts; similar considerations of unconscious expressions and actual efforts apply to the therapist. The patient's associations often contain representations of the prevailing mode of cure in operation for both patient and therapist. These allusions usually involve descriptions of efforts to deal with and solve all kinds of problems and dilemmas. At times, they touch upon the patient's wishes and fantasies in this area, though most often they represent the actual state of the curative process for the moment. Modes of relief and cure are closely related to, and factors of, the state of the frame and mode of relatedness between the patient and therapist. Because they involve basic styles of communicating, they will be discussed in Chapter 15 along with that topic.

4. *The mode of communication in use by both patient and therapist.* Each participant to therapy adopts an empirically recognizable mode of communication within the therapeutic interaction. The polarity here is that of expressing and recognizing activated truths or creating lie-substitutes for and barriers against these truths. Each style is defined by specific criteria for the patient and therapist. The extent of interactional pressure involved in the communicative expression is also considered. This level of observation is studied in Chapter 15.

5. *The dynamic and genetic implications of the patient's material.* The interactions with the therapist arouse responses fraught with dynamic and genetic meaning in the patient. The first area involves a full consideration of intrapsychic and interpersonal conflict, aroused unconscious fantasy and perception constellations, id, ego, and superego considerations, and aspects of pre-Oedipal

and Oedipal issues including those related to the development of the self. The latter area pertains to the historic implications of the patient's material as aroused by the ongoing therapeutic interaction. An important polarity here involves the extent to which the patient's aroused memories involve connections inappropriately made between the present and past (transference) and connections made between now and then that are based on actual resemblance (nontransference). Activated dynamics and genetics are essential to an understanding of all of the dimensions of the treatment experience, and are considered in particular in Chapters 27-30 and 33. However, this level of information is but one of many that the therapist must monitor in the course of listening; much of prior therapeutic work has been overly concentrated in this area to the neglect of the other aspects of the listening-formulating process.

6. *To whom the main dynamic and genetic implications of the patient's material apply—i.e., whether the deeper meanings involve valid unconscious perceptions of the therapist or fantasy-based distortions from the patient.* In gathering information from the patient's associations and behaviors, the therapist maintains an open attitude and does not assume that the communications apply only to the patient and are essentially pathological and distorted (transference-based). Room is maintained for the realization that the most cogent meanings of the material may apply validly to the therapist in terms of the unconscious implications of his or her actions and interventions (nontransferences). In the latter situation, the dynamics reflected in the patient's associations tend to apply more meaningfully to the therapist than to the patient, although both may be involved. Genetic repercussions then entail actual repetitions of the pathogenic past, rather than distortions introduced by the patient on the basis of earlier pathogenic experiences. This level of listening and formulating is considered mainly in Chapters 27-30.

These six areas consistute the main informational or observational aspects of listening. In actual practice, the therapist tends to concentrate organizing efforts on the tripartite listening-intervening schema, delineating the main adaptive contexts (their representations and implications), the major indicators, and the patient's derivative responses. Simultaneously, the patient's direct and derivative images, and the therapist's sense of what may be important, guide him or her toward formulations in the observational spheres. Once or twice in each session the therapist should also run through the six observational categories as a way of catching implications of the patient's material that may have escaped notice.

Since the initial goal is to develop the listening process as it applies to the patient's communications, the stress here has been on attending to the material that the patient conveys to the therapist. However, as must be evident by now, the therapist must also attend to his or her own subjective state and interventions to the patient with the same two schema in mind. The tripartite schema for intervening serves the therapist as a guide to the extent to which he or she has met the criteria of sound interventions. In addition, the six-part observational schema helps the therapist to stay in touch with the dimensions of his or her own contributions and unconscious expressions in interaction with the patient. Attention to these areas enables the therapist to conceptualize valid efforts and functioning in the spheres of importance to the patient's therapeutic experience. In this way, the therapist stays in touch with his or her management and attitudes toward the frame, as well as with his or her mode of relating to the patient, the patient's unconsciously expressed preferred mode of relief or cure, and the therapist's own mode of communicating with the patient. The therapist's aroused and personal dynamic and genetic stirrings, and the extent to which he or she responds to the patient essentially in terms of the latter's communications through valid perceptions and formulations (noncountertransference) or on the basis of distortions and pathology within the therapist (countertransference), are all monitored. Thus the qualities of the therapeutic experience are organized spearately, and yet in interrelated fashion, for the patient, the therapist, and for their interaction, arising through vectors from both participants.

Material from Patients

With the exception of reported dreams, therapists tend to pay little attention to the avenues of expression utilized by their patients. There is some justification for this attitude, in that every manifest communication, whatever its nature, must be treated by the therapist as a potential carrier of both manifest and latent meaning. Nevertheless, various modes of expression are available to patients, and are necessary to an understanding of the nature of the data of psychotherapy.

The following excerpt is from a psychotherapy session. The patient is a young woman in psychotherapy because of problems in getting close to men and episodes of depression. The therapist is a woman. The session followed an end-of-the-year two-week vacation by the therapist.

Patient: Happy New Year. Last week, while you were away, I went with Sally to the museum and then to her house. She's not interested in me. She cooked and I listened to the hi-fi. We went to a bar where she knows some people. I tried to talk to this man, but he had nothing to say. I turned to another man, but he walked away from me. I'm not happy with my friends. They think I'm not interested at all in sex. They have their families and have little time for me. I pretended I was out when one of my friends called. I'm feeling lethargic now. *(The patient lets her body slip low in the chair, and her arms droop.)* I dreamt I was on a bridge trying to cross it. There was a piece missing. No one would help me get across. Then I was in Buenos Aires where I was born. I was with a man. He was bedraggled. My friend Toby was with a wealthy looking man. I felt I had no one. When I was a child, my mother used to tell me I would end up alone. I would feel depressed and get stomach aches. I just had this image of my mother standing over me frowning. I can remember times when I would come home from school and she wouldn't be there. She did it because she hated me. I just thought of our last session. You kept very quiet. While you were away, I had this weird experience where I imagined meeting you in a department store. You seemed upset when you saw me and you were very distant. What was strange was that I saw a television show that night, and it was about this woman who was in therapy. In the story, she and her therapist meet in this luncheonette and have coffee together. About a year ago I ran into an old college professor of mine at a movie and we had a drink together afterwards. I feld uncomfortable with him, somewhat anxious.

This session contains most of the kinds of manifest material that therapists confront with patients.

1. References to current and recent events, behaviors, actions, and interactions in the patient's everyday life outside of treatment.
2. The report of memories of relatively recent experiences and reactions.
3. Allusions to experiences, observations, and transactions that pertain to the therapeutic experience.
4. References to memories from past years and childhood.
5. Conscious fantasies or daydreams.
6. Night dreams.
7. Creative works, such as novels, movies, television, myths, etcetera.
8. Slips of the tongue.
9. The report of psychological and physical symptoms, subjective states, thoughts, and reactions.
10. Deliberate lies.

EVERYDAY LIFE OUTSIDE OF TREATMENT

The patient alludes to going to a museum and a bar with her friend Sally, and to other situations and conditions that exist in her outside life, such as her aloneness and the families that are available to her friends.

Allusions of this type may include references to symptoms the patient is experiencing, such as the feelings of depression described in this vignette. They may reveal maladative responses in the patient and other signs of emotional disturbance that are indicators for intervening (i.e., therapeutic contexts). The patient's behaviors and reactions may also convey indications of symptom alleviation and maturation, and reflect adaptive and constructive functioning. They may also reveal the status of the patient's outside mode of relatedness and his or her attitudes toward the frame and cure.

Material of this kind may also serve as an important carrier of latent meaning (i.e., as a derivative expression). Thus an incident with an outside person may be used to represent a disturbing intervention or adaptive context within the treatment situation in disguised form. For example, the patient alludes to a man who walked away from her when she wanted to speak to him. Through displacement and symbolic representation, this description of a recent experience probably serves as an encoded representation of the adaptive context of the therapist's vacation—itself a way in which the therapist became unavailable for the patient at a time of evident need.

The description of recent events and experiences also serves admirably, because of the inherent displacement involved, as a vehicle for the encoded (derivative) expression of responses to activated adaptation-evoking contexts. They therefore often form an important part of the derivative complex. Taking the therapist's vacation as one adaptive context for this session, and in light of the implied abandonment, the patient's allusion to the man who walked away from her at the bar may be seen to contain an encoded perception of the therapist's departure. Later in the session, the patient describes pretending that she was out when a friend called. This behavior implies an introjective identification with the abandoning therapist, and an effort through displacement to have revenge in kind on the therapist. This action seems to have qualities of acting out (i.e., the living out in an external relationship of an unconscious perception or fantasy that pertains to the therapist), and the behavior appears to be maladaptive in that it is false and seemingly unnecessarily hurtful. If the patient had stated that she had created a fight with one of her girlfriends and had walked out on her, this particular expression would have conveyed these postulated implications in far clearer form. Here, however, the patient's behavior is (1) encoded and (2) based unconsciously on fantasies and perceptions related to the therapist and creating an emotional disturbance. Thus both meaning and behavioral consequences are involved—both derivative complex and indicators.

Particular attention is paid to the patient's behaviors in her description of recent events. Such behaviors may reflect emotional disturbance and serve as indicators for intervening. They may involve unconscious perceptions and introjects of the therapist, and may also reflect the living out of unconscious fantasies. Their actual meanings and functions can be understood only in light of the specific activated adaptive contexts at hand and the nature of the behavior itself, although the patient's other associations may clarify the implications of a particular action. Thus it is important to understand the manifest implications of the patient's description of recent events and behaviors and, in addition, to treat such material as possible carriers of derivative or encoded meaning. There has been an unfortunate tendency to think of descriptions of such realities in simplistic terms and to accept them at face value. They are, to the contrary, often an extremely important means of unconscious communication.

MEMORIES OF RELATIVELY RECENT EXPERIENCES AND REACTIONS

The patient remembers meeting an old professor in a movie and having a drink with him. This type of material tends to reflect the past adaptations and maladaptations of the patient, and to reveal something of earlier object relationships. It also may serve as a means of derivative expression, through which the patient can represent in encoded form either an activated adaptive context or some aspect of the derivative complex. Thus the particular memory cited appears to serve here as a response to the adaptive context of the therapist's vacation. It seems to reflect a reactive wish within the patient to undo the separation and to achieve some type of closeness with the therapist. It may also imply a wish for a pathological symbiosis—an outside contact with the therapist with direct oral gratification—or it may have sexual overtones. Other material from the patient is necessary to clarify these tentative—*silent* (i.e., not passed on to the patient)—formulations or hypotheses. As a representation through the opposite, the unexpected meeting with the professor may be seen as a heavily disguised representation of the therapist's absence.

ALLUSIONS TO EXPERIENCES AND OBSERVATIONS THAT PERTAIN TO THE THERAPEUTIC EXPERIENCE

The patient mentions that the therapist had been away, and she recalls that the therapist had been quiet during the previous hour. There is also a manifest fantasy of meeting the therapist in a department store. These are, of course, direct allusions to the therapist and the therapeutic experience. Patients sometimes describe detailed recollections of what the therapist did or said, and conscious fantasies (daydreams) about the therapist that often are more elaborate than the one reported here (see "Conscious Fantasies or Daydreams," below).

There is thus a wide range of possible direct allusions to the various aspects of treatment and to the therapist that may take a variety of forms: observation, speculation, feeling, fantasy, thought, etcetera. It is important, however, to treat all such manifest contents in a manner comparable to the way that the therapist listens to and formulates other types of material. There has been a tendency among therapists to immediately think of such expressions as *transference*, using that term to imply some type of pathological or pathology-related allusion to the therapist. In terms of their derivative functions, manifest references to the therapist may indeed reflect unconscious transference fantasies, but they also may portray unconscious nontransference perceptions or, as is frequently the case, may prove to be poor carriers of encoded meaning. The key lies in approaching manifest material about the therapist and therapy with the same basic listening process that is applied to all material. Organization of derivative meanings in terms of prevailing adaptive contexts is essential.

Allusions to relatively recent transactions in treatment may, on a manifest level, contain indicators—therapeutic contexts that point to the need within the patient for an intervention from the therapist. They may do so by referring to ways in which the patient has behaved inappropriately or symptomatically in his or her hour, or by touching upon ways in which the therapist has behaved or intervened erroneously and in a fashion that disturbed the therapeutic hold and experience. These errors create an actual or potential emotional disturbance within the patient. Indications for intervening encompass both the manifestations of disturbance and error in the therapist that serve to create therapeutic needs within the patient, and signs of internal disturbance or resistance in the patient himself or herself (see Chapter 9). It should be noted, however, that disturbing behaviors and communications from the therapist are only sometimes represented manifestly in the patient's material through direct representation. Quite often, they are alluded to by the patient in encoded form, either through a reference to another aspect of the therapist's behavior or by complete displacement, through a reference to an outside figure or to the patient himself or herself. This last is, on the whole, a most unsuspecting and highly useful vehicle within which the patient may disguise threatening perceptions of the therapist in particular. Decoding direct allusions to the patient and to the therapist is therefore always essential.

Direct references to the therapist and to the treatment situation

are the only means through which a patient can manifestly repre-
sent an activated adaptive context. Because of this, the therapeutic
work is greatly facilitated by such representations. Ideally, the
adaptation-evoking intervention is alluded to directly and in passing, and the patient moves quickly to other subjects, thereby developing a meaningful derivative complex through displaced and
symbolic representation. The therapist needs a direct allusion to the
adaptive context as a sign that the patient is prepared to connect
derivative reactions to a specific intervention by the therapist. This
link, which overcomes a denial barrier and defense, facilitates
intervening and the development of a sense of conviction in the
patient. The absence of a direct representation of this kind is
usually a sign of communicative resistance and defense. This is
usually reflected in responsive denial when the therapist attempts to
bridge this defensive gap (by tying the material to the therapist
when the patient has not done so), and to connect derivatives to
adaptive contexts that have not been directly represented in the
material from the patient. Toward the beginning of this hour, for
example, the patient mentions in passing that the therapist had
been away. This brief mention is sufficient to link the patient's
subsequent derivative communications to this particular adaptive
context through associative proximity.

As noted, manifest allusions to the therapist and to therapy
often involve important signs or indications for intervention, and
are the essential means through which patients represent activated
intervention contexts directly. Such associations may serve as well
as carriers of *derivative* (unconscious) fantasies and perceptions that
pertain to the therapist. These manifest allusions are encoded
derivatives, and they must be reduced to underlying raw messages—
perceptions or fantasies—in light of the prevailing adaptive contexts. Therapists too often accept manifest references to themselves as
containing inherently dynamic meaning. They fail to treat such
allusions as surface manifestations of underlying encoded messages.
All associations must be subjected to efforts at decoding in light of
adaptation-evoking stimuli. Because of the absence or minimal
degree of displacement involved, it appears clinically that direct
allusions to the therapist and to treatment are, in general, poor
carriers of derivative meaning. In contrast, direct references to the
patient himself or herself tend to be good carriers of derivative
implications—especially of valid unconscius perceptions of the
therapist.

The allusion to the therapist having been away appears to convey little in the way of encoded meaning. The fantasy of meeting the therapist in the department store and of the therapist being upset also seems thin in respect to encoded images. Inferences can be made from this manifest material that the patient wished to meet the therapist in order to undo the separation, and that she felt that the therapist would be upset by such a meeting, or instead that the patient herself would be upset and projected this onto the therapist in her fantasy. These formulations are essentially Type One derivative formulations that involve inference decoding. In this process, manifest material is examined for evident implications. There is little or no consideration of symbolic image representation and, instead, the stress is on inference and intellectualized formulations. In general, this type of formulation, unrelated to a specific adaptive context, does not meaningfully illuminate the unconscious basis of an emotional disturbance. This is the type of inference that is typically available in direct references to the therapist. Only on rare occasions will a manifest fantasy or memory about the therapist function as an encoded representation of an entirely different perception or fantasy—i.e., function in true symbolic fashion.

REFERENCES TO MEMORIES FROM PAST YEARS AND CHILDHOOD

On a manifest level, allusions by the patient to childhood may reflect earlier modes of relating and functioning, adaptive and maladaptive. They may represent directly important childhood experiences that have some bearing upon the patient's present emotional disturbance. The manifest allusion does not, however, illuminate the unconscious implications of these experiences in the past or in the present. Such genetic connections must be understood in light of activated adaptive contexts, and must be subjected to the decoding process—i.e., treated in part as screen (encoded) memories (Freud 1899).

By and large, the recollection of early memories have their greatest import in terms of their latent implications. They frequently serve as an important means of derivative communication that must be decoded in light of activated intervention contexts. The early recollection has been stimulated by the actualities of the therapeutic interaction, and serves as a commentarty on this interaction. It tends to represent the genetic experiences and interactions that have a bearing upon the here and now in therapy (Gill 1979). As such, the main dynamic meaning may imply either transference (displacements and projections from the past onto the therapist in the present, which are without substantial basis and reflect aspects of the patient's psychopathology and unconscious fantasy-memory constellations) or nontransference (the genetic counterparts of the therapists actual behaviors and their implications, usually in the form of an inappropriate pathological repetition by the therapist of a past pathogenic Neurosis-creating interaction). Thus allusions to early life experiences tend to introduce the genetic element into the listening process. They form the genetic aspect of the derivative complex. Considerable caution is necessary, however, in understanding the true nature of the connection between the past and present. This is feasible only in light of a full understanding of the implications of the therapist's interventions.

On occasion, an early memory may be used to represent an indicator or an adaptive context in encoded form. For example, the patient recalls her mother's absence when she returned home from school. In light of the activated intervention context of the therapist's vacation, it may be formulated that this particular manifest memory is an encoded representation of the adaptation-evoking context. Included in this representation is the implied connection between the therapist and the mother. In light of the nature of the adaptive context, a largely nontransference quality would be assigned to this derivative representation (for now): the therapist has in actuality left the patient much as her mother had done in earlier years.

Next, however, the patient states her belief that her mother did this because she hated the patient. If the therapist were to carefully examine her subjective feelings toward the patient, and to analyze the basis for her decision to take a vacation (and further, to analyze the implications of her other interventions), and conclude with some level of clear self-knowledge and certainty that she feels and has expressed no sense of hatred toward the patient, this particular memory would be seen as the derivative expression of a distorted unconscious perception of the therapist. It would be understood functionally as a transference-based expression, and displacement from the mother onto the therapist would be postulated. The associative element would also be hypothesized to contain an unconscious fantasy that in all likelihood expresses the patient's own hostility toward the therapist, and is therefore based on both further displacement and projection. Through the total recollection the patient displaces and symbolically represents an unconscious perception of the therapist who has left her and her own unconscious hatred toward the therapist for doing so.

CONSCIOUS FANTASIES OR DAYDREAMS

These expressions may reveal the patient's affective state directly, and may at times contain indications of emotional disturbance. Depending on their manifest content, the fantasy could also represent directly or indirectly other types of indicators. If the fantasy involves the therapist, it may touch upon one or another of the therapist's interventions, and thereby represent an activated adaptive context directly.

Conscious fantasies serve as a vehicle for encoded expression and as elements of the derivative complex. Depending on their specific contents, they may reflect important dynamics and genetics, which must, however, be organized around activated adaptive contexts in terms of unconscious perceptions and fantasies. It is important not to accept a conscious fantasy as a meaningful statement per se. Conscious mental products are neither the language of emotional disturbance nor the means through which the unconscious basis of Neuroses are revealed. They are not the medium of *unconscious* communication. To the extent that they are carriers of derivative meaning, then, they must be subjected to the decoding process.

For example, the patient reports a conscious fantasy about meeting the therapist in a department store. It has already been suggested that the fantasy reflected a wish in the patient to undo the separation, and was a disguised way of representing her (the therapist's) absence, and that the suggestion that the therapist would be upset by such a meeting might have involved a projection of the patient's own sense of upset over the therapist's absence. By and large, this particular conscious fantasy serves as a means of encoding a representation of two indicators (the patient's sense of upset and the therapist's absence), an adaptive context (the therapist's absence), and the patient's own derivative response (the wish to undo the separation). All three elements were thereby served through a single vehicle of expression.

NIGHT DREAMS

Both day and night dreams tend to be strong carriers of encoded communications. It must be recognized, however, that they frequently portray important valid unconscious perceptions of the therapist. In addition, they may serve to express important unconscious fantasies, including their dynamic and genetic aspects.

Freud (1900) offered a basic model of human functioning in which it was recognized that manifest dreams are prompted by day residues—events of the day of the dream. This model of reality stimulus and intrapsychic response has served as the cornerstone of the listening process developed in this section. In place of the day residue, the term adaptive context has been used to emphasize the adaptation-evoking qualities of the stimuli for the patient's experience, reactions, and communications. For the dream, the entirety of the patient's free associations has been substituted. In addition, meaning has been assigned to the surface of the patient's material, as well as to its latent implications.

In principle, the therapist listens to dreams in a manner comparable to that with which he or she attends to all of the patient's material. On a manifest level, depending on the nature of its contents, a dream may reveal important indicators or may represent an activated intervention context through some direct allusion to the therapist. In terms of its derivative functions, a manifest dream may serve as a strong carrier of derivative meanings—dynamics and genetics, perceptions and fantasies.

The patient's dream concerns trying to cross a bridge. There is a reference to returning to her native city. She is with an inadequate man, while her friend is with a successful one. No one will help her to reach her goal of getting across the bridge.

The latent meanings of a dream—perceptions and fantasies—can be identified only in light of activated intervention contexts. Thus, by making use of the adaptive context of the therapist's absence, the patient appears to have unconsciously perceived her loss in terms of a gap that would make it difficult for her to achieve her goal—here, by implication—of completing treatment. The absence appears to have reminded the patient that she has left the city of her birth, and in the dream she returns to that location. This particular manifest element could represent the raw message of a wish within the patient to be reunited with her home city and with her mother (who appears in the next association), as it connects to wishes to be reunited with the therapist.

The balance of the dream could reflect some type of feeling of inadequacy within the patient or a search for a man in the absence of the woman therapist. It could also reflect an unconscious perception of the therapist as having behaved in some masculine way and of being inadequate. Without knowing the nature of the therapist's active and verbal interventions, it is impossible to decide whether these representations are primarily valid unconscious perceptions or distorted unconscious images and fantasies.

Many dreams are filled with evident dynamic and genetic images. Some dreams are, of course, relatively barren of potentially meaningful elements. However, the rich dream has tended to lead therapists toward Type One deriviative formulations of intrapsychic dynamics and genetics, which do not take into account the adaptation-evoking stimuli from the therapist and the context of the therapeutic interaction. There has also been a tendency to consider dreams entirely in terms of unconscious fantasy formations, to the unfortunate neglect of the ways in which they may portray valid unconscious perceptions in encoded form. At times, the pertinent perception or fantasy is stated with little disguise, and the only substantial defence is the use of displacement in order to avoid the direct realization that the raw message involves the therapist.

CREATIVE WORKS

Allusions to the patient's own creations or to those of others tend, by and large, to serve in important ways as carriers of meaningful derivative expressions. Depending on their contents, they may also from time to time directly represent an indicator or an activated adaptive context. They should be subjected to the listening-formulating process.

For example, the patient mentions a television play in which a woman had coffee with her therapist. In the adaptive context of the therapist's absence, this particular communication appears to serve as another encoded representation of the patient's wish to undo the loss of the therapist and to be with her in some type of feeding context. The raw message—the wish to be with and perhaps fed by the therapist—has been subjected to displacement and symbolic representation. There may be additional underlying (encoded) wishes represented here—e.g., a vengeful cannibilistic wish to devour the abandoning therapist. In addition, this particular manifest element may express, in encoded form, an unconscious perception by the patient of the therapist in terms of the latter's own wish to undo the separation experience. Such a perception would have been based, of course, on conscious or unconscious implications of the therapist's interventions. For example, had the therapist suggested a make-up hour, this particular communication regarding the television show would have been an apt symbolic portrayal of the therapist's offer.

SLIPS OF THE TONGUE

Slips of the tongue, not illustrated in the session described, must be subjected to the listening process and understood in light of activated intervention contexts. Both the patient's manifest intention and the erroneous statement must be subjected to analysis and to a search for derivative implications. Quite rarely, a slip of the tongue will represent an indicator or an activated adaptive context. Most often, it serves as a carrier of some derivative meaning, though typically these are difficult to interpret to the patient in light of an activated adaptive context.

PSYCHOLOGICAL AND PHYSICAL SYMPTOMS AND THE PATIENT'S SUBJECTIVE STATE, THOUGHTS, AND REACTIONS

Reports of symptoms tend to constitute one important group of indicators. They do not, however, reveal the unconscious basis for the emotional disturbance. This is especially true for symptomatic responses, which are poor derivative vehicles—perhaps the poorest of all.

Subjective thoughts and reactions may, of course, contain important encoded messages. These may be arrived at through the basic listening-formulating process.

DELIBERATE LIES

Conscious attempts by the patient to falsify and to lie must be noted. Such behaviors are, of course, therapeutic contexts. Sometimes the content of the lie touches upon an image of the therapist that can serve as a means of representing an activated adaptive context.

There are both derivative and nonderivative lies. The former serve as a meaningful vehicle of encoded communication in response to activated adaptive contexts. The latter are relatively devoid of derivative meaning, and serve mainly as barriers to the truth.

SUMMARY AND CONCLUSIONS

The main verbal-affective means through which patients express their therapeutic needs, the adaptation-evoking stimuli that create these needs, and the unconscious meanings and genetic basis for the emotional disturbance involved, have been identified. With all this stress on meaning, it must be recognized that there are some patients who do not express themselves in a manner designed for positive communication. Instead, they make efforts to suppress indicators. They fail to represent important adaptive contexts directly or through derivatives. They associate in a manner virtually devoid of derivative meaning. Such patients wish, then, to destroy meaning and understanding. They prefer either to continue to suffer from their emotional disturbance or to find *relief* through some means other than insightful adaptive structural change.

Behavioral Communications

The therapist, in addition to monitoring the patient's cognitive-affective verbalizations, monitors and examines the nonverbal qualities of the patient's associations and the patient's actual behaviors. In the session just described, for example, the patient slips down in her chair and droops. This suggested to the therapist a sense of depression. Her voice quality alternates between flatness and sadness, further suggesting a depressive affect. At times, the patient fidgits, suggesting the presence of anxiety.

The patient's verbal communnications are experienced in terms of their speed, tone, inflection, syntax, accompanying affect, etcetera. The therapist observes (listens to) the patient's manner of dress, gait and posture, and bodily movements as he or she sits in the chair or lies on the couch. All possible nonverbal qualities are recognized and given a cognitive representation by the therapist.

In addition, there are the patient's overt behaviors. The patient may miss a session or walk out on one. The patient may attack or

attempt to seduce the therapist, or may show or report a symptomatic act. Behaviors with others outside of treatment are also examined. Considerations of both the quality of expression and of the
living out of some aspect of the patient's unconscious fantasies and
perceptions as they pertain to the therapist and therapeuetic interaction are also important.

These actions may serve as a mode of manifest and latent
expression, and must be analyzed in keeping with the usual considerations of manifest meaning and derivative function. In addition,
such actions serve to gratify a variety of unconscious fantasies and
to portray various unconscious perceptions of the therapist. They
satisfy the patient's Neurotic needs, and they may interfere with
other types of expression, especially those that involve verbalization.
As such, then, these actions may have important resistance implications that must be appreciated by the therapist. Thus, in addition to
applying the usual listening-formulating process to these behaviors,
their interpersonal and intrapsychic functions must also be understood.

One final realm of listening-experiencing must also be examined—the interactional and interpersonal pressures generated by the
patient directly and indirectly on the therapist. There may be direct
pressures for the therapist to behave or relate in a particular manner
or to experience himself or herself in a particular way. There may
be implied or latent and encoded pressures on the therapist to adopt
a particular role or self-image. Through indirection, latent meaning, and the accumulated effect of a sequence of associations, the
patient may generate pressures on the therapist to behave in a
particular manner or to experience a particular aspect of the patient's inner mental world. These pressures should be experienced
by the therapist, processed or metabolized to the point of cognitive
formulation, and silently validated through the patient's continuing cognitive associations (see Chapters 13 and 14).

The Means through which the Therapist Listens and Formulates

The therapist experiences the patient in order to generate
responses that will shape the best possible therapeutic relationship
and generate cogent and dynamically meaningful, accurate formulations. These latter are developed at first silently within the

therapist, and tend to involve considerations of two interrelated spheres of intervening: the creation and management of the ground rules and boundaries of the therapeutic relationship (the frame) and interpretation-reconstructions of the patient's material. The patient requires a healthy symbiotic mode of relatedness with the therapist in order for the interpretive work to have its intended effects related to insight and cure. The basic framework-securing (holding) and interpretive efforts are most vital to the formation of a therapeutic symbiosis. A secure background relationship and the sound application of the listening process are essential components of a healthy therapeutic symbiosis.

An attitude of openness, concern, relatively unencumbered experiencing, and neutrality are basic to the therapist's listening process. Part of the mind of the therapist must enter each session without desire, memory, or understanding (Bion 1967, Langs 1978). In this sphere, the therapist's listening is passive and as naive as possible, and the patient is permitted through free associations to promote both recall and fresh formulation. Another part of the therapist's mind, however, enters every session with a background knowledge of the patient, of psychoanalytic theory, and of the therapeutic process. With some sessions the therapist will be aware of an unresolved adaptation-evoking context and anticipate to some extent that the patient will be working over the relevant unsettled issues.

It is difficult to maintain a balanced mode of listening and to properly execute these two contradictory functions (Fenichel 1941). When the therapist's listening begins with relative emptiness, there is the danger of critical delays in recognizing the patient's important manifest and latent communications, and in missing a necessary framework-management or interpretive response. On the other hand, when the therapist enters the session with preconceived ideas, there is the danger of missing activated adaptive contexts and meanings contained within the patient's manifest and latent associations that pertain to issues other than the one on which the therapist is focused. It is therefore especially important to develop careful means of *silent validation* for any formulation developed by the therapist before or during a session, and to protect against the inevitable narcissistic investment therapists have in their own ideas. Interventions to the patient should not be made without such ongoing validation. In addition, the therapist must have the means of deciding upon the extent to which an intervention that is actually offered to the patient obtains confirmation or fails to do so.

Ideally, every session should be its own creation, and the therapist should make use of nothing from previous hours when intervening. In this way the therapist can safeguard against undue influence from preconceived notions, and whenever possible freshly discover both the psychodynamics and genetics of his or her patient's emotional disturbance and the psychoanalytic theory that has been derived from such individual clinical observations.

The listening process is essentially visual and auditory, although it may involve touch, either inadvertently or with a rare but appropriate handshake, such as at the time of the first meeting with the patient. Listening also involves nonsensuous impressions and the experience of interaction with the patient.

Although the listening process is directed primarily to the patient and his or her expressions, it must also be directed toward the therapist's own subjective experiences and interventions. The main goals in listening are to understand the status of the core therapeutic relationship, to be in touch with the patient's emotional disturbances and their manifestations, to prepare and offer interpretations of the underlying factors in this disturbance, and to monitor qualities of the therapist's inner state and work and of the therapeutic setting and hold in order to maintain the therapeutic environment in optimal form. Such efforts require an understanding of both the surface and the depths of the patient's and therapist's communications. All intaking processes and experiences within the therapist should be ultimately metabolized or processed into cognitive understanding and formulation The main means through which the therapist attends to the material from the patient are (1) direct observations of the patient; (2) empathy (emotional knowing); (3) intuition (a form of immediate knowing); (4) the subjective experience of interactional and interpersonal pressures from the patient; and (5) responsive feelings, thoughts, and other reactions.

DIRECT OBSERVATIONS OF THE PATIENT

The therapist observes the patient's behaviors and manner, posture, and style of free associating. This aspect of listening has already been previously discussed above, and will not be pursued further here.

EMPATHY (EMOTIONAL KNOWING)

The therapist attempts to or unconsciously engages in temporary identifications with the patient, which involve the patient's own inner state and the state of internal and external objects (as they are experienced by the patient), including the therapist. The therapist endeavors to stay in touch with the patient's inner state, both affectively and cognitively, including the conflicts, dynamics, genetics, and all aspects of the therapeutic interaction that are of concern. However, a true empathic response involves more than being in touch with and sharing aspects of the patient's surface communications. In psychoanalytic psychotherapy, empathy must also involve the patient's unconscious communications and state, which is often at a variance with conscious expressions. A great deal of the therapist's empathic experiences are accessible immediately to conscious awareness, while other aspects of empathy are experienced more automatically and not immediately understood. However, all such experiences must consistently be processed cognitively by the therapist and metabolized into an understanding of the patient, and secondarily, of the therapist. In principle, all manifest experiences and reactions within the therapist should be understood for their immediate meanings and, in addition, self-analyzed in order to determine additional unconscious and derivative implications. The therapist should not accept surface experiences at face value and as the totality of the implications of inner transactions. The therapist must also arrive at their latent meanings and functions (see below). Further, all such impressions must be subjected fully to the validating process (see Beres and Arlow 1974, Kohut 1959, and Shapiro 1974).

INTUITION (A FORM OF IMMEDIATE KNOWING)

Through temporary identification and other sensory and non-sensory avenues, the therapist develops hunches or experiences a sudden insight into the patient's material. All such formulations should be understood in terms of manifest meaning and then subjected to self-analysis for latent implications. Validation is essential (Beres and Arlow 1974).

THE SUBJECTIVE EXPERIENCE OF INTERACTIONAL AND INTERPERSONAL PRESSURES FROM THE PATIENT

The therapist will experience aspects of the patient's inner mental world—fantasies, defenses, etcetera—that the patient attempts interactionally to place or dump into the therapist through projective identification. All such experiences have manifest meaning, but must be subjected to self-analysis and a search for deeper implications as well. The effort must be made to sort out that portion of the therapist's subjective experience that derives from efforts of the patient and that aspect that is experienced primarily because of the therapist's own internal fantasies and needs. All such experiences are clearly interactional products of varying proportions in regard to these two sources. In addition, the specific meaning of the experience for both the therapist and the patient must be arrived at through self-analysis. In all such efforts, it is important to attend to the adaptation-evoking context and the patient's behaviors and associations, and to make use of both the patient's ongoing material and the therapist's own subjective efforts to arrive at a correct and validated formulation. Of special importance is the confirmation of these subjective impressions in the manifest and especially latent (derivative) material from the patient.

The patient will attempt to establish a particular mode of relatedness with the therapist. In addition, efforts are made to have the therapist behave in certain ways, adopt particular roles, and experience himself or herself in terms of a variety of self-images. The patient may express these pressures directly, as when a patient specifically asks the therapist for advice and support; however, they may also be expressed indirectly and thorugh derivative communications, as when a patient becomes relatively nonfunctional, and thereby implicitly pressures the therapist to assume a so-called supportive role. The therapist should experience these pressures as signal experiences that do not evoke responsive behaviors and projective identifications. These signal experiences should then be metabolized and understood in terms of their sources within both participants to treatment, and in terms of their manifest and underlying meanings and functions. Sound interpretive and framework management responses should follow when needed.

RESPONSIVE FEELINGS, THOUGHTS, AND OTHER REACTIONS

While listening to the patient the therapist may experience a particular affect or an intrusive thought or fantasy. The therapist may move in a certain way or have a particular impulse. At times he or she may even act in idiosyncratic fashion. All such reactions are a part of the therapeutic interaction. They must be processed and understood in terms of their meanings for the therapist and for what they reveal about the therapeutic interaction and the patient. No matter how disturbed or disturbing such a response may be on the surface level, since it is in some measure a reaction to adaptation-evoking stimuli from the patient, it can be processed to yield some measure of understanding of the patient's inner state, relationship with the therapist, and cognitive communications.

The Basic Model of Self-analysis

When the therapist experiences an intrusive thought or fantasy subjectively, these should be submitted to self-analysis. Both their manifest attributes and latent implications are then used to understand and resolve possible countertransferences, and especially to understand material from the patient. Here, too, efforts at validation are essential (Beres and Arlow 1974). Release into action should be avoided if at all possible, though the use of language (words) for action-discharge is sometimes difficult to control.

Through a synthesis of information derived from all possible incoming sources, the therapist begins to develop a silent formulation of the most cogent meanings of the patient's material. At the same time, these experiences are used to identify and to formulate the underlying basis for possible countertransferences and, in addition, for indications of sound and effective functioning within the therapist. The basic model of self-analysis is applied to all silent cognitive formulations and interventions of the therapist. The essential steps are these:

1. *A review of the manifest meanings and implication of the formulation, intervention, or subjective experience at hand.*
2. *An in-depth evaluation of the adaptation-evoking qualities of the patient's material.* Stress is placed on the most immediate precipitants for the therapist's formulation and inner experience.

3. *The use of the patient's ongoing associations and their manifest and latent contents as commentaries on the intervention, formulation, or experience.* Even when the therapist has not intervened, the patient's continuing associations are in some way in interaction with the therapist's subjective state and thinking. In particular, the derivative implications of the patient's material, understood in light of adaptation-evoking contexts from the therapist, can provide important sources of supplementary insight into the therapist's own thinking and experiencing. In addition, the offer of a specific intervention constitutes an adaptive context to which the patient reacts in terms of both validation or its lack, and with an extensive conscious and unconscious commentary on the implications of the intervention. Properly understood, then, the patient's material serves as an important source of information regarding the therapist's own inner transactions.

4. *The cognitive evaluation and reevaluation of the therapist's subjective experiences.* The therapist brings to bear his or her understanding of the patient, of himself or herself as therapist, and more broadly, of and psychoanalytic thinking on the formulation or inner experience. These are supplementary tools to further the therapist's conception of these inner experiences in light of the ongoing therapeutic interaction. At times, the therapist will note cognitive errors and other deficiencies in his or her thinking. At other moments, the therapist will discover cognitive support in unexpected quarters that must, of course, be supplemented by derivative support from the patient. Still, the therapist engages in continual cognitive reappraisals of all silent formulations and actual interventions, as well as of any other subjective experience.

Critical to these efforts is the application of the validating process to all silent formulations and interventions to the patient. Nonvalidation must serve as a signal for reformulation. In addition, any sense of subjective disturbance calls for a reexamination of the therapist's cognitive understanding, as well as for a search for unconscious countertransference constellations.

Summary and Conclusions

As is true of every aspect of psychotherapy, the listening process is an interactional product with sources in both the therapist and the patient. The therapist's capacity for unencumbered listening is founded upon the personal resolution of countertransferences, and the ability to create a healthy therapeutic symbiosis and secure therapeutic setting with and for the patient. These same qualities help to determine the nature of the communications from the patient that the therapist will have available for listening and formulating. In turn, the therapist's specific interventions further influence the patient's associations, while the nature of the patient's material will, in turn, influence important qualities in the therapist's listening and formulating.

Although the therapist must therefore bear the greater responsibility for his or her listening-formulating capacities, the patient too plays an important role in this regard. There are some patients who foster the therapist's use of empathy and intuition, and his or her ability to generate valid formulations and interventions. Others greatly disturb these capabilities through their behaviors, the nature of the basic relationship they seek, and the types of associations they offer. Similarly, there is much in the therapist's basic approach to the patient that will influence both how the patient communicates and the ways in which he or she responds to the therapist's interventions.

The patient makes use of a wide variety of expressions, verbal and nonverbal or behavioral. In psychoanalytic psychotherapy, all such expressions must be understood in terms of both manifest and latent meanings and functions.

The therapist makes use of a wide variety of capabilities in listening to and formulating the material from the patient. These must be geared, however, to both the manifest and latent implications of the patient's expressions.

The basic listening-formulating process may be characterized as (1) listening-experiencing and intaking, through which vague and general impressions, verbal and nonverbal, are experienced (a period of random and unorganized taking-in that may be accompanied by fragmented efforts at formulation and understanding); (2) attempts at synthesis and formulation (involving the generation of a silent hypothesis that must then be subjected to silent validation— i.e., to a study of whether the patient's continuing associations offer direct and especially derivative support for the formulation at hand); (3) a definitive silent and tentative formulation-intervention, once validated silently, which may be offered by the therapist at an appropriate moment to the patient; (4) examination of the patient's material for responsive indirect (Type Two derivative) validation or its lack (this material is also taken as a commentary on the therapist's intervention; the focus is primarily on the patient's derivative expressions, and they are taken first as sound and valid perceptions and reactions to the therapist's effort, and second, there is a search for distorted responses to the intervention on the manifest and derivative levels); and (5) fresh, open listening if an interpretation has been validated (or listening geared to reformulation if nonconfirmation has taken place). These efforts have been separated artificially for purposes of exposition. They may occur sequentially in a session, or the therapist may shift repeatedly back and forth from open listening to attempts at synthesis and formulation.

The listening process should also be geared to an examination of the manifest and latent meanings and functions of the therapist's subjective reactions, inner thoughts and fantasies, cognitive formulations, and interventions to the patient. It is essential that these not be taken simply at face value, and that they be understood in terms of their functions as a carrier—more or less—of derivative messages and meanings. In this way the therapist is able to understand both the conscious and unconscious communications that he or she offers to the patient. It is then also possible to identify those ideal formulations and interventions that are sound on a manifest level and that convey relatively little in the way of contradictory unconscious communications.

In psychotherapy, the goal is to enable the patient to express himself or herself meaningfully on both the manifest level and derivative levels. To the contrary, the therapist strives to express himself or herself meaningfully on a manifest level to the greatest extent feasible, leaving little to disruptive unconscious communication. The therapist requires the patient's derivative communications in order to intervene, while the patient's therapeutic needs are best served by meaningful manifest interventions from the therapist that are not in any major way contradicted through unconscious expressions. Thus the therapist must not only be correct in his or her formulation and intervention, but also must relate to the patient and express himself or herself otherwise in a manner that creates a healthy background therapeutic symbiosis.

The therapist's constant search for meaning and for an understanding of both the patient and of himself or herself must be pliable enough to leave room for the recognition of situations in which the patient is expressing himself or herself in a manner that is designed for the absence or destruction of both meaning and understanding. Similarly, the therapist should be capable of recognizing those of his or her own formulations and interventions that serve functionally to destroy meaning and understanding, and that are designed as lie-barrier systems to obliterate disturbing underlying truths. The development of a sound listening-formulating process with specific criteria for meaning and its absence enables the therapist to more readily identify interludes in which destruction of meaning plays a significant role.

Chapter 7

Manifest Contents

Psychotherapy is founded upon the unique and adaptive capacity of the human mind to express a multiplicity of meanings simultaneously through a single manifest communication. On the therapist's side, psychotherapy tends to be hindered because the human mind also tends to operate as simply as possible and to adhere to surface meanings. This tendency requires of the therapist a special capability of shifting from concrete to abstract and metaphorical thinking, and to develop understanding through indirect rather than direct formulations.

The Roles and Functions of Manifest Contents

The patient's manifest associations carry information of considerable importance to psychotherapy. They contain the manifestations of the patient's emotional disturbance and adaptive resources, and other types of data that the therapist hopes to monitor. Although the surface material does not reveal the unconscious implications of such data, these surface landmarks provide the critical indicators of disturbance that point the therapist toward areas in need of deeper understanding. In a sense, many of these surface phenomena are like the tips of icebergs that signal areas in need of deeper probing.

The following excerpt is taken from early in the hour of a first session with a young man in his late 20s who made the appointment for his first session at a clinic with the therapist's secretary.

Patient: I feel agitated, anxious, and unhappy. I've got this job I don't like, but I'm sticking with it for now. I don't like my boss. His secretary runs the show. I bought this car and it was damaged. I've been having problems with my wife. Her sister keeps interfering in our business. *(Becomes silent.)* I don't feel much like working. After I called you, I went to see my girlfriend. I'm not happy about having affairs. My father had a mistress for many years. My wife is a cold fish. I get angry with her pretty easily. Your secretary sounded cold on the telephone. I want therapy, but I may decide to just get the hell out of this city any day now. Why are you so quiet? Why don't you ask me some questions?

The evident meanings of this manifest material should, of course, be considered. However, an attempt must also be made to identify the encoded messages. Both aspects of the material are analyzed in the following sections.

SURFACE EXPRESSIONS OF EMOTIONAL DISTURBANCE AND NEUROTIC FUNCTIONING

In a given session, allusions by the patient to characterological disturbances become the therapeutic contexts that serve as second-order organizers of associational material. These are active expressions of emotional disturbance, and the goal in a particular hour is to identify the adaptive context that has evoked the Neurotic response and the derivative complex that explains its unconscious basis.

The most evident and symptomatic expressions of the patient's emotionally maladaptive reactions are relevant. This is an important group of indicators for intervention. It includes both psychological and emotionally-founded somatic symptoms, and other types of evidence of major characterological difficulties. It involves as well behaviors with evident disruptive qualities for either the patient or others. In this context, the identification of Neurotic symptoms and behaviors involves necessary clinical, subjective judgments by the therapist.

In the session above, this type of manifest content is illustrated in the patient's allusions to feeling agitated, anxious, and unhappy. It is suggested in his visit to his girlfriend, especially in light of his own dissatisfaction with his involvement with her. It appears too when he mentions getting angry easily, and is suggested in his thoughts of sudden flight from the city in which he is living.

REFLECTIONS OF THE PATIENT'S CHARACTER STRUCTURE, EGO FUNCTIONING, DRIVE EXPRESSIONS, SELF-IMAGE, PERSONALITY, AND ADAPTIVE OR POSITIVE FUNCTIONING

To the extent that these factors are nonneurotic, they do not require intervention. Nonetheless, the therapist must monitor the patient's capabilities as reflected in the surface descriptions of inner feelings and daily interpersonal transactions. However, attention also must focus on the patient's nonmanifest (and usually unconscious) capabilities, and on the capacity for unconscious communication—attributes latent to his or her manifest associations. The therapist must be aware of the patient's positive capabilities, areas within which ego functioning is sound, and ways in which the patient is functioning adaptively both in outside life and within treatment—the latter usually subsumed under the concept of the therapeutic or working alliance. These important surface attributes must be identified without losing sight of their unconscious components and basis.

The patient mentions that he continues to work even though he doesn't like his boss. This is a sign of some measure of ego resource. His evident cooperation with the therapist and ability to maintain a flow of seemingly meaningful communication on the surface are other positive signs.

THE SURFACE ATTRIBUTES OF THE PATIENT'S RELATIONSHIPS WITH THOSE OUTSIDE OF THERAPY

On the surface, there is often considerable information regarding the patient's basic mode and level of object relationship with persons outside of therapy. The therapist must study the patient's manifest material for signs of healthy and pathological symbioses, autistic withdrawal, parasiticism, and commensal modes of relatedness (see Chapters 13 and 32). Other important dimensions of object relatedness include the degree of the patient's consideration for others, his or her handling of the framework and boundaries of relationships, the type of instinctual drive gratifications involved, the state of his or her capacity for delay and for indirect satisfactions, etcetera. The therapist must then integrate these observations with those related to the patient's relationship with himself or herself (see below).

The patient describes problems with his wife—an evidently conflicted object relationship. There is a sense of either parasiticism or pathological symbiosis in the allusion to his affair, qualities that would require clarification based on additional material. The patient's object relationships appear to involve immediate discharge of both sexual and aggressive instinctual drive wishes, as reflected in his affair and in his easy anger with his wife. There may also be a sense of a disregard for the needs of others (e.g., his wife) as reflected in his affair, and some type of problem in maintaining extended object relationships in his thoughts about leaving the city. All of these impressions would require clarification and validation, since the present material is insufficient for clear-cut formulations in this regard.

To the extent that the patient's object relationships are disturbed and infused with psychopathology, their manifestations in a given session are important indicators for intervention.

THE STATUS OF THE PATIENT'S LIFE SITUATION AND EXTERNAL REALITIES

The patient's manifest associations provide considerable information in regard to the other people in the patient's life.

At times, life crises form important indicators, in that the patient will respond with emotional disturbance or other maladaptive reactions. Contrary to common belief, patients seldom react to external traumas and crises with encoded communication that is meaningfully related to their Neuroses. By and large, such material serves mainly as carriers of encoded or derivative expressions. On occasion, a major life trauma, such as the death of a family member, may prompt meaningful derivative communication. As a rule, however, interpretations pertinent to the patient's Neurosis may be made only when the patient's reactions to the outside trauma are linked up in some way to an activated adaptive context within the treatment situation.

In this session, the patient refers to his job problem, his damaged car, and his thoughts of leaving the city. These all touch on his external life circumstances.

ALLUSIONS TO PAST ACTIONS, BEHAVIORS, AND RELATIONSHIPS, INCLUDING EARLY CHILDHOOD EXPERIENCES

There is, of course, importance to the patient's past life and early childhood experiences. However, manifest references of this kind are surface allusions, and tend to be available as isolated genetic elements. At times, their connection to an emotional disturbance within the patient is self-evident. This is illustrated in the present session when the patient reports his own affair and then recalls the affairs of his father. The connection between the two is transparent on the surface.

It has been difficult for therapists to recognize the linear and manifest qualities of this type of genetic material, and of the connection between present behaviors in the patient and past behaviors in others. Although there is clearly a tie between the present and past in these situations, realizations of this kind do little to help patients find symptom relief. The insights involved are highly intellectualized, entirely manifest, and divorced dynamically from the therapeutic interaction that is mobilizing the patient's meaningful responses to adaptive stimuli. They are attractive transparencies, which serve mainly as lie-barrier systems directed against the more threatening derivative meanings and functions embodied in such material. The internal mechanisms that create emotional disturbances within patients, and the means by which they communicate about these difficulties, are always encoded and subjected to primary process mechanisms. They do not appear on a manifest level or emerge through self-evident inferences. This is also true when the patient makes a manifest statement about the therapist and then makes a comparable statement regarding an earlier genetic figure.

In all, then, this type of information is of importance in developing a general appreciation for the early sources and manifestations of the patient's Neurosis. However, the manifest listening to this kind of association does not reveal its derivative meanings nor the unconscious basis for emotional disturbance. It therefore cannot be used as the basis for interpretation or framework-management responses by the therapist.

Most often, allusions to genetic figures of this type serve the derivative function of identifying the earlier person who is connected to an ongoing interactional experience with the therapist. This link-up, however, may take one of two forms: either (1) the therapist is currently behaving in a manner comparable to the earlier person (nontransference); or (2) the therapist is behaving quite differently from that person, and the patient, through intrapsychic need and distortion, is nonetheless inappropriately viewing the therapist in such terms (transference). Simple surface considerations will virtually never enable the therapist to make this absolutely critical distinction.

DIRECT COMMENTS ABOUT THE THERAPIST, THE TREATMENT SITUATION, PERSONS RELATED TO THERAPY, AND OTHER COMPARABLE MATTERS

Patients will comment frequently or infrequently on the therapist and the therapeutic experience. They will also react directly to the therapist and behave in a variety of ways in their sessions. This material may be monitored as a means of determining the status of the *manifest* alliance between the patient and therapist. Such allusions reflect the nature of the patient's object relationship with the therapist, and may include observations by the patient of how the therapist in turn is relating to him or her. There may be direct comments regarding a noticed difficulty in the therapist or about an apparently helpful intervention. There may be other direct perceptions or manifestly stated fantasies. These are manifest allusions to the therapist. As such, they are devoid of encoding, and do not constitute communications through which the underlying basis of an emotional disturbance within the patient may be clarified and understood. Thus such allusions, considered manifestly, are not transference, since that particular category of reactions is based on *unconscious* and distorted fantasies about the therapist, which appear in the patient's material in encoded form. Similarly, they are not inherently nontransference manifestations, since valid perceptions of the therapist that relate to the patient's Neurosis also tend to be encoded by the patient.

On the surface, manifest allusions to the therapist and therapy serve as a guide to the surface alliance, and to the patient's *conscious* perceptions of and fantasies about the therapist. They may involve signs of evident disturbance in the patient who on the surface appears to be reacting in strange or inappropriate ways to the therapist—a subjective evaluation that must be clarified in light of the therapist's own interventions and the unconscious interaction. This type of manifest material may also reflect ways in which the patient has consciously detected difficulties within the therapist. These realizations of disturbance, whether within the patient or within the therapist, are among the most important indicators for intervention to appear in the course of a session. Still, the interpretive or framework-management response by the therapist requires the use of derivatives, and must extend beyond the manifest level.

A special group of behaviors in the patient and reactions to the therapist may be identified as part of this category of manifest material. They involve gross behavioral resistances: manifest behaviors of the patient that are disruptive to the goals of therapy and to the treatment process itself. They appear as silences, lateness, absences, and the like, and may include direct opposition to the therapist's interventions. It is important, however, to determine the unconscious basis of gross behavioral resistances, since these obstacles to therapy are often interactional products with important contributions from the therapist. Whatever the underlying basis, gross behavioral resistances are important indicators for intervention. Quite often, they involve efforts by the patient to alter the basic framework of the therapeutic relationship and treatment process.

Manifest allusions to the therapist and therapy serve a critical function. They are the means through which the patient may refer directly and in passing to an activated adaptive context that is a determinant of both an emotional disturbance and a highly meaningful derivative complex (which, in turn, helps to clarify the underlying basis of the symptom). This type of manifest allusion provides the critical link between the patient's displaced and derivative expressions, which on the surface usually do not at all refer to the therapist, and the adaptation-evoking context that has evoked the Neurosis-related communicative and symptomatic reactions within the patient. Without this essential element, the therapist has no choice but to remain silent or to become engaged in a selected playback of derivative reactions to the unmentioned adaptation-evoking context. It is a sign of low resistance when a patient alludes to the adaptive context manifestly and in passing.

In this session, the patient refers directly to the therapist's secretary, who had made the appointment with him for the first session. In this way, he represents manifestly a critical adaptive context: a third party to the treatment. Had he not done so, the therapist would have been left with only encoded representations of this context, as seen in the allusion to the sister of the patient's wife who interferes with their marriage. On a more disguised level, the patient's girlfriend may also represent the therapist's secretary. These are encoded representations that could be used in a playback of selected derivatives, though by themselves they lack a definitive and ideal manifest connection or link to the therapist and the treatment situation.

The patient also mentions the therapist directly, referring to his failure to ask questions and to his relative silence. There is also a gross behavioral resistance when the patient himself becomes silent. Each of the manifest allusions to the therapist and treatment situation are important indicators. However, only the therapist's relative silence and the allusion to the secretary are representations of adaptation-evoking contexts; the balance of the material in this hour could well be organized as derivative expressions that reveal the patient's responses to these important intervention contexts.

Summary and Conclusions

The patient's manifest associations provide a large measure of storage information (as contrasted with dynamically active information, which involves the ongoing therapeutic interaction). They reveal a great deal of the patient's present and past functioning, object relationships, self-image, etcetera.

Manifest contents may also reveal surface or evident links between the manifest elements themselves, and between the present and the past. A reading of manifest communications may also generate highly apparent inferences that could easily obtain a consensus of agreement among observers. Although these manifest connections and direct implications have some measure of meaning, they tend to involve quite general and highly intellectualized formulations. They may reflect signs of emotional disturbance, but do not reveal its underlying basis.

There appears to be a human tendency among patients and

therapists alike to attend to, formulate, and react in terms of manifest exchanges. The hypotheses involved tend to be simplistic and easily stated. In general, they serve both participants to treatment as lie-barrier systems, designed to defend against and cover over the more complex, threatening, and latent meanings of the patient's material. There is strong evidence that the patient is protected in this way from highly disturbing unconscious perceptions and fantasies; similarly, the therapist is protected against the more primitive and frightening aspects of the patient's expressions, and against painful realizations related to his or her own psychopathology and countertransference-based inputs into the treatment situation. Because of these tendencies, a therapist must engage in considerable self-scrutiny, self-analysis, and conscious effort to maintain a therapeutic approach that involves the patient's manifest associations as a point of departure for the therapeutic work, and moves then into a sound comprehension of the implications of the patient's derivative material.

Beyond its general informational value, then, there are three main functions of the patient's manifest material in psychotherapy:

1. *To convey directly the presence of an emotional disturbance within the patient or therapist, or within the therapeutic interaction.* These are manifest expressions of indicators for intervening—therapeutic contexts. The therapist's interpretive efforts are consistently geared toward identifying the adaption-evoking stimuli that either simultaneously also constitute an indicator (i.e., when there is an expressed disturbance in the therapist) or that have prompted the emotional disturbance of the patient. To this is added the patient's derivative reaction, which explains both the unconscious basis for the emotional disturbance as perceived or experienced by the patient, and the patient's reactions to the activated intervention context.

2. *To represent activated intervention contexts.* Such representations facilitate the therapist's interpretive and framework-management responses. They provide a fulcrum for these efforts and a clear link between the derivative material and the therapeutic interaction and relationship.

3. *To function as carriers of encoded or derivative communications from the patient* (unconscious dynamics, genetics, fantasy-memories, and perceptions)—the unconscious basis for emotional disturbance.

Psychotherapy that takes place on a manifest content level fails by definition to deal with unconscious processes and contents within the patient. As such, it does not meet the definition of psychoanalytic psychotherapy (despite its common usage). This type of therapeutic effort tends to be manipulative, seemingly supportive, quite superficial, and to involve self-evident links to the past. It tends to involve highly intellectualized and simplistic formulations, and often makes use of clichés. It tends to be focused primarily on manifest intrapsychic processes within the patient, and virtually never considers the therapist and the ongoing therapeutic interaction. When it does attend to these factors, it does so in terms of manifest expression, and excludes unconscious factors within the therapist and the unconscious communication between the two participants to treatment. This type of treatment effort is often designed as a pretense for therapy, and involves the use of massive lie-barrier systems designed to exclude the unconscious dimension of treatment that exists within the patient, therapist, and therapeutic interaction. As such, it may at times actually provide the patient with temporary symptom relief. It cannot, however, do so on the basis of insight into unconscious conflicts, fantasies, and perceptions.

It is encumbent upon the therapist to examine first the level of communication at which his formulations are made. When these are developed in terms of the patient's manifest associations, the therapist can be only dealing meaningfully with signs of disturbance (indicators) and representations of adaptation-evoking contexts. At such moments, he or she is not attending to underlying and unconscious factors. A second and critical step is required: attention to the patient's derivative material.

CLINICAL EXAMPLE

The patient is a young woman who has shown marked improvement in her depressive symptomatology during therapy. The therapist, and to a lesser extent, the patient herself, has begun to consider the termination of her treatment. The therapist shares a waiting room with Dr. A., and the two of them also share a secretary.

Patient: I'm depressed and mad at you. I don't feel like talking. (Silence.) You keep pushing me toward being independent.

You won't discuss things with me on the telephone, and you tell me to wait for my session. You took away the Kleenex so I won't cry. Instead of calling you, I ended up talking to myself. But then I wanted to take a few drinks. Dr. A.'s wife must have a cleaning woman so she can go off and do what she wants. I clean my own house, hold down a job, and pay for my own therapy. We should eliminate therapists and doctors. We should solve our own problems. I wish I could meet someone in the waiting room who would ask me about you. I'd tell them to go away and save their time and money.

In each session the therapist must scan the manifest contents of the patient's associations and pay considerable attention to the presence of indicators and representations of active-adaptive contexts. Other types of storage information also must be monitored. These efforts alternate with those that involve decoding the manifest elements in respect to their derivative meanings.

In regard to information storage, it may be recognized that this patient is, on the surface, struggling with consciously perceived pressures from the therapist to establish a state of relative autonomy, and it seems likely that issues of separation and individuation are active at this time. There is some indication of the patient's sound capacity to cope in her allusion to talking to herself, and more so in the references to the way in which she cleans her house, holds down a job, and pays for her own therapy. There is also her comment about how people should solve their own problems. No genetic material is available in this excerpt.

Signs of emotional disturbance and indicators include the patient's depression, her anger at the therapist, her wanting not to talk, and her actual silence—a gross behavioral resistance. There is a sense that the surface alliance between the patient and therapist has been disrupted. There are thoughts of getting rid of the therapist and of wanting to carry out some type of vengeful action toward him—the wish to tell everybody in the waiting room to go away and save their time and money. Finally, there is a sense of jealousy or envy of Dr. A.'s wife, a disturbance indirectly related to treatment.

In all, the patient is conveying manifestly a sense of conflict, struggle, and symptom within herself, and is suggesting directly that there is some problem in what the therapist has been doing. These are powerful indicators, in that they involve signs of emotional disturbance in the patient and suggestions of countertransference difficulties in the therapist. However, on this level, it is impossible to tell whether this conscious and direct perception of the therapist as having difficulties is well-founded or greatly distorted by the patient's own pathological needs. In one sense, then, it is impossible to tell whether this is a series of essentially nontransference-based or transference-based expressions. The manifest observations of the therapist and a fantasy about him are there, but the unconscious meanings of this material are not in evidence.

In attending to manifest content, the therapist will often make self-evident inferences in terms of the meaning of the patient's material and the connection between one element and another. For example, in this session, the patient may have been frustrated by having had to wait and in being unable to discuss things with the therapist on the telephone. Her wish to take a few drinks indicates that she was upset, and the allusion to Dr. A.'s wife suggests that the patient was either jealous or envious. The presence of pride in the patient's achievements and anger in her thoughts about eliminating therapists and doctors are noted. There is a sense of opposition to independence at the beginning of the hour, and of an acceptance of relative autonomy toward the end of the session, when the patient alludes to how people should solve their own problems. Finally, the wish to tell another patient to go away and save his or her time and money speaks for vengence against the therapist.

These relatively transparent inferences may be rather simple or more complex. If strict distinctions are maintained, these inferences must be termed *nonmanifest messages,* and therefore part of the latent content of this material. However, shadings extend from the surface into the first level of inference, and the term *inference derivative* is more appropriate for those manifest elements treated in this way to yield self-evident or speculative implications. Although, strictly speaking, manifest content listening is restricted to the surface of the patient's material, in actual practice, it is virtually always accompanied by some small or large measure of inference-making.

The same line of thought applies to direct associative links. This patient's depression might be connected in some way with her anger toward her therapist. This in turn would be connected in some way to issues of dependence and independence. All of this would be connected to the patient's wanting to take a few drinks and to her resentment of Dr. A.'s wife, who has a cleaning woman. All of this would then be connected to ways in which the patient functions well, to her thoughts of eliminating therapists, and to her need to solve her own problems. Finally, there is a connection in some way to wanting to tell another of the therapist's patients to go away and save his or her time and money.

In all, it is possible to suggest some seemingly meaningful manifest connections in this material. For example, the connection between the patient's depression and her anger at the therapist, which is directly stated at the beginning of the hour, hints at a common psychodynamic factor in depression: the turning of aggression toward others against the self. Similarly, a connection between pressures from the therapist toward autonomy in the patient and the patient's reaction of both depression and anger may be identified. These in turn could be used in a surface way to understand the patient's wish to drink, though here more extended speculation would be necessary as to the meaning of the drinking—i.e., whether it constitutes a turning of aggression against the self, a way of becoming dependent and needy, an expression of depression, or whatever.

These are the type of formulations made by therapists who work in terms of manifest contents, their most evident implications, and the apparent links between surface associations. They have a certain dynamic quality, and tend to be rather intellectualized, superficial, and simplistic. The reasoning involved tends to be linear, and often fails to distinguish between stimulus (adaptive context) and response. Yet, it may at times, as in this vignette, make use of such sequential thinking, though it does so in a very limited fashion. The interpretation of these superficial dynamics does little if anything to insightfully resolve a patient's Neurosis.

Chapter 8

Latent Contents

The resolution of a patient's Neurosis requires a complex mode of treatment that takes into account both the manifest and latent levels of the patient's associations and behaviors. In many ways, the proper and timely decoding of the patient's derivative communications is the most difficult and yet one of the most important tasks that a psychotherapist must face.

Type One and Type Two Derivatives

THE ABSTRACTING-PARTICULARIZING PROCESS

The patient's communications pertaining to emotional disturbance virtually always entail adaptive reactions to the therapist and to the therapeutic setting and experience. Thus all truly meaningful efforts at decoding the patient's derivative communications must be carried out in light of the ongoing therapeutic interaction. It is quite possible to engage in types of decoding that do not take this interaction into account; however, these endeavors cannot reveal the presently active dynamic-genetic meanings of the patient's Neurosis. They may at times touch upon such meanings in an isolated, nondynamic, type of statement; if so, they require an identification of the adaptive stimulus within treatment for completeness. More often, however, formulations developed without due regard for the therapeutic interaction are isolated statements of little or no pertinence to the *active* unconscious conflicts, fantasies, memories, perceptions, and introjects that form the actual unconscious basis for an ongoing emotional difficulty within the patient. These conceptions are sometimes quite inaccurate and erroneous. At other moments, they may be truthful statements of psychodynamic and genetic propositions that serve the therapist *functionally* within the therapeutic interaction as fictions, lies, and barriers to the truth. Such statements are inherently attractive in that they involve otherwise truthful propositions, are easily arrived at through psychoanalytic theory and through postulates that involve the psychodynamics and intrapsychic state of the patient, and because they serve admirably as a means of denying disturbing and pathological, countertransference-based adaptation-evoking stimuli from the therapist and the patient's consequent unconscious perceptions. Their existence serves as a warning that psychodynamic statements and formulations may serve either as a way of departing from the interactional truths of the moment in psychotherapy or as a basis for moving toward and correctly identifying such truths. This last is possible only when the entirety of the therapist's attitudes and interventions are taken fully into account.

Technically, then, the fact that a therapist has generated a dynamic formulation in no way guarantees its validity. The same group of associations from a patient can be formulated by a therapist as reflecting an intrapsychic fantasy, a valid unconscious perception of the therapist, or a specific response to an intervention context. Each of these formulations receives its ultimate test when it forms the basis of an actual intervention to the patient. Only those efforts that begin with the conscious and unconscious implications of the therapist's interventions, and then organize the specific derivative meanings of the patient's material as responses to these adaptation-evoking contexts, obtain indirect, Type Two derivative, psychoanalytic validation when offered to patients. Further, it is this type of indirect confirmation that leads to symptom relief based on true insight. Because of this, the crucial distinction between isolated formulations of dynamics and genetics (Type One derivative formulations) and propositions made in light of the therapist's interventions and the therapeutic interaction (Type Two derivative formulations) must be established.

CLINICAL PERSPECTIVE

The difference between Type One and Type Two derivative formulations may become apparent through the vignette presented at the end of the previous chapter. It is possible to suggest a number of different Type One derivative formulations based on that particular excerpt. First, a series of inference derivative formulations of the kind cited at the end of the previous chapter could be constructed. For example, the patient's impression that the therapist won't discuss things with her on the telephone may be seen by her as a form of rejection, and possibly even abandonment. Her proposal that therapists should be eliminated could imply anger toward the therapist, and perhaps murderous feelings as well. It could also imply thoughts by the patient of leaving therapy, just as the fantasy about telling another patient to go away implies vengence on and desertion of the therapist.

Each of these formulations attempts to describe some aspect of the patient's intrapsychic state, her feelings and impulses, and in some limited way, her fantasies. Much of this work is highly intellectualized and lacking in *specific images*. Almost all Type One derivative formulations involve the patient's inner mental world and fantasy-memory constellations. They are virtually never developed around encoded perceptions of the therapist, though it is possible to do so. Such a Type One derivative formulation would therefore involve the therapist, but would state the formulation in terms of the patient's inner needs and the perceptions that they cause. It would not be developed in terms of the stimulus of an adaptive context and the patient's unconscious perceptions on the basis of the implications of the intervention context; to do so would involve a shift to Type Two derivative formulations.

Even when Type One derivative formulations involve feelings and fantasies toward the therapist, they are not organized around the details of the ongoing therapeutic interaction. Instead, they are statements of the patient's intrapsychic state as directed toward the therapist and treatment. This quality renders them noninteractional and nondynamic, and available to serve as lie-barrier systems.

Other Type One derivative formulations involve image derivative hypotheses. These impressions are stated in terms of specific unconscious fantasy-memory constellations. They are often founded on a knowledge of psychoanalytic theory, and may include some understanding of the personal life history of the patient. These formulations are therefore couched in the type of unconscious language that is characteristic of the unconscious basis of the patient's emotional disturbances. Nonetheless, they are not valid formulations, in that they omit any consideration of the adaptation-evoking context from the therapist. Because such formulations have been so attractive to therapists and are so prominent in the literature, it is important that their true nature and functions be understood. A careful distinction must be maintained between this type of hypothesis and a Type Two derivative formulation.

In the vignette, a Type One derivative formulation might be generated to the effect that this patient is split: on the one hand, she is striving for independence and autonomy (as represented by the allusion to the way in which she cleans her house, holds down a job, and pays for her own therapy); on the other hand, she is frightened by such autonomy and stands opposed to it (as reflected in her anger at the therapist for pushing her in this direction). As a representation of the patient's intrapsychic state, the manifest allusion to the patient's resentment of the therapist for pushing her toward independence may be formulated entirely in self-representational terms: part of the patient is pushing herself toward independence and part of her stands opposed to it. This would then be postulated as a form of intrapsychic conflict.

Another Type One derivative formulation would suggest that the patient is also divided in regard to her wish to cry. The tears could be proposed to represent a urinary fantasy of soiling the therapist or the patient herself. The allusion to drinking liquor could similarly symbolize oral incorporative wishes that have self-destructive qualities. The reference to the cleaning woman and to the patient cleaning her own house could be postulated to involve anal impulses involving cleanliness and the repudiation of dirt. The image of meeting someone in the waiting room and telling the person to go away could symbolize an intrauterine fantasy of meeting a rival within the claustrum and wishing to destroy him or her.

In each of these Type One derivative formulations, no attention is paid to adaptation-evoking stimuli from the therapist. Instead, these hypotheses take the form of formulations related to the intrapsychic state and dynamics of the patient. If, in addition, it were learned that the patient had a sister who was three years her junior, a genetic dimension could be added to some of these derivative formulations. For example, it could then be suggested that the intrauterine rival is specifically the patient's sister, and that the material reflects hostile and envious wishes directed toward her. This thesis might even find support in the patient's envy of Dr. A.'s wife. However, studies show that all such formulations, unless they are linked to the ongoing therapeutic interaction, involve theoretical truths, which serve functionally as lie-barrier systems that conceal a more pertinent and dynamic set of truths pertaining to the therapeutic interaction.

Type One derivative formulations rely upon selected facets of the more valid Type Two derivative decoding process. In Type One derivative decoding, the main underlying thesis is that the patient's manifest associations reflect and contain representations of intrapsychic conflicts, fantasies, and memories in disguised form. The use of symbolic representation, displacement, condensation, and considerations of representability is acknowledged. The decoding process therefore requires that the manifest elements be decoded. Surface associations are understood to represent different underlying meanings. With inference derivative formulations, the underlying message is readily implied from the manifest associations. With image derivative formulations, the manifest elements are treated more as symbolic representations of the underlying message. It is through this latter form of decoding in particular that the therapist strives to arrive at hidden (unconscious) raw messages by undoing possible displacements and symbolic representations, as well as the condensation of several raw fantasies or images into a single manifest element.

A Type Two derivative formulation of the material under consideration would begin by identifying an activated intervention context. Since the specific interventions made by the therapist in the previous hour are not known, this formulation will be limited in terms of available knowledge. The known intervention contexts involve deviations in the ideal therapeutic framework. These alterations are among the most powerful adaptation-evoking contexts to which patients respond through derivative communications related to their Neurosis. In the session, these deviations pertain to the waiting room and secretary, which the therapist shares with Dr. A. Through self-directed efforts designed to analyze the possible implications of these two deviations, and with the assistance of the patient's material, some of the latent meanings of this particular intervention context must be identified. Thus the therapist's need to share the secretary and waiting room with Dr. A. could be perceived unconsciously by the patient as reflecting an excessive need for inappropriate gratification, as a defense against anxieties related to separation and loss, as an impairment in relative autonomy, and as an expression of, and defense against, homosexual fantasies and wishes. These particular raw-message attributes of the intervention context are then used as a way of organizing the meanings contained in the patient's encoded associations.

This particular approach to decoding must be complemented with a second effort in which as many possoble potential symbolic meanings for each associative element are identified. This is done in terms of likely or potential representations, by developing generalizations and by abstracting possible meanings. These abstracted and generalized themes are then reviewed, and those specific meanings that fit the implications of the adaptive context are selected.

In principle, the development of Type Two derivative formulations begins with the recognition of the best representations of the adaptation-evoking contexts. In the session, the patient alludes directly to the waiting room in her manifest associations. As noted before, this is an ideal representation, one that would facilitate rectification and interpretive interventions. On the other hand, the adaptive context of the presence of a shared secretary is probably most clearly represented through the reference to Dr. A.'s cleaning woman. Since this is a disguised and encoded representation, it seems likely for the moment that an intervention could be more readily organized around the implications of the waiting room arrangement than around the presence of the secretary.

Once a represented context is identified, the next task involves identifying the encoded valid unconscious perceptions which the patient has selectively developed and conveyed in his or her material. (A subsequent step is the recognition of responsive derivative fantasies.) Thus, if we do indeed use the shared waiting room as the central adaptation-evoking context for the moment, the patient's allusion to being depressed and mad at the therapist would be formulated as involving several interrelated meanings in light of this particular context. The patient's sense of depression could represent an unconscious perception of the therapist as defending against his own depressive difficulties through the waiting room arrangement. As a deviation in the ideal frame, the shared waiting room exposes the patient inappropriately to other patients, an aspect mentioned in these associations toward the end of the hour in the allusion to meeting someone in the waiting room. The deviation may well be seen unconsciously by the patient as an expression of the therapist's anger—his being mad at his patients (to make use of the patient's initial associations). Through condensation, the same initial element may reflect the patient's own sense of depression and her anger at the therapist because of his deviation.

In conceptualizing the implications of this association, the depression and anger must first be accepted at the manifest level at which they have been represented, and as pertaining to the patient herself. In addition, however, the decoding process is utilized in order to derive a second level of meaning that involves an unconscious perception of the therapist. In this effort, the postulated operation of displacement is undone by treating an association that alludes manifestly to the patient as containing in encoded form a raw and latent message that alludes to the therapist. Thus the presence of some type of introjective identification by the patient with the therapist is proposed. Simultaneously, needs of defense and communication are served. As already noted, this is an extremely common means through which threatening, raw perceptions of the therapist are disguised in the material from patients.

Some further, especially meaningful, associational elements include the patient's manifest allusion to the therapist not discussing things with her on the telephone and his taking away the Kleenex, and the reference to talking to herself. All are, in part, encoded versions of raw messages directed toward the therapist. In light of the two adaptation-evoking contexts, they contain important models of rectification. Through displacement and symbolic representation, they are a way of telling the therapist that he should be less dependent on others and should rely upon himself. The same type of underlying raw message appears in the image of eliminating therapists and solving one's own problems. There is another related encoded message in the patient's wish to tell another patient to leave.

As long as the therapist behaves in a manner that supports the patient's image of him as having actual difficulties in maintaining a strong sense of his own identity and an appropriate degree of relative autonomy, the patient will have unconscious justification for a Neurotic maladaptation in which mergers are effected as a way of coping, even though they interfere with her own relative autonomous functioning. For this reason, countertransferences of this kind must be resolved and interpreted to the patient in terms of her unconscious perceptions before the patient will be capable of analyzing and modifying her own difficulties in this area. In keeping with this precept, the patient will tend always to deal first with unconscious perceptions and introjects of the therapist before clearly delineating his or her own psychopathology.

The abstracting-particularizing process is used in this sequence: A repetitive theme is identified in the material that touches upon issues of independence and pressures toward autonomy (e.g., not talking to the patient on the telephone, taking away the Kleenex, and other signs of relatively independent functioning). Directives are discovered about eliminating therapists and sending people away. An admonition is heard that people should solve their own problems. In this way, a series of general themes contained within the specific elements of the patient's associations is abstracted. A certain commonality is noted in these themes, and then a specific formulation is suggested in light of the implications of an activated adaptive context. This latter step is the particularizing aspect of this part of the listening process.

In sessions with patients, the therapist tends to abstract generalized themes of this kind while listening. In a manner comparable to an antigen and antibody, there is a fit between the implications of an intervention context and the patient's derivative responses. They are like the interlocking cogs of two wheels. Because of this, the therapist can use the meanings of the intervention context as a guide in decoding the patient's derivative communications. In addition, the therapist can generate abstractions and generalizations of the themes evident in the patient's material, and use these themes as a way of suggesting the presence of unrecognized intervention contexts. Here the therapist searches for a particular adaptation-evoking stimulus that could account for the shape of the patient's derivative expressions.

In its essence, then, the abstracting-particularizing process involves the identification of general and broad themes and images implied in the patient's material. There follows a selection process in which definitive themes are identified from within these initial groupings, using the adaptive context as the primary guide.

CHARACTERISTICS OF TYPE ONE AND TYPE TWO DERIVATIVE FORMULATIONS

TYPE ONE DERIVATIVES

The patient's manifest associations are treated as disguised or encoded carriers of isolated latent meanings and functions. Manifest elements considered in this way are termed Type One derivatives.

The raw message that has been encoded and that the therapist attempts to arrive at through decoding procedures is usually postulated to be an unconscious fantasy or memory. In this type of decoding, no consideration is afforded to the ongoing therapeutic interaction and the specific implications of the therapist's silences and interventions. Instead, the disguised material is viewed as relatively isolated intrapsychic contents within the patient.

This type of decoding assumes the use of primary process mechanisms for the encoding and disguising of latent fantasies into a defended form that permits conscious expression. The belief is held, however, that the danger situation and anxiety that prompts the encoding process is entirely intrapsychic. The thesis is advanced that threatening unconscious fantasies about the therapist (i.e., unconscious transference fantasies) or others are subjected to encoding because of inner anxieties. Thus this type of isolated decoding procedure is believed to lead to meaningful dynamic and genetic formulations. However, efforts of this kind, which are divorced from considerations of the stimuli from the therapist (adaptation-evoking contexts), tend to produce formulations that falsify the actual dynamic inner state of the patient, despite any measure of theoretical truth in the statements generated in this way.

In Type One derivative decoding, displacement is usually postulated as operating from the past into the present. Thus allusions to the therapist are believed to represent unconscious fantasies regarding earlier figures. Because of the flaws in this type of decoding (see Leites 1979), it is also postulated that references to early childhood figures may encode unconscious fantasies regarding the therapist. Symbolic representation, condensation, and secondary elaboration with considerations of representability (i.e., the need to maintain a logical flow of surface free association) are also considered as factors in the production of the patient's manifest material.

There are several sources of Type One derivative formulations:

1. Evident cognitive implications in the manifest material.

2. Imagery inferences formulated in terms of unconscious fantasy elements. These may allude to psychodynamics, to genetic experiences, and to aspects of the patient's personal history. They are, however, couched in terms of specific fantasy and memory elements rather than intellectualized concepts.

3. Inference and image meanings that are evident from the clusters of themes and thematic threads.

4. Inferences based on the sequence of the material and the postulate of some measure of relatedness between contiguous associations, and in addition, between all associations in a given hour.

To generate Type One derivative formulations, themes and images are abstracted and generalized from the patient's manifest associations. Often, the underlying (unconscious) raw message is seen as simply displaced from one figure to another. At other times, symbolic representation and disguise are understood to be in full operation and a translation process is invoked.

Type One derivative formulations may involve the therapist. They are, however, usually couched in terms of the patient's unconscious fantasies, though they may be stated in the form of unconscious perception. However, they are the result of a general monitoring of the thematic material, and do not take into account the implications of specific intervention contexts.

TYPE TWO DERIVATIVES

All formulations are organized around, and given specific meaning by, the conscious and unconscious, manifest and latent, explicit and implicit, meaning and functions of the activated adaptive contexts constituted by the therapist's interventions. Depending on the nature of the intervention context, the formulation will be stated in terms of a derived unconscious perception of the therapist or a fantasy-memory constellation that pertains to the therapist—or both.

All Type Two derivative formulations are stated in terms of specific imagery to which more intellectualized implications may be added. This is in keeping with the nature of unconscious expression, which, as it applies to emotional disturbance, always takes place in the form of imagery elements related to raw perceptions and raw fantasies.

The first step in the decoding process is, as noted, the abstracting-particularizing process. Through it, the therapist identifies general and abstract themes evident in the material. In this way, the therapist undoes the mechanism of symbolic representation by formulating the nature of underlying, general, raw messages. Following this abstracting process, through particularization, the therapist postulates the presence of specific themes in light of the implications of the prevailing adaptive contexts.

The presence of displacement is assumed to be in operation at all times. Its influence is such that manifest material is always seen as having been displaced away from an underlying raw message. As a result, if there is a manifest allusion to the therapist, it is nonetheless considered to be displaced from the main unconscious raw message. Allusions to outside figures are understood as representations displaced from the therapist as well. The specific operation of displacement is undone in light of an understanding of the adaptive context that reveals the original, nondisplaced (raw and unconscious) message.

The patient's use of condensation is recognized, and undone or decoded, through the identification of two or more intervention contexts. A single manifest element will often condense responses to both contexts. All material also consistently condenses allusions to both the patient and therapist (the me/not-me interface of the patient's associations). A patient's use of secondary revision in light of a need for representability is undone by taking the material from the patient as separate elements and subjecting each component to the decoding process. Psychic determinism and the unconscious links between associative elements are taken into account by organizing the patient's material in terms of stimulus (adaptive context) and response (derivative complex). Similarly, the patient's material is examined first for direct and encoded representations of the adaptive context itself, and second, for possible encoded reactions to this context—perceptions and fantasies.

Type Two derivative decoding always begins with and centers around the implications of the adaptive contexts—the therapist's interventions. It consistently takes into account the therapeutic interaction and contributions from both participants to treatment. With the here-and-now of treatment central—actualities filled with manifest and latent implications—dynamic and genetic influences are traced out from that particular central point. In the presence of an essentially nonpathological adaptive *context*, the genetic component, as it pertains to emotional disturbance, will tend to function as a pathological influence, and to effect distortions of the patient's perceptions of and reactions to the therapist (transference). If the adaptive context is essentially pathological, the genetic allusions will tend to reflect ways in which the disturbed and disturbing interventions of the therapist resemble past pathogenic interactions in the life of the patient (nontransference). Thus the adaptive context always initiates the sequence, and then touches upon the present and past in terms of aroused fantasy-memories and perceptions that are either projected by the patient into the therapy situation and onto the therapist (transference), or introjected from the therapist's interventions by the patient (nontransference)—or both.

Type Two derivative formulations consistently refer to activated conflicts and the unconscious dynamics and genetics of the patient—and secondarily of the therapist—as aroused by the specifics of the therapeutic interaction. As such, they involve the truth of the patient's Neurosis as aroused at a specific moment in therapy in response to the therapist's silences and interventions. They are therefore interpersonal-intrapsychic statements that pertain to the inner- and outer-directed adaptive efforts of the patient. As such, they appear to be the most comprehensive and accurate formulations that can be developed in respect to the actual implications of the patient's material.

CLINICAL EXAMPLE

The patient is a young woman whose hour had been changed by her therapist (also a woman), and who paid for her therapy with both insurance and money from her father. In the previous session, the therapist asked the patient to change the time of their session two weeks hence. The patient was being seen on a once-weekly basis. She began the hour after the therapist's request as follows:

> Patient: I can make the later time you requested quite easily. Can you change the hour for me next week?
> Therapist: Yes. How is 10:20 A.M. on Wednesday?
> Patient: Fine. *(A long period of silence.)* I don't know why I am afraid to talk to you. I keep thinking of how I don't trust people who compliment me. Sometimes what you say helps; sometimes it doesn't.

In general, the material from the patient should be approached by first searching the manifest contents for indicators and other types of storage information. Next, direct representations of known adaptive contexts are sought and, from there, encoded representations of the same context. Finally, Type Two derivative formulations may be generated, beginning with unconscious perceptions of the therapist.

In this brief excerpt, the manifest contents initially involve two changes in the fixed frame (i.e., shifts in the times of the patient's sessions). There is then a gross behavioral resistance in the form of the patient's long silence, and a comment by the patient regarding her fear of talking to the therapist.

Next, there appears what seems to be a symptomatic form of mistrust: it seems irrational to be suspicious of people who compliment you. However, a final decision regarding evident symptoms should never be made prior to a full analysis of the unconscious basis of the emotional disturbance. Often, important inputs into the problem will be discovered from other persons, especially the therapist. Further, the symptom may involve an unconscious meaning or function that renders it less malignant than would appear on the surface. Finally, the excerpt concludes with a manifest comment regarding the ways in which the therapist is sometimes helpful and sometimes not.

In terms of indicators of emotional disturbance and indicators for intervention, all alterations of the basic therapeutic environment serve as first-order therapeutic contexts (indicators). Deviations invoked or participated in by the therapist simultaneously constitute important intervention contexts. Thus the two changed hours are among the major indicators for this session.

There is an additional indicator in the form of a gross behavioral resistance reflected in the patient's silence. There is also the patient's subjective fear of talking to the therapist and her mistrust of others. The allusion to how the therapist sometimes is not helpful may constitute an indicator by alluding to the existence of a countertransference difficulty in the therapist or by expressing a resistance within the patient—or both. In either case, it is a therapeutic context that the therapist would hope to illuminate in terms of its unconscious basis. The same applies, of course, to the remaining indicators: the signs of emotional disturbance in the patient or therapist, and of the disruption in the ideal therapeutic environment. In each instance the therapist would hope to conceptualize the underlying factors that are contributing to the difficulty, doing so in terms of activated intervention contexts and the patient's derivative responses. These formulations could then lead to rectification of the impaired frame if necessary, and to an appropriate interpretive intervention.

There are two main adaptive contexts in this excerpt: the therapist's request of the patient to change an hour, and the therapist's compliance with the patient's request to change the time of a different session. Adaptive contexts are always stated in terms of interventions by the therapist.

Once an adaptive context is identified, the next step is to search for representations of the context. In general, the single best representation is sought, looking first on the manifest level and then in terms of encoded derivatives. Here the patient alludes directly to the therapist's request to change the hour. In addition, the therapist's participation in the second shift of time took place during the session at hand. This too is a direct manifestation of an adaptive context, though it takes the form of a manifest behavior of the therapist carried out in the presence of the patient. In all, then, the first context is represented directly in the patient's association, while the second is evident in the behavior of the therapist in the session at hand.

In the actual session, the therapist would next move to develop Type Two derivative formulations. For the purposes of the present discussion, Type One derivative formulations will be identified before moving on to Type Two derivative efforts. Type One formulations tend to rely heavily on knowledge of the patient and of psychoanalytic theory. In the absence of the former, the presence of a paranoid trend in this patient might be suspected. It might be proposed in highly tentative fashion that, in the presence of a woman therapist, this patient has feelings and fantasies toward the therapist of a homosexual nature. The main clue is the allusion to compliments and the patient's mistrust of those who favor her. This could well be a projection of the patient's own positive and homosexual feelings and fantasies toward the therapist, which in turn create a sense of mistrust. This mistrust might then be linked to the patient's fear of talking to the therapist—this last, based on associational affinity. Finally, the patient's comment that the therapist sometimes helps and sometimes does not could be formulated to reflect a split image of the therapist. It might also in some way involve a split image of the patient herself.

In the main, then, this sparse material suggests a tentative Type One derivative formulation of unconscious homosexual fantasies directed toward the therapist, and through the use of projection, of mistrust of the therapist as well. It seems likely that there actually is some truth to such a formulation, but a Type Two derivative analysis of this material will locate the main underlying homosexual needs in the therapist for the moment, rather than in the patient. In this light, the Type One derivative formulation of unconscious homosexual fantasies in the patient, and of some type of internal split within her psyche, appears to be true, though not dynamically active within the patient as understood in light of the ongoing therapeutic interaction. It is essential to maintain a definition of truth in psychotherapy in terms of the ongoing therapeutic interaction, and of the actualities to which the patient is adapting. All other statements, no matter how truthful, serve dynamically as departures from the truth of the therapeutic moment and of the actively dynamic truths within the patient at a given juncture. As such, they function as derivative and lie-barrier defenses designed to cover over the more compelling dynamic and interactional truths that are actually pertinent to the activated aspects of the patient's emotional disturbance and Neurosis.

How then would Type Two derivative formulations be generated from this material? First, general themes would be abstracted: a fear of communicating with the therapist; a sense of mistrust; a fear of those who compliment her; the helpful therapist; and the non-helpful therapist.

Next, these general themes would be particularized in light of the implications of the two adaptive contexts. They are comparable in nature—both involve a decision by the therapist to change the patient's fixed time for her sessions. Therefore the patient's derivative responses may be expected to condense reactions to both contexts. (In order to simplify this discussion, the focus initially will be on the therapist's original request of the patient to change an hour.)

In the actual session, those direct and implicit meanings of the therapist's intervention that are likely to have been communicated to the patient are identified subjectively, and the patient's material is scrutinized to discern if the patient also represents these meanings. In actual practice, the therapist does both simultaneously.

Here, the patient's material will be examined first. Her allusion to her fear of talking to the therapist, particularized in light of the therapist's request that the patient change the time of her session, may now be seen to represent (in encoded form) an unconscious perception and introject of the therapist's own fear of talking to the patient. This reading is in keeping with the finding that all deviations in the ideal framework are indeed actions, and consistently constitute forms of acting-out by the therapist. As such, they involve pathological modes of gratification with adaptive value for the therapist. Actually, they constitute maladaptive responses or adaptive failures. They are therefore an alternative to maintaining the secure therapeutic environment and hold with the patient, and to working in an entirely interpretive fashion (i.e., through talk geared to insight). This very formulation is implied in the patient's derivative element, which alludes to her fear of talking. This manifest association acquires some measure of symbolic representation by the recognition that it expresses an unconsciously perceived fear within the therapist—an image that is supported by other interventions from the therapist that have not been reported here.

It is possible also to suggest a broader generalization from this association. Thus the patient's allusion to her fear of talking to the therapist may indicate the presence of a basic problem in their communicative relationship, much of it initiated by the therapist in light of the adaptive context at hand.

As expected, there is reason to believe that displacement is in operation, here from the therapist onto the patient. Thus the raw message (an unconscious image and perception) is to the effect that the therapist is afraid to talk to the patient. Through displacement (and introjection), the patient's manifest association is that *she* is afraid to talk to the therapist. Displacement is basic to this change, as is the mechanism of reversal. Condensation is in operation, in that the therapist's fear of talking to the patient (i.e., of working interpretively) is reflected in both adaptive contexts (i.e., in both changes in the time of the session). In addition, the patient has condensed her own manifest fear of talking to the therapist with an unconsciously perceived fear on the part of the therapist to talk to the patient.

Finally, considerations of representability have been taken into account, in that the patient on the surface is attempting to comment upon her own long period of silence during the session. Her manifest communication is therefore an attempt to respond to that silence on the surface, while simultaneously, through its capacity as a derivative, the same element reveals the unconscious basis of the patient's very fear of talking. This is indeed a remarkable combination of manifest and latent meaning. However, it is not at all unusual to find this type of manifest and encoded communication condensed into a single message.

Still another unconscious meaning may be found condensed in this particular manifest association. In view of the adaptive context of the therapist's change in the patient's hours, the patient's surface comment that she doesn't know why she is afraid to talk to the therapist takes on a specific meaning. Here the patient makes use of negation to indicate that she senses some reason why she is afraid to talk to the therapist. The patient also does not link up her fear of talking to the therapist's actual intervention. It is this connection to the adaptive context that is repressed, so that as an isolated statement the true meaning cannot be identified. This can be accomplished rather simply by connecting the negated statement to the adaptive context and undoing the negation. The resultant raw message would read, "I do know why I am afraid to talk to you: it is because you changed my hour (and altered the fixed frame)." Studies have shown that patients are consistently fearful and mistrustful of therapists who do not securely maintain the ground rules and boundaries of the therapeutic relationship and setting.

The second element in this segment is the patient's mistrust of those who compliment her. In light of the second adaptive context, the patient is indicating through an encoded derivative that the therapist's agreement to change an hour is seen as a compliment. (The patient's agreement to change the time at the request of the therapist has a comparable quality.) As seen with this patient, such compliment-gratifications are a source of considerable latent mistrust. Further, based on associative contiguity, the patient's mistrust of compliment-gratifications may be understood as providing an additional clue through which to account for the patient's silence and general fear of talking to the therapist. In this way, the disturbing implications of an adaptive context as reflected in the patient's own derivative complex makes it possible to explain the unconscious basis of a gross behavioral resistance. Such a silent hypothesis would readily lend itself to interpretation. It is an understanding of these kinds of implications of the derivative complex in light of an activated adaptive context that is most important in the development of Type Two derivative formulations and interventions.

Clinically, the therapist must evaluate the extent to which the change in the hour is validly perceived by the patient as some type of compliment. The therapist must also abstract implications of the image of being complimented to take into account instinctual drive representations. It is important to include id-based formulations in the abstracting-particularizing process, since there is some tendency in therapists to overlook unconscious and derivative instinctual drive expressions. In this situation there are strong indications that the theme of compliments implies some type of gratuitous seductiveness—an unconscious homosexual threat.

Although this particular exercise of listening and formulating begins in a manner similar to that which leads to the development of Type One derivative hypotheses, the critical second step of particularizing and selecting definitive implications in light of a specific adaptive context is a distinguishing characteristic of Type Two derivation. Only in this way is it possible to correctly locate the major source of danger or threat within the patient, and to specify whether it arises mainly from pathological inner fantasies and memories, or from valid unconscious perceptions of others, and of the therapist in particular.

Thus, in the present situation, the gratuitous and unanalyzed agreement by the therapist to change an hour at the request of the patient is indeed in some way a form of inappropriate gratification and seductiveness. In light of this unconscious implication of the second change in hour, the patient's mistrust is appropriate rather than Neurotic.

As can be seen, the therapist must continually engage in clinical judgments regarding the unconscious implications of his or her own interventions and the patient's readings of these implications. Here, the sense of compliment appears to be a valid perception of the intervention. The therapist's response was noninterpretive, and therefore afforded both herself and the patient a pathological mode of relatedness and instinctual drive satisfaction. The former takes the form of a pathological symbiosis and of parasiticism—initially of the patient by the therapist, and subsequently of the therapist by the patient. The latter touches upon unconscious homosexual satisfactions.

There is virtually always an inappropriately seductive element to deviations in the ideal framework. This particular factor is the basis for considerable mistrust of therapists by patients. In this instance, the seductive implication of the adaptive context has been taken and used to develop a specific meaning chosen from the general implications of the particular associational segment. The principle of developing material first in terms of valid unconscious perceptions, and of assigning to the category of distorted unconscious fantasies only that which cannot be subsumed in this first area, is also employed.

As noted above, it may well be that this patient has seductive fantasies toward her therapist. This is reflected in some measure by her wish to change an hour and by her agreeing readily to change the hour at the request of the therapist. However, it is critical to first identify that which belongs to the therapist. In formulating, stress should be placed on these valid, unconsciously perceived components. As the material permits, it is then essential to add an understanding of contributions from the patient to this initial formulation. The main technical point is that the therapist must be careful not to deny the existence of these perceived dynamics within himself or herself, or to overstate their existence within the patient.

A correct approach here would lead the therapist to implicitly accept the patient's unconscious perceptions of her seductiveness, to rectify the framework in keeping with the need to correct this aspect of the therapist's interventions in actuality, and to interpret these perceptions to the patient with implicit acceptance of their validity in light of the intervention context. In addition or subsequently, the therapist could then, as further material permitted, identify the ways in which this particular seductive effort corresponded to and supported similar needs and fantasies within the patient. Finally, it would prove possible to interpret the patient's own wishes in this area, though only after the therapist had rectified the expressions of her own needs along these lines.

In light of the two adaptive contexts, this same derivative element—the patient's mistrust of compliments—may also reflect an unconscious perception of some type of mistrust in the therapist, perhaps in part because of the patient's compliance with her initial request to change an hour. It may be noted that, in our first formulation (of the patient's unconscious mistrust of the therapist who asked and agreed to changes in the sessions), a displacement from the therapist to people in general is postulated. The mistrust remains that of the patient, and the defensive operations involve a disguise of the object and nature of the mistrust. Thus the patient represents the raw message of the therapist's seductive changes in the hours with the vague image of a compliment. In our second formulation (of some introjected or unconsciously perceived mistrust within the therapist of people who compliment *her*), there is an additional displacement from the therapist onto the patient, and from the therapist again onto people in general.

The final segment—the comment that the therapist sometimes says helpful things and sometimes says things that do not prove helpful—may now be considered. In light of the adaptive contexts, it may be suggested that the change in the hour is helpful to the patient in some ways, while in other ways it is not. It might also be suggested that the patient is reacting not only to the change in session, but to other interventions in the previous hour, unknown to us, which would account for a split image of the therapist. Under those circumstances, it might be postulated that the deviation is not helpful, while the therapist's other interventions had been of use to her.

In any case, some measure of truth can be found in the formulation that an alteration in the fixed frame is both helpful and unhelpful. On the surface it tends to gratify the patient pathologically, and this immediate satisfaction is sometimes experienced rather positively. However, in the depths such deviations are always disturbing and disruptive for the patient, and quite unhelpful in the long run.

In this formulation, the patient's allusions to what the therapist says are taken as conveying two related meanings. The first meaning is a reference to all of the therapist's interventions. As such it proves unnecessary to invoke the use of displacement (a rare exception); instead, the patient's main defense may involve a failure to identify specifically the interventions that have and have not helped her. Second, the use of a general comment of this kind may represent the two specific deviations invoked by the therapist. Here a generalization is used to convey and encode two specific issues and adaptive contexts. At times of relatively low resistance, the patient's main defense may involve a separation of a derivative element from its true adaptation-evoking context.

Summary and Conclusions. In all, then, a series of Type Two derivative formulations are proposed for this small excerpt. The importance of first determining the unconscious implications of each pertinent adaptive context while considering and shaping the implications of the patient's derivative material has been demonstrated. How the nature of the context determines much of the true meaning of the derivative complex, especially whether such encoded material is to be thought of in terms of fantasy or perception constellations, has been shown, as well as how the implications of an adaptive context helps to highlight selected meanings of the patient's derivative material.

A second factor in generating these formulations involves a consideration of the patient's own unconscious needs to perceive selectively and to experience a particular intervention context in personal terms. As a rule the total active meaning of the patient's material involves vectors from the adaptive stimulus and from the patient's intrapsychic set. The identification of the latter elements is possible, however, only in light of a full comprehension of the unconscious implications of the therapist's own interventions.

Although a Type One derivative formulation is, on rare occasions, merely an incomplete version of a more integrated Type Two derivative hypothesis, quite often there is a sharp discrepancy between the two types of hypotheses. This leads, of course, to rather different interventions by Type One and Type Two derivative therapists, including the considerable lack of framework-management responses by the former, and an overriding emphasis on transference and distortion in their interpretive efforts. By and large, the Type Two derivative therapist works in the areas of both framework management and interpretation, and offers far more balanced interventions in terms of valid and distorted components. The influence on the patient and the course of therapy is considerable.

Differences Between Type One and Type Two Derivative Psychotherapy

The therapist's level of listening and the nature of his or her formulations is one of the major determinants of the therapeutic approach and the nature of interventions. A series of distinguishing characteristics are presented here that compare Type One and Type

Two derivative listening-therapy to further the understanding of the errors inherent to Type One derivative formulating.

Type Two derivative formulations consistently take into account the input from the therapist and the therapeutic interaction. Formulations are made entirely in terms of the conscious and unconscious implications of the therapist's interventions. These are understood as the adaptation-evoking stimuli to which the patient is responding, particularly as a patient's reactions pertain to his or her Neurosis. Because of this, all of the therapist's efforts at deciphering derivative meaning from the patient's manifest associations and behaviors are carried out in light of the adaptive stimuli that have, in actuality, shaped the patient's encoded response.

In contrast, Type One derivative formulations either totally disregard the implications of the therapist's interventions or treat them in a general, superficial, or nonspecific manner (e.g., as when it is formulated vaguely that a patient is reacting to a therapist's vacation). There is thus no guarantee that a particular effort at this type of decoding will yield a raw message that is dynamically active within the patient or therapist at the moment the formulation is made. There is considerable risk that the impressions developed will involve statements of true psychoanalytic propositions, which serve functionally in the actual therapeutic situation as lie-barrier, defensive systems designed to seal off underlying interactional truths.

Both Type One and Type Two derivative formulations involve genetics and dynamics. Type One derivative therapists consistently assign these qualities to the patient. In contrast, the Type Two derivative therapist first considers whether these dynamics and genetics apply in some way to himself or herself in light of the implications of his or her interventions. Those dynamics and genetics that do not appear to apply in this way are then assigned to the patient. Thus the question as to who it is that a particular dynamic and genetic constellation belongs is seldom asked by the Type One derivative therapist and, in contrast, is an ever-present question in the mind of a Type Two derivative therapist.

With rare exception, the Type One derivative therapist shapes decoding around postulated unconscious fantasy-memories constellations and pathology-related transferences. The possibility of valid unconscious perceptions and nontransference responses is seldom considered. On the other hand, the Type Two derivative therapist makes a consistent effort to distinguish between transference and nontransference, valid encoded perceptions and distorted, unconscious and encoded fantasy-memories. The therapist is aided in this effort through a full characterization of the implications of his or her adaptation-evoking interventions.

For the Type One derivative therapist, genetic material virtually always implies transference (an allusion to a past person and experience that is a distorting and distorted influence upon the patient's perceptions of and reactions to the therapist). For Type Two derivative therapists, genetic allusions may involve such transferences or, instead, may constitute a reference to a past traumatic figure who had behaved in some comparable fashion to actual traumatic behaviors of the therapist. Again, the nature of the genetic link is determined through an analysis of the implications of the adaptation-evoking interventions from the therapist that have aroused the genetic material within the patient.

Truth in psychotherapy must be defined for the patient in terms of the adaptation-evoking stimuli that generate the inner dynamic and genetic expressions and give them their specific meanings and functions. Inherent to this definition of truth is an understanding of the communications from the therapist and the extent to which they touch upon the therapist's own inner dynamics and genetics, or those of the patient. All statements of truth in psychotherapy must have both an interactional and an intrapsychic dimension. It follows then that the Type One derivative therapist does not engage in the decoding of manifest contents in a manner designed to identify consistently the activated truths of the patient's emotional disturbance. It is only the Type Two derivative therapist who can arrive at these truths and interpret them accurately.

For the Type One derivative therapist, either little effort is made at validating interventions, or confirmation is taken in terms of the patient's subsequent manifest associations or direct elaborations of the interpretations offered by the therapist. Virtually any response which extends to the intervention, no matter how thin, self-evident, or repetitious, is seen as confirmatory. In contrast, the Type Two derivative therapist accepts as validation only those responses from the patient that uniquely extend an interpretation and involve encoded-derivative communications that shed new and unexpected meaning on the patient's previous material.

Type One derivative decoding is often utilized in the service of countertransference, and involves considerable defensiveness on the part of the therapist, who consistently denies both his or her role in the patient's communications and the extent to which the dynamics and genetics involved in the patient's material pertain to the therapist. On the other hand, the Type Two derivative therapist has the potential to operate relatively free of countertransference, and to readily accept that which belongs to him or her, and to distinguish it from that which belongs to the patient—always in light of the implications of the therapist's interventions.

In all, manifest content therapy has been designed to avoid unconscious expressions and meanings. Type One derivative therapy creates the *illusion* of dynamic and genetic understanding. In actuality, unfortunately, it operates through self-serving fictions from the therapist that have some measure of truth as theoretical psychoanalytic statements, but little or no measure of truth as they pertain to the true meaning of the patient's derivative material and of the patient's (and sometimes, the therapist's) dynamic inner state. Type Two derivative therapy is designed to rectify these errors and to produce true statements regarding the nature of the therapeutic transactions between the patient and therapist, and of the inner state of both.

CLINICAL EXAMPLE

A situation was presented in which both the patient and therapist asked for and obtained a change in the time of the sessions. The session presented here followed the last hour described above. The therapist was five minutes late to this session. Once in the consultation room, the patient began to speak.

> Patient: I am paying you in cash today. *(Gives the therapist the money, which the therapist accepts.)*
> Therapist: I'm sorry I was late. Can you stay an extra five minutes? .
> Patient: That's fine. *(Long period of silence.)*
> Therapist: Why don't you tell me what's going on in your mind and what happened over this last week?
> Patient: I keep asking myself why I can't tell you things. I expect you to know what I am thinking. My parents live nearby me. They come over every day and drive me crazy. My father is so inconsistent, so unreliable. He demands things but won't give. I never know what to expect from him. He's

inherited some money, but it ends up being self-defeating. One moment he's nice, the next moment, he's so provocative. I get so angry with him. My mother takes it from him, but I won't. He respects that, but he prefers my brother. I wish I could stand up to him more than I do. I had a fantasy of stabbing him with an ice pick. That reminds me, I also had a dream last night that he came to me saying my mother was making him unhappy. He asked me to do him a favor, to help him find another woman. I said I'd do it if he gave me part of the money he inherited. It all connects to how angry I am with him these days and how my mother doesn't know how to handle him.

This longer excerpt illustrates the complexities of a patient's associations in a given hour. In looking first to the manifest content of this material, the indicators of emotional disturbance, whether in the patient or therapist, and indicators for intervention, are particularly noteworthy. Manifest representations of an activated adaptive context should also be examined. The remainder of the available information should be noted in passing and placed into storage.

Indicators present include: (1) payment of the fee by the patient in cash (the ideal form of payment is by check, though the therapist's deposit of the money is a slight alteration in total confidentiality); (2) the patient's silence in the session (a gross behavioral resistance); (3) the patient's comment that she expects the therapist to know what she is thinking (a possible symptomatic expression); (4) an allusion to difficulty in telling things to the therapist (a disturbance in the manifest therapeutic alliance); (5) a problem with the patient's parents (a troublesome life situation); (6) an apparently disturbing and hostile fantasy of stabbing her father (a possible sign of poor ego defenses); and (7) a sense of anger toward the father who prefers her brother (another aspect of a disturbing life situation). In addition, (8) the therapist's lateness must be taken as a sign of disturbance, since it will function for the patient in this way regardless of the actualities—certainly creating some measure of disturbance and therapeutic need within the patient. Similarly, (9) the therapist's acceptance of cash payment without exploration is an indicator that suggests the presence of countertransference; it will also create a therapeutic need within the patient. Finally, (10) that this particular session is taking place at a time different from the usual meeting hour is an indicator for intervention, since it is a modification in the fixed (frame) arrangement between the patient and therapist. The earlier changed session is also a background therapeutic context.

In all, then, there are strong signs of actual and potential disturbance in the patient and of noticable disturbance within the therapist, who has in several ways modified the ideal therapeutic hold. Under these conditions, if the material at all permits, the therapist is likely to intervene with both rectifications of the framework and interpretations.

What kind of Type One derivative formulation could be made from this material? It is inviting to begin with the self-interpretation that this patient developed for herself and the therapist in the session at hand. It is formulated in terms of Type One derivatives, the typical level at which patients carry out such work, and it makes use of a scanning of the available manifest themes in the hour and a study of the sequence of this surface material. Thus the patient suggests that her father's inconsistency and demands, his preference for the patient's brother and his unreliability, are all factors in the patient's conscious fantasy of stabbing him, and are somehow related to the dream of helping him to find another woman. Undecoded (direct) manifest elements are used in this way in an attempt to explain the patient's anger with her father.

It must be stressed, however, that this is a simplistic and linear explanation, well within the realm of the patient's conscious awareness. It involves an essentially nonneurotic response, in that anger at someone who has the attributes described for the patient's father is by no means inappropriate or inexplicable. Much of the so-called therapeutic work that is carried out on a manifest content level deals with this type of nonneurotic response.

Other Type One derivative inferences can also be identified in this material. The description of the father's self-defeating behaviors may be formulated as a projection of the patient's own masochism. The father's preference for the patient's brother may imply sibling rivalry and envy within the patient. There is some support for this thesis in the patient's conscious fantasy of stabbing her father with an icepick. A strong sense of hositility and murderous impulses toward the father is inherent to and may be derived inferentially from this image. The patient's expectation that the therapist would know what she is thinking is another inference derivative, and implies magical expectations. Then too the patient's dream could be viewed as some form of Oedipal triumph. However, all these *inference derivatives* are highly intellectualized and quite theoretical. They allude entirely to the patient, though inferences could also be made regarding her parents. They have a static sense, and are isolated and not actively dynamic.

Type One derivative *images* include the suggestion that the patient's stabbing of her father with an ice pick involves a phallic self-image, as well as a picture of her father's phallus as an attacking and piercing weapon. In addition, the patient's dream can imply the presence of an unconscious fantasy of wishing to go to bed with her father, represented through disguise in the effort to help him find another woman. The reward of the money could symbolize an anal fantasy of fecal reward, as well as an anal-phallic image in which the money represents the father's phallus, now given to the patient. If, in addition, the patient recalled a memory of being in bed with her father, this particular dream might be postulated to represent the actual experience with the father as well as the patient's fantasied response. As such, it would have a clear configuration of a fantasy-memory constellation.

Each Type One derivative formulation has taken a manifest element—here a fantasy and a dream—and arrived at the raw message that it is purported to represent. In each case, this raw message is considered to be an intrapsychic fantasy and wish.

Through decoding, the patient's use of displacement and symbolism has been undone (e.g., the use of the icepick to represent the phallus and the use of another woman to represent the patient), and concerns for secondary revision and representability (e.g., the manner in which the encoded messages are part of the patient's ongoing, logical surface associations) have been taken into account. The presence of condensation in respect to the fantasy of stabbing the father with an icepick has also been proposed in the suggestion that it represents specific images that the patient has of herself as well as encoded images of the patient's father and his penis.

Each of these formulations concentrates on an intrapsychic fantasy-memory constellation that is purported to exist within the patient. They are developed either in isolation or seen as responses to current provocative behaviors by the father. At times, Type One derivative therapists will consider material of this kind as pertinent from the therapist and represents *wishes* symbolically directed to themselves (i.e., as the expression of unconscious transference fantasies). Then the use of further displacement and condensation would be proposed, and the fantasy of stabbing the father with an icepick would be suggested to represent (in some way) an unconscious impulse-fantasy directed toward the therapist. The dream of the patient's father asking her to help him find another woman might be seen as representing an unconscious homosexual fantasy directed toward the therapist. Similarly, the allusion to the mother's ineptness could be viewed as a wish to render the therapist ineffectual.

In each of these instances, it is postulated that the material is encoded in a fashion that displaces the manifest associations away from the therapist and represents *wishes* symbolically directed toward the therapist—wishes for which both the dynamic attributes and genetic sources are portrayed. Still, such formulations see the driving source of the patient's material as her own intrapsychic fantasies and needs, rather than as a mixture of factors that specifically include the interventions and stimuli from the therapist. In being wish-oriented, they serve admirably as a means of denying or sealing off valid unconscious perceptions of the therapist and the role that the therapist plays in the patient's responses and material. In part, the manner in which Type One derivative formulations serve the defensive needs of the therapist helps to account for their wide, though generally erroneous, usage.

What are the possible Type Two derivative formulations? They are the central adaptive contexts for this session, and the patient's manifest associations must be decoded in light of their manifest and latent implications. The change in the hour at the therapist's request is one adaptive context. It implies a disregard for the patient's holding needs, as well as seductiveness and manipulativeness on the part of the therapist. It appears to be best represented manifestly in the allusion to the father's inheritence. The therapist has been given something (a gift) by the patient.

Using the abstracting-particularizing process, the balance of this material may now be decoded in light of this particular intervention context. The patient's associations imply that the change in the hour interferes with her freedom to communicate openly with the therapist (cf. the allusion to not being able to tell the therapist things). It is seen too as a confusing intervention designed to drive the patient crazy. It is also a reflection of inconsistency and unreliability in the therapist, represented in this material through an allusion to the patient's father. This particular element simultaneously suggests that the therapist's actual behavior in some way replicates comparable behaviors in the patient's father. The deviation is also seen as a demand and as something unexpected. The therapist obtains the change in the hour, but it is self-defeating. It is also provocative, and suggests a preference for someone else other than the patient. It evokes fantasy (wishes within the patient that she could stand up to the therapist), as well as reactive rage (the allusion to wanting to stab the father is viewed as an encoded representation of hostile impulses directed toward the therapist). Through condensation, this same conscious fantasy element reflects an unconscious perception of the therapist's request to change the hour as a hostile attack. Finally, the change in hour is represented in the patient's dream as a request for a favor for which the patient wishes some payment in return. As the reader may recall, in the actual transactions, the patient herself requested a change in the hour at the very moment that she agreed to the therapist's request to shift the time.

These formulations have taken the material as stimulated by the therapist's intervention and as consistently displaced from the therapist onto others—especially onto the patient's mother, father, and the patient herself—and postulated several instances of condensation. The symbolic representations have been represented largely in terms of valid encoded unconscious perceptions of the therapist based on implications inherent to her request that the patient change an hour. It may well be that the patient is overly sensitive and exaggerates the implications of this request, and thereby introduces effects derived from her own pathological fantasies (transference). However, since nothing of the nature of the therapist's additional interventions is known, the extent to which this material reflects valid perceptions of the therapist or distorted fantasies cannot be further clarified.

The adaptive context of the therapist's lateness is best represented here in the allusion to the father's inconsistency. This manifest material can then be organized to yield derivative meanings in light of that particular context. In brief, this particular break in the fixed frame also disturbs the patient's ability to communicate with the therapist, and creates a seemingly powerful and omnipotent image of the therapist (cf. the references to the patient's being unable to tell the therapist things, and her expectation that the therapist will know what she is thinking). It is viewed as part of an effort by the therapist to drive the patient crazy in a manner not unlike her parents. Through the patient's comments about her father, the patient, by means of displacement, conveys her perception of the self-defeating qualities involved. The reference to the patient's anger with her father condenses the hostile qualities of the therapist's lateness with the patient's reactive anger. The patient then suggests that she wishes to protest because she unconsciously views the therapist's behavior as expressing a preference by the therapist for someone else. The displaced fantasy of stabbing her father with an icepick represents both the therapist's and the patient's violence as simultaneously connected with this context.

The therapist's acceptance of payment in cash for the day's session is best represented in the allusion to the father's inheritence of money and in the patient's demand for money in her dream of her father. The patient's reactions to this context are condensed with those to the other adaptive contexts (the therapist's request to change the hour, the therapist's participation in the patient's request to change an hour, and the therapist's lateness). Thus the general theme of why the patient can't communicate with the therapist is a commentary on the way in which the therapist's acceptance of cash interferes with the relationship. It drives the patient crazy and is seen as a form of unreliability. It is characterized as self-defeating and as a hostile gesture, to which the patient responds with hostility of her own. It is seen too as a special form of gratification, and possibly as a reward that has homosexual implications. Again, these formulations tend to involve encoded perceptions far more than encoded fantasies. This is because of the traumatic and countertransference-based nature of the prevailing intervention context.

Certain trends are now in evidence in regard to Type Two derivative formulations, especially as compared to those that revolve around Type One derivatives. In the former effort, there is a careful consideration of the therapist's interventions. Many of the patient's associations are then viewed as valid unconscious perceptions, though room is left for extensions into distortion and excessive sensitivity or selectivity. Many of the associations that would be formulated by the Type One derivative therapist in terms of the patient's unconscious fantasies and wishes are actually stated in dynamically meaningful terms by the Type Two derivative therapist as involving valid unconscious perceptions based on aspects of the actual therapeutic interaction. Clearly, the Type One derivative therapist would consistently deny many, if not all, of his or her own inputs into the patient's experience, as well as the patient's valid representations of the unconscious implications of the therapist's interventions. There would be much direct and indirect blaming of the patient, and the patient would be held accountable for much of what more correctly belongs to the therapist's sphere of responsibility. Type One derivative therapy often exploits the depressive and masochistic trends within patients, and sometimes evokes a form of misalliance relief or cure through the therapist's unconscious punishment of the patient. In contrast, Type Two derivative formulations attempt to give a fair accounting to both participants to treatment, and to place the responsibility for moments of both disturbance and clinical improvement exactly where it belongs.

Summary and Conclusions

There are many possible encoded meanings in a patient's manifest associations. The approach presented here is designed to help the therapist select those meanings that are likely to be most cogent and active at the time for the patient (and secondarily, for the therapist). In listening to a patient's free associations and in engaging at efforts at decoding, a therapist should feel free to engage in both Type One and Type Two derivative formulations. Through the former type of effort, symbolic representations may be formulated that suggest activated intervention contexts that the therapist has missed. The remainder of the Type One derivative formulations may be stored away as informative if not immediately relevant. Eventually the therapist will organize decoding efforts around the implications of recognized adaptation-evoking contexts that stem from his or her own interventions. As noted, however, the therapist must make constant efforts to safeguard against the fixation of formulations, and must always remain open to new impressions and derivative meanings unrelated to those already identified.

In this way the massive amounts of potential information encoded in a patient's manifest associations will be subjected to a careful selection process that provides the therapist with the most compelling derivative reactions to the adaptive contexts contained in the patient's material. These will then be shaped in light of the implications of the intervention context as possible encoded representations of the context itself, of reactive perceptions and fantasies, and of emotional disturbance in either the patient or therapist. By means of this selectivity, the therapist is more easily in a position where an interpretive response to the patient's material can be developed, or the framework can be properly managed in light of the patient's derivative communications.

A fair portion of the information contained on a manifest and latent level in the patient's associations has been assigned to the area of storage and passing impressions. Neither the storage nor intervention-oriented information has been organized in terms of the six basic categories of listening that were introduced in the previous chapter (the state of the frame, mode of relatedness, mode of cure, mode of communication, dynamics and gentics, and to whom they belong). Instead, those aspects of listening have been chosen that most directly involve the transition from formulation to actual intervention. In an ideal (relatively resistant-free) session, both the indicators and adaptive context will be touched upon briefly and in passing in the patient's manifest associations, while the balance of the patient's material will organize into a coalsescible and diversely meaningful derivative complex. It is in this latter sphere that much of the information gained through the use of the six-part observational schema is funneled into the formulating and intervening processes.

Chapter 9

The Network of Communications: Indicators

The distinction between Type One and Type Two derivative listening shows the need for a basic revision in the nature of psychoanalytic listening in the direction of adaptive context formulations. With this point established, the three basic components of a Type Two derivative formulation and intervention (indicators, contexts, and derivatives) will be studied. Together they constitute the network of communications (communicative network) through which the patient expresses himself or herself, or fails to do so. Not unexpectedly, this network contains within its confines an activated representation of the patient's Neurosis, its sources in the therapeutic interaction, and its unconscious basis as evoked by the therapist's interventions. Thus it has within its province all of the basic information that the therapist needs for managing the ground rules and for interpreting to the patient, and thus for insightful cure.

The therapist's goal is two-fold: first, to define his or her framework-management responses, and second, to generate interpretation-reconstructions of the patient's material. The first of these efforts is undertaken on the basis of a recognition of the patient's encoded directives in this sphere, carried out in light of known adaptive contexts and indicators. The second task begins with the recognition of an indicator, and requires the identification of the intervention context and derivatives from the patient that have stimulated and explain the therapeutic context at hand. Thus the therapist's relatively unstructured listening and initial discrete formulations eventually require synthesis into a meaningful and dynamically active whole, shaped in terms of stimulus and response in light of the ongoing interaction. On this basis it becomes possible for the therapist to intervene in terms of either framework management or interpretive response.

As noted, the network of communications identifies the three components of a synthesized formulation and intervention: (1) indicators or therapeutic contexts, (2) activated adaptive contexts, and (3) the derivative complex. The study of this network begins with a careful consideration of the signs of disturbance within the therapeutic context.

A Classification of Indicators

Indicators for intervention by the therapist, or therapeutic contexts, involve signs of disturbance in the patient, therapist, or therapeutic interaction. In terms of the listening process, they are therapeutic contexts in the sense that the therapist's treatment efforts will be directed toward their explanation and rectification. They are second-order organizers of the material from the patient, the first-order organizer being the adaptive context. They are the immediate and active expressions of the patient's Neurosis and, secondarily, of the Neurosis of the therapist. They are the manifestations of emotional difficulty that the therapist hopes to help the patient understand in both conscious and unconscious terms. Positive introjective identifications are thereby generated with a helpful therapist, and the cognitive insights through which the patient is best able to resolve his or her Neurotic maladaptation are identified.

Virtually every single session contains one or more indicators expressed in the material from the patient. They are quite often alluded to manifestly and directly. At times, however, especially when the major disturbance is within the therapist, they may be conveyed in the patient's material through encoded, derivative expressions. In a sense, they are one fulcrum of the therapeutic work, in that they constitute the manifestations of emotional illness that call for therapeutic responses from the therapist.

Indicators of disturbances within the therapist tend in general to create more powerful therapeutic needs within the patient than those involving difficulties within the patient. This is so because they tend to reinforce the patient's own Neurotic adjustment. They also are signs that the therapist is having difficulty in carrying out the therapeutic work, an experience that is introjected on some unconscious level by the patient. They tend to create mistrust and uncertainty, and disturbances in the patient's mode of relatedness and interaction with the therapist. For these and other reasons, therapeutic contexts that involve difficulties within the therapist must be resolved before the patient can expect an effective therapeutic effort in respect to those aspects of his or her own emotional disturbance that derive primarily from within. The resolution of these indicators through both rectification and interpretation tends to foster the patient's own motivation to change by depriving the patient of support for Neurotic maladaptation, and promotes the patient's wish and ability to meaningfully express the critical aspects of emotional difficulties and their underlying basis. In principle, then, the therapist's image and functional capacities must be sound and intact as a basis for therapeutic work with the patient's more intrapsychically-based difficulties.

This first group of indicators, then, involves the countertransferences of the therapist, which tend in actuality to unconsciously express a wish for a pathological mode of relatedness and other pathological needs that are comparable to those conveyed in the patient's own emotional disturbance. Until these are rectified, verbal interpretive work is undermined and proves to be ineffectual. These indicators therefore involve difficulties within the therapist that impair the therapist's basic maturational mode of relatedness with the patient, as well as the therapeutic alliance, the therapist's necessary holding and containment of the patient, the communicative properties of the therapeutic relationship, and the essential efforts directed toward cognitive and insightful resolution of the patient's Neurosis. It is for all of these reasons and more that indications of disturbance within the therapist tend in general to be weighted more heavily than those that involve or are expressed by the patient. This particular type of therapeutic context requires two types of intervention from the therapist: (1) rectification of the error or disturbance and its manifestations in the therapeutic interaction, and (2) interpretation of the patient's responsiveness, unconscious perceptions, and fantasies.

Indicators that pertain to emotional disturbances within the patient are, of course, also of considerable importance. Although the patient's emotional disorder may stem primarily from disruptive inputs from the therapist (and therefore prove to be capable of being resolved based on rectification-interpretation efforts that center on these disturbing adaptive contexts), quite often the therapist is dealing with difficulties within the patient that reflect mainly the latter's own inner mental suffering. Of course, here too the unconscious basis for the symptomatic disturbance located within the patient may derive from vectors within the therapist as well as the patient, but the direct manifestations of the therapeutic context must first be identified as reflected in the patient's associations and behaviors.

This second category of indicators involves all types of symptomatic disturbances within the patient, ranging from anxiety to suicidal and homicidal fantasies and actions. This group of indicators may at times reflect a rather strong need within the patient for an active intervention from the therapist. At other times the basic symptoms that brought the patient into treatment may be involved. Correct interpretation, which is always carried out in light of activated intervention contexts, provides the main means by which the patient gains insight into the unconscious structure of his or her Neurosis. Thus insight therapy is the systematic understanding of the unconscious basis of indicators as revealed through activated adaptive contexts, their implications, and the patient's responsive derivative complex.

Therapeutic contexts often involve disruptions of the therapeutic process, and yet, they provide the therapist with compelling opportunities for active therapeutic work. The presence of indicators in virtually every treatment session creates the potential for each hour to become a minianalysis. The accumulation of these interrelated minianalyses will lead to the proper completion of a psychotherapy.

There is a distinct advantage in rating indicators on a scale of one to ten. The low end of the scale involves sessions in which the therapeutic needs within the patient, based on active disturbances within the patient or the therapist, are relatively low. The higher end of the scale characterizes situations in which this therapeutic need is quite intense (e.g., a suicidal threat or sudden, unexpected wish to terminate). A rating of ten would involve situations in which the therapeutic need is of such proportions that the therapist *must* intervene in some active way if at all possible.

By and large, the strength of the indicators is set against the clarity of representation of the adaptive context and the degree of meaning of the derivative complex. In the ideal, low-resistance network, the adaptive context is represented manifestly or with minimal disguise. In addition, the derivative complex is highly meaningful, and coalesces around the activated intervention context in a manner that reveals many facets of the meaning of the represented therapeutic context. This type of interplay facilitates sound interventions by the therapist. In general, powerful therapeutic need unconsciously motivates most patients to express themselves meaningfully, and to provide the therapist with the elements for intervening which he or she and the patient requires.

In principle, then, the therapist will tend to weigh the intensity of the indicators against the availability of meaningful material for framework management and interpretive responses in each session. The stronger the indicators, the more likely the therapist will intervene with less clear material. In the presence of weak indicators, the therapist will usually wait until the material is relatively clear. It is because of this important balance that a rough measure of the weight of indicators is necessary in every session. Thus the therapist establishes the intensity of therapeutic need within the patient, an evaluation that influences the decision regarding active intervention.

The Rank Ordering of Indicators

The major groups of indicators of both emotional disturbance and a need within the patient for intervention by the therapist are presented in order of importance. There may be an indicator of such power in any category that it is more compelling than those in any other category for the moment. There are thus always two levels of consideration: (1) a very specific weighting of each individual therapeutic context, and (2) a general weighting of the categories of indicators, which helps to establish broad orders of precedence and a general sense of the level of need within the patient for intervention.

ERRORS BY THE THERAPIST

Errors by the therapist, especially major deviations in the basic ground rules of therapy, involve the greatest degree of therapeutic need within the patient. Of late, analysts have become aware of need systems that arise through the patient's object relationships and stem from disturbances in these objects (e.g., Sandler and Sandler 1978). In psychotherapy, the most important of these motivational systems are derived from the patient's object relationship with the therapist. Thus the patient's pathological instinctual drives and unconscious conflicts may be mobilized not only by internal fantasy-memory constellations, but also through the emergence of specific outside stimuli—adaptive contexts and their consequent stirrings and introjects. Id, ego, and superego responses are also created.

On some level all of the therapist's interventions will create some measure of therapeutic need within the patient—i.e., every adaptive context is also an indicator. Validated interventions tend to have a paradoxical effect in evoking envy, guilt, fears of the therapist's powers, and other responses that require therapeutic understanding and intervention.

For the moment, however, the focus will be on the manner in which the therapist's errors create critical therapeutic needs within the patient. These mistakes may involve incorrect interpretations and reconstructions, the use of noninterpretive interventions (a term that is used to allude to all verbal-affective interventions by the therapist that are not essentially interpretive and/or reconstructed, and that do not involve any aspect of the ground rules and boundaries of the therapeutic relationship), and the framework-management responses. They may also involve erroneous measures in the handling of the basic therapeutic environment—deviations from the fundamental ground rules of treatment.

The errors of the therapist create therapeutic needs within the patient for several reasons. First, the patient will tend to introject aspects of the therapist's psychopathology that, once internalized, may lead to symptomatic disturbances within the patient. These pathological introjects and symptomatic disorders require both rectifying and interpretive responses.

A second basis for therapeutic need in the patient involves the impaired fundamental hold and image of the therapist experienced as a consequence of the therapist's error. There is an accompanying disturbance in the basic therapeutic mode of relatedness, with a shift from a healthy therapeutic symbiosis (when it has been present) to a pathological mode: autistic, symbiotic, or parasitic. These qualities are especially intense when the error involves a deviation from the ideal therapeutic frame. There are also concommitant disturbances in the mode of cure (errors lead to the use of action-discharge for relief), the therapeutic alliance, the communicative relationship, and in the basic trust that the patient should have of the therapist. The rectification and interpretation of these fundamental sources of disturbance within the patient is clearly a first-order therapeutic task. The patient reacts powerfully to unconsciously and consciously perceived disturbances in the therapist and to the introjects generated internally.

At times, a major disturbance is evident in the therapist, though as a rule consequent impairments appear as well in both the therapeutic interaction and within the patient. Wherever the major locus of manifest disorder may be, the patient will experience a powerful need for interventions by the therapist. As noted several times already, these interventions, in the presence of an error by the therapist, must involve first a rectification or correction of the manifestations of the error (and its underlying basis), and then the interpretation of the patient's responsive unconscious perceptions, fantasies, and other direct and derivative reactions.

The therapist's errors are actualities with conscious and unconscious, direct and indirect, implications. As noted, they always constitute both therapeutic and adaptive contexts. This implies that they are the adaptation-evoking source of the patient's derivative reactions, as well as a form of Neurosis-related disturbance. In a sense, then, they are both a *type* and *source* of emotional or interactional disturbance.

CLINICAL EXAMPLES

A young man was in therapy for two years at the time of the session. The patient had been responding well to the efforts of the therapist to secure the previously loose ground rules and boundaries of the therapy, and to the therapist's occasional interpretations.

The patient cancelled the session prior to the one presented here. He telephoned the therapist and told him that, because of a city-wide transportation strike, he would be unable to make it to his hour. He said that he had spent four hours hitching one ride or another, and he was still at least an hour away from the therapist's office. He concluded by indicating that he expected to see the therapist the following week. The therapist responded by saying that it was all right, and that he would see him the following week.

The patient then arrived 45 minutes late for a 50-minute session. The following took place in the short time remaining.

> Patient: I'm sorry to be late. I left even an hour earlier today and I just got here. This transportation strike is really something. I see my time is up. I'll pay you for both sessions now.
>
> Therapist: I'm not going to charge you for last session.
>
> Patient: Thanks. *(Writes out a check for one session and gives it to the therapist.)*

At the beginning of the following hour, the patient spoke as follows:

> Patient: I'm furious with my boss. He broke our contract, his commitment to me. He said if I worked on Saturday, I could have Monday off. Now he wants me to work both days, and says its supposed to be good for me. He violated our agreement, and I don't care if I earn some more money, it's not fair.

The main indicator is the therapist's decision not to charge the patient for the first missed hour. Despite the realities involved, the therapist modified the ideal therapeutic contract, which calls for the patient to be responsible for all of his sessions. In addition, the therapist violated the implicit ground rule that all decisions regarding the framework will be subjected to analytic exploration and will be based on the patient's derivative communications as supplemented by his or her manifest responses. Since an intervention by the therapist is involved, this particular indicator is also an adaptive or intervention context.

It has been consistently found that any deviation in the ideal therapeutic framework creates an important measure of inner disturbance and therapeutic need for the patient. This arises because of the inherent damage to the basic holding and containing qualities of the therapist's relationship with the patient, and because of impairments in the patient's image of the therapist in regard to his or her capacity to tolerate frustration, to delay, and to analyze.

There is a characteristic shift to action-discharge, and therefore to noninsightful modes of relief. There are also seductive and hostile qualities to these deviations. Finally, all deviations express efforts by the therapist to effect a pathological mode of relatedness—here, a pathological symbiosis.

The patient does not directly represent the indicator-adaptive context of the therapist's decision not to charge him for the session that he missed. In general, indicators that involve errors by the therapist tend to be represented on a derivative level rather than manifestly. It is alluded to in encoded form when the patient speaks of how his boss broke their contract. Here is the operation of the typical encoding mechanisms to which raw messages are subjected when they are matters of threat. Thus the raw unconscious perception is to the effect that the therapist inappropriately and destructively modified the basic ground rules of the therapy. Through displacement onto his boss, and through symbolization, the patient alludes to a broken contract and a broken commitment. In this instance, there is a small measure of symbolization and the strong use of displacement. The patient appears to be intensely working over the implications of this deviation. He states quite clearly through a displaced derivative, which also contains some degree of symbolic representation, that he remains upset about the violation of the therapeutic pact, even though it gave him more money. He states in plain but displaced language that this is not fair.

The therapist's interpretive and noninterpretive errors fall on the scale of intensity of therapeutic contexts at about the six to eight level. The patient seldom represents them manifestly, so intervening will depend on the extent to which the derivatives coalesce around this type of erroneous intervention. Often, the best technical approach is to understand the meaning of the patient's unconscious communications and to benefit from them by *silently* rectifying the erroneous technical measure to the greatest extent possible.

Deviations in the ideal therapeutic frame tend to be eight to ten level indicators, and are especially high when they involve the fixed-frame arrangements (see Part III). Under these circumstances, the patient will sometimes allude to the deviation manifestly, and will virtually always provide the therapist with highly meaningful derivative material. This tends to include representations of the perceived implications of the deviant intervention context and expressions of the patient's reactive fantasies; encoded directives to the therapist to rectify the damaged frame are also typical. Patients tend to be extremely active on a derivative level in response to this type of disturbance—breaks in the ideal treatment relationship and setting—a finding that indicates the powerful extent to which these deviations create within them powerful therapeutic needs. In general there is a strong correlation between the degree to which an internal or external stimulus disturbs the patient in the realm of his or her Neurosis and the extent to which the patient engages in meaningful communications, both manifestly and latently (i.e., the degree to which the patient provides the therapist with a full and meaningful network of communications).

The following brief vignette serves as a further illustration. The patient is a young woman who has been in psychotherapy for about a year-and-a-half. During this time, the therapist had adopted a number of measures to rectify a highly damaged frame, which included the presence of a secretary, shared office space, and the release of information to third parties. At the time of this session, the therapist had his own consultation room, but shared a waiting room with a therapist (Dr. B.) with whom the patient had been in treatment some years earlier.

> Patient: I saw Dr. B's patient in the waiting room. He's a man with a scoliosis. I wish I could end up like that. I was very upset yesterday. Someone stole my credit card and used it before I could notify the Master Charge people. I got a call from the doctor and felt humiliated. They want to do a mylegram for my spinal problem, and I'm afraid of the procedure. I'm worried it will make me worse even though it's supposed to be helpful. The doctors don't seem to know what they're doing. They seem to have made a good diagnosis, but there is also some confusion. I'm afraid they will only tell me part of the truth and that they will lie to me. I thought cf asking you to call them, but I'm afraid that you will also only tell me part of the truth. I had my dining-room table refinished. It came back looking beautiful, but there was a small flaw. Somehow, the flaw upset me more than it should have.

There appear to be a number of indicators, including the patient's stolen Master Charge card, the damaged dining-room table, and in particular, a work-up that was carried out on the patient because of a suspicious spinal column lesion. These classes of indicators are examined later in this chapter. First, however, the subject remains the indicators that involve a flaw in the ideal therapeutic holding environment—here, that the therapist shares a waiting room with another therapist who also happens to have treated the patient for a period of time. The patient represents this deviation manifestly at the beginning of her hour. Much of the material that follows may be organized around unconscious perceptions of the therapist based on the meanings of this deviation. The patient's upset regarding the theft of her credit card and her suspicious lesion are logical and understandable, and on the surface do not appear to be inappropriate or neurotic. It remains to be seen whether the patient responds to these difficulties on a derivative level that links up meaningfully to her Neurosis. In general, this is seldom the case. On the other hand, the flaw in the fixed frame will tend to evoke derivative responses that meaningfully influence the patient's Neurotic difficulties. Much of this reaction will be founded upon valid unconscious perceptions that reinforce the patient's own Neurotic adjustment. They will be expressed often in encoded messages that manifestly pertain to life issues outside of the therapy.

In the present session, the patient encodes a number of unconscious perceptions of the deviation. Her material reflects her view that it creates conditions of compromise and establishes a situation in which total cure is not feasible (cf. the patient's allusion to settling for some measure of scoliosis). It is a dishonest setting that steals something from the patient (often, patients feel unconsciously that the therapist is taking money from them under false pretenses and conditions). It is also seen as a reflection of confusion in the therapist, and produces a mixed image of him, in part based on his having secured other aspects of the frame while maintaining this particular deviation. This raw message (perception) is encoded in the patient's allusion to her other physician. As the patient also indicates, this type of deviation creates a therapeutic relationship in which lies rather than the truth are likely to be expressed. In one sense, the deviation itself is an expression of an unrecognized lie by the therapist—i.e., it belies the therapist's implicit offer to the patient of an ideal therapeutic relationship and setting. The deviation leads to a sense of basic mistrust in the patient, and is seen as an offer of a pathological symbiotic mode of relatedness from the therapist. These flaws are critical indicators and intervention contexts. Patients will respond quite intensely to them, and they therefore constitute high-level indicators for intervention. In this regard, much of the therapist's effort should concentrate on rectification of the frame at the behest of the patient's derivative communications, and on interpretations of the patient's unconscious perceptions of the implications of the deviation, to which may be added any fantasies and distortions that emerge subsequently.

THE PATIENT'S ATTEMPTS TO ALTER THE GROUND RULES OF THERAPY

In contrast to the first category of indicators, which involve disturbances within the therapist that tend to interfere with the therapeutic experience, the second category of indicators involve emotional difficulties within the patient that lead him or her to attempt to disrupt the treatment process through some modification in the ideal therapeutic setting and rules of treatment. This particular group of indicators constitutes forms of gross behavioral resistances, and they have been separated out from other resistance indicators (see below) because of their considerable importance.

Therapeutic contexts constituted by the patient's efforts to alter the framework of treatment are one of the most frequently observed indicators among those that involve the behaviors of, and disturbances within, the patient. While they tend to express a wish to disturb the therapeutic process and to engage the therapist in pathological modes of relatedness, communication, and cure, they nonetheless constitute important therapeutic opportunities for framework management and interpretive responses by the therapist. Thus, although they express needs within the patient that are pathological and antithetical to insightful cure, they do provide the therapist with a group of indicators that tend to have the potential for highly meaningful therapeutic work.

This category of indicators includes all attempts by the patient to modify the basic ground rules of treatment in any way. As such, they tend to suggest the presence of important underlying emotional disturbances. These may, as with all indicators, derive primarily from within the therapist or from within the patient, but they always stem in important ways from factors within the therapeutic interaction. Quite often, the adaptive context for such an indicator involves a break in the frame on the part of the therapist, a form of counterresistance to which the patient responds resistantly with efforts to modify the frame. Paradoxically, at times these indicators may also arise in response to adaptive contexts constituted by the therapist's securing of the frame, at which point they are characteristically based on distorted unconscious transference fantasies.

The patient's attempts to modify the ground rules of therapy tend to reflect wishes to achieve a framework-deviation cure—symptomatic relief derived from pathological defenses, modes of gratification, modes of relatedness, and the like—that the patient experiences as a consequence of the deviation itself and without constructive cognitive insight. As a rule, then, such efforts at deviation involve the wish to engage the therapist in a pathological mode of relatedness and to gratify specific pathological instinctual drive needs and superego expressions. In essence, they are designed to satisfy the patient's Neurotic needs rather than to insightfully modify them. They are therefore high-level indicators, tending to fall within the seven to ten range in most cases.

These efforts to alter the ground rules of therapy may take place unilaterally or with the implicit or explicit support of the therapist. In the previous chapter, a situation was presented in which a patient responded to a therapist's request to change an hour with a request of this kind of her own. In this situation, the original disturbance was within the therapist and therapeutic interaction. The patient then responded by requesting an alteration of the fixed frame, and the therapist acquiesced. This mixture of adaptive context and indicator evoked powerful derivative responses within the patient.

In general, patients will respond to deviations effected by the therapist with deviations of their own. On the other hand, in situations where the therapist secures an ideal and proper holding environment, patients may become disturbed internally and attempt to unilaterally alter the basic conditions of treatment. There are underlying paranoid and phobic fantasy-anxieties behind these latter efforts at framework-deviation cure. Since they are essentially maladaptive, Neurotic, and uninsightful efforts, they are high-level indicators of disturbance, and reflect a need in the patient for intervention.

The therapist's response must be to maintain the framework to the greatest extent feasible, and to interpret a particular indicator in light of an activated adaptive context and responsive derivative complex. It is quite critical technically to use the patient's efforts at deviation as second-order organizers of the patient's material, and to consistently relate these endeavors to activated intervention contexts. These latter tend to be of two types: deviations by the therapist or efforts by the therapist to secure the frame. The derivative material will usually organize quite well around the implications of the particular context involved, permitting proper interpretation and rectification when needed.

OTHER RESISTANCES EXPRESSED BY THE PATIENT

A variety of gross behavioral resistances are signs of disturbance within the patient and indicators for intervening. These tend to fall into the middle and upper range of the scale of indicators, and at times may be quite disruptive for the patient and the treatment, and obtain a rating of nine or ten. Included here are forms of acting out that do not modify the fixed frame, such as an involvement in an outside relationship that is distinctly pathological and through which the patient is living out responses to the therapeutic situation that interfere with the ongoing therapeutic work. Another type of resistance is rumination and a retreat into relative noncommunication on the surface. Then too, the patient may not attend to or even listen to the therapist's interventions, or may dispute them manifestly to a degree that interferes with the ongoing therapeutic work.

Disturbances in the ideal network of communications serve as indicators for intervention whenever possible. This group of indicators involve unconscious opposition to therapeutic progress, and thus are of critical importance. The activated adaptation-evoking context to which these resistances are related must be identified. At times they are based on disturbances within the therapist that must be rectified if the resistance is to lessen. In contrast, this type of resistance may arise in the context of effective therapeutic work and a sound holding environment; sources then tend to be located within the patient in terms of unconscious transference fantasies, and require interpretation. In principle, the analysis of counterresistances takes precedence over the analysis of resistances, while those resistances that involve the fixed frame are in general stronger indicators than resistances that have little to do with the ground rules of therapy.

SYMPTOMS WITHIN THE PATIENT

Physical and psychological symptoms experienced by the patient constitute indicators of disturbance, and reflect a need in the patient for intervention. Here too, the therapeutic work must be carried out in terms of activated intervention contexts. At times, there are important sources for symptoms within the patient in disturbing interventions from the therapist and in the consequent unconscious perception-introjects so generated. Within a secure frame and in the presence of valid therapeutic work, symptoms will appear primarily on the basis of the patient's own pathological fantasy-memory constellations. These too must be interpreted, however, in light of the positive qualities of the therapist's interventions—the adaptive context.

This category of symptomatic disturbance embraces all types of psychologically founded physical and emotional symptoms. Included here are suicidal and homicidal fantasies, impulses, and behaviors, which may be of such intensity to reach the level of nine or ten on the indicator scale. Other symptoms tend to obtain ratings that are variable and depend on their specific nature. Psychotic, interpersonally disruptive, and severe neurotic symptoms tend to be stronger indicators than milder neurotic symptoms such as limited degrees of anxiety. Acute psychosomatic and depressive symptoms tend to be stronger indicators than milder disturbances. This group of therapeutic contexts involves internal difficulties within the patient, though they may have important sources within the therapeutic interaction. All forms of acting out are also included in this category of indicators. It must be recognized, however, that this particular evaluation is highly subjective on the part of the therapist, who must distinguish pathological behaviors from those that are adaptive.

LIFE CRISES AND OTHER DISTURBANCES IN THE PATIENT'S LIFE

Emotionally laden life experiences constitute the final group of indicators. Extreme situations, such as a serious physical injury or a death in the patient's family, may create relatively strong indicators, though on the whole this particular group tends to be the weakest of all signs of therapeutic need within the patient. In general, these indicators take on importance as the life trauma links up to some issue in the therapeutic interaction.

Patients tend to express themselves manifestly or through Type One derivatives in response to such disturbances, and only rarely make use of Type Two derivative communication in light of an activated intervention context. Characteristically, these outside traumas are used as a vehicle through which the patient expresses derivative unconscious perceptions and fantasies regarding the therapist as they pertain to some specific adaptation-evoking context within treatment. The patient's response to a major outside trauma rarely occurs on a sufficiently Neurotic and derivative level to permit intervention with minimal attention to activated adaptive contexts. In general, such a response occurs only in the presence of a major trauma. The therapist must remain mindful that, in general, such material is most meaningful for the psychotherapeutic experience and for the illumination of the patient's Neurosis through the ways in which it serves as a vehicle for the patient's derivative expressions.

Summary

Indicators or therapeutic contexts are expressions of emotional disturbance within the patient, the therapist, and the therapeutic interaction. Most critical indicators involve the treatment experience, although on occasion they may pertain to the outside life of the patient.

At the heart of an indicator is an emotional disturbance within the patient, though its primary source may lie within the patient's inner mental world or in an unconsciously perceived and introjected disturbance within the therapist. Thus indicators reflect a therapeutic need in the patient for intervention by the therapist. The latter involves interpretation when the therapist's contribution to the therapeutic context is relatively small, but requires both rectification of the therapist's contribution and interpretation when the input from the therapist is of some significance.

In order of importance, the five categories of indicators are: (1) errors by the therapist, especially major deviations in the ground rules of therapy; (2) alterations in the ground rules of therapy by the patient, or efforts on the patient's part in that direction—the most common form of gross behavioral resistance; (3) other resistances expressed by the patient; (4) symptoms within the patient; and (5) life crises and other disturbances in the patient's daily life.

All adaptive contexts (interventions) from the therapist are indicators, though not all indicators are adaptation-evoking contexts. The presence of indicators in virtually every session offers a potential therapeutic opportunity for both patient and therapist through which an activated expression of the patient's emotional illness, or of some factor within the therapeutic interaction and therapist that is contributing to that illness, can be interpreted and, where necessary, rectified. All such work is carried out in terms of the activated intervention contexts that have contributed to the indicator itself, and to the derivative complex that forms the unconscious basis of the indicator and reveals its encoded meanings. Involved in the latter are both unconscious perception-introjects and unconscious fantasy-memory constellations.

In intervening, the therapist must weigh the power of the indicators against the clarity of the patient's material. With intense signs of therapeutic need within the patient, the therapist must intervene even in the presence of poor representations of the adaptive context and derivative responses that are highly disguised and have been subjected to strong resistances. In the presence of less pressing indicators, the therapist would tend to intervene only when the material is quite clear. In general, powerful indicators reflect pressing therapeutic needs within the patient, and tend to lead the patient to modify his or her defenses and resistances so that there is highly meaningful interpretive material.

By carrying out therapeutic work in terms of activated indicators and their unconscious meanings and functions, psychotherapy is constituted as a series of minianalyses whose total effect should be that of a successful treatment, which produces an insightful resolution of the patient's Neurosis. Indicators mark the emotional disturbance of the patient and its sources within the therapeutic interaction. Proper interpretive and framework-management responses create the necessary maturational mode of relatedness and therapeutic framework, and the essential cognitive insights, through which the patient is able to knowingly resolve the basic maladaptations that have led to a symptomatic disturbance.

Chapter 10

The Network of Communications: The Adaptive Context

The adaptive context lies at the heart of the patient's manifest and latent reactions as they pertain to his or her Neurosis and its resolution. This is the adaptation-evoking stimuli to which the patient is responding. The therapist's interventions are nearly always the critical adaptive context. Thus adaptive context, adaptation-evoking context, and intervention context may be used interchangeably. A true understanding of the patient's manifest and latent (derivative) responses and expressions is possible only in light of a full conceptualization of the manifest and latent implications of the adaptive context. Thus much of the listening-formulating process is a study of the adaptive context.

The therapist has five interrelated tasks: (1) identifying each manifest activated intervention context; (2) determining the best representation of the adaptive context in the patient's material, as well as supplementary representations; (3) identifying the patient's conscious and (especially) unconscious perceptions of the meanings and functions of the adaptive context, and his or her image of the therapist who has intervened in this manner; (4) recognizing other possible meanings of the adaptive context not represented for the moment in the patient's material; and (5) understanding how the intervention context serves as a stimulus for the patient's symptomatic responses, and how it functions to organize the patient's manifest and (especially) derivative associations.

144

Identifying the Manifest Intervention Context

The therapist's first task is to state simply and directly the manifest interventions that constitute the adaptation-evoking contexts for the patient. The therapist does so in plain terms without suggesting the implications of these contexts or the patient's representations and perceptions of them. This direct effort at naming provides the therapist with a point of orientation from which the listening-formulating process may be used.

In the actual clinical situation, the therapist will sometimes enter a session already mindful of a number of specific adaptive contexts drawn from the previous hour or from some other contact with the patient, such as occurs with a telephone call. Other contexts will occur to the therapist as he or she listens to the patient's material, allowing himself or herself to be guided by the patient's manifest allusions to the therapist's efforts and by the encoded material. On the derivative level, the therapist has two guiding forces: first, derivative representations of the intervention context itself; and second, the manner in which a constellation of derivatives will suggest the presence of an unrecognized intervention context. This latter is based on the recognition that it is the adaptation-evoking context that stimulates the derivative complex. Thus the shape of the derivative complex can provide important clues to an active intervention context.

In principle, every intervention by the therapist is an adaptive context. Aspects of the fixed setting and of the therapist's basic attitude and approach to the patient may function at times as activated adaptation-evoking contexts, especially when they are pertinent in some special way. By and large, however, the main adaptive contexts for the patient's material take the form of the therapist's extended silences and active interventions—interpretive, noninterpretive, and in regard to managing the ground rules and frame. The therapist must therefore take each intervention as an activated adaptive context, affording special emphasis to adaptive contexts drawn from the previous session and, especially, from the session at hand.

Highly traumatic adaptive contexts tend to have a persisting influence, sometimes for months and even throughout the entire duration of a treatment experience. This is especially true of breaks in the basic framework that are part of the therapeutic pact.

However, long-standing adaptive contexts may be used as the organizers of the patient's material only when there is some immediate adaptation-evoking stimulus to which it is related, or a situation in which the earlier traumatic intervention is repeated.

The therapist has two sources through which to identify activated intervention contexts. The first involves the therapist's own subjective realizations and the specific identification of the presence of a meaningful silence or active intervention on his or her part. The second derives from the patient, and is based on a continual monitoring of the material from the patient for direct and encoded representations of the intervention context.

All direct allusions by the patient to the therapist, the therapeutic setting, and the nature of the therapist's interventions should be examined as possible direct manifestations or representations of intervention contexts. Although these manifest elements may also yield derivative meaning in light of other intervention contexts, it is most important to first consider the possibility that the manifest association is serving as a direct representation of an activated adaptive context. In addition, each derivative element should be tested out as a possible means through which the patient is representing an intervention context from the therapist. Only subsequently are the same manifest elements examined as potential representations of indicators or for possible derivative meaning.

As a rule, in low resistance sessions, patients tend to represent activated intervention contexts early in the session directly or with little disguise. When they fail to do so, it is quite likely that the adaptive context will not receive a readily identifiable representation, and it may be postulated that the patient has resistances against this representation. On rare occasions, a patient will provide the therapist with a rather meaningful derivative complex and offer a good representation of the adaptive context at the very end of a session. Sometimes this occurs as the patient is leaving the hour, such as is often seen with the presentation of an insurance form that the therapist is expected to fill out. However, manifest and especially derivative listening is facilitated when the patient provides the therapist with a direct but passing representation of the adaptive context early in an hour. Such sessions are likely to lead to interpretation and framework-management responses by the therapist.

Most sessions have two or more activated intervention contexts.

The exceptions arise in clinical situations in which the patient is afforded a secure therapeutic environment, setting, and relationship, so that a basic, healthy, therapeutic symbiosis has been established. At such times, the therapist either maintains a holding position or interprets the patient's derivative material in light of the latter's response to the securing of the therapeutic environment. In these instances, the main adaptive context is the therapist's offer of a sound holding relationship and correct interpretations.

When one or more modifications are present in the ideal therapeutic environment, or when the therapist engages in noninterpretive and erroneously interpretive interventions, there is usually a conglomeration of several active intervention contexts. Thus it is helpful to have an understanding of those adaptive contexts that are likely to promote the greatest level of therapeutic need within the patient.

It is important to distinguish between countertransference-based silences and interventions and those that are not based on error and poor technique. In general, countertransference-based intervention contexts are more powerful indicators and organizers of the patient's material than those in which countertransferences are not reflected. Similarly, it is important to evaluate the extent to which an adaptive context is traumatic and hurtful to the patient, and the degree to which it is essentially constructive and helpful. Sound interventions tend to deprive the patient of pathological modes of relatedness, and generate a wide variety of narcissistic and other hurts. At times they are essentially helpful and constructive, and create little pain for the patient.

In general, the more traumatic, frustrating, and depriving an intervention context, the more intense is the therapeutic need created within the patient, and the more strongly does the particular intervention serve as a prime organizer of the patient's material. Interventions that involve the basic relationship between the patient and therapist, its ground rules and boundaries, since they are fundamental to the patient's therapeutic experience, tend to be more powerful adaptation-evoking contexts than those unrelated to the fixed frame.

In practical terms, this means that any type of deviation in the ideal framework will be a more powerful adaptive stimulus than the paradoxically threatening and frustrating contexts related to the secure frame, and even more powerful than an absence by the therapist for vacation or for other reasons. This latter is a necessary though hurtful part of the ideal therapeutic environment, in that it proves essential that the therapist at times separate from the patient in order to prevent pathological merger or undue dependence, and in order to afford the patient an opportunity to work over and analyze universal separation anxieties. Similarly, a break in the frame, such as the therapist's lateness to an hour, will take precedence over the frustrating but necessary holding approach in which a therapist, at the behest of the patient's derivatives, decides not to change an hour despite the patient's request to do so because of some important external reason. The painful holding qualities of the frame are less powerful intervention contexts than actual deviations and breaks.

Determining the Best Representations of the Adaptive Context

The ideal, resistance-free representation of an activated adaptive context is a direct and manifest allusion by the patient to a particular intervention, whether the reaction is conscious or unconscious. This type of allusion is made relatively briefly and in passing, and the patient then shifts to talk about other surface matters—the latter providing the necessary displacement that enables the patient to meaningfully communicate encoded reactions to the adaptive context. Should the patient dwell upon the manifestly represented intervention context through extended surface associations, the therapist is usually faced with a situation in which the intervention context has been represented directly, but the derivative complex is quite poor.

In those situations in which the patient does not manifestly allude to the intervention context, the next best mode of representation is that of a thinly disguised derivative. While direct representations facilitate full interpretation, derivative representation enables the therapist to play back a series of selected derivative responses organized around the close derivative representation of the adaptive context. Important supplementary representations should also be identified. This endeavor overlaps into the therapist's next task: identifying the patient's conscious and unconscious perceptions of the meanings and functions of the adaptive context. Thus the therapist is immediately in touch with the patient's gross resistances, and gets a sense of the ease or difficulty of the intervention.

The issue of *representation* is separate from the nature of the dynamics and genetics contained within the represented material. When representations are poor, interpretations will be difficult; when they are clear and relatively resistance-free, interventions (where necessary) are facilitated. These propositions are true regardless of the dynamics and genetics involved, and regardless of whether the material organizes primarily as unconscious perceptions or unconscious fantasies of the therapist and the intervention.

CLINICAL EXAMPLE

A woman patient is being seen by a therapist who shares his waiting room and his secretary with two other therapists. At the time of this session, a number of issues regarding the ground rules of therapy had arisen and been explored. However, rectification of the two deviations identified had not taken place. In the session prior to the hour excerpted, the therapist had not intervened.

> Patient: When I came in, I could smell coffee brewing. It smelled good. I would like to have a cup. I guess your secretary made it up for you. I'm beginning to understand more about myself; my anxiety has lessened. I decided to leave my job at the abortion clinic. The other day, while I was in session with a client, my boss walked in and sat down and stayed for the entire hour. I was furious. Therapy should be intimate between two people. Her presence was disruptive. Afterwards, she wanted to talk to me about the patient. There was nothing I wanted to say to her. I dreamt about having sex with my husband. There was something pleasant about it, but something was wrong. I'm thinking of going to a hypnotist so I can lose some weight. I should be able to do it on my own without that kind of assistance. With my first husband, we had this scene when he found out I was having an affair. But then I found out he was having an affair too. There were such lies and deceit between us. We tried to do something about it, but he really didn't understand me.

There are compelling implications here regarding many aspects of psychotherapy. However, the two immediate tasks are: (1) identifying the adaptive contexts for this hour, and (2) determining the ways in which the patient has represented these contexts, including the best specific representation of each. The therapist's silence in the prior hour is the first adaptive context for this session. Other contexts include the shared waiting room and the shared secretary.

Having simply stated the manifest definition of each of these three contexts, the next task is to determine their relative hypothetical power. In doing so, one must be prepared to find that a particular context is especially strong for a particular patient. In principle, however, the two breaks in the frame—the shared waiting room and the shared secretary—would be expected to take precedence over the therapist's silence. It would be important to know whether this silence constituted a validated intervention or a missed intervention—i.e., whether the therapist had overlooked a necessary interpretation or framework-rectification response, or had maintained an appropriate measure of silence in light of the indicators and the patient's derivative and manifest material. Still, each of the three contexts must be examined to determine how it is best represented in the patient's material.

How, then, is the therapist's silence most clearly represented in the patient's material? There is no direct allusion to it in the patient's associations. There is, however, a moderately disguised derivative representation in the patient's statement that there was nothing that she wanted to say to her boss after her boss had sat in on the patient's session with her client. Using displacement from the therapist to the patient herself, the patient symbolically represents and specifically characterizes the therapist's silence in the previous hour as reflecting a way of pulling back from the patient and not wanting to talk to her. In this particular representation, there is a suggestion of maladaptation and a hint that the silence was experienced as reflecting some measure of emotional disturbance (countertransference) and hostility.

Are there other, more disguised, representations of the adaptive context of the therapist's silence? The only one that can be readily detected is the patient's allusion to her decision to leave her job at the abortion clinic. Through displacement, condensation, and symbolic representation, the patient may well have represented her unconscious raw perception of the therapist's silence and its implications as his way of giving up on his job and, perhaps, of abandoning the patient as well. The representations of the adaptive context begin to shape an understanding of the patient's unconscious perceptions of their meanings.

Next, how is the adaptive context of the shared waiting room represented in the patient's material? On the manifest level, there is a vague and minimal direct allusion to this context in that the patient says something about smelling coffee brewing. In actuality, this refers to the brief period of time during which she sat in the waiting room. However, since there is no direct mention of the waiting room itself, this reference to the period when she came into the therapist's office would have to be considered an encoded representation of the waiting-room adaptive context—i.e., as a general allusion to an aspect of the treatment experience that serves as a disguised representation of a specific adaptive context. Perhaps the most meaningful and best representation of this particular intervention context is the encoded allusion to the presence of the patient's boss during the patient's session with her client. This representation touches upon a specific meaning of the shared waiting room—the exposure to third parties. Other representations include the reference to the clinic, the thought of going to a hypnotist (i.e., another therapist or third party), and the allusion to having an affair. Each of these representations illustrates the use of displacement and symbolic representation of the raw image of the shared waiting room, and some of the implications are readily apparent.

Finally, how is the adaptive context of the shared secretary represented in the patient's material? There is a direct and manifest representation of her presence—the patient mentions her directly. There are also a number of supplementary representations, many of them overlapping (condensed) with those that pertain to the shared waiting room. Both the secretary and the waiting room introduce third parties into the patient's treatment situation. The presence of the secretary may also be represented by the reference to the boss who sat in on the session with the client, as well as through the allusions to the clinic, the hypnotist, and the affair.

In the course of listening, the therapist selects the best and most meaningful representation of the most important intervention contexts as a fulcrum through which to organize the balance of the patient's derivative material. The therapist will be inclined to intervene in respect to these contexts rather than others. The therapist will also attempt to select no more than one or two important and interrelated, highly active intervention contexts as a basis for active therapeutic efforts (using the patient's material as the main guide). In the present session, the therapist would be likely to organize this material and intervene in terms of the presence of the secretary far more than in terms of the shared waiting room, and especially far more than in terms of his earlier silence. It would be possible for him to secondarily touch upon the issue of the shared waiting room, since the material condenses and overlaps in this area. However, the main focus would be on the most clearly represented intervention context, which also proves to be the context that most meaningfully organizes the patient's derivative responses.

Establishing the Patient's Conscious and Unconscious Perceptions of the Therapist and the Interventions

Although a patient occasionally comments consciously and directly on an intervention by the therapist, these manifest responses have little bearing on the patient's Neurosis. These manifest reactions tend to be highly distorted either by overidealization or undue suspiciousness and criticism. As a result, their direct implications are open to question, and their most compelling meanings involve their function as derivative expressions. Only when the therapist has been involved in a blatant error does the patient prove capable, and then only rarely, of recognizing such gross dificulties and commenting directly upon them. Because of the patient's own defensive needs and the interpersonal anxieties involved in reporting responses to the therapist on a direct, open, and manifest level, the vast majority of important perceptions and areas of understanding of the therapist are communicated in encoded form.

In principle, then, the therapist should attend to and understand the immediate (direct) implications of manifest responses to interventions. It is essential, however, to be certain, in addition, that these manifest expressions are subjected to the decoding process in light of the implications of the most immediate intervention contexts. These may correspond and be identical to the one regarding which the patient is commenting, though the most active intervention context is quite often a different intervention from the one to which the patient is responding manifestly. The displacement is from one intervention to another, and the usual decoding proceddures must be applied.

The therapist must monitor all of the material from the patient following interventions as a *commentary* on the intervention. The basic assumption is that the patient's derivative expressions will contain a series of valid unconscious perceptions of the implications of the intervention. In addition, of course, there may be extensions into pathological fantasy and distortion, and at times— especially when the therapist has intervened in a manner that is validated—these distortions may be predominant.

An essential component of the patient's commentary reactions to an intervention involves the unconscious perceptions and introjects considered here. The distinction between valid perception and distorted fantasy is possible only through a full evaluation of the implications of the intervention at hand. The therapist's self-knowledge and understanding of the nature of his or her silences and interventions prove to be the most critical factors in the therapist's capacity for listening and formulating. Because of the dangers of countertransference-based influences, the therapist's own subjective evaluation of the implications of an intervention should always be checked against the patient's direct and especially derivative communications. In general, the patient's associations on a derivative level tend to be rather perceptive, accurate, and truthful. Although unconsciously distorted perceptions of the therapist are possible, they are not especially common. Because of this, they should not be formulated unless the therapist has carefully checked and rechecked the nature of his or her interventions and found the patient's unconsciously expressed view clearly in error.

The patient's unconscious perceptions and introjects of the therapist, and of the implications of the therapeutic efforts, are an important part of the derivative complex. Since they involve realities filled with unconscious meaning, these impressions tend to take precedence over the patient's own primarily intrapsychic pathological fantasies. Further, since they involve the therapist's communicated inner state and capacity to intervene and maintain the holding environment, they are of critical importance. Thus the therapist's first task is to identify representations of the adaptive context, while the second task is to identify unconsciously perceived implications of these same contexts. These two tasks often go hand in hand. Only after these issues have been carefully studied, can other aspects of the derivative complex (e.g., reactive pathological fantasies, other types of adaptive and maladaptive reactions, genetic connections, etcetera) be considered.

CLINICAL EXAMPLE (CONTINUED)

Some of the patient's unconscious perceptions of the three intervention contexts have already been identified. An examination of this manifest material for derivative commentaries on the therapist's silence leads to the association of the patient to a decision to leave her job at the abortion clinic, which suggests through the undoing of displacement and symbolic encoding that the patient had perceived the therapist's silence as an abandonment of his job and possibly as an effort to disturb or abort the therapeutic process. This particular derivative meaning implies that the therapist probably had missed an important intervention in the previous hour. Although this particular thesis cannot be documented, it offers an illustration of the ways in which the derivative decoding of manifest material may suggest specific intervention contexts and particular implications for the contexts. Thus, in listening to this session relatively openly, the images of leaving a job and of an abortion clinic could readily conjure up, through abstraction and generalization, the themes of separation, abandoning a job (which may have a variety of meanings, some that need not be pathological), abortion in the sense of premature ending, and the clinic with all of its many implications of exposure, inexperienced therapists, low fee, etcetera. Through the particularizing process, the specific meanings that seem to fit the known adaptive context are then selected.

The manifest material regarding the presence of the patient's boss in the session with the client, as organized as a commentary on the therapist's silence, suggests a possible perception or fantasy within the patient that it is the presence of third parties that in some way has led the therapist to be silent. The reference to being furious could suggest an unconscious perception by the patient of the therapist's silence as a consequence and reflection of anger and rage. The allusion to intimacy implies either that the silence was an effort unconsciously on the part of the therapist to arrange an appropriate intimate relationship, or that it reflected a fear of such a relationship.

The element that involves the patient's wish not to talk to her boss because she had intruded on the session with the client has already been discussed in terms of the way in which it serves as a representation of the intervention context of the therapist's silence. It also suggests that the patient unconsciously perceived some type of upset and intrusion as a factor that influenced the therapist's failure to intervene.

In each instance of attempting to identify an aspect of the patient's unconscious perceptions of the therapist and his intervention, the material is treated entirely in terms of either introjects of the therapist or valid representations of attributes of the therapist. Of course, the same material on a derivative level may also represent aspects of the patient and representations of herself. In principle, all of the patient's associations are applied to the therapist, in an attempt to shape them as valid unconscious perceptions and introjects, before they are applied to the patient in terms of fantasies and distortions. This process has been described as the use of the *me/not-me interface*. (This particular term has been developed as a way of indicating that the manifest associations from a patient serve as an interface that reflects introjects and unconscious perceptions of the therapist in one direction, and realizations regarding the patient in the other. All decoding of derivatives should be carried out in terms of both of these aspects.)

Therapists inevitably experience considerable resistance in accepting all of the patient's material as containing, on some level, derivative and valid unconscious perceptions and introjects. Although there are certainly exceptions to the veracity of these communications, and distorted unconscious perceptions do get expressed from time to time, there is considerable truth in these expressions. They are far more readily recognized when the therapist attends to the unconscious implications of his or her own interventions rather than limiting consideration of his or her own efforts to manifest intentions and their surface meanings. For the patient, the derivative and unconsciously communicated meanings of an intervention are far more powerful than the manifest effects. In addition, interventions have their intended constructive effects only when the manifest and latent implications are syncronous and constructive.

The patient's dream of sex with her husband suggests an unconscious perception of some type of sexual conflict as contributing to the therapist's silence. The allusion to the hypnotist implies that the patient also experienced the therapist's silence as an effort to merge with her. In this regard, it can be stressed that this particular introjected formulation (in terms of an unconscious perception of the therapist) must take precedence over the suggestion that the same derivative reflects an unconscious wish-fantasy within the patient to merge sexually with the therapist. Certainly, through condensation, in light of the activated intervention context, both formulations may be true. However, to the extent that the patient has accurately perceived pathological needs within the therapist, these must be rectified and interpreted first, before the patient's own comparable wishes can be fully expressed, analyzed, and resolved.

The next derivative, regarding the way in which the patient should be able to lose weight on her own without hypnotic assistance, gives the therapist's silence a positive tone. It is the patient's reading here that the silence reflects a wish on the therapist's part that the patient function relatively autonomously. However, this particular implication of the silence is short-lived. Next, the patient returns to the theme of sex and of having affairs, and of lying and deceit. In this way, the patient is suggesting again that the therapist is experiencing underlying sexual conflicts and fantasies, and that he is defending himself against them through his silence. The patient also indicates that she believes unconsciously that the therapist used the silence as a form of deceit.

Finally, the patient indicates, through a displaced derivative related to her husband, that she experienced the silence as reflecting a lack of understanding within the therapist. This is in keeping with Freud's (1900) conceptualization of primary processes and unconscious communication: the material from the patient may contain a series of rather different derivative characterizations of a particular intervention context. Similarly, the patient may reflect a variety of unconscious perceptions of the therapist based on particular therapeutic efforts. At times these may be quite contradictory. Contradiction emerges as a rule because of mixed qualities that can be attributed to the intervention context itself. No silence or active intervention by the therapist is entirely correct or incorrect; the inevitable presence of some degree of intermixture of both valid and destructive efforts is likely to produce a series of mixed unconscious perceptions and introjects within the patient. It is the therapist's job to identify the patient's major impressions, to validate them subjectively, to develop formulations on the basis of his or her particular evaluation of the patient's material, and eventually—when the time is right—to offer an interpretation on the basis of his or her listening-formulating efforts. Indirect and derivative validations of such an interpretation would suggest if the therapist's formulations were essentially correct.

In this type of listening, the therapist silently expects the patient to characterize his or her impressions of the therapist's most recent interventions. The therapist accepts all of the manifest material as an encoded commentary on his or her efforts. The therapist understands every allusion, whether to the patient, himself or herself, or others, as characterizing either one of the therapist's personal attributes or some possible unconscious motive for the particular therapeutic effort. By checking out these unconsciously conveyed impressions against the therapist's own subjective appraisal of the manifest and especially latent implications of the interventions, the therapist is able to decide on the extent to which the patient's commentary has validity.

In the session much of the decoding process would involve an attempt to understand the derivative implications of the associations as they pertain to a particular adaptation-evoking context—in this case, the sharing of a secretary with two other therapists. Its centrality for this material has already been established, and thus the therapist would be likely to concentrate his listening-formulating efforts in this direction. However, it is essential that, at the same time, he in part maintains an open mind and is prepared to identify other activated adaptive contexts that could help to account for the patient's encoded messages.

Had the therapist established prior to the session a silent hypothesis that, of late, the intrusion of the secretary as a third party to this treatment situation was of especially compelling importance, the material in this hour would have provided him with silent validation. The patient's direct allusion to the secretary at the beginning of the hour is a favorable sign, in that this type of early direct representation often indicates that the patient is prepared to work over this particularly disturbing intervention context through derivatives. The presence of an additional, especially clear derivative representation—the allusion to the intrusive boss—also points to this issue as an important unconscious problem that the patient is presently working over. In that light, the patient's unconscious perceptions of the deviation and of the therapist may be reviewed. Each representation and specific commentary will tend to express a separate aspect of the patient's total reading or evaluation of the deviation. Together they form a coalescible network of unconsciously perceived meanings and functions.

Thus the patient first assigns a meaning to the therapist's use of the secretary that involves his feeding and nurturing. Her own manifest wish to have a cup of coffee—i.e., to share in the oral gratification—is a surface, and possibly derivative, reaction to the perceived meaning of the intervention context; as such, it belongs to the remainder of the derivative complex that is presented in the following chapter.

The next encoded unconscious perception of an implication of the presence of the secretary is developed manifestly in terms of the patient's decision to leave her job at the abortion clinic. In this way, the patient is communicating her perception of the deviation as a means through which the therapist himself has abandoned his function as a therapist and has tended to abort the treatment process with the patient. Since secretaries usually imply to patients the existence of pathological symbiotic needs in their therapists and modifications in total confidentiality and privacy, their presence does indeed preclude the possibility of cognitive understanding in regard to certain aspects of the patient's Neurosis. The possibility of a truthful therapeutic experience is abandoned or aborted.

A further representation of the presence of the secretary is formulated through the manifest allusion to the patient's boss who sat in on her session with a client. The reference to the patient's sense of fury suggests that the alteration in the frame is seen by the patient to be based on some unresolved hostility within the therapist. The same derivative also contains the patient's displaced reaction toward the therapist for including the secretary in the basic setting of his work. This second, condensed meaning belongs to the balance of the derivative complex, and not to the important area of representation of the implications of the adaptive context itself.

The patient's comment that therapy should be an intimate experience between two people reveals in a displaced and only minimally encoded form that the patient has an unconscious perception of the disruption in the necessary one-to-one relationship created by the presence of the secretary. The patient herself alludes directly to these disruptive qualities, and then goes on to indicate the way in which this particular deviation interferes with her wish to communicate openly with the therapist. This is, of course, a critical implication for this particular deviation: it evokes and expresses defensiveness and thrusts directed toward noncommunication.

The patient then alludes to the dream of having sex with her husband. In this way, the patient portrays the unconscious sexual implications of the therapist's need for the secretary. It is gratifying, pleasant, but wrong. The allusion to the hypnotist suggests the unconsciously perceived merger qualities involved in the therapist's need for the secretary. The use of the hypnotist to lose weight as an alternative to doing so through insight gained through treatment implies a perception of the deviation as offering an alternative mode of cure through fusion rather than insight for both the patient and the therapist.

The patient's comment that she should be able to lose weight on her own without that kind of assistance is a clear model of rectification. As such, it bridges the patient's unconscious representations of the implications of the adaptive context and that part of the derivative complex that contains the patient's reactions to what she has perceived.

Next, the patient alludes to her own affair and the discovery that her husband too was having an affair. Here the patient represents the deviant adaptive context as implying again a break in the usual frame (a sexual liason) and, quite importantly, a means by which the therapist expresses himself in an inappropriate and pathological manner, which suggests to her that he shares maladaptive and Neurotic problems with her.

Finally, the patient alludes to the lies and deceits between her and her husband. Through displacement, she rather cogently indicates that under the conditions of a third party to treatment the therapy itself is characterized as a form of lie therapy. The patient may be suggesting here that, while the therapist sincerely professes to wish to help the patient understand herself and gain insight, the manner in which he has created the basic framework for treatment belies these intentions. As such, the deviation gives lie to the therapist's stated or otherwise implied intentions. This is a common unconscious perception under such conditions.

The patient's last comment, about trying to do something

about the relationship with her husband and the way in which he did not really understand her, is probably not so much a representation of the adaptive context as a reflection of the patient's unconscious awareness that, on some level, she has been attempting to help the therapist to rectify this frame, and has found him to be refractory to her efforts. As such, it too belongs to the reactive aspects of the derivative complex.

Each of these derivative elements touches upon a different aspect of the implications of the adaptive context to which the patient is responding. There is, of course, some measure of selection, since certain qualities will have special cogency and meaning for the patient in light of her own history, needs, pathology, and assets. The particular unconscious perceptions and meaning assignments that the patient affords an adaptive context are an interactional product that depends on the nature of the intervention itself, the attitudes and behaviors of the therapist in other areas, and a host of factors within the patient. There is a tendency for a given patient to accentuate selected meanings of an intervention context in terms of those implications that have especially compelling power for that particular patient. Thus the meanings assigned to a particular adaptive context may be classified as: (1) universal (those meanings and implications of an intervention context that exist for all patients), and (2) personal (those particular meanings chosen from the universal meanings that are experienced in light of highly individual factors within the patient).

In the session, the assigned meanings involve unconscious conflicts and dynamics. In a later hour, the patient spoke of a brief affair she discovered between her mother and a neighbor. At this point the unconsciously perceived genetic element emerged in the material. In terms of the therapist's use of the deviation, this particular recollection may be seen as an offer by the patient of an unconscious perception of the possibility that the therapist adopted this particular kind of arrangement because of some deviant behavior that occurred in his relationship with his mother (a general unconscious interpretation offered by the patient). Of course, on another level, the same derivative undoubtedly reflects an aspect of the patient's own sensitivity to this issue and its personal meaning for her. It is important, however, to always begin with a characterization of such material in terms of unconscious perceptions of the therapist. It is often these perceptions that bridge over into a patient's unconscious interpretations to the therapist of possible dynamic and genetic factors that have motivated him or her to deviate or to otherwise err.

Recognizing Possible Meanings of an Adaptive Context Not Represented in the Patient's Material

Whenever a patient alludes manifestly or through a thinly disguised derivative representation to a particular intervention context, the therapist should engage in an extensive reevaluation of the nature and implications of his or her own efforts. While listening to the patient's material for additional clues, the therapist must engage in a period of reassessment and self-analysis. The therapist may examine such attributes of the intervention as its correctness or validity, timing, and a variety of other qualities of this kind, including unconscious meanings and functions. When an intervention is viewed as essentially correct, the therapist can search out the small measure of countertransference and error that will be reflected even then. On the other hand, when the therapist begins to discover that he or she has made an error, the focus will be more clearly on the factors within the therapist that have contributed to the mistake.

In regard to the valid aspects of the intervention, the therapist will have little need for further exploration of the motives for intervening. The main focus will be on the positive impact that the intervention has had on the patient and the search for possible paradoxical and threatening consequences.

In addition, the manifestations of the therapist's inevitable or preponderant countertransferences—that aspect of the therapist's intervention that is in error to a minor or major degree—must always be formulated. Because of the important ways in which this erroneous quality effects the patient, the therapist must then carry out a number of additional subjective tasks. The nature of the therapist's mistake and its timing must be carefully identified. The therapist must look to the patient's prior associations and to the state of the relationship with the patient (and secondarily with others, within and outside of his or her professional life) for the antecedent factors that prompted the error. Since every mistake constitutes a pathological unconscious communication from the therapist, the therapist must also engage in self-analytic efforts in order to determine the unconscious messages that he or she has expressed. The possible pathological meanings and functions that can be attributed to the therapist's intervention, and that the therapist has attempted in reality to actualize in the relationship with the patient, must also be identified. The therapist must also privately engage in efforts at self-analysis in order to identify the unconscious countertransference constellation that accounts for the mistake. The therapist must attempt self-understanding, both dynamically and genetically, and to identify the interplay between these intrapsychic factors and the relationship and interaction with the patient.

In all, then, the therapist must engage in a variety of efforts at self-evaluation, self-analysis, and reexamination of the implications of the interventions in an effort to identify what has been communicated to, and imposed upon, the relationship with the patient. There must be a consistent interplay between the therapist's understanding of the implications of the patient's material in these areas and the therapist's own self-realizations. Each will increase the therapist's sensitivity to the other. As comprehension of the nature of the intervention context grows, the therapist will also be in a position to recognize areas in which he or she has been relatively defensive and unaware, and aspects of the adaptive context to which the patient is most and least sensitive. Thus the therapist is able to develop a clearer picture of his or her own defenses and resistances, as well as those of the patient.

In principle, all of the therapist's private evaluations of a particular intervention context should be tested out in the material from the patient, especially through its encoded implications. Subjectively founded silent hypotheses must always find support in the patient's own communications before being adopted as a basis for intervening. Every aspect of the listening process should have at least one form of independent verification, one essential effort to safeguard its veracity and validity. Formulations derived from the patient's associations should be validated through both the therapist's own subjective appraisal and from additional material from the patient, especially in terms of its encoded messages. Conversely, subjective impressions and evaluations from the therapist should find support in the therapist's subsequent private formulations; but in particular, support must be sought in the patient's ongoing material—especially on the derivative level.

The Adaptive Context as the Organizer of the Patient's Material

As the attributes of a particular intervention context become clear, the therapist must make attempts to relate the meanings and implications of the patient's additional associations to the adaption-evoking context. A particular adaptive context must be understood in light of its meanings and functions so that it may help to account for the unconscious basis of an indicator (a symptom within the patient, a resistance, or some type of disturbance within the therapist). The therapist must also attempt to understand the patient's associations (especially those that are latent) as responses to the adaptive stimuli contained within the intervention. Thus the therapist makes use of adaptive contexts to shape an understanding of the patient's derivative material.

The meanings of the adaptive context become the key to unlock the specific secrets within the patient's manifest associations. The dynamic and genetic implications that the therapist formulates with the patient's material are assigned a specific meaning in light of a particular adaptation-evoking stimulus. Thus the therapist is able to continually establish the extent to which these assigned dynamics and genetics apply, both to the therapist and the patient (i.e., the degree to which unconscious perceptions or unconscious fantasies are involved). Once the adaptive context-derivative complex constellation has been dynamically and correctly formulated, the yield of understanding may be used as a framework for conceptualizing the unconscious basis of an activated indicator.

Summary and Conclusions

Adaptation-evoking stimuli are fraught with conscious and unconscious meaning, which is, by and large, experienced and introjected on both the conscious and unconscious levels by the patient. Much of this process as it pertains ultimately to the patient's Neurosis takes place quite unconsciously, and involves derivative and encoded messages from both the therapist and the patient. Thus the first task in decoding the patient's communications involves decoding those from the therapist. This is perhaps the most crucial aspect of the listening-formulating process.

In studying an adaptive context, the following additional determinations must be made: (1) the extent to which the intervention context involves framework issues; (2) the type of mode of relatedness that the therapist is attempting to effect with the patient through the intervention; (3) the type of curative process reflected in the therapist's intervention; (4) the style of the therapist as reflected in the adaptive context; and (5) the extent to which countertransference factors are reflected in the intervention, including their specific precipitants and nature.

In examining the patient's representation and derivative characterizations of an adaptation-evoking context, the extent to which these expressions are relatively resistant-free or instead highly defensive must be determined. The presence of interpretable material, weighed against the intensity of the indicators, determines when the therapist should intervene in a particular session.

Chapter 11

The Network of Communications:
The Derivative Complex

The derivative complex contains all of the patient's encoded and disguised (unconscious) reactions to an activated intervention context. It includes both unconscious perceptions and unconscious fantasies generated in response to the therapist's efforts, as well as a wide range of additional reactions to activated intervention contexts within the therapeutic interaction—some maladaptive and pathological and others adaptive and nonpathological. The aspect of the derivative complex that involves the patient's unconscious perceptions and introjections of the therapist's interventions was presented in the previous chapter. That particular aspect has overriding importance as a first level of derivative listening.

The Nature of the Derivative Complex

Intrapsychically founded responses to the therapist's interventions take place on both a manifest and latent level. Surface reactions may be adaptive or maladaptive, sound or unsound. They may involve conscious fantasies, feelings, or thoughts about the therapist that, upon analysis, are appropriate to the nature of the stimulus, or they may involve surface responses that are distinctly inappropriate and unrealistic. These latter reactions are surface indicators of disturbance within the patient, and their unconscious basis must be determined.

In general, conscious reactions to the therapist's interventions are not related to the underlying basis of the patient's Neurosis or emotional disturbance. They are direct, linear, simplistic, and self-evident. They function mainly as ways of sealing off underlying chaotic responses to the therapist's interventions, organized mostly in terms of valid unconscious perceptions of the implications of the adaptive context itself. On occasion, however, these conscious reactions to the therapist's interventions, whether valid or not on the surface, serve as important carriers of derivative responses to the adaptation-evoking context. Thus, in the face of manifest complaints about treatment, it is essential that the therapist subject such material to the decoding process in light of activated intervention contexts. At times, these comments may actually constitute encoded representations of the adaptive context itself. On other occasions they may involve either unconscious perceptions of the intervention context or encoded fantasied reactions. Here, of course, the focus is on the latter function of such material.

In principle, the most meaningful intrapsychically founded reactions to activated adaptive contexts take place in encoded (and therefore derivative) form. Those derivative responses that are determined primarily by the context itself, and only secondarily by factors within the patient, were the subject of the preceding chapter. Here, the study shifts to the other end of the continuum, to those responses to intervention contexts that are determined primarily by factors within the patient, and only secondarily by the nature of the stimulus.

The former constellation involves primarily valid unconscious perceptions of the therapist based on his or her interventions, and falls mainly into the realm of nontransference. In contrast, the latter constellation involves distorted and distorting unconscious fantasy-memory constellations, and tends mainly to be responses to non-pathological intervention contexts—to the presence of a secure framework and to valid interpretive efforts or silences by the therapist. These reactions tend to fall into the realm of transference, and require interpretive interventions from the therapist. (Non-transference requires rectification and interpretation.) It is not unusual to find intermixtures, with primarily valid and perceptive responses spilling over into distortion and transference. Similarly, any reaction to an intervention context that is primarily transference-based will have additional nontransference elements. Here, however, the focus will be on the preponderant quality of a particular communication.

CLINICAL EXAMPLE (CONTINUED)

The session presented in the previous chapter provides a clinical basis for the present discussion. The therapist had made it a practice to change the patient's hours upon her request or when the time of her session came into conflict with some other need of her own. There were times when hours were extended and when sessions were made up because the patient had to miss an hour due to illness or because the therapist took a holiday. There were also many noninterpretive interventions. Virtually all of these types of deviations had been rectified in the two months prior to the session reported above. In light of this particular group of adaptive contexts, the patient's manifest associations must be examined for derivative responses. In this regard, the allusion to the good-smelling coffee can be decoded as an evoked unconscious fantasy of being properly nurtured by the therapist. The oral qualities of this fantasy are in evidence. The reference to understanding more about herself and to the decrease in anxiety suggests that the adaptive context of securing the frame has created the conditions for greater insight and has produced a relatively secure hold through which the patient has lessened her sense of anxiety. It also suggests some measure of conflict resolution without indicating what this may entail.

The patient's decision to leave her job at the abortion clinic may reflect, first, the patient's own capacity to secure the frame and to adapt well to disturbing situations. The material suggests that the job at the abortion clinic was a poor one in important ways and, at this level, the patient's decision to leave was adaptive. On the other hand, the allusion to abortion could also refer to anxieties and distorted fantasies within the patient evoked by the therapist's securing of part of the frame and her dread that instead of being held well she will be aborted. The same manifest elements may reflect a masochistic fantasy-wish to be destroyed or, in some way, to annihilate the therapist. The boss's presence in the patient's session with a client could, in light of this particular adaptive context, reflect a wish within the patient for a third-party protector who would interfere with her intimacy with the therapist. This image follows the derivative allusion to abortion, and may well constitute a defense against the patient's anxieties evoked by her fantasy of harming the therapist or being harmed by him. The patient's mention of her own rage is in keeping with these formulations.

Next, the patient suggests that therapy should be intimate between two people. This would constitute her own wish for privacy in light of the therapist's capability to provide a measure of such privacy. The subsequent manifest elements, which have to do with the disruptive qualities of the boss and the way in which they interfered with communication, would again constitute wishes within the patient to disturb the increased intimacy between herself and the therapist.

The patient then provides additional derivative material through which her fears of intimacy with the therapist appear to be further clarified. On this level, the manifest dream of having sex with her husband suggests unconscious sexual fantasies toward the therapist. There is some allusion to guilt in the suggestion that there was something wrong with having sex with him. The patient next shifts to a nonsexual form of merger in her reference to the hypnotist, after which she proposes functioning on her own.

The final material regarding the affair of the patient's first husband and her own affair would reflect, in the adaptive context of the therapist having secured aspects of the framework, the patient's own unconscious wish for sexual involvement with the therapist, and her wish that the therapist himself also wanted to have an affair with her. The allusion to lies and deceit pertains here to the patient's *wish* for something inappropriate and corrupt. Her final comment about not being understood would also involve some wish to keep from achieving insight.

These particular readings of the unconscious implications of this material may seem rather forced because the adaptive context of the therapist's efforts to secure the frame remains overshadowed and contradicted by the deviations that still exist in this treatment situation. Nonetheless, the reading provides a model through which the variety of elements in this particular derivative complex are formulated. They include unconscious fantasy constellations, adaptive and maladaptive reactions and behaviors evoked in re- sponse to the intervention context, symptomatic fluctuations that could be related to the context, signs of introjective identification with the therapist, and a variety of instinctual-drive wishes and superego responses. Although this particular derivative complex does not contain a genetic allusion, in a later session (as noted above), the patient referred to an affair that her mother had had. Had this particular derivative appeared in this session, it would have been formulated as a type of identification between the patient and her mother to help account for her unconscious sexual wishes toward the therapist. On another level, the same association might imply the presence of an underlying homosexual unconscious fantasy toward her mother, which would also constitute a basis for the patient's sexual wishes toward the therapist. In light of the adaptive context of securing the frame, the earlier fantasies and wishes directed toward the mother are now being experienced with and projected onto the therapist.

Thus much of the patient's derivative complex is constituted by reactions to an intervention context that receives a major impetus from within the patient. Shaped by the nature of the adaptive stimulus, the overridingly important contribution derives from the patient.

Major Constellations that Constitute the Derivative Complex

THE PATIENT'S RESPONSIVE UNCONSCIOUS FANTASIES EVOKED BY INTERVENTION CONTEXTS

Representations of the id, ego, and superego, as well as the reality of the intervention context, are coalesced by the ego into an unconscious fantasy constellation. In response to a particular adaptive context, the patient may experience fantasy-wishes on all psychosexual levels, as well as wishes related to the merger or fusion and to narcissistic entitlement.

These fantasy constellations may be pathological or non-pathological. Thus they may entail adaptive responses to an intervention context and be constituted by fantasy systems that do not produce Neurosis. On the other hand, they may involve pathological unconscious fantasy constellations with forbidden instinctual drive wishes, pathological narcissistic and superego components, and manifestations of ego dysfunctions including failures of defense. These unconscious fantasy constellations are the underlying elements of intrapsychic conflict, and similarly, they help to account for the unconscious basis of all indicators. Thus a pathological unconscious fantasy constellation, as evoked by a specific adaptive context, creates a highly meaningful activated basis for a patient's emotional disturbance or Neurosis. As such, it becomes a critical component of the interpretation of such emotional difficulties.

UNCONSCIOUS MEMORIES EVOKED BY INTERVENTION CONTEXTS

As a rule, unconscious fantasy constellations are meaningfully linked to unconscious memory constellations. The two together are often referred to as unconscious fantasy-memory constellations as a way of showing their intimate connection. It is through the derivative and encoded expression of unconscious memories that the patient works over and utilizes earlier genetic history and experiences in adapting to current intervention contexts. In general, most derivative complexes will contain encoded memories. However, these are seldom recognizable without some specific manifest allusion to an early family figure or early life event. It is this particular manifest element that alerts the therapist to the genetic implications of the balance of the encoded material. In the absence of such a link, the tendency is to formulate the material in terms of unconscious fantasy and to await the specific link-up to genetic elements.

All meaningful memory constellations are evoked by immediate adaptive contexts within the therapeutic interaction. Thus the listening-formulating process, even when it deals with the genetic factor, should always use the adaptive context as its organizer and focal point. It is insufficient to simply identify a memory that a patient consciously recalls at a particular point in a session. It is quite essential to (1) identify the adaptive context that has produced this conscious recall; (2) make every effort to decode the implications of the conscious memory in light of the activated intervention context; and (3) remain alert to encoded and derivative expressions of early memories, which are virtually everpresent in the patient's ongoing material.

In those situations where the therapist's countertransferences and errors predominate, the evoked unconscious memories in the patient serve two functions: (1) to identify those aspects of the patient's pathogenic past that are now being repeated in some way, usually unconsciously, by the therapist in interaction with the patient; and (2) as an unconscious attempt to alert the therapist to possible genetic factors in the therapist's life that could account for the countertransferences.

Matters are somewhat different when the adaptive context involves a positive and constructive intervention by the therapist. These interventions tend to evoke genetic stirrings that are in consonance with the positive introjective identification that the patient makes with the well-functioning therapist, as well as responsive distortions based on the anxieties caused by the therapist's sound holding and interpretive functions.

The material contained in the derivative complex reflects the patient's efforts at adaptation and communication. Unconscious fantasy responses involve intrapsychic efforts to cope, and constitute a basis for the patient's behavioral reactions. Unconscious memories are conjured up as a way of drawing upon important experiences from the past, of developing comparisons between the past and the present, and of mobilizing adaptive resources and responses to adaptation-evoking stimuli. The specific nature of the adaptive response can be identified only through a full assessment of the adaptive context.

The therapist must make a distinction between derivative perceptions and derivative fantasies and memories by knowing the implications of the interventions and testing them against the patient's expressions. Similarly, a therapist is able to identify the functional nature of genetic material, manifest and encoded, only through a full conceptualization of the adaptive context. Errors by the therapist tend to repeat past traumas and to call them up on the basis of similarities. Sound interventions tend to distinguish the therapist from past traumatic figures, and to bring the latter to mind, both in contrast to and as a reflection of a continued internal need within the patient to inappropriately attribute aspects of past pathogenic figures to the therapist. In all situations, a full evaluation of the derivative material must be founded on a conceptualization of the implications of the adaptation-evoking contexts.

OFFERING CONSTRUCTIVE MODELS OF FUNCTIONING TO THE THERAPIST AND THE PATIENT, INCLUDING MODELS OF RECTIFICATION

An important aspect of the derivative complex involves the patient's adaptive responses to intervention contexts in terms of the offer of corrective models. These responses are most clearly seen in

reaction to traumatic intervention contexts. In responding to deviations in the ideal therapeutic environment and to errors by the
therapist, the patient often quite directly, though more typically
indirectly, offers corrective models. When these involve breaks in
the frame, the typical response will contain commentaries to the
effect that deviations in ground rules and basic compacts are inappropriate and should not be continued. Behaviorally, the patient
may handle some type of framework issue by maintaining the
ground rules and boundaries of an established relationship, thereby
offering a model to the therapist in light of an activated intervention context. Allusions to the need to learn something, to handle
matters differently, to understand better, and to correct wayward or
destructive ways may also appear. All of the behaviors of the
individuals to whom the patient refers in free association, and all
possible images that may contain directives of this kind, must be
understood in light of activated intervention contexts.

In the session presented in the previous chapter, in the adaptive
context of the presence of a secretary, the patient stated that therapy
should be intimate between two people. This manifest statement,
which referred to the patient's own work with clients, contained a
moving derivative corrective communication to the therapist regarding the presence of the secretary. This message was treated mainly
to displacement, and not especially symbolized. It was an encoded
statement to the effect that the therapy should be totally private and,
by implication, totally confidential.

Later in the same session, when the patient thought of going to
a hypnotist to lose weight, she stated that she should be able to do it
on her own without that kind of assistance. In the adaptive context
under study, this too was a derivative model of rectification through
which the patient proposed to the therapist that he function without third parties and develop a capacity for relative autonomy. To
the extent to which the patient herself is inappropriately dependent
on the therapist and on pathological gratifications in the therapeutic relationship, this model of rectification certainly applies to
herself as well. However, in the presence of an erroneous or deviant
intervention by the therapist, the first level of meaning always
involves the correction of the therapist's own mistakes.

Behaviorally enacted models of rectification account for many
interludes of apparent symptom alleviation and characterological
change that take place in the course of a psychotherapy that is

dominated by the therapist's countertransferences and technical errors. Such therapists tend to take these actions at face value, and to account for them as some type of positive consequence of the treatment experience. However, careful evaluation of the implications of the prevailing intervention contexts reveal consistently the extent to which these behaviors are adaptive responses to traumatic and countertransference-based intervention contexts through which the patient is attempting to cure and change the therapist, and to offer constructive role and image models. It is therefore important to consider all such behaviors in light of the adaptive contexts that have prompted them, and to consider carefully the possibility of the presence of a reactive model of rectification or of constructive functioning.

Whenever such positive functioning and images appear in response to a sound intervention or in reaction to a secure therapeutic hold, they imply positive introjective identifications with the well-functioning therapist. In these instances, it is the therapist who has in actuality provided the constructive model and the patient who has functioned through introjection. When the therapist's countertransferences predominate, the therapist offers a poor model, and the patient may react by repudiating the destructive projective identifications of the therapist and offering a constructive model of his or her own.

The consistency with which models of rectification and constructive functioning appear in response to the therapist's countertransference-based interventions enables the therapist to restore a damaged framework and to add a correct interpretive intervention, all at the behest of the patient's derivative communications. In the presence of an error by the therapist, this level of attending to the derivative complex is of considerable importance.

OTHER EFFORTS AT ADAPTATION

The patient's behaviors in the course of therapy can be understood as derivative expressions of adaptive responses to activated intervention contexts. These behaviors may involve treatment and the therapist, and may range from the revelation of new and illuminating material to wishes to terminate the therapy. They may involve actions with outside persons of virtually any type. These behaviors function as (1) actualities through which the patient attempts to adapt, and (2) vehicles for communication in the relationship with the therapist. Both types of meanings and functions must be understood through a decoding process carried out in light of the implications of the prevailing adaptive contexts.

In the session of the previous chapter, the patient's decision to leave her job at the abortion clinic is an example of such a behavioral response. In light of the adaptive context of the presence of a secretary in the treatment situation, this particular behavior reflects an apparently unconscious thought within the patient that she might, should the deviation continue, decide to terminate the treatment. Since the third-party intruder significantly limits the therapeutic potential of the treatment situation, this particular decision has strong adaptive value. In the patient's own encoded language, it would constitute a decision on her part to leave a treatment situation in which the likelihood of abortion is considerable.

Another adaptive behavior that appeared in this material is the patient's decision to say nothing to her boss. Here the patient, through derivatives, is expressing the way in which the therapist's deviation increased and justified her resistances to the point of noncommunication. In addition, the patient is expressing quite understandable tendencies not to communicate with a therapist who evidently leaks information to a third party. Here, again, the noncommunication appears to serve relatively sound and adaptive functioning.

In principle, then, each of the patient's behaviors, inside and outside of therapy, must be taken as a derivative response to an activated intervention context. At times, of course, these behaviors reflect valid unconscious perceptions of the therapist's intervention. As such, they would belong in that aspect of the patient's derivative complex that is organized around the patient's unconscious perceptions and readings of the adaptive context itself. On the other hand, when the behaviors reflect adaptive and fantasied responses to intervention contexts that arise primarily from within the patient, pathological or nonpathological, they should be assigned to the particular aspect of the derivative complex that is the focus of this chapter.

UNCONSCIOUS EFFORTS TO CURE OR HARM THE THERAPIST

The derivative complex often contains encoded efforts by the patient to respond either curatively or hurtfully to the therapist. In general, countertransference-based intervention contexts will evoke a mixture of curative and hurtful reactions. Similarly, sound interventions will tend to evoke either acceptance or paradoxical efforts to hurt the therapist, based on envy or a distorted belief that the therapist's sound functioning will not continue or that it covers over hurtful intentions.

The therapist can silently and inevitably benefit considerably from the patient's unconscious curative efforts, including the patient's unconscious supervisory endeavors and efforts at unconscious interpretation (i.e., encoded attempts by the patient to identify the adaptation-evoking stimuli to which the therapist is responding idiosyncratically, and to indicate in some general disguised fashion possible genetic and dynamic factors in the therapist's errors).

In the session in the previous chapter, the patient's comments regarding the necessity for intimacy between the two participants to therapy has a curative thrust. It implies an unconscious interpretation of some type of fear of intimacy within the therapist. Further, the patient's image of going to a hypnotist in order to lose weight implies the presence of a therapeutic need. In the adaptive context of the presence of the secretary, it may be viewed as an unconscious interpretation of the therapist's inappropriate need for the protection of, and merger with, his secretary.

The patient's comment that she should be able to lose weight on her own without that assistance is a directive designed to push the therapist toward greater autonomy. The allusion to an affair can be seen as an unconscious interpretation through which the patient indicates that the therapist's involvement with his secretary is tantamount to having an affair, and has unconscious implications along these lines. As such, it constitutes an unconscious interpretation that identifies a deviant adaptive context and assigns it a dynamic meaning. The patient's later allusion to her mother's affair would then be an unconscious genetic interpretation that would suggest to the therapist that his need for the secretary is in some way derived from a disturbance in his relationship with and perceptions of his own mother.

In order to recognize the patient's unconscious therapeutic measures, it is essential that the therapist understand the implications of his or her own interventions. Once the therapist is able to formulate their pathological elements, it becomes quite feasible to recognize the patient's unconscious therapeutic endeavors. At times, the general interpretations, confrontations, and directives offered by the patient can lead the therapist to important insights that might not otherwise be reached. However, the therapist should not in any way directly request therapeutic help from the patient, nor should treatment become the therapy of the therapist. Most of these interludes involve expressions of inevitable countertransference that are part of essentially sound interventions or occasional lapses, to which the patient reacts with curative responses. The patient's unconscious curative efforts should be accepted and understood silently and without direct comment by the therapist, though they can be alluded to in the course of an interpretation of the patient's Neurotic and maladaptive responses to the disturbing adaptive context to which the patient has reacted with curative effort.

On the other side of the ledger, patients will sometimes respond to pathological intervention contexts with highly disturbing, disruptive, action-prone reactions that are designed to hurt the therapist emotionally, and sometimes even professionally and physically. On occasion, these efforts may be quite subtle and involve major resistances and other types of obstacles to treatment. There may also be attacking derivative communications and harmful thrusts toward others, which are designed on some level to hurt the therapist. All such hurtful actions must be traced to the therapist's activated intervention contexts, and understood as derivative communications in that light. In most situations, they involve responses to hurtful interventions by the therapist, and will require both rectification and interpretation.

RESPONSES TO THE STATE OF THE FRAME, MODE OF RELATEDNESS, MODE OF CURE, AND COMMUNICATIVE STATE OF EACH PARTICIPANT TO TREATMENT

In respect to the six-part observational schema, it has already been indicated how the derivative complex contains responsive unconscious fantasies and memories, and may reflect the dynamics of the patient, and secondarily of the therapist. Concerning the other four areas of information that the therapist monitors for derivative meanings, there are two possibilities: (1) the patient may actually behave in a fashion designed to influence one of these spheres and to actualize a particular break in the frame, mode of relatedness, or form of cure; or (2) the patient may represent images that pertain to the therapeutic frame, the mode of relatedness, the mode of cure, and the state of each participant. In this latter regard, in general, when the therapeutic frame is secure, these representations tend to express the patient's fantasies and wishes. On the other hand, when the frame is broken, these representations tend to convey actualities and valid unconscious perceptions of the therapist and the patient's own disturbances in respect to the ground rules, mode of relatedness, mode of cure, and communicative relatedness. Thus, in considering the derivative complex in each of these areas, the therapist studies the actualities that prevail consciously and unconsciously between the therapist and the patient and, in addition, the representations of the patient in each of these spheres. Because of the complexities involved, in the actual clinical situation, a therapist might carry out an evaluation of this kind once or twice in a given hour. Although it is complex, the therapist is by and large richly rewarded in undertaking it, since the effort generates realizations that might not otherwise surface.

Summary and Conclusions

The derivative complex contains reactions to intervention contexts that derive from the nature of the evocative stimulus and the patient's own inner mental world and life history. The forms of expression include behaviors, affects, and verbal associations. The derivative meanings involve unconscious perceptions, unconscious fantasy and memory constellations, models of rectification, behavioral adaptive efforts, and endeavors to either help and cure or harm the therapist. These expressions also reveal critical dynamic and genetic aspects of the patient's functioning as they pertain to the patient's adaptive resources and efforts to cope with the therapist's intervention. Failures to adapt lead to symptom formation. Similarly, the patient's symptoms are sustained and founded upon the introjection of implications of the therapist's interventions and the patient's own derivative reactions.

The therapist's listening-formulating endeavors therefore center upon the recognition of these critical unconscious perceptions and fantasy-memories as they illuminate the implications of and reactions to an activated adaptive context and clarify the unconscious basis for an indicator. In the realm of the derivative complex, the patient expresses intrapsychic and self-identity conflicts, efforts to establish a basic mode of relatedness, disturbances in psychosexual, ego, and superego development, and unconscious conflicts. These are the means by which the patient's own inner mental functioning and introjects of others contribute to the patient's emotional disturbances and Neurosis. Thus the interpretation of the derivative complex provides the patient with critical insights into the nature of activated emotional ills.

CLINICAL EXAMPLES

The young male patient who missed two sessions, and who was not charged for one of the missed hours, was introduced in a brief excerpt from the session that followed the therapist's decision regarding the fees. It will be remembered that the patient then cancelled the following hour because of a commitment at work, and left a message with the therapist's answering service. The following excerpt is from the hour that followed:

> Patient: I was afraid you wouldn't get my message, that you wouldn't understand why I had missed the session. My father has been disturbing me a great deal lately. He's depressed and he tries to be nice, but he only upsets me. He seems to feel guilty for having been a bad father in the past, and now he overindulges me. I don't like that either.

First the adaptive context for this segment of material should be identified. Then the best representation of this context in the patient's material should be formulated. (In this way, the initial communicative issue is addressed before considering dynamics and genetics.) Next, other encoded unconscious perceptions of the therapist and his intervention context should be identified. Once these tasks are accomplished, the effort can be made to identify the patient's additional derivative responses—the derivative complex.

The main activated adaptive context for this hour may be stated as the therapist's decision to forego the fee for a missed session because of a transportation strike. Applying the sequence developed for the listening process, the *best representation* of this context must be identified. First the patient's manifest material is examined to see whether the intervention has been alluded to directly. Clearly, this is not the case in this particular segment. Next, the least disguised encoded representation of the context is sought. In this instance, it appears to be the allusion to how the patient's father tries to be nice and overindulges him. This particular representation is relatively well disguised, and provides neither a bridge to therapy nor a clue to the money issue inherent to the intervention context. On the other hand, it already includes a characterization of an important unconscious attribute to the therapist's decision: that it was an attempt to be nice that constituted a form of overindulgence.

The next task is to identify other derivative representations and unconscious perceptions of the intervention context and of the therapist in light of his interventions. Since the excerpt is brief, each communicative element should be considered separately. The patient first alludes to his fear that the therapist would not get his message. In the adaptive context cited, this suggests that the therapist had in actuality, as perceived by the patient, missed the patient's communications regarding how the fee issue should be managed. Another possible condensed meaning suggests that the therapist's deviation created conditions under which communication would be impaired. The next segment involves the patient's comment that the therapist might not understand why he, the patient, had missed the session. In the adaptive context of foregoing the fee, the patient offers the unconscious characterization that this is an action that lacks understanding. He adds too that something was missed and that, in a way, the oversight might well have contributed to the patient missing an additional hour. A characterization of the adaptive context as an unconscious effort to disturb the patient may be present in the allusion to how the patient's father has been disturbing him a great deal lately. Some sense of projective identification is hinted at here. The subsequent allusion to the father's sense of depression indicates that, unconsciously, the patient views the deviation as a reflection of, and an effort to cope with, a depressive syndrome within the therapist. Further characterizations imply that the patient sees the deviation as an effort to be nice, and yet as a reflection of a state of upset within the therapist, the last alluded to in terms of how the patient himself gets upset.

There is a reference to feeling guilty over having been a bad father in the past, which decodes as a suggestion that the therapist made the deviation out of guilt over his poor interventions earlier in treatment. This is followed by the characterization already noted of the way in which the deviation overindulged the patient.

Modifications in the ideal therapeutic framework are powerful intervention contexts. This small segment of an hour several weeks after the deviation is filled with encoded unconscious perceptions of the nature of the deviation, of the therapist in light of the deviation, and of the therapist's possible (unconscious) motives for altering the frame. There is a rich, diverse, and full characterization of the implications of the deviant intervention context. All that is wanting is a manifest allusion to the break in the frame, which could form the basis for an interpretation of the main indicator of this hour—the missed session. In this regard, the material suggests that the patient missed the hour in an effort to get some distance from the overindulging and seductive therapist.

A number of the formulations of the implications of the adaptive context in this situation bridge over to aspects of the derivative complex. The patient provides a genetic link between his father and the therapist. In the adaptive context of the therapist's deviation, the genetic connection is constituted as a means by which the therapist in some fashion is repeating a pathogenic behavior of the patient's father (a form of nontransference). Both have created suffering for the patient through overindulgence.

Unconscious fantasies are overshadowed here by unconscious perceptions. However, there are distinct efforts by the patient to be curative toward the therapist and hints at models of rectification. Thus the patient suggests through derivatives that the therapist should get his message and understand why he has missed the session. He then interprets unconsciously to the therapist that the therapist's overindulgence disturbs rather than helps the patient. He offers the additional unconscious interpretation that the underlying motive involves a depressive core within the therapist—a point that the therapist himself was able to confirm in his supervisory session with this author. Similarly, the patient offers still another interpretation that unconscious guilt regarding past errors had prompted the need to overcompensate the patient in the present. This unconscious commentary has all of the major hallmarks of an interpretation: it identifies an indicator-adaptive context for the therapist, and attempts to illuminate its unconscious basis. Here too the therapist felt that the patient had offered a valid unconscious intervention.

The patient's adaptive response (missing a session) contains an alteration of the framework that also serves as a representation of the activated intervention context. It may well have been designed unconsciously to bring the disruptive qualities of his own deviation to the therapist's attention. It may also constitute a maladaptive (acting-out, symptomatic) reaction to the seductive and threatening qualities of the adaptive context. In addition, it may express some of the underlying hostility involved in the therapist's efforts, as well as the patient's own reactive anger.

Another brief excerpt is drawn from the psychotherapy of a young married woman with one child. The session took place several months after the patient had attempted to introduce the use of insurance into her therapy. She had produced material that indicated through derivatives that this factor would essentially destroy the therapeutic work, and had decided to forego the use of the insurance payments. In the previous session, the therapist had not intervened.

> Patient: My husband says that I'm like my mother and that worries me. I never drove a car. She's fearful of letting someone else drive, afraid they'll have an accident. My father would go on these drinking binges and she wouldn't take care of him. I would have to be the one to put him to bed. It went all right but it was messy. Sometimes he'd be exposed, and that bothered me. I went out with a lot of fellows as a teenager. I'd feel trapped, and the relationship would never last.

There is a rather low level of indicators in this material. Later in the hour the patient described some sense of anxiety before coming to her session. It is not uncommon to find a low-level of indicators in the presence of a secure hold by the therapist and a basically interpretive and nondeviant approach.

The main adaptive context here is the therapist's silence. In supervision, it was evaluated as appropriate to the material (no rectification of the frame or interpretive intervention appeared to be called for in the previous hour). Further, the patient had seemed to respond positively to the therapist's holding efforts. The therapist's capacity to secure and maintain the framework may be seen as an implied aspect of appropriate silence.

The derivative complex must be examined in light of this adaptive context. The patient first mentions her mother, who is afraid of driving and who also fears driving with others. In the setting of a positively toned intervention context, the material reflects (1) an unconscious projection of aspects of the patient's mother's anxieties and incapacities onto the therapist, (2) a projection of comparable qualities within the patient onto the therapist, and (3) an expression of the patient's own anxieties regarding the holding relationship and a fantasied fear that some disaster will befall her (cf. the allusion to the fear of an accident).

These elements distort the patient's perception of the therapist and help to account for the anxiety that she experienced before the hour. The raw message is that the therapist is in some ways ineffectual like the patient's mother and that, as someone who is in control of (or managing) the treatment situation, he will make a mistake—have an accident—and the patient will be harmed. This is an unconscious transference fantasy constellation that reflects a pathological introject within the patient of her maternal figure, as well as some type of sadomasochistic fantasy system. Through encoded derivatives, this material may also reflect unconscious recollections of interactions between the patient and her mother, as well as possible reactive unconscious fantasies within the patient— these also heavily colored with sadomasochistic qualities. The therapist's constructive holding capacity, which in reality stands in contrast to the mother's ineffectuality, is the adaptive context that has evoked the patient's anxieties and fantasy-memory derivatives.

Next, there is the material regarding the manner in which the mother failed to care for the father while the patient took over these responsibilities. The reference to the father being exposed undoubtedly refers to his genitals. This segment, in light of the adaptive context, reflects an introject of the positive qualities and sense of responsibility reflected in the therapist's holding and interpretive capacities. The image of his failing the patient in a manner comparable to her mother must be taken here as an anxiety-evoked, transference-based distortion, a reflection of an unconscious fantasy-memory derived from experiences with the patient's mother and displaced into the relationship with the therapist. The allusion to the father's alcoholism must also be taken as a displaced projection onto the therapist of a fear within the patient that the therapist will lose control as had the father, and become unmanageable and, in addition, require her care. The reference to the exposure of the father's genitals may be taken as a reflection of an unconscious sexual fantasy-memory of a voyeuristic nature. The shift from the ineffectual mother to the exposed father also suggests an activated Oedipal constellation stimulated by the positive qualities of the therapist's holding efforts.

In making formulations of this kind, the therapist must check out the possibility that some measure of unconscious perception is in evidence. Formulations regarding fantasy-memory constellations and distortions must be put to the test with efforts to determine, for example, whether the therapist has indeed missed an intervention, behaved in some ineffectual manner, lost control in some way, and inadvertently exposed himself or herself in a manner that could be unconsciously seen by the patient as somewhat sexualized. When these questions were raised with the therapist in supervision, he was led to recall that he had intervened several sessions earlier in an unduly forceful manner, which might help to account for some of these qualities in the patient's material. The intervention he had made had obtained some measure of indirect validation, and this had lulled him into neglecting the small, but apparent, measure of countertransference reflected in his work.

All of the material from the patient is *transversal*—it will contain a mixture of encoded unconscious fantasy and perception, transference and nontransference, fantasy and reality. The mixtures may be relatively equal, and the therapist, if intervention is appropriate, should adopt a transversal approach in which he or she alludes to both dimensions. When the mixture is heavily weighted in the direction of either valid unconscious perception or distorted fantasy (the latter prevails in this excerpt), then the therapist's listening, formulating, and intervening should concentrate on the major attribute. It is especially important to account for the unconsciously perceptive aspects of the patient's material before touching upon the realm of distortion. The therapist should neither over-blame and overdump into the patient, nor take overblame. A balanced approach is essential.

The final segment of material alludes to the patient's fears of being trapped in dating relationships. In the adaptive context of the therapist's capacity to offer a sound holding relationship, this

184 / Psychotherapy: A Basic Text

particular manifest element may be decoded as reflecting some type of unconscious romantic fantasy toward the therapist and the emergence of some measure of anxiety that intimacy with him is dangerous. The earlier associations regarding the possibility of a car accident seem to point to an underlying sadomasochistic fantasy-memory constellation, though additional material would be required to validate this particular hypothesis.

This particular derivative complex emphasizes the fantasy-memory (genetic) constellation aspects of such material. There is also evidence of a positive introjective identification with the therapist. There is little in the way of behavioral efforts at adaptation or endeavors to harm or cure the therapist.

A truly meaningful derivative response by the patient will consistently involve a multitude of unconscious readings by the patient of the implications of the therapist's interventions. Such a derivative reading will touch upon unconsciously perceived as well as unconsciously evoked gentics, a variety of dynamics, and a wide range of additional attributes. Such a derivative response is a coalescible derivative network, and it is a sign of a high level of expression and a low level of resistance.

Derivative-adaptive reactions that are determined primarily from within the patient's own inner mental life must also be examined for a coalescible derivative complex that touches upon genetic issues, as well as a variety of dynamic, frame, object relationship, and mode of cure considerations. This variety has the potential for enriching the patient's self-understanding, and provides the therapist with promising material for intervention.

When therapists talk of a rich or meaningful session, they are usually alluding to an hour in which both critical indicators and a direct representation of the adaptive context appear relatively early. They are referring also to material rich in genetic and dynamic implications, filled with vivid imagery that can be given true meaning in terms of both unconscious perceptions and unconscious fantasy-memory constellations.

A listening-formulating process that is organized around the unconscious implications of the therapist's interventions is the only means through which the activated and interactional truths of the patient's emotional disturbance or Neurosis can be identified. Only Type Two derivative formulations are expressions of intrapsychic and interpersonal truths. Manifest content and Type One derivative formulations constitute lie-barrier systems that may either be opaque to the underlying and more chaotic truths of the therapeutic interaction (i.e., nonderivative lie-barrier systems) or derivtives of these underlying truths (i.e., derivative lie-barrier systems). However, it is the responsibility of the therapist to state the truths of the patient—and secondarily of the therapist—as they pertain to the patient's emotional disturbance in direct and fully conscious terms. Such statements must take into full account the contributions of both the patient and the therapist to the patient's emotional disorder. Genetic repercussions must be traced out from the here and now of the therapeutic interaction (Gill 1979). Type Two derivative listening and formulating is the essential means through which this is done.

Chapter 12

The Validating Process

An intimate relationship exists between the listening-experiencing, formulating, intervening, and validating processes. Thus a full appreciation of the nature of validating responses from the patient is not possible without a full understanding of the nature of the therapist's interventions. However, the validating process must be introduced here because even the basic listening-formulating process itself must be subjected to efforts at validation. Therapists must have some process through which particular formulations can be tested. They must also have a systematic means to determine if a particular formulation or *silent hypothesis* is in error (i.e., if derivative support is absent in the patient's continuing associations). Thus all silent efforts at listening and formulating must be subjected to efforts at *silent validation* as an integral part of the listening process.

The ultimate test of a therapist's formulation lies in the use of the therapist's impressions as a basis for intervention—whether it be interpretive, noninterpretive, or if it involves a management of the ground rules and frame. At the moment an intervention is offered, the patient is exposed to the therapist's conscious thinking and the way in which the therapist has synthesized or otherwise responded to the patient's material. The patient responds to this experience both consciously and unconsciously. The patient's reactions constitute a *commentary* on the therapist's intervention, and are filled with valid unconscious perceptions and introjects, and at times, reactive distortions. True validation involves responses from the patient in both the cognitive and interpersonal spheres. In the cognitive sphere, a unique derivative communication emerges, which gives new meaning and insight into the patient's previous material (*a selected fact;* Bion 1962). In the interpersonal sphere, the patient's derivative associations reflect a positive introjective identification with the well-functioning therapist. These encoded and derivative responses, which are the hallmarks of psychoanalytic validation, are then supplemented by some measure of conscious working over and working through.

Silent Formulations and Silent Efforts at Validation

Without a validating clinical methodology, psychotherapy is bound to be overrun by the prejudices and idiosyncratic thinking of the therapist. Errors will go undetected, since most therapists assume that they are working in correct fashion with their patients except on rare occasion. The therapist's narcissistic investment in his or her own ideas is likely to blunt his or her capacity to detect interventions to which the patient has not responded favorably. Thus sound psychotherapy cannot exist without a validating process.

In current practice, little attention is paid to the patient's material following an intervention except to note ways in which the response may extend the therapist's comment. Much of the therapist's attention is directed on a manifest level to a search for direct agreement or self-evident elaboration. Therapists who make use of Type One derivative interventions accept any new memory or response from a patient that extends the original intervention as confirmation. The unconscious implications of such material is rarely analyzed; rather, it is taken immediately and at face value as an elaboration of the therapist's intervention, and therefore as a sign of validation. The focus tends to be on the manifest contents of both the patient's associations and the therapist's intervention. Little attention is paid to the unconscious communication conveyed by the therapist in his or her therapeutic efforts, nor is the patient's responsive material analyzed in this light. The seemingly rare, obviously erroneous intervention is simply discarded, and the belief is adopted that the intervention had little influence upon the patient (Freud 1937). The patient's associations are regarded as overridingly reflecting transference and distortion, and little credence is afforded to their other manifest and latent implications. Thus the patient's derivative associations are not recognized as a reliable basis for confirmation.

In contrast to these attitudes, the therapist who makes use of Type Two derivative interventions treats the material following an intervention as a commentary on the therapist's conscious and unconscious expressions as reflected in the intervention. Such a therapist studies the manifest and especially latent material for the patient's impressions as to the accuracy and relevance of the intervention, and for ways in which it generates unique and illuminating responses from the patient. The patient's associations following an intervention are carefully investigated for introjective identifications of the therapist, and for a wide range of perceptive and fantasied derivative reactions. This particular approach has led to the development of specific criteria for the evaluation of every intervention, and to a comprehensive study of nonvalidation and its implications.

The hallmark of psychoanalytic validation involves a supportive, encoded, derivative response from the patient. Direct agreement, surface elaboration, and the repetition of familiar material in no way validates an intervention from the therapist. The emergence of new material in and of itself is not confirmatory, since its implications must be understood in light of the conscious and especially unconscious implications of the therapist's intervention.

Seemingly rich material in and of itself has little bearing on the evaluation of whether an intervention has been confirmed or not. One way of evoking rich and sometimes new material from a patient is to intervene incorrectly, especially through an unneeded deviation in the basic ground rules. Such material, upon analysis, consistently conveys the patient's unconscious perceptions of the therapist's error and working over of unconsciously perceived and introjected difficulties within the therapist. These responses cannot be viewed as a means of validating a particular intervention, since their essence is basically nonvalidating, and often involves attempts to correct the therapist's error. True validation involves a Type Two derivative response that sheds new light and meaning on previously disparate material. It is nonmanifest and unique, though eventually it enables the patient to consciously recognize aspects of his or her Neurosis that were previously unconscious.

The therapist has two basic checkpoints at which to evaluate the extent to which validation has occurred for a particular hypothesis, whether the hypothesis is silently maintained or offered to the patient. The first occurs relatively early in the course of a session as the therapist silently listens to and experiences the patient's material and attempts to generate formulations. The second takes place after the therapist has offered a specific intervention, including that of an extended silence. At both of these points, the therapist must make use of subjective sensitivities and cognitive understanding, as well as the implications of the material from the patient.

VALIDATION OF SILENT LISTENING AND FORMULATING

The therapist enters each session with a divided mind: unencumbered in one part, and prepared with known adaptation-evoking contexts in the other. As the therapist listens, he or she accepts impressions from all possible sources and in all conceivable states of development. Still, even as the therapist experiences this cognitive-affective data, meaning and function must be assigned to the accumulating impressions. Thus the therapist will pause from time to time and attempt to generate a formulation that takes into account the most essential meanings of the patient's material. A silent hypothesis is developed that may propose either a general or specific set of unconscious meanings for the patient's associations and behaviors.

The ultimate goal is to formulate as specific a silent hypothesis as possible. The therapist must attempt to understand the manifest and latent implications of the patient's material in terms of the elements of the network of communications: indicators, activated adaptive contexts, and derivative reactions. At times, the therapist may quickly shape a series of specific silent formulations or hypotheses in light of a known intervention context and its implications. When the intervention context is less clear to the therapist and not well represented in the patient's material, the therapist may develop a series of general impressions, monitoring the patient's material first for unconscious perceptions of the therapist and his or her interventions and, second, for reactive fantasy-memory constellations.

The therapist's ultimate goal is to develop a formulation that can be translated into an actual intervention to the patient. In this regard, there are two possibilities: (1) the use of the patient's manifest and especially derivative communications to develop a framework-management response; or (2) the development of an interpretation. With these goals in mind, much of the listening-formulating process unfolds around framework issues, while most of the balance of these efforts involve the identification of important indicators and their understanding in light of the implications of activated intervention contexts and the patient's derivative material. In all, there tends to be a transition from early global and general silent hypotheses to those that involve specific framework management and interpretive responses. These processes take place silently within the therapist.

In addition to open and unencumbered listening, the main task is to identify activated intervention contexts, and then to identify a clear, direct, or minimally encoded representation of the context, if it is present. An attempt is then made to decode the patient's derivative unconscious perceptions and to assign meaning to the therapist's intervention. Finally, efforts are made to decode the implications of the patient's material in light of the patient's fantasy-memory responses and other adaptive efforts.

The development of silent formulations may unfold quite smoothly or prove difficult. Ideally, the patient will allude manifestly and early in the hour to important indicators, and mention, in passing and on a manifest level, the critical intervention context for the session. The therapist may then focus on the patient's derivative readings of the intervention context and personal or idiosyncratic derivative reactions. A coalescible derivative network is developed; important unconscious implications of the intervention context itself and a variety of adaptive reactions from the patient are thereby communicated.

Hypotheses regarding the framework are in general to the effect that the patient is unconsciously expressing a need to have the frame secured, or else they involve the unconscious implications of the therapist's participation in a deviation. Formulations of the patient's cognitive material center around the identification of the adaptive context-derivative complex meanings and functions, which account for the unconscious basis of an indicator. All other types of formulations, such as those that relate to the patient's manifest contents and those shaped in Type One derivative terms, may be used for storage information. They are of some interest, but are not pertinent to the activated truths within the therapeutic interaction as they pertain to the patient's emotional disturbance. Although their understanding is of some value to the therapist, they should not constitute the major silent hypothesis in any particular hour. These hypotheses must involve either framework mangement or interpretive issues.

The therapist attempts to develop a specific silent hypothesis as early as possible in a session. In carrying out this work, the therapist will develop a series of incomplete silent hypotheses. Eventually, they will coalesce into a major silent hypothesis, which will be either a statement of a necessity to secure the frame and of the unconscious implications of a deviation as it pertains to the patient's emotional disturbance, or an interpretation of an adaptive context-derivative complex network that accounts for the unconscious basis for an indicator. Each of the therapist's minihypotheses must be subjected to efforts at confirmation in the patient's ongoing material and in the therapist's subjective reappraisal of the formulation. A similar process is applied to a major silent hypothesis once it has been developed.

What then are the hallmarks of *silent validation?*

1. Silent validation is recognized when an initial silent hypothesis finds encoded and derivative support in the patient's ongoing associations. In this way, a formulation based on one set of derivatives finds additional evidence for its validity in another set of derivatives.

2. Silent validation also occurs when the therapist is able to unite a series of minihypotheses into a meaningful whole. This coalesence of disparate hypotheses into a meaningful statement lends support to each of the minihypotheses themselves.

3. Validation is also seen when the therapist develops a silent hypothesis and then unexpectedly remembers an aspect of the patient's previous material, particularly from earlier in the session at hand, that supports the hypothesis generated on the basis of other data.

4. Some measure of silent validation is obtained when the therapist finds support for the formulations from the patient's material that is recalled from previous hours. Some small measure

of validation is also afforded an hypothesis when it appears to be in keeping with previously validated psychoanalytic hypotheses. This last is an impersonal form of validation, however, and must always be supplemented with highly personal and specific derivative validating material from the patient.

As with any aspect of the psychotherapeutic process, silent validation is open to unnoticed countertransference influences. A therapist must develop a capability for skepticism when it comes to his or her own formulations and sense of confirmation, and an attitude of self-doubt until proven otherwise through surprising derivatives. These attitudes must be adopted in order to counter the more natural tendency to overinvest in formulations and to be unwary of their more erroneous aspects.

Thus the therapist must develop an ear for unique Type Two derivative expressions; he or she must have a sense of the way in which derivatives coalesce, revealing now one meaning and then another. The therapist must develop an understanding of the ways in which the patient's encoded messages will first represent and clarify a genetic aspect and then an unconscious perception, only to move on to an unconscious fantasy. There must also be a sense that the patient's assignment of meanings to an intervention context through derivatives will touch first upon one implication and then upon another. This diversity of meaning and implication provides the basis for silent validation, in that the hypothesis at hand must be able to afford unified understanding to the patient's different derivative communications.

The therapist should not offer an intervention to the patient if it has not obtained a significant measure of indirect silent validation. This is a safeguard for both participants to treatment. It may protect the therapist from premature and erroneous interventions, just as it protects the patient from undue exposure to the therapist's errors and countertransferences. It creates a treatment atmosphere in which the therapist must prove the validity of a formulation by being capable of immediately understanding and integrating a surprisingly unique association filled with derivative meaning. It also establishes a set of criteria through which the therapist can develop a sense of likelihood that a formulation is correct or incorrect. It therefore enables the therapist to develop a reasonable and sound measure of confidence in formulations before offering them to the patient.

CLINICAL EXAMPLE

A young married woman is being seen in psychotherapy at a clinic. She had been referred to treatment by a friend, Nancy, who had also been in psychotherapy with the therapist. The patient's complaints concerned depression and dissatisfaction with her husband and with the affairs in which she was involved.

In the first weeks of this therapy, the therapist adopted an extremely active approach. He made many comments regarding the patient's manifest associations, and offered many direct suggestions. He would typically initiate each hour with a question, comment, or suggestion. Under the influence of supervision, he had decided on a dramatic modification in his basic technique: he planned to remain relatively silent, at least at the beginning of the next hour, and to attempt to work with the patient's derivative material.

To pause in order to comment briefly and to develop a number of *preformed silent hypotheses,* the therapist might well approach a session of this kind with an attitude in part of being without desire, memory, or understanding. And yet, because of his own major decision, he would in all likelihood also already have developed some impressions of the implications of his planned intervention context (the introduction of a major measure of relative silence). As the hour begins he might then identify other implications of this intervention, both through his own subjective appraisal and through the patient's unfolding associations and their derivative implications as she experiences the change in the therapist. The therapist's initial silent hypotheses might well have been developed at the time when he decided to change his style of listening and intervening. What implications might this shift contain? How might the patient unconsciously perceive the therapist in light of his decision?

This is a highly preliminary effort at silent formulation. The possibilities are, of course, legion. It is best to organize them in terms of the six basic informational categories for listening—the frame, mode of relatedness, mode of cure, communicative issues, dynamics and genetics, and the prevalance of fantasy or perception. Thus it might be anticipated that the patient would unconsciously perceive the modification in technique as a securing of the ground rules and boundaries of the treatment situation, and as a sign of increased control and management capacity within the therapist. The new attitude would involve a shift from some form of pathological mode of relatedness—autistic, symbiotic, or parasitic—to the offer of a healthy symbiosis. Then too there would be a change in the therapist's expressed use of a mode of cure from action-discharge to a search for cognitive insight.

The shift might be perceived unconsciously by the patient as a change in the therapist's preferred mode of expression from the Type B-C mode of dumping and destroying meaning, to the Type A mode of working interpretively and symbolically (see Chapter 15), through which the therapist appropriately holds and contains the patient until he or she is able to make a sound interpretation-reconstruction.

The patient might well unconsciously perceive a lessening of the therapist's seductiveness, hostility, and need to overwhelm or devour the patient. Genetic connections to constructive parenting experiences might well emerge. Finally, the shift would initially reflect unconscious dynamics within the therapist, though it would soon create the conditions under which the patient's own dynamic-genetic psychopathology could come into focus. With this in mind, this patient, who has accepted therapy under the conditions of a modified frame and pathological symbiosis, would be expected to be quite threatened by the implications of the unconsciously perceived changes within the therapist.

Silent hypotheses of this kind should be loosely held. Those hypotheses to which the patient's derivative material points should be added. Those formulations that are not reinforced by the patient's manifest and especially derivative associations should be discarded. If the patient's material does not begin to coalesce around encoded expressions in keeping with these initial formulations, the entire conception should be discarded, and a search should be made for an entirely different silent hypothesis.

The actual session is presented here bit by bit.

> Patient: One of my girlfriends has a facial paralysis. A group of us got together. Her husband let her drive. My husband and Nancy's husband wouldn't let me do that. My girlfriend felt good about driving, but was concerned because she lacked any depth perception.

The allusion to the facial paralysis appears to be a highly encoded derivative of the patient's unconscious perception of the therapist's decision not to initiate the session. It has a number of possible encoded implications, including a view of the therapist as ill and not speaking, as well as a concern that the patient's psychopathology would quickly surface under these conditions.

The adaptive context is the therapist's silence at the beginning of the session—a truly unique response on his part. The me/not-me interface represents this association as a possible unconscious perception and possible unconscious fantasy. Should it emerge that the therapist has voluntarily maintained his silence out of health rather than illness, the patient's image of him would then be understood as an unconscious misconception—a product of internal distortion.

The main focus, however, is in generating and validating silent hypotheses. The patient's first association suggests an unconscious perception of the therapist's silence. It is constituted by a symbolic representation of that silence through the image of paralysis and through an allusion to the face. Although it is a remote derivative, and one that does not call for definitive confidence in the preformed formulation, it nonetheless offers a surprising sense of indirect fit. Although it may be wondered if the patient could so quickly unconsciously perceive this change in the therapist, it is sufficient encouragement to move on to the patient's continuing associations for a further examination of their derivative implications in light of the budding silent hypothesis. (In the actual session, the image of the facial paralysis might also be evaluated against other known intervention contexts, and used to determine if new intervention contexts are suggested.)

The next major derivative is to the effect that the sick woman's husband let her drive. This particular image suggests responsibility, autonomy, and control. It is in keeping with the silent hypothesis that the therapist's relative silence would reflect his own constructive functioning and offer the patient a healthy form of symbiosis and an opportunity to direct the session in an appropriate manner—the patient's derivative material should always lead the way. The image suggests an unconscious perception of the therapist's silence as affording the patient these opportunities.

Next, the patient alludes to how her own husband will not let her drive, nor would the husband of the woman who referred her to treatment. This particular derivative does not appear to characterize implications of the therapist's new-found silence, though in some heavily disguised manner this could refer to a raw message (unconscious speculation) to the effect that the therapist, given a clinic setting, was being held back from his natural propensities by his supervisor. Perhaps the most likely implication of this derivative element involves an expression of an unconscious perception of the therapist based on his previous technical approach, and specifically on the manner in which he accepted the patient into treatment—a patient referral implies pathological symbiosis or parasiticism and the loss of an independent therapeutic space. The former factor also may have been represented at the beginning of the session when the patient alluded to her girlfriend's facial paralysis.

The hypothesis of detrimental factors in the therapist's technique is now lent additional support when the patient alludes to the absence of depth perception. Pathological symbiotic and parasitic modes of relatedness that are based on manifest content and Type One derivative listening and intervening create therapeutic experiences that are distinctly without depth.

The preformed formulations and some of the specific silent hypotheses that were developed through first one and then a second derivative are subsequently finding support in this reading of the implications of a third encoded element. Nonetheless, in the interest of caution, these conceptualizations should be reexamined to confirm that they are strongly evident in the patient's material rather than the result of a particular bias that has restricted or prejudiced the understanding of the patient's derivative material.

Along the way, the therapist should sit back and severely test out his or her burgeoning formulations. Blind spots or too intense an investment in a particular formulation must be avoided. This problem arises in the present session when the patient describes the mixed qualities in allowing the sick woman to drive: on the one hand, she felt reassured, but on the other, she was somewhat endangered. In response to this material it might first be asked if the therapist's initial silence was in some way inappropriate and a means of pathologically endangering the patient. Such a consideration seems unlikely, but must be checked out. The preformed silent hypothesis embodies some expectation that the patient will feel somewhat endangered by the possibility of a secure holding relationship with the therapist. Apparently it is this anxiety that has been translated into an unconscious fantasy of bodily harm—the possibility of an accident—that appears to be represented here.

In the actual session, the patient next mentioned feeling good and handling a dinner party quite well. This association seemed to support the silent hypothesis of an unconscious perception of the therapist as functioning well in light of his decreased unnecessary activity.

As the session unfolded, the therapist did press the patient to associate and asked a number of questions, though his rate of intervening was dramatically reduced. Toward the latter part of the session, the patient spoke as follows:

> Patient: I've been able to talk more to my husband lately. He's handling things differently. A friend of mine remarked about how confident I seem. At work, this belligerent woman came into my office and I was able to handle her quite well. My son did well in school. He seems less frightened now.

These manifest associations, treated as derivatives, organize quite well around the adaptive context of the change in the therapist's style. These associations are in keeping with the positive introjective identifications or unconscious perceptions that had been anticipated from the patient. The patient encodes an unconscious image of the therapist now as confident, handling matters well, less anxious, and behaving quite differently. The patient also expresses an ability to talk more openly, and even adds an unconscious allusion to herself as a belligerent woman whom the therapist must manage, and whom he is managing far better than in the past. These encoded communications are in keeping with the initial silent hypotheses, and appear to extend them in a number of directions. A meaningful derivative network is shaping up, much of it involving the patient's positive unconscious perceptions of the therapist in light of his change, and a small part of it in terms of the patient's reactions to this shift in style. Although there is no genetic-memory dimension to this material, such derivatives might well emerge in a future session if the therapist maintains his new stance.

For purposes of illustration, the end of the session will be represented as the following:

> Patient: I was with my lover. He treats me like such a baby. He can't stand on his own two feet. I really don't feel like talking to him. He seems always to be out of control.

This material, treated first, as it must be, as encoded expressions of unconscious perceptions of the therapist, is distinctly out of keeping with the silent hypotheses. It suggests a rather different image of the therapist, as someone who is still quite seductive, who breaks the boundaries (the reference to the affair), who infantilizes the patient, and who is himself quite insecure and out of control. This derivative material therefore runs quite contradictory to the budding formulations. It is important to experience this lack of support and to accept it as a signal to reformulate. Certainly, if these associations had appeared toward the end of the session, there would be little basis for confidence in the initial silent hypotheses. The therapist would therefore be compelled to search for a new and unrecognized adaptive context, and to determine whether the material organizes meaningfully around that particular precipitant. Simultaneously, he would consider the possibility that this material is primarily distorted and fantasy-based, though he would have to await further material from the patient before clarifying the nature of these difficulties. In principle, the absence of silent validation and the emergence of material that is distinctly contradictory to a silent hypothesis calls for serious efforts at reformulation.

SUMMARY OF TECHNICAL PRINCIPLES OF SILENT VALIDATION

In the early part of the session, the therapist engages in unencumbered listening and in efforts to develop silent formulations of the patient's material. Once these silent formulations have been crystalized in terms of indicators, adaptive context, and derivative complex, they should be subjected to a silent testing-out (a validating process) in terms of the patient's ongoing associations.

Silent validation occurs when the patient's continuing associations support the original hypothesis and extend it in unexpected and meaningful ways. This type of extension may occur through a direct representation of the adaptive context that the therapist had presupposed, or it may also involve the emergence of new and encoded derivatives that extend the therapist's thinking. The emergence of diverse derivative material to form a coalescible derivative network (i.e., encoded unconscious perceptions, unconscious fantasies, genetic repercusions, adaptive reactions, etcetera) is especially significant.

The therapist should not press formulations or attempt to force meanings into the patient's associations. Silent validation is best obtained through strikingly compelling derivative implications.

The therapist must maintain an open mind and a readiness to recognize nonvalidating associative segments. Although not every portion of the patient's material must necessarily add to a silent hypothesis, seemingly meaningful derivative associations that fail to support the therapist's formulation should be taken as a sign of the need for reconsideration. The absence of derivative elaboration over an extended portion of the session must be taken as a clear signal for reevaluation of the initial silent hypothesis and the search for new and different formulations. The key to the development of an alternate formulation often lies in the recognition of a previously unrecognized adaptive context that, upon analysis, proves to be a more powerful organizer of the patient's material. At times the problem may lie in a failure to appreciate important unconscious implications of a known intervention context. Any sense of uncertainty calls for continued silence and reassessment. In principle, the therapist should not offer an intervention to the patient that has not obtained a significant measure of indirect silent validation.

Direct Validation

Once an intervention has actually been offered to the patient, the patient's responsive behaviors and associations must be examined along three basic lines: (1) for the presence of derivative cognitive validation; (2) for the presence of interactional or interpersonal validation; and (3) for the presence of some measure, however small, of unique conscious insight and subsequent working through. In addition to these aspects, central to the issue of validation or its lack, the patient's material is also treated as a *commentary* on the therapist's intervention: responsive unconscious perceptions and fantasies in light of the manifest and latent meanings and functions of the therapist's effort.

For an intervention to be considered correct by the therapist, it must obtain both cognitive and interactional validation, and lead to some degree of conscious understanding and working through. The essential hallmark of validation involves uniquely elaborating cognitive derivatives and derivative representations of the introject of the well-functioning therapist. Only conscious insight that follows upon this type of derivative validation can be viewed as genuine and truly adaptive.

Derivative-cognitive or interpersonal validation alone may be considered a form of partial validation. Apparent conscious understanding in the absence of derivative confirmation is highly suspect and seldom genuine.

No matter how certain a therapist is of a particular intervention (management of the frame or interpretive), the patient's derivative response most remain the criterion of its actual validity. In some situations, the patient may offer an initial and even fragmentary form of derivative cognitive (and more rarely, interactional) validation, only to move quickly toward communications that fail to support and elaborate upon the therapist's intervention. Some of these patients are responding with negative therapeutic reactions to valid interventions. However, in all such instances, there must be some initial sign of derivative validation before the patient's shift to nonconfirmatory material. Only then should the therapist begin to develop hypotheses as to why an essentially valid intervention is being defensively refuted by the patient. Except for this rare type of occurrence, all instances in which the patient's derivative associations fail to support the therapist's intervention in unique and surprising ways should be taken as a sign of *interventional error*. Rather than attempting to formulate this type of nonvalidation in terms of the defensive needs of the patient, the therapist should spend the effort in accepting nonconfirmation and developing new and different hypotheses.

DERIVATIVE COGNITIVE VALIDATION

Derivative cognitive validation of framework management or interpretive interventions takes the form of new material that has been previously repressed by the patient. This cluster of associations has uniqueness both in terms of its manifest meanings and its latent implications. Often the patient simply recalls a thought, fantasy, or incident that took place just prior to the session or sometime recently. On occasion, the recall may involve a previously forgotten dream. More rarely, it will involve an early childhood memory filled with direct and encoded new meaning.

As a rule, the conscious recollection adds in some unexpected and surprising way to the therapist's intervention, and the derivative meanings extend the therapist's formulation. The essential quality of a validating segment lies in its uniqueness, and especially in the way in which it serves as the vehicle of unanticipated derivative expressions pertaining to previously unrepresented, unconscious perceptions and fantasies. These in turn serve to further illuminate the area that has been managed or interpreted.

This type of encoded or indirect confirmation is termed *Type Two derivative validation*. In essence, this term implies the emergence of entirely unique *encoded* material. Contained therein are disguised implications that shed new light on the material at hand and on the patient's Neurosis. Bion (1962) terms such a communication a *selected fact*. It involves a realization that serves as an unanticipated constant conjunction, meaningfully unifying previously disparate observations. A selected fact, or Type Two derivative validation (the terms are synonomous), provides synthesis where none had previously existed. On both the manifest and latent levels, it integrates diverse observations into a new and meaningful whole.

Clearly, the patient's direct agreement with an intervention is not Type Two derivative validation. Such a manifest response may be followed by derivative validation or may not. Similarly, direct disagreement with an intervention cannot form a basis for deciding on its validity. Clinical experience, however, indicates that direct negation of this kind is most often followed with nonvalidating derivative responses.

Direct elaboration of an interpretation without a unique derivative expression is another type of response that does *not* imply validation. Even the recall of early memories, when they are previously known or when they do not shed unique light and perspective on the material at hand and do not extend the therapist's intervention in surprising ways, cannot be accepted as confirmatory. Therapists have all too often mistakenly accepted seemingly dynamic communications or the recall of any early memory as a positive response to their efforts. In actuality, these are Type One derivative reactions, and do not constitute a true form of cognitive validation. The therapist must be clear that the dynamic material or early recollection serves as a unique selected fact that elaborates the intervention before accepting the patient's response as a form of validation. True validation involves both encoded meaning and unique and unanticipated discovery.

It is important to approach the question of derivative cognitive validation with considerable caution. The tendency of therapists to have strong investments in their formulations and interventions is well known. All too often, there is an attitude of undue certainty or an implicit assumption of the correctness of a hypothesis, especially once it has been offered to the patient. Frequently, no special effort at validation is undertaken. Alternately, the search is for the slightest sign of agreement or elaboration, and disagreement is treated as a sign of the patient's defenses rather than a signal that the therapist might well have been in error.

In light of these biases, rather stringent criteria of validation must be maintained. The therapist should, as a rule, *remain quiet* for some time after intervening, allowing the patient a full play of response. In the absence of strikingly significant derivative cognitive validation, strong efforts at reformulation should be undertaken.

In general, derivative validation is the basis for insightful structural change.

INTERACTIONAL OR INTERPERSONAL VALIDATION

A patient will usually respond to a sound intervention with some derivative allusion to a positively functioning or helpful person, sometimes himself or herself. Thus there will be material that involves ways in which the patient is able to function well or ways in which some other person had done something constructive. Images of positive attributes, such as good impulse control, the absence of anxiety, sound management capacities, and other forms of effective coping, will appear. Quite rarely, the patient will allude to a constructive effort by the therapist. However, this type of allusion must be indirect and derivative for it to be taken as a sign of validation. A manifest response to an intervention, such as the comment that the therapist is being helpful, cannot be taken as a sign of interpersonal validation. Since the essential process in this type of confirmation is entirely unconscious, it must be reflected in encoded representations.

While derivative cognitive validation forms a basis for specific insights and conflict resolution, interactional validation signals an *inevitable, unconscious introjective identification* with a well-functioning therapist (i.e., a therapist capable of securing, maintaining, and interpreting the therapeutic environment). Thus it is only when the therapist fulfills his or her basic functions as the manager of the ground rules of the therapeutic relationship and as the interpreter of the patient's material that the patient will derive unconsciously positive, constructive, helpful introjects.

Although there may be some measure of insight inherent to these incorporations, their main influence appears to involve the patient's internal object- and self-representations and his or her introjected inner mental world. It is there that many pathological, destructive, inappropriately seductive, highly defensive, and otherwise disruptive introjects have their influence. Some of these introjects are ego-syntonic so that the patient is identified with them; while others are ego-alien, leaving the patient to feel persecuted by them or to experience behaviors motivated by need systems involving these introjects, which are felt to be alien to his or her own wishes and best interests.

This inevitable and unconscious positive introjective identification with the therapist is generally ego-enhancing. It also has a specific function of modifying the patient's pathological introjects and lessening their disruptive influences. It must be stressed, however, that this type of ameliorating effect does not occur when a therapist attempts to deliberately (consciously) behave in a "good" fashion or as the result of direct, so-called supportive interventions. At such times, the patient tends to respond to the unconscious implications of such efforts, and these tend to be quite negative— destructive and infantilizing. Thus, the essential basic functions of the therapist and distinctly unconscious processes and effects must be involved. In addition, these particular consequences of a sound intervention must be supported and extended by the ultimate development of specific cognitive insights.

CONSCIOUS INSIGHT AND WORKING THROUGH

Basic derivative validation of an intervention should be followed or accompanied by unique conscious insights on the part of the patient. This understanding may be quite restricted, and the surface working through may be rather limited. In some situations the conscious insight may extend and be elaborated upon, and include a considerable period of conscious working over and working through—efforts by the patient to apply his or her new self-understanding to the relationship with the therapist and those outside of treatment. Trial actions, the testing out of symptoms, and the use of new adaptational responses may be involved.

It is not uncommon for the patient to experience only a minimal degree of conscious understanding. In such instances much of the insight and reworking will take place through encoded derivatives, and therefore on an unconscious level. However, in all instances of effective readaptation, there should be some element of unique surface realization. By and large, validating responses on a derivative level that do not lead to conscious understanding tend to be flawed. On the other hand, apparent conscious insight that is not accompanied by cognitive and interpersonal Type Two derivative validation is virtually always spurious. Such apparent understanding tends to constitute functional falsifications—false insights—designed to avoid the true area of disturbance and chaos. Self-interpretations by patients tend to be expressed on the manifest content or Type One derivative levels, and seldom entail Type Two derivative formulations. As such, they tend to constitute false insights and lie-barrier systems that may or may not nonetheless prove to be adaptive.

CLINICAL EXAMPLE

A young woman in psychotherapy met her therapist at a health spa before entering treatment with him. Once therapy began, the issue of whether it could be carried out successfully in light of the prior and continued personal contact between the patient and therapist came up several times.

The session presented here took place after six months of once-weekly psychotherapy. In the previous hour the therapist had offered a highly pressured, extended intervention about the difficulties for both himself and the patient that had arisen because of their relationship at the spa. Making some use of the patient's derivative material, the therapist introduced a number of associations of his own, and suggested that the problems involved raised serious doubts about the viability of the therapy. The therapist was aware that he had made little use of the patient's associations, and that he had intervened largely because of pressures within himself to deal quickly with the situation and to rectify it.

Patient: I have nothing to say today. I left work early because my boss gave me nothing to do. I don't think the new job is going to work out. As a child, my mother was like an animal in pursuit. I felt trampled. *(Pause.)* Ask me questions today. You were pretty rough on me last session. You looked friendly at the spa talking to that other girl when I saw you there on the weekend.

Therapist: You are saying that last session you experienced me as trampling you as your mother had done in your childhood. This leads you not to want to talk to me and to question whether treatment will work out. Your doubts are also connected to seeing me at the spa.

Patient: I've had enough about the spa unless you're suggesting that treatment can't work out because of it. I've had this fantasy I never mentioned to you. It's about being a stripper and undressing all over the world. I also imagine men exposing themselves to me. When I see how horny men are, I don't feel so bad about myself. There is this guy at the spa who is different. He's an executive and very sharp. He's sensitive to other people's feelings.

The validating process cannot be considered in the absence of a formulation of the material prior to the therapist's intervention in terms of indicators, activated adaptation-evoking contexts, and derivative complex. On this basis, a silent hypothesis may be developed as to whether the patient will confirm the therapist's intervention or not. In an actual session with a patient, this type of evaluation would begin as soon as the therapist had finished intervening.

In brief, the main activated intervention context for this material is the therapist's pressured and erroneous intervention in the previous hour. The major background intervention context involves the decision by the therapist to accept a person into therapy with whom he had a prior personal social relationship, however minimal it may have been.

What are the unconscious implications of these two interventions? The first intervention has qualities of a projective identification, a dumping into the patient, through which the therapist projects his uncontrolled anxieties, his failing defenses, and his inability to deal with the personal contact that existed between himself and the patient at the spa. There is an implied sense of wanting to terminate the patient, to get rid of her. There are distinct qualities of attack, hostility, and loss of control. The mode of relatedness appears to be a pathological symbiosis (mixed with some sense of parasiticism), based on the therapist's wish to rectify a damaging therapeutic situation and relationship, while doing so in a destructive manner. The mode of cure is by action-discharge.

Among its many meanings, the second context—the prior social contact—implies a lack of necessary boundaries between the patient and therapist. It conveys the need to exploit or parasitize the patient, and a sense of seductiveness. Dynamically, there are inappropriate qualities of both exhibitionism and voyeurism. A basic mode of maladaptation and cure through action and framework deviation is also conveyed unconsciously in this decision.

The indicators for this particular session include the therapist's erroneous intervention, the background but fundamental flaw in the framework and, once the session began, the patient's feeling that she had nothing to say to the therapist.

What now of the derivative complex? First, there are the derivative implications of this material in light of the therapist's pressured intervention. As always, the patient's unconscious perceptions and assignment of meanings to the intervention must be the first consideration. That the patient had nothing to say to the therapist implies a perception of the therapist as having said nothing to the patient. It suggests too a perception of the therapist as wishing to destroy meaningful relatedness with the patient. Next, there is the allusion to leaving work early, a derivative representation of the way in which the therapist left his job by intervening as he had done. The reference to the patient's boss giving her nothing to do conveys an additional unconscious perception of the therapist in light of his intervention, to the effect that he wishes to do all the work and to allow the patient little in the way of functioning. This appears to relate to his need to introduce his own associations into his comment, and his failure to allow the patient to offer him the derivatives he needs for intervening. In this way, he also took away the patient's job in therapy.

Next, the patient alludes to her belief that the new job is not going to work out. This appears to be an unconscious perception of the therapist's failings. There follows a rather striking genetic connection and derivative representation of the patient's unconscious image of the therapist: like the patient's mother, he was an animal in pursuit. The patient's allusion to feeling trampled involves an unconscious perception of the intervention as an effort by the therapist to trample her.

The initial silent hypotheses regarding the implications of the therapist's intervention in the previous hour are borne out in the patient's ongoing derivative material. A highly meaningful and coalescible set of derivative unconscious perceptions of the therapist are present. They include a genetic link that could be translated primarily in terms of nontransference: the therapist behaved in an uncontrolled manner comparable to the patient's mother in her childhood. By implication, experiences of this kind contributed to the patient's Neurosis, which took the form of depression and some degree of sexual promiscuity.

On a second level the same material contains derivative expressions of the patient's responses to the intervention context. She herself withdraws and wishes not to communicate. Then too she conveys an encoded message that reflects thoughts of leaving treatment prematurely and her belief that therapy will not work out. Finally, along different lines, she asks the therapist to do something constructive for her, however defensive it might be—to ask her questions.

The patient's allusion to the therapist's rough treatment of her during last session is, of course, a direct representation of the adaptive context. It is followed by another direct representation, this time of the second adaptive context: the relationship between the therapist and patient at the spa. The first representation further characterizes the therapist's roughness on the patient; the second adds an allusion to third parties as part of the deviant conditions to treatment. In addition, it alludes to ways in which the patient is able to observe the therapist outside of treatment, and conveys a derivative hope that the therapist will be able to lessen his hostility toward the patient—i.e., be friendly.

The patient's associations may also be organized as derivative unconscious perceptions of the therapist and responsive reactions, based on the adaptation-evoking context of the personal relationship at the spa. In essence, the material implies that this relationship interferes with the openness of the treatment relationship, that it interferes with the therapeutic work, and that therapy will not work out because of it. This deviation also generates an image of the therapist as someone in pursuit of the patient, someone who also may see the patient outside of treatment. The patient feels trampled or harmed by the deviation.

The therapist makes use of the adaptive context of his interven-tion of the previous hour. He interprets to the patient in light of that particular indicator-context that she experienced him as tram-pling her as her mother had done in her childhood. Without further addressing additional unconscious perceptions of the therapist on the basis of his intervention, the therapist then shifts to the patient's reaction to his intervention: her not wanting to talk and her questioning whether treatment will work out. He then connects these doubts to her seeing him at the spa—i.e., to the second adaptive context.

Before hearing the patient's response during supervision of this therapist, the present author evaluated this particular intervention as incomplete, but essentially correct. Its main shortcoming was a failure to spell out carefully the patient's unconscious perceptions of the therapist in light of his intervention and to more fully characterize this aspect of the patient's derivative communications. It omitted some of the important derivatives, and yet touched upon the most compelling encoded communication—the allusion to the mother who had trampled the patient. Even there, however, the animal quality is omitted, perhaps because it involved an assigned image to the therapist with which he was uncomfortable (see Chapter 13). In all, partial validation was predicted.

In the patient's response to the intervention, there is first a conscious comment that appears to be a surface working over of the possibility that treatment cannot work out because of the outside personal contact. This conveys the element of conscious insight that has been identified here as part of the validating process. However, this material should not be accepted as a sign of true validation without derivative confirmation.

The patient's next association constitutes an almost ideal form of Type Two derivative validation, the report of a fantasy that had not been previously mentioned to the therapist. It suggests the modification of a repressive barrier and of the patient's defensive alignment as a consequence of the therapist's interpretation. Fur-ther, it implies a willingness to communicate meaningfully in response to the therapist's effort. These are highly positive signs of validation, though not definitive. The revelation of a derivative selected fact that will provide new meaning to the material at hand and to the patient's Neurosis is still absent.

The content of the patient's previously repressed or suppressed fantasies must be examined. The first is that of being a stripper and undressing all over the world. Heretofore, the patient had said little of the exhibitionistic, voyeuristic, and distinctly sexualized, aspects of the therapist's manner of intervening and of the deviation from the ideal therapeutic relationship. Through an *encoded* communication, these elements are now expressed in striking form. In regard to the therapist, both his erroneous intervention and his social contact with the patient are forms of exhibitionism. They involve a sense of grandiosity, in that the intervention implied great knowledge within the therapist, and the deviation implied an unwieldy sense of power. These images are reinforced by the patient's fantasy of men exposing themselves to her. Also implied within this sequence is a valid impression within the patient that both she and the therapist are alike in important pathological ways. The reassurance afforded to the patient on this basis is reflected in her next communication: when she sees how horny men are, she does not feel so bad about herself. This is indeed a form of misalliance cure—cure through nefarious comparison—without insight. It is one form of symptom relief available to the patient prior to this interpretation.

Each of the patient's associations contain critical derivative implications that serve as selected facts to help give new meaning to the patient's associations not only in this hour, but in many earlier sessions. The new material also illuminates the patient's Neurosis, in that her mother's lack of control and evident sexual problems (she had many affairs of which the patient knew a great deal) had been factors in the patient's chronic sense of depression and promiscuity. The therapist's errant intervention and acceptance of this patient into therapy under deviant conditions served to unconsciously justify and support the patient's Neurotic mode of adaptation in a manner comparable to its early beginnings in the context of the patient's relationship with her mother.

At this point the role of the patient's own unconscious sexual fantasies and needs cannot be detailed. They can emerge only when the therapist rectifies his error and the basic framework of this treatment so that his actions and interventions no longer confirm this particular image that the patient carries of him.

This initial material has an indirect quality, and functions as Type Two derivatives that illuminate the disturbances in this therapeutic interaction, as well as the nature of the patient's Neurosis. In encoded form, the material conveys fresh and highly meaningful, previously unexpressed perceptions of the therapist and of the treatment situation. This is a sign of extensive derivative cognitive validation.

Finally, the patient concludes this segment of the session with an allusion to the sharp executive at the spa who is sensitive to other people's feelings. This constitutes a positive introjective identification with the therapist, who has been capable, perhaps for the first time, of offering this patient a sound interpretation and strong hints in the direction of rectifying this permanently damaged framework. Here too the material is encoded and derivative. The introjects of the therapist developed on this basis could prove quite ego-enhancing for the patient. Similarly, the specific cognitive insights that could eventually be developed from these derivatives could serve to help the patient more adequately understand the nature and basis for her Neurosis.

An essentially valid, though incomplete, intervention has been presented. The power of the patient's confirmatory response may have been based in part on the therapist's failure heretofore to offer sound interpretations. In any case, this patient showed a highly meaningful derivative cognitive response to the intervention, and evidenced interpersonal validation as well. There was also a conscious realization that the deviation in this treatment might preclude its successful completion. Later in this session and in the following hours, the patient extended her sphere of conscious understanding considerably, and ultimately worked with this therapist toward an insightful but necessary termination.

The Presence of Validation

In the presence of validation, the therapist will generally sit back and begin to formulate the implications of the new material emerging from the patient. It is here that the commentary qualities of the patient's associations are taken into account. The new adaptive context is the correct intervention and its implications. Some small measure of countertransference is inevitable, and will lead to areas of nonvalidation with efforts to represent perceptions of the therapist on this basis. The substantial area of validity will lead to further derivative and conscious elaboration of the insights involved. In addition, there will usually be a paradoxical response to the threatening qualities of a well-functioning therapist. This involves, in part, ways in which a positive introject disturbs the denial defenses directed against negative and hurtful introjects within the patient's inner mental world. In addition, the knowledgeable therapist is often seen as frightening and omnipotent, and as dangerously entrapping. The therapist's knowledge suggests a sense of power that leads the patient to mobilize anxieties and transference-based fantasy-memory constellations. On this basis, the therapy continues in meaningful fashion, further illuminating the patient's Neurosis. By and large, both conscious and derivative cognitive insights lead to the direct understanding of previously unconscious conflicts and pathological unconscious perception and fantasy constellations. As a result, there are modifications in the patient's adaptive resources and revisions in the use of pathological defenses. Such insight fosters growth and leads to symptom alleviation and characterological change.

The initiation or continuation of a healthy symbiotic mode of relatedness is inherent to this curative process. The incorporation of this mode of relatedness and the patient's experience of its qualities helps to foster the use of healthy modes of relatedness in outside relationships. Through these effects there are, as well, modifications in many aspects of the patient's pathological id, ego, and superego functioning.

In essence, then, the mode of relatedness and cure inherent to a sound intervention, and the insights and introjects so generated, lead to symptom alleviation in the patient through a variety of means. The offer of a sound mode of healthy relatedness, usually in the form of a healthy symbiosis is perhaps the most fundamental. There are also a variety of constructive changes in virtually every sphere of mental functioning.

The Absence of Validation

Nonvalidation is the absence of both a derivative cognitive selected fact and the derivative expression of a positive introject in response to a therapist's intervention. Certain signs of nonconfirmation deserve specific mention.

First, there is the manifest refutation of an intervention, the patient's essential disagreement with the therapist. A related response occurs when the patient manifestly ignores the intervention and there is little sign as well of derivative response. Although a patient's direct and manifest agreement with an intervention has no bearing on validation (it may be followed by derivative validation or its absence), in most instances a negation of the therapist's intervention is followed by the absence of derivative confirmation. Thus surface disagreements should be taken as a sign that an intervention is likely to have been in error. It is, however, essential to study the patient's further responses in order to detect those rare occasions when this type of negation proves to be highly defensive and is followed by Type Two derivative validation.

The appearance of new material in itself, while encouraging, is not a sign of Type Two derivative validation unless it clearly extends the therapist's formulation as it has been conveyed to the patient. At times such new material is presented not so much to extend the therapist's correct comments as it is to unconsciously help the therapist to identify an unrecognized error, as well as its nature and source. The new material is often designed to redirect the therapist's thinking and to cure the therapist's expressed countertransferences. Similarly, seemingly productive or meaningful associations that appear to have important dynamic and genetic thrusts are often prompted by erroneous techniques; they are not *per se* a sign of sound therapeutic work. Traumatic and erroneous adaptive contexts are often evocative of extensive manifest and derivative communications from patients. All such associations must be consistently evaluated in light of activated intervention contexts stimulated by the therapist's interventions.

Surface agreement with an intervention, as well as the direct extension of its evident implications, does *not* constitute psychoanalytic validation. Similarly, the recall of highly familiar material that does not shed new light on the associations at hand cannot be viewed as confirmatory, even if it involves themes that have not been reported for some time. The recall of previously repressed early memories are not confirmatory *per se;* they too must be evaluated in light of their conscious and especially unconscious implications as responses to specific intervention contexts. The same principle applies to previously repressed conscious thoughts or fantasies about the therapist. Any material, no matter how fresh, must be organized as manifest and especially derivative responses to the implications of adaptation-evoking contexts. It is only on this basis that validation or its lack can be established. Much of present-day material from patients, however lively, is constituted as nonvalidating and derivative commentaries on erroneous interventions by therapists. Stringent criteria of confirmation must be applied at all times.

The situation is further complicated by the patient's unconscious investment in erroneous interventions and mismanagements of the framework. On the one hand, the patient will accept these errors for their defensive and other pathological value, and tend to exploit the therapist's error. On the other hand, however, the patient will also have a need to eventually pick up on the error, usually on a derivative level, to help the therapist recognize its basis and the means by which it can be rectified. Such efforts can be recognized because of the absence of Type Two derivative validation and the presence of extensive commentary by the patient. The key, as always, lies in the therapist's appreciation of the unconscious implications of the interventions, and therefore of the patient's responses to them.

There is an ever-present danger of establishing an intellectualized, defensive, seductive, or hostile sector of misalliance based on the extension of erroneous interventions. Some patients tend to support this type of effort by the therapist on the surface. The therapist who continues on without subjecting silent hypotheses and the patient's responses to actual interventions to a test of their validation allows highly fanciful but erroneous formulations to become barriers and defenses against hidden interactional conflicts within the treatment situation, and within both participants to therapy. The therapist's only protection against the various types of misalliance involved is a repeated application of the validating process in both of its phases—silent and open.

Finally, the appearance of a harmful, hurtful, negative figure, such as someone who is frustrating, destructive, seductive, infantilizing, or in any other way threatening or nonfunctional, is a common sign of erroneous interventions. It suggests an essentially pathological introject of the therapist based on errors in intervening. Similar principles apply to allusions to all types of unhealthy, exploitative, and stultifying object relationships. As a rule, these involve reflections of the patient's unconscious perceptions of the basically pathological mode of relatedness established through the therapist's errors. Images of efforts to find relief from an emotional or other types of problems in exploitative or otherwise inappropriate ways are also derivative indications of therapeutic error. These last reflect the action-discharge pathological mode of cure (sometimes through the use of words for evacuation instead of understanding) that the therapist has offered through his mistake.

These signs of nonvalidation are to be contrasted with a situation where the patient initially expresses a derivative positive introject and then moves on to deal with more harmful figures. Here there is an initial sign of validation, usually accompanied by validation in the cognitive sphere, after which the patient works over mobilized negative introjects and other pathological aspects of his or her own inner mental world and object relationships. In all such instances, clear signs of validation must be detected first.

It is useful to assume some greater or lesser degree of error in every intervention, in part because of the inevitability of some measure of countertransference-based influence, and also because of the previously alluded to tendency toward narcissistic investment by the therapist. By establishing stringent criteria for validation and insisting upon clear-cut positive introjects and uniquely meaningful derivative expressions after an intervention, the therapist can safeguard against unrecognized misalliances and the development of attractive but deceptive lie-barrier systems that are shared unwittingly by himself or herself and the patient.

CLINICAL EXAMPLE

The patient is a saleswoman who travels; because of this, her once-weekly session is on different days each week. In addition, the treatment is covered by insurance. In the previous session, the patient, who is single, talked about her considerable upset with Bill, a man with whom she had become involved. She was highly critical of him, especially of the way he talked and dressed. She recognized that she tended to carp and pick at him incessantly. The therapist, who had intervened somewhat critically a number of times earlier in the session, suggested at the end of the hour that the patient had shown a consistent pattern in which she picked on anyone toward whom she was attracted. Because of this, the therapist suggested that the patient lost out on many good times and relationships. The patient responded by agreeing that this was true.

The next hour begins as follows:

Patient: I'm really depressed. I want to end my relationship with Bill. He has really become a burden. He's never helpful, and he doesn't seem to want to hear me out. Then I don't want to talk to him. He doesn't seem to understand me.

In the presence of an intervention offered at the end of a session, the material with which the patient begins the following hour must be examined for validation or its lack. On a manifest level, it is possible to suggest that in addition to the patient's initial agreement, she was continuing in the next hour to pick on Bill. This would then mistakenly be taken as confirmation of the therapist's intervention, since it is a further elaboration of the therapist's comment. It is this type of self-evident, manifest extension that has been used to maintain the practice of manifest-content psychotherapy. It involves flat and linear thinking, and lacks any sense of unconscious processes and communication.

A rather different impression would be derived from this material through a consideration of derivative validation. It would be recognized that the patient's initial manifest agreement has been followed by material that lacks unique manifest or cognitive validation. Clearly, derivative signs of a positive introjective identification with the therapist are not present. Instead, there is ample evidence of negative introjects—the allusion to someone who is a burden, not helpful, who does not want to hear her out, and who does not understand her. In all, there is a distinct absence of derivative validation and strong signs of error.

The basis for the patient's derivative response—her use of encoded allusions to the therapist displaced onto her boyfriend Bill—is evident from an evaluation of this therapeutic interaction. In brief, this therapist—a woman—had been intervening on a manifest content level with a high rate of unnecessary activity. The patient was treated as the person within the bipersonal field who contained all of the psychopathology. No use was made of adaptive contexts and their implications, or of the patient's derivative material.

In this light, the patient's associations in the preliminary session appeared to contain valid unconscious perceptions in light of these interventions. The therapist then responded with an intervention that moved away from these encoded perceptions of herself, and especially from her own difficulties. Instead, the patient was confronted with a problem that in many ways actually, for the moment, belonged to the therapist. This attempt at confrontation and seeming interpretation is distinctly defensive and in error.

The patient's derivative responses support this initial formulation. Her depression is both an unconscious perception of the therapist's depressive state and a reaction to the therapist's assaultive and blaming interventions. The wish to end the relationship with Bill alludes both to the absence of a true treatment situation under these conditions and the patient's responsive wish to terminate. The subsequent material reflects the patient's experience of the therapist as a burden, not helpful, not hearing her, and not understanding her. The therapist herself is not speaking meaningfully to the patient, and the patient, of course, does not wish to communicate with the therapist under these conditions.

The patient's associations organize and coalesce quite well as a derivative commentary on the therapist's intervention and its unconscious implications. Had the therapist reflected upon her effort, she might have begun to identify some of the qualities of her mistakes. She could have easily developed a silent formulation that would have been borne out early in this hour. On that basis, both interpretation and rectification might have been feasible. In this way, the hurtful and destructive therapeutic interlude could be turned into a more constructive experience.

In the absence of clearly and uniquely validating derivative material, the therapist should make every possible effort to reformulate the thinking on which the prior intervention was based. The therapist should be guided in these efforts by the patient's manifest and especially derivative associations, and by subjective efforts. The therapist should remain silent and should be careful, in particular, to avoid extensions of, insistance upon the correctness of, and direct repetitions of the intervention. All too often, rather than accepting a nonvalidating response as a signal to reformulate, therapists attempt to clarify their meaning to the patient or to otherwise extend an initially erroneous effort. It is far more advisable to sit back under these conditions, and to silently hold and contain the patient and the material until new understanding has been generated. It is often then possible, using the adaptive context of the erroneous intervention, for the therapist to shape a correct interpretation of the entire sequence of material at hand, and to silently or, when necessary, openly rectify the mistakes involved. In this way, an initially disruptive and countertransference-dominated interlude is changed into a constructive and essentially noncountertransference-transference experience for the patient.

Summary and Conclusions

Efforts at validation are fundamental to a sound application of the listening-formulating process. No type of material is taken as confirmatory per se. All of the patient's associations in response to the therapist's silences, managements of the framework, and verbal-affective interventions are evaluated for their manifest and derivative implications in light of the similarly manifest and derivative implications of the therapist's interventions. The process is certainly a complicated one, though principles are available as a guide. Reflections of derivative and unconscious positive introjects are relatively easy to detect. The ideal cognitive confirmation involves a previously repressed piece of material that has unique qualities on both the manifest and latent levels.

The validating process described in this chapter involves the pursuit of the truth of the patient's Neurosis as activated by the therapist's interventions within the spiraling interaction of psychotherapy. These truths have, therefore, a secondary bearing on the truth of the therapist's efforts as well. On this basis, cure through insight and structural change can be effected. The constructive consequences of positive introjects add to these effects.

It is well, however, not to underestimate the highly threatening and painful qualities involved in facing the truths within the therapeutic interaction as they apply to both the patient and therapist. This process is by no means simply cognitive, and is deeply emotional and often highly disturbing. *Truth therapy* depends upon the therapist's fulfilling the basic functions of establishing a healthy therapeutic symbiosis with the patient, affecting a sound holding and containing relationship through the establishment of appropriate ground rules and boundaries, and the capacity for appropriate silence and for interpretation-reconstruction when necessary. This implies, of course, that the therapist is different in very important ways from the patient's past pathogenic figures and current pathological introjects. It implies as well that the therapist has a special capability for both holding and understanding. Cure through insight asks a great deal of both the patient and therapist, though it offers both much in return.

In this light, it is not surprising that there are many forms of psychotherapy that lack a validating methodology and operate on manifest content or a Type One derivative level. These forms of *lie therapy* may offer much in the way of immediate relief, but at considerable expense to both participants. The type of validation described in this chapter is essential to truth therapy. Failure to apply these principles inevitably leads to one form or another of lie therapy, and to a distinctly different form of cure—something other than true insight and structural change and growth.

Among the many characteristics of the sensitive therapist is the ability to quietly search for, recognize, tolerate, and respond to nonvalidating responses. In the course of a therapist's daily work, there can be a refreshing quality to nonconfirmation. It promises, among other things, to afford the therapist a special opportunity to learn something about the patient and himself or herself, and perhaps even about the psychoanalytic theory of Neuroses and of therapy. It thus creates a moment for potential growth in those who are prepared to experience it in just that way.

Chapter 13

The Object Relations Sphere of Listening

It is the therapist's goal to translate all experiences and the understanding of their implications into cognitive terms. With a strong foundation in this area, the therapist is better able to deal with other areas of listning and formulating that are critical, though somewhat difficult to define.

The object (person) relationship between the patient and therapist, and the interpersonal interaction that unfolds on the basis of their ongoing relatedness, is the core dimension of psychotherapy. This mode of relatedness is primary to all other dimensions of therapy. Its main determinants are the therapist's and patient's use of the ground rules and boundaries of the therapeutic relationship, including the conscious and unconscious goals and intentions of each participant. In turn, the mode of relatedness influences the nature, meaning, and functions of the communications of both patient and therapist. It is also a critical determinant in the actual mode of cure established for a particular treatment situation. Should the ground rules vary, the mode of relatedness will change, as will the implications of the communicative exchanges and the nature of the therapeutic effort shared by patient and therapist.

As a fundamental dimension of psychotherapy, the vicissitudes of the object relationship between the patient and therapist is an important area for listening and formulating. It involves a whole that is greater in important ways than its individual parts. It therefore requires the monitoring of specific factors or elements, as well as an integrated totality.

The Elements of Object Relatedness in Psychotherapy

There are, of course, many definable qualities to the object relatedness between the patient and therapist. These can be characterized separately for the patient and the therapist, though in addition, it is also possible to identify the attributes of the amalgam that they create together. The following categorizations are among the many possible:

1. The level of maturity or immaturity, including the extent to which the other person (object) is experienced as part of the self and afforded little separate consideration—i.e., treated as a self-object (Kohut 1971, 1977) or a separate and distinct individual.

2. Outstanding characteristics—e.g., anaclitic, dependent, hostile, seductive, etcetera.

3. The extent to which relatedness is to the whole person or to part objects.

4. The extent to which the relationship is basically constructive or therapeutic, as compared to destructive and antitherapeutic.

5. Such qualities as dominance and submissiveness, activity and passivity, and realistic or fantasy-dominated.

6. The extent to which the relationship is lasting, strong, and solid, with a clear sense of object constancy, as compared to temporary, weak, uncertain, and confused.

7. The extent to which the mode of relatedness is action-oriented and impulsive as compared to thoughtful and characterized by delay.

8. The extent to which the relationship is need-satisfying as compared to need-frustrating, though the type of needs involved—and whether they are pathological or nonpathological—must be specified.

Each of these dimensions is important to the therapeutic experience and to its outcome for the patient. However, because of the complexity of the object relationship between the two participants to treatment, it becomes necessary to seek out ways in which these various dimensions can be organized into integrated categories that form a more usable framework for listening and formulating. At present, the following dimensions of the therapeutic relationship appear to be the best organizers of the therapist's listening efforts:

1. The extent to which the relationship is geared to the therapeutic needs of the patient and, secondarily, to the appropriate needs of the therapist.

2. The nature of the instinctual drive gratifications, superego and ego ideal expressions, and ego functions, including defenses, that are characteristic of the relationship. By implication, this would require a definition of the nature of the frustrations involved.

3. The holding and containing qualities of the relationship for each member of the therapeutic dyad, and the extent to which the mode of relatedness is *inherently* ego supportive.

4. The specific nature of the role and underlying self-image adopted by each participant to treatment. In addition, the efforts by each to evoke role-responses and self-images in the other.

5. The *maturational mode of object relatedness* sought by each participant to treatment. This final categorization, which will be described in detail below, proves to embrace most of the other significant dimensions of the object relationship between the patient and therapist, and is the main classification used here.

Each of these spheres can be monitored in two ways: (1) in terms of the actual behaviors of each participant to treatment, and (2) through manifest and especially derivative representations in the patient's material. In the latter effort, the therapist monitors the characterizations and implications of all *object relationship allusions* in the patient's associations, whether they manifestly involve the patient himself or herself, the therapist, or outside figures. In keeping with basic principles of listening, this particular type of formulation must be made in light of prevailing intervention contexts, and in terms of both the manifest and derivative implications of the patient's material.

The clinical appraisal of the meanings of such associations or of the patient's direct behaviors with the therapist (and the therapist's with the patient) relies in turn on two factors: (1) the understanding within the therapist of the attributes of the ideal therapeutic relationship, and therefore of the specific role and functions of each participant to treatment; and (2) the patient's conscious and more especially unconscious commentaries on the nature and function of the basic mode of relatedness between the patient and the therapist as reflected in the patient's associations and behaviors. In light of established principles of listening and formulating, the therapist should accept only those formulations that obtain initial silent Type Two derivative validation, followed eventually by direct Type Two derivative validation in response to an intervention from the therapist based on the object-relationship hypothesis that has been generated. In principle, too, all formulations should be developed in terms of actualities and tested out as such, before considering the element of the patient's fantasies.

Role Responsibilities in Psychotherapy

In a sense, this entire volume is devoted to the delineation of the responsibilities, gratifications, and frustrations that accrue appropriately to patients and therapists in the course of a psychotherapeutic experience. Here, then, only the essence is presented.

THE PATIENT

The patient's role consists of the following:

1. A wish for help with an emotional problem.
2. A desire and ability to work with a therapist with some measure of cooperation.
3. An ability to communicate in a manner relevant to his or her Neurosis in terms of both manifest and latent expressions.
4. The capacity to tolerate the ground rules and boundaries of the therapeutic relationship, or alternatively, to subsequently explore and analyze modifications in these ground rules as imposed upon the therapeutic situation by the patient and, at times, the therapist.
5. A willingness to listen and to attempt to understand the therapist's interventions, and to respond with communications that contain, when necessary, manifest and derivative meanings.
6. An acceptance of those gratifications that pertain to the holding qualities of the therapeutic relationship and to the cognitive insights into the nature and functions of his or her Neurosis. An ability to renounce pathological gratifications, inappropriate superego sanctions, and pathological defenses or, alternatively, to analyze their implications when expressed or actualized in the treatment relationship.
7. A willingness and capacity to work with the therapist toward an understanding of the unconscious basis of the Neurosis or,

alternatively, when refractory to such efforts and interested instead in action-discharge and riddance, to eventually subject these expressed needs to analysis and insightful modification.

The essence of the patient's role in psychotherapy is to accept the conditions of treatment as offered by the therapist, to work through the use of free associations within these conditions, to accept the holding qualities of the therapeutic relationship offered, and to communicate intermittently in a manner that permits proper framework-management and interpretive responses from the therapist. However, any of these requisites may be temporarily unfulfilled by the patient, since the lack of fulfillment is an important means through which the patient expresses his or her psychopathology. Such exceptions are therefore an acceptable aspect of the patient's role and functions in psychotherapy, but there is a particular qualification: the patient must at some point be prepared to bring the deviation under control and subject it to analysis. Failure to do so at some juncture involves a refutation of the patient's role in psychotherapy.

The therapist should monitor the patient's behaviors and associations in an effort to understand the extent to which the patient accepts or refutes the ideal and necessary role requirements outlined here. This requires attention not only to the patient's verbal-affective associations, but also to actual behaviors with the therapist and outside of treatment. This involves attending to the patient's responses to interventions, to the surface and deeper (communicative) alliance sectors of the relationship, and to the patient's representations of relatedness and mode of cure in his or her associational material. In principle, any indication of disturbance in respect to the patient's acceptance of his or her role in treatment is a first-order resistance and therapeutic context—an indicator for intervening. It is essential, of course, to identify the activated intervention context to which this resistance is a response, and to trace out its unconscious meanings and functions on that basis—doing so in terms of both unconscious perceptions and unconscious fantasies.

THE THERAPIST

The role requirements of the therapist may be stated as follows:

1. To establish a therapeutic relationship and setting with definitive boundaries and ground rules.

2. To attend to, listen to, and interact with the patient in a manner geared toward the therapeutic needs of the latter, with only secondary and appropriate gratifications for himself or herself—i.e., and appropriate fee, the satisfaction of helping another person, the gratification of formulating a correct intervention and having it validated, etcetera.

3. To adhere to the basic responsibilities of maintaining and managing the framework and the holding aspects of the relationship to the patient. In addition, the fulfillment of the responsibility to offer sound interpretation-reconstructions called for by the patient's material.

4. To forego all possible types of pathological, instinctual-drive gratifications, pathological superego sanctions, and pathological defenses as expressed through erroneous interventions and mismanagements of the frame. Should the therapist inadvertently deviate, the error must be silently rectified, the framework of the treatment relationship must be restored when necessary, and the patient's material must be interpreted in terms of the latter's responsive uncounscious perceptions and fantasies.

5. To monitor the therapist's own silences and interventions as a way of determining the status of his or her object relatedness with the patient and the mode of cure that the therapist is seeking. In this regard, the therapist is guided by his or her own subjective experiences and evaluations, as well as by the manifest and especially derivative implications of the patient's behaviors and associations. The therapist's goal is to offer to the patient a healthy symbiotic mode of relatedness and an opportunity for cure through insight.

The type of relationship that the patient is attempting to establish with the therapist and that which the therapist wishes to maintain with the patient must be characterized separately. They may coincide or overlap, or be quite discordant. It is generally possible to identify efforts *directed toward* a particular mode of relatedness and, in addition, to characterize the *actual* qualities of the therapeutic relationship at a particular moment. In addition, the patient's (and therapist's) fantasies of how he or she wishes to relate may be detected. However, depending on the adaptation-evoking context that must be faced, there can be striking shifts in actualized and fantasied tendencies in this sphere.

Therapists' tendencies toward developing a pathological mode of relatedness with their patients (defined empirically as any departure from their basic role and responsibilities) are often diffcult to recognize and even more problematic in regard to their resolution. The achievement of a therapeutic approach that consistently offers the patient a healthy therapeutic symbiosis requires considerable insight and mastery by the therapist. Nevertheless, this type of self-analytic work is essential to the creation of the necessary mode of relatedness and framework that offers the patient the best opportunity for insightful structural change.

For the patient, too, the ideal mode of relatedness is that of a healthy symbiosis. However, it is to be expected that the patient will from time to time express a need for healthy periods of autism, at which juncture the therapist's response should also be a healthy autism. Because expressions of psychopathology are inevitable, the patient will also unconsciously attempt to engage the therapist from time to time in a pathological mode of relatedness. Although somewhat disruptive to smooth therapeutic work, these object relationship pressures create important therapeutic opportunities for interpretive and framework-management responses by the therapist, including the insightful understanding of the implications of the patient's efforts to create the pathological mode of relatedness itself. Such interpretive work tends to involve all of the other dimensions of the therapeutic experience, including those that pertain to both the tripartite schema for intervening and the six-part observational schema through which the therapist comprehends the therapeutic experience.

A Classification of Maturational Modes of Relatedness

HEALTHY AUTISM

The autistic mode of relatedness is defined clinically as one in which the *meaning link* (the K link) between the patient and therapist has been severed (Bion 1962). The patient is using the Type C communicative mode (see Chapter 15), in that he or she fails to clearly represent an activated intervention context and/or does not produce a meaningful and coalescible derivative complex. Healthy autism, then, involves periods in psychotherapy, such as the middle or lying-fallow phase, during which there is no meaningful activated intervention context and the patient makes no effort to create one. This is a period of holding and containing, during which the patient generally engages in Type One derivative self-interpretations that appear to soften and modify the pathological elements of derivative and nonderivative (lie-barrier) defenses. Most patients in the course of a successful psychotherapeutic experience require some period of healthy autism.

PATHOLOGICAL AUTISM

Here, an active intervention context is in existence, but the patient fails to represent the context in a manner that lends itself to interpretation, and/or does not produce a meaningful and coalescible derivative complex. In this way, the patient withdraws from meaningful relatedness with the therapist in a clearly pathological and defensive manner. The mode of relatedness therefore reflects the patient's use of pathological defenses, and may at times entail pathological modes of gratification as well. Pathological autism may refer to gross behavioral withdrawal by the patient; but it may also allude to a patient who is cooperating with the therapist and free-associating, though failing to respond to activated stimuli within the therapeutic interaction with a meaningful network of communications.

For the therapist, pathological autism involves inappropriate silences that constitute failures to intervene. This mode of relatedness is also reflected when he or she intervenes without a full consideration of the implications of an activated intervention context and the patient's derivative complex. Such interventions typically involve highly abstract, intellectualized, and theoretical manifest and Type One derivative inferences that are unrelated to the true meaning of the patient's material; instead, they reflect the conscious and unconscious fantasy and perception systems of the therapist. Many erroneous interventions reflect the pathological autism of the therapist.

THE HEALTHY SYMBIOTIC MODE

The healthy or therapeutic symbiosis involves the patient's acceptance of the ground rules and boundaries of the therapeutic relationship and of his or her basic role responsibilities in the psychotherapeutic relationship. This mode of relatedness is reflected in meaningful Type A (symbolic) communication (see Chapter 15), through which the patient represents all important activated intervention contexts, and responds as well with meaningful coalescible derivative material to these precipitants. While the pathological autistic mode tends to imply cure through defense and lie-barrier system, the healthy symbiotic mode usually reflects a wish to achieve the cure of the patient's emotional disturbance through a sound holding relationship and the insights derived from the therapist's interpretations and reconstructions. Thus, in the healthy symbiosis, the *meaning link* between the patient and therapist is maintained, the patient's therapeutic needs are uppermost, and a variety of pathological defenses and satisfactions are renounced. This difficult mode of relatedness therefore forms the basis for truth therapy or cure through genuine understanding.

For the therapist, the wish for a healthy symbiosis is characterized by the establishment of ideal ground rules and boundaries for the therapeutic relationship, appropriate use of silence, and an offer of framework management and interpretive responses in keeping with the manifest and latent implications of the patient's material. In this way, the therapist places the patient's therapeutic needs uppermost in the treatment relationship, and accepts the role as the *primary symbiotic provider*. The therapist renounces his or her own tendencies toward pathological modes of relatedness, gratification, and defense, and accepts those measures of inevitable satisfaction that are accrued as the symbiotic provider-therapist. It is the offer of a healthy symbiosis that makes the therapist available to the patient for inevitable and uncounscious positive introjective identifications, and as a sound holding and containing figure. This mode of relatedness also provides the only relationship that does not contradict apparently sound interpretive interventions. It is therefore essential that the therapist offer the patient a healthy therapeutic symbiosis as the foundation for a successful therapeutic experience.

PATHOLOGICAL SYMBIOSIS

Pathological symbiosis is an unbalanced relationship that may involve either the patient or therapist as the symbiotic provider. Pathological forms of merger are characteristic, as are pathological satisfactions and forms of collusiveness that are inimical to understanding, insight, growth, and individuation. The quest is for immediate and inappropriate gratifications on an interpersonal and instinctual drive level.

For the patient this mode of relatedness is typically expressed through a failure to adhere to the essential role requirements described above. In particular, all efforts on the patient's part to modify the ground rules and boundaries of therapy, and to obtain gratifications from the therapist beyond interpretations and appropriate managements of the ground rules, may serve to express a wish for this type of relatedness. Through these means, the patient achieves a variety of pathological interpersonal and intrapsychic satisfactions. The therapist expresses needs for pathological symbiosis, usually as the symbiotic recipient, through modifications in the ground rules and boundaries of treatment, and through noninterpretive interventions. Pathological satisfactions comparable to those obtained by the patient are the result.

When a pathological symbiosis is effected, the patient's associations and behaviors are designed for pathological gratification and action-discharge rather than for understanding insight. Even though it may seem on the surface that the patient is seeking comprehension, the effective, functional implication of his or her associations involve the search for merger, and for a variety of pathological satisfactions. Under these conditions, of course, the therapist who seeks to maintain a healthy symbiosis must in actuality frustrate these inappropriate wishes and interpret their implications. Should the work with the patient proceed on a manifest content level in terms of the evident (though false) meanings involved in the patient's associations, the therapist will on some level pathologically gratify the patient and contribute to the pathological symbiosis. This particular type of interaction constitutes a common form of lie-barrier therapy through which the true implications of the patient's associations and behaviors are bypassed.

In a similar vein, the therapist who attempts to actualize a pathological symboisis with a patient—and most patients are prepared on some level (usually manifest, but not latent) to participate in this mode of relatedness in order to maintain their Neurosis and a Neurotic mode of relatedness—will express these relationship needs through erroneous interpretations and alterations in the framework. Although often afforded the trappings of efforts at support, so-called flexibility, and the like, the main functions of such efforts are not at all directed toward insight and understanding. Instead, they seek to engage the patient in a pathological symbiosis in which, as a rule, the therapist is the symbiotic recipient. The qualities of this type of interaction are consistently represented in derivative form in the patient's associational material, usually through allusions to disturbed interpersonal interactions of one kind or another.

THE PARASITIC MODE OF RELATEDNESS

In symbioses, there are distinct manifest nurturing qualities, whether pathological or healthy. In the parasitic mode of relatedness, there is no sense of nurturance and, instead, there are expressions of wishes to exploit, harm, destroy, or otherwise damage the other person. On a manifest level, there may be seductive, hostile, or overly dependent qualities to the interaction, though the main feature is an underlying sense of misuse of the other person and a disregard for that person's reasonable needs.

In patients, this mode is expressed through efforts to exploitatively modify the ideal ground rules and boundaries of treatment and to otherwise exploit the therapist. This appears in such forms as requests of the therapist to communicate with others regarding the treatment situation, other deviations that exploit their therapist, and attempts to press the therapist into a wide range of noninterpretive interventions. This mode is also expressed when the therapist attempts to exploit the patient through breaks in the frame, which serve primarily to gratify the therapist's pathological needs and to otherwise misuse the therapeutic situation. This is exemplified by such deviations as tape-recording sessions, physical contact with the patient, and a variety of self-serving noninterpretive intervention.

THE COMMENSAL MODE OF RELATEDNESS

The commensal mode accords relatively equal satisfactions to both participants in keeping with the healthy needs of each. The ideal therapeutic relationship is a healthy symbiosis, but the patient's therapeutic needs far outweigh the satisfactions of the therapist: thus any shift toward a greater measure of satisfaction for the therapist constitutes a pathological symbiosis. In this light, the commensal mode of relatedness must be seen as the ideal form of interaction outside of treatment, whereas the healthy symbiosis is the ideal within the therapeutic situation.

CLINICAL EXAMPLE

Patients tend to be split in regard to the type of relationship they wish with their therapists. The general trend involves a surface clamor for a pathological symbiotic mode of relatedness, accompanied by consistent derivative communications that indicate the patient's unconscious awareness of the inappropriate qualities involved. On this derivative level, the patient tends to repudiate the pathological wishes and to propose models of rectification and representations of the more ideal mode of relatedness to both himself or herself and the therapist. Based in part on similar split tendencies, therapists have been misled by the patient's conscious and direct pressures into participating in many forms of pathological symbiosis. Patients then tend to respond with conscious appreciation, though with derivative disillusionment, efforts at rectification, and even unconscious efforts at interpretation—all based on a negative image of the therapist who has succumbed to their pressures.

The therapist must monitor both the direct attributes of the therapeutic relationship and the patient's conscious and unconscious representations of the existing mode of relatedness—and sometimes their wishes in this regard. Monitoring of the patient's derivative material for encoded representations of the prevailing mode of relatedness at a given juncture is especially important. Such efforts involve every dimension of the listening-formulating process as attuned to the unconscious expressions of both the therapist and the patient.

The following session involves a 31-year-old homosexual woman who had met her therapist socially at a country club and later entered treatment with him. At this point in the therapy, the therapist had been offering the patient direct advice regarding difficulties she was having with her present woman lover.

Patient: I saw a movie in which a mother, a woman who seemed to love her children, suddenly murders them. My own mother still needs to keep me as an infant. She binds herself to me for her own benefit so she won't kill someone. *(Alluding to the therapist's note-taking):* What did you just write down? My girlfriend and I are from different backgrounds. She wants one thing while I want another. I get furious with her when she tries to use me.

Therapist: This must be connected with your rage at your mother.

Patient: My father never understood me. I have fantasies of begging a man to rape me until he finally does it. Last time, your face intruded into the fantasy. I had the thought I ought to get out of here.

Formulations regarding the actual maturational mode of object relationship between the patient and therapist should be developed consistently in light of prevailing intervention contexts. Wished for modes are given secondary consideration. In this therapeutic situation, there is the deviation in the ground rules of the prior personal relationship between the patient and therpist. There is also the therapist's noninterpretive interventions,—his use of directives. Finally, there is the therapist's note-taking. Each of these deviations imply a pathological mode of relatedness between the patient and therapist. For her part, the patient's choice of the therapist under the conditions described suggests needs for a pathological symbiosis, and perhaps, to be exploited as well—a parasitic mode of relatedness. The therapist too, in light of these contexts, is reflecting a mixture of pathological symbiotic and parasitic needs. The advice-giving, which the patient encouraged and accepted manifestly, seems to point toward a mutually satisfying pathological symbiosis as well. With both of these deviations, it would be possible for the patient and therapist to alternate as to who adopts the role of symbiotic recipient and symbiotic donor. The note-taking is distinctly parasitic in serving pathological needs of the therapist at the expense of the patient. While there may well be a faint symbiotic quality in the therapist's wish to review his notes in order to better understand the patient, the pathological incorporative qualities, along with the hints of lack of privacy and confidentiality, tend to be experienced by the patient as highly parasitic. Note-taking is typically accepted on the surface, often in the service of pathological masochistic gratification, while its destructive attributes are worked over on a derivative level.

232 / Psychotherapy: A Basic Text

These silent formulations must not, of course, overly bias the listener to this material. Part of the mind must approach these associations without desire, memory, and understanding, and allow them to characterize the therapeutic relationship. In this manner the first characterization is of a woman who seems to love her children but suddenly murders them. This derivative clearly portrays a most devastating form of concealed parasiticism. It must be formulated first as an unconscious perception of the therapist and, second, as a possible reflection of needs within the patient. In light of the specific adaptive context, it is the therapist in this situation who must bear the primary onus as the parasitic murderer. In general, as long as the therapist behaves in a parasitic manner, the patient's own tendencies in this direction cannot be fully identified, and certainly cannot be explored and interpreted.

The next derivative element alludes to the patient's mother and her need to keep her daughter (the patient) as an infant in order to avoid killing someone. Here the patient's derivatives characterize a mixture of pathological symbiosis and parasitism. On the first level, the patient sees herself as the symbiotic donor and parasitic victim. On another level, the patient herself may well have needs to infantilize the therapist and to maintain an immature relationship with him as a means of obtaining pathological gratification, which protects her from her own murderous impulses. In light of the prevailing intervention contexts, it appears likely that there is some validity to both formulations. Specifically, the therapist infantilizes the patient through his deviations, and binds her to him as a willing victim. It is the patient's unconscious interpretation that defensiveness against underlying murderous hostility is involved.

Since the next association involves the therapist's notetaking, it appears that this particular deviation is especially cogent to the preceding material, and may well be the most immediate and critical adaptive context to which the patient is responding through these derivatives.

Patients tend to characterize, manifestly and especially through derivatives, the existing mode of maturational object relationship between themselves and their therapists. Clearly, there are many other supplementary formulations that could be made regarding this object relationship, but they will not be pursued here. Instead, the patient's comment that does *not* characterize an object relationship, about how she and her girlfriend are from different backgrounds, is noted. This comment alludes to the attributes of two individuals, illustrating that not every derivative communication regarding other persons will be couched in object relationship terms.

Finally, the patient alludes to her own sense of rage when her girlfriend tries to use her—another derivative unconscious perception of the therapist and the parasitic mode of relatedness. When the therapist treats this material in terms of its manifest contents and offers an inference Type One derivative intervention, connecting two manifest themes, the patient's immediate response to this adapation-evoking context is to the effect that her father never understood her. While this association contains a valid unconscious perception of the therapist in light of his intervention, it does not involve a characterization of the maturational mode of relatedness. However, further allusions of this kind do appear in the patient's image of begging a man to rape her, into which the therapist's face intruded. This is a cogent representation of this parasiticism in which, for a variety of pathological and dynamic reasons, with genetic repercussions, the patient is indeed the main victim. In some sense, each participant to treatment is both the parasitic perpetrator and the parasitic victim. Unable to manage the pathological mode of relatedness and its devastating implications, the patient responds with thoughts of taking flight from treatment.

The mode of object relatedness has genetic meanings for both the patient and therapist. In general, patients will attempt to interpret to the therapist, through derivative expressions, their impressions of these childhood factors as they contribute to the patient's—and therapist's—adoption of a pathological autism, symbiosis, or parasiticism. The patient will also represent through derivatives both unconscious perceptions of the earlier parental figure whom the therapist now resembles and the genetic factors in the patient's own evocative or responsive participation.

In the present session, the patient's mother looms quite large as a parasitic and pathologically symbiotic figure to whom the patient submitted, and who also helps to account for the patient's participation in this mode of relatedness with her therapist. Toward the latter part of the excerpt, the father was seen to play a role, first, in light of the therapist's failure to understand his patient and, secondly, as the figure behind the rape fantasy—the male person whom the therapist resembled when parasitizing the patient. The implications appear to be that both the patient's mother and father related to her in a manner comparable to the pathological ways in which the therapist is now doing.

Formulations regarding the maturational mode of object relationship tend to involve, and intermingle with, cognitive hypotheses regarding defenses, instinctual drives, superego factors, genetics, and the like, for both patient and therapist. Attention to the relationship sphere is critical since, as this material strongly implies, as long as the therapist maintains a basically pathological autistic, symbiotic, or parasitic mode of relatedness with the patient, there will be no true understanding and no insightful therapeutic work. Often, gratification of the therapist's pathological, sadistic, and other wishes, which correspond to the patient's masochistic and other pathological needs, will be the main medium of cure, affording the patient pathological satisfactions and sometimes relief, though often creating considerable distresses as well. In the present session, even the therapist's sincere effort at (erroneous) interpretation is experienced by the patient as an assault—a rape—as well as a failure at understanding. These efforts to state meaning, since they do not involve the truth of the patient's Neurosis as activated by the therapeutic interaction, serve as lie-barrier systems with strong defensive and assaultive qualities—here, mainly in the form of blaming the patient and placing all of the sickness within her, thereby entirely sparing the therapist of such qualities.

Efforts at Role, Image, and Relationship Evocation

Another aspect of listening and formulating involves efforts by the patient, and secondarily by the therapist, to create a particular mode of relatedness, to have the other participant adopt a role, or to have the other person experience a particular type of self-image. These endeavors may be expressed directly and consciously, or by implication and unconsciously. Similarly, they may be experienced by the recipient on a conscious or unconscious level. Any actualization of this kind must be studied for sources in both the perpetrator and recipient, and must be understood as an interactional product in which both inner need and outside pressure are factors. Thus a particular self-image experienced by the therapist may derive primarily from the conscious or unconscious efforts of the patient, or may arise mainly from the therapist's own inner needs in response to a minimal stimulus from the patient. All such experiences require a careful sorting out as to their sources and meanings—an effort based on the therapist's subjective evaluation and on guides available in the patient's manifest and especially derivative associations.

Efforts at evocation may involve wishes for pathological modes of relatedness and interaction, or may instead entail pressures toward health and sound functioning. Depending upon the patient's pathology, he or she may attempt to engage the therapist in a repetition of past pathogenic interactions, or may pressure the therapist to experience negative self-images. Similarly, the patient may attempt to engage the therapist in a pathological symbiotic or parasitic mode of relatedness. An additional common source for such efforts derives from pathological inputs from the therapist to which the patient responds by attempts to extend the pathological qualities involved.

On the other hand, based on the patient's inevitable wish to get well, the patient may attempt to engage the therapist in a healthy symbiosis, or may try to create positive interactions and self-images in the therapist. The latter tend to appear largely in response to the therapist's actual sound interventions, though they may also emerge as intense corrective efforts in the light of countertransference-based interventions by the therapist. These positive qualities may be part of the patient's efforts unconsciously to cure the therapist in light of his or her expressed countertransferences, or at other times a response to signs of health in the therapist.

The area of *relationship evocations* involves *actualities* that the therapist experiences subjectively, though the patient will often *represent* these pressures manifestly and in derivative form. Because of the subjective factors involved, the therapist must develop the best possible *silent* hypothesis as to the sources of the subjective experience in both himself or herself and the patient, and extensive cognitive validation of the formulations must be obtained in the therapist's further subjective responses and primarily in the patient's derivative associations. This type of silent validation is essential before intervening on the basis of any subjective experience within the therapist.

Pathological evocations are designed by the patient for the following reasons:

1. To gratify pathological instinctual drive wishes, defenses, and superego expressions.

2. To repeat past pathogenic interactions.

3. To enact and gratify, and find support for, aspects of the patient's Neurosis in a form that is designed for pathological satisfaction rather than understanding.

4. As a means of expressing aspects of the patient's Neurosis that may well lend themselves to interpretation and framework-rectification responses in light of activated intervention contexts.

5. To in some way thwart or harm the therapist, to disturb and disrupt the therapist's functioning, either in response to a sound intervention or an error.

Because of his or her own pathological needs, the therapist too may create relationship pressures on the patient as an inappropriate way of pushing the patient toward experiencing pathological roles, self-images, and modes of relatedness. Every intervention by the therapist must be examined for this level of meaning and function.

Efforts at positive and constructive relationship evocations tend to represent the curative wishes of the participants to therapy. While necessary to understand and formulate, they seldom require intervention by the therapist.

CLINICAL EXAMPLES

In the session presented in the preceding section, when the therapist gave his patient direct advice, on the surface she was extremely pleased with his efforts. At that moment, the therapist had a positive self-image. Only after a supervisory discussion, did he review the session in which the advice was offered and discover derivative allusions to highly destructive persons. At that moment his self-image changed considerably and took on highly unpleasant qualities. This particular experience demonstrates the extent to which therapists tend to accept manifestly idealized images of themselves, while resisting not only surface negative images, but most importantly, the evocation of negative images in response to a patient's derivative associations. At times, the latter may evoke negative self-images within the therapist of which he or she is quite unaware. These tend to surface in other contexts, and the therapist tends to experience difficulty in tracing out their sources.

In the session, the therapist maintained a conscious focus on the destructive qualities of the patient's mother. He soon realized in the supervisory session that, in this way, he had defended himself against a highly devastating self-image of himself as infantilizing the patient and destroying her. On the other hand, he felt troubled by the patient's image of the rapist, especially since his own face had intruded into the fantasy. Unfortunately, he did not trace out the sources of this particular self-image, but instead recalled aspects of the patient's father's forceful seductiveness, and attributed the patient's fantasy to experiences with him. In this way, as he soon realized, the therapist had once again defended himself against a highly troublesome self-image.

In principle, the therapist must accept every characterization of a person that appears in the patient's material as a form of self-image. These self-images should be experienced as *signal images* that are felt affectively but maintained in modulated form. They are important data for listening and formulating, and must be processed in the manner described above. The tendency to deny or fend off self-images that are contrary to the therapist's ongoing self-image must be recognized and its influence minimized.

On a second level, each image recognized by the therapist should be applied to the patient in terms of the therapist's own efforts to have the patient experience himself or herself in a particular way. Thus this therapist's advice in some ways destroyed the patient's autonomy, and involved a certain kind of murder. (Actually, this particular image was also derived from other, far more blatantly destructive interventions offered by the therapist.) Both the advice-giving and the note-taking tended to evoke an image within the patient of herself as a helpless infant. The intrusive qualities of both interventions contributed to the patient's image of herself as a rape victim, a self-image that stems more powerfully from the therapist's more hostile and aggressive interventions in previous hours (efforts not described here).

Each characterization of an individual, then, whether it alludes manifestly to the patient or therapist, to a family member or other figure, is monitored subjectively by the therapist as applied to himself or herself, and then as applied to the patient. In each instance, the sources of this self-image in pressures from both the patient and therapist are sought out. In addition, each of the patient's manifestly expressed self-images must be treated as *derivative* communications, alluding to both the therapist and the patient, and understood in light of activated intervention contexts.

This patient's search for direct advice from the therapist led him to adopt a deviant role that gratified a variety of pathological needs in both participants, and contributed to their basic pathological symbiotic mode of relatedness. Here, the therapist's role tended mainly to repeat aspects of the patient's mother's need to control and infantilize the patient. A number of pathological needs and aspects of the patient's Neurosis were also gratified, all in a manner that precluded insightful understanding.

The session presented below involves a therapist who had accepted an ashtray as a gift from a woman patient who was a medical student. Based on her derivative communications, he had rectified the deviation by returning the ashtray to her. The following excerpt is from the session that followed.

> Patient: I had this patient and the doctor insisted on giving him intravenous fluids. He was able to eat by mouth, and he finally insisted that he could do without IVs. He had been agitated and addicted to drugs. He was a manipulator. He began to eat on his own and grow stronger. It was easy for me to settle him down. .

On the maturational object relationship level, the allusion to the intravenous fluids suggests that the therapist's decision to accept the gift from the patient constituted a means of establishing a form of pathological symbiosis in which the therapist was the major symbiotic recipient. The patient herself seems to be represented by the doctor who insists on the fluids, demonstrating her own role and gratification in this symbiosis. However, the allusion to the sick patient's ability to eat by mouth reveals that the patient not only unconsciously perceived the pathological symbiotic qualities in the therapist's acceptance of her gift, but also recognized that it was quite inappropriate as well. At the same time this particular derivative implication involves a shifting unconscious perception of the therapist: accepting the intravenous-gift, only to recognize its inappropriate qualities and to rectify the situation.

The material illustrates the shift from the pathological symbiosis created by the deviation to the healthy symbiosis that followed upon the therapist's interpretive and framework-rectifying efforts. This is represented in the sick patient's capacity to eat on his own and grow stronger, a derivative image that implies that the intravenous fluids-gift is not only infantilizing but inimical to growth, while the return of the gift promoted autonomous functioning and maturation.

As for role evocations, the adaptive contexts for the patient's gift were a number of deviations that the therapist himself had undertaken in regard to the basic ground rules of this treatment— e.g., the presence of a secretary, a group practice, records, and the like. Much of this was rectified at the same time that the therapist returned the gift to the patient. Nonetheless, these deviations represented the therapist's wish for a pathological symbiosis with the patient and possibly some measure of parasiticism. The patient's offer of a gift, then, was an attempt to extend the pathological symbiosis and to permit the patient to temporarily shift from the symbiotic recipient to the symbiotic donor. The therapist was pressed into a role in which he accepted inappropriate gratifications from the patient and responded noninterpretively to her communications (here, the offer of the gift). The patient, for her part, was permitted the role of directly satisfying the therapist, and of being pardoned for the moment from her responsibilities as a patient.

Subsequently, mainly through derivative associations, the patient unconsciously pressured the therapist to rectify the frame and to shift to a role as a sound framework manager and interpreter of her material. These pressures also involved a shift from a pathological to healthy symbiosis. Similarly, the therapist created implicit pressures on the patient to communicate meaningful derivatives as a basis for cure, rather than engaging in a framework-deviation cure without insight.

The excerpt presented conveys in derivative form the patient's unconscious perception of the therapist's pressure upon her to engage in a pathological symbosis and in unhealthy satisfactions (cf. the allusion to the intravenous fluids). Simultaneously, it portrays the patient's efforts toward the therapist in a comparable direction. It is the doctor's insistence on the fluids that confirms the evocative qualities of this interaction.

Then, through the sick patient's insistence that he could do without the IVs, the derivative pressures from the patient and the manifest efforts by the therapist in the direction of rectifying the frame and establishing an interpretive relationship and healthy symbiosis are represented in this material. The role of the well-functioning therapist and well-functioning patient is similarly conveyed in the allusion to the sick patient's ability to eat on his own and grow stronger, and the ease with which the medical-student patient was able to settle this man down—here again alluding to the constructive holding quality of a secure frame.

Finally, as for image evocations, the therapist had at first felt positively inclined toward himself when the patient offered him a gift. However, when her derivative material became distinctly negative, he began to recognize underlying negative images. In this regard, he experienced acceptance of the gift as permitting himself to be seduced, manipulated, and shifted away from his role as a therapist. As a consequence, he entertained a set of negative self-images, some of them under continued pressure from the patient's negative derivative communications. With rectification, his self-image changed considerably, as evoked by the patient's material and as experienced subjectively.

In this session, the first communication from the patient suggested a self-image to the therapist of insisting upon merging with and infantilizing his patient. Similar possibilities were entertained for the patient. Next, there was a positive self-image reflected in the sick patient's ability to eat by mouth and his insistence that he could do without the IVs. The therapist also applied this to both himself and his patient.

The allusions to being agitated and addicted were taken as valid images of the therapist, which enabled him to recognize that his acceptance of the gift was an effort to allay certain anxieties in his work with his patient, and that it did indeed reflect a disguised addictive tendency on his part. In keeping with the patient's next associations, he realized too that he had permitted himself to be manipulated and, in a sense, had manipulated the patient in turn. Here too, on a second level the therapist saw that these images could also be applied to the patient in light of the therapeutic transactions.

Finally, the vignette concludes with several positive images that the therapist accepted for himself in light of his having rectified the frame and interpreted the patient's material in a manner that received Type Two derivative validation. Similarly, the patient's acceptance of the return of the gift, and her shift to meaningful communication, could be used to account for evidences of positive self-images of her own.

Summary and Conclusions

Much of the effort of listening to and formulating the patient's material in the object relationship sphere relies on the therapist's subjective experiences of the relationship with the patient and on the patient's own derivative representations of relationships and interactions in associational material. In addition, there is the patient's direct efforts to engage the therapist in some type of mode of relatedness, although the more indirect pressures in this regard deserve special emphasis.

The object relationship between the patient and therapist, the structure of their interaction from moment to moment, is a core factor in the therapeutic experience. As such, it is an important arena for listening and formulating that should lead to silent hypotheses couched in cognitive terms. As always, these should be organized around prevailing intervention contexts, with their conscious and unconscious implications, and should be subjected to Type Two derivative silent validation before forming the basis for an actual intervention with the patient or silent rectification by the therapist.

Most of the important dimensions of the object relationship between the patient and therapist may be characterized in terms of the maturational or developmental mode of relatedness. Both the patient's manifest object relationship pressures and derivative material are monitored for characterizations of the mode of relatedness between the two participants to treatment. All such material is treated first as valid unconscious perceptions and characterizations, and only secondarily as wishes—this last, only in the face of evidence that the represented mode of relatedness has not been actualized by the patient and therapist.

When a mode of relatedness has been identified, its existence must be understood in light of adaptation-evoking contexts. The expressed relationship needs of both the patient and therapist must be formulated. In this regard, the derivative communications of both are critical.

Relatedness is a spiraling process and must be understood interactionally, with contributions from both participants. If a pathological mode of relatedness is recognized and its existence validated, the therapist must respond in keeping with the patient's material by both interpreting its sources and meanings, and rectifying his or her own participation. The goal is to establish a healthy symbiosis by modifying existing pathological modes of interacting. The healthy symbiosis is essential to insightful therapeutic work and growth.

The second area of interpersonal listening and formulating involves efforts by the patient to create a particular mode of related-ness with the therapist, or to have the therapist adopt a particular role or experience a specific self-image. In general, these pressures are recognized through the subjective experiences of the therapist. All such formulations arrived at through the subjective impressions of the therapist must obtain silent Type Two derivative validation from the patient's material before they are accepted with any measure of confidence.

Relationship evocations may occur directly on a manifest level, or be implicit to the patient's communications. Even when they involve direct pressures on the therapist, they should also be sub-jected to efforts at decoding in light of prior adaptive contexts. The therapist's own interventions must also be monitored for pressures on the patient to adopt a deviant mode of relatedness, a patholog-ical role, or a pathological self-image. Because of this, all role and image representations in the patient's material are applied first to the therapist and second to the patient. Pathological pressures are often a critical unconscious implication of erroneous interven-tions—framework mismanagements and noninterpretive comments. The relationship pressures and images that the patient creates for the therapist are often a response to pressures that the therapist has created for the patient. Relationship evocations by the patient or therapist may be pathological or healthy. The former tend to require intervention, while the latter do not.

There appears to be an inevitable tendency within therapists toward some measure of pathological symbiosis with their patients and toward the avoidance of the recognition of self-images of a pathological nature that are contrary to their usual self-image. Because of these trends, the therapist's own contribution to a pathological mode of relatedness and to the experience of an evoked self-image may be missed. As a safeguard, the therapist should accept on a temporary and trial basis as valid and self-pertaining all possible evocations reflected manifestly and latently in the patient's material. In light of activated intervention contexts, efforts must be made to pursue the silent hypotheses generated on this basis and to search for silent validation.

The application of the listening-formulating process to the object relationship between the patient and therapist is clearly one of the most important and difficult tasks that confronts the therapist. Both evaluations in this sphere, and actual participation in interactions with the patient, are open to countertransference influence. A pathological mode of relatedness in itself tends to detrimentally effect the very application of the listening process in this important area and in respect to other spheres as well. The therapist must therefore do all that is possible to safeguard the basic structure of the relationship with the patient by maintaining a manner clearly defined for functioning as the sound therapist. All pressures to depart from this basic stance must be subjected to considerable scrutiny for sources within and from the patient. Still, the analysis of efforts by the patient to establish a basically pathological mode of relatedness with the therapist, when undertaken without the actual participation of the therapist, provides an exceedingly meaningful arena for therapeutic work. Critical technical problems emerge with patients who insist upon a pathological mode of relatedness as a prior condition to any work with the therapist. It is here that actualities loom large and influence all other elements in the therapeutic experience.

Chapter 14

The Interactional Mechanism Sphere of Listening

The interactional mechanism sphere of listening is the third basic sphere of the listening-formulating process. As with aspects of object relatedness, it involves the subjective impressions of the therapist. Because of this, the principle of validating such impressions in the derivative cognitive material from the patient is once again an essential aspect of the listening process.

Listening to and experiencing interactional pressures, those from the patient and from the therapist, involve processes that are highly vulnerable to countertransference. Therapists readily err in both directions: toward failing to recognize the presence of interactional projections, especially in their own interventions, as well as overstating the presence of such pressures, especially when they come from the patient.

Actualized interactional pressures are somewhat different from, though overlapping with, relationship evocations. Projective and introjective identifications are involved. The former influence the intrapsychic state and interactional functioning of the other person to generate some type of complex introject within the other participant, and place into him or her aspects of the subject's inner mental world. The process may be designed for gratification or defense, and as a way of disrupting or enhancing the functioning of the other person. Involved too is the interactional dumping into the other person of the subject's own unconscious introjects, conflicts, perceptions, and fantasy-memory constellations, *in toto* or in fragmented form. The functions and contents projected in this manner have been called *the contained*, and their recipient, *the container* (Bion 1962).

The recipient of a projective identification or interactional projection (the contained) may be open to these interactional mechanism pressures (prepared to contain) or refractory (refusing to contain). In most instances, however, it appears that both patients and therapists lend themselves readily as containers of the projective identifications from the other participant to treatment. Refractoriness is rare, and tends to occur only after repeated pathological projective identifications, which exhaust the containing functions of the recipient.

Based on pathological needs, virtually all patients will, from time to time, engage in efforts at pathological projective identification. In doing so, they adopt *the Type B mode of communication* (see Chapter 15). Such efforts at dumping or riddance may take place within the framework of a healthy therapeutic symbiosis, and be designed simultaneously for action-discharge and evacuation on the one hand, and cognitive understanding on the other (the B-A mode). In contrast, there are patients who engage in pathological projective identification as part of a pathological symbiosis or, more often, as a means of parasitizing the therapist. Their efforts at interactional projection are designed to obliterate and destroy meaning, to evacuate inner tensions with an utter disregard for the appropriate needs of the therapist, and are conveyed without any effort toward understanding and mastery (the Type B-C mode).

In principle, the therapist should remain open to all pathological (and healthy) projective identifications from the patient. Bion (1962) has termed this a capacity for *reverie*, an ability to contain, metabolize, and detoxify the patient's pathological projective identifications. Such an effort implies the subjective processing of these interactional mechanisms toward cognitive understanding in light of activated intervention contexts. At times, these pressures are in response to pathological projective identifications from the therapist. However, in a patient so inclined, they may reflect destructive interactional pressures that are evoked by the therapist's efforts to secure a sound therapeutic setting and relationship. For these patients, a nonpathological mode of relatedness and secure frame are experienced as depriving, threatening, and persecutory. The sources in adaptation-evoking contexts of all efforts at pathological projective identification by the patient must be carefully identified, as should those factors within the patient.

Thus *projective identification* is an actual interactional effort to place or dump into, and to interactionally arouse in the object, some aspect of the subject's inner mental world and functioning. The term *identification* in projective identification is used in a somewhat unusual manner: it is usually applied to incorporative processes, but here is used to refer to matters of extrusion. However, *identification* is used because, first, it implies that the subject is still *identified with* the contents or mechanisms that he or she is attempting to place into the object, and secondly, because of the realization that the subject is attempting to *evoke an identification* with some aspect of himself or herself by the object. Thus *interactional projection* involves the dumping into an object contents and mechanisms with which the subject remains identified, and with which he or she hopes the object will identify.

Projective identification can be distinguished from *projection*, in that the former constitutes some type of actual interactional pressure and effort, while the latter is essentially an intrapsychic mechanism. Thus, in projection, the subject intrapsychically attributes something that belongs to himself or herself to the object. No effort is made to have the object experience its content or function. Were this to occur, it would constitute a *projective identification*.

The Patient's Projective Identifications

Interactional projections are adaptive and maladaptive efforts by the patient designed to have the therapist interactionally experience some aspect of the patient's disturbed or troublesome (and at times healthy) inner mental world. The major motives for the use of projective identification vary considerably. They may include efforts by the patient to be rid of highly disturbing and conflictual (toxic) fantasies and/or perceptions, to help the patient get rid of bad and destructive introjects, to place into the therapist good parts of the patient for safekeeping against the patient's own inner destructiveness, to have the therapist experience and respond to and manage (i.e., metabolize and reproject) aspects of the patient's own troublesome inner mental world, to reproject into the therapist pathological projective identifications which the therapist had placed into the patient through his other erroneous interventions, or to come to the aid of a therapist who has consciously or unconsciously demonstrated failings to the patient and a need for some type of constructive introject.

Thus projective identifications by patients may be designed to disturb or harm the therapist, or to help in a constructive, ego-building manner. They are also often designed to place into the therapist disturbing aspects of the patient's instinctual drives, pathological superego and ego ideal, and pathological defenses, so that the therapist may take these over and rework them, thereby offering the patient an opportunity to reintroject and identify with the therapist's more adaptive capacities. As such, these interactional pressures may be seen as efforts to evoke a *proxy* response in the therapist (Wangh 1962), and then to benefit from the therapist's (ideally) better ability to contain and manage the pertinent aspects of the patient's inner mental world. Much of this gain is accrued through a sequence in which the patient's pathological projective identification is faithfully introjected by the therapist, metabolized toward conscious understanding, and interpreted in a manner that produces both cognitive insight and a constructive introjective identification in the patient—both thereby modifying the patient's own tendency toward pathological projective identification. Both consciously and unconsciously, patients will tend to monitor and incorporate the therapist's responses to the patient's interactional projections.

The complementary process to projective identification is that of *introjective identification*. In incorporating interactional pressures, the recipient will always respond in keeping with both the nature of the projective identification and his or her own inner mental world, as well as the specific conflicts and other reactions stirred up by a particular interactional projection. As a result, an introjective identification may be essentially faithful to the projected contents and functions, or may considerably distort that which has been interactionally projected. In addition, the subsequent working over of an introjective identification may be essentially adaptive and nonpathological, or highly pathological.

Projective Identification and Technique

In principle, the therapist should be open to, and prepared to contain, all interactional projections from the patient. The therapist should be capable of introjecting them to the fullest extent possible in terms of their intended meanings and functions, and of processing them toward conscious understanding (i.e., of *metabolizing* them toward insight). This requires of the therapist the freedom to experience interactional pressures, to become consciously aware of their nature and implications, and to respond primarily with understanding rather than through action or countertransference-based pathological projective identifications of his or her own.

An essential aspect of this processing endeavor—listening and formulating interactionally—involves the validation of all subjective impressions of interactional pressure from the patient in the patient's ongoing cognitive associations. In a manner similar to the handling of subjective impressions of role and image evocations, the therapist should attempt to sort out his or her own inner contributions to a subjective experience of interactional pressure from those of the patient. In addition, ways in which the therapist has provoked the use of pathological and nonpathological projective identifications in the patient must be formulated. The utilization of all such mechanisms within the patient are part of the spiraling interaction, and must be understood in that broad context, especially in terms of activated intervention contexts.

Difficulties in identifying and processing the projective identifications from the patient may arise when the therapist pays little attention to this area. They may occur too when the therapist is unable to bring the nature of the interactional projection being experienced into conscious awareness, including the influence of the therapist's own introjective and metabolizing reactions. Frequently, the result is a responsive pathological projective identification—a projective counter-identification (Grinberg 1962)—from the therapist, who thereby dumps back into the patient the latter's own pathological interactional projection along with some aspects of the therapist's own psychopathology. This type of response in the therapist can be seen clinically when a patient generates interactional pressures on the therapist, attempting to dump into the therapist an inner state of chaos, unmanageable aggression or sexuality, and the like. The therapist then intervenes with some type of chaotic intervention, or with comments and behaviors that dump back into the patient, in a still raw and unmetabolized form, the unmanaged aggression or sexuality. Such therapists lack the capacity of *reverie* (Bion 1962)—the ability to contain and metabolize pathological projective identifications—and prove unable to properly manage the inner disturbance created in them by the patient and to generate interpretive responses that help the patient to understand the nature of what is happening on the interactional level.

Under these conditions, the therapist fails in functioning in two important ways that are unconsciously perceived and introjected by the patient: (1) cognitively, by proving *incapable of interpreting* the implications of the patient's interactional pressures in light of activated intervention contexts and the patient's cognitive, derivative associations; and (2) in *containing functions* as recipient of the patient's pathological projective identifications. This latter function is an essential aspect of the holding-containing qualities of the therapeutic relationship, and is basic to a healthy therapeutic symbiosis. In general, impairments of this kind often reflect an autistic mode of relating by the therapist; they tend to shift the maturational mode of relatedness toward a pathological autistic, symbiotic, or parasitic form.

Some therapists are quite refractory to their patients' interactional projections. They intervene prematurely in order to interrupt or fend off these interactional pressures, and fail to incorporate, experience, and work over the contents and functions toward interpretation and framework-management responses.

It is important to monitor and conceptualize any subjective sense of interactional pressure from the patient. Because these experiences are so vulnerable to countertransference-based influence, the therapist must maintain consistent efforts to ascertain the sources of such subjective impressions in both the patient and himself or herself and, as indicated, to validate the formulations derived in this way through both further self-analysis and hypothesis formation, and through the use of the material from the patient.

While most inappropriate or pathological expression involves some degree of projective identification, certain patients (and therapists) are especially prone to utilize this mechanism. In addition, its use may be especially prominent under particular interactional conditions. Thus it is important for the therapist to recognize those sessions in which projective identification becomes a critical dimension of the spiraling interaction. Measures must then be taken to identify the initiators of a sequence of this kind, searching out the interactional pressures of the therapist's interventions and silences, as well as factors in the patient. The therapist must be prepared to find that he or she has been the instigator of a sequence of pathological projective identifications because of a faulty intervention. Whenever the therapist feels hard-pressed and tense because of aspects of the patient's communications, dumped into and such, this type of sorting out endeavor is mandatory.

CLINICAL EXAMPLE

A young woman patient had been in couples therapy for herself and her boyfriend with the present therapist. The therapist had been selected because he was a member of her country club. The session described here is a session with the patient alone (the boyfriend had terminated). It followed a missed hour because of a legal holiday, and antedates the therapist's summer vacation by two months.

> Patient: I felt sad yesterday because there was no session last week. I felt no immediate relief today in coming to my hour. I expect you now to mention your vacation. I was at the country club and felt I lied to myself: actually I look fat in the mirror and won't accept it. I played golf with this man and had a lot of fantasies. I dreamt I was on a train and met a pilot. He was going to teach me how to fly. We got to the station and people were laughing because I was hoodwinked. I have to clean up my apartment. I feel I'm getting nowhere in these sessions these days.
>
> Therapist: You've been mentioning the country club, but denying that it has anything to do with how you came into treatment with me. Yet you keep coming back to it, and now complain that you're getting nowhere in therapy. This must relate to how you began treatment and how you now feel helpless, feeling that you have changed some but will change no more. You played golf with this young man and had fantasies, and this must imply that you are having fantasies about me and can't distinguish between reality and fantasy

because of the absence of clear boundaries. In the dream, you meet a pilot on a train rather than in his office, which also must have to do with how you met me. You feel cheated and want to clean up your apartment, and this ties to therapy as well. Your comment about expecting me to announce my vacation reflects your feeling that under these conditions, we must work toward termination.

Patient: I hate you so much, I don't know what to do about it. You lied to me when we started treatment, and this whole thing is your fault. You're a fraud, and now you're trying to get rid of me. I don't see how knowing you at the country club interferes. You'd better tell me. I don't want to speak. *(Silence.)* I felt good about playing golf with the man, because I found that when he talked to me, I wouldn't panic. Give me some answers already.

In this situation, the therapist was feeling considerable internal pressure to rectify a rather contaminated therapeutic situation, and to work with the patient toward termination. This led him to the premature intervention described here. It was based on highly tentative material, and became a means through which he projectively identified his own unmanaged anxieties and guilt about the collusive qualities of the therapeutic arrangement; his sense of helplessness; his difficulties in knowing what was appropriate and inappropriate, real and fantasied; his anger with both himself and the patient; and his need to get out of the situation because of the unbearable pressures it was creating for him.

Initially, the therapist failed to recognize the interactional pressures he had generated for the patient. As he monitored the patient's subsequent associations, however, he began to experience an intense sense of being dumped into, of being frustrated and without interpretive recourse. He felt that the patient was attempting to dump into him a somewhat disorganizing sense of interactional pressure and unmanaged aggression. With that, he initiated efforts to formulate the sources for the patient's interactional pressures, and to validate their presence in her cognitive material.

In the following hour, the therapist again felt intense interactional pressures from the patient with her announcement of immediate termination. She was angry with the therapist, attacked him directly, and for a while, refused to talk in the session. She had dreamt of a teacher who kept interrupting her, and of being in the water with dangerous lobsters while in the presence of a man who wouldn't help her. Her direct hostility left him helpless, and he felt again that the patient was dumping a strong sense of unmanaged aggression and disorganization into him. In light of the therapist's intervention—the adaptation-evoking context—the patient's dream of a teacher who kept interrupting her was seen as an unconscious perception of a therapist's efforts, and an accurate portrayal of his role and image. He was also able to sense the disruptive qualities of these interruptions, especially in light of the second dream of the dangerous lobsters and the man who wouldn't help the patient. In light of the intervention contexts, he recognized more clearly his own hostile and unhelpful projective identifications into the patient. Later in the second hour, it proved possible for the therapist to interpret aspects of this sequence.

In terms of interactional projections, the patient's response to the therapist's intervention reflects an introjection of the hateful qualities of his pathological projective identification. She states not only that she hates the therapist so much—an introjective identification—but also that she does not know what to do about it. This latter represents through a cognitive derivative an unconscious perception and introject of the therapist's own failure in containment in regard to both his own impulses and the communications and interactional projections of the patient. The allusion to a lie is not uncommon in response to an erroneous intervention, and the patient's efforts to hold the therapist at fault appear to mirror a comparable interactional projection by the therapist—to some degree, his intervention overly blamed the patient.

The therapist had intervened consciously intending to generate understanding, but had mainly dumped into the patient. In this sense, his intervention was a lie and he was a fraud. The allusion to his attempt to get rid of the patient contains within it, on an interactional level, an unconscious perception of the dumping qualities of the intervention.

The pathological aspects of the patient's response to the therapist's pathological projective identification are first manifested when the patient became agitated and then continued to pressure the therapist for answers that would be difficult for him to provide. Her announcement to terminate appears to be an effort of her own to dump into the therapist the failed sense of containment and the hostile disorganization that the patient had been pressured to introjectively identify with by him. Similarly, her refusal to talk in this session was designed to place the therapist under interactional pressure, with little recourse available for interpretive mastery. As noted, many of these formulations obtain silent Type Two derivative validation through the material of the patient's two dreams.

However, a second trend in the patient's response to the therapist's pathological interactional pressures must be noted: the patient shows a capacity to contain these interactional pressures and metabolize them toward some effort at understanding, even though this occurs on a derivative and unconscious level. Thus she alludes to feeling good with the man with whom she played golf because, when he talked to her, she did not panic. In encoded fashion, the patient indicates that talking—and by implication, understanding—would help to contain the anxieties that the therapist is dumping into her, and that she in turn is dumping back into the therapist. She offers something of a model of rectification in this way, as she does in her quest for cognitive answers.

Similarly, the patient's derivative representation of the interrupting qualities of the therapist's interventions, their attacking qualities (cf., the allusion to the dangerous lobsters) and their unhelpful attributes, reflect a healthy measure of containing and metabolizing on her part. Patients very rarely are able to metabolize the therapist's pathological projective identifications to the point of conscious understanding, though they are capable of sound efforts in this regard on an unconscious (derivative) level. Therapists should *silently* benefit from these endeavors, and utilize the cognitive material for understanding and intervening.

Subjectively, in the second hour, the therapist felt very much put upon and dumped into. He experienced a sense of guilt, helplessness, victimization, and ineptitude. He was able, however, to process these subjective experiences toward understanding by realizing ways in which his own subjective experiences reflected qualities of the interactional projections contained in his own intervention of the previous session. This in turn helped him to better contain the patient's pathological projective identifications in this next hour. By silently sitting back and not responding with an immediate pathological projective identification of his own, he created conditions under which the patient was able to communicate in a more meaningful cognitive and derivative fashion. On that basis, interpretation proved feasible—an effort that reflected not only a new sense of cognitive understanding within the therapist, but an ability to properly contain and metabolize the patient's interactional pressures. The results were quite salutory for all concerned.

This same material reveals efforts at role and image evocation on the part of both the patient and therapist. In respect to the patient's interpersonal pressures, the first session contains a distinct attempt, largely in response to the therapist's countertransference-based interventions, to have the therapist see himself as deceptive, guilty, inadequate, and helpless. This was mainly done quite directly, though some of it was by inference. On a more unconscious and indirect level, the allusion to how the patient herself would not panic may well have been designed to have the therapist recognize and alter constructively an image of himself as someone out of control and in a state of panic. In the second session there are further efforts to have the therapist experience himself as quite inadequate and helpless, and as failing the patient in major ways. Some of this was carried out directly, some of it by indirection, and some of it through the underlying implications of the patient's dreams.

Once such pressures are identified, the therapist should also attempt to ascertain the degree to which the evoked image is in keeping with the actual quality and nature of his or her efforts with the patient. Thus some attempts by the patient to evoke an image in the therapist are discordant with the latter's actual behaviors, while other such efforts are designed to help the therapist to become aware of apparently unrecognized qualities to interventions and interactions with the patient.

It is important to determine the *sources* of the patient's interactional efforts, whether in the sphere of projective identification or that of role and image evocations. In the sessions described here, the patient's efforts were mainly designed to have the therapist experience himself consciously in ways that would be consonant to his actual behaviors (i.e., to help the therapist to realize directly the role and images of which he seemed to be unconscious, and which were involved in his countertransference-based interventions). Although there may well be significant pathological aspects to these interactional mechanisms as used by patients, they also have constructive and adaptive qualities. They often constitute unconscious efforts by the patient to help the therapist achieve important conscious realizations that seem to be lacking and would help to better manage and resolve the therapist's countertransferences. These efforts are part of distinctive unconscious therapeutic efforts by the patient toward the therapist, whatever additional destructive and pathological components may exist.

In principle, then, the therapist attends to any sense of interactional pressure experienced in the work with patients. In addition, however, it is critical that the therapist listen as well for projective identification qualities in his or her own interventions. Virtually every erroneous intervention—verbal or in regard to framework management—contains an element, large or small, of interactional projection. As such, they often serve as initiators of unmetabolized and uninterpreted sequences in which patient and therapist exchange pathological projective and introjective identifications without understanding or detoxification.

Summary and Conclusions

The therapist should monitor his or her subjective experiences for indications of interactional pressures from the patient. When such pressures are experienced, the therapist should determine how much of the subjective feeling derives from factors within himself or herself and how much is indeed responsive to the projective identifications of the patient.

All subjectively based formulations of projective identification should be validated through representations in the patient's ongoing associations. The therapist should have a capacity for reverie, an openness to containing and metabolizing (processing toward interpretation) the patient's interactional projections. The therapist's response, however, should avoid the use of reactive pathological projective identifications. Instead, the patient's interactional pressures should be contained until interpretation is feasible or a proper framework-management response effected.

The patient's projective identifications are an aspect of the spiraling interaction. Their sources must be ascertained in both participants to treatment. While certain patients are especially prone to the use of this mechanism, the effort must be made in all instances to identify the adaptation-evoking contexts involved. These may prove to be highly pathological and a means by the therapist of pathologically projectively identifying into the patient, or may involve essentially sound interventions that threaten certain types of patients, in particular those inclined toward strongly pathological symbiotic and parasitic modes of relatedness.

Finally, in evaluating therapeutic interventions, the therapist should be alert for the possibility of pathological projective identifications of his or her own. Virtually all erroneous interventions and mismanagements of the framework entail some measure of pathological interactional projection by the therapist into the patient—a placing into the patient of some aspect of the therapist's own psychopathology.

The therapist should function, to the greatest extent humanly feasible, as a barometer who responds to the patient's interactional pressures. With some patients, especially those with a particular constellation of borderline or ambulatory schizophrenic pathology, a notable portion of the therapeutic work is done in the area of interactional pressures. With all patients, from time to time, these issues arise as a focus of the therapeutic work. Similarly, there are many therapists who, quite unconsciously, express themselves toward their patients with powerful interactional pressures and projective identifications. Sensitivity in this area depends on the therapist's awareness of this level of expression, and on the development of the necessary sensitivities and safeguards for proper listening-formulating-experiencing in this realm.

Chapter 15

Styles of Communication and Modes of Cure

Until the present chapter the discussion of the listening-for-mulating process and styles of communication have concentrated on the manner in which the patient or therapist functions as a *sender of messages*—the *expressive* side of communication. Here styles of *receiving* messages will also be considered. There may be a consonance or dissonance in regard to the style of communication within a given patient as it pertains to sending and receiving messages. The same may, of course, apply to the therapist, though by and large there tends to be a greater correlation in this area on the therapist's part as compared to patients.

The two basic expressive of communication styles are the Type A, which refers to communications directed toward meaningful expression, and the Type C, which is designed to destroy meaning and understanding. The empirical basis for this fundamental classi-fication lies in the extent to which the patient meaningfully repre-sents an activated intervention context and responds with a coalescible derivative complex. In general, those patients who provide such meaningful material fall into the Type A group, while those patients who do not do so are Type C.

The Type A Expressive Mode

The clinical criteria for the Type A expressive mode are those of a clear, manifest, or relatively undisguised representation of an activated intervention context, and the related communication of a meaningful, responsive, coalescible derivative complex. The Type A communicator will allude to a prevailing adaptive context in passing, or afford it a disguised representation that is easily decoded and manifestly recognized upon playback. In the same session, before or after this representation, a series of associations are conveyed that yield compelling implications in light of the intervention contexts. The Type A patient will represent the important therapeutic contexts or indicators for each particular hour manifestly or through thinly disguised derivatives.

The Type A communicator wishes to—and does—self-express and understand himself or herself through meaningful derivative communication. He or she relates to the therapist through such meaning, usually through a healthy symbiosis, and consciously and unconsciously expects to be helped to understand the implications of the material. When inevitable resistances appear in the associations from such a patient, they can rather quickly be understood in terms of their own derivative meanings, and often they are spontaneously resolved by the patient. Such resistances have a sense of depth and complexity, and are themselves based on meaningfully communicated unconscious perceptions and fantasies.

Recent clinical observations suggest that all but a few patients become Type A communicators when under intense stress within the therapeutic interaction. Thus, in the presence of an acute break in the framework, a major erroneous verbal intervention from the therapist, or their own active internal conflicts and anxiety, most patients shift to the Type A mode of communication. Once the framework or intervening error has been rectified, or the anxiety or other symptom insightfully resolved, they are likely to shift to Type C expression for longer or shorter periods of time. In the absense of an activated intervention context, the shift to the Type C mode is essentially healthy.

Patients of all types of diagnosis and character structure may make use of the Type A mode. Even those who demand the development of a pathological symbiosis or parasitic mode of relatedness will from time to time express themselves in this fashion—though those who are inclined toward parasitism tend to do so through Type B-A expressions (see below). They will consistently do so in response to major breaks in the framework, though long standing impairments in the frame may also lead to a shift toward Type C expression. On the other hand, in situations where the frame is secure and a healthy symbiosis prevails, patients will adopt a Type A mode from time to time in order to work over the anxieties and distorted unconscious fantasies evoked by a therapist capable of such a mode of relatedness and cure.

The Type A therapist is someone who secures and manages the ground rules of therapy, and who otherwise offers almost entirely interpretive interventions when they are called for by the material from the patient. In this way, the therapist expresses a basic ability to hold and contain the patient and his or her communications, and to understand the meaning and truth of the interaction as it becomes available in the manifest and especially latent contents of the patient's associations and behaviors. The Type A therapist is capable of demonstrating these meanings to the patient through conscious and direct interventions when the material permits. On an object relationship level, the therapist is able to offer and accept a healthy therapeutic symbiosis with the patient, to effect the necessary renunciations, and to develop a curative process that relies on inevitable postitive introjective identifications and insight. Any departure from the therapist's two basic responsibilities to the patient (securing and managing the framework and interpreting-reconstructing) will reflect either the Type B or Type C communicative mode, and the search for cure through action-discharge, pathological gratification, and lie-barrier defense.

The bipersonal field that has been secured by a Type A therapist, and to which a patient responds with Type A communications, may be characterized as a Type A field. It is a space of illusion, a kind of play space in which healthy imagination, symbols, and sound perception have full play. There is ample opportunity for the patient to express himself or herself safely and meaningfully through derivatives that also convey expressions and manifestations of his or her psychopathology. For the therapist it is a space that facilitiates appropriate framework management and interpetive efforts. This type of bipersonal field may also be thought of as a transitional space, one in which the patient may meaningfully traverse both reality and fantasy, sickness and health.

CLINICAL EXAMPLE

Most of the clinical examples to this point involved patients using the Type A mode of communication. The reader is likely to benefit from reviewing these excerpts. It would seem best to begin by identifying the main activated adaptive context, and determining whether the patient alludes to it manifestly or represents it with minimal disguise. A consideration of the derivative complex should follow, through which the presence of coalescing and meaningful derivatives can be ascertained. These are, of course, the hallmarks of the Type A style of communication, and the reader will notice that it is evoked by blatant breaks in the ground rules, striking errors, and at times, even by a secure frame and correct interpretations. It is adopted in the presence of powerful and emotionally meaningful stimuli for the patient, and it reveals the unconscious basis of evident indicators and Neurosis.

The following example is another instance of Type A communication in a patient. The session involves a young man whose therapy was being paid for by the state. It occurred after the therapist had taken a two-week vacation, during which he had grown a beard.

> Patient: I've been thinking about my body image. I hate the way my body is. I'm too boney. Glad you're back. You look like an Iranian militant. I've moved to a half-way house. I could get free housing, but I haven't done it. I don't like being obligated. Oh, here is your check.

There are three intervention contexts here (a not uncommon finding): (1) that the patient does not pay for therapy on his own, (2) the therapist's vacation, and (3) the beard the therapist had grown. In this brief excerpt, the patient has represented each of these contexts either directly or with an easily decipherable representation. The fee situation is best represented when the patient hands the therapist a check from the state. The vacation is best represented when the patient states that he is glad that the therapist is back. The beard is represented in the patient's comment that the therapist looks like an Iranian militant. Thus the patient fulfills the first criterion of the Type A style: the presence of manifest or minimally disguised representations of the prevailing adaptive contexts.

Does the patient meet the second criterion—the development of a meaningful, coalescible derivative complex? Since the excerpt is brief, the number of derivatives is small. Nonetheless, when the me/not-me interface is applied in respect to the fact that the state is paying for the patient's therapy, the manifest content regarding the patient's unhappiness with his own body image may be taken as a disguised, derivative representation of some possible unconscious perception of the therapist's discontent with the basic conditions of treatment (in actuality, the therapist had been attempting to interpret the implications of this arrangement and to explore whether rectification of this frame was in any way possible).

Having identified a "not-me" implication for this material, the "me" aspect of this interface may be applied to suggest that the patient as well, on an unconscious level, is also unhappy with these basic arrangements. The association also suggests that the free therapy leads the patient to feel inadequate and to entertain unconscious perceptions of a basic inadequacy in the therapist because of his decision to accept the patient under these conditions. Although these are heavily disguised, remote derivatives, they nonetheless can be meaningfully connected to the no-fee arrangement. The presence of a fee is basic to the sound therapeutic symbiosis necessary for insightful therapy.

Using the fee arrangement as the adaptation-evoking context and organizer, what other disguised meanings could be detected in these manifest associations? The patient's comment that he has not sought free housing can be seen in light of that particular adaptive context to be a *model of rectification,* a derivative suggestion that the free therapy should be abolished. This implies the patient's unconscious awareness that this arrangement places him in pathological symbiosis—a helpless, overly dependent situation against which he is now rebelling. There is thus a notable adaptive response reflected in this element of the derivative complex.

The adaptive context of the therapist's vacation is represented in thinly disguised fashion by the allusion to the patient having moved to a half-way house. This is a mixed communication, in that this change was seen as a positive step, since the situation at home was quite chaotic, and yet there was some compromise involved because the patient did not find his own apartment. Later in the session, he spoke of plans to get a job and to find his own housing, manifest associations that organize as derivatives implying a constructive reaction to the therapist's absence.

The manifest comments about the patient's poor body image may also be organized as derivatives pertinent to the therapist's absence and to the patient's feelings of inadequacy under those circumstances. Along the me/not-me interface, it may well be that the patient perceived the therapist's vacation as a reflection of something inadequate within the therapist, but the material does not permit clarification.

In the adaptive context of the therapist's new beard, the patient's comments regarding his discontent with his own body image could be seen along the me/not-me interface to represent an unconscious introject of the discontent within the therapist that led him to grow the beard. Along the "me" side of the "not-me" interface, there may be a corresponding problem within the patient, though for the moment that which exists within the therapist is clearly uppermost.

The association regarding the therapist looking like an Iranian militant (holding Americans captive at the time) should not be taken at face value, nor thought of in terms of the obvious inferences regarding the threatening image of the therapist. It must be given derivative meaning in light of each of the specific intervention contexts. Thus, in respect to the absence of the fee, the patient may be reflecting his unconscious perception of himself as being held captive, and conveying as well an image of the extent to which the therapist is perceived as dangerous under these conditions. In the context of the therapist's vacation, this derivative element may reflect wishes by the patient to be held captive by him and to undo the experience of the separation. Finally, in the context of the therapist's decision to grow a beard, the patient may be indicating through this derivative that such a basic change in the therapist is perceived as dangerous.

This patient has directly or with little disguise represented three major adaptation-evoking contexts for this hour. He has also manifestly alluded to several major indicators, including the symptom of disliking his body, the important framework deviation of the absence of a fee, the hurtful aspects of the ideal frame as reflected in the therapist's vacation, and the therapist's decision to change himself by growing a beard. In addition, he has conveyed a derivative complex that tends to support the initial silent hypotheses through Type Two derivative elaborations, and appears to meaningfully coalesce as responses to each of the critical adaptive contexts at hand. It would be possible to make use of this network of communications as a way of rectifying the frame and interpreting the other major indicators present in this hour. Thus there is strong evidence for the Type A style in this patient.

The Type A mode of communications facilitates the proper management of the ground rules and the therapist's ability to offer interpretations. Patients tend to make use of it when the therapist breaks the frame, alternating between Type A communications designed toward its rectification and toward the recognition of the unconscious implications of the break, and the use of the other two modes of communication (B and C).

In essence, the Type A communicator (sender) unconsciously is seeking to express the truth about his or her Neurosis as it is activated within the spiraling interaction. These truths involve both unconscious perceptions and unconscious fantasy-memories. There is a search for meaning and understanding—not consciously, but outside of awareness and in a manner that is actually beyond the conscious control of the patient.

As for the *truth receiver,* he or she usually employs the Type A expressive mode. When a correct interpretation is offered, the receiver validates it both cognitively and interactionally with a derivative selected fact and indirect expressions of a positive introject. The receiver will then produce additional associations that yield further meaning, ultimately deriving considerable conscious insight in the course of this process. Often, the response will include meaningful representations of the adaptive context of the correct intervention made by the therapist and the production of a further coalescible derivative complex that shows the meaningful ways, both positive and negative, that the receiver reacted to the sound intervention. Eventually, the receiver will trail off into the Type C mode of communication, returning quickly and powerfully to the Type A mode if a major issue arises within the therapeutic interaction.

The main characteristics of the Type A communicator, then, is the clarity with which he or she represents an activated adaptive context, and the power and complexity of the multiple derivatives with which he or she responds to these contexts, and which provide the therapist with a highly coalescible and meaningful derivative complex. The true Type A communicator is also a Type A receiver, and responds to a correct intervention from the therapist with Type Two derivative validation and with meaningful elaboration and conscious insight. When the therapeutic interaction is quiescent, these patients tend to shift to the Type C mode of communication, and enter a quiescent or fallow phase of therapy.

The Type C Style of Communication

When patients unconsciously express a need to destroy meaning, to not understand, and to break the meaningful relationship
link that could exist between themselves and their therapists, they
are engaging in the Type C mode. Few analysts and therapists have
recognized the existence of patients who wish *not* to understand and
not to convey meaning. They seem aware that certain patients, such
as psychopaths and overt liars, court remands, and such, may enter
a therapeutic situation with little conscious intention of carrying
out meaningful therapeutic work. Usually, the therapist believes
under these circumstances that if the patient stays in treatment,
there will be some possibility of meaningful effort. There is virtually no recognition that, on an unconscious level, many other
patients do not wish to express themselves meaningfully. Nonetheless, in contrast to the truth-seeking, truth-expressing Type A
patient, the Type C patient wishes to avoid or destroy the truth.
The Type C patient is best characterized as lie-seeking, or as
wishing to effect lie-barriers that will obliterate disturbing underlying truths. The clinical hallmark of the Type C patient is the
failure to manifestly represent, or to represent with thinly described
derivatives, an activated intervention context, and/or the failure to
produce a coalescible derivative complex.

Patients tend to have a predominant or basic style of communication. Nonetheless, this style may shift in response to inner needs
and interventions by the therapist. The Type A patient will tend to
self-express meaningfully only in response to acute and activated
intervention contexts, and will shift to a healthy form of the Type C
mode in the absence of such a context. On the other hand, the Type
C patient will tend to shift to the Type A mode in response to an
acutely disturbing intervention context, expecially a modification of
the fixed frame of treatment.

The distinguishing characteristic appears to be the extent to
which these two groups of patients create framework issues and
pressures on the therapist to make mistakes, and the degree to
which a patient will meaningfully work over a long-standing or
background intervention context. Thus when the Type A patient
requires an intervention from the therapist, in order to understand
an acute conflict and the like, he or she will tend to behave in a

manner that calls for an intervention from the therapist. This initiates a sequence of fresh adaptive contexts and meaningful derivative responses that may lead to considerable insight. In contrast, the Type C patient is less likely to create such issues, and far slower than the Type A patient in dealing with long-standing, background adaptive contexts. Recent evidence indicates that the Type A and Type C modes are on a continuum, and a highly resistant Type A patient and a patient who makes basic use of the Type C mode are essentially comparable.

There are several types of Type C or lie-barrier patients. One group fears the establishment of a secure and holding therapeutic environment; they experience the secure frame as a dangerous setting within which they will be destroyed. They show distinctive claustrophobic responses to the therapist's efforts to define the conditions of treatment, and experience these endeavors as persecutory and dangerous. They repeatedly attempt to modify the conditions of therapy in one way or another, and often do so without providing the therapist with meaningful interpretive derivatives. Many of these patients are *lie-dumpers*, Type B-C patients who engage in action-discharge and projective identification in the absence of meaningful derivative material.

Another type of lie patient will accept the therapeutic environment, raise little in the way of issue, and simply settle into the therapeutic situation and nonmeaningful communication. They do so not only through ruminative associations, but also by engaging in extensive narrative communications that lack a clearly represented intervention context or meaningful derivative complex, or both. These patients are *Type C narrators* or *lie narrators*. They accept the therapist's sound holding efforts as long as meaning and meaningful relatedness—a true therapeutic symbiosis—are not developed. In this sense, their maturational mode of object relatedness is that of a pathological autism.

There are three basic forms of Type C communication. Although Type C patients tend to repeatedly adopt one of these forms, they may also shift from one to the other. In the first, the patient will represent, directly or with little disguise, an activated intervention context, but then fail to generate a meaningful or coalescible derivative network. The derivative complex is flat, empty, or fragmented; it cannot be organized into a meaningful whole. The second Type C style involves the communication of seemingly meaningful derivative expressions in the absence of a clear representation of the pertinent intervention context. The third Type C style involves patients who fail both to represent an activated intervention context in a relatively direct manner, and to provide a meaningful derivative complex as well.

Truth and meaning within psychotherapy require of the patient a clear representation of an activated intervention context and a meaningful and coalescible derivative complex. The Type C patient, then, will destroy one or both of these elements in an effort to destroy the meaningful relationship-link with the therapist. As already noted, however, the distinction must be made between the use of the Type C mode in the presence of an activated adaptive context and its use in the absence of such interactional pressures.

The Type C patient who is relatively unresponsive to an activated intervention context is often attempting to deal with an agitated psychotic core or a highly disturbing and primitive internal and/or interpersonal conflict, including terrifying unconscious perceptions of the therapist. The patient creates relatively impervious barriers that are not constituted in a fashion that will yield derivative meaning. In contrast to defenses generated by the Type A patient, which are indeed meaningful derivative expressions, the defenses seen with the Type C patient are *nonderivative* in nature, and constitute relatively impenetrable lie-barrier systems. Often, the central motivating anxiety involves fears of annihilation and other persecutory fantasies and perceptions, and depressing perception-introjects and fantasy-memories.

This kind of Type C patient, rather than attempting to meaningfully express the nature of an activated unconscious disturbance, attempts to seal it off with nonderivative barriers through the use of nonderivative defenses and resistances. These are efforts at obliteration rather than at disguised expression. The purpose is to destroy meaning and access rather than to convey it. For these patients, access to the truth is viewed as terrifying and potentially overwhelming, and the truth—perception or fantasy—must be closed off at all costs. Any aspect of the patient's relationship with the therapist that embodies truth and meaning as it pertains to the patient's Neurosis must be destroyed.

The therapist must constantly formulate and reformulate the material from the Type C patient in the search for a clear representation of an intervention context or a derivative implication of the patient's behaviors and associations. This is a trying task, and often the therapist feels hard pressed, uncertain, and even incompetent. The Type C style of communication is designed on one level to disturb or even destroy the therapist's sense of understanding and effectiveness, especially when the Type C style is invoked in the face of an acute intervention context. This aspect is less prominent during the *lying fallow Type C phase,* which comprises much of the middle period of many psychotherapeutic experiences.

The psychoanalytic and psychotherapeutic literatures indicate that most therapists utilize one or another form of the Type C mode in their work with patients. The use of psychoanalytic concepts and jargon (terms) as meaningless clichés is quite common. Every alteration in the basic therapeutic environment, regardless of cause or possible justification, and every intervention that does *not* constitute a validated rectification or establishment of the framework, or an interpretation-reconstruction, is an expression in part of a lie-barrier system. This is true of all questions, clarifications, and confrontations, as well as all manipulative, directive, and so-called supportive interventions. It is true as well of efforts at so-called interpretation based on manifest contents or Type One derivatives.

It is not surprising, then, that therapists who work in this fashion have difficulty in recognizing patients who utilize this mode. More broadly, therapists and analysts have failed to recognize the presence of many patients who enter psychotherapy with little conscious or unconscious interest in understanding themselves and in obtaining symptom alleviation through insight. Patients tend to seek *relief* from emotional suffering, and appear to lean quite spontaneously toward obtaining this relief through action-discharge, the use of lie-barrier systems, and various ways of avoiding rather than comprehending the terrible truths of their Neurosis. It is therefore quite important to identify efforts by the therapist that are unconsciously designed to destroy a meaningful relationship-link with the patient, and to understand as well the Type C mode of communication when it appears in a patient. All too often, through unconscious collusion and misalliance, a Type C patient obtains Type C interventions from his or her therapist and, as a result, attempts to effect symptom alleviation through the collaborative development of one or another lie-barrier system that will preclude genuine insight. Both patient and therapist are involved in a pathological autistic mode of relatedness in which meaningful ties and the appropriate needs of the other person are set aside. This mode of relatedness prevails, even though on the surface one or both participants to treatment may consciously profess to seek out or impart meaning. There is a failure here of adaptive context communication on either or both sides.

There are several variations of Type C communicators. Some are silent, and their overall associations are quite barren; while others express themselves vividly and imaginatively in sessions that are filled with fantasies, dreams, and anecdotes (the Type C Narrator), which nonetheless are lacking in the presentation of a definitive network of communications. Another group of Type C patients will make repeated efforts to modify the framework, while still others will show considerable affect in the absence of integrated cognitive meaning.

Most Type C senders also use the Type C style in receiving messages. This receptive mode will also be found in some Type A communicators. The Type C receptive mode is characterized as a response to a correct interpretation with an initial fragment of Type Two derivative validation that is developed, as a rule, in only one of the two spheres of confirmation—cognitive or interactional. There then follows a rather extensive fragmentation of the network of communications, and a failure by the patient to consciously or unconsciously meaningfully utilize (and extend) the understanding that has been imparted, acknowledged, and validated in his or her indirect associations. Often, there is also an intensification of the prevailing lie-barrier system that the patient has been using. The therapist has a distinct sense that the hard-earned bit of insight that could have been available to the patient has been obliterated. It is the Type C receiver who has the greatest need to destroy both generated understanding and the security of the therapeutic environment, especially when it has been possible for the therapist to intervene soundly in either or both spheres. A therapist capable of holding and containing, and of understanding, poses a considerable threat for such patients; paradoxically, such a therapist is experienced as a persecutory object. The Type C response is therefore designed to destroy the therapist's capabilities in this regard.

CLINICAL EXAMPLE

The patient, a Type C sender or communicator, had not paid his fee for several months, and this problem had been under discussion in the sessions. At the time of the hour excerpted here, payment of the fee was again due (it was the beginning of a month). In the previous hour, the therapist had attempted to interpret the patient's desire to continue therapy without payment in terms of wishes to nurse at his mother's breast.

> Patient: I felt stirred up last session. I also felt persecuted. One of my employees at work wants a raise, and I'll give him part of it. I have a sick relationship with him. He's like my brother, incestuous and disturbed.

Next, the patient ruminated in some detail about the level of raise to be offered, the job this individual does, and some general worries he has in respect to his own responsibilities in the business. He then went on to ruminate about wanting to nurse at a breast, and after a while said that he must be boring the therapist. He then described some details in respect to his job and a meeting that he must arrange for a group of people. His various responsibilities were mentioned repeatedly.

To analyze this material, the partial raise he will offer his employee is a disguised representation of his indebtedness to the therapist. The remainder of the associations, however, do not organize meaningfully around the adaptive context of the therapist's continuing to see the patient without having received his due fee. On the surface, the material is empty, and in terms of derivative valence the yield is very thin. There are only fleeting or fragmented hints of meaning, such as wanting to pay the therapist part of his fee. There is a derivative representation of the parasitic mode of relatedness effected by the patient's failure to pay the therapist, which takes the manifest form of the patient's own feelings of persecution. There are also hints of an unconsciously perceived level of pathological symbiosis in the patient's allusion to the sick relationship he has with his employee. In this regard, some genetic link to the patient's relationship with his brother is indicated, and it may well involve a first level of nontransference meaning that pertains to the adaptive context of the therapist's continuation of treatment without current payment. Finally, allusions to boredom are common when the Type C mode is being used.

In terms of listening, the *patient's* failure to pay his bill is an *indicator or therapeutic context,* while the *therapist's* acceptance of the deviant situation is a *primary adaptation-evoking stimulus* for this material. Despite these fragments of meaning, there is little sense of substance to these silent hypotheses, and they do not coalesce meaningfully around the main intervention context.

The following excerpt is from the next hour:

> Patient: I'm not here to work, just to masturbate. Money's the issue, and I guess I want treatment for nothing. I had these dreams. In one, I'm playing sandlot baseball and my brother is there. He's some kind of a clown performing, and I feel ashamed. He's making a fool of himself, and I go over and take him in my arms to comfort him. The dream reminds me of my son, who is now in college. It probably has to do with being deprived of care from my mother. It must also have something to do with my own need to exhibit myself. It's a shame dream. I had another dream in which I was arranging a conference like the one that took place yesterday. I thought I had it all under control, but ended up making a bunch of mistakes. I didn't make much sense either.

In the remainder of the session, the patient produced a number of additional dreams. There were some hints as to the latent homosexual implications of the therapist's acceptance of the non-payment situation, but beyond that the elements were so scattered that it was impossible for the therapist to synthesize the material in any meaningful way. The presence of dreams in this material should serve as a reminder that Type C patients may well include them in their associations. While often meaningful, dreams can sometimes be part of efforts by a patient to destroy meaning, as seen when their derivative implications have no essential revelance to the prevailing activated adaptive context.

On the whole, the therapist must maintain silent holding in the presence of the Type C style of communication. The style speaks for major resistances, although all patients need to use it for periods of lying fallow Type C communication.

The Type B Mode of Communication

The Type B communicator expresses himself or herself through action-discharge, projective identification, and other types of interactional pressures. He or she is a dumper, attempting to get rid of accretions of disturbing inner stimuli.

There are, however, two distinctive types: (1) *the Type B-A communicator,* the patient who dumps and creates interactional pressures, but does so with an accompanying meaningful cognitive network of communication that fosters frame management and interpretation; and (2) *the Type B-C patient,* the dumper and evacuator who creates usually intense interactional pressures on the therapist in the absence of cognitive meaning. This last group of patients is perhaps the most difficult. They are usually borderline or ambulatory schizophrenic patients who enter therapy with powerful unconscious needs for a parasitic or pathological symbiotic mode of relatedness. They wish for pathological forms of merger, and show unconscious needs to destroy the therapist's capacity to manage the ground rules and to maintain an interpretive approach. They prefer instead to dump their toxic and pathological contents and unconscious fantasy-memory constellations into the therapist while creating highly destructive lie-barrier systems designed to seal off the underlying factors in these efforts. These deeper issues may involve either highly disruptive and pathological interventions of the therapist or the rather agitated and poorly defended psychotic core with which these patients struggle.

In listening to and experiencing the Type B patient, it is important for the therapist to remain open to, and repeatedly assess the basis for, experiences of interactional pressures and being dumped into. Some therapists are especially sensitive to any measure of pressure from a patient, and will experience projective identifications quite readily. Other therapists absorb a great deal before sensing the presence of interactional projection. The therapist can be aided by the patient's cognitive associations which, in the presence of significant projective identification, represent in some derivative form the patient's efforts at evacuation and discharge. Certainly, no intervention should be offered to the patient on the basis of this type of subjective experience without supportive material in the cognitive sphere.

On the whole, the Type B patient is under considerable pressure from within, which is markedly aggravated if the therapist too engages in pathological projective identifications through mismanagements of the frame or erroneous verbal interventions. These patients tend to be struggling with highly primitive unconscious fantasy, memory, perception, and introject constellations. Quite often, they have been acted upon and dumped into in their own primary childhood relationships, especially by their parents. In turn, they deal with others in a comparable manner, as is seen with therapists who engage in efforts at pathological interactional pressures of their own.

These patients have little tolerance for a secure therapeutic environment, because it interferes with their efforts to projectively identify indiscriminately into others, especially the therapist, and because it disturbs their need to effect a pathologically symbiotic or parasitic mode of relatedness with the therapist. These patients are also threatened by the therapist's capability of securing the ground rules and boundaries of treatment, although they *unconsciously* appreciate the therapist's sound capacities for containment and ability to metabolize their highly threatening and agitating projective identifications (even though they often find it necessary to destroy them).

These individuals, then, are quite divided; wishing on one level for a cure through evacuation, projective identification, and the psychological destruction of the therapist; yet on another level, they hope to find in the therapist someone capable of reverie and containment, so that cure may be effected through the metabolism of their pathological projective identifications toward understanding and the insightful resolution of the patient's Neurosis. This wish is especially prominent in the Type B-A communicator, who engages in the active use of pathological projective identifications, while meaningfully representing important intervention contexts and providing a coalescible derivative complex to the point where specific activated indicators and the patient's interactional projections may be interpreted. Nonetheless, in developing these concepts from the vantage of the patient, one must always be mindful that his or her communications and style of communication are interactional products with important inputs from the therapist. (Many projective identification efforts by patients have important origins in comparable pathological interactional projections by the therapist.)

In dealing with projective identifications, it is the therapist's responsibility to contain and metabolize them toward interpretive understanding. All too often, therapists respond to these interactional pressures with projective identifications of their own. Many therapists have their own strong tendencies toward interactional projection, and may be described as Type B communicators. Some engage in interactional projection in the context of otherwise sound interpretations and managements of the framework, though most therapists of this type engage in interactional projection through erroneous interventions and mismanagements of the ground rules. In these instances there is a mixture of evacuation and the destruction of meaning—a Type B-C expression. Virtually all technical errors have some measure of interactional projection within them, and many express such propensitities with considerable force. This is especially true of deviations in the ground rules and verbalized confrontations.

The most serious form of projective identification communication is expressed in the Type B-C mode. This is most ominous when it occurs in a patient with a tendency to directly attack or seduce the therapist, or to disturb him in some other way, especially when this takes place early in treatment. Usually, the patient attempts to attack and destroy the ground rules and holding-containing environment, and proves to be a Type B *receiver* as well. Since the interest of such patients is almost entirely concentrated on dumping pathologically into the therapist and destroying both meaning and relatedness, the therapist has little possibility of reaching this type of patient with a meaningful intervention. Such patients are quite disturbing and draining for the therapist, who must respond with holding and containing until some interpretation, however crude, is feasible. This can often be done in light of the adaptive context of the therapist's offer of a secure framework, which is experienced by such patients as dangerous and persecutory. Type B-C receivers tend to noisily refute and fragment virtually all of the therapist's interventions, including those that obtain momentary Type Two derivative validation.

When the intervention context from the therapist is in some measure a form of pathological projective identification, it is generally impossible to modify a patient's own Type B propensities, whether expressive or receptive, without first substantially correcting these tendencies in the therapist. The Type B mode usually implies a wish for a parasitic form of relatedness, though sometimes it may involve a highly pathological symbiosis. The therapist's use of this mode of communication unconsciously supports its utilization by the patient. Rectification of the therapist's own propensities in this regard must be carried out in order to establish a healthy symbiosis with the patient. On this basis, and with supplementary interpretive work, the therapist enables the patient to insightfully resolve his or her own pathological modes of communication and relatedness, and to develop a capacity to contain inner disturbances.

CLINICAL EXAMPLES

A young woman in psychotherapy had had insurance forms signed by the therapist. In response to derivatives that indicated this act violated the patient's privacy and the confidentiality of treatment, and served to preclude the expression of separation anxieties and their analysis, the therapist suggested that she no longer complete and sign these forms. On one level, the patient's derivative response tended to support this decision, in that it was represented as a frightening opportunity to attain a true sense of autonomy and independence. On the other hand, on a manifest level, the patient continued to object to the elimination of the insurance form, showing considerable threat regarding any effort to truly secure the therapeutic situation.

> Patient: There, I'm going to take one of your tissues and keep it. Do me something. I don't give a damn about this therapy. Fuck you. I saw my boyfriend yesterday. He's my insurance policy. I saw this other fellow and told him I wouldn't see him any more, that I had a steady boyfriend. I'm tired of having two boyfriends and of being unfaithful all the time to one of them. He was furious, but he understood. For the first time in years, I could tolerate not hearing from my regular boyfriend for one day. But anyhow, I'm really furious with you. Why don't you say something? All that stuff about not signing the insurance form, explain yourself. I dreamt someone was being tortured. I don't know if I was the one who was being tortured, or if I was torturing someone else.

This is a complex sequence, and only those aspects that are relevant to identifying the Type B style of communication will be selected.

In this situation, the therapist felt himself to be under intense interactional pressure. He felt that the patient was placing into him her own sense of helplessness, her feelings of persecution, a sense of anxiety about securing the framework, and even her fear of being tortured by the therapist and the truth within herself under these conditions. He also realized that the decision not to sign the insurance form, which was undertaken at the behest of the patient's derivatives, and which obtained Type Two derivative validation, might be seen on a more superficial level as a deprivation, and therefore as a form of torture, though he did believe that the situation was more complex and meaningful on the other levels described. Still, he felt quite frustrated, and sensed that he was being tortured in some way. He therefore perked up when he heard the patient's dream about someone being tortured, taking the dream as a confirmation of his subjective experiences of interactional pressure. There was as well an attempt to evoke self-images and roles within him, such as that of someone who should feel guilty for depriving the patient and for harming or torturing her, and as someone who should adopt the role of apologizing and responding manifestly with direct, compensatory explanations.

It can be seen, however, that this patient was utilizing the Type B-A mode of communication. After breaking the frame by taking the tissue and wishing to keep it, and dumping into the therapist by challenging him, rejecting therapy, and cursing him, the patient represented the adaptive context of the insurance not being signed with a direct allusion to an insurance policy. Later in the hour, the patient represented the therapist's decision not to sign the form quite directly.

In addition, the patient produced a meaningful derivative complex in light of the therapist's effort to rectify the damaged frame. This reveals her persecutory anxieties in the absence of a pathological symbiotic tie to the therapist and a fear of a secure therapeutic space. There is also a strong sense of appreciation for the therapist's decision reflected in the patient's allusion to being understood and in her capacity to tolerate some degree of separation from her boyfriend for the first time in her life—a derivative that also represents the loss of the type of pathological symbiosis and merger effected in the presence of an insurance payer in the therapy.

The patient indicates that there should be just one and not two boyfriends—an encoded representation of the importance of a private therapeutic space with a single therapist. There is a derivative representation of the sense of betrayal experienced by the patient when the therapist released information to the insurance company, as seen in the patient's comment about being unfaithful. In addition, the patient includes several models of rectification, such as when she expresses being tired of being unfaithful all the time and indicates her decision to maintain a single, serious relationship with one boyfriend and to tolerate periods of separation from him.

The patient's use of the idiom of the boyfriend to represent her relationship with the therapist has both perceptive and distorted qualities; the latter is accentuated by the efforts by the therapist to rectify the frame. This is typical of situations in which there has been an alteration in the basic framework. This association may therefore represent transversally both an unconscious perception of the seductive aspects of the therapist's interventions, especially his signing of the insurance form until recently (the nontransference element), and an unconscious erotic fantasy of wishes to be involved socially and sexually with the therapist (the transference element).

In the adaptive context of the rectification of this frame, the patient's dream of being tortured most likely represents an unconscious transference-based fantasy that reflects the patient's dread of being alone in a secured and therapeutic space with the therapist. In addition, this dream undoubtedly reveals her own masochistic needs (and those of the therapist?), and her wish to torture him.

This material includes a clear representation of a critical adaptive context and a meaningful derivative complex that reveals a number of unconscious perceptions and fantasies pertaining to the therapist, evoked by the intervention context of the therapist's decision to no longer sign the insurance forms. There is no evidence that this decision constituted a projective identification by the therapist, since it was carefully carried out at the behest of the patient's earlier derivative communications. Thus this particular style of communication is largely the responsibility of the patient, and constitutes a means of attempting to evacuate disturbing inner contents that began to emerge in a more sound therapeutic space.

The following session illustrates the Type B-C style of communication. A patient who had failed to pay his bill for the previous month was presented with an ultimatum from the therapist to terminate treatment if the bill remained unpaid. The patient began the session by sitting on the couch instead of lying down as he usually did in this three-times weekly treatment situation.

> Patient: I don't want to lie down today. I'm distraught. Therapy is going nowhere. I didn't pay my bill, but I don't want to terminate. I don't know what to do. I wish you'd tell me what to do. I wish you'd do something. You just sit there and stare at me. Where do we go from here? What should I do? Maybe I should quit now and return when and if I can pay. *(The patient gets up to leave.)* I've had enough for today. If I'm here next time, that means I'm continuing. If I don't show up, then I've terminated. See you. *(The patient stood and waited silently.)*

In the adaptive context of the therapist's ultimatum, which was formulated in supervision as a form of pathological projective identification with aggressive and controlling qualities, the patient responded here with a pathological projective identification of his own. He attempted to dump the introjected rage from the therapist back into the therapist and to create an ultimatum of his own. The action-discharge qualities were highlighted when the patient threatened to leave the hour prematurely, doing so in a manner that rendered the therapist uncertain as to whether the treatment would continue. The highly impulsive, threatening, guilt-provoking qualities of the therapist's own projective identification are interactionally projected back into him.

In all, the patient carried out these measures with a network of communications in which he failed to directly represent the therapist's ultimatum, though he did so through a highly disguised derivative conveyed through his own threat to the therapist. This might well have facilitated an interpretation had there been a meaningful derivative complex. However, these particular manifest associations were repetitive and yielded little in the way of indirect (derivative) meaning. The therapist was at a loss to intervene on an interpretive level, and his effort to deal with the patient's threat on a manifest level (not described here) had no influence on the patient, who eventually left the session early.

As a rule, powerful pathological projective identifications express a parasitic mode of relatedness. This is in evidence in the therapist's ultimatum and in the patient's response. These interactional projections are also an expression of, and accompanied by, role and image evocations. Here the patient made some effort to have the therapist feel guilty and helpless and to see himself as having persecuted the patient, much of this based on the implicit meanings of his actual interventions and the patient's unconscious valid perceptions. There is also an implied wish that the therapist would intervene actively and noninterpretively in order to prevent the patient from terminating prematurely. There is as well some effort to render the therapist quite helpless. The therapist reported experiencing all of these feelings and images during the hour, though the material provided little opportunity for their cognitive validation and interpretation.

The difficulties inherent in metabolizing projective identifications, especially when they are derived from the Type B-C mode, are apparent here. This type of working introjective identification and working over toward understanding is facilitated only when the patient provides meaningful cognitive associations. In their absence, the therapist usually experiences a sense of violence being done to himself or herself, and has the task of containing this experience and not responding with retaliation or noninterpretive interventions.

The *Type B receptive mode* is characterized by an almost immediate fragmentation of the valid meanings contained in the therapist's correct interventions, and by a responsive interactional projection. Thus, after an appropriate framework-management response or interpretation, the patient will offer an element of Type Two derivative validation and, following that, attempt to further fragment the ground rules of therapy or the understanding so derived. The patient tends to place the therapist under almost immediate interactional pressure. The Type B-A patient will then associate in a manner that generates additional meaning, while the Type B-C patient will not do so at all and, instead, will fully destroy the insight that had existed only a moment earlier.

Modes of Cure or Relief

In his writings on technique, Freud (1914) established a critical polarity for the patient (though not the therapist or analyst): cure through insight into unconscious processes and contents, as opposed to cure through acting out. The latter was seen as a way of repeating aspects of past pathogenic interactions rather than subjecting them to the analytic process. Freud (1919) invoked the rule of abstinence as a means of avoiding interventions through which the analyst would directly satisfy the patient's pathological needs and fantasies, and thereby interfere with the patient's efforts toward insightful recovery.

Freud's insights are extended when a means is offered through which patients who are not acting out on a gross behavioral level, and who nonetheless do not wish to achieve cure through insight, can be identified. By offering specific criteria for meaningful communication by the patient, and for sound and valid interventions by the therapist, it becomes possible to recognize efforts by both participants to treatment to help the patient to obtain relief from emotional disturbance by some means other than insightful understanding. Unconscious collusion of this kind has been termed the development of a *therapeutic misalliance;* when it involves relief through alterations in the basic ground rules and boundaries of the therapeutic relationship and setting, it is a *framework-deviation cure* (see Part III).

These two extremes of the continuum on which the curative process in psychotherapy may be categorized are termed *cure through insight* and *cure through action-discharge and barrier formation.* The first term implies a search for the truth of the spiraling therapeutic interaction as it pertains to the activated unconscious basis of the patient's Neurosis. In the object relationship sphere, the term implies the presence of inevitable positive introjective identifications with, and the generation of ego-enhancing inevitable benefits from, the efforts of the well-functioning therapist. Cure is through validated insights derived from interpretations and framework-management responses that pertain to sound therapeutic efforts by the therapist (see Part III and Chapters 34 and 35).

For the patient, the wish for this type of cure will find genuine expression primarily on an unconscious level. Its hallmark is a Type A style of communication, through which the patient clearly represents an activated intervention context and generates a meaningful and coalescible derivative complex in response to that context. Implied too is an acceptance of the ground rules and boundaries of the therapeutic relationship and of the other basic role responsibilities that accrue to the patient in the course of the psychotherapeutic experience.

Cure by action-discharge and pathological gratification and defense may take many forms. Each involves a type of lie-barrier therapy through which genuine insight and constructive introjective identifications are set to the side, and some other method of symptom relief is sought. There are strong and natural tendencies in both therapists and patients to avoid the highly painful and threatening mode of cure through insight and truth, and to seek instead some type of uninsightful relief. While cure through insight requires a considerable measure of delay and renunciation, and a tolerance for highly threatening realizations, cure through action-discharge tends to be relatively immediate, highly defensive, and pathologically satisfying.

In general, the Type B-C communicator typifies the patient who wishes to destroy both meaningful relatedness and the possibility of genuine insight, and to obtain relief through action-discharge, evacuation and riddance, and pathological projective identification. Although this type of patient gains some measure of lie-barrier protection, the main thrust is toward dumping and riddance, efforts that usually involve a parasiticism of the therapist. There is usually an absence of meaningful material; the possibility of meaningful communication is so threatening to these patients that they intensify their efforts at patholocial projective identification and action discharge in response to all efforts by the therapist to secure the framework of treatment and to generate understanding through interpretation. For these patients, truth and insight are highly persecutory and dangerous; rather than viewed as providing relief, they are seen as highly disruptive and disturbing, and as to be avoided at all costs.

This type of patient tends to be caught up in a "catch-22" situation: they cannot permit themselves to function as truth receivers, since the acceptance of any type of meaningful intervention from the therapist threatens to destroy totally their mental equilibrium. Thus their main unconscious model of cure involves fantasies of and actual efforts to dump into the therapist aspects of their highly primitive and disturbing inner mental worlds in the hope that some type of magical riddance will provide them with a measure of relief. Responding effectively to these patients requires considerable holding and containing by the therapist, and concentrated interpretive efforts designed to deal with their inordinate dread of meaningful expression and understanding.

The second major group of patients who seek uninsightful means of relief involve Type C communicators who attempt to destroy the meaningful relationship link with their therapists. Patients in this group unconsciously fail to generate meaning in the face of activated intervention contexts, and rely on the development of mainly nonderivative defensive formations for symptomatic relief. Often, these lie-barrier systems involve highly elaborate narrations and extensive manifest content and Type One derivative self-interpretations. Although unrelated to truth and genuine insight, such efforts, especially if they are reinforced by the therapist, may indeed provide the patient with momentary periods of respite. However, because of the absence of genuine insight, these patients then require relationships designed to maintain their defensive position, and they lack a sound basis for growth and individuation.

Any therapeutic intervention that departs from the adaptation-interactional model of a valid interpretation or framework-management response reflects some measure of an effort on the therapist's part to achieve cure through either action-discharge or lie-barrier formation. If the intervention involves blaming and dumping into the patient, and is highly critical or manipulative to the point of parasiticism, the therapist's effort is best characterized as an effort at self-cure through action discharge—one in which the patient's therapeutic needs are essentially disregarded. On the other hand, if the intervention is designed to projectively identify and blame others, and to reinforce the patient's own use of pathological interactional projection, the therapist's effort may be seen as an attempt to support the patient's own use of this particular mode of cure. Failure to interpret the patient's use of action-discharge, and responses by the therapist to the patient's interactional pressures with pathological projective identifications, also unconsciously reinforce this particular mode of relief for the patient.

Similarly, interventions that lack strong interactional pressures, but are nonetheless erroneous, tend to reflect both the therapist's own need for pathological lie-barrier systems as a way of resolving his or her own countertransferences and Neurosis, and the wish to offer this particular mode of cure to the patient. The lie-barrier and defensive systems offered by the therapist often serve unconsciously to reinforce similar mechanisms in the patient. At times the specific nature of the lie-barrier system used by the patient and therapist are in conflict, and the patient will either adopt the defensive system of the therapist or refute it—sometimes by leaving treatment.

Manifest content and Type One derivative interventions, including those with elaborate metapsychological formulations, even though offered in the name of insight, tend in the actual therapeutic interaction to offer the patient an opportunity for cure through fictionalized lie-barrier formations. Their use by the therapist can be identified empirically through an analysis of his or her interventions to determine whether an attempt has been made to help the patient understand the unconscious basis of an indicator or therapeutic context in light of an activated adaptive context and derivative response. As noted, all departures from this fundamental model offer the patient some mode of cure other than that through genuine insight.

In respect to the listening-formulating process, the therapist observes and monitors the patient's associations and behaviors in two ways as a means of identifying the mode of cure sought after by both the therapist and the patient. Thus the direct nature of the patient's behaviors and efforts are observed in order to determine whether they are geared toward insight or action-discharge. Of course, the therapist must make similar observations of his or her own therapeutic endeavors.

In addition, the therapist should pay careful attention to the patient's manifest and derivative material. Quite often, in the course of free associating, a patient will characterize efforts to obtain relief, cure, help, or the solution of a particular problem. Such communications tend to convey in derivative form the patient's unconscious perceptions of the actual mode of cure in operation in the present treatment situation, as well as the patient's (and therapist's) wishes in this regard. Thus, through both direct observation and an understanding of the patient's derivative communications in light of activated intervention contexts, the therapist is able to keep track of the prevailing mode of relief in the treatment situation. In this way, the therapist will be prepared to intervene with both rectifying and interpretive responses as need be, though always in light of the patient's derivative material.

A review of the clinical examples presented in this chapter illustrates this aspect of the listening-formulating process. For example, with the first patient it was possible to formulate his use of the Type A mode of communication. Direct observation of his efforts suggest an unconscious wish on his part for cure through insight. The therapist's silence in the context of meaningful communication from the patient, but with no immediate indication for intervention, could well imply a similar interest on his part. Clearly, this particular evaluation would become far more substantial with a study of the entire session and the nature of his ultimate response to this material The patient's allusion to moving to a half-way house suggests an effort to solve the problem of separation-individuation in a constructive, though incomplete manner. It speaks for both a search for insight and the wish for defensive protection. On the other hand, the patient's mention that he could have had free housing but has not accepted it suggests a capacity for delay and renunciation that would tend to accompany the search for true meaning and insight. The patient's comment that he does not like being obligated has similar implications, though in the main it appears to be an effort to repudiate the pathological symbiotic mode of relatedness offered by this therapist through a psycho-therapy for which the patient had no responsibility for the fee.

Direct observation of the patient who used the Type C mode of communication indicated that, on an unconscious level, he was attempting to maintain defensive lie-barrier systems designed to seal off the possibility of insightful understanding. The mode of relief represented in the patient's material is characterized by the allusion to the employee who wishes for a raise, and the decision to give it to him suggests a type of constructive solution that would tend to accompany a search for insight and understanding. (It is not uncommon for a patient to behave in a manner in keeping with the search for one type of cure, while representing the possibility of its opposite in his or her association.) On the other hand, the patient's image of wanting to nurse at a breast suggests cure through pathological (infantile) gratification. This is in keeping with the actuality of the patient's nonpayment of the fee, a mode of symptom relief that involves action-discharge, pathological gratification, and pathological defense.

The therapist who stopped signing the patient's insurance forms was attempting to shift the mode of cure for this patient from action-discharge to meaning and insight. In the session extracted, the patient clearly protested against the latter possibility by taking a tissue from the therapist and keeping it. Here the cure was by action-discharge and immediate pathological gratification. This occurred on a gross behavioral level, and was then represented in the patient's material. However, the representations in the patient's associations soon changed their characterization. The patient described a problem of having two boyfriends and being unfaithful to one of them all the time. She proposed a solution through renunciation, and referred to how the boyfriend whom she stopped seeing was furious but understood. In this way, the patient alluded to cure through insight, despite its hurtful qualities. Having expressed herself in this manner, the patient soon shifted again to direct behaviors designed for action-discharge, and to representations that reflected her search for uninsightful cure. She asked for noninterpretive interventions from the therapist, and for self-revelations. She generated interactional pressures that proved difficult for the therapist to manage. In all, then, both behaviorally and through her representations, this patient revealed an intense conflict regarding her own wishes in respect to mode of cure: at first her allegiance was to action-discharge, though she then shifted to insight and understanding, only to return to a quest once more for action-discharge.

There is some evidence, however, that the therapist had sufficient material for an interpretation during the interlude when the patient was expressing herself in favor of the renunciation of pathological modes of gratification and the quest for insight. It may well be that his failure to intervene unconsciously reflected an inability to effect an insightful cure for this patient. In light of that particular intervention context, the patient's shift back to the action-discharge mode of cure is an interactional product with inputs from both herself and the therapist. In principle, of course, this is always the case: the preferred mode of cure expressed by both patient and therapist is under the influence of the entire therapeutic interaction.

Finally, in the session that involved the unpaid bill and the therapist's ultimatum, there is strong evidence that both patient and therapist wished to cure their own respective difficulties through action-discharge and that, in addition, the therapist unconsciously preferred this mode of relief for the patient as well. The patient's gross behaviors and efforts involved further expressions of the wish for cure through action-discharge, dumping, and pathological gratification. There is no evidence of a meaningful network of communication, and the patient actually left the session early. These are clearly uninsightful efforts at symptom relief (framework-deviation cures), though here too they found a measure of support in the therapist's own propensities in this direction, and in his failure to intervene interpretively. In all, both behaviorally and through his derivative communications, this patient expressed a strong preference for cure through action-discharge.

In summary, it is essential that the therapist monitor his or her own behaviors and interventions, as well as the material from the patient, for activated efforts at cure and for representations of the mode of cure being effected by each of the participants to treatment. In particular, the patient's associations, understood in light of activated intervention contexts, will tend to reveal the nature of the therapist's endeavors in this regard, as well as the propensities of the patient.

It is important not to assume a genuine, conscious, and especially unconscious preference for cure through insight in either the patient or the therapist. Cure through true insight is an extremely painful and sometimes terrifying process (see Chapter 38). Based on inevitable residuals of countertransference and on the patient's own psychopathology, there are strong needs in both participants to treatment for uninsightful modes of cure. The therapist must constantly monitor his or her own interpretive and framework-management efforts and the material from the patient for the extent to which they adhere to the Type A mode. All departures from this mode of expression will simultaneously involve a shift toward a pathological mode of symptom relief. These latter tend to involve action-discharge, as well as pathological gratification and defense. A patient's effort to invoke a deviant mode of cure creates important opportunities for therapeutic work by the therapist. However, these endeavors can be effective only if the therapist has unconsciously and consciously renounced deviant modes of symptom relief and is capable of responding with insightful interventions.

Correlations between Modes of Communication, Relatedness, and Cure

Certain evident patterns and correlations emerge in respect to the patient's (and therapist's) activated mode of relatedness, mode of cure, and mode of communication. The manner in which each participant deals with the ground rules and framework of the psychotherapeutic situation also tends to correlate strongly with these three factors. In general, breaks in the frame will correlate with pathological expressions in all areas, while securing the frame provides a basis for healthy responses in the other two spheres. Regarding modes of relatedness, cure, and communication, the following correlations seem most consistent:

1. The Type A communicative mode, cure through insight and understanding, and a healthy therapeutic symbiosis.
2. The Type B communicative mode, and in particular the Type B-C style, cure through action-discharge, and the parasitic mode of relatedness.
3. The Type C communicative mode, cure through nonderivative defenses and lie-barrier formations, and the pathological autistic or pathological symbiotic modes of relatedness.

As a rule, interventions designed to modify the pathological factors in one of these spheres will help to ameliorate disturbances in the other two. Such efforts tend to involve the rectification of breaks in the frame and the correction of other areas of erroneous intervention by the therapist, accompanied by sound interpretations offered in light of the intervention contexts at hand.

Mode of Relatedness: Some Final Comments

An analysis of the extent to which the patient manifestly represents both indicators and activated intervention contexts, and provides a coalescible and meaningful derivative complex, leads to two basic styles of communication: Type A and Type C. An additional style, Type B, involves expression through projective identification.

The style of communication of both patient and therapist is an interactional product, receiving vectors from both participants to therapy. Still, the specific modality of communication may vary from session to session depending on the nature of the intervention context and a variety of other factors within both patient and therapist. In principle, the patient's immediate mode of expressions must be understood in light of intervention contexts from the therapist, including his or her own style of communication.

The Type A mode as used by the patient is characterized by a direct but thinly disguised representation of the important indicators, and especially of the most critical activated intervention contexts, and by the presence of a meaningful derivative complex. Defenses and resistances as expressed by such patients have depth and derivative meaning, and tend to lend themselves to analytic resolution through interpretation or rectifications of the frame; these last are carried out in terms of the patient's meaningful derivative communications.

The Type A therapist maintains a secure therapeutic environment, and responds with silent holding and containing until it is possible to make a sound interpretation or framework-management response in terms of the patient's derivative responses to activated intervention contexts.

The Type C patient can be recognized by the meaningful representation of an adaptive context in the absence of a meaningful and coalescible derivative complex, or by the presence of a seemingly meaningful derivative complex in the absence of a represented adaptive context. At times, these patients destroy meaningful representation in respect to both the intervention context and the derivative complex. These patients wish to destroy meaning, possible understanding, and a meaningful relationship-link with the therapist. They attempt to generate relatively impervious defenses and resistances without depth and derivative implication. These are *Type C barriers* or *lie-barrier systems*. They can be modified primarily when the therapist rectifies his or her own contributions to such nonderivative defenses and, on rare occasions, when the patient conveys derivative representations of the actual use of barrier systems and their unconscious meanings in response to an activated intervention context. Common metaphors for the Type C mode include references to tanks, walls, and vaults.

The Type C therapist consistently fails to intervene in terms of the unconscious implications of an activated intervention context. Such a therapist may be a framework changer, may use psychoanalytic clichés in the form of Type One derivative interventions, or may defensively utilize genetic reconstructions that are divorced from the ongoing therapeutic interaction. In essence, each of these interventions is designed as a falsification and as a lie-barrier system that will seal over the patient's unconscious perceptions of the therapist and the chaos within the spiraling interaction as it pertains to the patient's Neurosis. (Interventions that pertain to outside relationships of the patient serve a similar purpose.)

The Type B patient may be either a Type B-A communicator or a Type B-C communicator. The Type B-A patient will generate pathological interactional projections into the therapist, but in the context of a meaningful network of communications. The Type B-C patient will pathologically projectively identify into the therapist in the absence of meaningful cognitive-affective expressions.

The Type B therapist is characterized by disruptive, erroneous interventions and mismanagements of the framework, work undertaken with full neglect of the implications of activated intervention contexts. All errors by the therapist offer the patient lie-barrier systems, and constitute pathological projective identifications of aspects of the therapist's own psychopathology (the therapist's countertransferences).

Patients may also be classified as Type A, B, or C in regard to the receiving of messages, the incorporative aspect of communication. The Type A receiver offers Type Two derivative validation for a correct interpretation or framework-management response of the therapist, and then both consciously and unconsciously works over the implications of the interventions. He or she makes use of direct and derivative communications to develop in-depth insight into an aspect of his or her Neurosis.

The Type C receiver will offer momentary Type Two derivative validation of an intervention by the therapist, but then become impervious to its implications. He or she fails to work over the newly won insight, and immediately constructs Type C barriers against further understanding.

Finally, the Type B receiver will offer momentary Type Two derivative validation of a correct intervention by the therapist, only to immediately fragment the subsequent derivative complex, dissipate the sense of understanding present just a moment ago, and shift toward the renewed use of pathological projective identification, which further obliterates any meaningful use of the previously validated insight.

The recognition of distinctive styles of communication prepares the therapist for interludes where a particular style of communication may be utilized by the patient that is rather different than that in use by the therapist. All interventions must be shaped with an understanding of the patient's style of communication, and this must include the realization that at certain moments, as with certain Type C and Type B-C patients, it will prove impossible for the therapist to intervene interpretively in terms of the Type A mode. Shifts to holding and containing, and efforts to interpret the nature of these resistances, must then take place, since simplistic efforts to impart meaning, even when done in light of activated intervention contexts, will seldom lead to Type Two derivative validation under these conditions. In keeping with the principle of analyzing resistances before dealing with contents, interpretive and framework-management responses must be first directed toward modifying pathological styles of communication; followed by analysis of unconscious fantasies and perceptions in other spheres. Resistances expressed as communictive dysfunctions, then, must be analyzed and modified (including any contribution from the therapist) before other types of efforts at intervening are attempted.

The correlation between style of communication, mode of cure, and maturational mode of relatedness similarly points to a need to carry out therapeutic work in these three spheres before undertaking the more usual type of dynamic and genetic interpretations. Since the state of the ground rules and boundaries of treatment are basic to both style of communication and mode of relatedness, it is often in this area that the therapist must first intervene.

Chapter 16

Some Precepts of Listening

This chapter offers some cogent clinical precepts on the listening-formulating process. They are presented in the light of supervisory and direct clinical experiences, which have indicated where the listening-formulating process is most vulnerable to countertransference-based influence and error. The chapter is not meant to be a comprehensive synthesis, but, rather, highlights the most clinically useful aspects of the listening process.

The *adaptive context* is the key to the patient's conscious and unconscious stirrings, adaptive responses, and communicative expressions. It is therefore pivotal in the therapist's interventions and in the decision whether or not to intervene. It follows, then, that a large portion of the listening effort must concentrate on attending to adaptive contexts and their implications as reflected in the patient's material. This involves the separate tasks of subjectively identifying all existing adaptive contexts in a given hour, recognizing the best representation of the most important of these contexts in the patient's material, and identifying the main unconscious perceptions of the therapist by the patient based on the implications of these contexts. Only then should the therapist consider the patient's reactions to these unconscious perceptions. Both dynamic and genetic considerations are inherent to these efforts, though valid perception implies a repetition by the therapist of a past pathogenic interaction (nontransference), while distorted perception and reaction implies a constructive and distinctive intervention by the therapist that is different from earlier figures (transference).

Communicative tasks should be separated from those that are *dynamic* and *genetic*. In regard to the adaptive context, the communicative effort (which is always primary) involves identifying the clearest representations in the patient's material of the contexts at hand. The ideal representation is, of course, made manifestly and in passing. The clearer the representation, including thinly disguised derivative expressions, the more likely it is that the therapist will be able to intervene.

A manifest representation of an adaptation-evoking context is a signal from the patient that his or her dynamic use of what is termed *the denial barrier* has been significantly lessened or eliminated for the moment. Thus a direct representation of an intervention context implies that the patient is prepared to meaningfully connect or relate defended, derivative communications to an intervention from the therapist. The absence of a direct representation of the adaptive context suggests a high level of defensiveness within the patient. The same applies to highly disguised, encoded representations of the context. In respect to thinly disguised representations, much depends on whether the patient offers some other allusion to therapy, a general bridge through which the therapist can connect the derivative material to aspects of his or her interventions and the treatment situation. In the absence of a manifest representation of the adaptive context or of a general bridge to therapy, it is highly likely that the patient will maintain communicative and dynamic defenses through which to *deny* meaningful connections between the implications of the therapist's interventions and his or her own adaptive-derivative responses.

While the patient's manifest contents are examined for direct references to intervention contexts and indicators, the encoded implications of the material must be consistently searched for all sense of meaning as it applies to the patient's emotional disturbance. In this sense, manifest contents are not psychoanalyticaly meaningful; their use for *explanation* serves mainly to generate fictions and lie-barrier systems. Even on the rare occasion when a manifest statement represents a breakthrough of a previously unconscious insight, its most cogent dynamic meaning lies in its derivative implications.

There is a natural tendency in the mental functioning of all persons, including therapists, to think in terms of manifest communications and to resist the decoding process. This is especially true in respect to encoded expressions of valid unconscious perceptions of themselves. The natural defense is to think manifestly and about the fantasies and reactions of others. Because of this, the therapist must take pains to subject all of the patient's associations and behaviors to the decoding process, treating them as potential derivative communications. Essential here is the abstracting of general and symbolized themes, and the reduction (particularization) to specific image-themes of perception and fantasy, in light of the implications of an adaptation-evoking context.

The therapist must learn to think in terms of images, fantasies, and perceptions. Efforts at formulating the patient's material should be essentially devoid of theoretical concepts and intellectualized inferences. Instead, the therapist should operate as if writing a novel or a play—thinking of scenes, images, human emotions, and human conflict and struggle. In substance, this is the language of unconscious expression and communication. All such themes and images must be organized in light of adaptation-evoking stimuli.

Similarly, the therapist should make efforts to avoid or lessen his or her investment in intellectualized inferences and other Type One derivative formulations made from the patient's material. Type One derivative image formulations may serve the therapist in some preliminary fashion when one is uncertain of the activated adaptive context. Such speculations, couched first in terms of perception and then in terms of possible fantasies, often provide clues to a missing adaptive context, since they are usually shaped in part by the precipitant.

Another major area of resistance in therapists involves the necessity of developing an extended series of hypotheses relevant to the patient's unconscious *perceptions* of the therapist and the unconscious readings of the implications of intervention contexts. In principle, only those images that are not in accord with repeated assessments by the therapist of the implications of his or her interventions should be formulated as derivative material based on unconscious fantasy-memory constellations.

The listening-formulating process, open in its initial stages, ultimately should be organized in terms of two basic schema. The intervention schema involves the identification of indicators, adaptive contexts, and the dimensions of the derivative complex. The six-part informational or observational schema involves broadly listening in terms of cognitive, object relationship, and interactional mechanism considerations. These observations are organized into six categories of meaning and implication, stated first for the therapist and second for the patient. At times, a particular category may also be thought of in terms of the interaction between the two participants. In developing these formulations, the therapist relies upon both direct observations of himself or herself and the patient, and the manifest and derivative representations in the patient's material. In rough order of importance, the six categories involve the frame (the ground rules and boundaries of the therapeutic relationship), the basic mode of relatedness, the mode of cure, the state and style of communications, represented dynamics and genetics, and the question of to whom they mainly apply—to the therapist through unconscious perceptions, the patient through unconscious fantasies, or both.

The therapist should have *faith* in the patient to represent and place into the therapist the material that he or she requires for formulating and intervening. Similarly, the therapist should have faith in the patient's capacities for defense to become resistant when it is necessary for the patient to lie fallow or to move along at a somewhat slower place.

Each session should be its own creation, and the bulk of formulations should be based on the material from the particular hour at hand. While these efforts may be bolstered by recollections of prior sessions, the therapist should intervene entirely on the basis of material in the immediate hour. In this way, the therapist is protected against the natural tendency to see in the patient's material that which he or she already knows, and to add to interventions selected material from prior sessions that is culled out mainly on the basis of prejudice and countertransference-based needs.

The therapist should have little or no confidence in a silent hypothesis or offered intervention unless it obtains rather dramatic Type Two derivative validation. Forced and overly convoluted formulations should be avoided, as should those that are direct, straight-forward, rather obvious, theoretical, intellectualized, repetitious, flat, linear, and nondynamic. A diversely meaningful coalescible derivative network and a Type Two derivative validation response have an inherent air of the unexpected, uniqueness, and excitement, which is one of the hallmarks of a sound formulation or intervention.

Formulations that are relatively devoid of instinctual drive representations should be avoided, as well. In sessions where powerful derivatives appear, a sound formulation virtually always integrates their meanings into the main hypothesis at hand, doing so in terms of activated intervention contexts. When genetic figures appear, this dimension should be added to the working formulation. It is well to treat all of the patient's communications as transversal. They traverse allusions to the patient and the therapist, and therefore convey meanings along the me/not-me interface. They also traverse reality and fantasy, transference and nontransference, present and past, and transactions within and outside of treatment.

In principle, a therapist should formulate nontransference before transference, perceptions before fantasies, his or her own dynamics and genetics before those of the patient, and reality before fantasy.

Virtually all of the dimensions of the treatment experience and of the listening-formulating process are on a continuum, as exemplified by such polarities as transference and nontransference, contributions from patient and therapist, valid and distorted, reality and fantasy, and the like. Neither extreme ever exists in pure form. Thus there is some measure of *transversal* quality to all of the patient's associations. It is nonetheless critical to identify the vast majority of expressions that fall mainly toward one of the two ends of a particular continuum, because at some point on these scales there is a definitive cluster of meanings and implications that accrue to an expression and experience of the patient that can be identified by recognizing the major characteristics involved. For example, while there are intermixtures of reality and fantasy in all of the patient's associations, those that are primarily realistic have a rather different configuration and set of properties from those that are mainly fantasied. As long as it is recognized that both ends of a continuum involve extremes that never exist in a pure state, this type of clear-cut delineation proves highly serviceable clinically.

The ideal formulation, as is true of the ideal intervention, integrates disparate derivative expressions around an organizing adaptive context as a way of explaining the unconscious factors in an indicator. Aside from this shaping in the form of a statement or image of cause, effect, and explanation, little else is provided by the therapist.

In the presence of technical errors, including deviations from the ideal therapeutic environment and relationship, attention must be focused almost exclusively on the patient's unconscious perceptions of the therapist and on the patient's offer of models of rectification. Almost all of these communications are made on a derivative level, and can be understood only in light of the deviant intervention context.

The truth of the patient's neurosis is virtually always expressed on an unconscious level through derivative expressions. In psychotherapy, these truths are defined as the unconscious basis for the patient's emotional disturbance as stimulated by the interventions of the therapist, and as they unfold in the course of the therapeutic interaction. By implication, then, the truth of the patient's Neurosis can only be defined through a full consideration of the manifest and latent meanings of the communications of both participants to treatment. In efforts geared toward identifying and modifying the actual underlying basis of a patient's emotional disturbance, it is these truths that must be determined by the listening-formulating process. Any error in this regard—any formulation that departs from these interactional truths—can then be termed lies or fictions, and can be viewed as derivative and nonderivative components of defensive and lie-barrier systems.

Both the insightful modification of the truths of the patient's Neurosis and the offer of lie-barrier systems may lead to an alleviation of the patient's symptoms. The advantages and disadvantages (risks) of each approach are considered in a later chapter. Truth therapy can be based only on interventions to the patient that obtain Type Two derivative validation; these in turn must be based on silently validated preliminary hypotheses. Every clinical psychoanalytic formulation and hypothesis—whether in a specific session with a patient or in an effort to derive a general clinical theory—must meet the criterion of Type Two derivative validation in a specific session with a patient with whom the relevant issues have been activated and interpreted through an intervention context.

In light of the critical importance of the patient's derivative communications, the therapist's use of empathy, intuition, and cognitive understanding is incomplete unless they operate on both the manifest and latent levels. The therapist must overcome tendencies toward simplistic and surface uses of empathy and intuition, and develop a sensitivity to the patient's unconscious representations and meanings. These automatic capabilities must eventually be metabolized into conscious experience and understanding.

Affects are manifest and surface communications. As such, they yield little in the way of derivative meaning. Similar considerations apply to somatic symptoms. In general, such phenomena are important indicators that reflect distinctive therapeutic needs within the patient. They are not, however, strong carriers of meaning. This can only be determined by an evaluation of the complex of communications within which they appear. Powerful affects may emerge in the context of any of the styles of communication—A, B, or C.

There is a strong, though defensive attraction to Type One derivative formulations. They find ready support in psychoanalytic theory and metapsychology. They protect the therapist from the implications of his or her own inputs into the therapeutic interaction and patient, especially those that are pathological. They therefore have considerable appeal, and afford the therapist a large measure of immediate protection and gratification. Since it is possible to manipulate and develop formulations of this kind for extended periods of time, they also have a self-sustaining quality. Further, since patients, for unconscious defensive reasons of their own, often manifestly elaborate upon this type of intervention, the therapist who uses it is likely to erroneously believe that he or she is engaged in validated and productive therapeutic work. The linear, simplistic, and self-evident qualities of these extensions tend to escape notice.

These shared misalliances and lie-barrier systems can be extended just so far. As a rule, at some point the patient will attempt in a major but derivative manner to rectify the situation. These interludes often have cataclysmic qualities. However, the regression and disturbance is usually ascribed to the patient's psychopathology, a position falsely supported by fresh Type One derivative hypotheses. For these reasons and more, it proves to be quite difficult to demonstrate to relatively experienced psychotherapists the flaws in manifest content and Type One derivative psychotherapy. Each therapist who has been taught to think and work in this manner should at some point take on the challenge of discovering and resolving these problems, and of working in Type Two derivative fashion.

While there are many exceptions, certain types of material tend to be used more often for Type A communication, while other kinds of behaviors and associations appear to serve well the Type C mode. For example, extended narratives with rich imagery, whether the recall of recent or past events or in the form of a dream or conscious fantasy, tend to be strong potential carriers of derivative meaning. On the other hand, manifest comments about the therapist, attempts by the patient at interpreting his or her own dreams and other material, direct complaints about therapy and conscious praise of the therapist, discussions of how therapy works, speculations about others, and behavioral and somatic responses, tend to be poor carriers of encoded implications.

A relatively neglected factor in adopting a sound listening-formulating attitude involves the therapist's capacity to tolerate ambiguity, frustration, and the build-up of tension within himself or herself and in the patient. There appears to be a strong tendency in therapists toward offering their patients some means, however pathological, of immediate satisfaction through one type of comment or another. This often involves noninterpretive and sometimes offhanded interventions. Such efforts reflect a difficulty within the therapist in establishing a therapeutic relationship and experience with the necessary and essential measure of frustration for the patient, which should not, however, be extended to the point where a necessary intervention is missed. Patients who require intervening from the therapist will place the needed elements into the therapist. In the absence of a clearly represented adaptive context and meaningful derivative complex, the therapist must in general refrain from intervening. Thus the therapist conveys to the patient a capacity for holding and containing, for delay and frustration tolerance, and for the necessary build-up of the tensions that lead the patient eventually to express himself or herself in meaningful fashion. To do otherwise is to pathologically gratify and support the patient's Neurosis, and to interfere with Type A communication, which arises in part because of strong needs within the patient to adapt and understand. Sound listening requires patience and faith in the patient, and a specific ability *not* to intervene in the absence of meaningful material.

In many sessions the therapist's listening-formulating capacities will be directed to two levels of issue. This arises in particular when the therapist has initially failed to deal with a framework issue and has missed a necessary intervention in this area. In this way, meaningful communicated material has either been ignored or misunderstood by the therapist, including the underlying unconscious issues involved, whether perceptions or fantasies.

Following such an interlude, the patient has two choices: (1) to express again through derivatives the original underlying framework issues that the therapist has mishandled, or (2) to express himself or herself in respect to his or her unconscious perception of the therapist as having made an error. In general, far more meaning accrues to the patient's material when he or she makes unconscious efforts to redirect the therapist's attention to the original mishandled issue than when the patient works over his or her unconscious sense that the therapist has made a mistake.

In keeping with this observation, when a therapist identifies themes of error and the like, it is important that the therapist scan the patient's material for indications of the specific nature of the mistake. Formulations that pertain in some general fashion to an error in technique by the therapist tend to be of only minor utility, while those that extend from the image of error in general into its specific nature have much more cogency.

By far, the largest proportion of the therapist's time spent in listening and formulating involves the job of identifying the activated adaptive contexts, their best representations in the patient's material, and the patient's unconscious perception of the therapist on the basis of these adaptation-evoking stimuli. The patient's valid and inappropriate reactions to these perceptions, ultimate distortions and misperceptions, and the patient's view of himself or herself in light of the therapist's efforts lend themselves rather readily to observation and formulation. In contrast, identifying and conceptualizing the implications of his or her own interventions meet with repeated resistances within the therapist. Thus the therapist must be mindful of these obstacles, subject failings in this regard to repeated self-analytic work, and maintain a conscious level of vigilance through which to identify any departure from this basic therapeutic requisite. Psychotherapy is by no means simply a cognitive effort; it requires considerable self-insight and mastery within the therapist.

Every aspect of psychotherapeutic technique stands or falls on the listening-formulating process of the therapist. Much confusion has arisen from the fact that a therapist may make many formulations and comments to the patient that are true in some other sense than sound realizations of the active state of the patient's Neurosis. Such statements, which depart in general from the ongoing therapeutic interaction, are *functionally* false. They are intellectual truths designed to serve dynamically as lie-barrier systems, which either express through derivatives or entirely seal off the interactional emotional truths that account for the underlying chaos within the treatment situation and in the patient—and secondarily the therapist. These meaningful, dynamic truths of the patient's Neurosis as they emerge in the therapeutic situation must be more clearly identified and the means by which the therapist can create the best set of conditions and relationship through which they can emerge must be discovered. For reasons that already may be self-evident, this further search must begin with a study of the ground rules and boundaries of the therapeutic relationship.

Part III

The Ground Rules and Boundaries of Psychotherapy

Chapter 17

The Nature and Function
of the Ground Rules

The setting, ground rules, and boundaries of the therapeutic relationship are among the most critical and yet most neglected aspects of psychotherapy. Shaped implicitly and explicitly by the therapist, with active or passive participation by the patient, this particular dimension of the therapeutic experience proves to be fundamental to virtually every other aspect of treatment. The shaping and maintenance of a framework for the transactions of therapy proves to be the single most important determinant of the background or core relationship established between the patient and therapist. This backdrop critically determines the nature of the foreground exchanges between the two participants to treatment, both in regard to form and meaning, as well as providing the means by which they will be handled.

Freud (1912, 1912a, 1913, 1914, 1915), with characteristic genius, afforded considerable attention to the ground rules of psychoanalysis. He viewed these tenets as a means of "safeguarding the transference," or of assuring that the analytic work would unfold at the behest of the patient's needs and psychopathology. Modern-day studies indicate that the framework is far more than Freud had imagined it to be; indeed, only under the conditions of an essentially secure framework to therapy can primary transference expressions emerge from the patient (see Chapter 28). This single tenet has proven to be the fountainhead for a series of critical realizations regarding the nature and functions of the ground rules and boundaries of treatment.

At the same time, however, Freud (1905, 1909, 1918) showed a distinct laxity in his applications of these tenets, as have most analysts. This attitude is the source of considerable confusion regarding both the nature and function of the ground rules themselves, as well as their proper clinical application. As a sign of these difficulties, it may aptly be stated that Freud had the genius of defining a set of valid ground rules and boundaries for the psychoanalytic experience despite the fact that he himself never made definitive use of them.

In this regard, it is well to recognize that the psychoanalytic literature in this area has been developed through manifest content and Type One derivative listening. This has led to many essentially false hypotheses, all the more so because of a typical split seen in patients in response to deviations in the ideal frame: *conscious* acceptance and gratitude in reaction to manifestly gratifying alterations in the ground rules, accompanied by *unconscious* (derivative) criticism and ingratitude.

In contrast, the observations and hypotheses to be developed here are based entirely upon Type Two derivative listening and validation. Every tenet proposed here has been subjected repeatedly to Type Two derivative confirmation. One of the more remarkable findings regarding psychoanlytic psychotherapy is that patients are exquisitely sensitive to the most minimal deviation in the ideal therapeutic frame. Their responses to such changes are powerful and universal, though they are in addition shaped by the specific nature of the deviation, the unconscious communications from the therapist, and the patient's own inner needs and tendencies.

The proposition that a single ideal therapeutic environment exists within which truth therapy (i.e., the pursuit of the activated truths of the patient's emotional disturbance within the unfolding of the therapeutic interaction) can take place has created a considerable stir among therapists. Nevertheless, this proposition has been subjected to ten years of Type Two derivative psychoanalytic validation. Each of the specific ground rules described here have been repeatedly tested. Responses to both deviations and adherence to a particular tenet have been studied. A search has been made for new or alternative ground rules, and for the possibility of dismissing one or more of these basic tenets. The ground rules described here have withstood these challenges, and appear to constitute the ideal conditions of treatment and the ideal ground rules for the treatment experience.

A number of metaphors have proved useful in conceptualizing this aspect of the therapeutic relationship. If therapy is conceived of as an interaction between a patient and therapist within the confines of a bipersonal field, the ground rules may be thought of as the *frame* of the field. They are the conditions of relatedness that give psychotherapy its distinctive properties, and the psychotherapeutic relationship its unique and therapeutic valences. Most important, however, is to think of these basic tenets as communicative expressions from the therapist of both rules of core relatedness and the statement of the basic contract under which insightful cure can take place. These rules need stating, managing, handling, and rectifying—actions that say a great deal about the therapist as well as the conditions of treatment.

An outline of the specific ground rules and boundaries of psychotherapy, and a delineation of the main meanings and functions of their collective expression, are presented in this chapter. Two basic modes of therapy—that which unfolds within a sound and secure frame, and that which occurs in the context of definitive deviations—are presented in the following chapter. In subsequent chapters, the implications and management of each specific ground rule are explored.

The Basic Ground Rules

A stable, single, relatively neutral setting. The patient and therapist are provided with a set of physical constants that imply a maximal degree of consistency, certainty, and stability based on the availability for each session of a constant, relatively impersonal, secure place within which the treatment experience can unfold.

A single, fixed fee. The monetary cost of therapy is defined for the patient, and affords the therapist an important measure of gratification and appropriate reward for his or her services. A singly stated and maintained fee precludes any image of either undue sacrifice or exploitation of the patient on the part of the therapist. It is therefore necessary that the fee be commensurate with the therapist's level of expertise and with fees charged within the community. A clear-cut fee is another part of the relatively *fixed* components of the ground rules and boundaries of therapy.

A specific and set time for each session, with a defined length for each hour (preferably 45 or 50 minutes). Regularly scheduled, defined time periods lend a maximal sense of stability to the therapeutic relationship, and are as well a part of the relatively fixed frame.

A full sense of responsibility for attendance at all scheduled sessions on the part of both patient and therapist. The patient is responsible for all sessions for which the therapist is available, and a reasonable vacation policy is set by the therapist, to which both patient and therapist must adhere. These are among the necessary stable attributes of the therapeutic contract that provide the patient with a strong sense of reliability, certainty, responsibility, and fairness. There is as well a necessary sense of commitment involved in the explication of this particular ground rule, which is also a part of the relatively fixed frame.

A regular location that affords privacy. With the exceptions of the initial telephone call and the therapist's greeting to the patient in the waiting room before each session, the transactions of psychotherapy should take place in the therapist's consultation room, which must be suitably soundproofed. These transactions occur with the therapist in his or her chair and the patient in a different chair or on the couch. The fixed positions of the two participants, and the confinement of interpersonal exchanges to the privacy of the consultation room, afford the patient a maximal sense of safety, stability, and security. These too are aspects of the fixed frame that involve the therapist's hold for the patient and the patient's hold for the therapist—the latter depending on the patient's acceptance of the fixed frame.

Free association. The fundamental rule of free association states that the patient expresses to the therapist everything that comes to mind—thoughts, feelings, images, and whatever. This rule is designed to maximize the conscious and unconscious expression of the patient's psychopathology, and to make available for interpretation the critical meanings of the patient's Neurosis.

The therapist's maintenance of free-floating attention, open role and image responsiveness, and a full capacity to contain the patient's projective identifications. These implicit attitudes, eventually reflected in the nature of the therapist's interventions, provide unconscious support for the open expressions of the patient.

The therapist's relative anonymity. By confining self-revelations to those *implicit* in the setting that the therapist creates, his or her manner of carriage and dress, and the nature of his or her interventions, and by avoiding all deliberate self-revelations, the therapist creates an atmosphere in which the characterizations of the patient constitute the main inputs into the therapeutic relationship. Relative anonymity not only provides full opportunity for projection by the patient, but also a sense of safety to the therapeutic relationship. Anonymity also reflects the therapist's willingness to forego and renounce pathological needs and to repel any tendency to misuse the relationship with the patient for pathological satisfactions.

The therapist's use of appropriate silence and valid, neutral active interventions. Interventions are confined to interpretations and reconstructions (and their variations), and the handling of the therapeutic environment at the behest of the patient's derivative communications. Here too the therapist expresses a commitment to the therapeutic needs of the patient and to renounce any pathological use of the treatment situation or patient.

A one-to-one relationship with total privacy and confidentiality. This relationship expresses the therapist's near-exclusive commitment to the cure of the patient's Neurosis. This single-minded, single-relationship therapeutic devotion creates a maximum sense of trust and the best possible opportunity for the patient to express his or her Neurosis and its underlying basis. The rule involves the patient's sense of safety, as well as the certainty that the treatment relationship has been designed almost entirely with the patient's therapeutic needs in mind. Misuse of the patient and the treatment relationship are thereby precluded.

The absence of any prior, concomitant, or post-treatment relationship between the patient and therapist, and the essential absence of physical contact. This too safeguards the therapeutic situation and relationship as a means of affording the patient the insightful cure of his or her Neurosis. It helps to preclude a wide range of extratherapeutic and nontherapeutic gratifications inimical to symptomatic alleviation through understanding.

The rule of abstinence. Extratherapeutic satisfactions for either patient or therapist are to be avoided. While listed separately here, this tenet is actually inherent to virtually all of the specific ground rules already stated.

Individually and collectively, these ground rules of relatedness and mode of cure constitute the basis for the ideal therapeutic interaction. They create the ideal therapeutic environment or frame. The therapist's capacity to establish and maintain these basic tenets, and his or her responses when under pressure to change them, are the vital factors in this therapeutic contract. The therapist's management of the ground rules contains within it a multitude of conscious and unconscious communications and expressions regarding the preferred mode of relatedness, mode of cure, way of interacting and communicating with the patient, and dynamics and genetics. The therapist's capacity to deal with and adapt to inner tensions, conflicts, and Neurosis is also reflected in these framework-management efforts.

Through these tenets, the therapist offers the patient the optimal set of conditions, basic mode of relatedness, and holding-containing environment within which the maximal expression and analysis of the patient's Neurosis and its underlying basis is feasible. These are a set of conditions that promise, to the greatest degree possible, to neither support nor gratify the patient's emotional disturbance, consciously or unconsciously, and to afford both patient and therapist a maximal degree of nonpathological gratification in the absence of satisfactions of pathological needs and defenses. Perhaps most crucial here is the manner in which these conditions permit and encourage freedom of communication in the context of a specifically healthy mode of relatedness—the ideal therapeutic symbiosis. Important too is the manner in which these ground rules foster the expression of the patient's Neurosis through words and affects rather than actions, while providing a means to the therapist of minimizing the manifestations of his or her own emotional ills. Finally, these ground rules secure a therapeutic situation in which words and behaviors are maximally utilized for positive communication, for meaning and the pursuit of understanding, rather than for action-discharge, destruction of meaning, and the search for immediate relief on the basis of defensive and riddance maneuvers.

The Basic Functions of the Ground Rules and Boundaries of Therapy

The following are the basic implications of the specific ground rules of psychotherapy acting in consort as a totality.

The offer of definitive rules of relatedness through which a healthy therapeutic symbiosis is constituted and maintained. This mode of relatedness implies a sense of safety and trust for both participants, as well as the nongratification of pathological id, ego, and superego expressions (satisfactions and defenses). Implied too is the pursuit of understanding, rather than some other, relatively pathological, means of relief.

A statement of the rules and mode of cure. The basic choice is one of two constellations: (1) frustration-tolerance, delay, the absence of pathological satisfactions, the presence of healthy satisfactions, the communication of relatively meaningful associations and behaviors, and the ultimate achievement of symptom alleviation and characterological change through validated insights and unconscious positive introjective identifications with the therapist; or (2) immediate satisfactions (most of them pathological), pressures toward action-discharge, the destruction of meaning, and relief through pathological defense, denial, and action. The secure frame creates movement toward insightful understanding, while breaks in the frame provide pathological and lie-barrier relief without insight. There is a basic choice of adaptation involved in adherence to or breaking the ground rules: cure or relief through insight or through action. The modification of the ground rules is per se a form of action and acting in or out; it constitutes the pursuit of uninsightful symptom alleviation through essentially pathological means.

Adherence to the ground rules. This is an essential or core component of the basic mode of adaptation. It involves thought, meaning, delay, and ultimate understanding. The breaking of one or more of the ground rules implies a different mode of adaptation with immediate discharge, action and riddance, and the like. These principles apply to both patient and therapist.

Providing a model. The therapist's creation and adherence to the ground rules of psychotherapy implicitly offers a basic model for adaptation, healthy functioning, and for the modification of emotional disturbance through understanding and insight. Similarly, the therapist's management of these ground rules reflects an inner capacity to manage his or her own mental disturbance as well as that of the patient, including pressures from within or without to adapt through deviation rather than understanding.

Boundaries. These rules define appropriate boundaries of the therapeutic relationship and the appropriate functions and roles of each participant.

Gratification. These rules specifically identify the nature of the gratifications and renunciations appropriate to the therapeutic experience.

Holding and containing. The rules are the basis for the patient's experience of the therapist's capacity to hold and contain himself or herself, inner mental content, and its expression. Similarly, they define a basis for the relatively smaller measure of holding and containing that accrues to the therapist from the patient under these conditions.

The expression of Neurosis. These rules are essential for the optimal meaningful expression of the patient's Neurosis and for its analysis. This includes the expression of anxiety-provoking, conscious and unconscious perceptions and fantasy-memory constellations, whatever their nature.

Alliance. The ground rules are fundamental to the alliance sector of the relationship between the patient and therapist, both in terms of manifest and surface cooperation, as well as latent cooperation—the communicative alliance.

Ego capacities. A clear delineation of the ground rules is essential as a means of supporting the patient's ego capacities. This includes the ability to maintain self-object differentiation, reality testing, nonpathological defenses, abilities directed toward understanding, and a capacity for synthesis and integration. Clear-cut boundaries of relatedness as defined by these ground rules support the healthy aspects of each of these capacities. In contrast, then, each deviation undermines these basic functions to some degree.

Pathological thrusts. The ground rules are the basis for a maximally noninstinctualized therapeutic relationship and environment, thereby providing a neutral space for the patient's own pathological thrusts. Deviations consistently express and gratify the pathological sexual and aggressive needs of those who participate in them. Similarly, the ground rules provide a basis for non-pathological superego and ego ideal functioning and expressions. Adherence to the ground rules also supports a relatively healthy self-image and sense of self. Deviations are disruptive in all of these spheres.

Interpersonal spheres. The ground rules enable the participants to maintain a proper measure of interpersonal boundaries with reasonable and healthy opportunities for empathy, intuition, and trial identifications. They also provide the participants to treatment with a proper sense of interpersonal distance—neither too close nor too far.

Autonomy. The secured ground rules are the only set of conditions under which true growth, separation and individuation, and relative autonomy can be accomplished. They are basically ego-enhancing and ego-strengthening, thereby providing an implicit means of support to both patient and therapist for the arduous task of pursuing insight and understanding. They are therefore the set of conditions under which the painful and anxiety-provoking task of insight psychotherapy can best unfold.

Relatedness. Ground rules establish a mode of relatedness and a therapeutic space in which the patient may express himself or herself as openly and freely as possible. Similarly, they provide the conditions under which the therapist may respond with appropriate interpretations and framework-management responses, and with silences. They offer the conditions within which it is most likely that the patient will experience a consistent set of implications to all of the therapist's interventions. Under these conditions, there is essentially no contradiction between the core, background mode of relatedness and the foreground of the therapist's active therapeutic efforts. The patient is most likely to comprehend and work through the intended insightful meanings and functions of his or her interventions.

Truth therapy. The ground rules are therefore the sole means through which the conditions for truth therapy, rather than lie therapy, can be effected. It is under these conditions that the patient will risk the necessary therapeutic regression needed for insight therapy, and tolerate dealing with the painful intrapsychic and interpersonal truths that underlie his or her emotional disturbance. These tenets also provide the therapist with inherent support and a foundation from which to pursue and analyze these truths, no matter how painful to the therapist or the patient—though always, of course, with suitable tact and timing.

The multiplicity of critical functions and meanings inherent to a sound and secure therapeutic environment attest to the over-ridingly critical nature and importance of the therapeutic contract. A secure frame offers the patient a wide assortment of inherently supportive and ego-enhancing qualities, and many other positive and constructive features. Nonetheless, since they constitute the rules for truth therapy, they are also a set of conditions that can evoke considerable threat and anxiety (see Chapter 18).

Clinical observation indicates that both patients and therapists contain with themselves major needs for deviation and pathological gratification-defense. A considerable measure of renunciation is required of both in order to effect and maintain a secure therapeutic setting and relationship. The natural thrust is toward immediate relief and satisfaction, and the detour necessary for mastery through understanding does not appear to be inherently attractive to either participant. Thus, despite all of the strongly positive qualities in the ideal therapeutic environment, there are powerful needs within patients and therapists for breaks in the frame and deviations.

Clinical evidence indicates that for both participants the absence of a pathological mode of relatedness and of the action-discharge form of relief has highly threatening qualities. Then too there are the dangers of experiencing the unconscious fantasies and perceptions that unfold under these conditions, as well as inherent fears of separation, individuation, and growth. Truth therapy requires both a core mode of relatedness and sound foreground inteventions. Lie therapy is effected with any flaw in the ground rules and core mode of relatedness, though more rarely it may be expressed in the face of a secure framework through erroneous verbal interventions. In general, a therapist who is capable of establishing and maintaining the ideal therapeutic environment proves capable of sound interpretative-reconstructive interventions. On the other hand, therapists who deviate tend to do so repeatedly, to lean toward noninterpretive interventions, and to make frequent interpretive-reconstructive errors.

CLINICAL EXAMPLES

Given the complexities of the implications of both securing and deviating from the ideal set of ground rules, the material presented here is solely for general introductory purposes.

An example from Chapter 15 involved a therapist who was attempting to secure the frame by no longer signing insurance forms at the behest of the patient's derivative material. The reader may recall that the patient responded by taking one of the therapist's tissues and keeping it. She stated she didn't give a damn about the therapy and that she used her boyfriend as an insurance policy. She also described terminating a relationship with a young man because she now had a steady boyfriend. She was tired of having two boyfriends and of being unfaithful to one of them all of the time. The jilted young man was furious, but he understood. The patient described being able to tolerate not hearing from her regular boyfriend for one day. Then, she expressed her fury with the therapist, and asked for an explanation of his not signing the insurance form. The patient had dreamt of someone being tortured—herself or someone else.

In this session, the adaptive context is a therapist's effort to rectify a framework damaged by modifications in the patient's privacy and sense of total confidentiality, and in the therapist's anonymity—on the insurance form it was necessary for him to state a diagnosis and other clinical opinions. The patient represents this deviation manifestly toward the latter part of the session. Early in the session, she represented it in disguise through the derivative behavior of taking one of the therapist's tissues and keeping it. This particular expression contains an unconscious perception of some of the qualities of the particular deviation at hand: it is a means by which the patient is able to incorporate something from the therapist and keep it within herself. This alludes apparently, first, to the therapist giving the completed insurance form to the patient and, second, to the insurance company then paying for 50 percent of this patient's therapy. Since the payments were made directly to the therapist, the same derivative involves a pathological incorporative gratification for the therapist under these conditions—the direct receipt of money from a third party.

In the face of an acute deviation in the frame, or efforts by the therapist to rectify a break of this kind, patients characteristically respond with very powerful manifest and derivative material. Typically, there is a deep and powerful split, one that reflects the patient's divided approach to therapy: on the one hand, wanting a secure frame and the conditions for truth therapy and all that it implies; while on the other, hoping to maintain a deviant frame and a form of lie therapy and to obtain immediate relief without insight. In general, the patient expresses the wish for a deviation on a conscious level, and appreciation for the therapist's participation. The patient objects directly to frustrating efforts to rectify the frame, and sometimes will oppose basically secure conditions to treatment. However, virtually without exception, the patient shows an extensive appreciation and wish for an ideal therapeutic environment on a derivative level, and on that level stands opposed to, and critical of, deviations.

Thus, in the present session, the patient manifestly expresses her anger at the therapist for indicating that he might no longer sign her insurance form. However, she then proceeds derivatively to characterize the signing of the insurance form as a form of action-discharge, a way of establishing a pathological sense of merger, and a type of uninsightful action-discharge cure—all of this in her taking and keeping one of the therapist's tissues. Through further derivatives, she indicates that behaviors of this kind reflect not giving a damn about therapy and an assault on the other person, both sexual and aggressive (cf., the patient's comment, "Fuck you").

Next the patient offers a compelling derivative model of rectification, one that reflects her appreciation for the therapist's framework-securing intervention. She describes having arranged to have a single boyfriend in order not to be unfaithful to one of them all the time. In this way, she portrays the need to be rid of the third party to treatment, while implying as well that the presence of the insurance payer had highly seductive overtones, and that it constituted a means by which the therapist betrayed the patient (and the patient betrayed the therapist). The patient's comment that the jilted young man was furious but understood is a derivative representation of her own rage and sense of understanding in response to the therapist's intervention. It also indicates that efforts directed toward understanding were initiated by the rectification of this deviation. Additional positive consequences are seen when the patient then describes being able to tolerate some small measure of separation from her boyfriend for the first time in their relationship. The manner in which a secure frame precludes pathological merger and implicitly speaks toward healthy symbiosis with appropriate distance is also reflected in this particular encoded communication.

Finally, the patient expresses her sense of danger under conditions in which the pathological symbiotic and parasitic qualities of the basic mode of therapeutic relatedness have been renounced. Her sense of separateness, her willingness to allow the build-up of tension and delay, her renunciation of pathological defenses and gratifications, and the anticipation of the emergence of derivative but truthful expressions of her emotional disturbance in the form of both unconscious perceptions of the therapist and unconscious fantasy-memory constellations all lead her to anticipate feelings of persecution (torture). However, the same derivative indicates the manner in which the signing of the insurance form is unconsciously destructive to both participants to therapy. As can be seen, there is danger for the patient under the conditions of a secure frame or a deviant one, though in the former situation there is an additional sense of security and safety that is lacking under deviant conditions. The intensity of this patient's reaction to the therapist's rectification of the frame is due in part to the initial contract for a basically flawed therapeutic environment and all of its implications in respect to relatedness, cure, and more.

Another patient, a male interior decorator in his late 20s, had been seen in consultation for chronic alcoholism. In arranging for treatment, the therapist (a woman) had reduced her fee in order to permit the patient to come on a three-times weekly basis. The patient made use of the couch. The following excerpt is from the second session:

> Patient: Shall I take my shoes off? *(Pause.)* I want to be fair. I know that you reduced your fee, and I want to pay you your proper fee once I take on some new clients. I know your time is valuable, and I'll pay you weekly. *(The patient falls silent.)*
> Therapist: Say whatever comes to mind.
> Patient: I've been thinking about this journey, therapy, and about sharing what I feel with you. It's very exciting. I'm

going to expose myself more than I ever have in my life, and
I'm very stimulated by it. Will you be asking me questions?

Therapist: Saying whatever comes to mind is often difficult at
the beginning of a therapy.

Patient: I don't understand how this works. It's like trying to
know the scenerio of a book I never read. I guess I'm
supposed to probe into my childhood.

The patient went on to ruminate in great detail about therapy,
the therapeutic process, his great excitement about being in treatment, his trust of the therapist, and his determination to give up the
use of alcohol when he experiences what he called his bizarre
moments and becomes restless. He spoke of taking a long nap in the
afternoon before the session, and wondered if the therapist wasn't
tired, since he was being seen late in the evening. At that point, the
therapist spoke.

Therapist: You seem to be expressing some doubts about your
therapy. You think that I may be tired, and you're expecting
to be asked about your childhood, and you have made note of
the fact that I have not done so.

Patient: I'm not aware of any criticism. On the contrary, I feel
that I can open up to you. I trust you and really like you. I
met this priest and got around to telling him I was entering
treatment. He asked me if you were an alcoholic. I said it
didn't matter to me. The woman who referred me to you said
that you dealt a lot with alcoholics, so I thought maybe you
are one, and that you would be more sensitive to my problem.

Therapist: I don't answer personal questions.

Patient: I feel like laughing at myself. Now I'm becoming
mentally constipated and feel myself in a state of limbo. Like
I only probe on the surface.

From here, the patient went on to describe how he had read
about the participation of multiple family members in the problems
of a given individual in the family. He spoke too of feeling blocked
and turned off, and of brief therapeutic experiences he had had with
a variety of therapists who attempted a wide range of therapeutic
procedures, each of which ended in disillusionment.

In the following session, the patient reported having fantasies of sleeping with the therapist. He described how important sexual contact was for him, though he added that he is not turned on by prostitutes. He then described his idealization of a number of creative individuals who are alcoholic, and added that he didn't care if he ended up killing himself with alcohol, or if they did so—being like them was quite aggrandizing.

This material illustrates some of the consequences of a basic flaw in the therapeutic contract—i.e., in the therapist's creation of the therapeutic hold and setting. The therapist elected to reduce her fee, rather than see the patient twice weekly at her usual and stated rate. This particular intervention context implied a seductive attitude toward the patient, a sense of indulgence, and an effort to effect a basically pathological symbiosis. In consequence, the patient was likely to be mistrustful of the therapist and fear open communication. These initial silent hypotheses are supported by the patient's utilization of the Type C style of communication at the beginning of the session. While other factors undoubtedly contributed, it is not uncommon for the patient to withdraw emotionally and communicatively in the face of a seductive deviation in the ideal therapeutic environment. In this instance, the patient manifestly represented the critical adaptive context at the beginning of the hour, but then offered a highly fragmented and thin derivative complex. The Type C style is represented in the patient's reference to napping and in his wish to have the therapist ask him questions.

The therapist's main intervention in this session, an attempt to identify doubts within the patient regarding therapy, is met with initial negation and subsequent Type Two derivative nonvalidation. Among the many unconscious communications expressed in this intervention is a sense within the therapist that she wishes to avoid the intervention context of the reduced fee. On this basis, it would seem that the patient then responded with a meaningful derivative complex that can be readily organized around the deviation in question. In essence, he indicated to the therapist that his conscious positive and idealizing feelings toward her were based on an unconscious sense of pathological symbiosis and merger, which were something like a religious contact. The fee arrangement also formed the basis for an unconscious belief within the patient that the therapist and he were alike in a significant pathological way: the patient through his use of alcohol, the therapist through her need to see the patient more frequently than would be reasonable with her regular fee. In each instance, there is an incorporative, seductive, pathological usage of the object or person. When the therapist modifies the basic ground rules and boundaries of therapy, this impression is always justified on some unconscious level: the patient and therapist are alike in important pathological ways (here, they are both alcoholics). The basic conditions of therapy, then, support the patient's pathological mode of adaptation and the essence of his Neurosis. With this established, verbal efforts at interpretation designed manifestly to help the patient renounce and resolve his use of alcohol would be contradicted by the therapist's communications as conveyed in the establishment of the therapeutic contract. In this way, the therapist's background expressions would undermine all foreground efforts directed toward the insightful resolution of this particular symptom.

Rather than understanding the patient's derivative communications in light of the intervention context of the reduced fee, the therapist interrupted the patient's flow of associations with the gratuitous comment that she would not be answering personal questions. On an unconscious level, this reflects not only a wish to put the patient off in respect to the question of her own "alcoholic" tendencies, but also a failure on the part of the therapist to understand and wish to hear more in the way of derivative communications regarding the fee issue. As a consequence, the patient responded with a series of vignettes pertaining to his unconscious perception of the therapist as wishing him to remain in a state of limbo and on the surface. The allusion to how family members share problems with one another is a further derivative expression of the underlying collusion. The patient and therapist have effected an idealizing misalliance as a way of gaining reassurance and taking flight from the inner basis of his (and the therapist's) Neurotic difficulties.

In the next session, the patient reported a fantasy of sleeping with the therapist. This transversal communication is based in part on a valid unconscious perception of the seductive qualities of the reduced fee arrangement. The patient then likened this arrangement to prostitution and commented upon the destructive aspects of this type of self-indulgence. Toward the end of this hour, the patient strongly indicated that he felt he should be able to handle his problems in some different manner—here offering to the therapist a model of rectification. He also spoke of the lies and deceptions used by alcoholics, and expressed a wish on his part to face the truth about himself. In this way, the patient was characterizing the lie-therapy qualities of the treatment situation that is constituted with a basic flaw in the therapeutic environment. The excerpts show how deviations made by the therapist are experienced as forms of action that tend to support a framework-alteration mode of adaptation (cf. the patient's question regarding taking his shoes off). The material indicates that deviations in the frame are unfair and need correction (cf. the allusion to the patient's wanting to pay a proper fee). Alterations in the framework support manifest forms of idealization of the therapist and seemingly cooperative work, though on a communicative level there is a disturbance in the alliance sector and negative images. Supposed conscious trust is accompanied by unconscious mistrust.

A therapist who deviates is perceived by the patient as having significant psychopathology and, in some way, sharing the patient's Neurosis. Deviations represent pathological interventions that in some manner also repeat past pathogenic interactions with early important figures of a type that helped to develop the patient's initial emotional disturbance. In several ways, deviations always provide the patient with support for his or her current maladaptation.

Deviations involve both pathological projective identifications and the offer by the therapist of Type C barriers to the patient. In the vignette discussed earlier in this chapter, the former was notable; while in the present case it is the latter that is most prominent. Deviations help to create a state of communicative limbo, and foster manifest content explorations and relatedness. Deviations promote a pathological mode of relatedness, ranging from an actual parasitisim of the patient by the therapist (or of the therapist by the patient; here the latter is in evidence) to forms of pathological symbiosis in which either participant to treatment is the symbiotic donor. Instead of a healthy mode of relatedness, there is the exploitation and pathology inherent to prostitution. Ultimately, as reflected in the patient's allusion to possibly ending up by killing himself, deviations are highly destructive to the treatment process, and to the patient and therapist alike.

Principles of Listening-Formulating vis-à-vis the Ground Rules

The state of the frame is the single most important and basic level of listening and formulating for the therapist. Thus the therapist's first job is to examine the status of the ground rules and boundaries of therapy and to determine whether he or she has in any way deviated from the ideal frame. Then the therapist must determine whether the patient has unilaterally or with the therapist created deviations.

If the frame is secure, the background adaptive contexts for this level of listening and formulating involve the therapist's creation and maintenance of the ideal ground rules and boundaries for the treatment experience. If there is an alteration in the ground rules, the deviation becomes a major adaptation-evoking context for listening to and understanding the patient's material. In principle, breaks in the frame take precedence over efforts to secure the ground rules. Long-standing and chronic deviations are background adaptive contexts that come to the foreground from time to time. Acute breaks in the frame are immediate intervention contexts to which patients tend to respond with powerful manifest and derivative reactions. They are therefore first-order organizers of the patient's material.

The patient's reactions to the secure or ideal framework tend to be polarized at the beginning of treatment, at times when the therapist rectifies a deviation, and at those moments when the patient attempts a unilateral break in the frame to which the therapist responds by maintaining the frame and interpreting the interlude in light of prior intervention contexts—doing so, of course, in terms of the patient's manifest and especially derivative associations.

While a deviation that the therapist initiates or participates in is always a major intervention context, unilateral breaks in the frame by the patient are *therapeutic* rather than adaptive contexts— i.e., are indicators of disturbance rather than adaptation-evoking stimuli for the patient. They are prompted by previous intervention contexts from the therapist, quite often in the form of the therapist's maintenance of, or deviation in, the ideal therapeutic environment. A unilateral break in the frame on the part of the patient is the single most common form of gross behavioral resistance seen in treatment (see Chapter 33). As such, they are highly important indicators for intervening.

When the therapist establishes and maintains the framework, the intervention context includes all unconscious implications of these efforts (see Chapter 18). On the other hand, when the therapist deviates, the intervention context includes all of the unconscious implications (meanings and functions) of the particular break in the frame. These tend to fall into three categories: (1) the universal meanings of all framework deviations; (2) the specific implications of the particular ground rule that has been modified; (3) the personal dynamic and genetic meanings that the deviation has for the patient, and secondarily for the therapist as communicated directly and indirectly to the patient.

In the presence of a break in the frame, all other levels of listening and formulating become secondary, and must be carried out in addition to an understanding of the patient's responses to the framework-deviation intevention context at hand. In formulating a patient's material in response to a deviation by the therapist, the latter makes use of the usual rules of the listening-formulating process. The therapist must first subjectively recognize the presence of the deviant adaptive context, and then identify the best representation of that context in the patient's associations. Next, the patient's manifest and latent responses must be examined, especially as they constitute a derivative complex in reaction to the intervention context. The latent and encoded implications of the patient's associations must be formulated in terms of valid unconscious perceptions of the meanings and implications of the deviation, and of the therapist, in light of the frame break. Under these conditions, all but a small portion of the therapist's formulation of the patient's derivative material will fall into this sphere of the patient's valid unconscious readings of the implications of the deviation. In addition, some small measure of listening should be devoted to the presence of any possible distortions, and for extensions by the patient of nontransference perceptions into distortion and fantasy-memory constellations. The therapist must also note the manner in which the patient reacts and adapts to the unconsciously perceived implications of a deviation, separating those with pathological implications from those that are essentially nonpathological.

An important part of the derivative complex in response to a therapist's break in the frame is the representation by the patient in encoded form of *models of rectification*—the need for and ways in which the framework break should be corrected. The therapist's eventual efforts at framework management and interpretation will follow the lead of the patient's derivative responses, which place into the therapist all that he or she needs for intervening.

As noted, there will be a split within the patient in response to the therapist's deviations. On the surface, there is usually acceptance and sometimes appreciation, while on a derivative level, there is nonacceptance, criticism, and efforts at rectification. Similarly, in the presence of a secure frame, there may be surface protests and their specific meanings and functions.

therapist to maintain Type Two derivative listening in the context of all breaks in the frame.

The state of the frame is essential to the maturational mode of relatedness established between the patient and therapist. Because of this, representations in the patient's material of modes of relatedness tend to convey important implications in regard to the status of the ground rules and boundaries of treatment. The consciously and unconsciously determined decision by a patient or therapist to work within the agreed upon boundaries and conditions of the therapeutic relationship, or to deviate, is a fundamental adaptive decision. This decision takes precedence over all dynamic and genetic implications of the behaviors involved, and actually affords these latter their specific meanings and functions.

In general, breaks in the frame reflect the countertransferences of the therapist and evoke primarily nontransference responses in the patient. Properly establishing and maintaining the frame tends to reflect the healthy functioning of the therapist and to evoke primarily transference-based reactions in the patient (see Part IV). Thus the formulation of a patient's conscious and derivative responses to the secure or broken framework must include careful evaluation of the degree to which the responses are appropriate and valid in light of the unconscious implications of the prevailing framework-intervention context at hand.

The state of the therapeutic environment and of the therapist's management of the ground rules and boundaries of treatment are of such high importance to the patient that he or she will respond with exquisite sensitivity to the least deviation in any of the ground rules. These intervention contexts tend to mobilize powerful derivative reactions and, on occasion, strong manifest responses as well. With a striking degree of consistency, then, patients respond in meaningful fashion to breaks in the frame, whatever the nature of their basic style of communication. These issues therefore provide the therapist with prime opportunities for listening and formulating, and for intervening.

Paradoxically, while the therapist's framework deviations tend to reflect his or her own propensities toward the Type B and Type C modes of communication, they elicit a mixture of communicative responses in the patient with qualities of all three types of expression—A, B, and C. Thus the patient may for a period of time join the therapist in an unconscious misalliance and utilize a mixture of the Type B and Type C modes. Nonetheless, on occasion, when the patient unconsciously wishes to understand the situation and to rectify the frame, highly meaningful Type A expressions will occur, though these will organize meaningfully only around the deviant intervention context.

Overall, whatever damage is done to the patient and to the treatment experience because of a deviation by the therapist, much can be repaired if the therapist engages subsequently in sound efforts at listening and formulating, and efforts at rectification and interpretation. The difficult subject of unrectifiable, and to some extent permanently damaging, deviations is discussed in Chapter 21.

Chapter 18

The Secure and Deviant Therapeutic Contracts

Qualitatively, all deviations share a great deal in common. As a rule, the therapist has no choice but to be committed to either maintaining or breaking the frame. In all but a few instances, decisions regarding a particular ground rule involve some type of all-or-none situation. The therapist either adheres to a particular tenet or deviates. The frame is either entirely secure or broken. By and large, it is the extent of the damage and the blatancy of the break that is the quantitative factor.

For example, the fee for therapy is either fixed or modified (reduced or increased); responsibility for a particular hour is either maintained or altered; and total confidentiality is either present or absent. With some ground rules, such as the therapist's neutrality, there is some measure of gradation. However, the continuum here is such that there is a point up to which the patient experiences an intervention as essentially neutral, correct, and based on his or her material and therapeutic needs. Beyond this line, an intervention is unconsciously, and more rarely consciously, experienced as distinctly erroneous and as containing significant inappropriate inputs from the therapist.

Overall, then, one may speak of the maintenance or alteration of each of the individual ground rules described in Chapter 17; however, one may also address the totality of the frame or of the therapist's holding and containing capacities as reflected in his or her handling of the ground rules and boundaries of treatment. The therapeutic contract and its maintenance functions as an entity in itself, with meanings and implications that derive from, and yet exist beyond, the specific functions of each individual ground rule. Because of this, one may talk of the issue of whether the framework or core holding relationship is secure and intact or broken and deviant. Although lesser breaks and minor infractions have a smaller total impact than blatant and major deviations, the presence of any small measure of alteration in the ground rules of treatment has extensive and significant influence on both the patient and therapist. A break in the frame detrimentally influences the basic maturational mode of relatedness adopted by the patient and therapist, the predominant mode of cure active in the treatment situation, the manner of communication adopted by both patient and therapist, the activated dynamics within both participants, the extent to which the patient is working over unconscious fantasies as compared to unconscious perceptions, and the fundamental nature of the relationship between the two participants to treatment.

In this light, then, therapists tend to be polarized into two groups in respect to the type of ground rules and boundaries that they offer to their patients. In the first camp are those who adhere to all of the fundamental tenets described in the previous chapter, and who offer their patient the ideal therapeutic relationship and setting. In the second camp are therapists who modify one or another of the basic ground rules, and therefore create a treatment setting that is basically deviant. In general, the therapists who belong to this second group tend to engage in a relatively loose type of management of the ground rules, and to deviate in one sphere or another depending on their own needs and the requests of their patients. There is a laxity to their approach to the framework, and virtually always a failure to engage in Type Two derivative listening in response to deviant intervention contexts. On a cognitive level, it is this particular failure in derivative listening that has led therapists for so long to maintain such a basically loose and inappropriate attitude toward the framework of the treatment experience.

These two camps constitute the extremes of the therapeutic continuum. Each arrangement offers something seemingly helpful to the two participants of treatment, though with distinctly different qualities. Each reflects motivational systems relevant to the wish for cure or relief, though the nature of the motives and the actual mode of cure are quite different. Each basic contract also, in addition to its manifestly positive attributes, creates anxieties and threat for both patient and therapist, though again these tend to be distinctive for the two contracts. Finally, each contract creates a set of conditions for a rather different type of therapeutic unfolding, and therefore requires somewhat different interventions, and tend as well to lead to rather different outcomes.

The Secure Contract and Frame

A therapist who offers the ideal therapeutic relationship and setting creates an optimal opportunity for cure through validated insight (truth therapy).

An offer of a sound hold and containment for the patient implies a setting and relationship under which the patient is able to trust the therapist and to experience an inherent sense of safety and protection. The secure frame offers the patient the safest and most open conditions for free and unencumbered communication. It is the basis for a relatively noninstinctualized image of the therapist as someone capable of maintaining proper instinctual drive and impulse control, and as having a healthy superego and ego, including essentially nonpathological defenses. It therefore implies a capacity in the therapist to control his or her countertransferences and to create the conditions and mode of relatedness best suited for the patient's therapeutic needs.

A sound frame also implies the opportunity to resolve the patient's symptoms through insight and understanding, rather than through a mode of cure designed for action-discharge, immediate relief, and pathological gratification and defense. It implies the presence of a therapist who can adequately manage inner and outer conflicts and tensions, fantasies, and perceptions, in order to maintain a core relationship and set of conditions under which the patient may safely and meaningfully communicate the manifest and derivative material through which his or her Neurosis may be insightfully resolved. Thus this type of contract implies a pursuit of symptom alleviation through verbal-affective communication and within the confines of the accepted ground rules and boundaries of treatment. It involves the renunciation of cure or relief through framework breaks and deviations, and in this way further emphasizes the therapist's commitment to understanding and truth therapy.

The therapist's ability to secure and maintain a sound therapeutic environment and relationship is based on a capacity to tolerate painful insights and to deal interpretively with the patient's communicated unconscious perceptions and fantasies, whatever their nature. It reflects the therapist's commitment to cure through understanding rather than action-discharge. It also provides a basis of core background communications that will in no way contradict the therapist's more active, foreground interpretive efforts. The secure frame therefore creates a set of conditions under which the patient will experience inevitable, unconscious, constructively positive introjective identifications with the therapist based on a capability for maintaining the frame and adopting a consistent therapeutic approach. Within the secure frame, the therapist's interpretations will convey their intended meanings without underlying contradiction, and they will be openly received and properly worked through by the patient.

The secure frame is the only means through which a healthy therapeutic symbiosis can be effected between the patient and therapist. It is also the specific set of conditions under which psychotherapy unfolds primarily in terms of the adaptive context of the therapist's capacity to establish and maintain a secure therapeutic environment. It is, of course, solely under these conditions that the implications of the patient's derivative material tend to mainly involve unconscious distortions and transferences, rather than unconscious perceptions and nontransferences. It is this mode of therapy, then, in which the analytic understanding and resolution of unconscious transference-based memory and fantasy constellations actually takes place. It is here, too, that genetic factors tend to account for *distortions* of the patient's perceptions of the therapist rather than constituting indications of actual pathological repetitions by the therapist of disruptive interactions from the patient's early childhood. Nonetheless, all such analyses of transference components are carried out in light of immediate intervention contexts related to the therapist's securing of the frame. In order to understand the threatening implications of the secure contract, and to have a perspective on the patient's transference-based fantasies and memories as evoked by this type of therapeutic environment, one must understand the threatening and dangerous qualities of this particular contract for both the patient and therapist (see below).

The secure frame is distinctly ego-enhancing for the patient. It provides a clear set of conditions that support the patient's capacity for mature object relatedness and reality testing, as well as reinforcing the healthy aspects of the patient's functioning in regard to instinctual drives, superego expressions, and defensive formations. In a sense, then, it is this type of frame that provides the inherent strength to the patient needed to risk the anxiety and disturbance involved in expressing the critical derivatives that pertain to his or her Neurosis and in generating meaningful networks of communication for interpretation by the therapist.

Finally, the secure frame offers the *therapist* the best possible conditions and mode of relatedness for therapeutic endeavors. It provides clear boundaries, with an inherent sense of hold and containment from the patient (however secondary), with a safeguard against an instinctualization of the therapeutic relationship and consequent acting in or out, and support for optimal and healthy functioning in regard to the management of instinctual drives, superego expression, and ego functions, including defenses. The therapist's capacities for reality testing, managing the frame, and interpreting to the patient find support in the safety of the conditions of treatment as effected in the defined ground rules. By offering the patient an optimal hold, the secure frame creates conditions under which patients are most likely to inherently hold and cooperate with the therapist. Because of this, the secure contract creates the most likely conditions for a sound manifest and communicative therapeutic alliance between patient and therapist.

THE THREATENING ASPECTS OF THE SECURE CONTRACT

Major sources of danger and anxiety accompany the secure therapeutic contract.

The optimal set of ground rules and boundaries creates a holding relationship that limits the patient's maladaptive options, significantly lessening the opportunity for flight, denial, and defensiveness. The patient experiences a sense of relative immobility and of entrapment. There is a strong claustrophobic quality to the resultant anxieties and fantasies, which also have distinct depressive, paranoid and persecutory overtones.

The ideal ground rules and boundaries of therapy tend to preclude pathological symbiosis and merger between the patient and therapist, and parasiticism and pathological autistic modes of relatedness. Patients whose survival has relied upon these types of pathological forms of relatedness are terrified by their absence. The lack of pathological gratifications and unconscious collusion create fears of annihilation and highly persecutory anxieties. Patients tend to believe that, in the absence of a basically pathological mode of relatedness, they will be unable to function or continue to exist.

The secure ground rules and framework of treatment create a type of relationship with the therapist and a treatment setting that fails to support the patient's pathological mode of adaptation and fails to reinforce the pathological introjects that populate the patient's inner mental world. As such, they place the patient under considerable pressure to experience his or her own psychopathology and maladjustment, and to express internal disturbance and its basis, directly and through derivatives. The positive introjective identification with the therapist that derives from sound management of the framework significantly alters the patient's inner mental equilibrium. It especially modifies the denial defenses that the patient tends to erect against realizations related to needed destructive objects and introjects. The internalization of a good object highlights the negative qualities of internalized bad objects and creates considerable conflict and turmoil for the patient.

Realizations of the therapist's capacity to manage the framework, and to adaptively handle inner and outer tension, conflict, and sources of anxiety, create a strong sense of envy in patients who are relatively unable to carry out these functions. This envy is both the cause of considerable anxiety and a basis upon which the patient attempts to attack and destroy these capabilities within the therapist. Paradoxically, then, the therapist's sound functioning can lead to highly destructive reactions within the patient. Similar attacks on the therapist and treatment situation arise because of the patient's rage over the lack of pathological gratification and the lack of pathological superego sanctions. Similarly, the therapist's capabilities in this regard create not only a strong and helpful image, but a fearful one as well. The therapist is viewed as highly powerful, and therefore as dangerous. Further, since the secure frame tends to create the conditions under which the patient will experience transference-based distortions, there will be additional sources of anxiety based on these genetically determined, threatening images of the realistically helpful therapist. In this regard, it is

330 / Psychotherapy: A Basic Text

well to recognize that there is always a kernel of truth in these transference-based, primarily distorted images. For the patient, based on his or her pathology and vulnerability, the secure frame does indeed pose many forms of actual threat—even though at the same time it offers the best possible conditions for truth therapy.

Another source of anxiety arises from the patient's reactions to forbidden and pathological wishes directed toward the well-functioning therapist. These may be envious and hostile, as noted above, but may also be highly erotic as well. They are the source of considerable guilt and disturbance for the patient, and a factor in many transference-based manifest and communicative resistances.

Virtually all patients who enter therapy suffer from superego pathology, which leads to the search for masochistic gratifications. In the absence of a small or large measure of punishment as conveyed through deviations in the ideal frame (and therefore in the presence of a sound and healthy holding environment), these patients experience a sense of disequilibrium and conflict. Paradoxically they feel persecuted by the absence of actual sadistic and persecutory framework-breaking behaviors by the therapist. They fear internal devastation in the absence of some continual measure of punishment and harm from the therapist.

The therapist who is capable of offering a secure hold and mode of relatedness to the patient offers a strong promise of sound symptom alleviation. Such hope typically generates fears of ultimate disappointment and betrayal. The therapist who is consciously and unconsciously perceived as good and strong by the patient is feared as someone who will turn into a bad figure sooner or later.

The security of the therapeutic environment and hold leads the patient to modify pathological defenses and to expose direct and derivative inner fantasies, conflicts, perceptions, and introjects—all in the hope of fulfilling the promise of achieving new and adaptive means of symptom resolution. The exposure of such material on direct and derivative levels is the cause of considerable, though usually temporary, anxiety, conflict, guilt, and resistance. The secure therapeutic environment creates conditions under which the truth of the patient's Neurosis will find expression in terms of both unconscious perceptions and fantasies. These truths, while necessary for growth and mastery, are inherently dangerous and threatening—which touches on the motives for their initial repression or denial in the course of symptom formation. The possibility of their exposure is a source of considerable pressure for the patient. In general, while patients unconsciously recognize that it is only the truth therapist who can provide them with new and lasting modes of adaptation, such a therapist is nonetheless experienced as dangerous and persecutory because of the pain involved in working with truth and meaning as it pertains to Neuroses.

THREATS TO THE THERAPIST IN THE SECURE CONTRACT

The secure frame offers a strong hold for the therapist as well as the patient. The patient's adherence to the ground rules and boundaries of treatment provides the therapist with an ideal working environment. However, the therapist too experiences a variety of anxieties and conflicts in response to the ideal therapeutic setting and relationship. These difficulties and dangers—and they are quite intense and prevelant—prompt many therapists to deviate as a pathological means of resolving their own inner disturbances.

The sources of anxieties and conflict for the therapist include: (1) the renunciation of pathological symbiotic and merger needs, of parasiticisms of the patient, and of the autistic mode of relatedness; (2) a fear of entrapment by the patient with resultant phobic and paranoid anxieties and fantasies; (3) destructive envy of the patient capable of accepting and maintaining the secure frame, and sometimes, through an internal split, an envy by one part of the therapist of the capabilities of another part of his or her personality; (4) fears of annihilation based on the absence of pathological gratification and merger where they have been a major (often unconscious) source of sustenance for the therapist; (5) fears of hostile and erotic wishes directed toward the well-functioning patient who is capable of accepting the ideal framework (if the therapist identifies with the pathological aspects of the patient, he or she may also develop fears of losing the patient because of the absence of a pathological mode of relatedness and some form of lie-barrier therapy); (6) responses to meaningful and truthful expressions of the patient's Neurosis, especially those that involve highly threatening valid unconscious perceptions of the therapist's own disturbances; (7) a dread of truth therapy, based in part on a preference for immediate discharge and the use of lie-barrier systems; and (8) a fear of the regression (usually limited, though sometimes extensive) that takes place in the therapist within the secure frame, including the mobilization of pathological defenses and needs.

Thus both patient and therapist tend to share a variety of anxieties, fears, conflicts, fantasies, and disturbances in respect to the secure frame. Because of this, both will tend to move toward deviations from time to time in the course of any psychotherapy. The therapist can be alert to such tendencies, manage them personally without enactment, and subject them to self-interpretation in light of adaptation-evoking contexts from the patient involved and from other sources. Verbalized tendencies and wishes on the part of the patient in this direction can be subjected to interpretation in light of activated intervention contexts. Similarly, actual unilateral deviations by the patient become important forms of resistance and indicators, and are subjected to rectification and interpretation in light of prior adaptation-evoking contexts and the patient's derivative material.

The therapist must have the means, through his or her own psychotherapy of self-analysis, of modifying his or her own pathological tendencies to establish and accept the appropriate ground rules and boundaries for therapy. On the other hand, because attitudes and behaviors regarding the frame are a basic means through which patients express their psychopathology, most patients will show some measure of intolerance for an ideal therapeutic environment. A crucial question arises as to whether these patients are prepared to express this intolerance through meaningful derivative associations and behaviors, and then to subject these expressions to analytic efforts geared toward rectification and understanding. Some patients are refractory to such endeavors directed toward insight; they insist upon framework-deviation cures, utilize breaks in the frame as means of riddance and pathological projective identification (the Type B-C communicative mode), and are refractory to the meaningful exploration of these pathological efforts. They insist upon a pathological mode of relatedness with the therapist, and will not accept conditions of treatment geared toward a healthy symbiosis and the pursuit of truth.

Some therapists have attempted to offer a compromised therapeutic contract with patients who appear to be of this kind. The results of such experiments have not been fruitful. The deviations tend to fix the expectations and efforts of these patients in the direction of pathological modes of relatedness and deviant modes of cure (maladaptations). Only rarely will they accept subsequent rectification of the frame and shift toward meaningful and insightful therapeutic work; instead, they insist on a continuation of the deviant arrangement. The factors that determine the presence of such attitudes in patients are presented in detail in Part VI.

Not all patients will subject these endeavors to achieve framework-deviation cures to analytic exploration. For those who do so, the interpretation and rectification of breaks in the frame become a critical source of insight and cure. As for those therapists who do not examine the implications of their deviant behaviors in this regard, there is a basic question as to whether truth or insight therapy is feasible.

COMMENTS ON TECHNIQUE

When the adaptive context is a secure therapeutic contract, the therapist will utilize mainly silences and interpretation-reconstructions of the patient's material (see Chapters 34 and 35). Much of this work will be structured around the patient's transference-based distortions as prompted by the anxieties evoked by the secure framework arrangement.

With the deviant therapeutic contract (see below), the therapist will make use of two main interventions: (1) *rectification* of the break in the frame, though always at the behest or direction of the patient's derivative material; and (2) *interpretation-reconstruction* of the patient's derivative behaviors and associations in light of the adaptive context of the deviant and rectified ground rule. In this work, the patient's material largely involves functionally valid, nontransference-based unconscious perceptions of the implications of the deviation and of the patient's view of the therapist in light of the break in the frame. At times, the patient's material will spill over into areas of distortion and transference.

Certain deviant contracts involve unrectifiable breaks in the frame. Therapeutic work under these conditions can be characterized as *unrectifiable framework-deviation termination therapy*.

In principle, framework issues are of utmost importance to the patient and therapist, and tend to mobilize responses in the former that are extremely pertinent to his or her Neurosis. Because of this, rectifying and interpretive-reconstructive efforts carried out in terms of adaptive contexts pertinent to the ground rules and boundaries of treatment, whether the secure or deviant frame, provide a critical means of approaching, interpreting, and constructively influencing the unconscious basis of the patient's emotional disturbance. In essence, then, a significant portion of therapeutic work will be carried out in light of frame-related adaptive contexts as they shed light on the unconscious fantasy and perception constellations that account for the patient's Neurosis.

CLINICAL EXAMPLES

A therapist attempts to secure a previously modified framework for a treatment situation. The deviations that are part of the initial deviant contract include a break in the frame that is unrectifiable: the patient is the spouse of another therapist with whom the treating therapist has both personal and professional contact. The patient herself had met the therapist's wife on several occasions, and had attended social functions in the presence of the treating therapist. In the excerpt presented here, the therapist has not as yet begun to initiate efforts to analyze and correct the deviation. He had become aware that he had engaged in excessively active interventions, and that he tended to begin each session with a question or comment of his own—not waiting for the patient to free associate and to set the course of the hour (which is, of course, the patient's prerogative and due). He had also engaged in many excessive, noninterpretive interventions, including extensive questioning of the patient and advising her on many matters.

After initiating supervision, the therapist decided consciously to allow the patient to begin the next session for herself. He became relatively silent, and did not respond with his usual barrage of questions and bits of advice.

This patient sought therapy because she was unhappy with several affairs she was having with men other than her husband. Though they were into the sixth month of psychotherapy, the patient had not been able to get these episodes under control. The following excerpt is from the session in which, for the first time, the therapist permitted the patient to initiate the interchanges of the hour.

> Patient: My friend developed a facial paralysis. She lacked depth perception. Her husband let her drive. My husband wouldn't let me do that. I've been feeling good lately. I don't know what to say.

Therapist: Tell me about feeling good.

Patient: I had a dinner party and got everything together quite well. *(Silence.)*

Therapist: Don't stop. Say more.

Patient: I've just been feeling good. I don't mind the calls my husband keeps getting from the Emergency Clinic and the interruptions in our lives. Lately, I've been able to talk to my husband, and he's handling things differently. I feel closer to him. He bought a new suit. Can you tell me where we left off last week?

Therapist: Why don't you continue to say what comes to mind?

Patient: A friend of mine wanted to quit school, but the teacher talked her out of it. The friend said I seemed to have some self-confidence lately. There was this very belligerent woman at my office the other day, and I handled her pretty well. I noticed my daughter is doing better. She's not as hyperactive as she had been, and seems less frightened. I've been offered a chance to do research on brain tumors and the prospect frightens me.

At this point in the session, the therapist reminded the patient of a prior discussion of her thoughts about quitting treatment and of her prior criticisms of her husband. He attempted to develop the theme of husbands who do not care for their wives, and to link it to the patient's concern about the ways in which he was treating her. The patient responded by saying that she couldn't see how the material connected to the therapist. She then complained about not being able to associate to the end of the previous week's session, and stated, "I can't associate backwards." When the therapist attempted to further his earlier intervention, the patient said that she could not connect with what he meant. She then spoke of her considerable conflict with society as a whole, and of ways in which she would like to change but then proves unable to do so. When the therapist suggested that she seemed to feel that he was doing something wrong and that she seemed to be wondering about his qualifications, the patient responded by saying that she really didn't care if the therapist understood her or not. She went on to say that there were times when she just wanted to quit treatment and do as she pleased—as a man, the therapist seemed to be unable to understand her—besides, she really didn't want to give up her affairs and didn't care to know what they meant.

In this situation, the patient showed an initial mixed response to the therapist's new silence (an effort to secure an aspect of the frame by establishing a greater sense of neutrality). On the one hand, there are allusions to facial paralysis; while on the other, an opportunity for autonomy. There then follows the reference to feeling good lately and being able to function well. There are allusions to the patient's improved tolerance of her husband and to changes she is seeing in him—derivatives that express the constructive unconscious perceptions of the therapist in light of his self-imposed, relative silence. In addition, the patient speaks of an improved sense of self-confidence and an ability to handle a hostile woman in her office. These suggest derivative introjects based on constructive unconscious perceptions of the therapist. There are similar positive qualities to the patient's image of her daughter, which serves as a derivative commentary on the therapist's improved functioning: she is less hyperactive and seems to be less afraid.

A number of positive introjects are based on the therapist's capacity to secure a component of this particular framework. However, once the therapist began to intervene again with excessively active and noninterpretive interventions, the patient unconsciously perceived him as regressing—as associating (i.e., moving) backwards. When the therapist recovered somewhat, the patient then refuted the pursuit of meaning and spoke in favor of framework-deviation cures—affairs.

In light of the prevailing intervention contexts, these images have mixed qualities: on the one hand, they reflect unconscious perceptions of the conflict within the therapist regarding a more secure frame and his continued need for deviations; while on the other hand, they convey transference-based reactions to the therapist's efforts to secure the framework of this treatment situation by wanting to destroy the possibility of control, delay, and understanding. There are also indications in this hour that the patient dreaded the possibility of exposing highly disturbing truths about herself and the therapist if the frame were to be further secured, as when the patient mentioned her fear of getting involved in a research study of brain tumors.

In all, then, the material indicates the positive qualities of efforts to rectify the frame, and the means by which they are supported by the patient through her *derivative* communications. However, in patients who have established an essentially deviant contract and a need for lie therapy, these tend to be followed by efforts to have the therapist break the frame in fresh ways, as well as expressions of the patient's own fears of the consequences of a more ideal therapeutic environment. Delay is perceived by these patients as dangerous, and both inner truths and valid unconscious perceptions are viewed as cancerously destructive. They cling to the therapist's deviations, and create deviations of their own in efforts to bypass these anxieties and to handle the threat involved. They are therefore usually split in their response to a therapist who begins to secure the therapeutic space: frightened and angry on the surface and appreciative on an unconscious level. Much then depends on the therapist's ability to interpret the basis of the patient's anxieties and fears of harm in the context of the securing of the framework, and on the patient's own capacity to tolerate the persecutory and depressive anxieties that arise in the context of more clearly defined boundaries and ground rules to the therapeutic relationship.

The next example includes a secure framework.

A young woman patient entered therapy because of depression. Deeply hurt by the discovery that her husband had been having an affair, she quickly introduced the possibility of payment through her husband's insurance program. Her associations after this proposal, however, went to her rage at the other woman who had been involved with her husband and her own wish for a safe and private place where she could work out her own rage and conflicts. The patient also stated that the woman had no right to come between herself and her husband and to interfere with the necessary honesty that they needed in order to have a sound marriage. When the therapist interpreted this material as derivative responses to the possibility that he might sign the insurance form, and showed the patient her own unconscious objections to this intrusive third party, the patient decided to get a part-time job and to pay for treatment on her own. Soon after this, the following material arose at the beginning of an hour:

> Patient: I get depressed when my mother meddles, but then I miss her when she's not around. I don't like driving her around, but I'm more afraid of an accident when she takes the wheel of the car. My daughter had to babysit for our neighbor's son, and I felt proud of her because she took the job. But then she got frightened of being alone in the

apartment with the little boy and their dog. Sometimes I
don't know what I really think or feel. I'm afraid I'll find out
that I don't love my husband and that I would love to have
an affair myself.

The positive qualities of the secure frame are reflected in this
material and in the patient's allusion to her daughter's capabilities.
There is, however, an additional expression of the patient's anxieties over being alone with the therapist who, through her transference distortion, is unconsciously misperceived as a dangerous
person similar to her mother, and someone with whom the patient
will have an accident. He is also misperceived or fantasied about as
the dangerous dog who will attack the patient in the seemingly
secure therapeutic space.

There was evidence that these transference-based fantasies were
based on erotic feelings and wishes, which the patient had developed toward the therapist in light of his capabilities for interpreting and managing the ground rules and framework of
treatment. These formulations were made after an extensive examination of the therapist's recent interventions, which revealed an
absence of dangerous and erotic qualities. For the most part, the
therapist had been holding the patient silently once he had offered
the interventions that helped to secure the framework of treatment.
In this instance, then, the patient appeared to be developing transference-based anxieties and conflicts based on her own pathological
needs in response to the therapist's sound framework management
and interpretive efforts. Such mixed responses are typical of reactions in patients to the secure therapeutic contract.

In the presence of an essentially sound framework, the patient
has a core relationship with a trustful and sound therapist—a
background of safety (Sandler 1960). Inadvertent breaks in the frame
by the therapist tend to be quickly recognized by both participants,
and both rectified and interpreted. Deviations carried out unilaterally by the patient tend similarly to be rectifiable and interpretable in light of prior adaptation-evoking contexts—usually in
the form of the therapist's efforts to secure and maintain the ideal
therapeutic contract. Constructive and insightful therapeutic work
may therefore be carried out in the context of a basic, healthy
therapeutic symbiosis through foreground interludes in which some
type of work unfolds that stands in striking contrast to that which is
undertaken in the context of an essentially deviant frame.

The Deviant Contract

A psychotherapy that is established in terms of a deviant therapeutic contract will involve significant impairments in each of the basic functions of the totally intact frame. In general, the most important qualities of a damaged framework of therapy are (1) an image of the therapist as requiring a pathological mode of related-ness with the patient—autistic, symbiotic or parasitic—the specifics depending upon the nature of the deviation (in general, deviations that pathologically gratify the patient are pathologically symbiotic, those that exploit the patient tend to be parasitic, and those that damage meaningful relatedness tend to be autistic); (2) a model of cure involving framework deviation, action, discharge, riddance, and pathological gratification and defense (efforts to ascertain the truth and to work with meaningful derivative communications are set aside); (3) an image of the therapist as someone who is unpredictable, out of control, dangerous, and not to be trusted (there is a sense of poor hold and poor containment); (4) commu-nicatively, alterations in the framework generate a mixture of pathological projective identifications and defensive Type C bar-riers; (5) the break in the frame reflects the psychopathology of the therapist and a significant measure of countertransference (this pathology tends to support the psychopathology of the patient, and to repeat his or her past pathogenic interactions with early genetic figures); (6) the deviant frame creates the conditions for lie-barrier therapy, and is inimical to truth therapy (interpretation without rectification is insufficient); (7) each specific and acute break in the framework provides a traumatic intervention context to which the patient responds both directly and through crucial derivative com-munications (typically, the patient's responses are split: on the one hand, designed to exploit the deviation for pathological gain; while on the other, designed as well to rectify the frame and to create a healthy mode of relatedness between the patient and therapist and the conditions for truth therapy); and (8) in the presence of an altered framework, the derivative unconscious introjects of the therapist are negative and destructive (they tend to support the patient's Neurosis and the therapist's own pathological introjects).

Misalliance and framework-deviation cures are attractive in their qualities of pathological gratification and defense, immediate relief, and as a way of bypassing the painful pursuit of truth and understanding. Qualities of action and riddance are also quite appealing, as is the support obtained by the patient for his or her Neurotic maladaptation.

Most expressions of psychopathology include some type of alteration of the framework of basic relationships. They involve as well basically pathological modes of adaptation and means of symptom relief. This basic constellation of pathological mode of relatedness and cure, through which pathological maladaptations are extended, is highly inviting to most patients and to many therapists. A capacity to modify the ideal therapeutic framework implies virtually omnipotent power, the ability to deny death (the boundary between life and death is the most threatening of all framework lines), and the illusion of being able to remain merged with the early maternal figure. Although pathological and mal-adaptive, these two are exceedingly attractive qualities. The renunciation of this type of need is quite difficult for both participants to treatment. Nonetheless, effective interpretive and rectifying therapeutic work built around actual flaws in the ideal therapeutic frame can have highly salutory effects for both patient and therapist alike.

In addition to the pathological gains for both the patient and therapist that accrue to them through a basically flawed therapeutic contract, there are a number of anxieties and dangers experienced by both patient and therapist under these conditions. For the patient, there is the loss of a sound sense of reality, since there tend to be strong contradictions between the therapist's background and foreground communications and between sequential communications as well. Deviations tend to produce pathological forms of merger and to blur self-object boundaries. They generate an appropiately mistrustful image of the therapist who behaves in an omnipotent and controlling fashion, and becomes both erratic and unpredictable in respect to both sexual and aggressive impulses. There is a strong sense of danger and persecution, as well as deep disillusionment in a therapist who proves incapable of securely holding the patient and containing his or her own pathological projective identifications. There is also the involvement in a pathological mode of relatedness, which on some level greatly disturbs both participants to treatment. Mistrust abounds, though much of it is quite unconscious.

Some measure of therapeutic work is possible under the conditions of a deviant therapeutic contract; however, there are several caveats. First, the basic background or core relationship is threatening and unsafe; the therapeutic work proceeds with a strong sense of peril within the patient. Second, almost exclusively, the only truths that will be meaningfully represented in the patient's material pertain to the specific deviations that constitute the adaptation-evoking contexts to which the patient is reacting. The basic flaws in the frame encourage resistances and impairments in the gross behavioral and alliance sectors.

The patient tends to utilize relatively well-disguised and remote derivative expressions under these conditions. Typically, the patient will fail to manifestly allude to the critical deviant intervention context. Often, the best derivative representation is highly defended and remote. Because of this, meaningful therapeutic work is slow and painstaking. In general, it requires an initial playback of the best available derivatives as organized by the missing framework deviation intervention context, without bypassing the patient's defenses by mentioning the context itself (see Chapters 34 and 35). Following such efforts, the patient often communicates clearer and more easily coalescible derivative expressions, which then permit a second and improved playback-interpretive intervention. As a rule, only then, and still with considerable resistance, will the patient directly represent the intervention context at hand and present derivative material that permits both rectification and interpretation-reconstruction. Because of the background of danger, such work is quite arduous. There are often periods of regression and acting out, and the therapist must take special pains not to participate when the patient wants to engage in a regression to further framework-deviation means of symptom relief.

CLINICAL EXAMPLES

A patient was referred to a therapist by a former patient, Al. The present patient was depressed and separated from his wife. In the initial hour, he described himself as a rug cleaner who was looking to change professions. He added that he was presently living in Al's apartment. Though divorced from his second wife, Al was currently living with her. The patient joked about the sense of confusion in his life. The therapist offered no interpretations; he accepted the patient for once-weekly treatment and established the other ground rules of therapy.

The patient was 15 minutes early to his second session. The therapist, who made use of a home-office arrangement, let the patient into the waiting room, but started the hour on time. In the session, the patient spoke of this rage at his wife when she would keep him waiting—one of the factors in their separation. He felt strange and anxious while in the waiting room. The therapist connected this anxiety to an underlying sense of rage, noting that he, as had the patient's wife, had kept the patient waiting until the time of his session. The patient responded that, while he could see the parallel, he didn't feel any anger toward the therapist.

The following excerpt is from the third session:

> Patient: I'm afraid to come on sexually to my wife. It is she who must approach me. I decided to tell Al's wife I want to sleep with her so I could get over my passivity. She felt flattered with the suggestion and told me not to feel bad about making it. She didn't give me an answer. With my wife, I feel inadequate. I prefer sexual fantasies and mastur-bation. I go into the bathroom while I'm working. I mastur-bate and then I feel badly about it. When I was younger I was involved with this mentally disturbed cousin, and we were caught while making out. Lately, I notice that I have been exposing myself and saying too much. I know this woman who is promiscuous like my wife. I try to tell her about it, and to tell her she ought to behave differently. Her other friend was listening, and I felt uncomfortable talking to her about it.

In this vignette, the patient expresses the sense of uncertainty about reality, the blurred self-object boundaries, and the basic sense of confusion that develops when there is a basic flaw in the frame— here, the lack of total privacy and reasonable anonymity that accrues because of the patient-referral and the inevitable sense of concern over the confidentiality of the treatment. Through deriva-tives, the patient characterizes this confusion through the fact that he is living in his friend's (the therapist's former patient's) apart-ment, and in his report that this divorced friend is nonetheless living with his wife.

The pathologically symbiotic and parasitic qualities of the mode of relatedness between patient and therapist that is based on this particular deviation is reflected in the patient's decision to attempt to have an affair with the wife of the referring friend. This derivative also conveys the unconscious homosexual gratification and instinctualization of the therapeutic relationship that accrues under these conditions. The patient described his plans as an effort to overcome his problem, and thereby demonstrated and represented the manner in which framework-deviation and action-discharge have been adopted as the mode of cure—here with the implicit approval of the therapist who behaves similarly. This material nicely illustrates the ways in which patients represent in their associations such aspects of the therapeutic interaction as mode of relatedness and mode of cure.

The additional derivatives point to the self-gratifying (masturbatory) qualities of this type of arrangement for both patient and therapist. The parasitic dimension is further reflected in the patient's seduction of an emotionally disturbed younger cousin. The fear of discovery by the third party present to this treatment is expressed in the patient's being caught in the seduction. The pathological instinctual drive satisfactions involved in the deviation are self-evident.

Finally, there is the mutually exhibitionistic-voyeuristic qualities to this deviation, and the manner in which the therapist expresses himself in a way that is comparable to the patient's wife— with the implication of some measure of pathology. The patient offers a model of rectification when he states that the friend who is like his wife should change. He also alludes to the manner in which the presence of third parties interfere with free expression.

The therapist's acceptance and implicit seduction of this patient render him similar in important pathological ways to the patient himself, and to his pathological introjects. These effects are an inappropriate means of diminishing the patient's guilt. It is evidently the patient's hope in seeking and gaining this type of deviant contract that his ability to seduce and be seduced by the therapist will enable him to overcome his underlying sexual anxieties, whatever their specific nature. The deviation creates a background of danger and exploitation. This helps to account for the patient's failure to directly represent the intervention context of the referral source in this particular hour—despite the presence of abundant derivative responses.

Early in the supervisory presentation of this material, this unrectifiable deviation was postulated to be a critical intervention

context. While the patient's derivative associations strongly supported a series of silent hypotheses regarding the implications of the
deviation, these formulations are offered in tentative and illustrative
fashion at this point, since they were not subjected to the ultimate
test of validation through an intervention by the therapist.
However, an attempt by the therapist to interpret the number of
sexual anxieties within this patient in a manner that failed to relate
them to this particular adaptive context was met with a nonvalidating response.

The next example is excerpted from the case of a young man
who was referred to psychotherapy by his father, who had himself
previously seen the therapist for a period of treatment. The patient
was severely anxious and worked infrequently. From time to time
he would work in his father's store. Without clear interpretation or
rectification, he owed the therapist the fees for a half-year's sessions.

At the time to be described here, the therapist had begun to
interpret the manner in which his laxity regarding the unpaid bills
had created barriers to effective treatment. The patient had responded with some anxiety and anger, although he also decided to
obtain independent work. For the first time in months, he began to
reduce in small amounts his indebtedness to the therapist. In the
hour in which he first made payment he spoke as follows:

> Patient: I've been working as a house painter and renovating
> this old house. I feel like I'm growing. I've decided to never
> return to my father's store. I thought it was a safe place,
> though I never did function there. I guess it wasn't safe after
> all. If I can keep working, my girlfriend and I can take our
> own apartment. I had no future in my father's place even
> though I was comfortable there. I guess I was hiding. It's like
> the bill situation here: I was unable to confront the problem
> and I hid from it. I went with my girlfriend to her therapist.
> After her session, her therapist came out into the waiting
> room. The therapist said I looked angry, but I didn't under-
> stand what she meant. I don't think I should have been there
> in the first place.

In this instance, the third party to therapy helped the patient to
constitute a therapeutic setting and relationship that supported his
own pathological, self-indulgent use of a deviant mode of maladap-

tation and cure through which he parasitized the therapist who lent himself masochistically as a willing victim. Avoidance (hiding) also became part of the mode of cure. As the therapist began to make attempts to interpret and rectify the frame, the patient responded by mobilizing his own adaptive resources and obtaining independent work. In an expression that contained a model of rectification, he renounced working at his father's store—here, a representation of the therapeutic space—which had been stultifying and infantilizing for him. Allusions to renovating a home and moving into his own apartment then followed. After a direct reference to the fee issue, the patient concluded this particular sequence by offering a minimally disguised derivative representation of the referral situation itself: he alludes to a setting in which a therapist modifies the framework of his girlfriend's treatment and intervenes to him in the waiting room, thereby including him in the therapy situation. This experience provides an impetus for a further model of rectification: the patient did not belong there in the first place. The implication is clear: his acceptance into treatment by this therapist was inappropriate and in error. It contaminated and extended the boundaries of treatment (cf. that the transactions took place in the waiting room). The patient implies too that the deviation leads to confusion, while rectification could lead to separation-individuation and growth-autonomy. Both behaviorally and communicatively, the patient initiated here what eventually became an unrectifiable deviation termination therapy.

In a subsequent hour, the patient reported a dream of being in his father's bedroom, where he did not belong. When the patient's perception of the therapeutic situation was interpreted to him in these terms—as his father's bedroom where he did not belong—and the need for rectification hinted at, the patient for the first time spoke of his concerns as to what would have happened to his own therapy if his father had become emotionally ill again. This led to further derivatives regarding the patient's resentment of the therapist who had not provided him with his own safe and secure therapeutic space. This material lent some measure of Type Two derivative validation to the hypothesis that the basic therapeutic environment in this situation was essentially flawed, as was the patient's image of the therapist because of the initial deviation.

One final note: prior to the therapist's efforts to rectify the fee situation with this patient and to explore the meanings of the referral source based on the patient's derivative associations, the therapist had gone through a long series of virtually incomprehensible sessions with this patient. He was at a loss to offer interpretive interventions, and the patient remained virtually immobilized and nonfunctioning. Exploration in the areas of the frame deviations—here, the acceptance of a nonneutral referral and the continuation of this patient's treatment in the absence of a paid fee—provided a series of highly meaningful sessions through which both interpretation and rectification proved feasible.

The Therapist's Fear of the Secure Frame

It is impossible to fully appreciate and study the ground rules and boundaries of therapy without an explicit recognition of the anxieties, conflicts, and other dysfunctions within therapists that lead them to fear the ideal therapeutic environment. The therapist who saw the patient described in the previous vignette consciously chose to deviate from the ideal therapeutic frame because of financial need, and in the belief as well that the referral source would have little influence on the course of the therapy. Similarly, he was fearful of securing the frame, even when the patient's derivatives pointed in that direction. He feared an abrupt ending of treatment by the patient, and did not want to interrupt the therapy until he could pay off his indebtedness. While mindful that these deviations seemed to be supporting the nonfunctional state of the patient, he was nonetheless loathe to intervene firmly even when the material from the patient pointed in such a direction.

Adherence to the ground rules and boundaries of psychotherapy entail a great deal of conscious and evident renunciation for a therapist. There are many patients whom the therapist will not accept for treatment because of deviant qualities to the referral source. There are some patients who, unable to tolerate a healthy symbiosis, will be lost to therapy despite the therapist's best efforts at interpretation, even as the therapist endeavors to maintain an ideal therapeutic relationship and environment at the behest of the patient's derivative material. There are also a wide range of additional evident anxieties and pressures that the therapist will experience and be required to manage if the ideal therapeutic setting is to be maintained.

There are many unconscious motives and reasons that prompt therapists to modify the ideal therapeutic contract. There is also a dangerous sense of potential regression in the patient, and perhaps less so in the therapist, under these conditions. For example, a therapist working at a clinic had rectified a variety of clinic-imposed deviations in the psychotherapy of a young woman who had had an incestuous sexual relationship with her father. The patient's response was highly salutory, in that she experienced a considerable diminution of her chronic sense of anxiety and guilt, and a new capacity to function relatively independently. Through derivatives, she also expressed a fear that the therapist might resume his use of deviations and become, once again, someone like her father. In an apparent effort to test out the security of the frame, the patient then asked the therapist if she could now address him by his first name. The therapist responded by saying that it would be up to her, thereby affording her implicit permission to do so. After using his first name, she brought fresh associations to the conditions under which her father pressed her into an incestuous relationship and the deep fear she had of giving up her terrifying tie to him. She spoke too of her early childhood anxiety of being alone in her dark bedroom, and of how destructive it had been for her parents to have simply allowed her to jump into their bed whenever she felt frightened. Lately, she was functioning in a more constructive and independent manner, but she was afraid of slipping back to her old ways.

The therapist was mindful of his error, though he did not interpret or rectify it. In the following session, the patient seemed deeply confused and spoke of mixed messages she obtained from others. The therapist began to recognize his own inner conflicts, and was able to discover a number of reasons for his deviation. Guilt over his attraction to this patient and earlier traumatic experiences with his own mother proved to be underlying factors. It was evident that he was fearful of a secure frame with this patient and the emergence of erotic transference material. Similarly, he had experienced a significant difficulty in establishing clear-cut boundaries with the patient and renouncing the unconscious and secret incestuous-like ties that he had established with her through his earlier deviations.

This particular sequence, in which a therapist proves capable of securing a previously deviant therapeutic contract only to quickly join the patient in a framework break in another sphere, appears to be common. These observations serve as a strong reminder of the inevitable human investment within each of us in deviant conditions to treatment. Unconscious needs are involved, regarding which the therapist must be in constant search. When in doubt, the best technical principle is to adhere to the frame except in dire emergency, and to deviate then only after holding the frame does not prove saluatory—as it often will.

Summary and Conclusions

The ground rules and boundaries of the psychotherapeutic situation and relationship have been introduced. This dimension of treatment is a major determinant of the basic mode of therapeutic relatedness and the essential process of cure. In part through the genius of Freud and in part through a process of unconscious selection, therapists have evolved a specific set of ground rules and boundaries for *truth therapy* (the genuine pursuit of insight and adaptive structural change through understanding and its accompanying inevitable positive introjects). Deviations from this ideal frame create the conditions for *lie* or *lie-barrier therapy* (shifts in the process of cure toward the development of lie-barrier systems and action-discharge).

Two therapeutic modalities have been characterized: (1) one that unfolds with the frame essentially secured and would be described as truth therapy; and (2) one that unfolds with one or more basic flaws in the conditions of treatment, and would be termed one or another form of lie-barrier therapy. Each set of conditions offers some type of relief to both the patient and therapist, while simultaneously creating a constellation of anxieties and conflicts.

With a secure frame, there is a safe and strong hold for both participants to therapy, a background of safety, and the potential for a healthy symbiosis and insightful cure. Inadvertent breaks in the frame tend to evoke strong and meaningful responses in the patient and to lend themselves readily to the two essential steps of *rectification and interpretation* at the behest of the patient's derivative material.

With a fundamentally flawed frame, there is a background of

danger, a poor sense of hold, and an essentially pathological mode of relatedness, with cure through lie-barrier formations and action-discharge. There are impairments in the qualities of the patient's material, and efforts by the patient to both exploit the deviation and to rectify it—the latter usually through highly encoded derivative expressions. From time to time the patient will meaningfully work over the long-standing breaks in the frame and any new and acute deviations. Under these conditions, however, the derivative response will tend to be more defended and more highly disguised than when also to show a conscious working through of the issues involved, directly to the framework intervention context in his or her associations; the initial intervention available to the therapist tends to be a playback of *selected*, though heavily disguised derivatives organized around the activated framework deviation, which has been poorly portrayed in the patient's material.

Under the first set of conditions, patients will tend to work actively and unconsciously toward the restoration of the frame. They will offer Type Two derivative validation of the necessary corrective measures and interpretations of the therapist as long as they are based on their own derivative associations. They will tend also to show a conscious working through of the issues involved, and move on from there—often with a phase of resistance now that the frame is secure and the major pathological inputs are to be derived from their own inner disturbance (rather than from the deviant therapist).

In contrast, patients who accept an essentially deviant contract with their therapists tend to have strong pathological needs for the mode of relatedness, type of cure, and communicative defenses that exist in such an interaction. They tend to have a strong investment in the pathological gratifications available in this type of setting, and to invest heavily in maladaptive, framework-breaking (framework-deviation cure) efforts. They therefore tend to work over the implications of the deviant frame with a notable measure of defensiveness, and to struggle against the therapist who begins to rectify and interpret the deviation issues in light of their derivative associations. Much conscious denial is usually in evidence, though Type Two derivative validation is virtually always assured—however brief and subsequently fragmented.

There is a fundamental question as to how such patients can be helped to tolerate a secure frame and truth therapy, especially those who make attempts to destroy the basic therapeutic contract in the initial hour and refuse to enter therapy under such conditions. Interpretive and rectifying efforts are experienced by these patients as highly persecutory and dangerous, though consistent work in this direction can enable some of these patients to begin to develop a capacity for delay and frustration tolerance, and to pursue an understanding of their depressive and persecutory anxieties and pathological relationship needs.

Frame issues appear to be most basic to the therapeutic relationship and work. With the ground rules and boundaries secure, the major adaptive context is the sound holding relationship offered by the therapist to the patient. On this basis, responsive anxieties and intrapsychic and interpersonal conflicts tend to be based on aspects of the patient's own psychopathology, and to constitute true forms of transference—i.e., distortions based on past relationships and unconscious fantasy-memory constellations evoked by the therapeutic relationship and pertinent to the therapist. On the other hand, in the presence of a deviation, the patient's responses tend to be largely nontransference-based, though with some degree of extension into transference. In the main, however, they tend to involve valid unconscious perceptions of the therapist and the deviation in terms of the extensive actual implications of the framework break. During such interludes, the therapist is behaving in some way in a manner comparable to a past pathogenic figure. Thus the past is being recreated in the present, rather than mistakenly attributed to the present by the patient, as in the case of the secure frame and transference reactions. These distinctions prove crucial when intervening (see Chapters 34 and 35).

Listening and formulating related to the status of the frame is the first level to which the intaking efforts of the therapist are directed (the others being the status of the relationship, the mode of cure, the communicative state of both participants, the presence of dynamics and genetics, and the person to whom they should mainly be assigned—patient or therapist). In the presence of a known deviation, the patient's material will tend to organize in a highly meaningful fashion as Type Two derivative responses to the break in the frame; virtually all of the implications will involve valid unconscious perceptions of the implications of the deviation and of the consequent image of the therapist.

In situations where there has been a break in the frame that has been missed by the therapist, the oversight can be corrected by monitoring the material from the patient for framework allusions. When these point to a secure and steady frame, it is likely that the framework of the psychotherapy is secure. When allusions to breaks in the frames and boundaries are in evidence, it is common to find that a violation in one of the ground rules of psychotherapy is involved.

CLINICAL EXAMPLE

A young woman was in once-weekly psychotherapy for depression. In the previous session, the therapist had attempted to help the patient understand some of her depressed feelings and fantasies, which he proposed to have been evoked by a brief vacation he had taken a month earlier. There had been little sense of Type Two derivative validation from the patient, however, and the therapist had sat back for the balance of the session. The following extract is from the hour that followed:

> Patient: Suddenly, I'm in love with my boss. I tried to connect it with my father, but it doesn't tie in. He hasn't done anything. Well, he did call me late at night about a problem with the books. Another time, he was saying something nice and patted me on the chin. He's been paying the truck drivers under the table and took some cash for himself. And I have to cover it over. I'm getting paranoid. It's like I'm too naive and don't know how to handle it. Somehow I'm reminded of the time my cousin molested me and I told my mother about it. Am I being set up for something?

When this material was presented in supervision, the therapist was at a loss to identify an activated intervention context that would give organization and meaning to this derivative complex. It was possible, however, for the supervisor to identify a number of representations of breaks in the usual ground rules and boundaries of relationships: the call from the boss at night after hours, the physical contact between the boss and the patient, the dishonest handling of the money, and the image of being molested. As a rule, the presence of so many representations of breaks in the frame suggest an unnoticed deviation in the therapeutic situation—most often one that involves the therapist. In keeping with this formulation, there is the patient's characterization of the dishonesty and exploitation of the job situation, and the sense of iatrogenic paranoia reflected in her associations. The represented relationship appeared to be one of pathological symbiosis or, more probably, that of parasiticism. There was a strong sense that the patient felt victimized. When these formulations were offered to the therapist, he suddenly remembered that for the past month, he had extended each of the patient's sessions by three to four minutes. Aware of the deviation involved, the therapist had nonetheless rationalized each of these extensions for one reason or another. The seductive, exploitative, molesting, and dishonest qualities of this unconsciously perceived deviation were now more than evident. The experience provided an excellent illustration of how an adaptive context shapes derivative expressions, and of how identifying a configuration of derivatives can lead to the discovery of an unrecognized context.

In the session, the therapist failed to intervene with a playback of these highly pertinent derivatives, but instead simply commented that the patient seemed to be protecting herself from her feelings of love. She responded with denial and then surface acceptance. Her thoughts went to a time at work when she had been wrongly accused of lying and when her boss had not trusted her. She would never tolerate an incident of that kind again. This last material is primarily a commentary on the lie-barrier qualities of the therapist's intervention, though it continues to convey the manner in which the unrectified framework deviation had made the patient basically mistrustful of the therapist.

THE FRAMEWORK FOR OBSERVING THE FRAME

There are three different sets of conditions under which the therapist applies the listening-formulating process in regard to the therapeutic frame. The first occurs in the presence of a basically deviant contract or an unrectified break in the frame. Under these conditions the patient tends *not* to represent directly the deviant intervention contexts, but will do so either through highly disguised derivative representations or virtually not at all. Similarly, the derivative complex is typically highly disguised and remote. The therapist must either wait for a particular session when the patient is unconsciously motivated to work over the deviation at hand and does so with more readily accessible representations and derivative material, or resort to an initial playback of the highly disguised derivatives as a means of initiating meaningful therapeutic work in this area. In principle, the therapist should wait for the patient's material to direct him or her toward the rectification of the frame before introducing the correction unilaterally. Occasional exceptions may be made, such as when a therapist is tape recording sessions or taking notes, though here too it is best in principle to do so through the encoded directives of the patient.

The second framework of observation occurs when the therapist begins to interpret the patient's unconscious perceptions of himself or herself and the deviation, and the possible measure of extension into distortion and fantasy, and when the therapist begins to move toward the rectification of the deviation at the behest of the patient's derivative associations. The material from the patient tends to become far more meaningful than under the first set of conditions. The representations of the deviant adaptation-evoking context tend to become far less disguised and, on occasion, there will be a direct allusion to the deviation at hand. In addition, the derivative complex usually involves closer and far more clear derivative expressions, and tends to be far more readily coalesced into a meaningful whole. The implications of the deviation thereby become far clearer, as does the therapist's opportunity for interpretation or its variation in the form of a playback of selected derivatives. Efforts directed toward rectification are easily carried out.

Finally, those situations where the rectification of the frame has been carried out (e.g., in the above clinical example, the therapist no longer extends the patient's sessions), there will be a tendency toward still greater clarity in communications from the patient. The adaptive context will, as a rule, be directly alluded to, and the derivative complex filled with new and fresh meaning. Only then will the therapist fully appreciate the extensive ramifications of the deviation, and its genetic and dynamic, and other, implications for the patient—and for the therapist. In general, once the therapeutic framework has been secured, there will also be a period of resistance because of the anxieties evoked by the sound holding relationship now offered by the therapist. However, the psychotherapy then proceeds with a background of safety rather than of danger, and new realizations are common.

In situations where full rectification is not feasible, the patient's derivative material will eventually point to the need for rectification through termination. (This particular problem is considered in Chapter 21.)

Chapter 19

The Setting

As a rule, the most stable aspect of the therapeutic environment is the physical setting. While there are some therapists, both in clinics and privately, who for one reason or another make use of two or more offices for a particular patient, the ideal therapeutic environment calls for a single setting without variation. Even a necessary move by the therapist of his or her office from one location to another is traumatic to the patient (and usually for the therapist as well), and will for some time create disturbances in the basic communicative relationship.

In-patient Office Settings

One of the many remarkable and ironical aspects of psychotherapy is that almost without exception, the beginning therapist is asked to work in a highly compromised therapeutic environment, despite the fact that he or she is attempting to learn the fundamentals of therapeutic practice. Many clinic administrators show little sensitivity to the role played by the therapeutic environment. As a result, in-patient and clinic practices are not only highly variable, but almost uniformly destructive. Direct awareness of many of the transparent problems involved, supported by the examination of material from patients for valid derivative commentaries, would lead to major reforms.

In treating in-patients with insight-oriented psychotherapy it is important to make use of a single office that in some definite sense belongs to the therapist. The office may be on the in-patient unit itself, or may be outside of the unit. However, a consistent therapeutic setting is extremely important for a patient whose illness is of such proportions that he or she requires hospitalization. This implies too that the therapist does not hold sessions in the patient's room—a modification in the ideal therapeutic environment with powerful detrimental consequences.

In an emergency with an extremely regressed patient who is immobilized in bed, it may prove necessary to see the patient in his or her own quarters. Nonetheless, in the presence of such a measure and afterwards, the deviation itself must be the primary focus of the therapist's interpretive work. This is facilitated by the finding that under such conditions patients will almost always offer a clear representation of the deviant intervention context and a meaningful, coalescible derivative complex pertinent to the alteration in the frame. In addition, a break in the frame must be repaired and *rectified* as quickly as possible, and the implications of both the alteration and rectification interpreted to the patient to the extent that his or her material allows.

As already noted, when it comes to the ground rules and boundaries of therapy, there are two technical measures required of the therapist: (1) *creating, managing,* and *rectifying the framework* when it has been broken; and (2) *interpreting* the patient's responsive unconscious *perceptions* and *fantasies*. Rectification is a prerequisite for meaningful interpretation, since all efforts at verbal intervention will fail unless the therapist has expressed himself or herself behaviorally as committed to the restoration of the frame. Since the conditions of treatment are actualities, the therapist has no choice but to respond when a patient requests that the therapist come to his or her room, change an hour, or extend a session. Interpretation is therefore an insufficient response, since the patient must know whether the deviation will be carried out or not. In principle, these decisions are made entirely through a reading of the patient's *derivative* communications, and are not based on manifest associations or pleas, or on arbitrary directives from the therapist.

As a rule, there are two critical adaptation-evoking contexts at such moments. The first is a prior intervention by the therapist, often one that itself involves the framework, which has prompted the patient to attempt to alter the basic ground rules of treatment. Most often, this prior context entails a deviation by the therapist; though more rarely, it is constituted by the therapist's efforts to establish and maintain the ideal frame. Prior deviations tend to reinforce the patient's own tendency toward framework manipulation and the search for symptom alleviation on the basis of framework-deviation cures. On the other hand, the establishment of a sound therapeutic environment poses considerable threat for some patients, who respond with unilateral deviations of their own or with efforts to involve the therapist in an alteration of the ground rules. In each sequence, it is essential to identify this *antecedent intervention context,* to seek out its representations in the patient's material, and to intervene—interpretively and in regard to the framework management—with an understanding of the patient's derivative communications in light of this context.

A second and more immediate adaptive context is based on the anticipation by the patient that the therapist will or will not deviate, a sense that is gained from the therapist's basic attitude and the initial approach to the patient's request. In this context, the patient's derivative communications virtually without fail will speak to the destructiveness of altering the framework—its pathological implications. Similarly, they will express the need to maintain the therapeutic environment when soundly constituted, despite the patient's conscious request to the contrary. As noted earlier, such a split is typical in patients (and in many therapists) when it comes to the ground rules and boundaries of treatment.

In principle, the therapist makes use of the patient's derivative communications to show the patient his or her own unconscious answer to the request. The same principles are applied after a shared break in the frame, since the patient's derivative expressions, organized in the light of the adaptation-evoking context of the therapist's participation in the deviation, will again uniformly speak for the need for rectification and the negative implications of the disturbance in the therapeutic hold.

As for the question as to whether these principles of listening, formulating, and intervening, and of managing the therapeutic environment, apply to psychotic patients, it appears that psychotic and borderline patients, more so than neurotics, have a deep need for a secure holding and containing environment, and of a safe person and space for their psychotherapy. These patients have usually experienced major failures in respect to the core aspects of their relationships with their mothers when they were children. A disturbed therapeutic environment repeats the very traumatic conditions and interactions under which these patients became seriously ill. On the other hand, a therapist's capacity to offer, and to maintain in the face of threat, a sound therapeutic environment and mode of relatedness provides the patient with a powerful relationship and unconscious introject that is inherently ego strengthening. It also provides unique conditions under which it is safe for the patient to undertake what is for the patient the highly dangerous yet integrating pursuit of the truth of his or her psychosis.

The key problem in offering a secure therapeutic environment to a psychotic patient is that on the one hand, the patient is in dire need of a therapist who can create conditions of this kind, while on the other, the patient has a deep dread of the inevitable therapeutic regression that takes place under such conditions. This shift tends to expose the highly primitive, psychotic parts of the patient's personality that must, however, be mastered in order to insightfully get well. In addition, the ideal therapeutic environment greatly diminishes the availability of pathological symbiotic and parasitic modes of relatedness between the patient and therapist, and these patients typically fear their own annihilation in the absence of such familiar though disruptive modes of interaction. Then too, the offer of a healthy symbiosis creates a constructive introject of the therapist that is internalized and greatly disrupts the denial defenses with which the patient has defended against the pathological introjects of his or her parental figures—based, in part, on their own holding failures. The result is a highly charged intrapsychic conflict whose analysis can produce considerable insight and integration for the patient, though the truths involved are quite disturbing.

Adaptive and maladapative responses that take the form of a modification of the usual ground rules and boundaries of everyday relationships are quite common with psychotic patients. This propensity arises in part because of the strong tendency in their parental figures to deviate in this regard, and in part because of the intensity of their own primitive needs and conflicts. Typically, these patients have related to others through autism, parasiticism, or pathological symbioses, and they are loathe to renounce the defensive and instinctual drive gratifications achieved on this basis. Nonetheless, if insightful cure is to take place, it can evolve only in a relationship with a therapist capable of offering a healthy symbiosis and maintaining the framework in the face of the many assaults on the ground rules and boundaries of treatment that are characteristic of these patients. This very basic capability to manage the therapeutic environment and core mode of relatedness with these patients inherently demonstrates to the patient that the therapist is able to contain and master his or her psychotic disturbance, and to work interpretively with its meanings and implications.

Finally, it is to be expected that in the opening phase of psychotherapy with psychotic and borderline patients, and during many interludes throughout their treatment, critical moments of holding, containing, and interpretive work will take place in response to efforts by these patients to modify the therapeutic environment and their mode of relatedness with the therapist. This type of therapeutic work is crucial to the insightful modification of the psychopathology experienced by these patients. The single most important factor in supporting their ego functioning, including reality testing and the ability to maintain self-object differentiation, is that of a therapist capable of creating clearly maintained ground rules and boundaries in the treatment relationship. The therapist's responses in this area are the key to the nature of the psychotherapy and mode of cure that will be experienced by these patients.

The Clinic Office

Similar principles apply to the clinic setting. The therapist should have his or her own office, and should use the same office with a particular patient. If possible, the same office should be kept with a sequence of patients, rather than shifting about in ways that inevitably raise questions for the patients involved.

All office settings should be soundproofed. Often, an inpatient office is not securely soundproofed, although the problem is usually greater in a clinic, where little has been done to seal off office space from leakage of sound—both incoming and outgoing. Offices that are in the waiting room areas of clinics are disasterous in this respect, though any office with an openness for noise from the corridors and/or from adjoining suites is similarly destructive. Clearly, this creates an untenable therapeutic environment, and must be rectified.

An office that lacks basic soundproofing is a *vested interest deviation*, an alteration in the ideal ground rules regarding which the therapist has a noticeable investment. In the presence of this type of deviation, no matter how evident the destructiveness for both patient and therapist alike, the patient will typically express himself or herself only through highly disguised representations of the deviant intervention context and with similarly disguised and fragmented derivative complexes. Because of the level of interactionally-based communicative defense, an unwary therapist who works on the manifest content level will tend to participate in the collusive bastion in which the basic framework issue is sealed off, denied, and goes essentially unrecognized. Dealing with framework issues of this kind requires considerable sensitivity to a patient's derivative communications, as well as considerable personal insight and a sound grasp of the nature and functions of the basic ground rules and boundaries of treatment.

In principle, leakage of sound impairs the communicative qualities of the therapeutic interaction, tends to establish a parasitic mode of relatedness between the patient and therapist (with the patient as the main victim), and generates a highly mistrustful and threatening image of the therapist. The deviation itself, as is true of virtually all alterations in the ground rules of treatment, expresses a pathological and disturbing projective identification from the therapist, which dumps into the patient the therapist's inability to secure a safe therapeutic setting and to provide the patient with a background of safety. This encourages the use of the Type B mode of communication by the patient. The deviation also indicates to the patient that it is unsafe to communicate meaningfully to the therapist on a conscious as well as unconscious level, and in this way promotes the use of the Type C mode and nonderivative lie-barrier, defensive systems.

Patients tend to respond in one of two major ways to this type of deviation. As already noted, they will on occasion, though with heavy defense and disguise, represent and work over this type of deviant intervention context. Most of the time, however, they utilize the Type B or Type C modes. Often, there is a Type B-C response, such as seen in a patient who fails to metabolize the pathological projective identifications from the therapist stemming from the leakage of sound, and reprojects these toxic and disturbing qualities back into the therapist through efforts at deviation and dumping. Such patients are typically challenging of the therapist, repeatedly questioning, frequently complaining about the treatment, and seeking out many additional deviations on their own.

In contrast, there is the second group of patients who quietly succumb to these destructive conditions, resorting to the use of Type C barriers to seal off their unconscious perceptions and realizations, which are related to the underlying chaos and truths of this type of therapeutic interaction. The greatest problem technically with these patients lies in the therapist's failure to realize the existence of the deviant adaptive context that is evoking the reactions in these patients. The difficult patients are passed off as being too sick to work in therapy, while the compliant group becomes engaged in an essentially lie-barrier form of therapy in which the critical truths of the therapeutic interaction, and experience (i.e., those related to the deviations at hand) are set to the side.

Some in-patient services and clinics have transparent glass on the doors to the office that their therapists use. This too is a way of making the psychotherapy public, and such practices clearly disturb the total privacy that should prevail. The consequences are not unlike those that take place in the presence of noticeable leakage of sound. Unconsciously perceptive exhibitionistic and voyeuristic themes abound, as do those of betrayal and lack of limits and boundaries.

CLINICAL EXAMPLE

A first session with a depressed, single, woman teacher was held in a clinic office. The therapist first telephoned the patient, who had applied to the clinic for therapy, and offered to see her in her private office because space was sparse at the clinic. When the patient refused, an appointment was made for an evening hour at the clinic. The therapist went to greet the patient in the waiting room, and then escorted her to the office in which the session would be held. However, they found the room occupied, and it was arranged for the patient to be seen an hour later. During that time, she sat in the clinic waiting room with several other patients and a group of therapists who were awaiting a conference to be held at the clinic. The office that eventually was used was only poorly sound-proofed, and voices could be heard from both the waiting room and the office next door.

In the session itself (which is extracted in Chapter 21), the patient had considerable difficulty in expressing herself. She felt overwhelmed, and believed the therapist thought she was crazy. She stressed the childhood roots of her problems and the need to care for herself. There were also images with a strong sense of isolation. In general, the therapist simply echoed the patient's manifest thoughts and feelings, though toward the end of the session she did attempt to comment on the patient's possible reactions to having been left alone in the clinic waiting room. Toward the end of the hour, the patient spoke of her fears of death.

As can be seen from this summary, despite the intrusion of clear voices into the therapist's office and the existence of other blatant deviations in the fixed frame of this treatment, the patient did not at any time in this first hour allude directly to the conditions of treatment, the delay of her session, and the intrusions into her therapeutic space. While the patient did make use of Kleenex from a box on the therapist's desk, there was no thinly disguised (close) verbal-affective derivative representation of these basic deviations. Further, the latent material from the patient organized only weakly around these deviant intervention contexts.

In the main, it appeared that the patient unconsciously felt unable to communicate with the therapist under these conditions, and that she recognized that because of the conditions of therapy, she would have to heal herself. The craziness of the setting was alluded to in disguised form in the patient's reference to her belief that the therapist will think that she—the patient—is crazy. The destructive qualities of the setting appeared through highly disguised derivatives related to the patient's fear of dying. (Death is a common theme in the presence of major form deviations.) In all, there appears to have been an extremely high level of resistances.

In listening and formulating, one must also consider the alternative hypothesis that the basic conditions of this treatment are of little consequence to the patient, although the purpose of this section of the book is to demonstrate that this is not the case. The situation described here is extremely unusual, though it can be stated that in the following hour the patient's derivatives began to organize more closely and meaningfully around the deviant adaptation-evoking contexts. It may be postulated that the major breaks in this therapeutic environment and in the therapist's hold of the patient were of such proportions as to render the patient unconsciously fearful of meaningful relatedness. The use of the Kleenex, and the presence of remote derivatives related to the craziness of the situation and its destructiveness, lend some minimal support to this hypothesis. The patient's dread of living alone may also be seen as an unconscious perception of the therapist who works with her patients under conditions that are so open to the presence of outsiders.

Still, it would be necessary to carefully analyze the material in the sessions that followed, and to explore the reactions of other patients under comparable conditions, before concluding that the most valid formulation of the implications of the patient's material as described here is that the deviations have created a set of conditions under which meaningful communication and relatedness have been seriously damaged.

On the face of it, the initial conditions of this treatment are so evidently disturbed that it seems likely that the patient's failure to meaningfully work over these basic deviations stem in part from a fearful image of the therapist and in part from her own highly masochistic, pathological needs as evidenced by her state of depression. The challenge presented by this material can only be met through an extended consideration of each of the basic ground rules of psychotherapy.

The Private Office

Departures from the ideal office tend to entail some measure of compromise in the basic mode of therapeutic relationship between the patient and therapist and in the holding qualities of the frame. When these compromises involve aspects of the fixed setting, and especially when they are not dramatic and blatant, the patient is prone to set them aside and to very seldom allude to them directly in a way that facilitates early interpretation and rectification. Usually, a series of interventions are required: first, the playback of pertinent derivatives organized around the unmentioned deviation context; next, with the direct representation of the adaptive context, the full interpretation of its implications; then, based on fresh derivative material from the patient, the essential step of rectifying the frame if at all possible; and finally, interpretations that relate both to the previous deviation context and to the adaptive context of the rectification of the frame once the ideal therapeutic environment has been secured.

Deviations regarding which the therapist has a special kind of investment (e.g., a home-office setting, an office shared by several therapists, or the use of a secretary) are vested interest deviations. Because of the therapist's special investment in their maintenance, patients are loath to communicate meaningfully, both directly and through derivatives, in respect to their existence and implications. In addition to reacting to the threatening and Neurotic, and sometimes seductive, image of the therapist generated by the deviation at hand, the patient is usually faced with a situation where the therapist is unlikely to modify the deviation involved. Because of this, the patient unconsciously realizes that his or her communicative and curative efforts will be wasted on the therapist. Often, there are cycles in which initially the patient attempts to assist the therapist in curing the underlying countertransferences or modifying the realities on which the deviation is based. Much of this is done through highly disguised and embedded communications and requires a knowing and sensitive use of the listening-experiencing process by the therapist. If, however, the therapist fails to appreciate the true implications of the patient's derivative expressions, and either remains silent or intervenes in some other area, and thereby offers the patient a lie-barrier and defense system, a period usually follows in which the patient is depressed and relatively noncommunicative. The situation is considerably aggravated when, as is often the case, the therapist is totally unaware of the importance of the deviation, its impact upon himself or herself and the patient, and the essential need for rectification. In general, vested interest deviations render therapists derivatively deaf.

The ideal office for the private practice of psychotherapy should be located in a professional building. It should also be a single office with a private waiting room, not shared by other therapists or physicians. It should have its own bathroom that may be used by patient and therapist (the luxury of a separate bathroom for the therapist, while perhaps even more ideal, is a practical impossibility). It should have an entrance to the waiting room and a different exit for the patient, so there is no contact in the waiting room between patients. A reasonable and workable compromise would involve a single door for entrance and exit to the office.

The office itself should be, of course, essentially soundproofed. Special measures must be taken to insure this. Use is usually made of double studding, with some type of padding and special ceiling. These sound barriers may be supported with some type of humidifier, dehumidifier, white noise machine, or a small fan that runs constantly in either the hallway or waiting room area, and perhaps as well in the consultation room itself.

The appointments of the office should be attractive, but as simple and neutral as possible. Plants are an option, though magazines tend to be diverting and self-revealing of the therapist and should not be included. Minor objects of decoration and inexpensive posters or prints are optional, since their absence creates a rather austere setting, while their presence must be understood to be minimally or sometimes more significantly self-revealing. If used, they should be kept in mind as possible intervention contexts.

Carpeting should be comfortable but not ostentatious. The therapist should have a private closet and a separate coat rack, preferably within the consultation room (for reasons of safety), for the patient. The consultation room itself should have a comfortable chair for the patient; a comfortable chair, possibly with an ottoman, for the therapist (and the two chairs should be quite different); and a couch if the therapist intends to make use of one. It is advisable to have a table between the two chairs and between the therapist's chair and the couch. The chair may be placed at a desk or not, though it is helpful to have a desk present to provide a sense of professionalism. However, there should be nothing on the desk that is self-revealing, and especially no papers, books, journals, or patient records—if such exist.

It is advisable that no notes be taken during sessions or written afterwards, except when a therapist must present to a supervisor in order to learn how to do psychotherapy. In that case, the notes must be made *after* the hour; none whatsoever should be made in the presence of the patient. There should be a telephone with a switch so it can be turned off during sessions with patients, though in any case, the therapist should not interrupt sessions by answering the telephone if it rings. An answering device is preferable to an answering service, since the latter involves third parties who are quite prone to insensitive and extraneous comments and mistakes. There should be an extension of the office phone in the therapist's apartment or house so that he or she will know when the telephone rings after hours, and *alone* should have the responsibility of answering it (if he or she happens to be at home during office hours). The extension should not be picked up after hours, but instead, messages should be retrieved after the call has been completed by whoever may have made it.

Such practices as sharing an office, sharing a waiting room, using two offices (usually one at home and one elsewhere), having an office in an apartment house rather than in a professional building, using any part of the therapist's home or apartment to see patients, and having an office attached to the therapist's home all constitute common alterations in the ideal therapeutic environment. Such practices flourish for many reasons: they inappropriately protect in some way both the patient and the therapist; they are especially convenient for the therapist; they are usually economical for the therapist; they are utilized without criticism by many therapists and analysts; they are seldom directly, though virtually always indirectly, questioned by patients; they are maintained by the prevailing therapeutic practice of listening on manifest and Type One derivative levels without due attention to Type Two derivative communication; and they find support in the belief maintained by many therapists and analysts that everything and anything can be satisfactorily analyzed.

This attitude is a *neurotic delusion*. Many such false beliefs exist in the field of psychotherapy and psychoanalysis. This particular attitude is based on the erroneous belief that a therapist or analyst can do virtually anything he or she wishes, and that it can then be resolved by so-called verbal, analytic, or interpretive work. Of course, such a belief denies the importance and relatively unmodifiable impact of the therapist's actual behaviors, and their conscious and unconscious implications on the patient. It denies too the realization that exists in all other spheres of life that how one behaves and what one actually is takes precedence over what one says—the latter may easily involve deliberate or inadvertent lies and falsifications. As the saying goes, actions speak louder than words—and words cannot very much change the implications of actions. There has been an unfortunate need among therapists and analysts to pretend otherwise.

In the ideal office setting, the patient is confronted with the adaptation-evoking stimulus of a solid and definitive physical setting for psychotherapy. This group of relative constants reflect only minimally the personality of the therapist, though they do reveal his or her capacity to secure the necessary physical space for the treatment experience. The physical setting then tends to become a silent dimension of the background and core relationship between the patient and therapist. In the absence of a deviation, allusions to the setting rarely emerge in a patient's material. In general, they become the physical component of a secure therapeutic space and hold that both safeguards and threatens the patient (see Chapter 18).

On rare occasions, the physical setting may lend itself to a framework-deviation issue. The patient may wish to present the therapist with a plant or ash tray for his or her office. If the therapist has magazines in the waiting room, or books in his consultation room, the patient may want to borrow some material from the therapist. At times, the soundproofing may decay, and sound leakage may become the issue. Then too, the therapist may decide to redecorate, a relatively innocuous and yet meaningful adaptive context.

In those instances where the patient wishes to modify the setting, the therapist should maintain neutrality and adopt an initially noncommittal attitude. This permits the patient to free associate without having effected a sector of misalliance and a pathological mode of relatedness through an implicit or explicit promise from the therapist to participate in the proposed deviation. In this way, the communicative qualities of the therapeutic relationship are maintained in a maximally open state. As a rule, the patient's derivative material will then direct the therapist to maintain the therapeutic environment, and will permit interpretation of the patient's effort at deviation in light of a *prior* adaptation-evoking context. With a solid setting, this context is often the secure frame itself and the threats it creates for the patient.

When the physical setting is not ideal, the patient's responses are likely to include a strong measure of communicative resistance.

CLINICAL EXAMPLE

The therapist, a woman, made use of an accountant's office. There was a space for secretaries, though no waiting room per se. The office was not fully soundproofed, though the therapist saw her patients in the evening when no one else was present, and she spaced the times of her appointments sufficiently apart so as to avoid complications.

The excerpt presented here is from a first session with a young accountant who had called the therapist and asked for a consultation appointment. He arrived early for his session and waited in a small foyer. The therapist came to escort him into her office; she introduced herself, as did he to her. While passing through the secretarial area, the patient made the comment "Hi Mel" as if he were greeting the accountant from whom the therapist rented her office. Once in the consultation room, the following exchange took place:

Patient: Have you been here long? I live in Great Neck, but I have my accounting practice in Garden City. *(The therapist's office is between these two locations.)* I grew up in this town. My job is getting to me. I can't make decisions, and I feel I'm cracking up. *(Pause.)* So where do I start?
Therapist: I think you have already.
Patient: Well, I'm married, but I'm separated. I'm not really sure. My wife still sleeps over at my house, even though she now has an apartment. I have a girlfriend and she's into this therapy thing. There was this confusion. I had a girlfriend and my wife had a boyfriend, and we each found each other out. It was pretty stupid. I find I have trouble looking directly at you. I feel like I'm making a presentation.
Therapist: You're feeling exposed.
Patient: I'm used to being on the other side: listening to other people talk. I may be an accountant, but they tell me all their problems. I can't decide between the two woman in my life. Generally, I prefer to be alone. This other kind of situation involves lies and deceit. I'm afraid I won't be truthful here. I don't like to hurt other people's feelings. I have to protect them. I wondered before I came here whether you'd be a Freudian.
Therapist: If I were, what thoughts would you have?
Patient: Somehow, I might already know why I can't make a decision. I should really tell both woman good-bye and set things straight. There are other woman too. I have this uncle who married his neighbor, but he doesn't live with her now. It's bizarre. Secrets.
Therapist: You seem to be wondering whether we have any secrets. How did you get my name?
Patient: My sister's friend heard about you. I went to the friend because I was afraid of cracking up, and she told me to call

you. I have a lot of friends who can give me approval. That's not what I need from you. My wife got involved with an accountant also. It's a mess. She said she might stay with me if I came to see you. That's not the only reason I'm here. I guess I should pay you now for this session. If your finances are as bad off as mine, you need the money. I'm concerned about paying for treatment because my rent is high. Sometimes I don't hear things the way they are said.

The therapist has many tasks in the first hour. Some extend well beyond the evaluation of the patient's psychopathology and assets, and involve an assessment of the patient's ability to work meaningfully in therapy. Also important is the determination of the presence of early resistances on a gross behavioral or communicative level. These must be understood, however, in terms of early adaptation-evoking contexts. Among these, the conditions of treatment and the therapist's manner of establishing the therapeutic contract loom large. In every session, including the first hour, the patient is responding adaptively to intervention contexts from the therapist. Even in the first hour, then, it is possible to discern meaningful *derivative* communication (as well as manifest meaning) and to intervene, when necessary, in a sound interpretive and framework-management fashion.

Briefly, in this session the patient began with a powerful derivative allusion to the contaminated qualities of the therapeutic setting: his comment, "Hi Mel," which he made in the waiting room. By making the remark in the secretary's area, the patient himself was extending the usual framework of treatment, which prescribes that the patient's communications (except for the initial greeting) take place in the therapist's consultation room.

Once in the therapist's office, the patient provided additional derivatives that reflected his evident concern regarding the therapeutic setting. He inquired as to how long the therapist had been using this particular office, and then spoke of his own decision to separate his practice from where he lived—i.e., to effect certain boundaries to his work efforts.

Most of the patient's associations can be organized as encoded unconscious perceptions of the therapist and of the deviant treatment situation. There is the patient's concern about communicating and about whether he can be honest under these conditions. There is the striking derivative regarding the uncertainty of his own marital situation and exactly where his wife resides. This conveys in meaningful fashion the patient's confusion regarding the treatment situation. Quite soon, the patient indicates that on the basis of the therapeutic setting he has been offered, he is able to establish an unconscious perception of the therapist as having difficulty in establishing clear-cut boundaries in a manner similar to both his wife and himself.

The patient repeatedly returns to the theme of discomfort over being exposed. As with the patient cited earlier in this chapter, he alludes to the advantages of privacy and aloneness. Contaminated and boundary-broken relationships are connected in his mind with lies and deceit. As if to account for the extent to which he has encoded his unconscious perceptions of the therapist in light of the deviations at hand, the patient also mentions his fear of hurting others and his need to protect them.

There then follows the question as to whether the therapist is a Freudian, which might well mean someone capable of establishing a secure therapeutic setting. There follows a *model of rectification* in which the patient states that he should disengage himself from both his poor relationship with his wife and a questionable relationship with a girlfriend. Another allusion to confused boundaries and ground rules follows in the reference to the uncle who married a neighbor and then left her. There is the patient's hope to achieve something more than approval—an allusion that may well contain his wish for insight rather than framework-deviation cure. The hour then concludes with a further derivative allusion to the setting of treatment and the patient's unconscious perception that the therapist may have chosen this particular setting because of financial pressures—an image that does indeed contain part of the truth of her motives.

In this situation, then, it is possible to develop a highly coalescible derivative complex organized around the implications of the deviations in this particular private office setting. One must realize, of course, that since the therapist did not attempt to interpret the patient's material in this light, these hypotheses can be accepted only as silent and tentative, and in need of validation. Highly tentative confirmation seems available in the extent to which this material can be developed into a meaningful derivative complex in light of the deviant contexts. The finding that the patient began and ended his hour with direct and derivative allusions to the nature of the setting also lends some tentative support to these formulations. In actual practice with other patients, interpretations based on hypotheses of this kind have obtained Type Two derivative validation.

One may speculate as to why this patient provided a far more meaningful communicative network to this therapist than that generated in the first hour by the clinic patient alluded to earlier in this chapter. Distinctive unconscious perceptions of the trustworthiness of each therapist may have been involved. Then too the patient's own communicative and other propensities may have been a factor. In this regard, the first patient appeared to be far more depressed and masochistic than the second patient, and therefore far more inclined to accept the deviant treatment conditions with resignation. The final factor probably involves the extent of the breaks in the frame. In the first situation they were blatant, extensive, and involved basic violations in privacy and confidentiality. In the second situation, despite the deviant aura created by the setting, the patient actually had a private office for his communications to the therapist. The closer a frame is to being secured, the greater the likelihood of meaningful direct and derivative communication from the patient.

These last considerations reinforce the factors to be taken into account when considering a break in the frame: the universal implications that are shared by all deviations; the specific implications of the particular deviation (here, the parasiticism and threat, and impaired sense of hold, created by the lack of total confidentiality and privacy, and by an uncertain physical setting); the specific implications of the deviation for the therapist (in the first situation, of being at the mercy of the clinic personnel, while in the second situation, the therapist's state of financial need—whatever additional emotional factors may have been involved); and the specific meanings of, and reactions to, a deviation for a particular patient. As each of these levels of meaning become available in the patient's manifest and especially derivative material, they can be interpreted and utilized for the process of rectification.

The Home Office

The home-office arrangement, another vested interest deviation, can be used to further illustrate some of the problems that exist and must be dealt with in the presence of a relatively fixed modification of the ideal therapeutic environment.

CLINICAL EXAMPLE

A young man was in psychotherapy for a year with a woman therapist who made use of an office in her apartment. From time to time, her young son would interrupt the patient's sessions when he eluded the baby sitter. On occasion too the therapist's husband was seen in the apartment by the patient. Two excerpts are presented here: the first from a time when several other framework issues had arisen; the second took place after the patient had seen the therapist's husband in the hallway of the apartment.

> Patient: I was in Pennsylvania on the weekend visiting my girlfriend's sister and her husband. They have a beautiful home and are quite wealthy. They promised to help me out when I started my business, but they never really did anything for me. They were in their bedroom fighting as if I wasn't there. I guess they don't care who's around; they do as they please. I was annoyed being there. It made me feel very competitive, especially with them having money and my having nothing. Sometimes I wonder if there is any point in my being here. I feel I'm getting nowhere in therapy.

Organized around the vaguely represented intervention context of the home-office arrangement (cf. the final two comments), the patient is expressing through derivatives the depressing, exhibitionistic, voyeuristic, selfish (for the therapist), and competitive qualities of the home-office arrangement. It generates within him a sense of disillusionment, which leads him to question the value of treatment.

> Patient: I'm annoyed. In a bad mood. Feeling unproductive. Everything here seems fucked up. I don't believe you're a God or that you're always right. Sometimes I think you miss things badly.

Therapist: Last session you mentioned a dream where you thought I was going to hurt or kill you.

Patient: It's not that I'm afraid of you, it's that everything seems so screwed up. I tend to ignore too many things. I don't feel well.

Here there are several fragmented and embedded derivatives that serve as a commentary on the apartment-office arrangement and the way in which it creates a sense of chaos within the therapeutic bipersonal field. The therapist knew from her husband that the patient had seen him in the hallway, but this particular intervention context found only highly disguised representation in this hour. The associations excerpted here convey the patient's unconscious perception of the therapist in light of these deviant conditions as unproductive, "fucked up," wrong, and missing things badly. The therapist's intervention unconsciously served to steer the patient away from the intervention context and his related derivative communications. The patient's responsive comment to the effect that he ignores too many things is a valid unconscious perception and commentary on the therapist's erroneous intervention—especially her need to ignore the disturbed therapeutic hold and environment.

The first excerpt included a less disguised, though still indirect representation of the intervention context of the apartment-office arrangement. The therapist could, in such an hour, intervene with a playback of selected derivatives organized around the unmentioned deviant adaptive context. This should be done with the best representation of the intervention context as the fulcrum for the therapist's comment. Thus the therapist could have pointed out to the patient that he's talking about someone's home setting and the way in which they have a great deal and he has nothing. He then spoke of having been promised help, but having received nothing, and of overhearing a disturbance. These thoughts are somehow connected with treatment, since his associations went to questioning his being here and his feelings of getting nowhere in therapy.

Validation of this intervention would take the form of the patient alluding either directly to the home-office setting and the recent disturbance created by the therapist's child, or through his representation of this issue with considerably less disguised derivative communications, and through the emergence of new and meaningful derivative expressions.

In principle, if the therapist maintains a vigilance for communications related to a vested interest deviation of this kind, he or she will be able to undertake therapeutic work initially through the kind of playback illustrated here. All interventions that depart from this critical intervention context, or do not in some way get linked up to the background deviation, will be experienced as a greater or lesser effort by the therapist to create a sector of misalliance or bastion through which the framework issue is sealed off from consideration and intervention.

If instead, the therapist initiates efforts at playback, the patient will experience both a sense of cognitive understanding and an introject of a therapist prepared to analyze and possibly even rectify the deviation involved. On this basis, the patient will generally respond with clear derivatives, and eventually shift from the common use of Type C communication to that of the Type A mode, to the point where both the intervention context and the derivative complex appear in a form that lends itself to both interpretation and rectification. This is usually a gradual and difficult process, since the patient is basically mistrustful of the therapist, and quite divided in respect to the deviation: consciously tending to accept its presence and the measure of framework-deviation relief it offers to him or her, while unconsciously objecting, angered, feeling endangered, and experiencing pathological introjects of the therapist. Further, should the therapist begin to interpret the patient's sound unconscious perceptions of himself based on the deviation, and yet fail to rectify the frame, the patient will experience a major split in the therapist and a strong sense of disillusionment: he or she is confronted with a therapist who seems to understand, but who does not take the necessary measures to correct the situation in actuality. Similarly, therapists who begin to make efforts to rectify those deviations that can be corrected, must be capable of interpreting the patient's derivative responses lest the patient experience a correction of the ground rules that is not supported with sound understanding.

Another patient, a young woman, was seeing a male therapist who also used a home office. With this deviation as a silent and insidious backdrop, the patient began to have sessions with another therapist for herself and her fiance. Typically, one deviation breeds another and framework alterations become the vehicle for "cure."

Furthermore, the therapist who is insensitive to one break in the frame will tend to be insensitive to others.

The following is an excerpt from a session that followed an hour in which the patient expressed a strong sense of confusion about the state of her therapy.

> Patient: My boyfriend says I need a check-up by a good doctor. I've been having fainting spells. It's probably psychological. We missed our session with Anne *(the other therapist)* this week. My boyfriend was at his college where he was confronted by several black teenagers. He was cornered, but kept answering them back. He got knifed in the arm and needed stitches. From there, he came to my apartment. It was a mess and left a bad impression. I've been having repetitive dreams like I had in childhood. I'm being pursued and the exits are barred, and I can't see my pursuer. Sometimes I think my boyfriend is after me. My mother called me. She's always tense and yells a lot. If I don't relax, I'll faint again. Oh, by the way, did you see the new fabric store downstairs in this building? I think there's a lot of items there you would like.

The thesis that this material relates on one level to the home-office arrangement receives some measure of support in the patient's allusion to her own apartment and to her final comment of the hour—a reference to the building in which the therapist has his office and an effort to modify the usual boundaries between herself and the therapist. If these derivatives are organized around the intervention context of the home-office arrangement, it could be formulated that the patient is suggesting that the therapist requires some kind of help because he has a problem. Pursuing additional unconscious perceptions and speculations as to the therapist's need for the home office arrangement, one might tentatively postulate that the patient believes that the therapist is fearful of a private office and of being trapped there alone with a dangerous patient. The home office provides a sense of the presence of third parties— family members—who in actuality often serve unconsciously as protectors for the therapist, and who are perceived in just that way by the patient. The availability of the home-office offers a ready means of escape, and family members are in some way similar to the second therapist: they serve to dilute the situation and provide both the patient and therapist a defense against paranoid and persecutory (being pursued) perceptions and fantasies, and an artificial means of decreasing other anxieties and pressures that might emerge in a more private one-to-one setting.

Patients typically see therapists who adopt a home-office arrangement as lacking in autonomy, fearing individuation, and as maintaining pathological symbiotic needs. They expect to be similarly gratified, and accept treatment under these conditions as a way of defending against, and setting to the side, their own anxieties related to separation-individuation, their own persecutory fantasies, and often their intense sexual conflicts, anxieties, and fantasies, which are more likely to emerge in a private setting. Then too, this arrangement is seen as a pathological expression of exhibitionistic needs in the therapist, both in respect to where he or she lives and with whom. There is, as a result, a strong primal scene quality to these actualities. In this respect, derivatives of transversal intermixtures of both perception and fantasy are not uncommon (cf. the allusion to the boyfriend being attacked and the patient's dream of being pursued with the exits barred). Many of these unconscious and actual implications for the home-office arrangement are universal to all deviations. Perhaps the main implication that most characterizes the home-office arrangement is the therapist's fear of being alone with the patient. The other meanings identified for this particular modification in the ideal therapeutic environment tend to be shared in general by most other alterations in the ground rules. As can be seen—and this is a fundamental principle—effective psychotherapeutic work typically deals with actualities within treatment and their unconscious implications (real and distorted).

Stress has been placed in these formulations on relatively valid unconscious perceptions and impressions of the therapist. It seems likely that the patient, too, is fearful of the secured therapeutic space, and is experiencing persecutory anxieties and fantasies for other reasons. Nonetheless, these should be developed as secondary formulations and utilized only sparingly or not at all in intervening in the presence of a significant break in the ideal therapeutic frame. Under such conditions, it is the therapist's psychopathology that is obtaining prime expression and to which the patient is reacting. These responses are essentially nontransference-based and soundly perceptive. The therapist must therefore implicitly accept the valid elements of these perceptions, and interpret and rectify the frame accordingly. It is only as the framework becomes secure that the patient's transferences and own pathological tendencies can be clearly identified and interpreted. There is, as noted before, a strong tendency within therapists to formulate material in terms of the patient's intrapsychic and interpersonal problems. In the presence of a framework deviation, these efforts must be placed to the periphery, since the patient's major reactions evolve for the moment mainly around the therapist's expressed psychopathology rather than that of the patient.

It may well be that there are therapists who adopt a home-office arrangement out of utmost financial necessity, and who do not have major countertransference problems. However, the realities of the conditions of the setting and its implications are such that the patient can in no way be convinced—nor does the patient have sound reason to believe—that his or her unconscious readings of the meanings of the setting are unfounded. Usually, these perceptions are quite justified, and lead to *unmodifiable* unconscious non-transference-based perception constellations that compromise therapeutic outcome.

Technically, a therapist who is involved in *any* deviation from the ideal therapeutic environment should take that particular intervention context and examine it for its conscious and unconscious implications. The therapist should maintain one level of the listening process in a way that organizes all of the patient's associations as derivative responses to the particular deviant intervention context at hand. The therapeutic environment is primary and basic for both patient and therapist, and any disturbance will to some degree preoccupy the patient on a derivative level as long as it is in existence. The patient's material will virtually never organize meaningfully around other intervention contexts unless they happen to involve additional breaks in the frame.

With patient listening, and with the strength not to intervene in respect to some other unnecessary area, the therapist will find that the patient eventually offers a direct or minimally disguised representation of the deviant intervention context. In such a session—a so-called *curative hour*, created unconsciously by the patient—there are usually several meaningful and coalescible derivatives (sometimes conveyed in a dream), and an interpretation of mainly unconscious perceptions is therefore feasible. Once it is made, the patient will usually respond with Type Two derivative validation and add derivative *models of rectification* if they have not as yet been presented. Should the therapist then interpret the expressed need to correct the situation, the patient will respond with still additional, previously repressed derivative revelations as to how he or she has been experiencing the particular alteration in the framework. If the therapist next proceeds to actually rectify the frame—in this instance, to move to an entirely private office—the patient will offer still further derivative (and often manifest) communications that reflect still more of the repressed unconscious perceptions that had been evoked by the previous arrangement, as well as their possible extensions into distortion and fantasy. Since breaks in the frame are uniformly repetitious in some form of past pathogenic interactions, the genetic meanings of the deviant arrangement will also eventually emerge in the derivative material from the patient. A sequence of this kind can turn a damaging deviation into a major opportunity for insight and for the patient's experience of the therapist as someone who can correct an error and secure the therapeutic hold even in the face of previous damage. Although some negative residuals will undoubtedly remain within the patient, this type of work is the best available under these conditions. It entails a shift from countertransference-nontransference, pathological mode of relatedness, and impaired holding and containing, to noncountertransference-transference, a healthy therapeutic symbiosis, and secured holding and containing. A great deal of sound therapeutic work can take place on this basis.

Any change in setting is, of course, a prime adaptive context and adaptation-evoking stimulus for the patient (and the therapist as well). As long as it is absolutely necessary and carried out with a full sense of responsibility, it will prove possible to interpret the patient's responsive unconscious perceptions and fantasies in a meaningful manner directed toward insight and therapeutic gain. Even in those situations where the therapist has deliberately or inadvertently altered the frame unnecessarily, there can be considerable therapeutic gain as long as the therapist first rectifies the deviation at the behest of the patient's derivative communications, and second, interprets all of the relevant material.

It should be realized again, however, that such deviations do produce a hurtful image and experience of the therapist that will not be entirely corrected by the act of rectification. Instead, there is an image of someone who has been hurtful, destructive, or seductive, and who is nonetheless capable of recognizing a mistake and modifying behavior. A period of self-analysis is often helpful during such interludes as a way of insuring that the therapist will not, under some different set of conditions, opt for a deviant response because of pressures within or from the patient.

On the other hand, the therapist who is able to maintain the framework in response to pressures from the patient to deviate is experienced by the patient quite unambigously as a good object on a derivative level, no matter what the surface complaints. Under these circumstances, the split is reversed from that which occurs when the therapist deviates. Here, the patient is sometimes consciously resentful of the therapist's maintenance of the ground rules, while showing extensive and deep appreciation on a derivative level.

These, then, are the essentials of the setting for psychotherapy. Ideally, there should be no books on the shelves, though in practicality, it is difficult for therapists to do otherwise. Should the therapist have written a book, it should *not* be in evidence, for the writing of books by psychotherapists create many framework problems that are beyond the purview of this volume.

Chapter 20

The First Contact: Whom To Treat

Having learned how to listen to manifest and derivative material, having created a sound therapeutic setting, and having acquired the other skills and knowledge necessary to do sound psychotherapy, the therapist is now ready for his or her first contact with a patient.

The In-patient Service

There are many troublesome problems with the first contact between a patient and an in-service therapist. Ideally, it should be this therapist who sees the patient in the emergency room and arranges the admission. This is in keeping with the principle that there should be one therapist for each patient. The same therapist should then manage the treatment of the patient, confining their contacts to the psychotherapeutic sessions. It is important for the therapist to limit deviations to those imposed entirely upon him or her by the patient and his or her psychopathology. There is a tendency among therapists on their own to move toward deviations in the ideal ground rules and boundaries of therapy under these conditions. This proclivity should be restrained as a way of offering the patient the best possible hold and insightful treatment experience. These principles apply to contacts between the treating therapist and family members, as well as between the treating therapist and nursing and other staff personnel. At times, the issue arises as to whether a supervisor should interview the patient directly (a practice that should be avoided), and there are many other pressures in an in-patient setting toward deviation and modification of the ground rules.

In principle, the ideal is to maintain a one-to-one relationship between the patient and therapist, excluding as much as possible all third parties to treatment. As noted earlier, psychotic patients often tend to adopt a framework alteration mode of adaptation and create considerable pressure on the therapist toward deviation. At times, of course, the therapist may have no alternative but to modify these ideal conditions. The therapist should not do so, however, unless absolutely necessary. Further, it should be remembered that these measures are modifications in the ideal therapeutic relationship and setting, and that the patient will have powerful direct and derivative responses to the unconscious meanings and communications involved. Among these, the treating therapist's fear of the patient and his or her inability to handle the psychotic or other disturbance loom quite large.

In this context, it is inadvisable for the treating therapist to perform a physical examination upon the patient. This violation in boundaries is often highly disruptive for the patient—and often for the therapist as well. It is also ideal for the patient to voluntarily seek treatment within the hospital setting; the therapy of a patient who has been committed to a hospital departs from the best possible therapeutic ambience. Again, these deviations should always be kept in mind as first-order intervention contexts throughout such a therapeutic experience.

Finally, it would be best if the in-patient therapist could continue with the hospitalized patient after discharge. Departures from this practice are highly traumatic for the patient and create many difficulties for the in-patient and subsequent out-patient therapy.

The Out-patient Clinic

Many of the principles that apply to in-patient treatment apply to out-patient clinics. Ideally, the patient should seek therapy, should be seen by a single therapist for both the intake procedure and actual therapy, and should carry through the treatment to its completion with the same therapist. Wherever possible, it should be the therapist who answers the initial telephone call rather than a secretary or an intake social worker. The practice of using one or more intake therapist who then recommends the patient to another therapist creates significant complications for the subsequent therapy, and constitutes a major break in the framework needed by the patient. The therapist alone should collect the fee and make appointments. Clinic therapists who have to cancel hours for any reason should make these calls themselves rather than relying on secretaries. As much as possible, psychotherapy in a clinic should take place privately between a help-seeking patient and a help-offering, single therapist.

Private Practice

The first contact with the private therapist is usually by telephone. The therapist should be cordial and should make the earliest possible appointment with the patient—doing so, however, only if able to offer ongoing therapy. The therapist should be sensitive to any hints of depression, and especially to suicidal trends, and should, if they are in evidence, address them during the conversation. For example, the therapist might ask the patient if he or she is depressed. If there has been some allusion to self-hurtful tendencies, the therapist might well inquire if there is any danger of a suicide attempt. If the therapist has any sense that this possibility exists, he or she should either arrange to see the patient that day or make it clear that he or she is available by telephone in any emergency or if intense self-destructive impulses should arise. The expressed sensitivity and availability of the therapist is usually sufficient to carry over such patients until the first session.

In keeping with principles already established, a therapist should not, as indicated above, see a patient if he or she does not have time for ongoing therapy. The practice of some analysts and therapists to hold consultation sessions with the purported purpose of recommending one or another therapist or of recommending psychotherapy or psychoanalysis, does not justify the deviation of involving a second therapist in the patient's treatment. There is an obvious hurt and a sense of exploitation experienced by patients who are treated in this way, much of it expressed through derivative communications rather than manifestly. There is no justification for such a practice, since any analyst who believes that a decision regarding therapy or analysis is in order can refer the patient to another analyst who has time available to offer whichever type of therapy the patient may need. In this context, it is well to mention the therapist's responsibility to treat all patients who enter his or her office. While a therapist does have the legal perogative to refuse to treat a patient, such refusal is highly hurtful and traumatizing to the patient, and runs counter to the basic responsibilities of therapists in light of their avowed profession.

As part of the initial telephone conversation, the therapist should specifically ask the patient how the therapist's name was obtained. This is necessary in light of the restrictions as to whom a therapist should treat. There are certain answers to this question that preclude even a consultation visit (see below). In order to spare the patient a traumatic and hurtful experience that will negatively color his or her image of therapists and of therapy, the therapist should deal with this question on the telephone. Should it be impossible for the therapist to see the patient, he or she should either offer a referral to someone known to have open time available or offer to make the necessary telephone calls in order to find a therapist with available time.

Some patients ask about the therapist's fee on the telephone. This is usually a poor prognostic sign in respect to the patient's commitment to therapy. The query is best handled with a response to the effect that the fee can be discussed during the initial consultation. If the patient insists on having this information, the therapist should state his or her usual fee and should be prepared to maintain that particular fee for the consultation session and for the psychotherapy itself. There is no justification for, and and considerable damage done by, the practice of holding a consultation session of any duration other than the usual 45 or 50 minute session that will be used throughout the treatment. Similarly, the therapist's fee for the consultation should be identical to that charged throughout the therapy.

During the first telephone call, the therapist should provide the patient with his or her full name and address. The therapist should not volunteer directions as to how to reach the office, unless it is in some rural settings where it may be necessary. In principle, it is vital always to safeguard and respect the patient's autonomy whenever possible.

Whom the Therapist Should Treat (I)

The therapist should treat anyone to whom he or she has personal anonymity. No therapist should treat friends or relatives or anyone with whom he or she has had an outside contact, whether socially, through a professional lecture, or in some other professional setting. The therapist should *not* treat individuals who are referred by present or past patients, since this violates his or her anonymity, and actually creates many difficulties for both of the patients involved.

There are many common violations of this particular ground rule. Type Two derivative listening makes it unmistakable that they are highly destructive and they preclude a sound therapeutic experience. The problem of these modifications in the ideal therapeutic environment cannot be effectively rectified, and therefore undermine the therapeutic relationship and experience. Under these conditions, the only possible basis for truth therapy and sound sectors of insight entails a working over of the deviation in question. This type of effort is often difficult. The pathological autistic, symbiotic, and parasitic qualities of the mode of relatedness established on the basis of an unrectifiable deviation, along with their pathological satisfactions and defenses, lead patients to attempt to establish sectors of misalliance and bastions with their therapist in respect to the alteration in the frame. Strong defenses and resistances develop under these conditions; the general degree of openness in respect to the derivative meanings of the patient's material tends to be considerably compromised because of the basic flaw in the therapeutic hold.

Still, from time to time, the patient will put together a session in which he or she meaningfully represents the deviant adaptive context and a relatively meaningful derivative complex that reflects the implications of the deviation as unconsciously perceived by the patient. On this basis, initial interpretive efforts prove feasible. Virtually without exception, once this type of work has been undertaken, the patient's *derivative* material will point the therapist toward rectification through the termination of treatment. On rare occasions, this decision may sometimes be effected within a few weeks or a month or two. However, largely because of the patient's (and therapist's) pathological investment in the deviant contract and the resistances it creates, more typically it takes six months to a year to work through an effective termination with such patients. Often, this period, which is concentrated on the analysis of the implications of the unrectifiable deviation and the need to rectify the frame through termination, provides the patient with sufficient insight to effectively resolve his or her Neurosis. This occurs because the patient's investment in the deviation, and unconscious perceptions of the therapist who has joined with the patient in the deviant contract, become interwoven with the unconscious factors in the patient's emotional disturbance. Should symptom resolution not take place, it is usually best to allow the patient to find his or her own second therapist in order to ensure an entirely uncontaminated second treatment experience. If there is no therapist available who understands the issues involved, it is sometimes necessary for the therapist to make a referral to someone whom he or she knows to be sensitive to these critical problems. Ideally, however, the termination should be complete and final, and the patient left to find his or her way from there. In all, this is the essence of an unrectifiable framework deviation termination therapy.

CLINICAL EXAMPLES

In Chapter 18, two brief excerpts were presented from patients who were seen on the basis of contaminated referral sources. As the reader may recall, in the first instance the referral source was a friend of the new patient who had previously seen the therapist in psychotherapy. The derivative material involved a strong sense of confusion as to who was living with whom, and included the fact that the new patient was living in the old patient's apartment. The new patient attempted to seduce the old patient's wife as a way of curing himself of his passivity and difficulties with women. This derivative underscored the parasitic and instinctualized (unconsciously sexual and especially homosexual) aspects of this type of referral. Allusions to masturbation brought out the self-gratifying qualities of the situation for both the patient and therapist, and an allusion to an earlier effort to seduce a mentally damaged cousin, and to being caught in the act, brought out further genetic implications and unconscious perceptions of the therapist. This particular derivative further emphasizes the inappropriately sexualized and parasitic gratifications involved in this type of relationship, as well as its thoughtlessness and its basis in ignorance. Finally, there were derivatives related to the patient's feeling that he was being exposed to others, material that hints at the manner in which this particular referral was experienced as a violation of both anonymity and total confidentiality.

Uniformly, patients unconsciously perceive this type of referral situation as a form of mutual exploitation—a means by which either or both the referring and the referred patient can avoid a meaningful therapeutic experience. It is also a situation in which the referred patient is seen as a gift by the referring patient, and a threesome is created that can serve to unconsciously live out a variety of unconscious fantasy-perception-memory constellations in relatively unanalyzable form, while simultaneously affording each participant a pathological form of sexual gratification and yet a third party defense against intimacy.

Another excerpt provided additional derivative material to support these hypotheses. There, in a situation where the therapist was attempting to rectify his continuing to see the patient in the absence of payment of the fee, the issue of the referral of this patient by his father, who had been a former patient of the therapist, served as the critical prior intervention context. In that regard, the particular means of referral created a situation in which the patient felt he would not have to function or take responsibility in his daily life or within treatment, and that he could exploit the therapist as the therapist was exploiting him. This latter translated into the patient's failure for many months to pay the therapist's fee or to work.

The example presented here involves a woman therapist who was seeing a young man in psychotherapy because of episodes of depression and difficulties in his relationship with women. The patient was living with a young woman whom he referred to the therapist for psychotherapy. The therapist had accepted the referral and arranged to see the girlfriend. The session excerpted here occurred after all of this had taken place.

> Patient: I'm upset with myself. I don't control what I eat and I'm getting fat. People bring in treats to work and I indulge myself. I don't know when to stop. It's a kind of sickness. I should have the will power to refuse. It's like losing control. Things are not going well at work this week. With our product, we sell more during a recession. [*The patient sells burglar-proof locks.*] When a depression comes, people steal

more. They get greedy. I don't like being at the office these days. There's too much gossip. Everyone's talking behind the backs of everyone else.

In the adaptive context of the therapist's decision to accept this patient referral, the referring patient is involved with a series of powerful, meaningful, and coalescible derivatives that organize quite well around the many unconscious implications of this decision. At the same time, the patient does not represent the adaptive context directly or with a disguised representation that lends itself readily to interpretation. There is no bridge whatsoever to therapy in this session, and the patient's resistances, which are *interactional* in nature (since they arise in part from the therapist's deviant intervention), are directed against the clear or direct representation of the intervention context. Perhaps the best such representation is the patient's allusion to the treats from others with which he indulges himself, or the reference to people being greedy and stealing. These are highly disguised (remote) derivatives at best.

In organizing the implications of the derivative complex when there has been a major break in the frame, the material to be formulated initially is understood mainly in terms of valid unconscious perceptions, with only minimal consideration of possible extensions into unconscious fantasy-memory formations. In this instance, the patient's derivative material lends itself readily to such perceived meanings, and constitutes an elaborate and coalescible derivative complex. There is a rather powerful unconscious commentary on the implications of the deviation at hand.

Thus the patient's associations provide images related to a valid view of the therapist in light of her deviation, as someone who lacks a sufficient capacity to restrain herself, as lacking in controls and self-indulgent, and in particular, as allowing others to inappropriately indulge her (cf. the allusion to eating the sweets from others). Through self-referential derivatives that imply unconscious introjections of attributes of the therapist based on her acceptance of the deviation, the patient indicates that the therapist has a sickness that she should be able to control with will power. This last constitutes a derivative model of rectification that implies that the girlfriend should be referred immediately to another therapist.

Through further derivatives, it appears that the patient unconsciously perceives the therapist as depressed and needy, factors that seem to help the patient account for the therapist's acceptance of this contaminated referral. This decision is also seen as dishonest, greedy, and as a form of stealing—themes that indicate the patient's unconscious perception that his own treatment is now constituted as a type of lie rather than truth therapy. Further, the therapist, in light of the deviation, is perceived as untrustworthy and as having created a situation where people will talk behind the backs of others. These last derivatives allude to the patient's sense of a loss of confidentiality and privacy because of the influence of the deviation on the patient's relationship with the therapist. This is a common form of iatrogenic paranoia, based on valid unconscious perceptions of the therapist, and developed in terms of the implications of this particular deviation.

This material organizes quite well as valid derivative commentaries on the unconscious implications of a deviation of this kind. The therapist's anonymity is compromised, and even when the therapist is capable of keeping the material from the two patients quite separate (itself a difficult task), the patient nonetheless experiences a sense of basic mistrust, a violation of privacy, and a belief that the basic safety of the therapy has been modified. These communications and impressions generate highly pathological introjective identifications with the therapist.

Later in this hour, the patient spoke of his brother, who had serious problems in controlling his appetite. In this way, he alluded to at least one genetic figure involved in the therapist's actual repetition of a past pathogenic trauma. In later sessions, the patient's depressed mother, who showed distinct narcissistic features and exploited her child, emerged as the critical nontransference genetic figure in respect to this deviation.

Many of the effects of this particular deviation are shared in common with all breaks in the frame. This includes the basic flaw in the therapist's holding and containing capacities, the negative images of the therapist, the basic sense of danger, the disturbances in the communicative qualities of the relationship, and the shift to a pathological mode of relatedness. The mode of cure becomes one of lie-barrier formations and framework-deviation relief. Breaks in the frame also consistently entail pathological gratifications for the therapist and a sense of inability to maintain adequate controls. The acceptance of a patient referral tends to extenuate those universal meanings of alterations in the ground rules and boundaries of treatment that touch upon self-serving, exploitative and parasitic, greedy and insatiable, and mistrustful qualities.

For this particular patient, the deviation involved a reenactment of a pathologically narcissistic and depressive interaction with his mother in his early childhood. Among the prior intervention contexts that prompted the patient to offer his girlfriend in referral, recent efforts by the therapist to secure this particular therapeutic frame were especially prominent. The patient had experienced these measures in part as a loss of a pathological symbiosis with a maternal figure, and his effort at deviation was an attempt through acting-out to recreate the pathological symbiosis that satisfied his Neurotic needs. A recent major illness in his mother further reinforced these wishes. By succumbing to them, the therapist fell into a sector of misalliance with this patient that reenacted aspects of his pathogenic past and supported his own Neurotic maladjustment and mode of relatedness. Only with rectification in the form of referring the girlfriend to another therapist would it be possible to insightfully understand the implications of these transactions, and to utilize them toward insightful structural change.

Each particular deviation as it unfolds between a specific patient and therapist has both universal and specific meanings. In principle, these can be determined when the therapist takes the particular deviation as an intervention context and, at first on his or her own, determines the unconscious implications involved. From there, it is necessary to organize the material from the patient as an essentially valid commentary on the breaks in the frame. Finally, idiosyncratic and distorted responses by the patient are considered. In this way, the more pressing and meaningful implications of each specific alteration in the therapeutic environment can be ascertained, and therapeutic measures carried out in terms of both broad meanings and the specific implications for a given patient.

Whom the Therapist Should Treat (II)

As indicated earlier, the therapist should not accept anyone for consultation with whom he or she had prior personal knowledge or contact. Referrals from fellow professionals are most ideal. Referrals from a clinic or a hospital are acceptable, though these should be carried out as simply as possible and without the many personal revelations regarding the therapist that clinic personnel are prone to offer. Referrals from personal friends must be evaluated individually, in that those that are likely to involve personal revelations or social contact, such as might occur with a close relative of the friend, should not be accepted. In general, referrals made by the relatives of the therapist should *not* be accepted, since there is an inherent modification in anonymity under these conditions (i.e., the patient knows a relative of the therapist).

The principle of not accepting any patient with whom there is any degree of contamination is fundamental. Patients are so strikingly sensitive to the least deviation in this regard that it is a disservice to accept anyone under tainted conditions. Often, when this is done, the patient will resort to communications based on highly disguised and embedded derivatives, and the therapist will be hard-pressed to maintain neutrality and to analyze and resolve the relevant issues—problems that actually undermine the basic therapeutic experience. In addition, as already noted, contaminations of this kind cannot be rectified: they constitute actualities filled with unconscious implications from the therapist that cannot be corrected, and certainly cannot be interpreted away.

In general, when a patient in psychotherapy requests a referral from his or her therapist for a relative or friend, the request should always be treated in part as a *derivative communication* and subjected to careful analysis in terms of prior intervention contexts. This type of request is often a signal that there is a major framework issue in the patient's own therapy that has not been rectified or analyzed. Sometimes—though as yet all too rarely—it may be a paradoxical response by a patient to the therapist's efforts to secure and maintain the frame. In principle, it is best to allow a patient to make such a referral through other means, using, for example, the resource through which the present patient entered treatment. For therapists who are concerned about the uneven qualifications of individuals practicing psychotherapy, referral to a particular training program registry, or to some other list of highly qualified therapists (where such lists do indeed exist) may be made as a final resort.

With patients who have telephoned the therapist for an appointment, and with whom it is discovered that there is some factor that precludes the initiation of treatment, it is acceptable for the therapist to refer the patient to a well-qualified colleague. However, in situations where a psychotherapy has reached a stalemate, or in which an unrectifiable deviation in the ground rules and boundaries leads to termination of the therapy before the patient has achieved symptom resolution, it is best to permit the patient to find his or her own subsequent therapist. A referral from the present therapist is highly tainted, in that it is offered by a therapist who has failed the patient in some significant way and in addition, actually impairs the rightful and autonomous search by the patient for a new and entirely separate treatment experience. It thereby interferes with the fresh beginning that is quite essential under these conditions.

In any situation in which a therapist makes a referral, it is best for the therapist to call the colleague to be sure that he or she has time available to see the patient. It is also advisable to give the patient that single name, and to suggest to the patient that he or she call back if any difficulties arise. Providing patients with lists of possible therapists is an inadvisable, traumatic, and frustrating practice that is usually hurtful to the prospective patient.

CLINICAL EXAMPLES

A 24-year-old woman whose mother had a large number of considerably younger siblings, so that the woman had two aunts who were just a few years her senior, was referred to the therapist by her Aunt Alice, who had been in treatment with the same therapist. The hour excerpted here had been randomly selected for presentation to the therapist's supervisor after the patient had been in treatment for about four months on a once-weekly basis.

> Patient: My Aunt Betty and I want to live together. I see advantages and disadvantages, but she's not ready yet. I need to leave home and yet I still can't do it. I'm feeling depressed. I need to buy a car, but I haven't done so. I'm afraid my father will find out about therapy and scream at me. He's really against my seeing a therapist.
>
> I had a dream. In it, I was coming to see you, but I had to wait until the time of my session. I was in some water and there were pieces of wood. The wood changed into sharks and I got frightened. I kept worrying about my father finding out I am in therapy and something awful happening to me. On the day after the dream, my boyfriend asked me if I talked

about him in therapy. He told me I shouldn't do it, and I got
angry that he wouldn't let me talk freely.

The issue of the referral source for this patient had not in any
way been subjected to exploration with this therapist, who had
worked with the patient mainly on a manifest content and Type
One derivative level. However, one can develop some further understanding of this type of referral situation by taking the therapist's
acceptance of the patient through a referral by a patient-relative as
the adaptive context. This is, of course, a powerful indicator and
adaptation-evoking context. Typically, there is, for the moment, no
direct representation of this indicator-context in this material. Perhaps the best representation is the allusion to a different aunt of the
patient and to living with her. This is a highly disguised and
remote derivative representation. Nonetheless, the material organizes quite meaningfully as a coalescible derivative complex pertinent to the unconscious perceptions and introjects of the therapist
based on his deviation and on the patient's adaptive responses. In
essence, the patient portrays this type of treatment arrangement as a
way of living together that may well hint at deeper homosexual
perceptions and fantasies, which are defended against for the moment. In any case, the patient also expresses her need for this
arrangement and her struggle against it, sensing that in some way
she loses out in her wish to gain individuation and autonomy.
There is a strong sense too of the pathological symbiosis effected
with the therapist on this deviant basis, as it repeats a comparable
mode of relatedness between the patient and her nuclear family.
Later material bore this out by revealing ways in which the patient's mother infantilized and clung to her.

It is not uncommon for patients who are experiencing a major
break in the frame to dream manifestly of their therapists. Here, the
patient also makes use of the metaphor of the water as an expression of the basic holding environment (see Balint 1967 for a comparable image), and conveys a shift in her unconscious perceptions
of the dangerous intrusion from something that is wooden and
inanimate, to something that is alive, devouring, and dangerous—
parasitic. There is also the patient's fear of discovery, a basic
concern regarding a lack of anonymity and confidentiality in this
treatment situation. Once again, the deviation then evokes a form of
iatrogenic or interactional paranoia—intense mistrust and suspiciousness created in part by the therapist's deviation, and also

reflecting to some unknown extent aspects of the patient's own paranoid core (cf. the allusions to the patient's father and the directive from the boyfriend). Finally, the patient rather movingly portrays the impairment in the communicative relationship that follows upon all departures from the ideal therapeutic environment.

Another brief excerpt involves a young woman who had taken an extension division course with an analytically trained psychotherapist. Upon completion of the program, she called up the therapist and asked him to see her in psychotherapy. Treatment was arranged, and at the time of this excerpt, had gone on for about a year. The therapist had been quite unaware of the possible ramifications of this particular aspect of his relationship with the patient. Through supervision, this changed, and soon he began to hear a multitude of embedded and well-disguised derivatives that organized meaningfully around the adaptive context of his prior contact with the patient. The situation crystallized when the patient herself, a professional in a related field, began to teach evening courses. She became involved with several men, and was considering having an affair with one of them. However, she felt she was being exploited, especially when she found out that one man in whom she was especially interested was having an affair with a close friend. In this context, it should be noted that the therapist had actually taken both this patient and another student into therapy after the teaching experience.

At the point of the excerpt presented here, the therapist had begun to play back some of the patient's selected derivatives, organizing them around the nonmanifest intervention context of the prior teaching contact.

> Patient: I don't want to be here. I have a new fantasy and don't want to show it to you. It's so obvious. It's about meeting a new student in a class I will begin to teach next month. He's an older man, and must be a psychoanalyst—a friend of yours. I know it's a way of making it with you. In the fantasy, he's interested in me. I mention to him that you're my therapist as a way of sabotaging my treatment. I have a feeling I have to make a choice between the man and therapy. I know I have to deal with it. Somehow I think of how treatment began and that I've been going in circles ever since.

Therapist: Perhaps that's because we never discussed the fact that you were formerly my student and that you know people who were involved with me.

Patient: Who should be learning from whom? The therapist has the power. I feel I'm in the position of strength when I'm the teacher. Perhaps there is an abuse of power. I'm thinking now of how my mother died when I was a young child, and how many times I've tried to replace her one way or another. Maybe I should be doing that in some other way, some way that makes better sense.

This therapist had realized that his prior involvement with his student had contaminated the therapy. For this reason, he had prepared himself to deal with the deviation with the patient. While he did wait until the present session before beginning his interpretive efforts, this particular intervention appears to be somewhat premature, in that the patient had not herself made a bridge between her fantasy about one of her own students and the fact that she had formally been a student of the therapist. In addition, the therapist made little use of this rich derivative complex. Nonetheless, in supervision, it was predicted that there would be a mixed response, and that some notable measure of Type Two derivative validation would follow, since the intervention was reasonably shaped by the patient's derivative communications and the therapist was now attempting to deal with a critical and neglected adaptive context.

The material that followed the therapist's intervention involves a form of Type Two derivative validation from the patient—the revelation of the critical genetic figure and experience that in part accounts for the patient's acceptance of the compromised treatment situation and for her unconscious image of the therapist on the basis of his participation. This information clearly extends the therapist's comment to the patient in a unique and previously unrecognized manner.

Through a commentary that reflects a mixture of both conscious and unconscious understanding, the patient indicates that her decision to seek out treatment with a therapist with whom she had prior personal contact was based on a pathological unconscious wish to search out—and possibly merge with—an inappropriate mother substitute. In a way, by modifying a basic boundary in the treatment relationship, the therapist may well have been gratifying the patient's omnipotent wish to undo the boundary between life and death, and to bring her mother back to life in a way that would maintain a pathological symbiosis and a sense of fusion, rather than having to face the loss and resolve her Neurosis. At the same time, through condensation, this derivative reveals that at the very moment that the therapist accepted the patient under these conditions, he was lost to her as an effective insight-producing, potentially positive introject and treating person. It is not uncommon to discover that patients unconsciously experience the loss (death) of the effective (interpretive and properly engaged in framework management) therapist in the presence of a major and especially relatively unrectifiable break in the frame.

One can hear the patient questioning who should be the functional patient and who should be the functional therapist, and indicating that she should be learning from the therapist, rather than the reverse. There is also an expression of the patient's realization that the therapist abused his position of power in accepting this patient for treatment, and a model of rectification: both patient and therapist should find a different way of dealing with the patient's loss of her mother, and on another level, along the me/not-me interface, the therapist's own depressive problems.

Before the therapist intervened, the patient began the session with an expressed wish not to be there, though on a derivative level this might well reflect her own sense that she is not present as an effective communicator, and that the therapist is not present as a proper interpreter and manager of the frame. The allusion to not wanting to reveal the fantasy to her therapist touches upon the impairment in the communicative properties of the therapeutic relationship under the deviant conditions. The reference to things being obvious may well allude to the framework break and its implications, an idea supported by the blatancy of the fantasy described by the patient. The fantasy itself is a derivative version of the therapist's decision to accept the patient, his student, into therapy. It is here that the patient makes use of close derivatives and a minimum degree of disguise: the student must be a psychoanalyst and friend of the therapist, a close derivative representation of the therapist himself. The involvement itself is an alteration in the usual boundaries of the student-teacher relationship, and is seen by the patient as a way of "making it." Here, the instinctualized—for the moment, sexualized—qualities of the deviation make their appearance, mostly in terms of unconscious perceptions. The specific pathological contributions from within the patient cannot be identified for the moment under these conditions. It seems clear, however, that the therapist's decision to function and adapt in terms of modifications in usual ground rules and boundaries has provided the patient with considerable support for her own propensities in this direction.

The patient then conveys an exquisite derivative related to sabotaging treatment, at this level thereby expressing her unconscious realization that the basic conditions of treatment have this quality. She then speaks of a necessary choice: between the man and the therapy, a disguised expression of a highly insightful realization that the patient must choose between the inappropriately gratifying therapist and pathological mode of "cure" available under present conditions, and the therapist who can create the necessary boundaries for a true insightful treatment experience. This is, of course, a derivative model of rectification. This thesis is borne out by the patient's comment that she has been going in circles ever since treatment began.

In principle, all deviations of this kind gratify the patient's Neurosis and preclude effective therapeutic work geared toward insight and structural change. As can be seen, this particular deviation could not be rectified, and eventually the treatment did indeed turn to an interlude during which, entirely at the behest of the patient's material, the patient was able to identify a multitude of unconscious perceptions and their implications based on the original deviation. These gratified the patient's Neurotic needs and maladjustment. Previously, they had neither been meaningfully revealed nor interpreted. Such work was feasible only because the therapist began to pick up the patient's directives in respect to rectifying the framework, and to indicate that he was prepared to do so through termination of the treatment.

Without exception, alterations in the basic therapeutic environment provide patients with pathological gratifications of the kind in evidence here. Their main influence falls into several spheres: (1) interfering with the derivative expression and analysis of the most threatening aspects of the patient's inner mental world, unconscious perceptions and unconscious fantasies; (2) providing the patient with pathological symbiotic ties that interfere with the analysis of separation anxieties, conflicts involving separation and individuation, and the ultimate development of individuation and autonomy; (3) the development of pathological and negative introjects of the therapist that, on an unconscious level, often become the locus of the therapeutic work for both participants to treatment; and (4) a concentration of the patient's adaptive and derivative responses on the deviation at hand.

Other Aspects of the First Contact

The first appointment should be made directly with the patient and not with a third party. At times, clinic therapists, parents, and even referring physicians and therapists will attempt directly to make an appointment for the patient with the treating therapist. In all such instances, they should be advised that this is the patient's responsibility. In a situation with an acutely psychotic or psychotically depressed patient who refuses to make the first telephone call, an initial deviation may be necessary as an emergency measure. However, accepting the patient under these deviant conditions will immediately compromise the therapeutic relationship and experience. Only a major emergency can justify such a step, which should be undertaken only after all efforts to have the patient call have been exhausted. In this type of situation, it is most important to maintain a listening attitude in the consultation session that takes the therapist's participation in the deviation as a critical adaptive context. As a rule, the prognosis for truth therapy with these patients is quite poor.

CLINICAL EXAMPLE

A homosexual man who had been in once-a-week psychotherapy for two years, and who left treatment because he obtained a better job in another city, wrote to the therapist on several occasions, including an inquiry as to whether the therapist would have time to see him again in treatment, since he was planning to return to the area. The therapist responded with a letter advising the patient to call him upon his return.

It is important to effect a clear and full termination with a patient, even when necessitated by external life circumstances. This implies the absence of follow-up visits, contact by mail, or other forms of interaction between the patient and therapist. Should a therapist receive such a letter, it should be read and returned to the patient, sometimes with a brief note acknowledging receipt. Involvements in this type of extra-therapeutic contact always entail bilateral pathological gratifications, and consistently undermine the patient's opportunity for autonomous functioning. In all instances, it is the therapist's first responsibility to a patient to respond to his or her communications in a manner best designed to serve the patient's *therapeutic* needs. This principle must be maintained both during and after a treatment experience.

Letters received in the course of the therapy may be opened and read or left unopened, depending on the therapist's knowledge of the patient. If there is any sense of suicidal or homocidal threat, it is best to read the correspondence, taking care always to return the letter to the patient by placing it on the desk or somewhere the patient can see it as he or she enters the session. These efforts by patients to modify the therapeutic framework are important indicators. The adaptation-evoking contexts are usually twofold: (1) a prior intervention by the therapist, and (2) the therapist's reading of the letter, or if he or she so chooses, his or her failure to do so. An additional context involves the therapist's efforts to rectify the frame by returning the letter to the patient. Often, these deviations by patients are a response to loose management by the therapist of the ground rules of therapy.

In this instance, it would have been advisable for the therapist to have simply returned the letter to the patient with a brief line to the effect that he had opened it and read its contents. It is self-evident that this patient understood that he was free to call the therapist either long distance or when he was in the area in order to make a specific appointment for consultation and for the resumption of therapy. There are therefore indications of pathological gratification here, though not having the patient in therapy would preclude their analysis. The return of the letter would, however, promote the patient's relative autonomy and efforts at sound self-analysis.

Some weeks later, the patient's mother called the therapist for an appointment. The therapist suggested that she have her son call him, but a week later, the mother called again and reported that her son said that the therapist could make the appointment with her, and that any time the following week would be acceptable to him.

The therapist then made the appointment with her and the patient later appeared for his session.

> Patient: I did a favor for my friend and picked up his dog on a farm near where my parents live. On the way, I stopped at my parents' house and my uncle gave me a hard time about my having moved out. I told him I didn't miss it, and that I preferred to get away from my mother. Mother complained I was leaving early, saying she felt my friend was more important to me than she was. We argued. Father wanted me to stay for a few days, but I said no. Mother lost control because of it, and I told her she needed a doctor too. She wouldn't talk to me directly and used my aunt as a go-between. Father offered me money, but it was like he was paying me off because I'm a hopeless case. A friend arranged for me to meet this gay man, and I went to bed with him, but the closer I get to someone, the more scared I get. I pull out and go to meet someone new. Then I feel they're talking behind my back and spreading rumors and lies.

A number of derivative themes appear repeatedly in the clinical examples that involve modifications in the ground rules regarding referral sources and the arrangements for the first session between the patient and therapist. One of the reasons for offering many different clinical examples is to provide the reader with an opportunity to experience the consistency with which these themes emerge under deviant conditions.

The adaptive context here involves the therapist's decision to make the appointment for this hour with the patient's mother. Once again, the patient fails to represent directly, or in thinly disguised fashion, the deviant intervention context. The unconscious basis for this resistance is expressed through the derivatives at the end of the sequence when the patient indicates his mistrust of others. Here again are the now familiar signs of iatrogenic paranoia and communicative disturbance. One can use this particular unconscious perception of the-therapist-as-untrustworthy as a means of understanding the unconscious basis for the resistances that so consistently attack the representations of deviant intervention contexts under these conditions.

On the other hand, the material is once again rich in derivative meanings and implications. These must be organized primarily in terms of the patient's valid unconscious perceptions of the deviation and of the therapist based on his alteration in the frame. The patient's encoded communications lend themselves readily to such formulations. Thus they indicate that the patient felt something like an animal who was being picked up for a friend, that he saw the therapist as favoring his mother over himself, that he experienced wishes from the therapist to capture or entrap him (wishes that reflected the therapist's own psychopathology and need for treatment), that he saw the therapist as accepting a go-between because of some difficulty in communicating directly with him—the patient, and that the appointment was arranged as something like a bribe because the therapist saw the patient (and felt himself, in part) as a hopeless case. This last derivative also alludes to the damage caused to the bipersonal field and the ways in which this type of appointment interferes with the therapeutic process. The patient also felt that something like a homosexual liason was being effected through his mother's arrangement of his hour for him. Finally, there is the already noted and quite common implication of the development of an iatrogenic paranoid response to the contact between the therapist and the patient's mother.

As a rule, one deviation begets another, and efforts to handle Neuroses through framework-deviation cures tend to fix both patient and therapist, and sometimes their families, on this particular deviant and uninsightful means of possible, though risky, symptom alleviation. (Once-weekly psychotherapy was arranged with this patient. However, within a month, the patient's father insisted upon a consultation for the patient with another therapist, which was carried out and further disrupted this particular treatment situation.)

Summary and Conclusions

The therapist should be cordial during the first telephone contact with the patient. The therapist should be sensitive to possible suicidal or homicidal potential, and should clarify the source of referral. No consultation should be offered if it is not possible for the therapist to see the patient in ongoing therapy, and the first appointment should be made at a time that would be feasible for the continuing treatment.

The therapist should accept for consultation and therapy only those patients with whom there has been no prior contact and with whom there is no basic flaw in the therapist's relative anonymity.

The initial appointment should be made directly with the patient—with rare emergency exceptions—and not with a third party to the therapy. In the presence of any type of third party to treatment or any flaw in the therapist's anonymity, intensely sexual and aggressive unconscious fantasy-introject constellations are common. In addition, therapist-evoked suspiciousness and paranoia are characteristic.

Most inappropriate referrals involve an unrectifiable deviation in the ideal therapeutic relationship and hold. Because of this, virtually all of the patient's *meaningful* communications will constitute adaptive responses to the deviation—a critical adaptation-evoking context for the therapy. Much of the time, the patient will either make use of Type C barriers to destroy the meaningful relationship link with the therapist (creating interactional resistances that are in part the responsibility of the therapist) or express himself or herself in the Type B mode. In this way the patient mirrors and introjects the Type B and Type C expressions reflected in the therapist's participation in the deviation.

The therapist must take care not to intervene in areas unrelated to the deviation at hand, since such interventions tend to constitute pathological projective identifications and the offer of defensive and distracting lie-barrier systems. Intervention should not be attempted until the derivatives begin to coalesce around the pertinent adaptation-evoking contexts. In response to such work, the patient will tend eventually to represent the intervention context with less and less disguise, eventually through a direct representation, and to further work over its disruptive meanings and functions. Derivative communications pointing toward the need to rectify the frame through insightful termination is the most usual outcome. This type of treatment, carried out at the behest of the patient's derivative communications, is termed *unrectifiable framework-deviation termination therapy*. As a rule, it will have highly salutory effects on the patient's Neurosis, and at times, provide sufficient insight for its resolution. It is, in any case, the only sound basis on which symptom alleviation can take place under these conditions.

Chapter 21

The First Session

The goals of the first session, the consultation hour, are to (1) establish the nature of the patient's emotional problems; (2) convey a sense of the therapist's competency to help the patient insightfully resolve these problems; (3) handle early resistances within the patient—or therapist—that might interfere with therapy, where indicated; (4) handle any initial breaks in the therapeutic frame; (5) establish the therapeutic contract, and thereby initiate the conscious and unconscious therapeutic alliance; and (6) obtain a sense of the patient's style of communication and capacity to work in therapy.

Techniques

There is much debate regarding whether a therapist should take a detailed history in the first session or simply allow the patient to proceed at his or her own pace, accepting whatever material is made available in that way and making mental notes of omissions and areas of uncertainty. The present volume advocates that it is best to structure the first session in a fashion consistent with the manner in which the basic treatment process is to be established. To do otherwise conveys unconscious communications to the patient that are uniformly viewed on an unconscious level as intrusive, destructive, and as a means of impairing the interaction.

In principle, then, the therapist should adopt a listening attitude that takes into account both the manifest content and surface of the patient's communications as well as their latent implications as organized around activated intervention contexts related to the

401

initiation of therapy. It is critical to recognize the presence of adaptive contexts in the first hour, and the extent to which they serve as organizers of the derivative implications of the patient's material. Listening must take place on both the manifest and latent levels from the outset of therapy.

On the basis of the initial telephone call and other intervening experiences, there may be a number of framework issues that prove especially pertinent to the patient as organizers of his or her material in the first session. It is striking to observe the extent to which, quite unconsciously, the patient is able to express simultaneously both manifest complaints and history, and derivative adaptive responses to intervention contexts, in the course of an initial interview.

If the frame is and will be essentially secure, the patient soon begins to sense this from the therapist's implicit and explicit attitudes and interventions. The sound holding environment and the initial offer of a healthy therapeutic symbiosis, and of a mode of cure through an analysis of the patient's derivative communications, are soon recognized unconsciously by the patient—along with other implications of the secure frame. This constellation then proves to be the critical intervention context for the initial and early sessions. In many patients, this context evokes extensive and powerful adaptive reactions and indirect communications. Thus, even in the initial session, the therapist is concerned not only with the patient's manifest complaints and history, but also with his or her derivative communications. The search for early resistances must be maintained on both the gross behavioral and communicative levels.

In practical terms, the therapist must respond appropriately to the patient's therapeutic needs. With a patient who is verbal and who essentially begins to free associate quite early in the consultation, all the therapist need do is sit back, listen, and attempt to formulate the material around recognized and discovered intervention contexts. The therapist thereby learns a great deal about the patient, and all that is needed to make an initial recommendation. Although specific historical facts may not be obtained for the moment—and major voids must be noted—nonetheless the therapist has available from the patient a great deal about his or her style of communication, the nature of his or her resistances and pathology, the extent of his or her capacity to reveal meaningfully and to work in therapy, and much more. Equally important, the information is gathered in a manner that tends simultaneously to offer the patient a therapeutic relationship and an environment that will be optimal for the therapeutic process. This particular approach is especially helpful in identifying the presence of early obstacles to therapy, and in making feasible the possibility of their interpretation (and rectification if necessary).

With patients who are silent and reluctant to communicate manifestly, the therapist should attempt to formulate the unconscious basis for such resistances in light of an activated intervention context and the available derivative complex. There is no substitute for the early interpretation of resistances in such terms; confrontations and the use of questions are poor replacements for a basic holding-interpretive approach. Nonetheless, when the material does not permit an interpretive response, considered efforts to engage the patient in expanding his or her communications by asking well-chosen questions stemming from the expressed material, or through the use of carefully selected playbacks of derivatives, will tend to further the work in this initial hour. However, such measures should be undertaken only when the patient is highly resistant on a gross behavioral level and reluctant to reveal himself or herself, and only when interpretive and rectifying responses are quite impossible. All such noninterpretive interventions will eventually have to be rectified, and their ramifications interpreted to the patient in order to create a workable therapeutic atmosphere and experience.

The therapist should enter the waiting room and greet the prospective patient by name (assuming privacy) and with a handshake. If the patient has brought along relatives, it is best to simply nod in their direction or to ignore them entirely and not become engaged in complicated introductions. If a patient asks that a relative be permitted to participate in the consultation, it will be necessary to respond directly with a rectification intervention to the effect that it would be advisable to begin the initial consultation privately and without the presence of the third party.

It is important to recognize, however, that this particular request is an effort to modify the frame. The therapist's noninterpretive response (directive) then serves as an intervention context that will organize the patient's subsequent adaptive and derivative reactions in the session itself. Virtually without exception, such material on a disguised level will reveal the unconscious motives for the patient's wish to compromise the basic therapeutic relationship and environment at the outset, as well as his or her responses to the therapist's efforts to secure the frame. It is quite likely that an interpretation along these lines will be feasible.

In shaking hands with the patient, the therapist should introduce himself or herself by name. The patient should be escorted into the consultation room, and should be allowed to lead the way and to select his or her chair. Should the patient move toward the therapist's chair, some comment will have to be made in the way of directing the patient to an appropriate place. Once both the patient and therapist are settled into their respective chairs (and the consultation should not take place with the patient on the couch), the therapist should begin the initial interview with a question such as, "How can I be of help to you?" or, "Perhaps you can begin by telling me something of the problems that have brought you to this consultation."

The question or comment is designed to indicate the therapist's preparedness to help the patient, and serves as a request that the patient communicate, manifestly and latently, the nature of the difficulties that have brought him or her to seek therapy. Once this first inquiry has been initiated, the therapist then should sit back and begin to observe and formulate. As already noted, the therapist's level of activity will depend upon the patient's directly and indirectly communicated therapeutic needs, and the level of gross and latent resistances. Efforts will be geared as much as possible toward an interpretive and rectifying-securing-the-framework approach.

ESTABLISHING THE PATIENT'S DIFFICULTIES

One of the first goals is to identify the patient's emotional and psychosomatic symptoms, and his or her characterological difficulties. The therapist wants to know if the patient's difficulties are ego syntonic or ego alien, and especially if there are any acute issues such as suicidal or homocidal possibilities, fantasies, and difficulties. The entire range of psychopathology and the conscious motivations of the patient in seeking help are involved. Issues of anxiety, depression, narcissism, and ego dysfunctions, which speak for borderline or psychotic problems, are among the most frequently seen syndromes.

On the whole, at the point where a patient actually seeks a

consultation—unless it is done under outside pressure and duress—
there are expressed symptoms and the presence of directly avowed
motivations to work in therapy. Patients who tend to be manipulative, psychopathic, and likely to act out; those fixed to pathological
symbiotic and parasitic modes of relatedness; and patients who are
in some way attempting to manage and seal off an intensely
psychotic or psychotic-like core are likely to fluctuate in the extent
to which they acknowledge having emotional difficulties, rather
than viewing their problems in terms of the maladjustment of
others.

Wherever possible, the therapist should make efforts to establish the presence of ego dystonic emotional difficulties and to
reinforce implicitly the patient's motivations for sound therapy and
insightful change. Those patients who tend to hold others accountable for their difficulties, and who are inclined to live out rather
than contain their problems, will usually show strong resistances
against entering treatment. Efforts should be made to interpret the
unconscious basis of such resistances in the light of prevailing
intervention contexts.

ESTABLISHING COMPETENCY AS A THERAPIST

The therapist's manner of conducting the consultation hour
expresses much in the way of his or her competency or difficulties
in being an effective therapist. The purpose in the first session is to
convey implicitly and explicitly to the patient something of the
therapist's capacity to create a sound therapeutic relationship and
environment, to hold the patient in a true therapeutic sense, to
contain if necessary his or her pathological projective identifications, to experience role and image evocations and relationship
pressures from the patient with sensitivity and understanding, and
to respond interpretively and with framework-management responses at the behest of the patient's derivative material if necessary.
There is a need to establish *rapport,* though it must be defined in
terms of appropriate therapeutic rather than social standards. Such
rapport involves sensitivities on both the manifest and latent levels.
Concern should be implicit, as should responsiveness to the patient's therapeutic needs. As is true of all aspects of psychotherapy,
the most important expressions of the therapist's preferred mode of
relatedness and cure are conveyed to the patient on an unconscious

level. In general, deliberate efforts at support, reassurance, statements of credentials and confidence, and the like tend to convey unconsciously needs within the therapist for pathological symbiotic or parasitic modes of relatedness, and for noninsightful means of cure—one or another form of lie-barrier therapy. Thus the therapist must be sensitive not only to the patient's communications in the first hour, but to his or her own expressions on this level as well.

Often, the therapist's sense of competency comes across in his or her management of initial pressures by the patient to engage the therapist in directly supportive interventions and modifications in the basic conditions of treatment. Much is conveyed in what the therapist does not do, especially when he or she is able to avoid possible errors and to maintain the quest for establishing a derivative mode of relatedness—a healthy symbiosis.

The therapist's sense of competency has little to do with his or her stated intentions to be of help to the patient or with sometimes overly exhibitionistic needs to engage in premature interpretations, which are usually carried out with a neglect of prevailing intervention contexts. Instead, competency entails a sense of implied strength, a capacity for patience, and a sensitivity to the critical conscious and especially unconscious issues that permeate the initial hour. It has little to do with highly complex formulations that parade in front of the patient the therapist's intellectual capacities, while latently confessing a sense of ignorance and disregard of the sensitive spiraling interaction between patient and therapist.

In essence, then, the therapist's professional capabilities are reflected in his or her ability to adhere to sound techniques while responding empathically (on both the manifest and latent levels), sensitively, and with tact to the patient's therapeutic needs. It must be recognized, however, that paradoxically, the patient responds to true competency in the therapist in a divided manner. On the one hand, the therapist's capabilities are welcomed in the hope of achieving insightful symptom resolution, while on the other, these talents evoke fear and envy as well. A competent therapist secures a therapeutic relationship and environment that frustrates the patient's pathological autistic, symbiotic, and parasitic needs and wishes for a deviant mode of cure, while favoring a healthy symbiosis and a setting and mode of relatedness designed for the unfolding of the sometimes terrifying derivative expressions that underlie and form the basis for his or her psychopathology. Thus the effective therapist creates the conditions for truth therapy, a pursuit that engenders in the patient both great anxiety and great hope for growth and structural change.

Dealing with Early Resistances

Several types of early resistances emerge frequently in first sessions. A major factor in their classification involves the extent to which the therapist is establishing a sound mode of relatedness with the patient based on a secure therapeutic contract, or instead, has become involved in developing a deviant therapeutic arrangement with the patient. As discussed in Chapter 18, the very presence of resistances depends on the nature of intervention contexts, most of which involve the basic conditions for treatment. Thus all early resistances must be considered in light of adaptation-evoking contexts from the therapist, especially as they pertain to delineations of the ground rules and boundaries of the therapeutic relationship and setting.

On a manifest or gross behavioral level, early resistances tend to be expressed by the patient through one or more efforts to modify the basic conditions of treatment. There will be periods of silence, conscious thoughts of not pursuing therapy, efforts to question the therapist, direct attempts to create a deviant therapeutic contract—e.g., not to be held fully responsible for all sessions, to have an arrangement where an hour may be readily changed, or to have the therapist agree to an active noninterpretive approach with use of so-called support and questions. Often, there are direct attacks on the therapist's implicit and explicit efforts to establish a healthy therapeutic symbiosis, and in particular a sound and basic therapeutic contract. These efforts constitute important indicators or therapeutic contexts that must be interpreted and rectified in light of activated intervention contexts and the patient's derivative material.

On a communicative level, early resistances may emerge especially with patients prone to utilize the Type B-C and Type C modes of communication. Such patients tend to wish to establish a pathological autistic, symbiotic, or parasitic mode of relatedness with the therapist, and to destroy the possibility of meaningful relatedness and insight therapy. At times there is sufficient representation of critical adaptive contexts and coalescible derivative material to make sound interpretive and framework-management interventions to the patient. The therapist's efforts should be geared in these directions whenever possible. Initially, gross behavioral resistances are more serious than those that involve communicative obstacles, though in the first hour the two tend to appear together.

Specifically, then, the patient's early resistances must be understood in light of the therapist's interventions, especially those that pertain to the implicit and explicit ways in which the therapist defines the ground rules and boundaries of the therapeutic relationship and experience. Any movement toward deviation will evoke powerful responses in the patient, some of which typically will manifest themselves as behavioral and communicative resistances. Such deviations reflect the counterresistances of the therapist.

On the other hand, if the therapist begins to develop a secure therapeutic frame, the patient may begin to express either type of resistance: gross behavioral, in terms of manifest opposition to, or disruption of, the therapeutic work; and communicative, in terms of disturbances in the communicative flow to the point where the patient fails to offer an interpretable network of communications or to clearly represent intervention contexts and provide a coalescible and meaningful derivative complex. Although all patients both welcome and are threatened by the secure frame, there are certain patients who are especially terrified by the healthy relationship and other deprivations that it creates, as well as the intimacy and other attributes that it possesses (see Chapters 17 and 18). Among the possible reactions to the development of the secure hold and frame, behavioral and communicative resistances are especially important in the first—and every—hour. Most interpretive and framework-management efforts in the initial hour will be developed in response to the emergence in one form or another of resistance to the sound therapeutic relationship and setting (see Chapter 33). As already noted, to the greatest extent feasible, the therapist's responses should be in the direction of maintaining the healthy therapeutic frame and hold, working toward the rectification of deviations unilaterally imposed upon the relationship by the patient, and interpreting the material in terms of the available implications of the communicative complex.

Virtually all resistances have contributions from both the patient and therapist, i.e., are in essence *interactional resistances*.

While the therapist's contribution may be quite minimal, it behooves him or her, in the face of evident obstacles to initiating therapy, to carefully explore his or her management of the framework, his or her comments (interventions) on the telephone and in the first hour, and the possibility that an important intervention required by the patient's material has been missed. Thus the therapist must first examine the therapeutic situation for ways in which he or she may be contributing to patient's resistances. The discovery of such contributions calls for silent rectification, so that the therapist desists in expressing this wish, need, and support for the patient's resistances. As the material from the patient permits, this step is accompanied by interpretation—at this level, carried out primarily in terms of the patient's unconscious perceptions of the therapist's countertransference-based role in the patient's resistance expressions.

The material from the patient must then be examined for reflections of sources of resistance that arise from the patient's own intrapsychic conflicts, pathologically narcissistic and symbiotic needs, conscious and unconscious dread of therapy and the therapeutic process, and such. It cannot be emphasized often enough, however, that all such interpretive work should be organized around the adaptive context that evokes the derivative material illuminating these conscious and unconscious motives for resistance.

In general, these early resistances are *relationship resistances*, with both transference and nontransference elements. They often prove interpretible in the first session, and such work tends to make feasible the establishment of a sound therapeutic contract with a reluctant patient. In keeping with the principle of analyzing defenses and resistances before contents, almost all interventions in the initial hour are made in this sphere.

CLINICAL EXAMPLE

A single woman teacher sought therapy for depression. She came to a clinic because her friend was seeing a therapist there, and she had an intake interview with the social worker in charge of patient selection. When assigned to the therapist (a woman), it proved necessary for the therapist to call the patient to arrange the initial session. Because the clinic schedule was overcrowded, the therapist offered to see the patient in her private office, but the patient refused. An appointment was arranged, but when the patient and therapist arrived for the session, they found the room occupied. After checking the schedule, the therapist offered to see the patient an hour later, and the patient agreed. The therapist explained that there had been an administrative error and apologized for the inconvenience. The patient then waited the hour in a waiting room occupied by several other patients and by a small group of therapists who were planning to attend a conference in the clinic. When finally ushered into the office, it was apparent to the therapist that voices could be overheard from the waiting room and from the office next door. The excerpt presented here is from the patient's initial session, conducted under these remarkable and yet not uncommon conditions.

> Patient: I don't know what to tell you. I've been so depressed, but I don't know why. *(The patient cried on and off throughout the balance of the session.)* Nothing like this has ever happened to me before. *(The patient took a Kleenex from a box on the desk.)*
>
> Therapist: It is difficult for you to put your feelings into words.
>
> Patient: I don't know what I'm feeling. I'm blank inside. Tonight has been a bad night. I feel ashamed. I don't cry and talk like this in front of my friends. I'm seldom home. I just feel horrible and overwhelmed. You must think I'm crazy.
>
> Therapist: It still seems difficult for you to put all of these feelings into words.
>
> Patient: It must come from my childhood; nothing's going on now. *(At this point the patient began to ruminate and repeat herself, emphasizing the vagueness of her complaints and revealing little more.)* I just suddenly feel afraid to live alone.
>
> Therapist: You are speaking of being alone with your feelings, of not sharing them with anyone, and it reminds me that you came here tonight and we couldn't get a room. I then left you alone, and you seem to be expressing concern about being left alone and whether you can be helped.
>
> Patient: *(Sobbing now.)* I've always had to take care of myself. I had an episode of pneumonia and was afraid of dying. I was afraid no one would find me. *(The patient then reiterated several times her sense that she was growing older and afraid of death.)*

Therapist: We must stop now for today. I will contact the director of the clinic and arrange a room, and will call you and tell you when we can meet again.

Patient: That's fine.

In this consultation, the patient reported significant depressive symptoms (symptomatic indicators). It was necessary, of course, for the therapist to determine the extent of the depression and to differentiate a psychotic from neurotic or reactive depression. Diagnostically, it is well to determine the specific nature of the patient's symptoms, his or her basic character structure and personality constellation, and the level of general functioning—psychotic, borderline, narcissistic, or neurotic (see Part I). These considerations are one determinant in recommending a particular treatment modality (e.g., psychoanalysis versus psychotherapy—the latter tending, with many exceptions, to be recommended for patients who fall toward the sicker end of the psychopathological continuum), though it should not influence the therapist's *basic approach* to the treatment experience. Yet, while the fundamentals are kept relatively constant, diagnostic considerations will influence variations within this essential framework, so that a patient with a psychotic depression, for example, would be likely to evoke more frequent interventions—though confined still to the interpretive and framework-management spheres—than a less depressed patient.

Diagnostic considerations also lead to anticipations in respect to central areas of conflict and the level and type of the patient's object relationships. They have some bearing as well on the patient's style of communication. In sum, then, diagnostic considerations are relevant to the recommendation of a particular mode of therapy and frequency of treatment, and to the nature and frequency of interventions, though they seldom call for an alteration in the basic therapeutic relationship and environment and in the fundamental aspects of the therapist's approach.

In this instance, the diagnosis was that of a neurotic depression in a patient with a schizoid character who was functioning, however, on a neurotic level (though she was showing some signs of deterioration toward a borderline adaptation). While clinic conditions did not permit the therapist to specifically structure and define the ground rules of this therapy—an unfortunate omission that is highly destructive to the subsequent treatment process and to the patient—it was deemed advisable to see this patient in twice-weekly

412 / Psychotherapy: A Basic Text

psychotherapy in an effort to help her resolve her depressive syndrome, whatever its causes. While her suicidal potential was evaluated as low, the therapist expected to continually monitor this aspect of the patient's problem.

As for gross behavioral and communicative resistances, one may begin, as one would in the session, by examining first this patient's gross resistances. They are in evidence in the relative emptiness of her associations and the sparseness of the information available to the therapist. Both consciously and as reflected in her material, the patient was reluctant to reveal herself and quite guarded. While cooperative in the sense of saying whatever came to mind, the yield of understanding was quite low. The patient appeared on the surface to be well motivated for therapy, largely because of her depression. She also showed a manifest wish to continue her work with the therapist. There therefore was little sense of resistance in regard to a recognized need for treatment and its continuation. Instead, the patient's resistance took the form of obsessive rumination with little in the way of evident meaning as it pertained to the nature and sources of her psychopathology.

It is important to evaluate the intensity of a resistance (or other) indicator as it emerges in the first hour. Clearly, any major threat to the continuation of treatment would rank as a nine or a ten, and would call for the best possible intervention available from the patient's material in the session. Lesser obstacles afford the therapist the option of managing or interpreting if the network of communications permits, or waiting for a later session if this does not seem feasible. In the meantime, the therapist should try to identify any way in which he or she has contributed to the patient's gross behavioral resistances and rectify its presence and influences. Often, this type of rectification enables a patient to resolve the factors within himself or herself that are also contributing to the resistance, and the gross behavioral resistance is significantly modified.

In the session under study, the therapist responded to the patient's resistances with a surface empathic intervention regarding the patient's difficulties in putting feelings into words. As can be seen, this did little to modify the gross behavioral resistance. This type of *surface* empathy is highly limited, in that it fails to respond empathically to the patient's *unconscious* needs and communications, and to the patient's deeper inner state. The empathic statement first used by this therapist—a type of intervention in common use today—indirectly revealed a basic insensitivity to the therapist's own contributions to the patient's difficulties in expressing herself. It is self-evident that because of this, while the patient might feel superficially understood, on some level she will also have a sense of being blamed and of a therapist who is quite out of contact with herself and the unconscious interaction. This is virtually always a major flaw in this type of so-called superficial empathic response.

Toward the end of the session, the therapist attempted an intervention that approached an interpretation of the unconscious basis for the patient's resistance—i.e., her difficulties in expressing and revealing herself. An ideal intervention of this kind would involve an identification of the indicators in terms of their best and most direct representation in the material. This would utilize some reference by the patient herself to her difficulty in speaking, or some thinly disguised representation of this particular therapeutic problem (resistance). Next, the therapist would identify the best representations in the patient's material of the intervention contexts that led to the patient's conscious and unconscious opposition to treatment. Finally, the derivative complex would be utilized to identify sound unconscious perceptions and possible pathological distortions that would account for the unconscious basis of the resistance at hand. In this way, a relationship resistance based on unconscious nontransference and transference factors would be interpreted to the patient. In addition, the therapist would make efforts to modify the nontransference factor—i.e., his or her own contribution to the patient's defensiveness.

Resistances emerge as adaptive and maladaptive responses to the therapeutic setting and the therapist's interventions. They must therefore be understood and evaluated, and eventually interpreted, in this light. Often, a patient's opposition is essentially non-pathological in view of the intervention context to which he or she is responding. At other times, the resistances are both transference-based and inappropriate, and may be interpreted as such. As always, an in-depth evaluation of the implications of the therapist's interventions is required to properly formulate the sources, motives, and unconscious basis for a resistance within the patient as derived from both the therapist's interventions and from within the patient.

In the actual intervention, the therapist picked up a concern in the patient about being left alone, rather than intervening around the resistance—the difficulties the patient was having in expressing herself. While this concern about being left alone and having to do the therapeutic work on her own (a latent implication) is related to the resistance, the intervention does not address the patient's defenses and resistances, but instead attempts to deal with one source of the patient's symptomatic concern. As such, the therapist went on to suggest that the material related to being alone had something to do with the intervention context of the therapist having left the patient alone for almost an hour before they were actually able to have the session. From there, the therapist generalized that the patient might have felt on that basis that she couldn't be helped, though this was not extended to account for the resistances related to her nonrevealing stance.

Although this intervention was an attempt to interpret material somewhat related to the patient's resistances, it did so in terms of only a single intervention context (and there were many more), and it made little use of the derivative complex. A more ideal intervention might have been stated as follows: "You are having a great deal of difficulty describing your symptoms and in expressing yourself in a way that begins to reveal their meanings and sources. You have commented several times about being ashamed and unable to communicate. You seem to hold yourself accountable for this difficulty, but indirectly you have touched upon problems in the clinic and things that I have done that also seem to be contributing to your hesitancy. For example, you said that tonight is a bad night. You also said that you don't like to reveal yourself in front of others. Now, while you have not specifically connected any of this to what has happened here tonight, you do show signs of wanting to avoid that very possibility. You kept stressing that your problems came from your childhood rather than from what is going on now. And yet, much of what you're saying suggests that a lot that has happened tonight has led you to feel inappropriately exposed, that you're in a situation where everyone seems overwhelmed, and that something crazy is going on. On that basis, you seem to have tried to protect yourself from me by closing yourself off."

In this particular first session, the patient did not specifically represent the major intervention contexts: the presence of a third party to therapy in the intake worker, the offer by the therapist to see the patient in her private office, finding the room occupied, sitting in a waiting room where therapists were talking to each other, and the lack of soundproofing for the office. One can only sense how absolutely overwhelming these modifications in the ideal therapeutic environment were for this patient, and postulate an enormous dread of dealing with some of their more horrendous qualities and what they implied regarding the therapist. The patient's comments about her fear of death and of being alone suggest a dread of giving up a pathological symbiotic tie to this therapist (and such a tie is more than promised through these deviations), while simultaneously reflecting in all likelihood a derivative realization that truth therapy, or any sound form of treatment experience, has been destroyed perhaps forever because of these initial conditions. One may postulate that the patient therefore turned to a defensive style of Type C communication through which she could maintain the pathological symbiotic tie with the therapist while defending herself against the overwhelming and crazy unconscious perceptions of the therapist and clinic with which she had been faced—and against her own fears of craziness as well.

Here then, is a moderately resistant derivative complex, with major resistances in respect to the representations of the adaptation-evoking contexts. Nonetheless, the interpretive intervention proposed here, which takes the form of identifying the best representations of the adaptive contexts and a playback of the most meaningful derivatives, could serve as a means of communicating to the patient the therapist's own awareness of the chaotic state of the therapeutic environment, and her understanding of how it contributed to the patient's gross behavioral resistances. Such an effort could well hint also at a preparedness in the therapist for rectification—a step that would be essential under these conditions.

This vignette highlights the extent to which deviations in the framework contribute unconsciously to essentially nontransference-based resistances in patients. It should be noted too that depressive patients tend to use the type of denial in evidence here. They become self-blaming and protective of the therapist, and absorb the "badness" within the therapist into themselves as a defense against underlying rage and the dread of the loss of pathological fusion with the therapist. In this instance, then, the diagnostic understanding of the patient helps to conceptualize the nature of her resistances, their manifestations in the first hour, as well as the patient's mode of interacting with the therapist.

The Patient's Style of Communication

It is important to identify the patient's basic style of communication in the initial hour. Patients who express themselves as Type A communicators tend to show relatively little in the way of resistances; while Type B-A communicators would be intermediate in this regard, since they express themselves meaningfully, but tend also to dump disturbing pressures into the therapist. Type C communicators are, in general, communicatively resistant, and Type B-C patients are highly so (and in addition, create unbearable interactional pressures on the therapist while giving little in the way of recourse toward interpretation and framework management).

In an initial session, the style of communication of the patient can be established by identifying the prevailing intervention contexts. In clinic settings, these usually involve, in part, violations in confidentiality and other aspects of the basic ground rules. In private practice, such deviations may be minimal with a therapist capable of securing a sound therapeutic setting and of maintaining an interpretive approach. Under these circumstances, the major intervention context involves the patient's experience and anticipation of a holding-containing environment and of a therapist with whom issues of separation-individuation and the exposure of primitive conflicts and contents become a problem.

Whatever the specific adaptive contexts, the Type A patient will usually represent them either directly or with little disguise, and provide a coalescible derivative network in response. The Type B-A patient will do the same, though he or she will also press the therapist in one way or another, usually by attempting to develop a deviation in the basic framework. The Type C communicator will either fail to clearly represent the intervention context or provide a poor derivative complex. The Type B-C patient will do the same, but in addition, violently attack the therapist and the basic framework of treatment.

There is some problem in deciding on the style of communication of the patient in the excerpt given above. The material suggests either a Type C or a highly defended Type A communicator (probably the latter). Thus the patient represents a number of the active adaptive contexts, but does so with considerable disguise. Nonetheless, they are alluded to in derivative form rather than entirely obliterated—a measure that would be taken by a Type C communicator. Similarly, there is a meaningful and coalescible derivative complex, though it is weakened again by the presence of derivative defenses. This patient might quickly shift entirely to a Type C mode because of her extensive use of denial and of lie-barrier systems. She has massively obliterated any conscious reference to—and perhaps any conscious awareness of—the flagrant violations in the framework of this therapy. Since she is likely to be under pressure to express herself meaningfully around these framework issues, she might well alternate between a highly defended Type A style and the use of the Type C mode.

In dealing with *communicative resistances,* the therapist's main intervention entails the rectification of any contributions of his or her own to the patient's expressive difficulties. More rarely, the patient will represent the obstacles to communication, and subsequently provide an interpretable network of communication that touches upon their sources. Such is the case in this opening session, since the patient's allusions to closing herself off can be taken as a representation of her resistances. The therapist's interpretation would be an attempt to explain the underlying basis of the patient's defensiveness on both the gross behavioral and communicative levels.

The therapist's attempts to understand the patient's style of communication must be made in light of known intervention contexts. This appraisal is related to the evaluation of the nature and level of the patient's gross behavioral and communicative resistances. These determinations involve issues that pertain to the development of a sound therapeutic alliance between the patient and therapist on both the manifest and communicative levels.

The assessment of the patient's level of resistances, especially those that are gross and evident, touch upon the basic issue of the feasibility of establishing a treatment situation with the patient. Threats to the initiation of therapy are therefore high level indicators or therapeutic contexts, major gross behavioral resistances that require framework management and interpretive interventions from the therapist based on the material from the patient. An identification of the adaptation-evoking contexts that are contributing to the style of communication and resistances of the patient, and the rectification of conscious and unconscious contributions from the therapist to a patient's disturbed mode of expression or state of resistance, are critical.

Interpreting and rectifying the pathological underlying sources of all early obstacles to therapy must receive first priority. This type of intervention is most common in the first hour, and implicitly and explicitly serves as an important means by which the therapist creates a therapeutic symbiosis with the patient and implicitly demonstrates his or her intention to utilize an insightful mode of cure. The analysis of early resistances and the definition of the ground rules and boundaries of therapy are the two most important active interventions by the therapist in the first hour.

Early Frame Issues

The therapist's manner and means of establishing the basic therapeutic contract, and with it the essential conditions of his or relationship with the patient and of the therapeutic environment, constitutes the core of the healthy and therapeutic symbiotic components to the therapeutic relationship. As such, it is fundamental to all other therapeutic work, to the mode of cure, and to the relationship between the patient and therapist per se. In addition, the therapist's behaviors and verbalizations in this sphere are such that they will tend to gratify and reinforce the patient's Neurosis when deviations from the ideal therapeutic environment are effected. In contrast, they will frustrate the gratification of the Neurosis in the therapeutic interaction, and thereby create the conditions for its expression in analyzable form when the frame is established and maintained.

Unconsciously, all patients have a sense of the importance of the framework of the therapeutic relationship. Because of this, they enter treatment with intensely divided wishes and efforts: On the one hand, they hope (mostly unconsciously) for the special conditions under which they can insightfully resolve their Neurosis; they therefore have every expectation of a truly ideal therapeutic environment and relationship. On the other hand, they wish to maintain their Neurosis and to create a therapeutic contract that will justify and support their pathological adjustment.

Both consciously and unconsciously then, patients enter treatment with a framework of their own, one that is usually mixed in its elements, containing attributes of a sound therapeutic contract mixed in with important deviations. As a result, it is quite common for patients to make attempts to establish a deviant contract with the therapist and to create conditions under which their Neurosis will actually prove unanalyzable and unresolvable through insight. The therapist must be alert to these endeavors, and yet allow the patient full play of these efforts short of knowing participation in the deviation. In this way, important expressions of the patient's psychopathology are realized within the framework of the therapeutic interaction, and interpretations and managements of the framework can be carried out at the behest of the patient's derivatives.

When a patient attempts to introduce a deviant ground rule or to modify those proposed by the therapist, it is important for the latter to respond initially with silence, and ultimately through interpretive and framework-management responses developed in terms of the patient's own derivative communications. All too often, therapists react to efforts of this kind on a manifest level, usually with directives, and tend to either accept or reject the deviant contract. It is quite antitherapeutic to respond so directly to efforts of this kind by the patient. It is important instead to realize that such endeavors are important expressions of the patient's psychopathology and pathological mode of relatedness; they require a full analysis.

A therapist should not respond to a patient's efforts to modify the basic mode of treatment with a deviation of his or her own in the form of a direct answer to a question or a directive, and especially through an acceptance of the patient's proposed deviation. Instead, the therapist should maintain a sound holding relationship with the patient until the latter has an opportunity to provide the therapist with a network of communications through which the patient's efforts at deviation can be understood and managed. Such work has a considerable influence on the patient's image of the therapist and on the basic issue of whether adaptation and symptom resolution will involve frame breaks or efforts at insight and mastery within the confines of necessary ground rules and boundaries.

It is to be expected, then, that the patient will experience anxieties and disturbance in response to whichever way the therapist constitutes the basic ground rules and boundaries of the treatment relationship. However, if the therapist secures the ideal frame, the basic hold is safe and sound, and the anxieties tend to derive from transference-based distortions. These involve the patient's fears, within the context of reasonable intimacy and a sound therapeutic symbiosis, of his or her annihilation and destruction. However, it is these very anxieties and unconscious fantasies (with secondary unconscious perceptions) that motivate the patient to express himself or herself in a manner that permits the interpretive resolution of the mobilized aspects of his or her Neurosis. Under these conditions, the basic introject of the therapist is constructive, and the threatening aspects are the product of pathological introjects and earlier pathogenic experiences—and the pathological unconscious fantasies and conflicts that they help to create and that underly the patient's symptoms. Thus the therapeutic work unfolds primarily in terms of the patient's inner pathology and transferences, expressions that cause the patient much anxiety and yet provide him or her with a sound opportunity for insightful, structural, and adaptive change.

In contrast, when there are basic flaws in the therapeutic setting, boundaries, and contract, the basic image of the therapist is highly charged with danger, and the holding environment is basically disturbed, traumatic, and inadequate. The patient's associations and behaviors are predominantly based on nontransference adaptive responses to the relatively nondistorted unconscious perceptions of the therapist derived from his or her deviations (countertransferences). The patient experiences some sense of immediate relief through the pathological symbiosis gained in this manner, and from the manner in which the therapist's psychopathology takes precedence over his or her own. In addition, the deviation will express in some form an unconscious support for the patient's Neurotic or maladaptive adjustment, and help the patient to set aside derivative confrontation of the truths of his or her own illness. And yet, despite the immediate pathological gratifications, the patient's derivative associations will be replete with realizations of the inadequacies and limitations of this type of framework-deviation cure and with efforts to correct the situation.

In the opening session, patients present an endless variety of proposed deviations to the therapist—and unfortunately, many therapists make similar presentations to their patients. The possibilities are legion. For example, a patient may ask not to be charged each month for one session because of a commitment to a monthly business trip, or he may ask for a monthly change in his hour for similar reasons. Then too, the patient may wish immediately to include third-party payers such as insurance companies, or may request that the therapist forego his or her fee for one or more sessions because of a vacation planned before the beginning of treatment.

In all such instances, these efforts to modify the ideal (though threatening) therapeutic environment and a basically healthy form of symbiotic relatedness should be taken as first-order indicators. The therapist must not respond directly when these requests are first made, and instead should either remain silent—implicitly encouraging free association—or simply suggest that the patient continue to say whatever comes to mind. With most patients this will provide an opportunity for the therapist not only to interpret and manage the framework in terms of the patient's derivative communications, but also to implicitly show the patient the way in which therapy will be carried out. This creates a strong thrust toward the establishment of an ideal therapeutic environment and Type Two derivative relatedness with its unique opportunities for insightful cure.

The Establishment of the Therapeutic Contract

About two-thirds into the first session, the therapist should take the responsibility for establishing the ground rules and framework of therapy. The therapist should introduce this particular step by simply indicating to the patient that he or she can be of help in enabling the patient to resolve his or her emotional problems. While there are many variations on how to proceed from there, much of it depending on what has been covered to this point in the hour, the therapist can then move on to indicate his or her fee. In principle, while each therapist should have a narrow fee range, only one fee should be stated to each patient, based on an evaluation of the patient's financial situation and the number of sessions per week that seem advisable (see Chapter 22).

Once stated, the therapist's fee should be maintained. Efforts by the patient to have it reduced should be subjected to full exploration, and will, as a rule, reveal derivative communications that point to the need to keep the fee as stated. In keeping with the typical split seen in patients in regard to most ground rules, patients under these conditions will protest their poverty and need for a reduced fee, while responding on an unconscious level quite favorably to the therapist's ability to maintain the frame as established. In principle, a patient should be seen once weekly for the stated amount rather than twice weekly at a reduced fee. Virtually without exception all reductions in the therapist's stated fee are seen by the patient as a sacrifice by the therapist and as a form of seduction. Because of this, this particular deviation has a detrimental influence on the therapeutic unfolding.

Once the fee is indicated, the therapist may move on to suggest a frequency of visits. Among the many factors that influence this recommendation, the patient's ability to afford more than one session per week looms large in actual clinical practice. Beyond that, there is the patient's motivation for treatment, as conveyed both directly and unconsciously in the first hour. Patients with highly questionable or tentative wishes for therapy are probably best seen once weekly, though on occasion twice-weekly sessions may be recommended. On the whole, more intensive therapy is unlikely to engage this type of patient in the treatment process, and is more likely to frighten him or her off and lead him or her to terminate treatment. In addition, there is often a scarcity of interpretable material with such patients, since they tend to be Type C communicators. The once-weekly treatment situation allows them a sufficient sense of protection and distance, while offering a set of conditions for treatment and a relationship that is sufficiently safe that the patient may risk meaningful communication and therapeutic work.

With a patient experiencing acute symptoms and an emotion-laden life crisis, twice-weekly therapy is probably ideal. Clinical studies raise questions as to the additional efficacy of more intensive therapy, especially in light of the commitment and cost, though far more clinical study is necessary before definitive conclusions can be made. Thus, assuming competence in intensive psychotherapy and in psychoanalysis, a therapist might recommend sessions three, four, or five times per week to those patients who show a combination of severe symptoms, distinct ego strengths, and strong motivation for treatment. Of course, such patients must also be able to afford intensive therapy, a factor that interacts with their degree of motivation and commitment to an insightful therapeutic process.

After recommending a frequency of visits, the therapist should allow the patient to respond. All decisions should be allowed their full play, and there is distinct advantage to permitting the patient to continue to free associate in order to have derivative commentaries on which the therapist may base his or her interpretations and framework responses.

Once the fee and frequency of sessions have been settled, the therapist should state the length of the sessions and arrange specific hours. It is best to use the consultation time for one of the sessions if at all possible, and to see twice-weekly patients with at least one or two days between their hours. There may also be some advantage in seeing patients who have three or more sessions per week on consecutive days, doing so as a means of concentrating the therapeutic experience and work.

Next, the therapist may indicate how the patient should go about paying for the sessions. In an ideal therapeutic setting, the patient is *not* handed a bill, largely because they are often used as pathological transitional objects and sometimes, as means of obtaining insurance reinbursements without the knowledge of the therapist. Instead, it is best to permit the patient to keep track of the number of sessions and to advise him or her to pay for each month's hours at the beginning of the following month. This ground rule is stated as such because asking the patient to pay for his or her sessions on the day of the last session of a particular month requires that the patient write out the check for a session that has not taken place—that he or she pay in advance or prepare to pay in advance for a session that has not as yet been held.

There is no need to state a particular date by which the fee must be paid, since to do so creates a sense of greed and rigidity, which patients seem to react against both consciously and on a derivative level. Instead, the patient is advised that payment is expected at the beginning of the new month for the sessions of the preceding month, and then any delay in payment is interpreted in light of prevailing intervention contexts in a fashion comparable to work with any other resistance as reflected in an alteration by the patient of the basic ground rules of treatment (the therapeutic contract).

It is next advisable to define for the patient the fundamental rule of free association. This is especially necessary with patients who have been noticably silent and reluctant to talk freely. It should be carried out simply, by indicating to the patient that it is best for him or her to say whatever comes to mind, no matter what it may be, and that the therapeutic work will unfold on that basis.

Next, the therapist may decide to deal with the position of the patient. If the recommendation is to maintain the face-to-face mode that has been used in the consultation hour, it is usually quite unnecessary for the therapist to make a specific comment in this regard. On the other hand, if the therapist plans to recommend the use of the couch, this should be done while defining the therapeutic contract. The therapist should indicate to the patient that it is preferable that he or she lie on the couch in subsequent sessions, adding that this tends to foster the therapeutic work. Clinical evidence indicates that even once-weekly psychotherapy is best carried out with the patient on the couch. This particular position has the advantage of diminishing reality cues from the therapist, of fostering freer communicative expression by the patient, and of mobilizing certain types of vulnerabilities, unconscious introjects, and intrapsychic conflicts that facilitate the therapeutic work in the opening phase.

Once a particular position has been recommended, it should be maintained as a dimension of the ideal therapeutic environment. Any wish by the patient not to comply or to change this condition should be taken as a major therapeutic context and subjected to therapeutic exploration. The therapist does not directly comment on the patient's wish or decision to change position. While neither sanctioning nor objecting to this decision, the therapist instead attends to the patient's material in an effort to understand the unconscious basis for this resistance-indicator.

As material permits subsequently, the therapist can then interpret the patient's decision in light of an activated adaptive context and derivative complex. Some borderline and ambulatory schizophrenic patients, though by no means all, are quite fearful of lying on the couch for reasons that include a dread of their own primitive fantasies and perceptions, and a need for concrete visual contact with the therapist, which forms a basis for a pathological parasitic or symbiotic mode of relatedness. Such anxieties, fantasies, and perceptions should be respected by the therapist, who should not pressure the patient or offer other forms of noninterpretive interventions, and who should maintain his or her interpretive stance in hope of rectifying this aspect of the framework when the patient is more comfortable and better able to manage its implications.

In patients who tend to be quite impulsive, it may be necessary to advise them that all major decisions should be subjected to analytic exploration before being explicated. By and large, it is recommended that this particular ground rule not be explicitly stated to the patient, since it is a directive that has manipulative qualities that extend beyond the inevitable minimum that accrues to any aspect of the ground rules. Instead, at those junctures where patients of this kind become involved in major life decisions, the therapist can respond with interpretive work that will serve the patient far better than a stated ground rule in clarifying the nature and basis for his or her choices, and in minimizing the risk of uninsightful acting out.

As a rule, the confidentiality and total privacy of therapy is conveyed by implication and remains one of the implicit ground rules. Their existence, which is essential for insightful psychotherapy, need not be specifically stated to the patient. However, in situations where there has been any type of complication in these areas, such as a request that the therapist fill out an insurance form or an expressed concern about total confidentiality, the patient should be directly assured that his or her sessions are entirely private and confidential. This cannot, of course, be stated to the patient unless it is true to the best of the therapist's knowledge and ability. This ground rule must be explicated and interpreted according to prevailing actualities.

In situations where breeches in confidentiality cannot be avoided, such as in clinic settings and when the therapist requires supervision, the absence of total confidentiality need not be stated directly to the patient. This type of direct self-revelation proves additionally destructive to the patient and to the therapeutic experience. Instead, the therapist should simply bypass offering the patient assurances of this kind, and work with an approach that implicitly takes into account the prevailing realities. Thus a patient's sense of the presence of a supervisor, when accurate and valid, should be handled as a manifest representation of an adaptive context or as a derivative communication in a manner that gives credence to the patient's belief. This is done without explicit acknowledgment and in particular, such work is carried out in a manner that avoids any implication that the patient is mistaken, distorting, and falsely deriving impressions based on past experiences. The therapist must also be careful to separate out the patient's valid conscious and unconscious perceptions from extensions into distortion.

In private practice, the therapist should never take or even make notes or discuss a patient with anyone at all. The only exceptions to this rule involve the therapist's continued need to learn through supervision or a difficult therapeutic interlude that requires supervisory consultation. The interactions between the therapist and his or her supervisor will implicitly influence the therapist's work with the patient, and may be detected unconsciously by the latter. Still, therapeutic work with the patient in this area must be carried out with the *implicit* acceptance of the patient's valid unconscious perceptions and without any form of inappropriate confession by the therapist. In principle, however, the overriding goal should be that of securing and maintaining the total confidentiality of the psychotherapeutic experience without exception.

In a clinic setting, total confidentiality is difficult to maintain, and usually quite impossible. Under these conditions, the therapist should not lie to the patient and promise a level of confidentiality that he or she cannot offer. Psychotherapy is founded upon truthful expression, and is badly damaged by any witting or unwitting lie or misstatement by the therapist. Thus, in clinic settings where confidentiality is, indeed, compromised, the therapist must recognize that he or she is working in a damaged bipersonal field, and that as a result, there will be many pathological elements in the patient's communications to the therapist that will prove unresolvable and uninterpretable. Under these conditions, the therapist can only hope to keep these deviations to a minimum and to work sincerely with the patient on the ramifications of the alterations in the ground rules as they influence the therapeutic relationship and interaction. As a rule, such a therapy will take place over a period of several months, during which both patient and therapist consciously realize at the behest of the patient's derivative communications the ultimate impossibility of effective, insightful therapy under these deviant conditions (the development of an unrectifiable framework-deviation therapy). The insight and positive introjects so derived prove curative for most of these patients, who will then often not need to be referred elsewhere. It is the failure to analyze the actual implications of these deviations that leads to many stalemated and sometimes catastrophic clinic therapies and to similar situations in compromised private therapies.

All requests by the patients for exceptions to these ground rules should, in general, obtain the response from the therapist that the patient should continue to say whatever comes to his or her mind. In this way, derivatives usually become available that will serve as a guide for the therapist's management response, as well as for interpretations. Virtually without exception, these derivative communications speak to the need to maintain the security of the framework.

For example, patients often come for the initial consultation with plans for a vacation sometime within a month of initiating therapy. They then request that responsibility for these sessions be waived because of the prior commitment. Permitting the patient to free associate consistently reveals that this arrangement is an unconscious resistance designed to gratify a number of pathological needs and fantasies, and that these range from the wish to be an exception to the wish to be certain that treatment can be interrupted if the claustrophobic and other pressures and anxieties become too great. Often, there are defenses against unconscious sexual and aggressive impulses and fantasies, and a need to deny symbiotic and merger wishes.

While many well-meaning therapists would accept the patient's framework and go along with the proposed deviation, derivative listening consistently reveals that such a measure runs counter to effective, insightful therapeutic work. It often speaks for the therapist's fear of securing the framework and of tolerating the inevitable direct aggression with which the patient responds. Further, on an unconscious level, it is experienced by the patient as a lack of commitment by the therapist in respect to the ideal therapeutic environment and to the pursuit of structural change based on insight and on a healthy therapeutic symbiotic mode of relatedness.

The Alliance Sector

The manifest and latent or communicative alliance sector of the relationship between the patient and therapist is grounded in the therapeutic contract. It is important in considering the therapeutic alliance to consider both surface and latent alliance attributes, as well as both manifest and latent factors in both patient and therapist as they influence this dimension of their interaction.

Thus the therapist must consider the patient's apparent cooperativeness and conscious willingness to engage in the pursuit of the therapeutic goals upon which both agree. In addition, however, the therapist must observe the extent to which the patient is also cooperative implicitly and latently in respect to achieving these goals. In particular, the therapist should develop a sensitivity to the extent to which the patient provides meaningful derivative material in light of activated intervention contexts. This is the sphere of the unconscious or communicative alliance, and the factors that influence it are largely unconscious, though within both patient and therapist. Quite unconsciously, patients may do much to disrupt effective psychotherapy even while apparently cooperating with the therapist. Similarly, many well-meaning, manifestly sensible (i.e., well-rationalized) interventions by therapists, most of them involving deviations from the basic ground rules and noninterpretive verbal efforts, convey to the patient (on an unconscious and derivative level) inputs that are disruptive to a sound therapeutic alliance.

Both the therapeutic contract itself and the alliance sector of the therapeutic relationship have manifest and latent dimensions. Further, they are explicated and developed only in part through the direct statements of the therapist. Much in these areas is shaped by the implications contained in the therapist's attitudes and behaviors, and by the nature of his or her interventions—which range, of course, from those that are interpretive and deal with the frame to those that are noninterpretive and manipulative. Thus, a therapist shapes an area of direct cooperation and an additional sector of communicative cooperation, doing so in the main through the manner in which he or she establishes the ground rules and boundaries of therapy and intervenes verbally. As expected, the secure frame and a basically interpretive approach produce the most effective type of therapeutic cooperation between the patient and therapist, both manifestly and latently.

Implicit Ground Rules

A number of additional ground rules and boundaries for the therapeutic setting and relationship are not stated directly to the patient. Instead, they emerge implicitly through the manner in which the therapist responds to the patient and his or her material.

For example, a therapist will seldom explicitly state to a

patient that there will be *no physical contact* between them other than the handshake with which the patient is greeted at the time of the initial consultation, and perhaps a handshake at the time of an extended vacation or at termination. Similarly, the therapist's *neutrality* through which he or she restricts himself or herself to intervening through silences, interpretations, and framework-management responses, without personal bias and such, is not stated to the patient at the outset of therapy. Instead, it becomes evident as the therapeutic work proceeds and as the patient perceives, consciously and unconsciously, the nature and qualities of the therapist's interventions.

Much in the way of the therapist's anonymity and neutrality is also conveyed in this fashion. The patient soon becomes aware that the therapist does not react to communications and pressures, and even to direct attacks or efforts at seduction, with counter-measures, but instead, maintains an interpretive-management stance. The patient soon recognizes the absence of self-revelations, personal opinions, and idiosyncratic responses from the therapist to the extent that this is humanly feasible. Some of this is conveyed in the initial consultation in the way the therapist works with the patient. Much of it unfolds in the course of subsequent treatment.

The therapist's creation and management of the ground rules and setting, and the nature of his or her interventions, make a major contribution to the alliance sector of the therapeutic relationship. Carried out in a concerned and human fashion, with due respect for the patient and with the utmost sensitivity and tact, this highly human though quite unique approach to the patient creates the conditions under which the derivative expressions of the unconscious fantasies, memories, introjects, and perceptions that form the basis for the patient's Neurosis emerge in the context of the therapeutic relationship and interaction in a form that lends itself to interpretive-analytic resolution.

The establishment of a Type Two derivative, healthy symbiotic, form of relatedness between the patient and therapist is inherent to this type of work. Further, it expresses the preparedness of both participants to deal with the patient's primitive conflicts and fantasy-perception constellations, as well as with issues of separation and individuation, of narcissism, disturbed self-system, and the like. It is a commitment as well for the therapist to experience some degree of necessary regression and to rework privately any unresolved aspects of his or her own Neurosis, which is reactivated in the therapeutic interaction with a given patient. Without fail, modifications of the basic ground rules create departures from this mode of relatedness and type of cure, and shift both patient and therapist into areas of unconscious collusion and bastion formation, through which symptom alleviation is pursued without true insight, individuation, and maturation.

Establishing the Patient's Style of Communication and Ability to Work in Therapy

As the therapist expresses his or her competency and preferred mode of communication and curative endeavor, so must the therapist make an assessment of the patient's communicative style and ability to work in therapy. Aspects of this evaluation have a bearing upon the patient's capability of participating in a sound conscious and unconscious therapeutic alliance with the therapist.

In every first hour the patient must deal with a number of activated intervention contexts, among which the therapist's efforts to establish and secure an ideal therapeutic environment may loom large. Patients who are likely to be able to work effectively in psychotherapy will be inclined to accept the therapeutic conditions and contract offered by the therapist with little or no effort to impose a deviant frame upon the treatment experience. If they do attempt to deviate, they remain expressive and prove receptive to the therapist's valid interpretive and framework-management interventions. Such patients, then, function as Type A communicators— senders and receivers—from the outset of therapy. Only later, once the initial adaptation-evoking contexts have been interpretively understood and rectified, will they shift to a Type C mode, when it is necessary for them to lie fallow and to carry out their own healing efforts.

In addition to these relatively ideal patients, there is a group of Type C patients who will show apparent resistances, but who accept the framework and soon settle into an ongoing therapeutic relationship. These patients require far more in the way of holding and containing than active, interpretive interventions. They will, from time to time, generate a frame issue or respond to an error by the therapist with somewhat defended Type A communication, only to return to their use of the Type C mode for long periods. However, some of these patients fail to produce clear representations of activated intervention contexts and meaningful derivative communications despite the presence of important adaptive issues within the therapeutic interaction. While some of these highly defended patients will continue treatment, many of them become bored and wary of the therapeutic relationship because of the therapist's relative inactivity. Since the therapist has no choice but to respond in this way, they often create a crisis in which the therapist has to chose between erroneous interventions or maintaing a stance within a secure framework and waiting to see whether the patient will then produce an interpretable communicative network. If the patient does so, the therapist is able to offer interpretations that tend to enhance the therapeutic alliance and promote the continuation of therapy. If the patient does not do so, there is often a shift to the Type B-C mode, with major efforts by the patient to disrupt the alliance sector, and to either effect a deviant therapeutic contract or to terminate.

Finally, Type B-C patients show powerful resistances in the face of mobilized intervention contexts. Although agitating to modify the framework in major ways, and often relentless in these efforts, these patients offer the therapist little in the way of an interpretive network of communcations. They appear highly determined to pathologically projectively identify distinctly primitive and disturbing inner mental contents into the therapist, to maintain some type of merger state with the therapist, and to create a deviant and pathologically symbiotic or parasitic contract. If they fail to do so, they destroy the therapist's efforts to secure the therapeutic environment by terminating their treatment prematurely. They show, then, little ability to work toward insight and structural change within a sound therapeutic environment and relationship.

It must be remembered that the patient's communicative style and ability to work in therapy is under continual interactional influence from the therapist. In general, the Type C therapist will tend to promote the use of the Type C mode in his or her patients, while the Type B therapist is likely to evoke responsive Type B projective identifications in his or her patients. On the other hand, the Type A therapist offers the optimal opportunity for the patient to express his or her own inherent communicative style and to convey to the maximal extent possible in the Type A mode.

In general, it is possible in the initial session for the therapist to have a strong sense of the patient's style of communication and ability to work in therapy, both on the surface and in regard to communicative relatedness. The patient's basic style of communication tends to be quite consistent over the course of therapy, with variations that depend on the nature of acute life crises, major intervention contexts, and the interpretive-management therapeutic work that the therapist is able to effect. In a sense, difficult patients remain difficult, while relatively easy and communicative patients tend to maintain their style until their acute problems are resolved. Ultimately, they terminate their therapy with an alternation between the Type A and Type C modes, which produces an insightful and yet holding termination phase.

In all, the therapist should be prepared to work with the valuable and pathological aspects of each person's communicative tendencies. Undoubtedly, the pathological elements of communication are an important means through which the patient's underlying emotional illness is expressed and clarified. Resistances are inevitable, meaningful, sometimes trying for the therapist, and yet they contain within them considerable potential for cure.

Summary and Conclusions

The main goal of the first session is to identify the patient's main emotional problems and to determine his or her degree of motivation for therapy. Important too is the need for the therapist to implicitly and explicitly convey a sense of competency, the ability to relate to the patient through a healthy symbiosis, and to indicate the possibility of effective and insightful treatment. In addition to a number of supplementary goals, a critical component of the initial session is the implicit and explicit delineation of the ground rules and boundaries of the psychotherapy (the therapeutic contract).

The basic approach to the first hour is to permit the patient to free associate and to keep questions to a minimum. Interventions with a relatively silent patient may initially involve questions related to material already presented, although the therapist should be prepared to respond interpretively or with framework-management responses to the patient's gross behavioral and communicative resistances as early as possible.

The therapist will also evaluate the patient's character structure and psychopathology, his or her style of communication, manner of working in therapy, and all assets and liabilities that pertain to the treatment experience. The therapist must be alert to acute symptoms, and to emergencies that involve suicidal or homicidal potential. A listening-holding stance should be maintained, and the therapist should be prepared to respond interpretively to such indicators. Only in extreme emergencies should it be necessary for the therapist to modify the usual interpretive framework-management approach in order to institute guarantees for the patient's safety. These should not if possible involve third parties, but should involve a viable agreement between the patient and therapist that will assure the safety of the patient and others.

The therapist's main interventions in the first hour involve interpretations of the patient's initial resistances and the offer of a definitive therapeutic contract. The former work is carried out consistently on the basis of activated intervention contexts and the patient's derivative responses.

With a therapist capable of offering the patient an ideal therapeutic relationship and setting, a major intervention context lies in the therapist's efforts to establish a healthy symbiosis with the patient. This approach creates a strong background of safety, and generates mainly transference-based anxieties and fantasies that reflect the patient's dread of entrapment, annihilation, and harm, somewhat based on the loss of a basically pathological symbiotic mode of relatedness. With a therapist who offers a basically flawed therapeutic environment, the patient may obtain uninsightful symptom relief (a framework-deviation cure), although his or her basic image of the therapist is greatly impaired. While many patients will accept such deviant arrangements, on a derivative level they make intense attempts to rectify the frame and resolve the therapist's—and their own—psychopathology, which has contributed to the situation. This response is in keeping with the typical split within patients (and many therapists) in regard to the therapeutic environment: often wishing consciously for breaks in the frame, while insisting unconsciously on its maintenance.

In principle, the first hour is approached as part of the spiraling interaction between the patient and therapist, and is understood in light of dynamic considerations. Since much of the future tone of therapy is established in this session, adherence to basic therapeutic principles with as little deviation as possible helps to establish the therapeutic relationship on a sound and secure basis.

Chapter 22

Fees and the Length and Frequency of Sessions

The Fee

The therapist should have a range of fees in keeping with his or her level of experience. The maximum fee should be charged with all patients whom the therapist believes are capable of paying it. In situations where the therapist senses that a patient cannot afford this fee, a lower fee should be proposed, though it should not be more than five or ten dollars less than the usual fee. The therapist should state the fee directly. The patient should not be told that there is a fee range or that he or she is being charged a maximum or minimum fee. The therapist should simply state that this is the fee per session, and the patient should be allowed to proceed from there. The same fee should be charged for the consultation session and for all other subsequent sessions. It follows too that each session should be of the same duration. As noted previously, the fee is often a factor in determining the frequency of visits. In principle, the fee should remain fixed, and the frequency of sessions should be determined by whatever is clinically indicated and what the patient can afford. It is inappropriate to propose a reduction in fee if the patient should wish to come more often than possible in light of the therapist's stated fee. This practice is especially common among analysts who prefer to see patients four or five times weekly in analysis, rather than in once- or twice-weekly psychotherapy. Any reduction in fee, or the proposal of a fee well below the therapist's usual range, is highly seductive and

435

infantilizing; it will mar the basic therapeutic relationship and environment.

The therapist alone should set the fee and handle the accounts. No third party should be involved. In a clinic setting, the responsibility for establishing and collecting the fee should belong to the therapist, and clinic fees should be set by the therapist in keeping with his or her level of training and the patient's ability to pay.

The stated fee should be maintained without change throughout the psychotherapy. A proposal by the patient that the fee should be less than that stated by the theraist, even when it is made in the first session, should be left open for exploration. Since the therapist's basic attitude should be that of maintaining the fee, the prevailing intervention context will be in keeping with that implied approach. In this light, the patient's derivative communications will consistently point to the necessity of keeping the fee as stated, since the sacrifice by the therapist involved in a reduction in fee will disturb the basic mode and properties of the therapeutic relationship. Those patients who realistically cannot afford the therapist's usual fee can be handled in one of two ways: The first alternative, once the reality is established, is for the therapist to reduce the fee, while interpreting from the patient's associations the implications of this measure. As a rule, the material will then lead to the conclusion that termination is necessary because of the seductive qualities and the lack of clear-cut boundaries between the patient and therapist. The second alternative is to refer the patient to a therapist who will establish a lower basic fee so that treatment can unfold without disturbance. As is true of all framework issues, the therapist must move beyond manifest-content listening and permit the patient's derivative communications to serve as a guide to both management responses and interpretations. Derivative meanings that involve unconscious perceptions of the valid implications of a reduction in fee take precedence over extentions into unrealistic and distorted fantasies within the patient.

Similar principles apply throughout treatment. Once a realistic and acceptable fee is established, the therapist should neither increase nor reduce it. Even when there is a striking increase in the cost of living or in the income of the patient, the agreed upon fee should be maintained. In principle, the therapist should increase fees for *new* patients, rather than doing so with ongoing patients.

The sole exception to this rule occurs when the patient has

been seen initially at an unduly low fee. This sometimes happens when a patient is transferred from a clinic setting to private practice when a therapist is first setting out. Although these low fees as a rule have detrimental consequences for the therapeutic experience, some of this may be rectified by an increase in fee when the patient's income permits. However, here too the basic principle of rectifying the frame entirely at the behest of the patient's derivative communications should be maintained. When such an increase is appropriate for both patient and therapist, the derivative associations from the former will consistently reveal the necessity for the increase, as well as the unconscious implications of both the low fee and the pending increase.

The ground rule regarding the fee should be stated as follows: "My fee is 'x' dollars per session. I will expect you to keep track of the number of sessions each month and to pay me at the beginning of each month for the sessions of the previous month."

Bills tend to be used secretly by patients as transitional objects and as ways of alleviating pathological separation anxieties. Affording the patient responsibility for keeping track of the sessions, and for payment at the beginning of each month for the previous month's sessions, fosters the patient's autonomy and gives the patient an opportunity to express underlying unconscious perceptions, fantasies, and conflicts in this area. The analysis of errors by the patient, of efforts to modify the frame in this area, and of delays in payment is usually quite revealing and a meaningful form of therapeutic work. It is essential, however, that these efforts be carried out in light of prior intervention contexts and in the adaptive contexts of the therapist's anticipation of payment early in each month and his or her not providing the patient with a bill.

A patient should not be permitted to accrue a large debt to the therapist. The payment of fees should be no more than a month or so late, and such delays require understanding and intervention. Situations in which the patient fails to pay the entire fee for longer periods of time consitute high level resistance-indicators for intervening. Efforts must be made by the therapist to discover the intervention context that helps to account for the payment failure, and to interpret the patient's derivative associations accordingly. In addition, it will usually be necessary to rectify the frame by terminating the patient either permanently or temporarily, though again doing so entirely at the behest of the patient's indirect associations.

Every effort should then be made to fill the abandoned hours and to offer the patient a different time upon his or her return. Whenever this is not feasible and the patient resumes his or her previous hours, the patient will maintain a conscious or unconscious belief that the therapist has made a sacrifice and has reserved the time for his or her return. Even when this is entirely untrue, this impression has a detrimental influence on the patient.

The patient should be told that he or she is responsible for the time that is leased to him or her and for which payment must be made as long as therapy continues—unless the therapist cancels an hour or is on vacation. The prerogative of cancelling hours and taking vacations belongs to the therapist, and is one of the necessary inequities (hurtful aspects) inherent to an optimal framework. This responsibility should be taken seriously, however, and the therapist should endeavor not to cancel single sessions except in a dire emergency or when there is an unmodifiable, major commitment. In general, the therapist should take two vacations each year, perhaps a month in the summer, and a week or two in the winter. While there is some latitude here, attention to derivative communications from patients will inform the therapist when he or she is behaving inappropriately and exploitatively in this sphere.

There are no exceptions to this requisite of responsibility for alloted time. Even when the patient is involved in a major life crisis, such as the death of a family member or hospitalization, if the patient wishes to maintain his or her time, then the patient must also accept responsibility for the hours. At times, it may be necessary to interrupt therapy rather than forego the fee and keep the patient's hours open. Failure to stand with this ground rule constitutes an unnecessary sacrifice on the part of the therapist for the patient, and will prove seductive and confusing to the latter, who is afforded direct and inappropriate support and gratification at a time of crisis. This measure unconsciously reinforces the patient's own use of pathological denial, tends to preclude the analysis of separation anxieties, and is likely to foster pathological symbiotic or parasitic ties. It may sometimes reinforce the patient's wish to be ill and to obtain other modifications in the framework that are similarly pathologically gratifying. The ground rules of psychotherapy, and the basic conditions of the therapeutic relationship, must of necessity have unique qualities that are at a variance with the proper hallmarks of social relationships. It is these very distinctive attributes of the therapeutic relationship, however, that are basic to the cure of the patient.

The patient should pay the fee by check, which should be endorsed by the therapist "for deposit only" so it is clear that the money has gone into the therapist's professional bank account. Although a check certainly modifies the total confidentiality of the therapeutic situation, it is nonetheless to be preferred to payments in cash, which foster fantasies and beliefs in the patient that the income is not being reported for tax purposes. It may well be that the ideal payment is cash, and that the patient's fantasies can be analyzed by a therapist who knows his or her own integrity quite well.

When a patient makes an error with a check, with cash, or in the timing of the payment, the therapist should *not* accept the altered fee, and should instead suggest that the patient explore the situation. Often the therapist discovers the mistake after the session in which it has been made. It is then necessary to hold onto the check until the next hour, when it should be out on the desk or on a table, so the patient can see it upon entering the session. From there, the techniques of rectifying the framework and interpreting the implications of the error are based on principles already established, and are founded upon the derivative communications from the patient in light of prior adaptive contexts. Some patients do not immediately accept the return of an erroneous check, and it therefore behooves the therapist to examine his or her interventions for possible mistakes, and to continue to hold on to the check so that it may be placed out in the open before the next session. It is important to intervene in this area as quickly as possible so that the therapist does not sacrifice too much for the patient by delaying receipt of payment.

Some patients attempt to hand the therapist a check for the month's session before the final session of that particular month. This constitutes payment in advance of services, and should not be accepted, and should instead be subjected to rectification and analysis. Other patients will attempt to give the therapist a postdated check, and this too should not be accepted, but again explored for implications. Such maneuvers often occur at times of separation, and serve as a way of pathologically fusing with the therapist and to undo separation anxieties at such times. Additional meanings will emerge in the context of the specific interventions from the therapist that have served to prompt this particular behavior in the patient.

The check for the fee should be made out and signed by the patient. Some wives have their husbands fill out and sign the check, while many adolescents will ask their parents to do so. With today's banks offering free checking to any responsible individual, it should be possible to analyze and rectify this intrusion of a third party into therapy in almost all such instances. However, a necessary requisite is the therapist's nonparticipation: a check of this kind must not be accepted so that full analysis is feasible. Acceptance of the check is seen as unconscious collusion and will interfere with the rectifying and interpretive work needed under these conditons. While there is still some influence upon the treatment when a spouse or parent is actually providing the funds for the therapy, having the patient pay for treatment with his or her own check offers the optimum degree of rectification possible under these conditions. The influence of the source of the money can then be interpreted in light of the therapist's participation in the deviation and other intervention contexts.

Receipts for payment made are in general unnecessary, since the patient's cancelled check can be used to document payment. A request for such a receipt deserves full exploration in advance of any decision. Should the realities be such that a receipt is necessary— and this is almost never the case—it will then be vital to utilize the prepared receipt as an intervention context that organizes the patient's subsequent derivative response. There is usually some shading of disturbance under these conditions.

The management of fees is a highly sensitive and difficult issue for many therapists. It involves the therapist's essential source of income, and needs of that kind can prompt countertransference-based responses and mismanagements of the framework. Fears of losing the patient and of not receiving fees create pressures within therapists toward deviation and efforts that are primarily self-gratifying rather than in the therapeutic interests of the patient. These measures are the basis for highly disturbing negative introjects of the therapist, and will disrupt the relationship between patient and therapist. The therapist should engage in extensive periods of self-analysis before deviating from the essential principles defined here.

CLINICAL EXAMPLES

The first situation involves the young man referred to in Chapter 16 who was in psychotherapy during a transportation strike. He had shown considerable improvement in both his job situation and his relationship with women during a year of once-weekly psychotherapy. The first week of the strike he called the therapist to tell him that he had been on line for special transportation for over an hour and he simply was not going to be able to make his session. The following week, he appeared 45 minutes late for a 50-minute session. He stated that he had left work quite early and that there had been many delays. He asked directly about the fee for the session of the previous week and the therapist said that there would be no charge. The patient then paid for his abbreviated hour and left.

The excerpt presented here is from the following hour.

> Patient: I'm really furious with my boss. He broke his contract with me. We had an understanding that if I came into work early, I could leave early. Now he won't let me leave early. He changed the rules. He violated our contract.
>
> Therapist: You seem angry that you are unable to have your sessions in the last two weeks. You may also be telling me that you saw my decision not to charge you for the missed session as a violation of our contract.

The session ended before the patient could respond. It later emerged that the patient had made insufficient effort to be on time for the missed session, a revelation that shed new light on the therapist's decision not to charge the patient for that particular hour.

In principle, the therapist violated the basic technical precept of managing the framework at the behest of the patient's derivative communications in light of activated intervention contexts. In the abbreviated session, when the patient asked him about the fee for the previous hour, the therapist should have responded in a non-commital manner and suggested that the decision would have to wait until the patient could explore the matter. It seems quite likely that in the following hour both interpretation and framework-management responses would have become available to the therapist on the basis of the patient's further and derivative material.

In the actual situation, the patient responded to the therapist's direct intervention with a shift of his own toward a manifest-content level of relatedness, and the therapist joined in, creating a bastion or barrier against derivative interaction. It may be hypothesized that this served to compensate the patient for his lost time by providing him with some measure of pathological symbiotic gratification, and that it afforded the therapist similar inappropriate satisfactions. It also helped to seal off the underlying issues and disturbance within both patient and therapist prompted by the missed and much abbreviated sessions.

The material organizes best around the intervention context of the therapist's decision to not charge the patient for the missed session. As derivative expressions, they indicate the patient's anger over the therapist's decision to violate their contract, a decision that he accepted on the surface with gratitude, but then described as an infuriating betrayal. This type of split is typical in both patients and therapists under these circumstances, especially when the latter manage the ground rules by deviating. The patient's associations contain an implied *model of rectification:* the original or basic contract should have been adhered to in order to create a clearly defined relationship between the patient and therapist.

The therapist's actual interventions, while sensitive to some of the meaningful implications of the material, failed to deal with the important need to rectify this framework. However, it is to his credit that the intervention stressed a valid unconscious perception of the therapist based on his deviation. In principle, in the presence of a break in the frame created by the therapist, it is essential to intervene in terms of this type of valid unconscious perception and introject before extending an interpretation, if necessary, into areas of distortion. In general, countertransference-based deviations lead to essentially nontransference reactions within the patient, whose material must be understood dynamically in such terms. The acceptance as well of derivative models of rectification is based on an approach that gives credence to the patient's derivative expressions where such is indeed deserved.

In a subsequent hour, the patient's derivative associations linked the therapist's behavior to the patient's depressed father, who became overindulgent because of a recent illness and his fear of death. In this way, the patient offered an unconscious interpretation to the therapist to the effect that his own separation anxieties had interfered with his proper management of the frame.

While part of this patient's absence was beyond his control, subsequent material also indicated that with necessary sacrifice, the patient could have made his hour. It is of interest too that on an unconscious level, the patient held the therapist responsible for his unavailability—an issue that emerged only after further exploration of this particular incident.

A more typical situation is presented in the case of a married woman who was in psychotherapy for over a year because of a schizophrenic illness with auditory hallucinations. The patient had apparently made an appointment with her internist that conflicted with one of her sessions, causing her to miss her hour. Without derivative material, the therapist told her in the following hour that he would not charge her for the missed session. Despite this error, the therapist could have established the patient's responsibility for her session at the behest of her derivative communications. Patients have such a firm *unconscious* grasp of the nature of a sound therapeutic hold and environment that, given the option, they will consistently point to its attributes and necessity in their disguised associations.

The patient entered the first session of the following month with a check that had been made out except for the dollar amount.

Patient: How much do I owe you?

Therapist: Based on our discussion, 210 dollars.

Patient: I figured 240 dollars because of that doctor's appointment.

Therapist: Let's see what comes to mind.

Patient: *(Writes out the check, hands it to the therapist, who leaves it on his desk.)* I feel funny with my husband away [*on a business trip to Mexico*]. I saw a movie of a woman dying of cancer. Death scares us. My husband is hurtful, and yet I miss him. He called and told me he bought me and the children a lot of presents. Doesn't he know that I don't want presents? I just want him to take me seriously. I had dinner with a psychologist who was so much like me. Her husband is a physician and he had an affair with a patient. Another friend told me how lonely she is. I didn't charge 30 dollars [*the patient's fee per session*], but I listened. Somehow I don't think she got anything from it. I read a book about a psychiatrist who hooked his patient on medication. I thought you would be more compassionate. The woman had to be hospitalized. My dancing instructor has problems. With all his studying, he has a lot to learn. My mother gave me this expensive oil painting. She insisted I keep it, but I want to sell it so she can't lord it over me. I feel my face twitching. When my mother beat me, her face would twitch. The voice in my head just said, "Shut up, don't tell him." I don't want to think that I'm crazy. I want to sweep it under the rug. The voice just said, "Let him keep his gifts." I want to hit somebody, maybe you.

Therapist: You seem angry about a gift that you feel forced to take. You were prepared to pay for your missed session, though I forgave it. You don't want your mother's gift of the painting, and you're talking about a therapist who addicted his patient to drugs. It sounds like you feel my gift of 30 dollars bothers you and that it makes you feel indebted to me and stifled, and you therefore want to strike out at me.

Patient: I feel I learned a lesson because of that session and my mixing up the appointments. I feel I should pay.

Therapist: You seem to feel I did not take you seriously when you offered to pay me, and that I was in effect insisting on your taking a present from me.

Patient: You're right. I will bring another check next week. I feel less tense now.

Through abundant derivatives, this patient indicates that she was prepared to pay for the missed session, and that the therapist's decision not to accept the fee involves an inappropriate present that did not take the patient seriously, infantilized her, and seemed to be in the service of lording over her. In addition, forgoing the fee was perceived as sexually seductive and as an error that indicated the therapist needed to learn more and is like the patient (in important sick ways). The forgiven fee is like medication that addicts the patient and binds her inappropriately (pathologically symbiotically) to the therapist. The net effect, especially when the therapist failed to interpret the available material, was to drive the patient crazy, to infuriate her and to prompt the two hallucinations. Relief followed upon interpretation and rectification.

Despite her schizophrenic illness, this patient offers an ideal form of Type A communication in response to the intervention context of the therapist's decision to forgo payment for the missed session. The patient represents the intervention context directly and in passing at the beginning of the hour. She includes an immediate model of rectification in proposing that she pay the full amount due to the therapist for all of her hours. She then shifts to indirect communication and provides the therapist with an extremely meaningful and coalescible derivative complex. The latter reveals the patient's unconscious perceptions of the therapist, her speculations as to the basis for his mismanagement of the frame, further models of rectification (e.g., that the therapist should not give the patient a gift, but should maintain the ground rules and take her seriously by holding her responsible for her hour), a series of responsive adaptive reactions, and a critical genetic link to the patient's mother. The latter must be understood as the patient's derivative way of indicating that the therapist has *in reality* behaved in a manner comparable to the patient's mother, thereby generating an essentially *nontransference-based* pathogenic interaction that repeats aspects of the patient's pathological present and past. The patient's efforts to generate an interpretive response in the therapist, and to provide him with clear models of rectification, are unmistakable. This serves as a strong reminder that even with a schizophrenic patient—and perhaps especially with such a patient—the maintenance of a secure frame is essential in providing a type of holding environment that he or she lacked in childhood, and that forms a foundation for the ego strengthening work that will enable the patient to express himself or herself in a manner that will then lead to specific cognitive insights and constructive structural change.

The patient arrived on time for the session that followed and saw that her check from the previous week was on the therapist's desk. She handed him an envelope containing a check for the fee for the missed session. The material from that hour is condensed here.

> Patient: I feel a bit tense and didn't want to come here today. I forced myself. I'm angry at Susie [*her present baby sitter*] because she's bossy. She picks up my daughter when she cries, but won't let her play in the grass because she gets dirty. She tells me when she has sex with her husband. Tanya [*her first baby sitter*] was more of a problem. But once I set her straight and was firm with her—she shaped up. I should be firm with Susie. You taught me the value of firmness. My

husband is back and I didn't let him be critical. He did some nice things for me while he was away and was very helpful when he got back. It's like he's doing too much. I learned a lot last session, like how gifts make me feel weak. I still want to sell the painting my mother gave me, but I know it would upset me if someone did that with a gift I gave them. I think I'll tell her how I feel about it, and tell her what I want to do. I shouldn't have accepted it in the first place. My father is afraid to be nice. He owes me some money, and I guess I'll have to get after him. The voice in my head tells me not to talk to you. My father was always superstitious, and felt that if you said certain kinds of terrible things, they might come true. I had a lot of superstitions and magical things as a child. Everything had to be perfect and clean, and nothing could be damaged. Everything had to be exactly in the right place or I would get obsessed. I haven't thought of these things in years. My voice tells me that I shouldn't get better, that it would have no place to go and that it wants to be with me. I've been ignoring it this past week. It seems more pathetic than crazy. I'm feeling really good and strong and direct today. Like I felt when I graduated from college. This woman had been after me, and I let her make love to me. When she was satisfied, she didn't want anything more to do with me. She lost interest, and then I got involved with drugs. The voice said *I* did these good things, not you. Funny that I should be thinking of these things for the first time in years, but I wonder about them rather than fear them.

The therapist's act of breaking and rectifying the frame produced a split image of him in the patient: as someone who had exposed his inappropriate needs initially, but who was then capable of strength and firmness, and of managing his own wishes in order to renounce the search for inappropriate gratification. The result is a positive introject and view of others, and derivative communications of a highly constructive nature, which were quite unique for this patient. In this material there are direct efforts by the patient to rectify the frame—i.e., her presenting a check for the fee for the missed session. There are also additional derivative allusions in this sphere, particularly as they pertain to the manner in which the patient felt she should handle the painting that her mother had given her. Quite specifically, the patient states that she should not have accepted her mother's gift in the first place—a strong derivative allusion to the therapist's initial erroneous decision regarding the fee for the missed hour. Similarly, the patient states that she will have to get after her father, who owes her some money—this too is a model of rectification.

This material lends itself well to Type Two derivative validation of the therapist's framework-management response (his decision to rectify the frame and his interpretation of the patient's unconscious perceptions of himself based on his previous decision to forgo the fee). At first, however, there is an allusion to the babysitter's bossiness, which appears to be a derivative unconscious perception of the manner in which the therapist rectified the frame—i.e., doing so through a directive rather than at the behest of the patient's derivatives.

Nonetheless, the patient then suggests the need for boundaries regarding sexual revelations (cf. the allusion to the babysitter and the importance of firmness). The positive image of the therapist based on his recent sound interventions is reflected in the patient's allusions to her husband. His constructive functioning is also taken in as an introjective identification, which is reflected in the patient's better perspective regarding the manner in which she should handle the gift from her mother. There are also allusions to a sense of getting better emotionally, the fear of having no place to go (a likely representation of the anticipation of the termination of her psychotherapy) and worry over the loss of her psychopathology in the form of her auditory hallucinations. In this segment of material the patient's separation anxieties are mobilized in response to a sound intervention by the therapist, and the patient's fear of getting well is expressed. The material also implies a sense of the manner in which a positive introjective identification with the therapist begins to threaten the patient's established pathological introjects.

Further positive effects of the therapist's interventions are seen in the patient's additional comments about her sense of strength and the diminution of her symptoms. The emergence of this material in this particular context also seems to imply a positive response to the therapist's sound interventions. This is supported by the finding that the patient's associations tend in some ways to further extend the implications of his efforts.

Finally, the patient's disappointment toward the end of the

hour, her feeling of being used and then abandoned, may well be a reaction to the therapist's failure to interpret this material in light of the intervention contexts of his rectification of the frame and his supplementary interpretation. The patient's derivative responses contain mobilized separation anxieties and genetic material, including important fears of separation and individuation, which call for such a response on this part.

Thus a favorable outcome was developed from a situation that began with a disruptive break in the frame in the area of the fee and in the need to maintain the patient's responsibility for her sessions. The patient eventually experienced an important measure of conscious insight (cf. her realizations regarding the need for firmness and the way in which to handle an unwanted gift), as well as widening other aspects of her scope of self-understanding. Through a sound framework management and interpretive response, whatever its flaws, a significant piece of therapeutic work was accomplished with this patient.

It is undoubtedly best for both patient and therapist for the latter to maintain the basic fee arrangements as established in the first hour. In situations where lapses occur, rectification and interpretation in terms of the patient's derivative communications can shift a disruptive and traumatic interaction into a constructive and therapeutic experience for patient and therapist alike. Although therapist-evoked, such interludes can be used in a meaningful fashion to illuminate and resolve a patient's Neurosis. Both specific insights and the restoration of a sound holding relationship (a healthy therapeutic symbiosis) are important in this regard. A great deal of effective therapeutic work is carried out around framework issues.

Length and Frequency of Sessions

In the consultation hour, the patient should be given specific hours of a stated weekly frequency, and of a 45 or 50 minute duration. The therapist should take at least a five-minute break between patients to rest, attend to personal matters, and respond to telephone calls and such. It is important that the therapist be on time, and if he or she is late, this is a critical intervention context. If the therapist's lateness is a matter of minutes, he or she can offer to extend the session. If it is for a longer period, either the time must be made up through extending a future session, or the fee reduced in proportion to the amount of time missed. Such deviations are highly traumatic for the patient—and often for the therapist as well—and are to be avoided if at all possible.

The therapist should be careful to end each hour on time, within 30 to 60 seconds of the appointed time. This should be done without apology, by simply stating to the patient that the time is up, or by using some other phrase that indicates the end of the session. Unless there is an absolutely dire emergency, there is no justifiable reason for extending an hour. Only if the patient's or someone else's life is at stake should such a deviation be undertaken, and even then, it will have mixed consequences.

If a therapist inadvertently extends an hour, he or she has no legitimate right to reduce the following session, though the patient will often be late to an extent that tends to equalize the two situations. An extension of this kind is a critical intervention context, and the therapist must be prepared to intervene in the following hour. The patient typically shows resistances in representing this particular high level adaptive context, and the therapist will often have to resort to a playback of meaningful derivatives around the unmentioned intervention context. It is important that the therapist attempt to analyze the patient's gross behavioral and communicative resistances under these circumstances, and to rely on the patient's direct and derivative associations, rather than introducing the issue ad hoc. However, it is equally important not to intervene in other areas until the implications of such an extension have been interpreted to the patient in some form or another. If there are additional activated intervention contexts, an intervention that combines the patient's reactions in both areas is to be preferred.

Twice-weekly psychotherapy appears to be the ideal mode of therapy, and once-weekly therapy is used when patients cannot afford this frequency. With those patients who can afford more intensive therapy, three or four times per week psychotherapy or psychoanalysis may be recommended. There need be no fear of attempting intensive therapy with borderline and schizophrenic patients, since this often offers them much that is constructive and symptom alleviating. However, clinical investigations are needed to determine what, if any, advantages accrue to the patient seen more than twice weekly.

The therapist should take one extended vacation so that the patient may do so as well. This vacation should be announced months in advance. For example, a therapist who takes off the entire month of August should inform his or her patient of these plans—and should have them made, at least in respect to the time and duration—at the beginning of the year. There should also be several months' notice for one- and two-week vacations.

Problems arise with patients whose company closes their offices for two or three weeks so that all employees can and must take their vacation at a particular time. When the business vacation period does not correspond with the therapist's vacation plans, the patient will often request that he or she not be held responsible for sessions during an extended leave of absence from the therapy. In principle, the therapist should not respond directly to such a request, but instead should permit, as always, full associative exploration, and generate a decision based on the patient's derivative associations. This material, virtually without exception, will indicate that despite the hardship involved, the appropriate response is to maintain the patient's responsibility for the sessions even under these conditions.

Such matters as seeing the patient always in the same office and of establishing a minimum of once-weekly therapy, are seldom mentioned as essential aspects of the ideal therapeutic environment. In a recent session, a patient who was being seen by her therapist on an every-other-week basis because of financial problems, offered the following associations:

> Patient: I feel so divided. The divorce and taking care of my daughter is upsetting me. She doesn't spend most of her time with me these days. I become anxious and depressed around her. I allow her to dump on me and carry on because I'm guilty I'm not spending enough time with her. It seems to me that she should go and live with one parent and have a one-parent relationship. Maybe it should be one-on-one with me, or maybe with her father. Any other way is hurtful.

The derivative implications for this every-other-week arrangement are unmistakable. The patient offers a clear derivative model of rectification, indicating that her hour should be her own rather than shared with someone else—in reality or fantasy. The therapist felt as well that the patient had unconsciously perceived some of his guilt for being unable to offer more frequent sessions to the patient, countertransference-based difficulties that led him to permit the patient to be more abusive than he might otherwise have done, since he often failed to interpret the implications of her rather destructive behaviors in the sessions.

It should be clear, then, that the patient's hours are set aside and that there is no valid basis to forgo the fee for a particular session—no matter what interferes with the patient's ability to appear. Of course, if the therapist cannot make an hour, there should be no charge for the session, *nor should the hour be made up,* since this too communicates unconsciously to the patient the therapist's need to inappropriately merge with the patient, the therapist's unresolved separation anxieties, greediness, a view of the patient as unable to function without him or her, and wide range of additional seductive, hostile, and infantilizing implications.

The secure and maintained frame asks of both the patient and therapist the tolerance to renounce and analyze pathological symbiotic needs, and to expose the inner pathology of both (though primarily of the patient) as it pertains mainly to the sickness of the patient. Simultaneously, it affords both participants the most secure and supportive conditions for such work, efforts that are filled with considerable anxiety and dread. Nonetheless, the ultimate gain for both participants can be considerable, and both can be provided with adaptive resources of lasting benefit.

CLINICAL EXAMPLE

The patient was young man in psychotherapy for homosexuality and alchoholism. He had planned a brief vacation overseas, and requested a change in hour so that he would not have to miss his session. Without exploration, the therapist agreed. There were many other inconsistencies in this framework, including the fact that the patient was also in group therapy from time to time, and that he would randomly shift from sitting up in a chair to lying on the couch. Treatment was on a once-weekly basis.

The shifted hour prior to the trip was filled with ruminations regarding the patient's resolve to meticulously arrange to avoid all alcohol during his vacation. The therapist responded manifestly with so-called support interventions that perpetuated the patient's ruminations.

When the patient returned from his vacation, he was seen at his regular time. He appeared drugged when he arrived for his hour.

Patient: I shouldn't be here. I took some downers. I didn't drink while in Europe, but I have since I'm back. *(The patient moves from the chair to the couch.)* I should have cancelled my session, but kept forgetting to call. My friend in Europe treated me like a baby, doing things at my slightest request and constantly protecting me from alcohol. I had a great sexual experience [*i.e., homosexual*], but felt all alone. He kept telling me everything about himself, and I pretended I was you, and just kept asking questions. I once asked my former group therapist how to stop being gay, and he told me not to expect to change and to accept my homosexuality. Somehow, even though I don't want a woman, I would like to have a family and children. The therapist had said there's a new form of shock therapy for gay men, but that's not something I want. *(At this point, the patient stands up and gets ready to leave his hour.)* I think I'll leave now.

Therapist: You're talking about being lonely and upset, and of turning to drugs and alcohol. Once again, you are not thinking things through but acting, and this includes your wish to leave the session.

Patient: *(Sitting down.)* That's true. Whatever you say. I want to go home in order to be alone. *(Gets up to leave.)* Can I have an additional session this week?

Therapist: I have no time available.

Patient: I'm leaving now. *(The patient leaves 15 minutes early.)*

This material may be taken as a *commentary* on this damaged therapeutic environment, and specifically on the therapist's decision to shift the patient's hour and not to firmly establish the patient's position during the sessions. The patient's associations and behaviors suggest that these deviations are seen as infantilizing, addicting, a form of immediate relief, pathologically symbiotically gratifying, and as substitutes for alcohol. They are highly seductive (cf. the reference to the sexual experience), but they destroy any hope for therapeutically founded change (the reference to the therapist who told the patient to accept his homosexuality). They therefore constitute an abandonment of the treatment process and the offer of a destructive substitute (the reference to the shock therapy). They lead the patient to disrupt his session and to end his hour early, and to request an additional deviation—a make-up session.

Although the patient accepted the make-up hour with gratitude, his derivative communications and behaviors are replete with its destructive implications. The patient unconsciously perceived the therapist's use of framework deviations as a means of adaptation—of seeking cure or relief—and responds, in part through identification and in part through his own pathological needs, by utilizing a comparable mode of cure. The patient's acting out/in by taking drugs before coming to the session serves here both as a way of conveying an unconscious implication of the therapist's shift in the hour (all deviations are a form of acting out/in by the therapist), as well as a way of demonstrating the behavioral consequences of failures to maintain a secure frame. The counterresistance-resistance aspects of all of the deviations by both patient and therapist are also in evidence. Unfortunately, the therapist's intervention in this hour failed to take into account the critical adaptive context that had contributed to the patient's further acting out by leaving the session early.

Chapter 23

Free Association, Position, and Free-Floating Attention

Psychotherapy should be founded on the *fundamental rule of free association* through which the therapist directly or implicitly asks or quietly expects the patient to say whatever comes to mind, regardless of its nature without censoring thoughts and feelings. The respective position of both the patient and therapist are clearly defined, and the therapist's basic attitude is that of unencumbered listening—so-called free-floating attention—with openness to role, image, and relationship evocations and to the patient's interactional pressures.

The Fundamental Rule of Free Association

There appears to be considerable confusion as to whether the fundamental rule of free association applies to psychotherapy. Some therapists believe that patients in therapy cannot free associate, while others are noncommital. Some of the difficulty in establishing a clear position involves a failure to comprehend the implications of the fundamental rule and its contribution to the ideal therapeutic environment. Establishment of open and unencumbered free association is an essential element of this environment and basic to insight therapy.

The fundamental rule can be explicitly stated to the patient during or toward the end of the first session through some comment to the effect that it would be best if the patient says everything that came to mind, and that on that basis, the therapeutic work will unfold. Quite simply, the therapist might indicate that the patient should express whatever occurs to him or her, without restriction. Sometimes, when a patient has not been especially silent and has offered a steady flow of associations in a first hour, it proves unnecessary to state the fundamental rule explicitly. However, should such a patient become silent in the following sessions, in addition to preparing to interpret the nature and function of this gross behavioral resistance, the therapist might once or twice advise the patient that it would be best for the patient and for the therapy to say whatever the patient is thinking and feeling no matter what it may be.

This fundamental rule creates an expectation that the patient will express himself or herself openly, without inhibition or censorship, honestly, directly, and as fully as possible. This *manifest* expectation actually carries over into the realm of *unconscious communication*. As a result, any modification by either the patient or the therapist in this tenet will disturb both manifest and latent expression and disturb both the surface and communicative alliance sectors.

The rule provides a standard by which certain gross behavioral resistances may be measured. In essence, it creates the opportunity to view all periods of silence, or the elimination of a specific association, as a form of surface resistance, which is a first-order indicator for intervention. It also provides a basis for the meaningful analysis of the implications of the patient's noncommunications, thereby providing an avenue for considerable potential insight.

Because of its implicit meanings, the fundamental rule also provides a standard for communicative resistances. The therapist's advice to the patient to say everything that comes to mind implies that the patient should express as well, in meaningful form, all necessary representations of activated intervention contexts and the derivative complexes with which they are associated.

Free association speaks to the definition of psychotherapy as based on the exploration of the patient's affectively toned verbal associations. It therefore suggests cure through understanding, rather than through action.

Finally, it serves as a guarantor that the patient will express manifestly all necessary indicators, including those of crisis proportions. Similarly, it pledges the patient to provide the therapist with an interpretable communicative complex where necessary.

Silence in Patients

Patients vary in the extent to which they comply with the fundamental rule of free association. Some show little tendency toward censorship or silence, while others are silent for long periods—sometimes even for entire sessions. The technical handling of such silences poses considerable difficulty for the therapist, and silence itself constitutes one of the more difficult gross behavioral resistances in psychotherapy. Quite often it represents an autistic mode of relatedness in which the patient attempts to destroy both cognitive meaning and meaningful relatedness. Because of this, it is seldom accompanied by a communicative network that clearly represents the antecedent intervention contexts to which the patient is responding or the meaningful derivative expressions that illuminate the basis for the gross behavioral resistance.

Although silence itself may have some minimal derivative and representational meaning, its implications are often quite ambiguous. At times it represents the destruction of meaning and relatedness. It may also represent an unconscious perception of a missed intervention by the therapist, a sense of the therapist's autistic withdrawal from the patient, as well as a reaction to either helpful or hurtful interventions by the therapist. Further, it must be kept in mind that silence is always an interactional product of the bipersonal field and therapeutic interaction. Any analysis of the underlying factors in its presence must begin with a search for inappropriate contributions from the therapist (which of course must be subjected to rectification), after which those from the patient receive full consideration.

As noted, silences are communications from the patient, and are often part of Type C barrier formations and efforts to destroy meaning and meaningful relatedness. They are a necessary expression of the patient's defenses and psychopathology, though more rarely, in the presence of significant expressed countertransferences, silence may be quite adaptive and appropriate to the treatment situation—though this must be weighed against the adaptive value of direct or indirect confrontation by the patient of the therapist and his or her problems.

Those silences that stem from countertransference-based difficulties require *rectification* of the therapist's problems, including breaks in the frame, as well as *interpretive* responses. This work must, however, be based on a represented intervention context and a meaningful derivative complex. Efforts at questioning, clarification, and confrontation, and directives to desist, tend to express further countertransferences within the therapist, and do not insightfully lead to the resolution of this particular resistance. Listening and holding patiently until an interpretive response can be made, along with the necessary rectification of the therapist's contributions, remains the essential technique.

CLINICAL EXAMPLE

A young woman patient was in treatment with a therapist who was seeing her at a low fee, had permitted extended indebtedness, had often changed the patient's hours, and had engaged in many noninterpretive interventions. In one session when much of this was still going on, the patient was ten minutes late. She was silent for a long period of time, and although sitting in a chair, would not look at the therapist. She took off her shoes and began to doze. She was then silent still longer.

Therapist: You took the trouble to get here, but you now sit silently. You must have mixed feelings about being here.
Patient: *(Continues to be silent for another 15 minutes.)*
Therapist: You seem to be saying by your silence that nothing can go on here, that we're both powerless here.
Patient: *(Silent for a while longer.)* I can't come for my Thursday session this week. Can I have a make-up? *(The patient now puts on her shoes.)*
Therapist: I can see you tomorrow at four p.m.

The next day, the patient called a little after four and asked if she could come later—she had been delayed. When the therapist said that he could not see her later, she asked if she were going to be charged for the session. When the therapist said that she would, she then asked for a make-up hour. The therapist then said he would discuss that question when he saw her next.

Here again is the kind of chaotic situation that evolves when the therapist modifies a number of attributes of the basic, ideal therapeutic environment. The therapist's confrontations, speculations, and interventions are more self-revealing than a reflection of the patient's communications, and had no influence whatsoever on the patient's use of silence.

It may be hypothesized that the patient's silence had been prompted by the therapist's deviations, some of which appeared to be both grossly seductive and blatantly hostile in nature. The seductive qualities are reflected in the derivative meanings of the patient's taking off her shoes. The patient's use of silence and of sleep appears to have adaptive value in erecting barriers between herself and the therapist, based in part on the therapist's own failure to establish secure and safe boundaries and conditions to therapy.

In later sessions, it became clear that the patient was deeply mistrustful of the therapist, and afraid to reveal anything to him lest it be misunderstood and misused by him. And yet, despite the evidence that the patient was somewhat terrified by the lack of sound therapeutic conditions, she requested a make-up session, which she then missed. This request lends some validity to the hypothesis that deviations in the framework have contributed to the patient's silences. To the extent that this could be confirmed, it is clear that the therapist would have to rectify the framework and his other contributions to the patient's silences, many of them based on his poor and countertransference-based interventions, before the patient would begin to modify this massive gross behavioral resistance and then provide the therapist with the communicative network he would need in order to interpret its meanings and functions. Massive silence of this kind often occurs when patients feel endangered and unsafe with their therapists.

The patient's failure to appear for the make-up session may be seen as an acted out model of rectification. However, the patient immediately shifts to further requests for deviations, revealing again the extent to which she has invested in the pathological relatedness, gratification, and defensiveness she is thereby receiving. Her continued efforts to have the therapist deviate further confirms the critical role that is played in this patient's behaviors, including her silences, by the therapist's deviations. It would appear from this material that the patient pressed the therapist to a point where, seemingly out of desperation, he finally maintained one aspect of this frame.

Silence is an action, as well as a form of resistance. Interactionally, it is often based on unconscious introjects of actions by the therapist and of his or her counterresistances. Silence can create interactional pressures for the therapist, and is often an un-metabolized, not understood reprojection of pathological projective identifications from the therapist. Thus silences tend to serve both Type B and Type C communicative functions. They appear anti-thetical to the Type A mode of communication.

In dealing with silences, the therapist must first identify and rectify any of his or her countertransference-based contributions to the silence. This usually permits the patient to communicate affec-tively-verbally in a somewhat more extended fashion, and this may then permit further interpretive and framework-management re-sponses by the therapist.

The Position of the Patient and Therapist

Traditionally, the psychotherapy patient has been advised to sit in a chair so that he or she may work face-to-face with the therapist, in contrast to the psychoanalytic patient who lies on a couch. In actual practice, however, many once- and twice-weekly patients are advised to use the couch, and there is some evidence that this is salutory to the therapeutic process. In any case, in the initial hour, the patient should be advised as to which position the therapist recommends, and this should be seen as a ground rule, which should then be adhered to as much as possible throughout the treatment. This implies that if a therapist selects the face-to-face mode, he or she will not later propose to the patient the use of the couch; while if the patient wishes to make such a shift, it will be subjected to full analytic exploration before being carried out. If the patient simply lies on the couch after having sat in a chair, this becomes an important indicator for interpretive and framework-management interventions. Directives to the patient should be avoided.

The patient's chair should be different from the one used by the therapist. Both chairs should be comfortable, and often the therapist has an ottoman, though as a rule, not the patient. Whatever their equality on a human level, there are important distinctions between the patient and therapist, and these should be conveyed implicitly through the furniture as well as in other notable ways.

It seems best, however, to advise all patients in psychotherapy to make use of the couch. Clinical evidence indicates that this constitutes a better and more viable therapeutic environment than the face-to-face modality with the patient in a chair.

Not every patient will immediately or even eventually accept placement on the couch. Nonetheless, even with these patients the recommendation that they use the couch becomes an important intervention context for interpretive therapeutic work. Responsive resistances are, as a rule, reflections of important and analyzable anxieties, defenses, fantasies, and perceptions.

The use of the couch tends to foster the patient's freedom in associating and ability to express manifestly and latently anxiety-laden contents and derivatives. By precluding visual contact, the couch tends to deprive the patient of an avenue of pathological symbiotic relatedness, and this deprivation proves to be a significant motivational factor (intervention context) that mobilizes important areas of conflict and disturbance. The patient's feelings of vulnerability intensify, and constellations related to entrapment, mistrust, and paranoid anxieties are revealed. There is an infantilizing, helpless quality to the position, which mobilizes anxieties in these important areas as well. The patient's inability to see the therapist fosters the latter's neutrality and anonymity by depriving the patient of facial cues; though of course, verbal and nonverbal auditory communication remains.

In addition to mobilizing important areas of anxiety and disturbance, the couch offers a sense of holding, privacy, and safety. It adds to that quality of the therapeutic environment that assures the patient of careful listening and interpretive response by the therapist without retribution. In all, then, the couch heightens the patient's sense of safety while simultaneously intensifying major areas of anxiety and vulnerability. The combination seems especially apt for the therapeutic experience.

Some patients will not lie on the couch. Among these, some will insist on sitting in the chair that they used for the consultation—and the consultation should always take place on a face-to-face basis. Others will sit on the couch, though not lie down. As a rule, these gross behavioral resistances stem from intense but pathological symbiotic needs, paranoid anxieties, and a dread of exposing both manifestly and through derivatives a disturbing inner mental world. Some of these patients develop intense persecutory anxieties when they are unable to maintain eye contact with the therapist, while others are action-oriented and fearful of letting their guard down so that unexpected expressions may emerge. In general, in the adaptive context of the recommendation of the couch and with the resistance-indicator of the patient's refusal to do so, there will be meaningful derivative material available upon which to base rectifying and interpretive measures.

Free-floating Attention

The counterpart of the fundamental rule of free association for the patient is the therapist's free-floating attention, role-responsiveness, and openness to interactional pressures. These attitudes are an important aspect of the therapeutic ambiance offered by the therapist to the patient. They imply, to the extent humanly possible, an openness to both the manifest and derivative implications of the patient's cognitive-affective material, as well as an ability to experience pressures toward modes of relatedness, role behaviors, and self-image evocations. These latter, and the experience of interactional projections, are experienced subjectively by the therapist, worked over or metabolized toward understanding, validated in the patient's cognitive associations, and are not acted upon through some counterresponse to the patient; instead, they are processed toward interpretation and framework-management responses. They are inherent to the therapist's neutrality.

Chapter 24

Neutrality and Anonymity

Four basic elements of the ground rules and boundaries of psycho-therapy apply mainly to the therapist, though they also involve the patient as well: the therapist's neutrality and anonymity, and the presence of total privacy and total confidentiality to the treatment experience. In respect to neutrality, the ground rule applies only to the therapist, though patients vary in the extent to which they directly and indirectly pressure the therapist to modify this basic component of fundamental attitude, emotional position, and stance in relationship with the patient. Anonymity, a factor closely related to neutrality, applies again entirely to the therapist, though here too patients vary in the extent to which they attempt to seek out personal information regarding their therapists. Total privacy and confidentiality are also basic responsibilities of the therapist, though the patient too, in an ideal therapeutic experience, will respect these important tenets.

While matters of fee and the length and frequency of sessions are aspects of the *fixed frame,* these four precepts tend to be part of the more *changeable or fluid framework* to the psychotherapeutic experience. Each tenet is, however, an essential component of the healthy therapeutic symbiosis necessary for a truthful therapeutic experience, and each is basic to an insightful mode of cure. While neutrality and anonymity are factors in every intervention made by the therapist, privacy and confidentiality tend to arise only under selected circumstances.

There tends to be interreaction and interrelationship between each of the ground rules to psychotherapy. In general, there is a correlation between the extent to which neutrality and anonymity are maintained by a therapist, just as there is a strong correlation between total privacy and total confidentiality. In addition, however, therapists who are likely to modify one of these four basic ground rules are likely to modify the other three.

Neutrality

Neutrality is founded upon the therapist's capacity to respond to the patient to the greatest extent humanly possible, based entirely on the latter's communications and therapeutic needs. This implies doing so in terms of interpretive and framework-management responses that are likely to receive Type Two derivative validation from the patient and generate sound cognitive insights and constructive introjective identifications as the basis for adaptive structural change in the patient. Neutrality is essential to the patient's sense of safety in the psychotherapeutic relationship, and is critical to the likelihood that he or she will engage in meaningful open, direct, and derivative communication.

Neutrality implies responding entirely in terms of the associations and behaviors of the patient, and adding nothing personal, biased, or otherwise introduced by the therapist except for the delineation of abstractions or implications to be found in the communications from the patient. Clearly, neutrality means the absence of personal opinions, self-revelations, directives, manipulations, and all other noninterpretive responses except for those that involve the establishment and management of the ground rules at the behest of the patient's derivative material. In this sense, neutrality and anonymity tend to overlap, since on some level, every nonneutral intervention reveals something personal and pathological about the therapist.

Neutrality does not imply indifference or a lack of concern. It also does not mean that the therapist is unduly cold and distant, or unavailable in the ways necessary for a sound therapeutic relationship and experience. All too often, writers have advocated a variety of noninterpretive interventions that are erroneously proposed as so-called efforts to establish the humanness and concern of the therapist and his or her availability as "an object" to the patient. These proposals, adopted either through manifest content listening or through simply setting aside the implications of the material from the patient, mistake attitudes appropriate for social relationships with those appropriate for the therapeutic interaction. They involve simplistic surface thinking, with a total neglect of the unconscious communications contained in derivative form in non-neutral interventions of this kind, and in the patient's responses to them.

Neutral and correct therapeutic measures offer a unique type of hold and gratification that is appropriate to a healthy symbiosis, individuation, growth, and cognitive insight. Adaptive structural change takes place only in the face of considerable renunciation and anxiety, and is difficult to achieve. Inappropriate *direct* gratifications that preclude this type of arduous effort toward insight appear inviting on the surface to most patients and to many therapists. They offer immediate satisfaction at the expense of understanding and sound structural change. They offer massive Type C barriers against the underlying chaos within the patient and the therapeutic interaction, while affording both participants a means of pathological projective identification and symbiotic gratification. They form the basis for therapeutic misalliances, and both misalliance and framework cures, all of which clearly set aside the more demanding task of insightful structural change and growth and individuation.

Although divided in respect to wishes to get well or remain ill, patients manifestly seek treatment in order to obtain *relief* from suffering. Almost automatically, they search for the most immediate means through which this goal can be accomplished. They seek a quick cure, with little in the way of tolerance for delay and indirect relief. Because of this, deviant interventions, which on the surface seem reassuring and supportive, seem to meet the patient's manifest wishes, although when this particular approach to symptom relief is adopted, the patient will virtually without exception experience and communicate its destructive elements on a derivative level.

For many therapists too, immediate satisfactions and relief, for their patients as well as themselves, are part of their basic *modus operandi*. Often, a surface search for understanding is used mainly as a facade to justify efforts at relief of the kind just described. In this light, one can appreciate the special capacities necessary in both the patient and therapist to accept a therapeutic modality in which understanding provides an *indirect* and delayed means for symptom alleviation.

The situation is not unlike offering a hungry person a few

lessons in how to find and cook food, rather than feeding him or her directly. In the long run, of course, the lessons will serve far better, though in the short run, his or her interests are centered upon the feeding. The analogy breaks down, however, in that the immediate feeding of patients by therapists, as represented in non-neutral interventions, has an inherently pathological or toxic quality. Although they may provide momentary relief, they do so at considerable cost to the patient. Nonetheless, with human functioning as it is, it requires a great deal of both patients and therapists to accept the more indirect and understanding avenue of symptom alleviation, and to renounce the deceptively attractive more direct routes.

Sound interventions may, of course, be imparted to the patient with due feeling, tact, timing, and concern. All too often, therapists have felt inappropriately guilty when they do not immediately and directly (pathologically) gratify their patients, and too often they see the interpretive and holding position as implying harshness, coldness, or destructiveness. Of course, any intervention or approach may be abused in these ways, but while the interpretive and holding position certainly may be frustrating in certain ways, it has a unique warmth and a constructive set of qualities absent in all other therapeutic endeavors. Much of what is carried out by therapists in the name of humanity, sympathy, and so-called empathy, involves derivative communications that are actually inherently destructive, seductive, and infantilizing, and are unconsciously perceived as such by their patients.

Neutrality implies the capacity to listen to the patient and to receive his or her interpersonal and role and image evocations, and interactional projections, in a manner that takes into account contributions from both the patient and therapist. It implies formulations that consider each of the macrostructures of both participants, though primarily the patient—id, ego, and superego. It also implies an understanding of the meanings and functions of the patient's associations and behaviors in the areas of narcissism, object relatedness, communicative interaction, and other intrapsychic meanings. Neutrality therefore implies a capacity to tend to all spheres of the patient's functioning (and of the therapist's as well), pathological and nonpathological, and to generate the most fair and compelling formulation, interpretation, or framework-management response called for by the patient's material and therapeutic interaction. Neutrality also implies, of course, the use of judicious silence in the absence of an interpretable communicative network.

In practical terms, neutrality means confining the therapist's interventions to silences, interpretation-reconstructions, and the establishment and management of the ground rules or framework. All other measures by the therapist are lacking in neutrality in important ways. This includes interventions such as questions, clarifications, and confrontations proposed as a means of fostering the openness of the patient's communications to the point where interpretation is feasible (i.e., as preparatory to interpretive responses). This is clearly not at all the case—these interventions interfere with the patient's own free associations and derivative communications, disturb the patient's communicative thrusts, and do not constitute appropriate responses to his or her therapeutic needs. They are essentially nonneutral and inappropriate. Each of these interventions implies selectivity, undue concentration, and focus on a particular associational element, and therefore bias within the therapist.

Beyond these measures lie all of the other noninterpretive interventions mistakenly used by therapists in present-day practice. The lack of neutrality in a directive, personal opinion, reassuring comment, or whatever, is well known. These violations of the fundamental tenet of neutrality are accepted for a variety of poor reasons. There remains no substitute for neutrality in the therapist, however, and no justification for its modification except in those rare situations, often contributed to in part by nonneutral interventions of the therapist, where, in an effort to protect the life of the patient or of someone else, and in the absence of interpretable material, a therapist must resort to a nonneutral intervention as an emergency measure. This type of interlude should be extremely rare and, despite its life-saving qualities, it will evoke within the patient a negative introject and a series of detrimental consequences common to all alterations by the therapist of the fundamental ground rules of treatment.

CLINICAL EXAMPLE

A young woman with one child who was separated from her husband had been seen by the therapist (also a woman) initially in a clinic, and with a shift to private therapy, she had signed permission for the therapist to obtain a copy of the notes that had been made on her case in the clinic. The session presented here followed a missed session for reasons that, upon telephone discussion with the therapist, did not seem to substantiate the need to miss the hour.

> Patient: I had a visit from the social worker attached to the court. My husband filed a complaint of child abuse against me, but the worker could not find my records. My husband had taken my son to the emergency room after he had been with me, and they could not find evidence of child abuse. My son hits and bites me. My husband wants me to provide him with a letter that would give him custody of the child. He doesn't want to pay child support.
>
> Therapist: In relation to the theme of child support, how do you feel about my charging you for the session you missed?
>
> Patient: That's all right. Sometimes you seem stubborn. I was confused about the time of my son's doctor appointment.
>
> Therapist: You should remember that I wasn't stubborn when you asked me if you could pay me toward the end of each month, rather than at the beginning.
>
> Patient: My husband was stupid to take my son to the hospital. The cat had scratched him and made him bleed. I didn't want the hospital visit on my son's record. Suppose he wants to be president some day. I showed my husband where my son bit me and told him I might need a shot, and he said he hoped I would die of rabies. I don't want to be used as a doormat all the time. If he wants custody of my son, he's going to have to take me to the Supreme Court. All he does is distort the truth. I can see now that he's not capable of working or of giving me child support; he's too sick. My son was supposed to go into therapy with a psychologist who seemed to me to be quite poor. I'm glad the psychologist hasn't contacted him. I'm beginning to realize how incapable my husband is of doing anything.
>
> Therapist: It must be painful to face that realization.

There are many ways in which this therapist violated the cannon of neutrality in this session. In brief, in her first intervention, the therapist introduced an adaptive context—the charge for the missed session—that had not been represented as yet by the patient in a form that would lend itself to interpretation or management response. The therapist asked a question that directed the patient toward her conscious feelings, instead of listening to the material as derivatives related to this and other active intervention contexts. The result was conscious permission for the therapist to make the charge, a conscious perception of some stubbornness, and an apology for the patient's confusion. At this level of manifest content relatedness, little derivative meaning emerges.

The therapist's second intervention, through which she reminded the patient of her own flexibility, is a powerful noninterpretive intervention, and constitutes a nonneutral attempt at self-defense. It is also self-revealing, in that the therapist's discomfort regarding the patient's conscious perception of her as stubborn is more than evident, suggesting that the therapist had a need to disclaim this direct self-image evocation. There is also an interactional pressure here, and a more neutral response would have been that of careful listening, the subjective experience of feeling criticized and dumped into by the patient, and an effort to determine the intervention contexts that would account for the manifest remark and reveal its derivative implications.

This defensive comment served as a powerful intervention context for the patient's subsequent derivative response. There are themes of stupidity, misguided treatment, being attacked and made to bleed, insensitivity to therapeutic needs, being a doormat, distorting the truth, being incapable of functioning well as a parent, and a poor impression made by a therapist. These are all-telling commentaries regarding the therapist that are of considerable validity, and are based on the patient's unconscious perceptions of the therapist in light of her interventions. There is a strong sense of harm, betrayal, and inappropriate care. There is also an allusion to distorting the truth—a derivative representation of the patient's realization that this therapist wishes to engage her in a form of lie therapy. The actual truth of the therapeutic interaction that is being set aside through the therapist's nonneutral interventions probably pertains to the existence of notes on this patient's session and the release the patient signed at the therapist's request so the therapist now has this material in her possession (cf. the allusion early in the session to records and to issues of confidentiality). This truth, among other interactional truths, was mainly set aside through these nonneutral interventions. As one can see, on a derivative level, the impact for the patient was quite devastating.

There are several allusions here to pathologically symbiotic and parasitic modes of relatedness. The deviations in neutrality contributed significantly to this type of relationship between the patient and therapist. Failures in metabolizing evoked roles and images and disturbing projective identifications tend to lead to nonneutral interventions by therapists that are exploitative and involve inappropriate gratifications and relatedness.

Anonymity

The patient's need for the relative anonymity of the therapist is another frequently misunderstood essential for the therapist's basic manner of relating to the patient and to the framework of treatment. Much confusion arises from the realization that anonymity can only be relative. Thus the therapist's appearance, the furnishings of his or her office, the way in which he or she dresses, and his or her manner of working with and addressing the patient, contain within them a variety of *inevitable* self-revelations. In this sense, of course, *total* anonymity is both impossible and absurd. However, the realization that total anonymity cannot be achieved has led many therapists to bypass *relative* anonymity and to develop weak justifications for engaging in deliberate self-revelations that extend beyond the inevitable minimum.

The type of continuum typical for virtually all factors in psychotherapy has, at one end, self-revelations that are inevitable, humanly necessary, and do not interfere with the therapeutic relationship and experience, and at the other end, a multiplicity of deliberate self-revelations that clearly disturb the ideal therapeutic environment and the relationship between the patient and therapist. A large number of deliberate and inadvertent self-revelations fall somewhere between these two extremes. This particular group of modifications in anonymity deserve careful consideration to a point where those that are distinctly disruptive to the treatment experience can be identified and rectified.

An example of this middle type of self-revelation involves the use by some therapists of magazines in their waiting rooms and art on their walls. An argument could be made for eliminating these items, as well as books on the shelves of the therapist's consultation room. Although this would further secure the therapist's anonymity, it may give the office such an austere tone as to be detrimental. However, such art and magazines should be as neutral and as generally popular as possible. All books should be professional in nature, and there should be no books or papers on the therapist's desk—items that often hint at a lack of total confidentiality and provide revelations as to the therapist's interests and reading habits. Further, no books or articles that the therapist has written should be visible, since these particular self-revelations fall clearly into the area of disruptive alterations in anonymity. In general, it is wise for therapists to lean toward maintaining rather than modifying their sense of anonymity, since unrecognized deviations tend to lead to *derivative deafness*—failures to organize and understand the patient's derivative material around the relevant self-revealing intervention contexts.

Various situations clearly contain a significant and unnecessary degree of alteration in this aspect of the therapist's presentation of himself or herself. The major and most common forms in which this particular tenet is violated by therapists include: (1) expressions by the therapist of personal opinions regarding issues and problems raised by the patient, personal and general, or regarding any other matter brought up by the patient (the very introduction of a subject by the therapist also modifies his or her sense of anonymity); (2) the revelation of personal attitudes, feelings, reactions, fantasies, and whatever, in response to the material from the patient, including personal reactions to the patient's manifest and latent feelings, fantasies, and perceptions of the therapist; (3) the revelation of any aspect of the therapist's personal life, vacation plans, political and other preferences, hobbies and interests, and all such personal information; (4) any information regarding the therapist in respect to his or her state of health or illnesses, the basis for a sudden cancellation of sessions, and such; and (5) any attempt to justify an aspect of therapeutic technique, a particular intervention, or the reasons for a particular attitude or reaction.

In sum, all revelations of a personal nature modify the necessary relative anonymity of the therapist. In general, these breaks in the frame serve to gratify pathological symbiotic and often parasitic needs within the therapist, to pathologically defend against separation anxieties and necessary separateness from the patient, to undo any sense of depression in the therapist by serving as a manic-fusion defense, to projectively identify a variety of needs and contents into the patient, to unconsciously pressure the patient to serve as the functional therapist in the treatment situation, and to develop a sector of misalliance as well. To these may be added a variety of pathological needs and defenses in keeping with the nature of the self-revelation, and its timing.

CLINICAL EXAMPLE

A young woman had been seen once-weekly in psychotherapy by a woman therapist for about a year. The therapist maintained a home office and used her living room as a waiting room. The therapist had a pet parrot, a cat, and a dog, and the patient often made verbal and physical contact with these animals. The session presented here took place after the therapist's extended winter vacation.

> Patient: I've been in great pain. I reached to get something in my closet and my back went into spasms. I had to call my parents, and they took me to the emergency room where I received medication. My father cooked dinner for me on my birthday.
> Therapist: I've found that sometimes a massage is good for that kind of back problem.
> Patient: Thank you. I think my pain had a lot to do with my father's plans to leave the city. He intends to sneak out without paying the rent. My mother is pretty angry about that. She's been crowding me lately, and I would like to get rid of her pressure. She ought to live her own life and not dump her problems into me. With my back pain, she insisted I share her bed with her, and my father slept in the den. My sister keeps complaining that my mother is a lousy mother. I told her she should have resolved her problems with our mother in her psychotherapy.

There is considerable evidence, not cited here, that the patient's back pain was a response in part to the therapist's vacation and reflected a notable failure in analyzing and resolving the patient's separation anxieties. The focus here, however, is on the patient's response to the therapist's self-revelation that she too had experienced back pain, and her recommendation for a massage. This intervention lacks neutrality and also modifies the therapist's anonymity.

In keeping with the typical split found in patients' reactions to deviations in the ground rules that are, on the surface, well-meant, this patient responded manifestly to the therapist's advice with conscious appreciation. However, her derivative communications, serving as a telling commentary on the therapist's intervention and its unconscious implications, show the patient to be expressing herself quite differently. The themes of separation, of dishonesty and deception, of mother's pressure, of wishing her mother would live her own life, of sharing a bed with mother, of poor mothering, and of how therapy should resolve a daughter's problems with her mother are all present. In the adaptive context of the therapist's intervention, these manifest associations organize meaningfully as a coalescible derivative network that indicates that the patient unconsciously perceived the therapist's intervention as a countertransference-based reaction to the recent separation from the patient. The patient perceives something deceptive and dishonest in the intervention, and experiences it as a pathological projective identification through which the therapist on some level is behaving in a manner comparable to the seductive and symbiotic pressure she is experiencing in actuality from her mother.

In the midst of offering a model of rectification (that her mother should live her own life and not make such inappropriate demands upon her daughter, the patient), there is the revelation of the latent homosexual and pathological symbiotic qualities of the unconsciously expressed needs contained in the therapist's intervention (the reference to sharing the bed with the mother). While the patient herself is undoubtedly suffering from unresolved pathological homosexual and symbiotic needs and fantasies, the therapist's expressed countertransference-based needs along these lines take precedence and have been forcefully placed into the patient by the intervention. The patient then indicates that this is a reflection of poor mothering (of poor therapeutic technique) and advises the therapist through a modified unconscious interpretation that she should have resolved these needs and difficulties in the course of her own personal therapy, and that they involve pathological fantasies and relatedness with the therapist's own mother.

This alteration in neutrality and relative anonymity repeats a past and even present pathogenic interaction, here between the patient and her mother. It reinforces this level of relatedness in the patient and serves to justify this mode of maladaptation. It creates conditions within treatment and within the therapeutic relationship and interaction under which no possible verbal interpretation could modify this sector of the patient's pathology, since it is being reinforced in actuality through the therapist's indirect communications to the patient. The nonneutral intervention speaks as well for the therapist's unresolved separation anxieties, and for her maladaptive efforts to seduce and merge with the patient as an inappropriate means of resolving conflicts and fantasies that exist in that area. This patient shows a typically mixed response, in that on one level she is prepared to join the therapist in this sector of misalliance, while on another level she unconsciously makes efforts to resist the therapist, call the misalliance to her attention, and have the therapist rectify the break in the frame.

This example serves as a reminder that many breaks in the frame cannot be rectified. A self-revelation cannot be made to disappear. At best, the therapist can rectify the frame by desisting in future self-revelations. While some harmful effects of the earlier deviation will remain with the patient, he or she will at least have had the additional experience of a sensitive, understanding therapist capable of change and mastery, and of rectification and interpretation in light of errors recognized with implicit (derivative) help from the patient. It is necessary to listen carefully to the patient's derivative material to discover whether a given permanent alteration in neutrality, anonymity, or confidentiality has so impaired the patient's image of the therapist and the therapist's hold of the patient to require unrectifiable framework-deviation termination therapy.

In the present example, the home-office situation may well meet such criteria. The material from this hour could also be organized as Type Two derivatives around this particular adaptive context, and reveals rather comparable unconscious implications and perceptions to those stimulated by the therapist's nonneutral intervention. The stress would be on the sneakiness involved, the therapist's failure to separate her personal from her professional life, and the confusion in boundaries that render it impossible for the patient to know whether there will be efforts at understanding or seduction—whether she will be seen in an office or in a bedroom. Here, too, the net effect is that of failed therapist-mothering, problems that the therapist should have resolved on her own.

Summary and Conclusions

The therapist's neutrality and relative anonymity are two inter-related aspects of the manner in which he or she relates to the patient that are essential to the basic therapeutic symbiosis upon which effective psychotherapy is founded. These tenets are therefore an important aspect of the ground rules, framework, and of the holding-containing qualities of the therapist's way of working with the patient. Modifications in neutrality and anonymity imply the offer to the patient of pathological defenses and Type C barriers, countertransference-based pathological projective identifications, and disturbances in the therapist's hold of the patient and openness to contain the patient's pathological interactional projections. They also imply a refractoriness to certain types of role-image evocations, and to certain types of manifest and derivative material. They therefore greatly impair the patient's own communicative range, and constitute forms of counterresistance in the therapist that tend to promote interactional resistances within the patient. A large proportion of resistances and counterresistances find behavioral expression through efforts by the patient or therapist, or both, to modify the basic holding environment.

Chapter 25

Privacy and Total Confidentiality

True insight psychotherapy is founded upon a totally private, one-to-one relationship, with total confidentiality. Essential here is the therapist's offer of a psychotherapeutic space that is exclusively the patient's, and into which no one else is permitted, directly or indirectly, to the greatest extent possible. This implies that actual intrusions of third parties, the offer of information to outsiders, and the acceptance of information from others, are all to be excluded. In this way, the therapist indicates to the patient that he or she is prepared to offer the safety of a totally private and confidential relationship, and that he or she is capable as well of being the sole individual who will attempt to cure the patient of emotional ills.

Privacy

Under some circumstances it is impossible to guarantee the therapeutic space in its entirety, and situations of this kind are not uncommon. They are exemplified when a child enters psychotherapy and a parent must pay for the sessions, or when a wife who does not work is in psychotherapy and the cost for the sessions is borne by her husband. Of course, there are also situations where patients are sent by courts or are seen in clinics where total privacy is all but impossible.

Recognition of these extreme situations should not imply an acceptance of many *entirely unnecessary* alterations of the total privacy of the relationship between a patient and therapist. In clinics, it should be possible for the therapist to carry out the initial consultation with the patient and maintain sole responsibility for the treatment process and the collection of fees. Since most clinics do insist upon some record of each session, however, it must be recognized that this particular alteration in the ideal framework immediately impairs the privacy and confidentiality of the treatment experience for the patient—and for the therapist as well. It is best to allow the patient's knowledge of these deviations to be as openly stated as possible, and to recognize this knowledge in the patient's derivative associations. The therapist should accept these realizations implicitly, without direct confirmation to the patient, because direct revelation of the existence of these alterations in the frame tend to be highly disruptive to the patient and the therapeutic experience. Nonethless, the therapist's framework management and interpretive responses must be designed to *implicitly* acknowledge and accept the existence of these breaks in the frame. These are mainly unrectifiable deviations that lead to some form of unrectifiable framework-deviation termination therapy. Although the result is a clearly limited therapeutic experience, the therapist who adopts this type of approach through the use of the patient's derivative communications, and does much of the therapeutic work in light of these deviant intervention contexts, can offer the patient the best possible treatment experience available under the conditions. This can then prove to be salutory for the patient.

In those situations where a spouse or parent is providing the funds for treatment, every effort should be made to minimize the actual influence and presence of the third party. For example, it is best if possible with adolescents and others not to accept a check written out by the third party, but instead, to work therapeutically toward the patient's use of his or her own checking account. Often, this type of effort may begin with a nonparticipating response from the therapist, conveyed by not accepting the check or by not cashing it and leaving it out for the patient to see and explore. This approach permits an optimal level of direct and derivative communication from the patient in regard to his or her proposed deviation from the ideal framework. Virtually without exception, the patient's disguised communications will then make it clear that he or she should take as much responsibility for payment of the fee as possible, should write the check on his or her own checking account (and even open up such an account if need be), and that the money should be given by the third party to the patient to avoid making the patient serve as a passive carrier of the fee. While there will still be some presence of the third party under these conditions, it is then at its minimal level. For some patients, this presence will nonetheless lead to a form of unrectifiable framework-deviation termination therapy, while for others, the more secure aspects of the framework, and the fact that the therapist has not participated actively in additional alterations in the ground rules (i.e., no sessions have been held with the parent or other third party), will enable these patients to benefit from a more extended psychotherapeutic experience.

Beyond this type of third party intrusion, without which there could be no psychotherapy for a particular patient, there should be no inclusion of outsiders in the patient's therapeutic experience. On the patient's side, this means that the therapist should not see relatives, should not talk to them on the telephone, and that the patient should not bring them to his or her sessions, even if they wait in the waiting room. It implies too that there should be no third-party payer such as insurance companies, and no consultation with other physicians or therapists at the request of the patient.

Clearly, a patient's wish to see another therapist in consultation modifies the privacy and one-to-one aspects of the therapeutic relationship and constitutes a major modification in the ideal therapeutic environment. Any effort by the patient along these lines, or any stated intention of this kind, is a prime indicator that must be managed and interpreted in light of prevailing intervention contexts from the therapist and derivative responses by the patient. While there are patients who enormously dread the one-to-one relationship and privacy of psychotherapy, experiencing it in a paranoid-phobic manner as a life-endangering entrapment, many efforts to modify this aspect of therapeutic relatedness are the result of deviations by the therapist that are based on comparable countertransference-based anxieties and conflicts. Pathological symbiotic needs as they exist in the patient or therapist, or both, are also at issue.

Modifications in the privacy of the therapeutic relationship by the therapist may take the form of wishing to have the patient seen in consultation, of imparting information to physicians or other therapists, and of efforts by the therapist to make contact with relatives and other persons known to the patient. It is important to realize that both privacy and confidentiality are modified when a therapist presents a patient to a supervisor. This measure should be undertaken only when it is clearly a necessity, as when it must be done in order to train the therapist or to help with an unmanageable crisis. It is best, however, not to directly reveal this deviation to the patient, and yet to be aware of the influence of supervisory interventions on the therapist and his or her manner of relating and intervening with the patient.

In clinic situations, patients consciously or unconsciously recognize the presence of the supervisor, and interventions in this area should be based on the *implicit* acceptance of this fact when it exists. The revelation of active supervision is a modification in neutrality, relative anonymity, as well as privacy and confidentiality, and has devastating effects upon the patient—and often the therapist as well. If such information has been imparted to the patient, *rectification* must take place through the *cessation of supervision* (of which the patient must then be informed), though at times this revelation will shift the therapy to an unrectifiable framework-deviation termination therapy at the behest of the patient's derivative communications.

These comments imply that seeing two or more patients simultaneously, family members or otherwise, and the use of more than one therapist, constitute major breaks in the ideal therapeutic environment and have extended consequences in keeping with all breaks in the frame. It should be recognized too that total privacy can be guaranteed only when a therapist does *not* take notes and does not write them after a session. In keeping with the principle of entering each session partly without desire, memory, or understanding, there is no need in the optimal therapeutic experience for note-taking or recording sessions after hours. Psychotherapy should be a fleeting interaction between patient and therapist that is not subjected to recording (an effort that often modifies the separation issues for both patient and therapist), and should unfold spontaneously in the interchanges between patient and therapist. Of course, where supervision is necessary, note-taking immediately *after* a session is usually necessary for process-note presentation. Under these conditions, total privacy is modified, and the consequences are extensive for both patient and therapist.

There is ample evidence of the presence of significant anxieties in regard to the one-to-one relationship in both patients and therapists. For the former, the sense of total privacy may stir up intense and disturbing fantasy and perception formations. There may be fears of activated dependency needs and anxiety-provoking sexual and aggressive fantasies. As long as the frame is essentially secure, these responses tend to fall into the realm of transference and pathological unconscious fantasy-memory constellations rather than that of unconscious perceptions.

The secured private relationship may evoke a variety of pre-Oedipal concerns and anxieties, such as fears of self-object boundary loss and merger, in more disturbed patients. The private relationship greatly intensifies the symbiotic needs of the patient and related separation anxieties. Both paranoid and depressive fantasies and anxieties also loom large.

The introduction of a third party to treatment by the patient or therapist on any level serves to temporarily bypass and alleviate these anxieties, conflicts, and difficulties. Sometimes it will lead to a form of framework-deviation cure. If the therapist participates in the deviation—doing so for inappropriate reasons rather comparable to those that exist within the patient—a sector of misalliance is effected, and insightful resolution, growth, and individuation are precluded.

Total privacy and the anonymity of the therapist imply that no referral will be accepted from a patient who is presently, or who has in the past, been in therapy with him or her. Even when the therapist attempts to keep his or her work with each of the two patients as separate as possible, there is a sense of third party presence—a violation in anonymity (each patient knows that the other is in treatment with the therapist, and in addition, there are often many other leaks in information)—and in neutrality (the acceptance of such a referral is seen as extremely self-serving for the therapist). This particular deviation usually evokes a series of valid unconscious perceptions of the therapist by both patients, which include images of the therapist's greed, a sense of betrayal, and a picture of the therapist as being fearful of being alone with a single patient. The therapist is experienced as having intense separation anxieties and pathological symbiotic needs, since with two patients, the therapist is less often alone than with a single patient. The deviation is also seen as reflecting the therapist's dread of the relationship with the referring patient and a fear of his or her manifest and derivative communications. The referred patient is often seen as a gift made to the therapist in order to deny hostility, undo separation anxieties, and as a means through which the referring patient removes himself or herself more or less—sometimes entirely—from his or her own therapeutic process. These implications are not uncommon in the presence of any type of violation of privacy.

CLINICAL EXAMPLE

A male patient had been in once-weekly psychotherapy for about a year when his woman therapist began to modify her rather loose handling of the framework and to rectify a number of previous deviations, while shifting toward a basically interpretive (rather than noninterpretive and so-called supportive) approach. In this general context, and soon after the death of his father, the patient proposed that the therapist take a young woman into psychotherapy with whom he was living. The manifest rationalization was that the therapist was in the best position to understand the problems he was having with the girlfriend, and she with him, and since the therapist had been so helpful to him, she would be similarly helpful to the girlfriend.

In the sessions that followed, the patient showed intense gross behavioral and communicative resistances. He was highly defensive and ruminative, but from time to time he provided meaningful derivative material that revealed his unconscious perceptions of the therapist because of her decision to see the girlfriend. These unfolded along the lines already described above. The excerpt presented here is from a session that followed the therapist's attempt to bring up this problem without sufficient derivative material. In response, the patient had maintained his denial that her seeing his girlfriend was having any detrimental influence upon him.

> Patient: I was angry with you after last session. I don't know why, but somehow I feel you've abandoned me. I've been angry with my girlfriend lately. She's too affectionate and seems to be closing in on me. She's selfish. Things are different here. You don't laugh at my jokes and talk to me like you used to. Maybe I'm angry with you because my father died. Somehow I can't talk about it here. When I talked to my relatives, it felt good. The same thing seems to be happening again: When a woman in my life begins to get

too close, I feel entrapped and leave her. Somehow maybe I feel you are one of those women, and that you can't be trusted. My girlfriend says that sometimes she finds it diffi-cult to talk to you.

In the adaptive context of the therapist's acceptance of the patient's girlfriend into therapy with her, an issue that had arisen in the previous hour, this material organizes as Type Two derivatives involving primarily unconscious perceptions of the therapist who, through the deviation, has abandoned the patient, been overly seductive, disturbed the communicative relationship, and joined the patient in a framework-deviation cure in regard to phobic-like anxieties and fears (of closeness and entrapment), which the patient began to experience in his relationship with the therapist as the frame was being secured. This image transversally may well con-dense paranoid-like transference fantasies (which were beginning to develop in response to the therapist's efforts to rectify the frame) with unconscious perceptions of the therapist's own dread of the secured privacy of the therapeutic relationship with this man.

Total Confidentiality

There is probably no dimension of the therapeutic relationship and its ground rules that is more controversial, misunderstood, and vulnerable to countertransference-based biases than the tenet of total confidentiality. This essential aspect of the framework requires of the therapist that no information whatsoever be released regarding the patient, even at the latter's request. Its modification bears with it the extensive consequences that have been seen for all deviations in technique, and leads to a compromise in the basic and communica-tive relationship between the patient and therapist, to negative introjects of the therapist, and to a variety of specific pathological incorporations of, and responses to, the therapist who does not adhere to this principle. In clinic situations where total confiden-tiality is an impossibility, and in those rare situations in which release of information is inherent to a private therapeutic relation-ship, the only resource available to the therapist is the adoption of a form of unmodifiable-deviation termination therapy, through which the most constructive outcome possible can be achieved.

In present-day practice, there are many breaks in total confidentiality that run contrary to the patient's therapeutic needs and derivative communications. They have dire consequences for the therapeutic process. It is evident too that adherence to this ground rule raises many social issues regarding psychotherapy for the indigent and for those with relatively low incomes. In addition, there is, of course, the manifest and conscious wish for patients who have insurance coverage for psychotherapy to obtain these benefits, even though it means that the therapist must release information about the patient.

It is here perhaps more than anywhere else that therapists have not understood the intense split within their patients—and themselves—in this regard. Characteristically, the patient manifestly professes a wish for the therapist to complete a particular insurance form, while his or her derivative communications without exception reveal the patient's unconscious realization of the destructive—and sometimes defensively and inappropriately protective—consequences of this measure. Influenced in part by financial anxieties and peer-group pressure, therapists tend to comply with these requests without any significant appreciation of their patients' derivative commentaries on these deviations and their actual implications.

In principle, if a patient in a first session requests the inclusion of a third-party payer into therapy (a violation of both privacy and confidentiality), the therapist should indicate that he or she is offering the patient a secure, private, and totally confidential therapeutic space, and that any request to alter these conditions should be subjected to exploration and analysis. If this issue arises in later sessions, the therapist's attitude should be that of silence and an implied expectation that the patient will continue to free associate, and to thereby explore and express himself or herself directly and indirectly in regard to the proposed deviation. In this way, the therapist does not immediately join the patient in establishing or enacting a proposed deviation. The necessary open communicative properties of the therapeutic relationship are thereby maintained, as are the possibility of a healthy symbiotic mode of relatedness and the therapist's own safe and intact image. Explorations can then proceed relatively unencumbered.

In the *therapeutic* context of the patient's proposed deviation, and in the *adaptive* context of the anticipation of the therapist's cooperation or lack of cooperation in this regard (to which may be added other prior activated intervention contexts), the derivative material from the patient, even in a first hour, unmistakably reveals the detrimental consequences of this deviation. As a rule, interpretations of these consequences are readily available, since the intervention context is usually directly represented, and the derivative complex both highly meaningful and coalescible. Virtually without exception, Type Two derivative validation follows these interventions.

The problem arises, however, with some patients who provide extensive interpretive, rectifying, and derivative validating material, and who also consciously acknowledge the implications of their associations and the therapist's interpretations. They subsequently deny, destroy, and attempt to invalidate these directly and indirectly realized insights. They have *expressed* themselves through the Type A mode of communication, responded temporarily with Type A receptivity, only to then shift to becoming Type B-C or C *receivers* who destroy and obliterate the chaotic implications of the understanding they possessed just minutes before.

With a patient of this type, the therapist is faced with a difficult dilemma. The patient continues to offer derivative communications that testify to the destructiveness of the completion of the insurance form, but continues to make conscious demands that it be completed—blatantly denying the realizations that he or she possessed earlier. Faced with the possibility of losing the patient, and in light of the overabundance of therapists who unwittingly accept insurance forms without exploration or clarification, the therapist is hardpressed indeed. As long as he or she is sensitive to the patient's derivative communications, signing the insurance form is untenable. And yet, as long as the patient will deny the evident (originally derivative) reasons not to do so, there is the danger of a premature termination. The outcome will vary depending on many factors, especially the therapist's holding and containing abilities and interpretive capacities, as well as the meanings of the patient's dread of a secure frame.

In respect to the latter, the signing of an insurance form powerfully gratifies the patient's pathological symbiotic needs, undoes critical separation anxieties, and shuts off the exploration of primitive and often terrifying derivative fantasies and perceptions, much of it related to the psychotic core pathology within the patient. The patient therefore has a considerable unconscious need and investment in a modified therapeutic environment and relationship, and often has little sense or wish to understand the negative consequences to this type of immediate gratification and defense. The unconscious lure is so enormous, and the direct gratification is so great, that gross behavioral resistances are often massive, though the communicative resistances, initially at least, are quite low, because the introduction of the insurance company is such a critical intervention context.

There are many breaks in total confidentiality that are strikingly self-serving for the therapist. These include not only insurance, but also any presentation of a patient that takes place as part of his or her training, or is offered for certification of any kind. While these breaks in the frame are sometimes necessary for the therapist's development, the negative consequences for the patient should not be overlooked.

CLINICAL EXAMPLE

In the previous chapter, a patient had signed a release so her therapist, who had first seen her in a clinic, could obtain a copy of her clinic records. As the reader may recall, in the adaptive context of this transaction, themes of abuse, poor care, the absence of support, physical damage, distortions of the truth, and an incapacity to function were discovered. The example presented here further illuminates the implications of violations in total confidentiality. It concerns a young man who had homosexual problems and had been involved in sexually molesting the young daughter of his girlfriend. In the session, he referred to expecting insurance coverage for the entire cost of his twice-weekly therapy.

> Patient: I don't like leaving my subordinates unsupervised while I'm here. In these sessions, I would like your advice. I would like to be told if I am doing something right or wrong. I'm having strange images of trees being cut down and of ships being swallowed up in stormy seas. I've lied to my girlfriend and told her I'm seeing a psychiatrist for personal problems, and even though she suspects I've been involved with her daughter, she's not sure. She is divorced, and the courts may turn her case over to the children's care service and declare her unfit as a mother. She might end up being blamed for what I had done.

Sometime later, when the patient discovered that the insurance coverage would be for 60 percent of his fee, the patient spoke as follows:

> Patient: I can't afford therapy. I may have to stop. The strain of money is the only thing I can't solve. I'm making plans, but don't want to tell you when I'm thinking of terminating. I was once jailed for child molestation. My former girlfriend had a therapist who wrote inaccurate and inflamatory things about her. She never trusted him again. My neighbor's daughter, who is a small child, was flirtatious with me. At times, I believe that I'm doing them a service by seducing them and opening them up sexually. It's easy for me to control my girlfriend, even though I know I should back off and let her live and act independently. *(Here the patient reads a letter to the therapist from his girlfriend's daughter, which he believed indicated that no harm had been done to her through their sexual contact.)* I don't handle being alone very well. I tend to go out and molest someone or to masturbate. My girlfriend is committed to the safety and protection of her daughter, rather than to me. She'd rather I stay away for a while because she feels I'm a bad influence. I don't think I have any more emotional problems, and I will probably stop my sessions very soon. Somehow I know I should be sensitive to the rights and privacy of others, but I tend to intrude because of my own needs.

If this material is organized around the adaptive context of the anticipation that the therapist will, as he had implied, complete the necessary insurance forms, these manifest contents would be taken as Type Two derivative commentaries related to the release of information and to the invitation, with the therapist's cooperation, for the third-party payer to participate in this therapy situation. On this basis, the following implications may be derived for the therapist's completion of the insurance form: It protects the patient from anxieties involved in being unsupervised (as it does for the therapist as well); it fosters manifest content, pathological symbiotic and parasitic types of relatedness between the patient and therapist; and it creates a sense of dangerous physical damage and annihilation (possibly the destruction of the therapy), as well as possibly protecting the patient from such dangers (and perhaps the therapist as well). It establishes too a dishonest, lie-dominated therapeutic situation and relationship in which denial and falsification will prevail. By participating, the therapist is seen as unfit. The insurance company will protect the patient from the therapist, from any sense of separation and loss in his relationship with the therapist, and from the chaotic inner mental world reflected in his fantasies about ships being swallowed up by the ocean and trees being cut down.

The presence of the insurance company promotes the patient's own needs to falsify and conceal, and to withhold information from the therapist (e.g., not to inform him of his plans for termination). This type of blatant disturbance in the communicative relationship—characterized as a disturbance in the communicative properties of the bipersonal field—is quite common under these conditions, and is best conceptualized as a disturbance in the communicative interchanges between patient and therapist.

The completion of the insurance form, most importantly, is seen unconsciously—and with considerable perceptiveness—as a form of molestation and self-gratification for both the patient and the therapist. It solves the financial problems of both participants at the expense of a disregard for the patient's rights and need for privacy. There is a danger of misstatement and defamation, and it entails highly seductive and inappropriate gratifications. On an unconscious level, it precludes the patient's experience of separation anxieties in his relationship with the therapist, while reinforcing his own perverted tendencies. It is a disturbance in the therapist's therapeutic commitment to the patient and a means of driving him away.

Each patient experiences the pathological mode of relatedness and gratifications, sectors of misalliance, superego corruption, and inappropriate defensiveness generated by the completion of insurance forms in terms of a series of valid unconscious perceptions of the therapist and secondary distortions in terms of the patient's own pathological needs and other aspects of his or her inner disturbance. The formulations just cited emphasize the patient's unconscious valid perceptions of the implications of this particular intervention context. Areas of distortion are impossible to determine for the moment, since so much of this material is justified in terms of the actual meanings of the therapist's proposed intervention.

This material also illustrates the highly selective influence of the patient's own psychopathology on those universal meanings of

a deviation he or she tends to respond to and emphasize. This is a most important dimension of patients' reactions to breaks in the frame, and is to be kept in mind when intervening. It is the aspect that provides one means through which a therapist may analyze the unconscious meanings of a patient's symptoms in light of valid unconscious perceptions of a deviant therapist.

One may note too the overall effect of this deviation. For this patient, the completion of the insurance form is an unconscious version of his own psychopathology—his perversion. Virtually without exception, each specific deviation involves an aspect of psychopathology that in some way supports the Neurosis of the patient. Since the emphasis here is on detrimental consequences, it should be noted that if the therapist is capable of recognizing the deviation and of rectifying its existence and influence, the patient's material would then provide important manifest and derivative elements that could permit the interpretive understanding of the unconscious basis of the patient's emotional disturbance in light of the activated intervention context. On the other hand, if the therapist fails to recognize the deviation and to rectify it, treatment conditions and a mode of relatedness are created under which the inner disturbance within the patient cannot possibly be insightfully modified because of the unconscious support from the therapist. The deviation enables the patient to view the therapist as a version of his sick self. The differentiating grade between the patient and therapist, which is so essential for sound insight and for positive introjective identifications, is eradicated. Self-object boundaries are also modified, and pathological autistic, symbiotic, and parasitic gratifications are abundant. The central separation anxieties that are a factor in this patient's illness are thereby set aside and rendered unavailable for therapeutic exploration and resolution.

Conclusions

The completion of an insurance form is an *actuality* that justifies a particular kind of unconscious image of the therapist, despite the rationalized realistic basis for this particular intervention. Although providing income for the therapist and an opportunity for treatment for the patient, the signing of the insurance form detrimentally influences the communicative relationship, the manifest and derivative expressions from the patient, the unconscious and introjected image of the therapist, and the course and outcome of the therapeutic work. The patient is therefore able to attend sessions physically; although on a derivative and unconscious level, his or her psychopathology is being reinforced rather than modified. As the derivatives from these patients so clearly testify, truth therapy is not feasible and lie therapy must prevail. The only possible area of truth therapy work would involve the deviation itself. Thus unmodifiable-framework-deviation termination therapy may prove to be successful with patients under these conditions. In private treatment, it is also possible to rectify the framework at the behest of the patient's derivatives and to eliminate the third-party payer. At times this will require a reduction in the frequency of the patient's sessions, although it should not involve a decrease in the therapist's fee, since this in itself would be a further detrimental deviation. There are many patients who wish to experience truth therapy as a way of adaptively resolving their Neurosis, and with whom this type of therapeutic endeavor can be carried out.

Manifest content and Type One derivative listening, and approaches that virtually ignore the patient's material when considering alterations in privacy and total confidentiality, have made it impossible to understand the implications of these two basic ground rules and their deviations. Adaptive context and Type Two derivative listening has revealed with remarkable consistency the extensive detrimental consequences to deviations of this kind, and they must now be carefully evaluated so that a fresh approach can be made to these extremely difficult problems. Simply enabling a patient to attend sessions is far from the goal of psychotherapy. Clearly, such attendance can be highly destructive for both participants if not undertaken in the presence of proper therapeutic conditions and relatedness. The social dilemmas involved should not lead therapists blindly into lies and distortions of their own. The approach presented here provides a means of therapy even under conditions of deviation, although these efforts must be properly carried out for the patient to achieve the best possible therapeutic outcome. Such must be the goal of the therapist despite hardships for both participants in therapy.

Chapter 26

Managing the Ground Rules: An Overview

The section concluding with this chapter has explored the nature and function of the basic ground rules of psychotherapy, which involves one of the most critical dimensions of the treatment situation. The ground rules are clearly among the most essential determinants of the modes of relatedness, cure, and interaction between the patient and therapist, and influence the entire unfolding of the therapeutic experience. These tenets are actualities filled with unconscious implications. The therapist's manner of defining the basic properties of his or her relationship with the patient, and his or her explication of these rules and boundaries, are replete with implications that are unconsciously perceived and introjected by the patient. This dimension of the therapeutic situation is so fundamental that it influences every other aspect of therapy. This includes the nature of the therapeutic or pathological symbiosis developed between a patient and therapist, the holding and containing functions of the therapist (and secondarily, the patient), and the nature and implications of all other communications between the two participants to treatment.

As fundamental actualities, the handling of these ground rules must be free of corruption, inappropriate gratification, and defense, and clear in the definition of relationship boundaries so that the patient is able, both consciously and unconsciously, to fully trust the therapist, to feel secure in revealing himself or herself, and to feel certain that any association or behavior in which he or she engages will be met with interpretive and sound management responses—and little else. The honesty, integrity, and insightfulness of the therapist and of the therapeutic experience depends upon the therapist's actual management of this dimension of the therapeutic relationship. Not surprisingly, it has also been found that it is in this very area that the patient most often meaningfully expresses his or her own therapeutic needs, and provides the therapist with important opportunities for framework management and interpretive responses. In sum, then, the ground rules and boundaries of the psychotherapeutic relationship is at the heart of the therapeutic experience.

In order to fully comprehend the nature and functions of these ground rules, the therapist must engage consistently in Type Two derivative listening around the conscious and especially unconscious implications of his or her framework-management responses. Working on this basis, it is possible to identify a wide range of implications to these efforts, and a series of basic techniques that may be applied in this sphere. The main points are briefly summarized here:

1. The framework should be established for the patient (and therapist) in the first session, after which occasional explication may be necessary, though always with additional interpretive efforts.

2. All framework-management responses should be developed in keeping with the patient's derivative communications (i.e., at the behest of the patient's unconscious guidance). Proper framework management cannot be effected on the basis of the patient's manifest associations or arbitrarily introduced by the therapist.

3. Much of the problem in establishing and managing the ground rules arises because of a typical split of patients in this sphere, a split sometimes shared by therapists. Thus patients tend as a rule to consciously request pathologically gratifying deviations in the basic conditions of the treatment situation and relationship, while their derivative communications quite universally point to the need to maintain a secure framework despite these conscious requests.

4. In principle, the therapist should establish a well-defined framework and set of boundaries for the therapeutic relationship, and maintain this frame throughout treatment.

5. If a patient requests an alteration in the ground rules (a therapeutic context), the fundamental approach is to permit the

patient to free associate, and to respond on the basis of his or her derivative communications, understood in light of activated intervention contexts. These derivatives will indicate that the fundamental decision should be that of adhering to the ground rules as established and *not* to modify the tenet in question.

6. Interpretations based on the patient's indirect associations will provide the patient with insight into his or her wish to modify the frame. It must be stressed—since this is so readily overlooked—that such interpretations must be based on prior intervention contexts, and only secondarily on the patient's anticipation that the therapist will maintain or modify the framework. It is these prior intervention contexts to which the patient is responding with his or her request for a deviation, and this effort must therefore be understood on one level as a derivative response to an earlier intervention of the therapist—if nothing else, to the securing and maintaining of the framework. Because of this, requested deviations are common at times of separation, such as when the therapist plans a vacation, though it must be remembered that such plans are a traumatic part of the established frame and do not constitute a deviation from the basic conditions of the therapeutic relationship.

7. If a patient unilaterally modifies the framework, the therapist must once again respond analytically in terms of the patient's derivative associations. These unilateral deviations are always responses to prior intervention contexts, not uncommonly in the form of some alteration in the framework by the therapist. In addition to the resultant interpretive work, rectification of the frame at the behest of the patient's derivative associations should take place as quickly as possible.

8. The ground rules are a dimension of the therapeutic relationship through which the patient often meaningfully expresses his or her psychopathology. Impingements therefore provide the therapist with important opportunities for interpretation and framework-management responses, efforts that yield considerable insight and positive introjective identifications for the patient. Patients also have a need to test the therapist's framework-management capacities and all that they imply.

9. In a well-run psychotherapy, an attempt to modify the ground rules is one of the few means through which a patient who is in need of an interpretive or management response from the therapist can evoke such a reaction. In this type of treatment, the

intervention context is usually the therapist's securing of the frame and the anticipation that he or she will maintain the ground rules, to which the patient responds with both efforts to evoke a deviation and with meaningful derivative associations.

10. Any tendency within the therapist to deviate calls for nonaction and self-analysis. In emergencies, an interpretive and framework-holding response is to be preferred to the use of a deviation. These last should be confined to situations where patients shift to the obliterating and pressured Type B-C mode of communication in the context of a therapeutic emergency such as a suicidal threat. Such situations are extremely rare and, further, while the deviation may be necessary to save the patient's life, they also have secondary detrimental consequences that will require both interpretation and rectification.

11. In principle, modifications in the ground rules are a major means through which patients express their *resistance* against insight-oriented therapy. A therapist's participation in deviations is an important form of *counterresistance.*

12. In all situations, rectification of the broken frame must take place before, or must accompany, interpretive efforts.

13. Breaks in the frame tend to have several alternating effects. They tend to generate Type A derivative and Type C nonderivative defensive barriers, as well as to constitute pathological projective identifications with extensive ramifications. In addition, however, as highly disturbing intervention contexts, they also create interludes of meaningful Type A communication by patients, with Type Two derivative responses that can be organized around the framework break and its unconscious implications in terms of valid unconscious perceptions, secondary fantasies, and often relevant genetic and dynamic links.

14. The ramifications of deviations in the ground rules of the therapeutic relationship are extensive. They have a wide range of detrimental influences on both the patient and therapist. For both, though sometimes mainly the patient, a deviation will interfere with the distinction between reality and fantasy, with established self-boundaries, with the trust of the therapist, with the implications of the therapist's other interventions, with the necessary therapeutic symbiosis, with a much-needed secure hold, with open communication, and with insightful and truthful therapeutic work. These deviations tend to repeat past pathogenic interactions, and to

reinforce and justify the patient's psychopathology. They create bastions and sectors of misalliance designed in part for framework-deviation cures.

15. Those deviations that cannot be rectified, or that generate lasting effects, create conditions under which the therapist, of necessity, must shift toward a form of unrectifiable framework-deviation termination therapy. Guided by the patient's derivative communications, limited rectification is attempted, and interpretive work is geared toward the ultimate realization that the basic elements of the therapeutic relationship have been damaged to the point where a broader form of insightful psychotherapy is no longer feasible. Important and critical insights may be gained by the patient into the implications of the deviation, though little else of meaning will unfold. The experience of an insightful therapist who is capable of an appropriate termination under these conditions (usually without referral so that the patient is free to either stop therapy altogether or to independently seek a new therapist) offers the patient the best possible type of insightful and introjective therapeutic experience available under these conditions.

16. Within limits, breaks in the frame, while damaging, also provide both patient and therapist with important opportunities for insight and inner structural change. When a therapist has a choice to deviate or maintain the frame, the patient's derivative communications will typically direct the therapist toward nondeviation. Thus any decision to modify the ground rules is traumatic for the patient. While the therapist may then recover and rectify the frame, and interpret the implications of the entire incident, there is a basically negative and hurtful aspect to this type of sequence. It stands in contrast to the entirely positive implications of an interlude in which the therapist maintains the frame and responds essentially interpretively to the patient's pressures to deviate. There is then no unconscious negative introject and no unnecessary trauma. While there are hurtful aspects to the frustrations and renunciations involved in maintaining the framework, the likelihood of constructive inner change without detrimental deterrents is greatest under these conditions.

17. Virtually without exception, all modifications of the ground rules provide both patient and therapist with pathological symbiotic gratification, and tend to set aside separation and depressive and persecutory anxieties.

18. Because of a wide range of pathological needs, both patients and therapists show strong tendencies toward seeking out the pathological gratifications, defensiveness, and modes of relatedness possible through alterations in the therapeutic frame. Such efforts often constitute attempts at *framework-deviation cure,* a form of uninsightful symptom alleviation based on an alteration of the ground rules and boundaries of the therapeutic relationship. While such efforts often fail to produce the hoped for relief, they sometimes prove effective, especially when developed through some type of conscious or unconscious collusion between the patient and therapist. The relief involved may stabilize, or instead, the patient may regress under the pressure of new adaptation-evoking contexts. Basic to this type of symptom relief, however, is the need to perpetuate a mode of adaptation that involves alterations in many of the usual boundaries and ground rules of the patient's outside relationships. The existence of framework-deviation cures serves as a reminder that the therapist must explore, in light of the patient's derivative responses to activated intervention contexts, the underlying basis of any interlude of symptomatic remission.

19. In the presence of a break in the frame, the therapist's formulations should concentrate almost entirely on the patient's unconscious valid perceptions of the therapist as reflected in his or her derivative material. This is in keeping with the actual dynamic implications of the patient's associations and behaviors at such moments. The additional measure of possible distortion tends to be easily recognized by the therapist, and should not be used to set aside the patient's more sensitive and accurate perceptions. In principle, in the presence of a deviation, the patient's material reflects primarily nontransference and perceptive responses. Interpretive work should therefore be carried out in these terms, much as the therapist's efforts to rectify the frame proceed on the basis of the patient's offer of sound derivative models of rectification. The inevitable selectivity of the patient's responses should also be given its due attention.

20. In general, framework deviations tend to correlate with the invocation of lie-barrier therapy, a pathological mode of relatedness, a deviant mode of cure, impairments in communicative relatedness and in the communicative styles of both participants, and the pathological dynamics and genetics of the therapist far more than of the patient.

21. Because the therapist's management of the ground rules and boundaries of therapy involves actualities, both *rectification* of the deviation and *interpretive* work are essential in this sphere.

22. A secure frame and a patient who adheres to the ground rules and boundaries of therapy offer the therapist the best holding environment and relationship, and the best conditions for his or her own listening and intervening efforts on behalf of the patient.

23. Whether the frame is secure or deviant, the therapeutic relationship and situation arouses significant anxieties and pathological fantasy-memory-perception constellations within the patient, enough to provide a major impetus to the therapeutic experience. With a secure frame, the patient's difficulties tend to be transference-based, founded on distortions, and interpretable in light of the adaptive contexts of the therapist's efforts to provide a sound holding relationship and environment. With a broken frame, the patient's response tends to be mainly nontransference in nature, unconsciously perceptive and valid, and in need of both rectification and interpretation in light of the deviant intervention context.

24. One must keep in mind the various levels of implication and reaction in a patient's response to a deviation and in the nature of the deviation itself: universal meanings and functions shared by all deviations, as perceived consciously and unconsciously by the patient; the specific but general meanings of the particular deviation for all patients, some of which will be selectively accentuated in the experience of a particular patient; the expressed or communicated implications of a particular deviation for the therapist, as reflected in his or her specific framework-management responses, silences, and interventions in this regard—and as consciously and unconsciously perceived by the patient; the specific meanings of the deviation for the patient, an experience based on an amalgam of the actual conscious and unconscious implications of the deviation itself and the patient's own propensities—pathological and nonpathological; the patient's specific unconscious perceptions of the therapist and the deviation based on the above factors; secondary distorted perceptions and fantasies in response to the deviation; and the patient's reactions to the deviation, including models of rectification, attempts at adaptation, unconscious therapeutic efforts on behalf of the therapist, efforts to exploit the deviation for Neurotic gain, efforts to correct the situation, and other dynamic and genetic responses.

Properly establishing and managing the ground rules of psychotherapy requires a great deal of the therapist: the major sectors of the therapist's own psychopathology must be resolved; an appropriate measure of separateness from the patient must be tolerated; the therapist's own inner mental world and moments of disturbance must be adequately managed; and a wide range of pathological satisfactions such as those in the symbiotic, instinctual drive, superego, and defensive spheres must be avoided. A sound set of ground rules creates the conditions for truth therapy, with all of its burdens and with its exceptional rewards. It is the *sine qua non* of effective insight therapy. Mastery of this sphere is not only essential, but also paves the way for effective therapeutic work in all other areas.

Part IV

The Therapeutic Interaction

Chapter 27

Nontransference

Traditionally, therapists have approached the therapeutic relationship in terms of relatively static concepts and with great stress on the patient's pathological or transference-based responses to the therapist. At times, the patient's relationship to the therapist is called "the transference," as if transference were the only component to this relationship, or at the very least, the overridingly critical aspect. Only lip service has been afforded to the patient's valid reactions to the therapist, and to the many intact and creative capacities that the patient manifests and utilizes in the course of therapy. Because of this, the manifest and especially latent manner in which the patient serves as an unconscious resource for both himself or herself and the therapist, and the patient's many sound ways of functioning, have been relatively neglected.

When the patient is considered to be a member of the therapeutic dyad in constant interaction with the therapist, the therapeutic relationship then becomes conceived of as the spiraling conscious and especially unconscious communicative interaction between the patient and therapist, and consistent attention is afforded the circular influence that each participant has upon the other. In this approach, few assumptions are made other than the presence of mutual adaptation and conscious and unconscious interplay.

Looking at the therapeutic dyad, one should recognize the nature of the formal characteristics that assign to one individual the role of *designated patient*, and to the other that of *designated therapist*. In general, the former individual is asking directly for some type of help, doing so voluntarily or involuntarily, and is usually prepared to pay a fee for the assistance sought—the relief of emotional suffering. It is the designated patient who states a complaint and is asked to free associate, and regarding whom the efforts directed toward conscious understanding are concentrated. On the other side, the designated therapist usually has an office, accepts the fee, tends to listen, and represents himself or herself as having the expertise with which to help relieve the patient of emotional problems.

These relatively fixed attributes vary among patients and therapists. On occasion, a designated therapist will function manifestly in a manner that suggests that he or she is operating as a designated patient. This is seen, for example, when a therapist consciously expresses aspects of his or her own emotional difficulties to the patient and seeks out the patient's advice or help. It may occur more subtly when the therapist does far more talking and reveals far more than the assigned patient. In response, on rare occasion, a patient will resort to interpretive and other interventions on a manifest level, through which he or she fulfills the role of the assigned therapist.

Beyond these surface manifestations, there is the manner in which the designated patient and designated therapist function on an unconscious level. The derivative communications of both participants to therapy must be examined, and their implications understood in light of activated intervention contexts—those from the therapist leading to reactions in the patient, and those from the patient leading to reactions in the therapist. This approach provides a more dynamic and true understanding of the actual functioning of each participant to treatment.

Thus it must be determined whether the designated patient is on an unconscious level functioning in keeping with his or her role responsibilities and with the usual expectations of a patient—i.e., whether the patient is also operating as the *functional patient*. The criteria here involve unconscious expressions of therapeutic need and manifestations of derivative communications that help to illuminate the underlying basis of the emotional disturbance at hand.

At times, of course, the designated therapist may express himself or herself unconsciously (or consciously) as a functional patient. This occurs when his or her manifest interventions prove to be in error and to express the therapist's own pathological tendencies and needs, and his or her wish for help from the designated patient. At such moments, quite typically, the designated patient becomes the functional therapist and responds with derivative interventions, such as unconscious interpretations, to the unconsciously perceived therapeutic needs in the designated therapist. In general, every erroneous intervention by the therapist (frame-management and verbal) conveys some measure of therapeutic need on his or her part.

Thus, for each therapeutic interlude, it is necessary to study the manner in which both the designated patient and designated therapist are actually functioning. In general, the countertransferences of the designated therapist convey to the assigned patient the therapist's therapeutic needs and place the therapist into the role of functional patient. On the other hand, the transferences of the patient tend to express the patient's own psychopathology and reflect his or her functioning as both designated and functional patient. However, because the roles and functions of the patient and therapist are under mutual interactional influence, as a rule, the designated patient will shift to the role of functional therapist mainly when the therapist has expressed himself or herself as a functional patient. Otherwise, the patient remains the patient on both the manifest and latent levels, and the therapist similarly remains both designated and functional therapist. Unconscious, functional role reversals tend to take place largely in response to expressed countertransferences from the therapist.

Conscious and Manifest Forms of Nontransference

On the surface, directly and sometimes consciously (though often quite unconsciously), a patient may show a variety of ego functions, capacities for relatedness, and more complex capacities that reflect essentially nonpathological communications and responses in his or her relationship with the therapist. Many of these abilities contribute to the manifest alliance between the patient and therapist, and some of them are essential for effective therapeutic work and progress. However, each of these capacities may be disturbed and require interpretive and framework-management interventions as a way of resolving the difficulties involved. These impairments must be understood as something more than simple ego dysfunctions, and recognized as being based on complex unconscious fantasy and perception constellations.

Nontransference functioning implies all aspects of the patient's relationship and interaction with the therapist that are essentially sound and nonpathological, and not based on distorting unconscious fantasy-memory constellations. While all such reactions fall on a continuum with transference at the other end and never exist in a pure form entirely divorced from psychopathology, they are in the main essentially valid, perceptive, and reasonable reactions. Their true nature cannot be entirely formulated in terms of manifest attributes, however, but require appraisal in light of prevailing intervention contexts. Thus a patient's refusal to accept a particular interpretation from his or her therapist may be a sound reaction when the intervention is, upon analysis, in error (nontransference), or it may be a form of unrealistic opposition to the therapist based on underlying pathological fantasy-memory constellations (transference). Only a full analysis of the conscious and unconscious implications of the intervention-adaptive context can enable the therapist to make this distinction.

Among the more common nontransference aspects of the patient's functioning within the therapeutic situation is the patient's conscious wish for help with his or her symptoms or characterological problems; his or her broad ability to cooperate with the therapist and to accept the ground rules, including the responsibility to free associate; the ability to remember, to describe and report, to be in touch with reality and yet to imagine, and to express himself or herself in some comprehensible way (on the surface) to the therapist; and the ability to understand the therapist's interventions, to work over and work through the interpretations and framework-management responses offered, and to accept and further the insights offered by the therapist. There is a related capacity to validate in some meaningful form the therapist's correct interventions, and to use the insights imparted to resolve his or her symptoms or to modify characterological disturbances.

All of this requires of the patient sectors of relatively autonomous functioning and a relatively nonpathological utilization of basic ego functions. Nontransference also involves the patient's capacity to relate meaningfully to the therapist, and to simultaneously accept a necessary degree of distance and boundaries—i.e., a capacity to develop a growth-promoting therapeutic symbiosis without the invasion of undue pathological symbiotic needs, and a wish for and ability to gain a separate identity and to individuate and tolerate the necessary separation and other anxieties involved in this experience.

Finally—and the list is by no means exhaustive—there is the patient's capacity to consciously and rationally perceive the implications of the therapist's attitudes, behaviors, and interventions, and to respond to them with logic and sensibility, and the ability to perceive and understand himself or herself, his or her own behaviors and communications, and to have some sense of their influence upon himself or herself, the therapist, and their interaction.

In sum, then, the direct or surface aspects of nontransference involve a variety of sound ego functions, an ability for some degree of effective and mature object relatedness, and a capacity to respond realistically to communications from within as well as those from the therapist. Clinical observations indicate that all patients, including schizophrenics, are capable of extensive functioning in the nontransference sphere.

Taking into account indirect and unconscious capabilities, one is led to conclude that in general—and, of course, with notable exceptions—only a small segment of the patient's communications and reactions fall outside of such essentially valid functioning and into the realm of dysfunction and transference. It is therefore important to realize the pervasiveness of the patient's sound capabilities, and to set aside the highly prejudiced view of the patient as entirely or mainly sick, continuously involved in distortions and transferences, and lacking most of the time in sound capacity. Careful observation and listening suggest that only under the pressure of acutely disturbing intervention contexts will most patients show major disturbances in their manifest functioning. This also implies, as stated before, that disruptions in the overall functioning of the patient must be analyzed in terms of activated intervention contexts and the patient's derivative responses.

In addition, a careful study of the manifest and latent implications of the intervention contexts to which a patient is reacting reveals that many apparent periods of dysfunction and so-called transference expression are in actuality relatively appropriate responses to disturbed efforts by the therapist. Beyond these, of course, lie primary expressions of the patient's psychopathology with only a minimal contribution from the problems of the therapist (all aspects of the patient's functioning are under interactional influence), though these too must be understood in light of activated intervention contexts.

In keeping with tradition, the realm of nontransference is defined here as all of the patient's sound and valid functioning. This implies a continuum with a pathological sphere at the other pole—transference responses in which the patient's reactions are distorted and inappropriate to the stimuli at hand. Often, at least for the term transference, the implication is that of a disruptive displacement from the past onto the present with the therapist. However, even though every inappropriate response to the therapist may ultimately be traced to a point where it involves some measure of displacement from the past, there are many inappropriate reactions to a therapist that derive mainly from present pathological dynamics and displacements from contemporary figures far more than from displacements from past and primary persons. Thus it must be stressed that *nontransference* and *transference* are used in this volume in their broadest but specific senses to allude to essentially healthy and unhealthy (pathological) functioning. Both of these kinds of responses derive in part from early relationships and may involve elements that are displaced from the past and influence the present—they may involve factors first developed in the past and then correctly applied to the present (nontransference) or misapplied to the contemporary situation (transference, when it involves the therapist). Clearly, genetic factors are but one component of the determinants of the patient's functioning in his or her relationship and interaction with the therapist. Genetic influence does not, however, necessarily imply transference; nontransference reactions also have important genetic antecedents and influences.

It is well to distinguish the patient's general capacities for ego functioning and object relating from those that arise in response to specific adaptation-evoking contexts from the therapist. In this way, it is possible to separate out many of the patient's basic tendencies as evoked in some broad way by the manner in which the therapist relates to the patient and creates the therapeutic ground rules and boundaries from aspects of the patient's functioning that arise in response to definitive stimuli from the therapist. These latter tend to be strongly colored by the conscious and unconscious implications of the intervention context involved.

In general, breaks in the frame and other forms of countertransference tend to evoke relatively sound, nontransference (unconscious, and sometimes conscious) functioning in the patient. In contrast, the sound interventions of the therapist, including management of the frame, tend to promote transference-based responses in the patient, accompanied by sound gross behaviors.

While the patient's general functioning and specific reactions tend to be strongly related, they nontheless deserve separate consideration. There is, however, far less correlation between a patient's manifest functioning and mode of relating and his or her functioning on an unconscious or derivative-communicative level. It is here that patients with rather disturbed manifest ego capacities, including evident impairments in thinking and reality-testing, often show highly sensitive derivative capabilities in response to counter-transference-based inputs from the therapist.

CLINICAL EXAMPLE

A young, depressed woman had interrupted her therapy soon after her therapist took a midwinter vacation. When his flight home was delayed, the therapist arrived quite late for the first session he was to have with this patient upon her return. The patient was very upset by this incident, and became acutely suicidal. She then missed two sessions, and the therapist wrote to her, suggesting she contact him. He indicated that if he did not hear from her in two weeks, he would consider the treatment terminated. When the patient did not respond, the therapist considered the treatment at an end, but for reasons unclear to himself, did not send the patient a final bill. Some months later, the patient called for a consultation session. The excerpt presented here is from the beginning of that hour:

Patient: I'd like a bill for what I owe you. I've been seeing a therapist at Mountainview [a local, county hospital]. They don't bill you, and then come chasing after you. My therapist went away and I saw a woman from Allendale [the clinic at which the therapist first saw the patient, before transferring her to private therapy]. She's an alumna from there. She didn't even bring up the fee with me. I had to ask her. She'd said we'd talk about it when I owe her 5000 dollars. I didn't have a session with her this week, and I didn't call her to let her know I wouldn't be in. It was my decision. I'm scared to make decisions. I usually paralyze myself. I thought of running away. That woman doctor finally sent me a bill for the sessions, but they really weren't productive hours. She got upset with what I told her and she would cry. I saw her as acting out. When she didn't hear from me, she wrote me a letter. My parents liked her because she sounded tough with me. They think I need structure. She said to me, "Fuck you or fuck off." I told her something and she said "Shit or get off the pot." I feel angry. My response is to not deal with things like that, and I stay stuck. I'm afraid to talk about things. I'm afraid you'll reject me because I'm not responsible about money. I'd like to start treatment again with you because I know I need help.

In this material, one may examine the level and type of object relatedness of which this patient seems capable, as well as her ego functioning. The patient's manifest attributes in these areas seem to indicate that the patient is attempting to create a healthy symbiotic mode of relatedness with the therapist through which she might obtain an insightful therapeutic cure. She appears to treat the therapist with respect, to be concerned about not having paid his fee, to be responding to him as a whole person or whole object, and to be doing so with considerable sensitivity. In regard to her ego functioning, the patient begins the hour by attempting to set straight a piece of unfinished business regarding her fee. Her associations are logical and quite in touch with reality. Her evaluations of others seem quite sensible and perceptive. While there is an allusion to a passing thought of taking flight, which indicates a potential for ego dysfunction and inappropriately defensive action, the patient does not in actuality do so. Instead, she acknowledges her need for therapy and seeks it out directly with the therapist, attempting as well to clarify and rectify the conditions of her relationship with the therapist and of the treatment situation.

On the whole, then, despite other evidence of severely depressive and perhaps even borderline psychopathology, her capacity for object relatedness and ego functioning as reflected in this excerpt appears to be quite sound. Such interludes were rather typical of this patient, who regressed and showed deterioration in ego functioning and object relatedness only at isolated moments—e.g., after the disruption in her treatment following the therapist's vacation. (Oddly enough, the behaviors of the woman therapist described by the patient offer reason to suspect poor ego functioning, a parasitic, or at the very least, pathological symbiotic mode of relating to the patient, and a possible disturbance in reality testing as it pertains to the nature of her functioning as a therapist. While such comments are, of course, highly speculative, their implications for needed investigations of countertransference in psychotherapists are worthy of note.)

The communications from this patient also prove to be replete with sound forms of functioning on a derivative or unconscious level. Among the adaptation-evoking contexts for this session, the most central appears to be the therapist's failure to bill the patient. Other contexts involve his letter to the patient and his lateness for the hour upon his return from vacation.

Applying the six-part observational schema, the therapist's failure to send a final bill may be characterized as a frame break, a form of pathological autism and symbiosis, an action-discharge means of obtaining and offering personal relief, a communicative barrier and projective identification (of some difficulty in separating from the patient and in accepting a fee from her), and dynamics that suggest seductiveness and separation anxieties in the therapist. The note to the patient and the decision to hold her hours available for two additional weeks also suggest difficulties in separating and in establishing clear boundaries, and in handling the patient's acting out. The lateness for the first session after his vacation implies poor planning—allowing himself too little lattitude in case of delay—and possible countertransference anxieties regarding the resumption of his work. There may also be an underlying thread of hostility and further reflections of separation problems and anxiety.

All of these adaptive contexts are also indicators. There is the important additional indicator of the patient's unexplained absence for the two final sessions, and her failure to respond to the therapist's letter.

To be selective (of necessity), it seems most pertinent to first examine the patient's handling of the major adaptive contexts—the therapist's failure to send the patient a final bill—as reflected in the material excerpted. The patient begins the hour with a manifest allusion to this particular intervention context, and her first statement also contains a direct model of rectification. The communication speaks for sound functioning on both the manifest and latent levels. The patient further represents the therapist's failure to bill her by mentioning a comparable failure of this kind in another therapist. She then expresses, through a relatively thinly disguised derivative, a second adaptive context—the therapist's letter to the patient (cf., the reference to the other therapist chasing after the patient). Next, the patient represents the therapist's vacation through an additional thinly disguised derivative. Less evident is the trauma of his late arrival for the patient's first session. Still, the patient's ability to represent three major adaptive contexts with this degree of clarity is a reflection of strong unconscious ego functioning and of sound communicative capacity.

Much of what follows belongs to the derivative complex. The patient refers to the clinic at which she first saw the therapist, thereby bringing up through derivatives an important background adaptive context: the transfer of this patient from a clinic to a private setting. Although such a transfer is often necessary and the best available treatment, patients nonetheless often experience it as highly seductive and exploitative.

The patient mentions how her woman therapist did not bring up the fee with her, and how she put the patient off when the patient brought it up herself. She then alludes to her absence from her other treatment situation without notifying the therapist, a derivative representation of the indicator of her absence from her sessions with the present therapist just before he terminated the treatment. Next, the patient expresses her difficulty in making decisions—an unconscious perception and introject of the therapist, whose difficulty in making decisions was reflected in his letter to the patient and in his failure to send a final bill. The avoidance involved is expressed in the patient's thought of running away. The nonproductive qualities of these deviations are alluded to through disguise when the patient comments on the lack of productivity of her other treatment. There follows an allusion to some type of emotional disturbance in the other therapist, one that suggests depression and poor controls.

At this point, it may be postulated that the patient is offering the therapist an unconscious interpretation to the effect that his own depressive and acting out tendencies must be understood in order to account for his deviations. This formulation is supported when the patient alludes to a letter from her other therapist, a clear additional derivative representation of the therapist's own letter to the patient. Another model of rectification is then offered: the patient needs structure. The hostility and vulgarity of the other therapist may well reflect the underlying hostile aspects of the therapist's lateness and his seemingly seductive deviations. The patient's own feeling of anger may reflect an unconscious perception of this very hostility on a derivative level.

Once again, the patient refers to her failure to deal with things and to stay stuck—another representation of a valid unconscious perception of the therapist. Her own fear of talking about things reflects the therapist's avoidance, while her fear that the therapist will reject her because she is not responsible about money is a highly sound unconscious perception of the therapist, and an interpretation to him regarding his fear of billing the patient because he was concerned he might lose her as a patient on a permanent basis. Finally, the allusion to the patient's need to start treatment again because she needs help is another sound unconscious intervention to the therapist: his deviations and errors reflect a need on his part for some personal therapy, either self-analysis or with someone else.

This analysis includes considerations of both the patient's manifest and conscious, and latent and unconscious, valid nontransference funtioning. At times there may be a distinct discrepency between the two, usually in a form in which the patient's surface functioning is impaired while unconscious functioning is quite good. Patients prove to be capable unconsciously of considerable sound perceptiveness and of meaningful communication even in the face of severe surface difficulties. In addition, however, many schizophrenic and borderline patients, who at times show evident thought disorders and difficulties in reality testing, will quite often function quite well in their sessions with the therapist. Regressions tend to occur in the face of countertransference-based inputs from the therapist, and more rarely because of major stresses in the patient's outside life.

In this particular session, the patient proved capable on a manifest level of offering the therapist a direct model of, or suggestion for, the rectification of an inappropriate break in the frame, which took the form of his failure to send her a final bill. She was able to afford considerable attention to the therapist's appropriate and reasonable needs, as well as to her own appropriate and therapeutic requisites. She was able to validly criticize the poor handling of the fee by her other therapist, and to raise reasonable questions regarding aspects of the interventions from this therapist that seemed to reflect poor technique and some type of personal difficulty. Her overall view of this therapist appears valid, though it would be necessary to have additional data regarding the actual transactions of the treatment experience in order to confirm this impression. The patient was also aware of her need for firmness, and able to verbalize a conscious insight into the existence of emotional difficulties within herself and in regard to her need for therapy.

The patient's nontransference functioning, then, covers a wide range of ego capacities. Some of these abilities contribute to the manifest alliance sector. Since therapists tend to concentrate their attention on the patient's disturbed functioning and transference manifestations, it is well to recognize the existence of extensive surface capabilities of this kind. On occasion a patient will directly distort his or her image of the therapist and reveal surface malfunctioning. As a rule, however, manifestations of transference involve *unconscious* distortions, which are communicated through derivatives rather than directly.

Indirect or Unconscious Nontransference Functioning

A patient may be unconsciously perceptive of attributes of the therapist and of the manifest and latent implications of his or her behaviors and interventions. The patient may also unconsciously attempt to harm or disturb a therapist who has been hurtful, and much of this can be appropriate and nondistorted. Or a patient may respond with unconscious therapeutic efforts in response to consciously or unconsciously expressed therapeutic needs from the therapist. There is also the patient's valid holding and containing capacities, though of course, these must not be exploited by the therapist but must remain an inherent and usually unconscious aspect of the therapeutic interaction.

The patient in the preceding clinical example showed an extensive array of sound unconscious capabilities. Communicatively, she was able to represent directly or with minimal disguise three critical adaptive contexts, and she was able to provide the therapist with a meaningful coalescible derivative complex pertaining to each of these contexts. Unconsciously, she concentrated her efforts on the most pressing deviation of the moment—the therapist's failure to provide her with a final bill. In that respect, she offered a sound unconscious model of rectification through her derivative expressions. She provided the therapist with highly sensitive and valid unconscious perceptions of the implications of his errors, and also attempted to indicate her impressions of the basis for the therapist's difficulties and touched upon implications for their relationship. She provided him with several helpful unconscious interpretations, and even offered to herself, on a derivative level, a number of encoded clues that could have readily been translated into conscious insight if she were capable of doing so.

As a rule, patients prove to be quite unable to translate these unconscious capacities into conscious understanding and into directly available modes of adaptation. One of the goals of psychotherapy, then, is to foster a transition from unconscious to conscious capabilities through the framework management and interpretive responses of the therapist. In general, meaningful conscious cognitive insight proves to be a critical factor in this type of transformation.

The well-functioning patient provides the therapist with the necessary representation of the intervention context, and with the coalescible and meaningful derivatives that the latter needs for interpretation and frame management. This kind of patient can provide the therapist with the elements necessary for understanding, but is unable to properly organize and order these elements consciously on his or her own. On an unconscious level, then, the capacity to generate a meaningful communicative network when necessary is a sign of sound ego functioning and an ability to participate in a healthy and therapeutic symbiosis with the therapist. Such capacities involve the natural propensities of the patient, as well as reactions to specific adaptation-evoking contexts from the therapist.

At the heart of the patient's unconscious nontransference capacities are valid perceptions and introjects of the therapist that take place outside of the patient's awareness, but are reflected in the derivative implications of his or her free associations and behaviors. The capacity to offer Type Two derivative validation for a sound interpretation or framework-management effort also falls into the nontransference sphere. It is these capabilities that form the foundation for the unconscious or communicative alliance between the patient and therapist.

In general, patients tend to respond on a nontransference level to the therapist's erroneous interventions and mismanagements of the framework. Under these conditions, valid unconscious perceptions and introjects prevail, and distortions (transference), if present, are secondary. In contrast, when a therapist offers the patient a sound holding environment, and directly manages the framework and offers valid interpretations, the patient is prone to respond with communications within which distortions (transference) are a significant element. This is true largely because the therapist's behaviors are essentially nonpathological, and the pathological elements are therefore introduced on the basis of disturbed intrapsychic and interactional mechanisms within the patient.

Empirically, all patients, including those who are psychotic, show strong capabilities for unconscious, nontransference-based functioning within the therapeutic relationship. This is seen most clearly when a therapist modifies the basic ground rules of the therapeutic relationship—an intervention context that universally evokes extensive and highly valid unconscious perceptions of the pathological implications of such deviations, and often, quite sound, though limited and unconscious therapeutic endeavors by the patient (i.e., expressed indirectly and through derivatives). Observations of this kind make clear again that one way of characterizing the goal of psychotherapy is to make the unconscious resources and capabilities within the patient available to the patient's conscious and direct functioning.

Many of the clinical examples already presented illustrate how valid unconscious perceptions and introjects, and other aspects of nontransference, play a significant role. In this realm, the patient is interacting with and responding to the therapist in keeping with the realities of the situation—actualities in the here and now as they exist between the patient and therapist that are filled with manifest and latent implications. Thus the essential definition of a nontransference-based reaction or communication from the patient involves as response that is appropriate to the direct and implicit meanings and functions of the therapist's behaviors and communications, and to the implicit and explicit nature of the therapeutic situation and interaction.

Finally, nontransference-based reactions have genetic connections, though their structure and functions (their dynamic state and implications) are different from those that pertain to primarily transference-based responses. These genetic ties or repercussions occur in two basic forms:

1. When the therapist makes a *correct* interpretation or a frame-

work-management response, the implications of his or her intervention will conjure up past figures who were constructive, helpful, and promoted growth and health in the patient's earlier life. The introjects within the patient based on experiences with these helpful figures (or constructive experiences with figures who were at other times hurtful) will be reinforced and elaborated on the basis of the therapist's sound functioning. Allusions to genetic figures under these conditions reflect the positively toned actual similarities between the therapist at the moment and the constructive figure in the past.

2. When a therapist makes an *erroneous* intervention—interpretively, noninterpretively, or in respect to the ground rules—he or she is behaving in actuality on some level (manifestly or latently) in a manner comparable to an earlier pathogenic figure in the patient's past life. A hurtful intervention and the negative introject it generates within the patient serve to reinforce the pathological introjects derived from these earlier traumatic experiences and to justify the patient's symptoms and other pathological modes of adapting (maladapting). Allusions to a family figure during such interludes help to identify the hurtful person in the patient's past whom the therapist now resembles in actuality.

This nontransference configuration is far different from a transference constellation. In the former, the therapist dynamically resembles an earlier pathogenic figure, while in the latter, the therapist is distinctly different from that person. In the former, the conditions under which the patient fell ill exist within the therapeutic interaction, while in the latter, they do not; instead, it is the patient who, through distortion, erroneously introduces a sense of similarity that cannot be substantiated through reality testing. In the former, then, the patient's response is relatively appropriate and undistorted, while in the latter it is essentially inappropriate and quite distorted.

The therapist's responsive interventions must take these differences into account. This is necessary not only because interpretations must be shaped according to existing actualities, but also because the therapist's contribution to a nontransference response requires a measure of actual rectification that is unnecessary in the transference situation. The neglect of the patient's nontransference-based reactions to the therapist has interfered with the realization of the importance of *rectifying* interventions in therapeutic work.

It is most critical, then, to realize that allusions to an individual or experience from the patient's childhood do *not* immediately imply the presence of transference. Instead, the basic meaning involves two possibilities: (1) that the therapist is behaving in some way comparable to the past pathogenic figure (nontransference), or (2) that the therapist is behaving differently from the past pathogenic figure, but is nonetheless being mistakenly perceived and responded to in keeping with that earlier relationship (transference). This means too that each manifest allusion to a genetic figure must be understood in light of the full implications of an activated intervention context, and the *functional capacity* (i.e., dynamic implications) of the genetic reference determined in light of the relevant adaptive context.

Clinically, the appraisal of the extent of the patient's unconscious nontransference functioning depends in large measure on a full comprehension of the manifest and latent implications of the interventions. This in turn depends largely upon the therapist's capacity for self-awareness, self-insight, and self-analysis. The therapist must have self-awareness before he or she can appreciate, integrate, and correctly evaluate, his or her impressions of the patient.

CLINICAL EXAMPLES

A married, female patient had been trained as a physician's assistant. She was being seen twice weekly by a therapist who had been intervening quite actively, sometimes rather quickly, with no use of prevailing intervention contexts. The basic treatment situation included many modifications in the ground rules. Before the session excerpted here, the therapist had changed an hour for the patient because of a family function. In the next session, the patient's associations included the following:

> Patient: I could have made the session. I don't know why I lied to you. One of the doctor's aides has mishandled some problem with medication and will probably lose her job. A social worker at the hospital is homosexually involved with another social worker. She gets quite sarcastic when she's asked about it.

During this session, the therapist made several comments regarding the patient's sense of guilt and her need to be deceptive. He did not, however, deal with the implications of this material for his decision to change the hour of this patient's session (a critical deviant intervention context), and for the patient's absence (an important resistance-indicator).

Even without the therapist's specific interventions in the previous hour, an important deviant adaptive context is present, to which the patient appears to be reacting: the therapist's decision to change the time of her session two weeks earlier. As a background context, there is the therapist's repeated interventions to the patient in terms of her own intrapsychic struggles, without any allusion to an adaptive context, the therapeutic interaction, and in particular, to his own contributions to the patient's behaviors and associations. Focusing mainly on the implications of the shift in the session, it is possible to tentatively propose several implications of the material from this excerpt.

First, the patient indicates that she could have made the hour. This appears to be a strong representation of the lack of consistent responsibility for the sessions that exists in both the patient and therapist. In a small way, it also contains an encoded model of rectification for the therapist regarding his earlier deviation—the prior change in session—directing him toward the maintenance rather than alteration of the basic therapeutic contract.

Next, the patient acknowledges having lied to the therapist. This particular derivative represents a valid unconscious perception of the implications of the therapist's deviation: it is a means by which he is able to create a lie-therapy relationship with strong parasitic, and some pathological symbiotic, qualities.

Unconscious lie implications are conveyed in the therapist's active interventions to the patient, which deny his contributions to her acting out and to her other resistances and symptoms. This is manifest content-Type One derivative therapy, and has all the hallmarks of a lie-barrier treatment situation. Clearly, the patient is also contributing to this therapeutic modality and mode of relatedness, though for the moment the implications of this derivative expression fall mainly within the realm of unconscious perceptions of the therapist and the nature of his deviations. In this context, it is well to remember the importance of organizing material in response to a deviant intervention context primarily around this type of unconscious perceptiveness, and to include as an afterthought any intermixture of fantasied and other adaptive reactions from the patient.

In keeping with this approach, the patient's next allusion—to the mishandling of a problem and the threat that someone will lose her job—must be noted. In the adaptive context of the change in the hour (and of the therapist's style of intervening and their contents), this derivative element suggests a valid unconscious perception of the therapist's error, as well as the possibility that the patient is thinking of terminating treatment.

The patient's allusion to a homosexual relationship between two social workers is another compelling derivative communication. It contains an unconscious perception of the unresolved and pathological needs of the therapist that prompt him to change the patient's hour and to intervene as he does. A poor sense of interpersonal boundaries and the presence of pathological symbiotic gratification are also suggested by this image. The patient's own pathological needs in these areas are embedded within those perceived within the therapist, and apparently complement them as well. In this respect, it appears for the moment that the lie-barrier systems of the therapist correspond in large measure to those within the patient.

Finally, the allusion to the sarcasm of the social worker when she is asked about her relationship with her friend suggests an unconscious perception of the therapist as someone who becomes defensive when intervening, and who also interferes with the communicative properties of the therapeutic relationship. The material strongly suggests the possibility that the therapist has responded with defensiveness and hostility to the patient. It appears too that the patient has tried, consciously and/or unconsciously, either manifestly or through derivatives, to alert the therapist to some of his difficulties in light of his manner of intervening and mismanagements of the ground rules and framework of treatment. Much of this material may be seen as an unconscious effort by the patient to confront and interpret the unconscious qualities of the therapist's manner of relating to her, of intervening, and of handling the frame. The allusion to homosexuality in particular may be an attempt by the patient to help the therapist recognize an underlying pathological sexual basis for his errors in technique.

In this particular clinical situation the patient responded to countertransference-based interventions and framework-management errors by the therapist with a manifest disturbance in her functioning, which took the form of missing a session that she

could have made and of lying to the therapist. There is a disturbance here in the manifest alliance sector, though not in the communicative sector of the alliance (see Chapter 31). The level of
functioning of those persons to whom the patient refers also appears to be infused with psychopathology and to be quite disturbed.

In evaluating evidence within the patient or his or her material
for impairments in ego functioning and in capacity for relatedness,
it is important to determine the underlying factors involved. There
will always be contributions from both the patient and therapist to
any aspect of the patient's functioning in a given hour. Thus these
signs of disturbed and transference-based functioning in the patient
must be understood in light of activiated intervention contexts and
the general nature of the therapist's function. As a rule, sound
manifest (and latent) functioning by the therapist tends to evoke
and support healthy functioning in the patient, even though, on a
communicative level, the patient tends to shift to transfence-based
expressions.

Despite the patient's poor manifest functioning, the material of
this hour indicates on a derivative and unconscious level that, in
response to the therapist's errors (including the break in the fixed
frame), she has expressed herself in a highly perceptive, sensitive,
and valid manner. This material is replete with valid unconscious
perceptions of the therapist and his interventions, with a moderately good model of rectification, and with a sensitive unconscious
reading of the likely unconscious implications of the therapist's
efforts. There are strong indications of unconscious confronting
and interpretive efforts by the patient on behalf of her therapist.
Thus, on an unconscious level, the patient is showing a substantial
capacity for sound ego functioning. As such, these reactions are an
important potential resource for both the patient and the therapist.
Essential, however, is the therapist's capacity to bring these resources into the realm of consciousness for both himself and the
patient. Virtually always, the patient lacks this ability, and these
resources will go untapped unless the therapist makes the transition
to conscious awareness through the necessary framework management and/or interpretive responses to the patient based on his or
her manifest and derivative material.

Rather typically, then, patients respond to the countertransferences of the therapist with unconscious nontransference
expressions of their own. The therapist's sick functioning invokes

unconscious healthy functioning in the patient. On a conscious level, however, the therapist's errors may either evoke healthy or pathological reactions within the patient. The more consistent nontransference responses to the therapist's errors fall into the unconscious realm.

On the day of the patient's next session, she called the therapist and asked for a change in the time of her hour. She said that she expected to be held up because of an emergency case on which the doctor for whom she worked had asked her to serve as an assistant. The therapist agreed to a later session that day. The following excerpt is from that hour.

> Patient: There was no traffic coming here at this hour. I had a dream that my husband did or said something and I suddenly realized that things are never going to change, that I will never be able to change him. I've been feeling depressed. I would like to know what's wrong with my husband. I try to get him to commit himself to me and he refuses. He's so inconsistent. I would like your advice. *(Pause.)* My mother's always been like that. She's nasty and sarcastic. I don't know how she says the things she does. She's so unsophisticated and crude. She blames me for her problems. She breast fed my sister, but told me that I pushed the breast away.

The main adaptation-evoking context here is the therapist's unanalyzed decision to again change the patient's hour. Later on in this session, it became evident that the shift actually was unnecessary, though the patient could not have entirely anticipated that the procedure on which she assisted would be completed as early as it was.

On a manifest level, the material in this hour reflects relatively sound functioning in the patient. The comments regarding her husband appear to be justified in light of all the therapist knew about both him and his relationship with the patient. Similarly, the patient's perceptions of her mother were apparently quite sound. Thus, on a surface level, the patient appears at this time to be functioning quite well. Specifically, in her relationship with her therapist, she is now cooperative and sensible, and there is no indication of disturbance. Much of her functioning therefore has the cast of nontransference.

In regard to the patient's unconscious and derivative functioning, the patient's material may be examined in light of the intervention context of the change in the hour. In this regard, the patient is correctly indicating through encoded messages that she has extensive evidence of the therapist's incapacity to manage the framework (cf. the husband's failure to commit himself to the patient, and his inconsistencies), and that he is unlikely to take care of the patient's therapeutic needs—an unconscious perception that found some measure of verification in supervisory discussion. Based on the therapist's repetitive errors and poor management of the framework, the patient further comments through derivatives that he has not been able to change either through self-analysis or through the unconscious interpretations that she has apparently offered to him throughout this therapy.

The patient also perceives the therapist's general inability to commit himself to her in terms of a sound and healthy therapeutic symbiosis and to offer valid therapeutic procedures. There are indications that the patient accounts for these difficulties on an unconscious level in terms of the therapist's unresolved depression—i.e., an inability to tolerate separation anxieties that would have been aroused if the patient had missed her hour.

The patient's wish for advice from the therapist is a model of the search for direct and pathological symbiotic gratification that unconsciously reflects the direct and noninterpretive ways in which the therapist has already gratified this patient—and himself as well. The introduction of the mother suggests that the therapist's failures to establish a sound interpretive and holding relationship repeats in some form the patient's mother's early maternal failures. The use of the image of breast-feeding suggests not only early oral conflicts within this patient, but a valid sensitivity to the core qualities of the ground-rule dimension of her relationship with the therapist and his basic failure to offer adequate therapeutic nourishment. The patient implies further that the therapist's interventions, which have centered around the patient's conflicts without any regard for inputs from the therapist, are a form of blaming the patient for the feeding failure, when in actuality, the therapist is contributing significantly to these difficulties.

Over all, this material reflects a series of valid unconscious perceptions of the implications of the therapist's erroneous verbal interventions and his mismanagements of the framework. It includes again unconscious therapeutic efforts on behalf of the therapist that can be appreciated only in light of a full comprehension of the activated intervention contexts. For the moment, there is no clear indication here of the presence of significant transferences or distortion, or of unmistakably inappropriate reactions to the therapist. There is evidence too that the missed session alluded to at the beginning of the vignette was prompted by seductive deviations and interventions by the therapist, adaptation-evoking contexts that prompted a need within the patient for actual distance from the therapist. While deviations are in actuality a form of acting out on the part of the therapist, the patient's response through acting out of her own must be properly understood as a mixture of nontransference and transference.

This last may serve as a reminder that the patient's reactions to the therapist are always a transversal mixture of valid and distorted elements. When nontransferences predominate, there will always be a segment of transference and an aspect of the patient's reactions that derive from the patient's own psychopathology, whether in the form of coloring the patient's unconscious understanding or behavioral reactions. A fully balanced view of the patient's associations and behaviors would take into account the contributions of both participants, and stress them in proportions in keeping with the implications of the prevailing adaptive contexts. The greater the validity of the therapist's interventions, the greater the extent to which the patient's communications will reflect the patient's own, rather than the therapist's, psychopathology. The greater the measure of error, the more the situation will be reversed and the therapist's pathology predominate.

The ideal and appropriate intervention in the presence of predominantly nontransference responses by the patient is somewhat different from those made in the presence of transference. As noted, such interventions uniformly require the *rectification* of the therapist's error, as well as interpretive efforts that are couched in a manner that *implicitly* acknowledges the validity of the patient's unconscious perceptions and responses.

For example, the following intervention might have been offered in response to the initial comment excerpted from the patient's session—confined to the adaptive context of the therapist's first change in the hour:

You have alluded to missing a session and lying to me. This implies that there is something highly deceptive and destructive taking place in regard to your hours. Your images involve someone who is mishandling therapy and someone who is sexually involved with another person. There is also a reference to someone getting sarcastic when questioned about that involvement. It would seem that you are experiencing some major mishandling of the therapy and feel it is based on some kind of sexual difficulty. Also, in your comment that you could have made this session, you seem to propose that whatever is being handled incorrectly should be handled differently and with a greater sense of responsibility.

This intervention implicitly accepts the patient's communications as involving valid unconscious perceptions and realizations. It is couched somewhat *transversally* to allow for the eventual inclusion of the patient's psychopathology, though its initial stress is on sound nontransference-based perceptions and introjects. It includes a model of rectification as offered by the patient, and therefore hints at the therapist's intention to correct his error. It remains within the confines of the patient's material of the hour at hand.

However, the intervention is not proposed as the one that actually should have been offered to the patient so early in this session. It would have been far better to permit additional associations to unfold, in the hope that the patient would more clearly represent the intervention context of the therapist's shift in the hour and provide him with still more compelling derivatives. It may nevertheless serve as a model of how the therapist intervenes in the presence of nontransference responses.

Nontransference reactions and introjects of the psychopathology of the therapist are important contributors to the patient's own psychopathology. Quite broadly, introjects of this kind contribute significantly to the development of emotional illness in patients. Thus therapeutic work with nontransference responses—rectifications and interpretations—is extremely important in psychotherapy. These responses are essential at all moments when the therapist has made a mistake, and have highly salutary effects both in terms of a shift from a negative to positive introject and of cognitive insight. The belief that psychotherapy must unfold mainly or exclusively around interpretations of transference is based largely on a misunderstanding of the patient's communications in which their nontransference components have been almost entirely overlooked. Acknowledging the strong intermixtures of both nontransference and transference in the patient's material, and specific situations in which nontransference predominates, leads to a more balanced view of therapeutic work.

The second excerpt from the patient contained no direct representation of the intervention context of the therapist's change in the patient's hour. At that point it is perhaps best represented in the patient's allusion to her husband's failure to commit himself to her. In the actual session, the therapist would have been well advised to wait for a more clear representation of this intervention context before intervening. However, the following might have been the therapist's tentative or *silent intervention,* one that he was preparing as the patient spoke, and to which he would add as the patient's material permitted:

> You began the session by alluding to the time of this hour. Your thoughts then went to disturbing things your husband does and his lack of commitment to you, and to your sense of disillusionment that he will never change. This connected in your mind to your mother and to the way in which you pushed her breast away. In some way, since you began these thoughts with a reference to the time of the session, they must have something to do with me. [*Of course, this is a very weak bridge, and in actuality, the therapist would have to wait for a clearer connection between this material and himself*]. It would appear that you are experiencing some things that I am doing as lacking in a commitment to you, as inconsistent, as behaving much like your mother, and as failing you in some basic and feeding way that leads you to want to pull away from me.

This intervention again shows how valid unconscious perceptions and impressions are implicitly accepted when the therapist intervenes in respect to nontransferences. Such material is not treated as inappropriate, distorted, unrealistic, and based through displacement only on actualities from the past. The genetic aspects of the intervention accept a similarity between the therapist and the patient's mother, rather than suggesting that the patient has misunderstood the therapist in some way because of her earlier experiences with the maternal figure. Thus the therapist may intervene in a distinctly different fashion from most present-day therapists who, should they interpret some aspect of the therapeutic relationship, will virtually always do so in terms of the patient's intrapsychic fantasies and distortions. Such efforts in the presence of essentially nontransference communications from the patient tend to undermine the therapeutic alliance, to confuse and accuse the patient, and to disturb his or her basic sense of* trust and reality-testing. They are often experienced as efforts to drive the patient crazy and to deny the therapist's psychopathology and the implicit disturbance in his or her erroneous interventions. Transferences can only be interpreted in the context of a sound holding environment and a basically correct interpretive approach by the therapist. Since both distortion and valid perception, transference and nontransference, play a role in the development and maintenance of Neurosis, both will require a full measure of interpretation (and rectification) in the course of a psychotherapy.

One further clinical example is offered. The patient was a married woman who had been in psychotherapy for about a year for a schizophrenic illness with auditory hallucinations. In the previous session, the patient had responded to a rectification in the frame with a direct representation of the intervention context and a series of derivatives that revealed that the patient had seen the therapist as quite strong, had herself begun to function more effectively and firmly, and had found a measure of freedom from her hallucinations and illness. Major separation anxieties had arisen, however, in that the voice within her head had told the patient not to get better, since he—the voice—would be lost without her. There was in addition a recollection of a time when the patient felt quite successful and became sexually involved with another woman who made love to her and then abandoned her. The patient had felt gratified but then deserted.

In supervision it was suggested that the therapist should have offered an interpretation that, in the (intervention) context of his having secured the frame by maintaining the patient's responsibility for missed sessions, the patient had taken in a considerable sense of strength, had begun to master her illness, but had then experienced intense anxieties over the prospect of developing sexual feelings toward him and of becoming well and eventually terminating her treatment.

The excerpt presented here is from the hour that followed:

> Patient: I felt out of it toward the end of last session. I became bored with what I was saying. My husband and I took the baby to the park. Some man kept talking, and I wished he would shut up. My husband, who had been nice, suddenly got nasty and critical. When you charged me for my missed session and when he made me organize the household, I felt great. But yesterday, I felt hurt and angry. I wanted to have relations with him but he had a business appointment. We started to make love and I said I'd finish up myself. He said he'd be back in an hour but did not return until quite late. I was furious, and I knew I had reason. I am furious with you too. I thought I saw you on the street. I think of you like a jack-in-the-box, and of hitting you on the head as you pop out. The voice in my head just asked, "What are you going to do now?" I had a dream of a friend's husband [*a man who was not working and had proven to be quite ineffectual*], and we made love and he satisfied me. He's the last one I'd choose. I feel I'm boring you.
>
> Therapist: You're bored and angry with me. Your husband dismissed your sexual needs. You dreamt of your friend's husband satisfying you. You mentioned that you imagined seeing me on the street. This suggests that your dream could have involved having sex with me as a way of making things more interesting and less boring.
>
> Patient: I don't feel like being Anne's [*her daughter*] mother this week. She clings to me and I get annoyed. I should understand it's her way of loving. I forget to be firm. I don't relate love to what you just said about sex.

Examining this material in terms of reflections of the patient's surface functioning, it is well to distinguish the patient's functioning in the actual session with the therapist from her functioning as reflected in the material that she presents. Briefly, it can be seen that there is, in regard to the patient's outside functioning, evidence of some measure of disturbance. The patient appears easily upset, confused, and unable to relate in a full and mature sense. These disturbances may be understood as a reflection of the patient's

structural dysfunctions (ego, id, and superego) in which unconscious displacements from the past (transference in its broadest
sense extended to include outside relationships) probably play a
notable role. It is in this regard that it is necessary to distinguish
transference-based influences and consequences from other aspects
of the patient's psychopathology.

Within the session the patient appears mainly cooperative and
reasonably logical (through there are some hints of breaks in logic
and the possibility of a thought disorder), though she does reveal an
experience of an hallucination. While some aspects of this disturbance can be immediately identified as reflecting the patient's
psychopathology, and as likely to be based in part on unconscious
transference constellations, other aspects require a clear sense of the
activated intervention context to which the patient is responding.
Disturbances within the patient that receive strong impetus from
the therapist, even when they occur in regard to his or her surface
functioning, must be understood to reflect important nontransference aspects. It is here that the distinction must be made
between nontransference-based functioning and the extent to which
the patient functions either by usual standards or pathologically
and idiosyncratically. This is necessary because nontransference
factors (through pathological introjects) can lead to psycho-
pathological functioning in a patient who might otherwise function rather well.

Thus the evident disturbance in this patient's functioning can
be seen to draw some of its impetus from the therapist's earlier
deviations. He had failed to charge the patient for a missed session,
though he then rectified this break in the frame; in addition, there
were other alterations in the ideal therapeutic environment that the
therapist was in the process of rectifying. It has already been noted
that mismanagement of the ground rules and boundaries of therapy
create pressures toward pathological functioning in the patient, and
may disturb such functions as drive management, the maintenance
of self-object boundaries, reality-testing, use of defenses, and the
like. The appearance of this type of ego dysfunction is an interactional product to be understood in terms of the inputs from the
therapist and the patient's own basic capacities. The greater the
vulnerability of the patient, the more likely it is that the countertransferences of the therapist will evoke relatively blatant ego
disturbances. Thus, while all patients are vulnerable, the extent of

regression and dysfunction depends on both the nature of the disturbing stimuli and the patient's own inner capabilities and failings.

Once again, despite the presence of some measure of surface dysfunction, the patient's material conveys a great deal of sound functioning on an unconscious or derivative level. Thus there is her unconscious perception of the therapist's missed intervention, represented in the material by the patient's feeling that she herself was out of it toward the end of the last hour. The patient also unconsciously perceives a shift in the therapist from having been helpful to being hurtful (represented through the patient's husband), and his basic failure to meet the patient's therapeutic needs (represented by the husband's sexual abandonment). In regard to this last derivative, there is considerable evidence of an unconscious erotic countertransference in this therapist, some of it reflected in the erroneous interventions cited above. One would therefore have to understand the patient's use of the sexual idiom to represent the curative process in psychotherapy as a *transversal communication*, with mixtures of transference and nontransference—i.e., of valid unconscious perceptions of the therapist and distortions based on the patient's own genetic past and her present psychopathology.

The patient went on to indicate her sense of justification for her anger, a valid derivative commentary on her disappointment in the therapist. The dream of the ineffectual husband satisfying the patient appears to represent in sexual terms the patient's wish that the therapist had intervened properly. The additional psychopathology contained in this communication must be recognized, much of it involving the patient's own poor capacity to manage her instinctual drive needs, and her tendency to sexualize and instinctualize relationships.

The therapist's intervention was not organized around an adaptive context, and was couched primarily in terms of transference. The therapist had in mind that the patient was sexualizing her relationship with him in a manner not unlike her mother's own blatant sexual behaviors with the patient and the patient's father. The intervention is couched entirely in terms of the patient's needs and psychopathology, and the possibility of valid unconscious perceptions and of the presence of an adaptation-evoking context is entirely ignored. The patient's commentary on this intervention is quite perceptive: It is a failure on the part of the therapist to function as a sound mother-therapist in his relationship with the patient. In all likelihood, his effort conveys certain counter-transference-based needs and conflicts related to his own erotic countertransference, an expression that the patient experiences as clinging and as loving in her own way.

Summary and Conclusions

This chapter has emphasized the patient's valid functioning and responses to the therapist, on both the manifest and latent (unconscious) levels. There is considerable evidence that this dimension of the patient's relationship with the therapist is primary with all patients, and that healthy functioning predominates in most. On a conscious and adaptively available level, the patient's basic level of functioning will, of course, reflect the nature of his or her psychopathology. The closer to the psychotic end of the psycho-pathological continuum a patient falls, the greater the evidence for structural (ego, id, superego) dysfunctions, impairments in object relatedness, and self-pathology. Nonetheless, even these patients show many sectors of sound functioning in their outside relation-ships and in their relationships with their therapists. These at-tributes should not be neglected through an overriding con-centration on a patient's psychopathology.

On a conscious and manifest level, there is a tendency for the dysfunctions and countertransferences of the therapist to heighten the dysfunctions and evident disturbances in his or her patients. In contrast, however, on an unconscious level, patients almost univer-sally tend to respond to the countertransferences of the therapist with sound, nontransference functioning of their own. It is there-fore quite critical to evaluate the patient's responses—both manifest and latent—to each intervention context from the therapist, es-pecially those that are erroneous and traumatic. Of course, a thera-pist's sound functioning will tend to have the opposite mixed effect on the patient: an enhancement of his or her own surface function-ing and the introduction of transference and distortion in uncon-scious responses.

On an unconscious level, all patients show a strong capacity for valid perception, understanding, sound confronting and inter-pretive efforts, and other healthy forms of ego functioning, which are expressed through derivatives. These abilities fall largely into the realm of nontransference, and can be recognized only through a full evaluation of the activated intervention context that evokes the patient's derivative reactions.

In principle the therapist should evaluate the patient's material in light of activated intervention contexts in order to first determine all possible valid conscious and unconscious perceptions, reactions, genetic connections, and the like. Only after this search has been completed can the therapist safely conclude that all that is left over belongs to the realm of distortion, inappropriate perception and response, and therefore to transference. This rule, then, points to considerations of nontransference before transference, and to the inputs from the therapist before those from the patient.

This approach is especially useful in counterbalancing the tendency among therapists to think primarily in terms of the patient's psychopathology, and to exclude from consideration their own difficulties and the sectors of valid functioning within the patient. However, care should be taken not to develop a bias in the direction of viewing the patient as essentially well and the therapist as essentially ill. The small islands of transference expressions in reactions of the patient that are predominantly nontransference-based must be identified and acknowledged. A full sense of balance must be maintained, although it appears for the moment that this can be achieved only by affording greater attention and appreciation than is the rule to the patient's nontransference functioning and expressions.

The patient should be understood as having a relationship with the therapist, with nontransference and transference components. *Nontransference* involves manifest and latent reactions to the therapist that are founded upon conscious and especially unconscious perceptions and fantasies that are appropriate to the therapist's attitudes and interventions. Thus, while founded essentially on unconscious constellations, these underlying complexes are essentially nonpathological and nondistorting.

The patient's nontransference functioning is reflected in sound manifest communications and behaviors, and in derivative communications that are appropriate to the manifest and latent implications of the therapist's interventions. All of the patient's communications to the therapist have relationship implications on some level, and all such expressions must be treated as derivative communications, and the nontransference components sorted out from the transference elements. This can be done only in light of a full analysis of the implications of the therapist's interventions, especially the unconscious needs and expressions that they convey.

All of the patient's associations and behaviors, no matter how seemingly inappropriate, must be carefully analyzed in light of activated adaptive contexts. Often, rather irrational behaviors are recognized to have important nontransference elements in light of the unconscious implications of the therapist's efforts. In general, there is a correlation between the therapist's valid interventions and (1) sound nontransference manifest functioning and (2) unsound, transference-based unconscious functioning. (There is a similar correlation between the therapist's erroneous interventions and (1) nontransference-based disturbances in manifest functioning and (2) sound unconscious and derivative functioning.)

The analysis of nontransference responses is of significantly curative value to the patient, and is an essential part of therapeutic work that must be carried out after an erroneous intervention. Such efforts must, however, include the *rectification* of the therapist's error, without which interpretive efforts are of little or no avail. These interpretations must *implicitly* accept the validity of the patient's unconscious perceptions and responses to the intervention context at hand, and will therefore be stated quite differently from a transference interpretation. Often, such efforts involve the interpretation of nontransference-based resistances (see Chapter 33). It is important, then, to interpret surface dysfunctions in light of disturbing intervention contexts from the therapist, and equally important to make use of the patient's unconscious resources when rectifying and interpreting derivative responses to erroneous interventions.

A good rule of thumb directs the therapist to search for the nontransference component of the patient's manifest and derivative communications before identifying transference elements. This is in keeping with the principle of taking into account reality before fantasy, and the therapist's errors before valid interventions. It is also a means of maintaining a balanced and basically interactional approach to the patient and his or her material.

Chapter 28

Transference

Transference or transference-based reactions to the therapist are founded upon pathological *unconscious* fantasy-memory constellations and pathological introjects derived from earlier pathogenic interactions. *Transference* refers to all reactions to the therapist on the part of the patient that are based primarily on these unconscious sources. Such reactions are prompted by the attitudes and interventions of the therapist (adaptive contexts) and are adaptive responses.

Transference, then, is *not* simply manifest allusion to the therapist. This may actually, upon analysis in light of intervention contexts, be either transference- or nontransference-based. Transference is not conscious fantasy about the therapist. Nor is it the totality of the patient's relationship to the therapist. Similarly, transference should not be equated with the unrealistic or unconscious aspects of the therapeutic relationship, as seen in the term *transference relationship,* and as used to contrast a so-called *real relationship* between the patient and therapist. As already noted, there are both unconscious and fantasied aspects of the patient's essentially nontransference responses to the therapist. There are also important reality stimuli to the patient's transference reactions. In addition, the patient's disturbed surface functioning may derive from transference or nontransference reactions to the therapist. Each of these determinations requires a careful evaluation of the conscious and unconscious implications of the adaptation-evoking stimuli from the therapist.

There is, then, but one relationship between the patient and therapist. It has realistic and fantasied aspects. It is stimulated by actualities with manifest and latent meanings, direct and indirect implications, and conscious and unconscious components. Both the realistic and fantasied responses of the patient are prompted by these realities, just as the patient's interpretation of these actualities depend upon both their own nature and factors within the patient—including the patient's capability to maintain contact with reality and his or her evoked fantasies. Further, it is necessary for the therapist to evaluate both the patient's manifest behaviors and functioning and his or her derivative communications, to determine the extent to which they are first, sound, adaptive, and in keeping with the implications of the prevailing actualities, and second, transference- and nontransference-based. It is the internal transference factor that disturbs the patient's manifest and latent functioning, although there is also an important influence from the therapist. Thus the therapist's valid functioning will tend to support healthy surface capabilities in the patient and unconscious derivative expressions of transference, while erroneous functioning will tend to undermine the patient's functioning—much of it, however, nontransference-based—while stimulating valid, nontransference-based unconscious responses in the patient.

Just as sound unconscious perceptions, valid introjects, and nonpathological fantasy-memory constellations are at the heart of nontransference, *pathological* unconscious fantasies, memories, and introjects (unconscious fantasy constellations) are at the heart of transference. As unconscious processes, contents, defenses, and such, their manifestations adopt many forms. These underlying constellations may therefore be expressed on the surface as daydreams about the therapist or about someone else, as behaviors directed toward the therapist or toward some outside person, as night dreams, as overt behaviors, and through any other form of expression available to the patient. These manifest communications function as *carriers* of *derivative transference expressions*.

In contrast to common usage and understanding, it has been found that manifest fantasies and other direct allusions to the therapist tend, by and large, to be poor carriers of *unconscious* transference fantasies. *Displacement* is a critical mechanism, which functions along with repression and other defenses in shifting the manifest locus of transference-based expressions to outside figures and often to communications involving the patient. This is, of course, a second-order displacement—the first being the displacement (usually carried out quite unconsciously) from the earlier figure onto the therapist. Thus a constellation from an earlier figure is displaced onto the therapist, but then usually (because of defensive need) finds representation in some further displaced form.

An *unconscious* fantasy and experience of a pathogenic nature in a relationship with an early childhood figure is at the heart of transference. This constellation is then attached to the therapist, and therefore pathologically influences the patient's perceptions of and reactions to the therapist. In the course of free associating, the patient then makes use of communicative vehicles to express the underlying fantasy, including both its source and its relevance now to the therapist. It is these communicative vehicles that tend to involve outside persons and the patient himself or herself. Thus the first displacement is from the parental figure onto the therapist, while the second displacement, carried out in the service of defensive and communicative expression, is usually from the therapist onto some other figure. Of course, there may be displacements from one aspect of the patient's relationship with the therapist to another, though at all times the essential transference fantasy is unconscious, and its expression is manifestly a reflection of encoding, disguise, and derivative formation. Any manifest fantasy regarding the therapist, then, must be decoded and treated as a derivative expression so that the underlying unconscious fantasy can be determined. Even when there appears to be a dramatic breakthrough of a previously repressed fantasy toward the therapist, at the moment it reaches consciousness it is functioning as a derivative of a different, still unconscious fantasy constellation.

Much confusion has arisen because of the error of treating conscious feelings, fantasies, and reactions to the therapist as "transference," and failing to attend to such material as derivative expressions of unconscious transference or nontransference constellations. In part, this has come about because of a failure to develop each and every formulation of the patient's material with the activated adaptive contexts that have prompted the patient's behaviors and associations. It is therefore important to be clear as to the implications of the prevailing intervention contexts in evaluating *all* associations and behaviors from the patient for reflections of transference and nontransference responses to the therapist. This failure to appreciate the therapeutic relationship implications in every communication from the patient has also led to much misunderstanding of the nature and manifestations of transference. As

already noted, it is best to identify all possible nontransference reactions first, and to consider the balance as transference-based as long as there is reason to justify such formulations. This implies that the patient is thought of as functioning appropriately and adaptively except when there is distinct evidence for clear-cut distortions and inappropriate and maladaptive reactions. Thus, the patient is viewed as healthy except where ill, rather than ill except where healthy. The former is a far more accurate and sensitive appraisal.

The Structure of Transference

The unconscious fantasy constellations that account for the patient's psychopathology involve early genetic and currently traumatic relationships and experiences. Present traumas and sources of maladaptation have important counterparts in earlier experiences, which sensitize the patient to maladaptive and symptomatic reactions to present traumatic conditions. Were it not for this earlier sensitization, the patient would, on the whole, be able to adapt without emotional disturbance.

As discussed earlier, the key to the patient's Neurosis lies in pathological unconscious fantasy (and perception) constellations. These may find expression in the patient's outside relationships or in the relationship with the therapist. Empirically, it has been found that the influence of these constellations on the patient's outside relationships, while important to his or her everyday living and at times, to symptom formation, do not form a viable source through which these constellations can be identified, analyzed, and resolved. While the patient may work over pathological aspects of his or her realtionship with an outside individual quite directly in that relationship, as soon as the patient becomes involved in a relationship with a therapist, it is this particular relationship that most cogently and meaningfully mobilizes these critical pathological unconscious constellations. Although the patient usually continues to operate in outside relationships, communications to the therapist about these particular manifestations are, in general, lacking in derivative expressions, and therefore fail to make the underlying fantasies accessible for interpretation. In contrast, reactions to intervention contexts tend to be convoluted and will, when

534 / Psychotherapy: A Basic Text

the patient is communicating meaningfully, contain the encoded derivatives that embody these underlying fantasy-memory formations.

In essence, then, the patient's relationship with the therapist, as constituted within the defined ground rules of the therapeutic interaction, unconsciously mobilizes the patient's investment of his or her pathological fantasies in the experiences with the therapist. Since empirical evidence indicates that it is only in regard to this interaction and the therapist's interventions that the unconscious fantasy constellations pertinent to the patient's Neurosis become available for interpretation, the psychotherapist has no choice but to interpret along these lines. The question as to whether the therapeutic work should involve outside relationships or that with the therapist is therefore answered unmistakably on an empirical basis in favor of the latter. This position has received repeated validation, in that the former effort does not evoke Type Two derivative confirmation, while the latter does. The therapist must interpret where dynamic meaning is available and cogent, and this emerges consistently in responses to the therapeutic interaction.

However, this position—that the therapist's interventions mobilize meaningfully the patient's unconscious fantasy constellations—only addresses the level of unconscious communication. The *manifest* vehicle for such expressions may pertain to any of the patient's relationships, present or past. Transference interpretations will be feasible only when the unconscious implications of an intervention context have mobilized a distorted response in the patient. This occurs mainly when the frame is secure and an interpretation proves to be valid.

This implies that transference does indeed become one of the central expressions of the patient's illness in the course of psychotherapy. However, this finding should not lead to a neglect of the role of nontransferences in the creation and perpetuation of Neuroses, in that pathological introjects appropriately preceived and incorporated can also lead to symptomatic responses in the patient. Here only those contributions to the patient's illness that derive from earlier pathological introjects and from residual unconscious fantasy-memory constellations that lead to distorting and maladaptive responses are being traced.

In summary, the patient's Neurosis originates in early childhood through pathological introjects and through intrapsychically-founded distorted and maladaptive unconscious fantasy-memory constellations. The entire constellation operates unconsciously, and leads to the patient's symptoms and characterological disturbances. When the patient enters psychotherapy, he or she responds to the therapist's interventions partly on a realistic level entirely separate from his or her Neurosis, and partly on an inappropriate level based on the pathological unconscious fantasy-introject constellations that account for his or her Neurosis—and therefore constitute the underlying basis for both inappropriate reactions to the therapist and for the Neurosis itself. It must be remembered, however, that transferences can emerge only when the therapist's interventions *do not justify* the symptomatic or maladaptive response or image from the patient. Where the therapist's behaviors correspond to a past pathogenic figure, the pathological reaction is in keeping with the actual nature of the therapist's communications. The dysfunction is therefore reinforced, and for the moment rendered unavailable for anlytic understanding and insightful change.

Transferences arise when the therapist has secured the therapeutic environment and intervened interpretively and correctly. The patient then, without external justification in the behaviors of the therapist, expresses a manifestation of an underlying pathological fantasy constellation. The patient may respond manifestly quite inappropriately to the therapist or unrealistically to an outside figure, or may experience a symptom or have a nightmare. Analysis of the associative material in the intervention context of a secure holding environment or correct intervention will reveal that the patient has responded with a need to distort his or her image of the therapist and to impose some aspect of pathological fantasy onto his or her perceptions and relationship with the therapist. Interpretive analysis of these derivative communications in light of the sound intervention context enables the patient to insightfully understand and alter the existing pathological unconscious fantasies and their influence on his or her symptoms and behaviors. This work constitutes the analysis of transference, and it will take place with some frequency in a well run psychotherapy. As can be seen, it is founded upon a sound image and the effective interventions of the therapist.

Types of Transference

There are two basic types of transference: (1) classical or displacement transference and (2) interactional transference. In the first, some aspect of a relationship with an earlier genetic figure, and sometimes a more recent figure whose genetic echoes are of secondary importance, is displaced onto the therapist. A fantasy, affect, or other type of response, as well as defenses against these expressions, is displaced from the earlier relationship onto the interaction with the therapist. These efforts do not arise de novo from within the patient, however, but always constitute maladaptive responses to the therapist's attitudes and interventions.

Interactional transference involves inappropriate efforts at projective identification or interactional projection on the part of the patient toward the therapist. These too are responses to sound intervention contexts that have received Type Two derivative validation. In addition, however, these responses evoke pathological interactional efforts directed toward the therapist. Of course, these pressures also derive from earlier relationships and have a distinct genetic dimension, and displacement plays a role, but they are separated out because of the particular form they take. Their existence implies that when under interactional pressure from the patient, the therapist must examine the activated intervention contexts at hand to determine whether the patient's pathological projective identifications are responses to pathological projective identifications from the therapist (nontransference), or arise primarily from pathological unconscious fantasy constellations that prompt the patient to create such pressures mainly because of his or her own inner needs (transference).

CLINICAL EXAMPLE

A clinical example is a useful starting point toward considering some basic issues of technique in respect to transferences. The patient was a young woman in psychotherapy for over two years. The therapist routinely vacationed from mid-August to mid-September, and in July, the patient would shift to a summer work schedule and ask the therapist to change her hours. When this was done—as it had been twice before—there were few if any indications in the patient's material of separation anxieties and other disturbed reactions to the therapist's vacations.

A sequence of sessions that took place before another summer break are presented here. It occurred at a time when the therapist had made efforts to secure the therapeutic environment and ground rules. The patient had responded with conscious protest, but also with extensive derivatives of positive introjective identifications of the frame-securing therapist that had greatly enhanced her functioning.

> Patient: Can I shift next week to early afternoon sessions?
>
> Therapist: You are asking for a change in the basic structure of therapy. Let's see what comes to mind.
>
> Patient: You've done it before, and I would appreciate it again. I don't like the way I've been behaving. I've been losing my cool and arguing with my fellow employees. My boyfriend Mark has been trying to calm me down. I feel tense about my vacation. I seldom concentrate on one thing for very long.
>
> Therapist: In light of your request to change your hours, you'll notice you were talking about not being able to concentrate and losing control. You also mentioned your vacation, which must connect to my being away. It sounds as if you're trying to handle some of your anxieties about my leaving by having me do something special for you so you would not have to face your anxieties about the separation.
>
> Patient: My fears are physical [*referring here to past recurrent bladder infections with hemorrhage*], but you feel they are mental. I am afraid I will hemorrhage and there will not be a doctor available. I hadn't thought about your going away next month. It's true I tend to set my anxieties aside. Why would your leaving affect me this year when it hasn't in the past? I've been more affectionate toward Mark, and it surprised him. I haven't mentioned it before, but I haven't been sleeping well recently. *(As she is leaving:)* What about next session?
>
> Therapist: You're implying that changing your routine drives you crazy and helps you to avoid things. I suggest that we keep to our structure.
>
> Patient: See you next week.

The main intervention contexts are the therapist's prior agreement to modify the frame by changing the patient's summer hours (and his recent efforts toward rectification) and the suggestion to the

538 / Psychotherapy: A Basic Text

patient that they see what comes to her mind regarding her request to change her hours at this time. Together, they clearly have contradictory implications: suggesting a likelihood based on past experience that the therapist will change the hour, though also hinting that he may not do so in light of his later efforts to secure the frame and his failure to immediately acquiesce to the patient's request.

In response the patient too shows indications of a split: on the one hand, she seems to have been disturbed by the therapist's failure to immediately satisfy her request; yet on the other, she appears fearful that he might do so—a response that she equates on a derivative level with losing control. With the frame held for the moment, the patient soon makes clear that the deviation would mollify some of her separation anxieties in response to the therapist's pending vacation, and create conditions under which her communications would be defensively scattered. As such, much of her initial derivative response falls primarily into the realm of nontransference.

The therapist's specific intervention is an effort at interpretation that implies the likelihood that he will maintain the frame. It is an effort with many sound qualities, and as such, it appears to shift the dynamic implications of the patient's material strongly toward the transference sphere. The intervention also enables the patient to reveal aspects of her psychopathology that would otherwise have continued to remain defensively concealed by virtue of the pathological symbiosis and misalliance that would have been effected again if the therapist had changed the hour. Sound interventions, then, intensify the transference implications of the patient's material, and create conditions for more open communication, including active expressions of the basis for the patient's symptomatic disturbance.

The material that followed the therapist's second intervention appears to reveal the patient's wish for a pathological symbiotic fusion in order to repair bodily-related anxieties mobilized by the anticipated separation from the therapist. In the absence of a framework-deviation cure, with its offer of a pathological symbiosis (or parasiticism), it seems likely that the patient experienced an actual sense of separateness from the therapist that mobilized her healthy and pathological needs and her adaptive communicative resources.

On one level, the therapist's interpretation, with its implied deprivation of pathological gratification, has evoked an essentially transference-based anxiety in the patient, as well as unconscious fantasies to the effect that the patient will be damaged physically by the failure of the therapist to merge with her and by his unavailability on this level. As can be seen, this appraisal can be made only in light of an evaluation of the indirect and unconscious implications of the therapist's intervention, which reveals a relative absence of countertransference and a relatively sound, though incomplete, effort to maintain the frame and to interpret the patient's wish for the deviation.

There is also an additional rectifying comment filled with nontransference-based perceptiveness—that breaks in the patient's routine drive her crazy. Then there is a shift to what is in all likelihood an expression of an additional unconscious transference-based fantasy—the allusion to the patient's greater capacity for affection toward her boyfriend. On one level, this reflects a positve introjective identification with a well-functioning therapist who is capable of appropriate therapeutic intervention and concern. On another level, it suggests the mobilization of unconscious sexual fantasies and wishes in response to the therapist's decision to maintain the boundaries between himself and the patient, and to allow her to experience fully the anticipation of his vacation.

No genetic figure emerges in this material for the moment. This may be accounted for, in part, by the fact that this therapist had only recently begun to secure the frame, and had not as yet gained the patient's full sense of trust. Additional resistances in respect to the genetic link may also have been present within the patient. This moment in the therapy appears to be a shift from predominantly nontransference-based derivative expression to those in which transference begins to play a significant role. However, it is possible to adopt this formulation only because the therapist's interventions do not on any level significantly justify the images reflected in the patient's material. This lack of correspondence between the unconscious implications of the therapist's interventions and the patient's derivative images is the empirical basis for a formulation of transference material.

The next session included the following material:

Patient: Last year I complained about being on vacation and kept having asthmatic episodes. I've been wondering what

I'll do now each Thursday [*the regular day of the sessions*] until I come here. Eddie called me. I hadn't seen him in years. I used to be taken with him. He's bright, sexually virile, and aggressive. He's more stimulating than Mark, but he never makes a commitment. We'd have sex and then he'd dump me. Somehow, I'm less interested in him now. Mark can make a commitment. I want someone who cares. Not one of these fly-by-night guys. Eddie's afraid of a commitment. When I was with him, I felt disloyal to Mark. But sometimes Mark hurts me sexually. He has a large penis, and sometimes I bleed. But still, he's considerate and tries to work things out. We had a good and close sexual relationship this past week.

In the intervention contexts of the therapist's previous deviations and his current effort to maintain the frame, the initial part of this material reflects sound surface functioning, and is filled with unconscious perceptiveness. This patient indicates—and this is not at all uncommon—that, in the presence of inappropriate alterations of the frame, there is a disturbance in the therapist's holding capacities and a regression to psychosomatic, rather than verbal-affective, communication by the patient.

Next, the patient rather exquisitely utilizes displacements onto her two boyfriends to portray her rather valid split image of the therapist: in the past, he was bright, sexually virile, and aggressive, but unconsciously used the patient to gratify his own pathological sexual and parasitic-symbiotic needs, and then abandoned her on some level such as when he took his vacation (in the first year of this therapy, the therapist had adopted a gestalt approach that included physical contact). The patient's unconscious interpretive comment is that the therapist was exploiting her and was fearful of commitment.

In contrast, the therapist who is now capable of maintaining the frame is seen as caring, concerned, and able to commit himself. In this context, the emergence of an image of the therapist with a large penis that would do damage to the patient can be understood as a reflection of an *unconscious transference-based fantasy* to the effect that appropriate intimacy with the therapist would lead to sexualized physical damage for the patient. Nonetheless, at the very moment that this fantasy is being expressed, the patient describes herself as capable of intimate sexual relations with her boyfriend in a fashion not previously possible for her. This patient had actually entered psychotherapy because she had been unable to have satisfactory sexual relations with a man, nor could she effect a long-term relationship. These difficulties had been modified in important ways in the recent months during which the therapist had begun his rectifying efforts.

There is evidence here that there is a positive introjective identification with the therapist that provides the patient with ego strength and with relationship capacities she had been previously lacking. To this was added some degree of insight, though the therapist had not as yet fully interpreted the patient's unconscious perceptions and fantasies as evoked by his prior deviations and his efforts at rectification. Even though the patient lacked full and definitive cognitive insight, there was evidence of considerable internal structural change and of the emerging resolution of the patient's major characterological difficulties.

It would appear that the derivative expression of this particular unconscious fantasy of damage enabled the patient to increase mastery despite the anxieties involved, largely because of the secure hold by the therapist. Later material linked this unconscious fantasy constellation to early sex play between the patient and her brother, and to primal scene experiences that involved her parents. These genetic elements had not emerged previously, and there was reason to believe that they were repressed in part because the therapist's actual behaviors and interventions in the early part of this treatment were experienced validly as nontransference-based repetitions of the traumatic aspects of these earlier genetic experiences. It was only when the therapist had rectified the frame and was no longer behaving in ways comparable to these early figures that the patient shifted to verbal-affective expressions and derivative communication. This shift itself reflects a greater level of mastery, and permits interpretive responses by the therapist.

The therapist's sound interpretations and efforts to rectify the frame had created a series of intervention contexts that prompted adaptive responses in the patient, including derivative expressions of primarily transference-based fantasy constellations. In the absence of any sign of seductiveness, hostility, or efforts to damage the patient on the part of the therapist, the patient's derivative associations that attribute such qualities to him (through misperceptions or fantasies) can be understood as inappropriate and distorted. They are based on unconscious fantasies that derive from the patient's experiences and fantasies vis-à-vis her brother and father.

Thus this case is an example of classical or genetic transference in which an earlier fantasy-memory-introject constellation involving the patient's brother and father created a fantasy constellation that found expression in response to a constructive intervention context from the therapist. This adaptive reaction is not expressed manifestly through a conscious fantasy or image involving the therapist, but instead found a derivative expression through a displacement onto the patient's boyfriend.

Although documentation is not possible here, other clinical experiences indicate that any interpretation of these fantasies that would restrict itself to the patient's relationship to the boyfriend, without treating the material as derivative communications pertaining to the therapist, would not find Type Two derivative validation even if the links to the patient's brother and father were suggested. The effort would be all too linear: the suggestion would be made that the fact that the boyfriend actually caused the patient to bleed reminded her of hurtful experiences with her brother and father. While there is certainly truth to this formulation, it would serve *functionally* within the psychotherapeutic situation as a derivative lie-barrier system and resistance designed to avoid the implications of this particular association as an encoded communication of a fantasy response to the therapist who has secured the frame and interpreted the patient's efforts to deviate.

The following excerpt summarizes the subsequent hour:

> Patient: I'm proud of myself. The agent who managed the building in which I have my apartment sent me a notice of a rent increase. I checked with the city and found out it isn't due until next year. I stood up to them and made them stick with my lease. I felt enormously excited that I could be so aggressive and take a stand like that; I could never do that in the past. I'm planning to go on a single's cruise while you're on vacation. I had a dream that you were naked and there was some sex going on. There was a party and there were people from my job.

This excerpt presents further evidence of a nontransference-based, positive introjective identification with the therapist who was capable of appropriately maintaining the ground rules (i.e., of

adhering to the therapeutic contract—the lease). With this acknowledged, and her surface functioning clearly sound, the patient then
shifts to the intervention context of the therapist's pending vacation. First, she is preparing to search for a single man, and then she
has had a dream that involves the therapist in some sexual way.
These manifest associations, treated as derivatives pertaining to the
pending vacation (a hurtful part of the established frame, but not a
countertransference-based deviation), suggest strong separation anxieties and a need to find a replacement for the therapist while he is
away (i.e., a need *in the patient* for a pathological symbiosis). There
is evidence too of transference-based sexual fantasies and wishes
toward the therapist that were not more clearly defined in this
particular hour. Later on, these too were connected to the patient's
brother and father.

In light of the intervention context, this material may be
considered as containing some type of derivative transference fantasies related to the therapist, based on the earlier experiences and
fantasies that the patient experienced in her childhood. It is of note
that the manifest dream of the therapist yields little in the way of
derivative meaning; it emerged in a session that made it difficult, if
not impossible, to determine the specific unconscious transference-
fantasy constellation.

In responding to a dream of this kind, it is well to approach the
material by attempting to determine any possible nontransference
aspect before concluding that the dream expresses some type of
transference fantasy. Thus the therapist would here ask himself if he
had exposed himself in any way to the patient and had been
seductive by deviating or by intervening inappropriately. In this
instance, the therapist was able to determine that this particular
dream had qualities of both transference and nontransference, in
that in the prior session, toward the end of the hour, he had made
an intervention regarding the patient's sexual fantasies without
tracing them to the specific intervention context that had evoked
them, and without including a recognition of certain nontransference elements derived mainly from his earlier techniques. This
intervention had been evaluated at the time as somewhat seductive,
and as reflecting unresolved sexual conflicts and anxieties within
the therapist, which prompted him to deny those aspects of the
patient's associations that were still perceptive and nontransference-
based.

It is common to find *transversal* derivative expressions of this kind, containing *both* nontransference and transference elements. With so many possibilities for interpretive, noninterpretive, and framework-management errors, a therapist must be quite clear as to the soundness and other qualities of his or her interventions before concluding that a particular derivative communication is essentially transference-based.

Summary and Conclusions

Transferences arise primarily in response to valid interventions from the therapist. This occurs first, because the therapist is expressing himself or herself in a manner that provides the patient with a secure holding and containing relationship and the ego strength to mobilize expressions of disturbing transference fantasy-memory constellations, and second, because the therapist is *not in actuality* behaving in ways that are comparable to earlier pathogenic figures. Because of this, distortion must be present when the patient experiences the therapist in this way.

Transference expressions are based on *unconscious* fantasy constellations and cannot be identified by a simple consideration of the patient's manifest associations. They are correctly conceptualized only when the therapist's interventions do *not* justify the particular image or reaction being expressed by the patient. This evaluation requires a full study of the direct and unconscious implications of the therapist's most recent interventions.

Transference expressions are *not* to be equated with manifest associations and reactions to the therapist. These responses are actually poor carriers of unconscious fantasy constellations and often serve primarily defensive rather than revealing functions. In a sense, every association from the patient pertains on some level to the therapeutic relationship. The key task for the therapist is to identify the full implications of the activated intervention contexts, and to determine the extent to which the patient's manifest associations and behaviors serve *functionally* as derivative expressions that pertain to valid unconscious perceptions (nontransferences) and how much is based on distortions introduced by the pathological inner fantasy constellations of the patient (transferences).

Pathological unconscious fantasy and perception constellations are at the heart of the patient's psychopathology. These are mobilized as adaptive and maladaptive responses to the therapist's interventions. Their presence therfore provides the therapist with an opportunity to interpret their nature and functions, including the patient's defensive efforts to protect himself or herself from their influence. When the intervention context involves maintaining the ideal therapeutic environment and correct interventions, the patient's surface functioning will improve, while unconscious and derivative functioning will shift toward maladaptive, distorted, and transference-based responses. Since the therapeutic focus is ultimately on the unconscious meanings and functions of the patient's resistances and symptoms, the interpretation of such material is an important factor in insightful cure. Fundamental to these efforts is the therapist's reasonable certainty, based on analysis of the adaptive contexts at hand, that the patient's derivative responses are inappropriate to the realities of the therapeutic interaction. Transference-based fantasies are therefore an important aspect of the derivative complex as stimulated by a particular intervention context and as a means through which the unconscious basis for the patient's Neurosis can be illuminated.

Both transferences and nontransferences contribute to the patient's emotional disturbance. Thus both types of interpretations and related rectifications will lead to symptom relief and constructive characterological change. The goal in therapy is to provide the patient with as few opportunities as possible for nontransference expression, and to maximize his or her transference-based communications. In actual therapeutic experience, under optimal conditions, these emerge for interpretation at selected moments in light of sound intervention contexts. Much of the balance of the therapeutic experience involves the patient's benefit from the therapist's capacity for secure holding and containing, and from interpretive efforts that involve the patient's nontransference-based responses to the therapist's countertransference-based interventions. In this last instance, a hurtful and uninsightful interlude is changed into a constructive and insight-producing experience based on the therapist's interpretive and rectifying efforts. This too is a common and important, even though not ideal, vehicle for insightful cure.

Chapter 29

Noncountertransference

In approaching the therapist's functioning in relationship with the patient, it is essential to adopt an unbiased attitude. Therapists, despite any measure of personal therapy and analysis, and despite the most abundant levels of self-knowledge, will inevitably tend to emphasize their own sound functioning. One is likely to think well of one's interventions in the absence of dramatic evidence to the contrary, and sometimes even in the face of nonvalidated responses and other pressures from the patient—one prefers to see oneself in general as functioning quite well. Of course, the truth of the situation may have an entirely different shading.

As has already been shown, the patient functions and expresses himself or herself quite soundly in many ways, especially on an unconscious level. Similarly, therapists, despite their best intentions, express many significant aspects of their psychopathology (countertransferences) in their work with their patients. However, just as the patient's valid functioning does not mask his or her distortions and transferences, the therapist's potential errors and essentially inappropriate functioning will not in any way disregard his or her many valid efforts. The particular emphasis adopted in this volume is designed to redress a distorted picture, and to stress for the moment those aspects that have been both underplayed and are nonetheless critical to the work carried out by the therapist.

Countertransference has been defined in the narrow sense as any unconsciously founded attitude, feeling, fantasy, intervention, and aspect of the therapist's work with patients that reflects a meaningful and notable measure of psychopathology. Thus noncountertransference alludes to those aspects of the therapist's efforts that have been developed essentially in light of the therapeutic needs of the patient (as confirmed through Type Two derivative validation) and reflect the healthy, relatively conflict-free capabilities of the therapist. These distinctions and determinations rely on a careful subjective analysis of the therapist's interventions before and after they are offered, the pursuit of Type Two derivative validation in response to each period of silence or active intervention of the therapist, and especially on a careful reading of the derivative commentaries contained in the patient's material in response to the therapist's efforts.

There are many aspects of the therapeutic relationship and the conditions of psychotherapy that lend themselves to—and even invite—expressions of countertransference. There are the therapist's isolation with the patient, his or her position as the expert, the ground rules of therapy, and the nature of the patient's associations—all of which have some potential for promoting regressive, and therefore pathological, responses in the therapist. Other pressures include the pathological component, small or large, that has motivated the therapist in choosing psychotherapy for his or her profession. Then too there is the unconscious need within the patient—again, however large or small—to have the therapist intervene inappropriately rather than validly. Thus many pressures on all sides can easily move the therapist toward error.

A therapist must know himself or herself quite well, undoubtedly in part by having gone through a sound therapeutic experience. The therapist must continually engage in self-analytic efforts, both of an immediate nature and through more lasting, quiet, ongoing endeavors. Attitudes, feelings, and interventions with a patient must always be anticipated and evaluated retrospectively, and the therapist must strive to understand the unconscious communications and expressions that they contain.

The therapist's basic attitude toward his or her work requires a delicate balance. It includes the acceptance of the inevitability of some measure of psychopathology *(inevitable countertransference)* in every intervention, an inescapable minimum that must be accepted and yet fought against at every turn. The realization that no one ever fully resolves the totality of his or her Neurosis cannot be used as license for error, and yet must be accepted as a perspective to modify the inevitable guilt that a therapist experiences on discovering mistakes and the underlying fantasy constellations on which they are based.

The therapist therefore strives to function as effectively as possible within the therapeutic interaction, is prepared for the occasional minor error, the hopefully rare major blunder (expressions of *preponderant countertransference*), and even for the occasional situation where major extended difficulties are experienced with a particular patient. There must be a commitment to self-analytic efforts to rectify and understand the therapist's problems, and to neither exploit their existence nor to deny their effects. The inevitable frustration of therapeutic work leads to situations in which even the therapist's best efforts can evoke paradoxical disturbances in patients (in addition to validating responses), so that the therapist is faced with efforts to undermine even the most effective of his or her endeavors. A therapist maintains his or her therapeutic commitment to the patient in the face of all pressures, knowing full well that at times this is enormously difficult to achieve.

Some Principal Noncountertransference-based Functions

The therapist's noncountertransference-based functioning, as noted above, includes all aspects of the relationship and work with the patient that are in service of the therapeutic needs of the latter and do not reflect more than the inevitable minimum of pathological disturbance. *Noncountertransference silences* and *interventions* are on a continuum with those that are predominately countertransference-based. This implies the therapist's functioning is never entirely free of psychopathology, and yet permits the recognition of a wide range of reactions that are essentially nonpathological. These are based on empirically derived, validated, sound technical principles, carried out in keeping with a strong sensitivity for the particular Neurosis and therapeutic needs of a given patient, and expressed in terms of the healthy individuality of each therapist.

The therapist's sound functioning tends to flow relatively quietly and smoothly, calling for little in the way of extended reflection and self-analysis. Instead, a sensitivity to indications of error and the influence of countertransference are required. Noncountertransference includes:

1. The capacity for neutrality and for free-floating cognitive

attention and listening. An ability to experience role and image evocations subjectively and to process them toward interpretation.

2. A basic capacity to secure the therapeutic environment and relationship properly, to establish the ground rules and boundaries, and to maintain them.

3. A sound capacity for securely and appropriately holding the patient, and for containing and processing his or her projective identifications.

4. An ability to take in all incoming information and interactional pressures without bias or prejudice.

5. An ability to formulate, integrate, and comprehend the totality of the communications from the patient.

6. An ability to organize and synthesize all incoming information into a silent intervention, and further, to have a sound sensitivity as to whether it is possible to offer the particular intervention to the patient. Involved here too is a capacity to appreciate moments during which the patient has destroyed meaningful expression and relatedness.

7. A capacity to intervene with sensitivity and tact, and at the proper moment (timing). This includes an ability to express understanding and framework-management efforts to the patient in a manner that is clear, concise as possible, appropriately toned with affect, and the best response to the patient's expressed therapeutic needs. These are the capacities relevant to the therapist's basic functioning in terms of securing the therapeutic situation, and then listening to, formulating the material from, and intervening to, the patient. There are many background attributes that serve the therapist in these endeavors.

8. A capacity to renounce pathological satisfactions and to manage pathological superego pressures. An ability also to forgo pathological defensiveness.

9. An ability to engage in trial identifications with the patient in order to understand the patient's inner mental world and those to whom the patient is related. These identifications may involve the patient, aspects of the patient's psychic functioning, and the others to whom the patient relates (objects).

10. A capacity for empathy, which must operate first on a manifest level, so that the therapist experiences along with the patient aspects of his or her manifest struggles. Empathy must also operate on a derivative level and involve unconscious communica-

tion. Here the therapist must temporarily share and immediately experience the patient's unconscious fantasy constellations, unconscious perceptions, and unconscious affects and conflicts. Most present-day studies of empathy have been naive, surface-oriented, and lacking in validating methodology. All seemingly empathic experiences should be silently validated and eventually translated into an understanding of the patient, imparted by means of an intervention where possible, and then validated through Type Two derivative confirmation in the patient's subsequent responses.

11. Sound intuition, a form of immediate knowing. Its use must also be subjected to validation, and especially to silent validation before it is used in intervening to the patient.

12. A strong frustration tolerance, a sound sense of patience, and an ability to tolerate separateness from (and yet appropriate intimacy with) the patient—the resolution of pathological symbiotic needs. The therapist must be capable of a relatively mature object relationship with the patient, since this serves as a basic backdrop for interpretive and framework-management efforts.

13. The ability to listen openly, without organization, impressionistically, and with fluidity. This must be accompanied by a capacity to shift from time to time to more discrete functioning, to efforts to generate definitive formulations, and the development of specific understanding and synthesis.

14. A capacity to forgo pathological satisfactions in the service of the small but significant measure of gratification that derives from helping a patient to resolve his or her Neurosis based on sound therapeutic work. This implies an ability to sacrifice and control many otherwise natural tendencies, needs, and forms of gratification, since they run contrary to the therapeutic needs of the patient. It requires an ability as well to conceptualize and carry out technical measures that offer the patient the best means of resolving his or her Neurosis at the least possible detrimental cost—i.e., a capacity to carry out truth rather than lie therapy. Involved here, then, is a capacity to tolerate the truth, conscious and unconscious, as it pertains to the ongoing therapeutic interaction, and as it includes aspects of disturbance within both the patient and the therapist.

15. Positive attributes and capabilities funnelled into the adoption of a basically concerned attitude toward the patient, and a sound holding-framework-management position that is accom-

panied by interpretive responses as called for by the material from the patient. The therapist's ability to maintain silence when indicated, to manage the framework, and to interpret when necessary forms the basis for ego-enhancing positive introjective identifications within the patient and cognitive insight with adaptive structural change.

These constructive capabilities are not simply tools utilized by the therapist, but pervade the entire relationship with the patient in ways that greatly influence the nature of the therapeutic interaction and the therapeutic experience of the patient—as well as of the therapist. In general, these positive consequences are experienced and integrated by the patient, much of it quite unconsciously, although occasionally through conscious realizations; they require no further or specific intervention by the therapist. It is only when a sound intervention evokes a pathological and transference-based response from the patient that further framework management and interpretive interventions by the therapist will prove necessary. It is therefore on many levels that the therapist's noncountertransference functioning has its salutory effects, primarily for the patient, although secondarily for the therapist as well.

The requirements are so unusual and demanding, so distinctive and difficult to achieve, that no therapist can expect to satisfy them in full with all patients at all times. There is no such person as a natural-born therapist, and the achievement of truly sound functioning as a therapist is a hard-won goal that runs counter to many natural tendencies. It is therefore essential to be aware of the extraordinary demands and requirements, and to consistently strive to meet them to the greatest extent feasible. Doing so provides the therapist with a unique sense of satisfaction that has qualities of gratification seldom available in any other endeavor.

No assumption is made as to the nature, quality, and level of the therapist's functioning. The patient's responses to each and every silence and intervention of the therapist are examined for both validation and commentary on the conscious and unconscious nature of the therapist's effort. It is only in the presence of derivative indications of positive introjective identifications with the therapist, and of Type Two derivative cognitive validation, that a therapist has a basis for feeling comfortable with the nature of his or her therapeutic work.

If the therapist is functioning smoothly, the patient's material should also represent a sound mode of relatedness and healthy symbiosis, as well as an insightful and truthful mode of cure. Communicative relationships should be relatively open, and the dynamics and genetics of the patient's material should center primarily on transference expressions and the psychopathology of the patient.

In the presence of a constellation of this kind, difficult to achieve and to maintain, the therapist may feel satisfied that he or she is functioning mainly in terms of noncountertransference efforts. Even then, it is essential to maintain a sense of vigilance for possible moments of regression and error, and to rectify and analyze all such interludes with the patient, based on manifest and derivative material. Cycles of smooth functioning, followed by brief periods of error and disturbance, are inevitable in psychotherapy. The therapist attempts always to master his or her countertransferences, thereby providing the patient with an important hold and introject. Still, at the moment of inevitable error, the ability to recognize the mistake and deal with it properly will serve both the patient and therapist quite well. In all, noncountertransference should not be assumed, but should be sought after and eventually rather automatically maintained, though always with a preparedness to find lapses.

Chapter 30

Countertransference

Countertransference is defined (narrowly) as those responses and tendencies within the therapist that are based on, and an expression of, the therapist's own pathological unconscious fantasy and perception constellations (psychopathology). There are many classifications of countertransference, but this volume considers only (1) those that are acute and have the potential for ready detection, and (2) those that are chronic, tend to be characterological, and prove difficult to identify. Since countertransference is founded upon *unconscious* constellations, self-analytic efforts are necessary to identify its manifestations in the therapist's silences (i.e., those that are inappropriate), basic attitudes, subjective responses, and interventions to the patient. An additional and critical effort is required first, to correct (rectify) the immediate expression of countertransference, and second, to engage in sufficient self-analysis so that the underlying countertransference fantasy-perception constellation can be resolved, as a way of forestalling further, however different, expressions of the underlying constellation.

The Detection of Countertransferences

Several means exist through which expressions of countertransference can be identified by the therapist. Since it is the therapist who ultimately must carry out this process and bring such realizations into conscious awareness, however, all of these measures are themselves open to countertransference-based influence, which can lead to a failure to recognize a particular sign of countertransference or to appreciate its implications and basis.

Any sign of subjective disturbance, of idiosyncratic reaction, of unusual response, and of any sense of anything different in the therapist's general and specific approach to, work with, and relationship with, a patient must be examined. Without cataloging the enormous range of possibilities, this implies that any sense of undue anxiety, hostility, sexuality, guilt, or other disturbance in the therapist's feelings toward the patient suggests a need to search for countertransference-based influences. It must be recognized, however, that minimal amounts of these affects and reactions may reflect role- and image-evocations by the patient, and if confined to small quantities (i.e., to signal experiences) need not reflect significant psychopathology within the therapist. Only a full exploration will reveal whether these controlled responses are essentially inappropriate, while more intense expressions along these lines are virtually always countertransference-based (no matter how provocative the patient).

In addition, any sense of conflict, any conscious fantasy about a patient, any dream about a patient (recognized manifestly or involving its latent content), any tendency to speak out or act inappropriately, and any other deviant impulse, feeling, or behavior, calls for an examination for countertransference-based factors.

All interventions—silence, verbal-interpretive and noninterpretive, and framework management—that do not obtain Type Two derivative validation call for an exploration for countertransference-based elements. Here the identification of the expressions of the therapist's Neurosis requires a sound grasp and ability to utilize the listening process, and a basic comprehension of sound therapeutic technique. In principle, all technical errors derive in part from countertransferences, though of course, other factors may also exist, such as lack of knowledge, poor training, and the like. Certainly, any knowing modification of sound technique calls for an examination of possible countertransferences. Beyond these immediately recognized errors, the absence of indirect validation in response to any intervention calls for such an exploration.

In addition, manifest and derivative communications from the patient that directly suggest or imply the presence of countertransferences must be examined. There are two types of situations in which a patient will sometimes manifestly suggest to the therapist that he or she is intervening incorrectly, or that the therapist has some type of Neurotic problem. In the first, the therapist's disturbance is blatant and the error is extreme. Some patients—but by no means all or even a majority—are capable under these circumstances of consciously and directly pointing out to the therapist the presence of some notable difficulty. More problematic are those patients who, even when faced with blatant, countertransference-based expressions, will not at all refer to them in any direct fashion. Some patients perceive these difficulties but suppress any reference to them, while others repress and deny their perceptions so that they themselves are quite unaware of these blatant disturbances.

Quite rarely, an especially sensitive patient may detect a less blatant countertransference-based expression and point it out directly to the therapist. However, this type of comment is made under two conditions: when the therapist is actually utilizing sound techniques, or when the countertransference-based errors are present though relatively minor. Often, a patient suggests manifestly that the therapist is intervening erroneously, although, there is no essential support for this evaluation in the patient's derivative associations and in the therapist's own careful subjective evaluation. These assessments indicate that the patient is in manifest error. Thus it is difficult to rely on a patient's *conscious* detection of an error or other kind of disturbances in the therapist. The patient's conscious judgment is often quite unreliable, and a final decision in respect to the patient's perceptiveness must be made through an evaluation of his or her derivative communications in light of activated intervention contexts, and in the therapist's own appraisal of the implications of the interventions.

Empirically, it appears that patients only rarely correctly identify and allude to a technical error by, or inappropriate attitude in, the therapist. Far more often, the patient's direct proposal that the therapist has been mistaken serves *functionally* as a *derivative communication* that conveys an entirely different meaning. At times, the intervention that the patient believes to have been in error has obtained indirect (unconscious) Type Two derivative validation and appears to be quite sound. Here the patient sometimes points to one error as a means of conveying the expression of a different error through derivatives. At other times, these efforts are transference-based and involve envious attempts to demean the therapist and his or her functioning. They may therefore be highly defensive communications and designed as derivative forms of protection. On the other hand, repeated complaints against the therapist, when unfounded in reality and when relatively devoid of derivative implications, often express powerful pathological projective identifications into the therapist and serve as strong lie-barrier systems in patients communicating with Type B or B-C modes of communication. Because of the extent to which manifest complaints about one aspect of treatment serve in a derivative manner to represent other technical errors by the therapist, criticisms and attacks of this kind should always prompt a search within the therapist for unrecognized expressions of countertransference.

The suggestion that the therapist has made an error is sometimes an aspect of an effort by the patient to obtain pathological gratification and relatedness, and a sector of misalliance, in response to an activated intervention context that threatens the patient in terms of either fantasy or perception constellations. Many such efforts are designed to obtain framework-deviation cures through direct and self-revealing responses from the therapist. Such responses also serve to create either a pathological symbiotic or parasitic mode of relatedness between the patient and therapist. Often, the pathological mode of relatedness and sector of misalliance will be used to create a Type C barrier designed to seal off other, more chaotic aspects of the therapeutic interaction and intrapsychic disturbances within the patient.

Thus, while the patient's conscious efforts to call the therapist's attention to his or her errors and expressions of countertransference have uncertain value, all such suggestions must be taken seriously, and must prompt the search for Neurotic manifestation from the therapist. At the same time, the therapist must carefully evaluate the unconscious nature and function of these manifest communications, and should not fail to understand their additional derivative implications.

There is, however, another level on which the patient monitors and points to expressions of the therapist's Neurosis: the patient's *unconscious* perceptiveness—the capacity to introject and sample the therapist's psychopathology (as well as the therapist's sound functioning), and to point to the vast majority of the therapist's countertransference-based efforts through encoded and derivative communication. Because of this, the therapist should continuously monitor the patient's associations for unconscious perceptions and introjects of this kind. Primary consideration should be afforded to all allusions to difficulties of any type, whether referring to the patient or to outside figures to whom the patient relates, as possible representations of the therapist's own problems. In addition, the therapist should evaluate the *commentary* responses of his or her patients to each intervention, including periods of silence, for ways in which the patient has unconsciously detected Neurotic manifestations and shows an appreciation, to whatever limited degree, of their implications and sources. In this way, the patient can serve a *secondary* role through the *inevitability* of his or her curative communications, as a resource through which the therapist can monitor and detect expressions of his or her own psychopathology. In this effort, the patient's commentary associations are used to direct the therapist back to recent interventions and to a reappraisal of their manifest and latent implications.

CLINICAL EXAMPLES

A young woman patient is in treatment with a male therapist for depression and problems in establishing a lasting relationship with a man. In the session that took place just two weeks before the therapist's vacation, the therapist had interpreted some material from his patient in terms of sexual fantasies and anxieties that had arisen when he had rectified the framework of her therapy and had not, as in the past, changed an hour at her request. Subsequently, the therapist had missed the representations of the intervention context of his pending vacation, which was arousing in the patient sexualized longings for closeness and for merger (pathological symbiosis) with him. He had failed to recognize that these unconscious transference fantasy-wish constellations had been expressed (acted out) when the patient had become involved sexually with a young man whom she did not know very well. In addition, the therapist's usual manner of intervening was in itself somewhat seductive, and his style reflected a remaining fragment of characterological countertransference that had found far more blatant forms of expression earlier in the therapy. The excerpt presented here is from the next session.

> Patient: I dreamt my mother was going on vacation. She asked me if she should wear a miniskirt. Both my mother and I are going on vacation, though separately. In the dream, she was asking my advice. She and her miniskirt don't go together.

In light of the adaptive contexts already identified (the therapist's seductive style, the pending vacation, and the missed intervention regarding the patient's erotic transference and nontransference constellations), this manifest dream seems to have been prompted by the day residues of the therapist's efforts in the prior hour. Thus the dream seems to reflect an unconscious perception of the therapist's countertransferences in terms of his unresolved exhibitionistic and seductive pathological needs. It is the patient's derivative suggestion—i.e., unconscious interpretation—that the therapist is having difficulty in these areas because of his own unresolved separation anxieties (represented here in terms of the mother's vacation). On this level, the patient's use of her mother to represent the therapist and his problems suggests the possibility that the patient is offering an interpretation to the therapist that these conflicts arise genetically from unresolved aspects of his relationship with his mother. Simultaneously, the allusion to the patient's mother indicates that the patient is experiencing a nontransference reaction to the therapist in terms of ways in which he has actually expressed himself in a manner that reflected sexual difficulties comparable to those the patient experienced in her mother. Although the patient's own erotic transferences and conflicts must also be condensed into this material, they would not be accessible for formulation and interpretation until the therapist rectified his own erotic countertransference and its expression.

In addition, the countertransference-based missed interventions are means by which the therapist attempts to become the functional patient and stresses his own therapeutic needs (cf. the allusion to the patient's mother asking the advice of her daughter). Under such conditions, the designated patient will often shift to an unconscious role in which he or she functions as therapist to the patient, an effort in evidence in this material—much of it designed to alert the therapist to his own unconscious sexual difficulties and his separation anxieties.

The final derivative element in this excerpt involves both an unconscious perception of the therapist and the offer of a model of rectification. In the adaptation-evoking context of the therapist's efforts to secure the frame, combined with his interpretive failures, the patient has indicated that these contradictory therapeutic efforts and blind spots do not go together. The derivatives suggest to the therapist that he should better manage his pathological exhibitionistic needs and find some other means of repairing and dealing with his separation anxieties.

Some of these derivative communications arise because the therapist had also actively intervened erroneously in the prior session regarding purported sexual conflicts within the patient. In principle, the therapist should monitor all allusions to therapeutic need, error, inappropriate behavior, and other images of this kind for possible implications from the patient that a technical error has been made. The unwitting therapist who has not, through retrospective analysis, recognized the expressions of countertransference in his or her recent silences and interventions should attend to the patient's associations in a manner that would foster a search for such mistakes.

Thus, in this particular clinical situation, upon hearing this dream, the therapist could have asked himself if he had in any way been seductive or exhibitionistic with the patient. He could have wondered too if he was experiencing undue separation anxieties and in some unconscious manner seeking help from the patient (i.e., placing her in the role of the functional therapist). Ultimately, the recognition of countertransferences relies on the dual resources of the patient's derivative communications and the therapist's own efforts at self-analysis. The therapist must detect the conscious and unconscious implications of his or her own interventions and where they are in error, and trace out the underlying roots to the point of insightful modification and resolution.

Another clinical example concerns a woman patient and a woman therapist. The latter had become engaged in direct suggestions and personal revelations to the patient. In the hour in which these had been offered, the patient responded with many unconscious perceptions related to the incorporation of the therapist's countertransferences. Seductive and fusion elements were strongly reflected in the intervention, in which the therapist had suggested that the patient should seek out a type of massage for her acute back pain, as she herself had done. The excerpt presented here is from the next session.

Patient: I'm obsessed now with Dr. Jones [*an obstetrician who was in attendance at a time when the patient had a miscarriage*]. He had me on the wrong medication. I would like to sue him. He's a terrible doctor. I want the money as reparation for the dead baby. He didn't take my cramps and spotting seriously. It's because of him I've suffered so much emotionally. In his guilt, he failed to send my new doctor his report. He'd be hard to reach, and would then try to do something nice to make up for it. I feel badly that I can't have a baby. I don't trust doctors; they make terrible mistakes.

When themes of poor medical, maternal, and other types of care are in evidence in a patient's manifest associations, they must first lead to a consideration that they are derivatively conveying valid unconscious perceptions of poor therapeutic (countertransference-based) practices by the therapist. However, it is insufficient to simply take such material as a general sign that something is amiss. Instead, the therapist must return to his or her prior interventions, evaluate their full implications, and carefully tease out all possible specific derivative implications in the patient's associations.

In this excerpt, the patient is indicating that noninterpretive interventions of the type made by this therapist in the previous hour create a form of negligent treatment that leads to the destruction (parasitism) of the patient and therapy. They are efforts that do not recognize and properly deal with the patient's symptoms, and fail to take seriously the patient's therapeutic needs. It is a type of mistreatment that should evoke guilt in the therapist and reflects a poor holding capacity. It renders the therapist untrustworthy because of her errors.

These are relatively straightforward derivative translations arrived at by removing the defensive displacement from the therapist onto the patient's former obstetrician. On another level, associations of this kind must always be considered in terms of both unconscious interpretations by the patient to the therapist, and representations of the therapist's needs as projected and projectively identified into the patient. In this respect, this material suggests that the patient is indicating on a derivative level that the suggestion regarding the massage was offered by the therapist in an attempt to provide the patient with reparation for the hurt of her recent vacation and for her destructive therapeutic practices—this, an inappropriate and countertransference-based form of repair. A more appropriate approach would be to secure the therapeutic environment and to respond interpretively to the patient's activated unconscious perceptions and fantasies.

The patient suggests also that the noninterpretive intervention is a product of the therapist's guilt for her previous errors. According to the patient, there is some type of nontherapeutic maternal need that leads the therapist to infantilize the patient and to make her into her own infant.

As can be seen, in principle, the therapist extracts all of the dynamic implications of a sequence of associations of this kind, and attempts to apply them in light of the unconscious implications of recent interventions. Quite naturally, the patient as a rule has only a limited range of communications from the therapist with which to make his or her unconscious assessments and interpretations. These are therefore usually restricted to general themes, though they often provide the therapist with important points of departure for his or her own self-analytic work. In the presence of an acute countertransference problem, this can be carried out privately in very brief spurts during a given session, although much of it must be done during moments of solitude in order not to interfere with the ongoing therapeutic work.

Throughout this volume, there are many illustrations of errors in technique. These reveal the patient's rather consistent unconscious perceptions of the therapist's countertransferences, and the presence of unconscious therapeutic efforts on the patient's part as well. While the patient must not be exploited for the therapist's own therapeutic needs, the therapist should nonetheless silently and implicitly accept these endeavors when he or she has placed some of his or her own pathology into the bipersonal field and into the patient. When it is possible for the therapist to understand his or her countertransferences, and to modify their direct manifestations and their underlying basis, the patient subsequently experiences a significant implicit change in the therapist. This results in an important unconscious therapeutic experience of considerable gratification, one that greatly enhances the patient's ego capacities and mobilizes the patient's resources toward further potential insight.

In this way, these unfortunately traumatic interludes can be turned to the gain of both patient and therapist, even though the pathology of the therapist in principle should not be the central basis of the therapeutic work. Here one is making the best use of a momentarily destructive situation. Although this is not the preferred route for insight, eventual positive introjective identifications (here, preceded by a destructive introject), and constructive structural change, it is far better to interpret and rectify experiences of this kind toward such gains than to allow them to go unrecognized and unmodified. It is under such uncorrected conditions that one may observe a stalemated psychotherapy, a seemingly inexplicable regression in a patient, or a chaotic therapeutic situation. All such interludes call for careful self-examination and a search for countertransference-based determinants.

The Search for the Unconscious Countertransference Constellation

At times the disturbance within the therapist affects his or her entire practice and has broader and more fundamental consequences. Many therapists soon become familiar with signs of the countertransferences that they have not been able to fully master. All therapists should remain sensitive to the slightest nuance that suggests internal disturbance, and should be prepared at the very least to check out the possibility of countertransference in the presence of any difficulty with a patient or within themselves.

It is, of course, quite another matter to develop the means of arriving at the unconscious fantasy constellations that are the source of the countertransference difficulties. Despite the obvious problems, certain principles prove helpful even for therapists who have had no experience with personal therapy.

In evaluating each and every extended silence or active intervention, the therapist should take care to identify the presence of at least a minimal sector of error. In this way, the therapist will be in touch with the *inevitable countertransference* that will influence all of his or her work. In addition, this search will make it possible to identify more blatant *preponderant countertransference-based expressions,* which have a significant impact upon the patient.

A major clue as to the unconscious basis for a countertransference-based intervention lies in the material from the patient that prompted the therapist's comment. Such material is, of course, the adaptive context for the therapist's response. Each intervention is a special form of adaptational reaction to the patient's material, an effort designed with the therapeutic needs of the patient in mind.

However, whenever this effort goes astray, it reflects the therapeutic and maladaptive needs, and pathological means of coping, of the therapist. These can therefore be best understood in light of the adaption-evoking context that contributed to the error. Countertransference-based expressions are a result of the interaction between adaptation-evoking contexts and tendencies within the therapist. In searching for these critical adaptive contexts, the therapist should look first to the material that immediately preceded a countertransference-based intervention (itself identified through the lack of Type Two derivative validation and by the presence of some sign of error or disturbance). The therapist should then formulate the unconscious implications of this material, and attempt to understand the meanings and functions of the idiosyncratic aspects of his or her intervention, and especially its role as a *derivative* response to the manifest and latent contents of the patient's material.

Additional and sometimes critical adaptive contexts for the therapist's error reside in the earlier associations of the patient, in previous sessions with the patient, in the meanings a particular patient has in general for the therapist, in interactions with other patients that lead to reactions displaced onto the patient at hand, and in the therapist's outside life and relationships, which may lead to similar displacements. Each of these factors may contribute to a countertransference-based intervention, although usually the material that immediately precedes such an intervention proves most crucial. A highly sensitive and self-perceptive therapist can often quickly identify the critical adaptive contexts for the erroneous aspects of his or her intervention and subject the responses to a form of immediate self-analysis. However, given the complexities of the situation, and the likely presence of continuing countertransference difficulties, a more extended type of self-exploration may well prove necessary.

By and large, some type of private free associating is required to arrive at validated self-insights through self-analysis. Direct inferences, especially if they neglect the activated adaptive contexts for the therapist, prove to yield either pseudo or false insights (i.e., defensive and derivative or nonderivative lie-barrier systems) or not to lead to any type of understanding at all. It is therefore essential for the therapist to engage internally in a form of free association that permits loose and derivative communication, intermixed with moments of integration and synthesis. This is, of course, possible during a session with a patient only to a limited extent. In the presence of any notable countertransference-based interlude, the situation requires that the solitary period be either in the therapist's office or at home, during which an extended period of self-analysis is possible. Often, the time before falling asleep proves to be propitious for such efforts.

The basic method of self-analysis begins with unencumbered free association. After a while, some effort may be made to identify and understand the implications of what appears to be the main adaptation-evoking context for the therapist's difficulty. The erroneous intervention itself must be examined for its manifest and especially latent contents and functions, as this constitutes the pathological unconscious communications made by the therapist to the patient. In addition to alerting the therapist to the nature of the intervention context to which the patient is reacting, this analysis enables the therapist to understand the nature of the communicated psychopathology that he or she has expressed to the patient—and to himself or herself.

Dreams often prove useful as starting points for free association, as do intrusive fantasies, selected memories, vivid incidents, and other more dramatic kinds of associations. At some point, the free flow is curtailed and an effort is made to integrate and comprehend. The therapist begins with his or her understanding of the adaptation-evoking context from the patient and others, and next organizes the derivative implications of his or her own free associations in light of those contexts. To this the therapist adds his or her comprehension of the unconscious communications contained in the erroneous intervention, and attempts to arrive at an integrated formulation of the dynamics involved. The associations should, from time to time, touch upon pertinent genetic links and permit in-depth understanding, and self-interpretation—with subsequent unanticipated validation.

The yield from these efforts reveals the true meaning of a countertransference, illuminating the influence of the therapist's unconscious fantasy constellations on his or her relationship and work with the patient. Countertransference implies that the patient is treated, either through displacement or interactional projections, in an inappropriate fashion that is in keeping with the unconscious constellation within the therapist, rather than in terms of the patient's communications and therapeutic needs. Thus the patient is responded to maladaptively as a figure from the past, and in terms of some internal representation of that figure within the mental world of the therapist rather than in terms of the actualities of the patient, the therapeutic situation and task, and the nature of the patient's communications. Through self-analysis, the therapist traces the unconscious roots of his or her maladaptive responses, and is thereby able to rectify these effects, promote internal structural change, and bring the countertransference constellations under greater mastery through conscious insight. Perhaps a positive introjective identification takes place within the therapist in terms of an incorporation of his or her own effective functioning.

On an object relationship level, countertransference implies a need for *pathological symbiosis, autism, or parasitism* in the therapist's relationship with the patient. The patient is used to alleviate the therapist's separation anxieties and fears of individuation, and as an object for fusion and merger or for exploitation. Much of this is accomplished through alterations in the ground rules and boundaries of the therapeutic relationship, measures that uniformly provide pathological symbiotic or parasitic gratification for both patient and therapist. Similarly, all noninterpretive interventions have invasive and pathological symbiotic qualities that express the therapist's countertransferences in this regard.

Efforts at self-analysis designed to resolve the inappropriate use of the patient by the therapist as a pathological symbiotic or parasitic partner must accomplish more than identifying the nature and level of the maturational object relationship effected through the therapist's erroneous interventions. They must lead to the specific unconscious fantasy, memory, perception, and introject constellations that account for the therapist's vulnerabilities, and to a form of self-analysis and renunciation that gives the therapist a genuine capacity for individuation and a clear tolerance for relative separateness from the patient. These efforts must be continued until the therapist has a strong sense of having resolved the underlying problem and has clear evidence that it is no longer significantly influencing his or her therapeutic work. At times, a single measure will suffice, while in other more difficult situations, a series of measures will be necessary.

Care must be taken not to become preoccupied with self-analytic efforts of this kind, since this will eventually prove detrimental to the therapeutic experience for the patient. The therapist's thinking must be concentrated on the ongoing material from that source. If a brief period of self-analysis does not lead to the understanding and apparent resolution of a countertransference difficulty, further efforts should be postponed until a quiet moment. In the meantime, the therapist should be alert to the nature of his or her error and its basis to the greatest extent possible for the moment, and should take special care to attempt to avoid its undue further influence on his or her further feelings and interventions.

Additional private efforts at self-analysis involve difficult and complicated processes, vulnerable to unconscious and conscious resistances. Such work requires considerable patience and sensitivity from the therapist. However, adherence to basic principles of listening and formulating can render these efforts highly insightful and constructive. It is important to avoid such pitfalls as intellectualizations, focus on manifest contents, repeated Type One derivative formulations, direct reading of inferences of associations, and other highly resistant self-interpretive efforts. The goal must be to permit free association and derivative communication, with only occasional efforts at formulation and synthesis.

In the presence of continued countertransferences, when faced with an inability to resolve the underlying difficulties and their manifestations in therapeutic work, the therapist must consider the initiation of psychotherapy or psychoanalysis, or a return for a hopefully brief period of treatment. Because of the many traumatic violations of the framework that are involved in referring a patient to a consultant, this particular measure is essentially contraindicated in the course of therapy. Whenever there is a stalemate that remains fixed and unresolvable, work toward termination is to be considered. Referral too is inadvisable, since the second therapist would be linked to the first. When all else fails, it is best to permit the patient to find his or her own therapist if this proves necessary after termination.

The best approach involves a period of supervision, during which a sensitive supervisor may well be able to help the therapist recognize more clearly the manifestations of his or her countertransference and better understand the unconscious implications of the patient's derivative communications in response to the therapist's difficulty. On this basis, the supervisor could then offer formulations regarding the therapist's countertransferences, taking care to do so primarily in terms of the *patient's* unconscious perceptions and therapeutic efforts. If required, available, and unmistakable, the supervisor could also quite tactfully add some of his or her own impressions.

Efforts of this kind should facilitate the therapist's attempts at self-analysis. If this proves to be the case, the therapist will be able to insightfully resolve the countertransference problem. If he or she continues to be unable to do so, serious consideration should be given to entering treatment

Characterological Countertransference

Acute countertransference manifestations are recognizable by a therapist who constantly monitors his or her therapeutic work for such difficulties. However, the problem is somewhat different for chronic countertransferences, those which tend to be characterological and embedded within the therapist's basic personality, and especially those that have implicit or explicit support within the profession (areas of shared countertransference). Access to these difficulties may develop when a therapist notices unconscious perceptions of some type of disturbance in the derivative implications of the associations from a number of different patients. Detection may also arise when a therapist begins to examine episodes of regression or stalemate with his or her patients for indications of some type of previously unrecognized personal problem. When acute countertransference-based manifestations do not emerge, the search can then concentrate on more characterological and unnoticed forms of difficulty.

The continuous monitoring of the patient's material for valid unconscious perceptions of disturbances in the therapist (as well as positive attributes) is basic to the pursuit of any type of countertransference, an approach that entails the acceptance of any negative image as likely to be valid until proven in error (i.e., a missed perception). All too often, self-critical comments by the patient, and comments regarding those to whom he or she relates outside of therapy, are taken at face value, or understood solely in terms of purported intrapsychic dynamics within the patient. The interactional approach requires that this material be treated first as potentially valid unconscious perceptions, and only second as possible reflections of unconscious fantasies and distortions pertaining to the ongoing therapeutic relationship.

Every instance of nonvalidation, whether of the therapist's silences and basic attitudes, or of active interventions, should prompt a search for both the intellectual-cognitive sources of the mistake and relevant countertransference factors. These may be highly personal or shared within the field, but the therapist who is open to this type of exploration in the absence of Type Two derivative confirmation of his or her efforts will discover a great deal about his or her own psychopathology and the blind spots of the field—as well as about his or her assets (i.e., the constructive aspects of his or her technique and functioning as reflected in positive Type Two derivative validation).

CLINICAL EXAMPLES

Many of the clinical examples already presented reflect areas of omission and commission that derive in part from individual and shared countertransferences. To add to this material, the case of a young married woman in treatment for a multiplicity of symptoms is presented. Her symptoms indicated an ambulatory schizophrenic illness. At the time of the session excerpted here, the therapist was having difficulty in interpreting her reactions to his pending vacation.

> Patient: I tried to be truthful with my husband, but he forces me to do all the work and to make all the decisions. I keep after him though. He's had his problems. He was left alone a lot as a child, and then his father divorced his mother, leaving him with her. It's left scars. My father owes me money and hasn't paid me, while my mother pretends she doesn't want to talk to me. I've decided to stop my dance classes, and feel afraid you'll get angry with me because I have no plan to discuss it with the instructor first. I just want to leave. I had to do all of the work there too. I've been feeling pretty good lately. My infant son smiles at me, but not at strangers. I don't want to revert to the old business of walking out on things I start. Actually, I've gotten all I can out of the dance class, and it's time to move on.
>
> Therapist: You've been talking about some of your husband's difficulties, and having to confront him. You're speaking too

of needing less and of leaving your dance class, feeling you've gotten all you can get. Your son doesn't smile at others, and you're concerned that I will be angry about your leaving the dance class.

Patient: I've been angry with my husband because he tried to discipline me as if I were a little girl. He's close-minded when I point out his problems to him. My son has a diaper rash, and my husband won't let me get proper treatment for him. I plan to think more about whether I will be leaving the dance class or not.

In principle, the therapist should have monitored this material in terms of possible valid unconscious perceptions of himself, and wondered whether in some way he had been failing to adequately carry out his role and functions as a therapist vis-à-vis this patient. With the references to divorce and being left alone, he might have wondered if his silence in the previous hour had constituted a missed intervention and an autistic abandonment of the patient. He might also have cast about for other possible separation-related adaptive contexts, and then recognized that, first, the patient was working over his vacation, which lay just one week ahead, and second, that she might also be working over possible thoughts of termination (there had been considerable constructive therapeutic work in recent months). The derivatives regarding the difficulties of the patient's husband in dealing with abandonment could also have readily been monitored as an indication that there was some possibility that the therapist was being perceived—again, one considers first the likelihood of accuracy—as having unresolved separation problems.

Much of the patient's material in this session is a response to the prior hour in which the therapist had, based on supervisory evaluation, apparently missed an important interpretation regarding the patient's reactions to his vacation, and had failed to detect derivatives that pertained to the patient's thoughts of eventual termination. (In such instances, the adaptive context is the expectation that the therapist will, if indeed appropriate, agree to termination.) The patient's initial associations in this hour propose through derivatives that the therapist had within him significant unresolved separation anxieties based on earlier separation traumas (a perception that the therapist amply confirmed when this was identified for him in supervision). Further, as the patient indicates, in situations where the therapist's countertransferences are having a significant influence on the therapeutic relationship and interaction, he becomes the functional patient. When he shows little or no capacity to modify the countertransference-based difficulty and its effects, the patient, primarily on an unconscious level (and more rarely consciously), must do all the work—i.e., become the functional therapist. She must work over and attempt to cure the therapist's psychopathology as well as her own.

The therapist's intervention in this hour fails to unfold from a well represented intervention context (here, his pending vacation, his missed intervention, and the likelihood that he would accept the patient's decision to terminate after a suitable period of working through). It constitutes a playback of *random* derivatives that are not selective and organized around a central, unrepresented, intervention context. It constitutes a rather scattered playback or confrontation, which fails to show a definitive appreciation of the extent to which the patient is working over the therapist's difficulties.

This intervention did not receive Type Two derivative validation. Instead, the patient responded primarily with a derivative commentary on how the therapist had a closed mind, in that he has failed to understand and appreciate the patient's derivative efforts to call the major problems within himself and within her to his attention. For the patient, this is rightly perceived as poor therapeutic care. Clearly, images related to close-minded people, to inadequate treatment of any kind, and all such negative communications must prompt a search within the therapist for countertransferences and their influence.

Another illustration is drawn from a first presentation by a supervisee of a patient with whom she felt treatment was moving along rather well. The patient was a young woman with severe sexual inhibitions, who was in intensive psychotherapy at a considerably reduced fee (she was referred by a clinic and was a supervised case; although the latter information had not been directly communicated to her). She was seen twice-weekly, and would pay for her sessions in advance. One week, about a month prior to the therapist's summer vacation, she made out the check to the wrong person and for twice the amount due to the therapist. The mistake did not emerge until after she had left the session that is abstracted here:

Patient: I will probably miss our session on Thursday because I am going to the shore with my boyfriend. He's totally indecisive and incapable of making up his mind, so we may or may not go. He suggested that I have an affair when I visit my brother in California later this month, so I can lose my virginity and we can then have sex. Even though he says he loves me, he's unable to have intercourse with me. The problem is all my fault because I'm so frigid and afraid. I won't let anyone get close.

Therapist: You really shouldn't blame yourself for the situation. It's not your entire responsibility, and it's a problem that you're working on.

The last intervention was made at the end of the hour, and the patient did miss the following session. At her next session, she spoke of the check:

Patient: Here's a new check; I realized the other one was wrong.

Therapist: Yes, I'm returning it to you.

Patient: I went away with Wally [*her boyfriend*] He was totally indecisive. It was a new experience for him, and he couldn't handle it. We eventually quarreled, and he stayed away from the cabin for a while. I was glad to be alone. I expected understanding, but it's asking too much of him. He's totally ineffectual. He was unable to get an erection, but masturbated himself in my presence. I wanted to tell him about my problems, but he was too preoccupied with himself. I eventually spoke about the death of my father, but he got upset and couldn't handle it. He gives a lot but it's all on the surface, and underneath he's entirely unstable. I never get the understanding I want. He's so split inside. I pulled back, and we got into a power struggle.

Therapist: The issue of a power struggle is an important theme for us to explore further.

Patient: I had that with my one other boyfriend. Is it all right if I pay you for this week next session?

Therapist: Yes.

The patient began the following hour by asking the therapist if she had paid her or not. She then spoke in detail about her boyfriend, his greediness and his exploiting others financially, and of a friend who was openly unfaithful to his wife and involved in threesomes.

It is the painful and difficult responsibility of the therapist to monitor all material initially in terms of potentially valid unconscious perceptions, replete with implications of unrecognized expressions of countertransference, unconsciously detected by the patient. Whenever a patient makes a mistake, the therapist must explore the treatment situation and his or her interventions for possible errors of his or her own. When there is some break in the frame or a representation of a pathological mode of relatedness, or when an issue is raised in therapy regarding the basic ground rules and boundaries of the therapeutic relationship, the therapist must investigate his or her management responses in this area—as should have been done in this treatment situation.

Thus, if the patient's errors as reported in this excerpt are treated as meaningful derivative communications that contain important valid unconscious perceptions, it becomes relatively easy to recognize that both the reduced fee and the acceptance of payment in advance are being experienced by the patient as reflections of difficulty within the therapist. Through several images, the patient implies that the therapist is engaged in a mixture of a parasitic and pathological symbiotic mode of relatedness with her. In addition to the many telling images that the patient experiences because of these deviations, by both paying more and delaying her weekly payment she offered clear models of rectification that the therapist could have utilized for framework management and interpretive responses in these areas.

This material is replete with valid unconscious perceptions of the therapist's difficulties, lack of clinical experience, inability to offer sound interpretations, and essential failure to function maturely and effectively in her relationship with the patient. There are derivatives that touch upon the therapist's pending vacation, but more importantly, this material must be organized around the alterations in the basic ground rules that reflect the therapist's countertransferences, relative incompetence, and the destruction of treatment—represented here through the death of the patient's father. These difficulties exist despite the therapist's well-meaning intentions and surface efforts to be supportive, much of it through noninterpretive interventions. The patient appears quite sensitive to this mixture, as reflected in her perception of a split within her boyfriend. There is also every indication that the patient realizes the presence of a supervisor, that she is being used as a learning case by the therapist, and that much of what is being done is designed to gratify the therapist's rather than the patient's needs. Despite the fact that the low fee is necessary for the patient, and that supervision is also necessary for both participants, the patient will inevitably experience these factors as countertransference-based, an impression that is supported by the therapist's difficulties in managing the ground rules and interpreting the patient's responsive unconscious perceptions and fantasies.

This example serves as a reminder of the extent to which therapists tend to have powerful needs to deny the presence and influence of countertransference difficulties in their relationships with patients. In this situation, primarily because the patient had not been able to relate at all to a man in the past two years, it was felt that she was making considerable progress. No effort had been made to monitor this material in terms of valid unconscious perceptions of the therapist. In keeping with the split so accurately perceived by the patient, the therapist herself accepted the patient's conscious praise at face value, and defensively split off onto others, including the patient, the latter's many negative feelings and perceptions.

Splitting is a major pathological mechanism used by therapists in their work with patients. Much of it involves well-meaning conscious intentions and notably hurtful, unconsciously effected interventions. Adaptive context listening can do much to resolve such splits. Clearly, however, the acceptance of much if not virtually all of the patient's derivative communications as first constituting sound unconscious perceptions can make the practice of psychotherapy, especially for those with continuing significant countertransferences, a most arduous task. In time, however, with proper personal treatment and through effective self-analysis, it is possible to achieve relative, though never complete, mastery over major countertransference problems, and to work relatively smoothly in unencumbered fashion with one's patients.

Summary and Conclusions

The attributes of the *designated therapist* cannot be taken for granted. It has been proposed that these qualities would center around the achievement of expertise as a therapist, and would have as their hallmarks the establishment of a sound and appropriate set of ground rules and boundaries to the therapeutic relationship, and a basically interpretive approach. It would include charging and accepting an appropriate fee, and accepting the basic role as interpreter of the patient's communications.

Clearly, there are many legitimate minor variations to these fundamental tenets that would not modify the therapist's assigned role to the point where he or she would no longer serve as both the designated and functional therapist. Nonethless, there are clear and important dividing lines. For example, at times the therapist may speak so excessively that he or she has assumed one of the main functions of the designated patient—that of free association. By and large, however, the designated therapist maintains enough of the role identity to meet the requirements of his or her assigned functions, and the main issue that arises concerns the carrying out of the role and functions as the designated therapist in sound fashion and in respect to the therapist's unconscious communications to the patient.

In addition to identifying the extent to which a given therapist meets and maintains the designated role, one must therefore examine the therapist's functioning in the therapeutic session in terms of whether it is in keeping with attributes of a functional therapist or that of a functional patient. Much of this is implicit and unconscious (see Chapter 32). At all moments when the therapist expresses himself or herself in terms of countertransferences, he or she is conveying a therapeutic need, and therefore operating as a functional patient. Reflected in errors in technique, countertransference-based interventions serve as a type of free association that reveals aspects of the therapist's psychopathology on both a manifest and latent level, and thereby implies a therapeutic need in the therapist. As a rule, patients tend to respond unconsciously to such inputs by shifting their *derivative* functioning in keeping with efforts that identify them for the moment as functional therapist.

These observations and formulations serve as a reminder that the therapist's functioning within the therapeutic interaction is neither a given to be taken for granted, nor a constant throughout a particular therapeutic experience—within a single session or from session to session. The therapist has a responsibility to monitor his or her functioning to determine the extent to which it is in keeping with his or her manifest and latent responsibilities as therapist, and to identify situations where, momentarily (one hopes), expressions to the patient place the therapist in the role of the functional patient. Determinations of this kind provide the therapist with a far greater sensitivity to the actualities, conscious and unconscious, of the therapeutic interaction, and permit rectification, framework-management responses, and interpretations that are highly attuned to the actualities of the spiraling interaction. Considerations of this kind implicitly reveal to the patient a sensitive therapist who fully appreciates the intricacies of the therapeutic experience, and foster in the therapist an ability to recognize countertransference-dominated interludes quickly enough to minimize their hurtful and detrimental consequences, and to maximize the extent to which they can be identified, corrected, and properly interpreted. In this way, a keen interest in and sensitivity to countertransference-based expressions becomes an important therapeutic instrument of benefit to patient and therapist alike.

Chapter 31

Reality and Alliance

There is considerable confusion regarding both the cooperative aspects of the patient's relationship with the therapist, and the realities that pertain to both patient and therapist, and to their interaction. The terms *working alliance* and *therapeutic alliance* have been used to refer to what is on the surface, the cooperative and working relationship between the two participants to therapy. Here *alliance sector of the therapeutic relationship* will be used in order to maintain the principle that there is but one relationship between patient and therapist, although it can be organized or subdivided into a variety of components, elements, interactional segments, or functional dimensions.

Similarly, there have been efforts to isolate a so-called "real relationship" between the patient and therapist, as if it were a separate entity from what is termed the "transference relationship." This conception not only violates the unity of the therapeutic relationship, but also fosters the mistaken notion that the so-called "real" relationship is relatively free of unconscious influence and exists as some type of autonomous, reality-oriented mode of interacting. As a result, therapists have been led away from interpretive efforts and toward direct manipulation based on surface considerations. Similar erroneous measures have also been derived from an approach to the *working*, or *therapeutic*, alliance that stresses the contributions of the intact functioning of the patient and therapist, much to the neglect of unconscious factors.

The Alliance Sector

The alliance sector of the relationship between the patient and therapist encompasses those qualities that pertain to the conscious and unconscious, direct and indirect, working together of the two participants to treatment in a manner designed for the insightful cure of the patient's symptoms or characterological disturbances (the patient's Neurosis). This implies the possibility of disturbance that may be either unilateral or bilateral, based on problems located mainly in either participant or on conscious or unconscious collusion between the two. The former may be referred to as a *disturbance in the alliance*, while the latter can be termed *sectors of misalliance*.

The alliance sector can be divided into two, somewhat interrelated, although sometimes independent, divisions: the *manifest* or *surface* alliance, which is the sphere of direct cooperation between the patient or therapist, and the *communicative* or *latent* alliance, which involves the extent to which the patient produces, when necessary, a meaningful communicative network and the degree to which the therapist is capable of interpreting its implications or managing the frame accordingly.

THE MANIFEST ALLIANCE

The overt sphere of cooperation between the patient and therapist is determined by two major factors, each under the influence of unconscious processes: (1) the relatively autonomous functioning of the patient, and (2) the relatively autonomous functioning of the therapist, including the ability to create a therapeutic setting and a relationship with appropriate ground rules and boundaries. This sector involves direct cooperation in the pursuit of insight and understanding. It therefore relies on the patient's ability to bring material to the therapist, and on the therapist's ability to offer the patient the appropriate interpretations of, and management responses to, this material—an aspect that overlaps with the unconscious or communicative sector of the alliance.

The alliance sector relies upon the patient's ability to work with and trust the therapist, and upon a therapist who deserves such trust and faith. It requires of the patient an ability to express and communicate meaningfully, some of it on a conscious and direct level. It asks of the patient additional capacities to attempt to understand the implications of his or her communications, and especially to attend to, work over, and integrate the therapist's interventions. Basic too is a capacity to form a meaningful relationship—a healthy therapeutic symbiosis—with the therapist.

The alliance sector requires of the therapist the capacity to relate maturely to the patient through a healthy symbiosis, to create a secure therapeutic setting and group of ground rules and boundaries for the therapeutic relationship, and to be able to carry out his or her responsibilities as a therapist with relative effectiveness (i.e., the ability to listen, formulate, interpret and manage the frame, hold and contain, and all of the other basic noncountertransference attributes identified in Chapter 29). These too are relatively autonomous functions under the influence of unconscious processes.

The manifest alliance sector of the relationship between the patient and therapist draws its importance in constituting a requisite for effective therapeutic work, and as a means of sustaining the treatment even in the face of momentary disturbances. The conscious sense of alliance between patient and therapist enables both participants to endure momentary difficulty and disorder, and to maintain an awareness of the purpose of therapy during disruptive interludes. The sense of cooperation is also a factor in assuring the continuation of treatment and in manifestly maintaining its stated purposes, goals, and methods. The sense of alliance therefore offers some degree of implicit support to both participants in the arduous work of psychotherapy.

Disturbances in the manifest alliance constitute important forms of *gross behavioral resistance,* and often take the form of threats to the continuation of the therapy or to the continued utilization of sound therapeutic procedures. This may be seen when a patient becomes consciously mistrustful and wary of the therapist, refuses to free associate, decides not to listen or consider seriously the interventions of the therapist, and otherwise directly opposes or attacks the therapist in his or her therapeutic endeavors. Similarly, the therapist may for brief or longer periods fail to listen carefully to the patient, to intervene properly, and to otherwise engage in the use of proper techniques.

The pursuit of understanding and insight is a major aspect of the alliance sector, and this is not a matter that can be taken for granted in psychotherapy by either the patient or the therapist: the

patient wishes for *relief,* and only sometimes for manifest understanding. The therapist, as attested to by the literature, endeavors to
offer such relief, though not always through a search for understanding and the establishment of a sound holding relationship.
There are many powerful unconscious motives within both participants to define a basic alliance, or major sectors of alliance, where
the basic configuration is not directed toward insight into the
unconscious factors of the patient's Neurosis. Although patient and
therapist work mainly in the verbal sphere, this is by no means a
guarantee that an alliance has been effected toward the pursuit of
insight. As noted by Bion (1962) and others, words may be used for
evacuation, projective identification, and discharge rather than for
the search for understanding. Thus the actual qualities of a manifest alliance may be determined only in light of a careful analysis
of prevailing intervention contexts, their conscious and unconscious meanings, and the patient's manifest and especially latent or
derivative responses.

When the alliance sector is afforded its basic definition in terms
of the pursuit by both participants to therapy of insight and
understanding, there is the implication that on the surface, this
aspect of the therapeutic relationship is disturbed when either
participant attempts to resolve the patient's Neurosis through any
other means. It is also disturbed whenever one of the participants
seeks to involve the other in some type of interaction unrelated to
the cure of the patient's symptoms.

For example, the patient may clamor for direct support, for
immediate answers, or for some type of seductive interchange or
contact, or may choose to directly attack the therapist in some
manner without any intention of understanding the implications of
his or her behaviors. The therapist may resort to noninterpretive
interventions, to modifications in the ground rules and boundaries,
and to such measures as efforts to cajole, advise, or direct the
patient, or to seduce or attack. Even the use of medication and
consultants are departures from the manifest alliance directed toward insight for the patient.

At times, these disturbances or ruptures in the alliance are
unilateral, in that they occur manifestly in either the patient or
therapist, but at other times they are bilateral and collusive, and
constitute manifest sectors of misalliance. This occurs, for example,
when a therapist offers advice to the patient and the patient accedes,

or when a patient directly attacks the therapist and the therapist attacks back. At times, these manifest forms of misalliance transpire outside of the awareness of both participants, although their influence and perception will virtually always appear in the patient's derivative communications.

All disturbances in the manifest alliance between the patient and therapist are based on conscious and unconscious factors. The resolution of these difficulties therefore relies on a basic understanding of these unconscious sources as they emerge in light of activated intervention contexts and the patient's derivative responses.

The alliance sector is established by the therapist in the first session, and in subsequent hours, through the therapist's manifest delineations, implicit behaviors, managements of the ground rules, and interpretations, especially as they pertain to disturbances in this sphere. The therapist need not—and should not (since it is noninterpretive)—directly appeal to the patient's cooperative side, but instead should establish the spirit of the therapeutic alliance by stating in the first hour his or her commitment and ability to help the patient resolve the patient's Neurosis, and by then delineating the ground rules and boundaries of the therapeutic relationship. Beyond that, *adhering to basic principles of technique* is by far the most crucial means of further creating and maintaining the alliance sector, though clearly, these efforts are carried out with due sensitivity and tact. In this way, the patient soon consciously and unconsciously comes to understand the nature of the alliance sector, including its direct manifestations.

In the face of disturbances in the manifest alliance, the therapist must maintain a basic framework management and interpretive approach. Direct appeals to the therapeutic alliance and for the patient's cooperation or understanding, and for any other type of cooperative effort, convey unconsciously failures in the therapist's ability to maintain the basic stance and a sound contribution to the alliance sector. They also convey unconsciously a sense of manipulation, interpretive and framework-management failures, disturbing projective identifications, and defensiveness, often with Type C barrier qualities. Because of these underlying attributes, the manifest appeal to the patient is undermined through a wide range of pathological unconscious communications and efforts to effect a pathological symbiotic or parasitic mode of relatedness with the patient. As a result, such efforts tend unconsciously to further disturb, rather than firm up, the alliance sector.

In principle, the therapist must look first to his or her countertransferences, and the patient's unconscious perceptions of their influence, in the face of a manifest disturbance in the alliance sector. In addition, these difficulties may arise in part from the underlying psychopathology of the patient, and from the patient's transference-based responses. As a rule, there is some intermixture of these two factors, although the former (countertransference and nontransference) often tend to predominate.

Paradoxically, with patients who enter treatment with a deviant type of alliance in mind, disturbances in the manifest alliance will arise when the therapist attempts to secure the framework and utilize an interpretive approach. These patients have little wish for insight and understanding, and instead demand direct symbiotic and other pathological gratifications of the therapist, doing so at times with relatively little in the way of accompanying derivative communications that could serve as a basis for an interpretation of these efforts. These patients wish to establish an entirely different mode of cure, much of it through action-discharge rather than insight. They respond with gross disturbances of the therapeutic alliance when the therapist does not join with them in these sectors of misalliance.

In sum, then, the manifest sector of alliance is founded on a healthy symbiotic mode of relatedness between the patient and therapist, and the genuine pursuit of insight and truth as it pertains to the patient's emotional difficulties. Disturbances in the alliance sector are a form of first-order resistance and require framework management and interpretive responses in light of prior activated intervention contexts and the patient's derivative responses. Although the manifest alliance sector is under the influence of unconscious factors in both the patient and therapist, the alliance itself has manifest and latent dimensions. Apparent surface cooperation does not guarantee a meaningful unfolding of the therapeutic work.

THE UNCONSCIOUS, LATENT ALLIANCE SECTOR

Actual cooperation between the patient and therapist in the pursuit of insight and understanding must exist not only manifestly, but also latently, implicitly, and unconsciously. There are three main dimensions to the patient's *unconscious* cooperation: (1) a capacity to accept, tolerate, or work toward a basic healthy symbiotic relationship with the therapist; (2) the ability to engage in meaningful derivative communication and to produce an analyzable communicative network in response to traumatic intervention contexts; and (3) an ability on an unconscious level to take in and work over toward ultimate conscious insight the therapist's valid interventions.

In a similar vein, this sector requires of the therapist a capacity for sound holding, listening, formulating, and intervening. Efforts with the patient must reflect an ability on the therapist's part to accept the healthy symbiotic mode of relatedness and to seek cure through insight. Thus both the manifest and latent implications of interventions must be directed toward understanding, rather than action-discharge or the creation of defensive barriers. Such sound efforts are founded on the therapist's basic capacity to function well within the therapeutic relationship and to accept the boundaries, limitations, frustrations, nongratification, and limited satisfactions that accrue to the therapist in the treatment experience.

The basic issue, then, as it pertains to the unconscious alliance sector, centers around the unconscious preferences in each participant as to the means by which the patient's Neurosis will be resolved. This involves as well a preferred mode of relatedness and style of communication. These unconsciously and often indirectly expressed needs are often at considerable variance with the patient's or therapist's conscious statements, intentions, and beliefs.

For example, there may be a wish in either or both participants to modify the necessary boundaries of the therapeutic symbiosis in order to alleviate Neurotic suffering through symbiotic and fusion mechanisms. Related to this is a need to maintain derivative and nonderivative defenses against the underlying chaos as it exists within the patient, and at times within the therapist and the therapeutic interaction. Since tendencies of this kind are universal, unilateral or collusive shifts in the nature of the unconscious cooperation between the patient and therapist will arise in all treatment experiences. They provide important interludes for therapeutic work. In addition, however, these pathological needs may undermine the basic communicative alliance to the point where it is fragmented or nonfunctional.

Disturbances in the communicative alliance are difficult to identify and resolve, since the problem lies either within the sphere of the patient's derivative communications or in the therapist's basic approach to the patient and to treatment, especially as it pertains to enhancing this level of expression within the patient. Much of present-day psychotherapy is constituted in a fashion that undermines the communicative alliance, since many therapists are entirely unaware of this particular level of cooperation and its attributes. A patient will, however, represent disturbances in the unconscious and communicative alliance sector in some disguised form—at which time interpretation and framework-management responses organized in light of prevailing intervention contexts can be carried out (see chapter 23).

CLINICAL EXAMPLE

The patient is a young man who is married and has a six-year-old daughter, Janet. He entered treatment because of periods of depression and a gnawing sense of dissatisfaction regarding his image of himself and his capabilities in work.

The material excerpted here emerged during the termination phase of the treatment. About a month earlier, the patient had brought in for the therapist's perusal a book on management problems in industry, an area of considerable concern to the patient himself. The therapist had accepted the book, though he later on had returned it to the patient and carried out some interpretive work regarding the deviation—much of it in terms of the therapist's own (and secondarily, the patient's) unresolved separation anxieties, which led the therapist to accept a temporary gift from the patient.

Soon after, the patient's daughter began to show problems in school, and the patient was invited to see the school psychologist. He agreed to do so, and the therapist questioned this decision. Nonetheless, the patient then saw the psychologist and reported this event in the session prior to the one excerpted here. In that hour, there were ample derivatives to indicate that the patient had identified with the therapist in attempting to alleviate the termination-related separation anxieties through a break in the frame and a deviation designed unconsciously to modify his own mounting separation concerns. However, despite a clear communicative network, the therapist had failed to intervene interpretively or to rectify the frame at the behest of several evident derivative communications from the patient that had reflected the inappropriate qualities of his consultation with the psychologist.

Patient: I guess I have to work out a termination now and

decide on a definite date for the end of treatment. All I have to do is work out my relationship with you and Sam [*his boss at work*]. At least I can see where I have to go and where I am heading. *(The patient then ruminates about his need for secure and consistent relationships both with the therapist and with his colleagues at work.)* Sam's wife was giving him a surprise party, and my wife didn't want to go. Sam's wife felt I would betray him if I didn't show up, so I went by myself. Sometimes Sam holds back and doesn't give me what I should be getting from him. I've been thinking a lot about ground rules and the need to hold them secure. With Janet, when I'm firm, things go well. When I get lax, things don't work out. Ground rules seem to be the most important thing. They're certainly very important here. I had the feeling I was breaking some kind of rule when I went to see the school psychologist. We have another appointment to see him next week. It was like it was going to interfere with termination or something. There was a hint of that kind of thinking in your comment two weeks ago.

Therapist: There are themes of withholding which you connect to treatment. You are also indicating that your seeing the psychologist will interfere with your working out a termination and your treatment here. It seems clear that it will be impossible for you to fully experience my loss if you continue to see him.

Patient: You're not telling me to not see the therapist, are you?

Therapist: I'm just clarifying the rules which we can best work by.

Patient: Thank you. Now I know where I stand.

In this session, the patient free associates on a manifest level in rather unencumbered fashion without any significant measure of silence. The issue of the termination of his treatment is at hand, and on a conscious level he is attempting to work it over and to master the associated fantasies, perceptions, conflicts, and anxieties. On the surface, there is also some indication that his seeing the school psychologist posed a threat for his psychotherapy, and he is attempting to understand this as well. Further, his sense of the therapist, his relationship with him, and his wish to cooperate all appear to be quite sound. In all, then, the surface alliance sector is intact except for the possibility that the consultation with the psychologist might interfere with the therapy.

What then of the unconscious or communicative alliance? There are several adaptation-evoking contexts for this session. There is the background context of the therapist's deviation in taking the book from the patient, as well as his rectification of that particular break in the frame. There are also the therapist's earlier, poor and incomplete interventions regarding the patient's decision to see the school psychologist. There is as well the therapist's missed intervention in the previous hour and the pending termination of the treatment—the adaptive context here being the patient's anticipation that the therapist will accept the end of therapy and of his relationship with the patient. Of these, the missed intervention and the pending acceptance of termination by the therapist are most immediate. Each of these adaptive contexts is also an indicator, as is the patient's visit to the psychologist. These too are represented with varying degrees of disguise: some are manifest and most are, of course, quite latent.

The listening-formulating process must be carried out to determine whether or not a meaningful communicative network exists. Thus the termination adaptive context is represented directly, while the missed intervention is represented with a displaced and only moderately disguised derivative in the form of the allusion to the ways in which the patient's boss, Sam, withholds things from him. In this respect, then, the level of resistance is quite low. However, the greatest degree of communicative resistances regards the patient's expression of derivatives. Much of what the patient has to say about each of the adaptive contexts is direct, conscious, and quite linear. There is little in the way of encoded and derivative communication in these associations. The patient has failed to generate a coalescible derivative complex.

It appears, then, that the patient is showing a strong (though possibly flawed) manifest therapeutic alliance, though a poor or highly resistant communicative alliance sector. At the very moment that he proposes to explore and understand the implications of both termination and the ground rules of therapy, on a derivative and unconscious level, he fails to express himself with meaning sufficient to clarify the nature of his unconscious perceptions and fantasies.

As would be expected, any combination of manifest and latent

alliance qualities is possible: manifest and communicative cooperation, manifest cooperation with communicative resistances and
opposition, manifest opposition with communicative cooperation,
and manifest disruptions in the alliance sector accompanied by
additional communicative ruptures (by far the most ominous of the
four combinations, and a reflection of the Type B-C communicative
mode). In the course of each session, the therapist attempts to
evaluate both his or her own and the patient's position in regard to
their cooperative therapeutic efforts on both the surface and on an
unconscious level.

The manifest intention of the therapist in the present session is
to further both the manifest and unconscious alliance sectors
through a rectification of the frame and a playback of the theme of
withholding—a way of acknowledging his previous error through
an implicit allusion. Unfortunately, the effort at rectifying the
frame was carried out as a directive and did not make use of the
patient's derivative material. The interpretive effort involved surface
elements and did not include a derivative complex. As a result, there
were major failings in both of these spheres, despite the therapist's
well-meaning intentions. Because the therapist did not offer a
sound intervention, both the surface and communicative alliances
are likely to have been undermined. This expectation is borne out
by the patient's response to the therapist's comment, through which
he points to the manipulative qualities of the therapist's effort and
attempts to establish a manifest content mode of relatedness. This
latter has pathological symbiotic, defensive, and pathologically
gratifying qualities that reflect further disturbances, now in both
the manifest alliance sector (the pursuit of insight is set to the side)
and the communicative alliance sector (the patient's use of nonderivative expressions are reinforced and continued).

THERAPEUTIC MISALLIANCES

Any mutually shared, collusive effort by the patient and therapist, consciously or unconsciously, to either set to the side the
insightful resolution of the patient's Neurosis, or to attempt to
alleviate it through other, essentially uninsightful means is a
therapeutic misalliance. Conscious sectors of misalliance can be
seen from time to time, especially in the work of therapists who
make extensive use of noninterpretive (i.e., manipulative and so-

called supportive) interventions, and who frequently modify the ground rules and boundaries of the therapeutic relationship. However, sectors of *unconscious misalliance* are far more common, and *misalliance cures* (temporary symptom alleviation through some uninsightful means) are far more prevalent than generally realized. The hallmark of misalliance is the absence of Type Two derivative validation for an intervention by the therapist. Its more detailed phenomenology and unconscious implications can be detected through a monitoring of the patient's material with representations of this type of collusion in mind. These efforts are carried out in a manner comparable to that applied to the search for countertransferences, and sectors of misalliance constitute one form of countertransference-based effect.

There are seemingly endless forms of misalliance. The following example was chosen because the therapist had some difficulty in recognizing its presence.

CLINICAL EXAMPLE

The patient was a young man living with his girlfriend, whom he had referred to his therapist. After some superficial exploration, the therapist agreed to see the girlfriend in treatment. About two months later, the therapist (a woman) had attempted to interpret the patient's resentment that she was treating both him and the girlfriend (without accompanying comments regarding the possibility of rectification, which actually could have been made based on the patient's associations). The patient responded with conscious denial of any concern, though with derivatives that implied that this arrangement provided the patient considerable pathological symbiotic gratification, reinforcement of his defenses against closeness with the therapist, and protection against some of his own inner conflicts and chaos. The excerpt presented here is from the subsequent hour.

> Patient: Ann [*the girlfriend*] has changed lately. She's been very nasty to me, especially after her last session with you. She pressed me about why I wanted her in treatment with you, the reasons for it and such. Did I think she was crazy? I said no, that I thought it would be helpful for her and for our relationship. I really don't want to talk about this. I noticed that you recently stopped taking notes. I guess you've finished your book, unless you have a silent, invisible pen.

Therapist: You're talking about Ann being different and angry after seeing me. You seemed confused and then discussed my not taking notes. Are you saying that you might be concerned and angry that I might confuse your sessions with Ann's?

Patient: I could say that, but I don't think so. Next year is an election year, and I was thinking about Eagleton and Ellsburg. I was bothered about confidentiality. I thought of using an assumed name in coming here. I've been realizing how suspicious I was about the note-taking. It's been difficult for me to confide in women. I must have been one of your first patients. I wasn't sure if you knew what you were doing and you seemed uncertain about how we should do things here. It's important that I learn to trust women. I keep thinking of how my mother died on me, and of how my father is acting as if he's mentally ill. He hasn't been able to take care of himself lately. He keeps making mistakes with bills and messing up his doctor's appointments. He accused me of cheating him. I'd like to help, but I don't think I should take over completely. He's not a father I can be proud of.

The manifest and latent alliance sectors between this patient and therapist reveal a mixed picture. On the one hand, the patient comes regularly to his sessions, apparently says whatever comes to mind, pays attention to the therapist's interventions, and has a sense of working with her in therapy. On the other hand, the patient states that there is something that he doesn't want to discuss. He later expresses his conscious suspiciousness of the therapist and his difficulty in confiding in her. He alludes as well to his uncertainty as to whether she knows what she is doing. All of this provides some indication of disturbance in the manifest alliance sphere. In addition, the patient's thought of using an assumed name in coming to his sessions also suggests some measure of surface anxiety and concern about treatment, and appears to be part of an effort to withdraw from meaningful interaction with the therapist.

In similar fashion, the therapist's earlier interventions, including her acceptance of the patient's girlfriend, pose a number of threats to the manifest sphere of cooperation between the patient and herself. The same qualities apply to her note-taking during the patient's hours, a practice that often undermines both the manifest and communicative alliance spheres.

In all, then, there are signs of unconscious collusion between this patient and therapist and a manifest sector of misalliance, constituted by the patient's offer, and the therapist's acceptance, of his girlfriend as a patient, and the therapist's note-taking and the patient's acceptance of this practice. The therapist's use of noninterpretive interventions, and her failure to interpret and rectify the deviation, further contribute to this sector of misalliance, as does the patient's direct protest that he had no concern about his girlfriend being in treatment with his therapist. There is strong evidence of both conscious and unconscious collusion.

On the other hand, the patient cooperates rather well in the communicative alliance sphere. The adaptive context of the referral of the girlfriend is represented, and a sufficient derivative complex is generated to permit an interpretive intervention by the therapist. In part, this appears to have arisen because of the therapist's previous efforts to interpret the deviation and to recognize the problems it is causing. In this way, the therapist herself has indicated a preparedness for a sound communicative alliance, and possibly for the necessary rectification of the frame that could be accomplished by terminating the treatment with Ann.

Thus the patient mentions Ann's therapy directly, and then produces a derivative complex that implies an unconscious perception of a change in the therapist's attitude (probably toward the deviation itself, which she accepted at first and now had begun to reconsider and interpret), the nasty and hostile qualities of the deviation, the sense of craziness that it reflected in the therapist, the manner in which it interfered with the manifest and communicative alliances (cf. the patient not wanting to talk about this subject), and the development of a disguised model of rectification (the allusion to the therapist having recently stopped taking notes during the sessions; as a derivative, this implies the termination of Ann's therapy).

In the presence of this strong indicator-deviant intervention context, the therapist makes a rather limited effort at interpretation regarding some of the patient's anxieties as evoked by the alteration in the frame. Although the interpretation falls short of establishing the patient's specific unconscious perceptions of the therapist, it does represent a clear effort by the therapist to interpret an aspect of the deviant situation and to hint at the possibility of rectification by mentioning that she no longer took notes. In all, then, the intervention represents an implicit effort to develop further surface cooperation with the patient, and a mixed message regarding the unconscious alliance sector: the wish for it to expand and yet only to a limited degree.

The patient's response to the intervention is replete with Type Two derivative validation. Both manifestly and through derivatives, the patient reveals his deep sense of mistrust of the therapist, his sense of her relative inexperience, and the need for rectification—it is important that he learn to trust a woman. He introduces a genetic element in revealing that the acceptance of the referral constituted the loss or death of the therapist, just as earlier he had lost his mother. This is in keeping with the implications of the derivative involving the assumed name, which implied the therapist's absence on an affective and effective level, and the development of an autistic mode of relatedness on both sides. The patient also characterizes the deviation as comparable to his father's mental illness, and as a consequence, of a failure on the part of the therapist to take care of her own personal needs. The parasitic qualities of the deviation are then reflected in the father's accusation that the patient is cheating him. The material concludes with a model of rectification through which limited help without manipulation or omnipotent control is offered. As matters stand, the patient cannot be proud of his therapist-father.

In all, while expressing some measure of disturbance in the manifest alliance, though nonetheless maintaining a cooperative attitude throughout, the patient firms up the communicative alliance with the therapist. This is an interactional product, in that he is responding to the sound qualities of the therapist's intervention and attempting, with her help, to resolve previously existent sectors of misalliance, especially those related to the therapist's seeing the girlfriend and the prior note-taking.

It is of interest that during the earlier phases of this therapy, at a time when there were distinct disturbances in the communicative alliance, both patient and therapist consciously felt that they were working well together. The evidence of sectors of misalliance, and of the patient's derivative and unconsciously expressed perceptions of these impairments, were virtually ignored. Only as the therapist became sensitive to derivatives, and began to secure the framework of the treatment and to rectify her more blatant deviations, did it become possible to effect a sound communicative alliance with the patient.

In the sessions that followed, the patient continued to alternate between meaningful derivative communication and resistances. On the surface, he was at first rather cooperative in pursuing the further implications of the therapist's acceptance of his girlfriend into treatment. However, he became difficult and uncooperative when the therapist, at the behest of the patient's derivative material, began to move toward the definitive rectification of this deviation (no doubt because of a pathological investment in the conscious and unconscious collusion).

In principle, one must remember that both patients and therapists have strong unconscious investments in the sectors of misalliance that they create together. Their renunciation requires considerable effort and insight on the part of the therapist and a sound grasp of valid techniques. Simiarly, the resolution of a sector of misalliance asks of the patient a willingness to maintain the unconscious communicative alliance to the point where sound interpretive and framework-management responses may be developed by the therapist. Interludes of this kind involve important aspects of the patient's defenses and Neurosis, and provide highly meaningful opportunities for insight and structural change. The therapist too may gain and grow considerably through the insightful resolution of a sector of misalliance.

It is the therapist's responsibility to identify and resolve through private self-analysis any sector of misalliance in which he or she participates. The patient will express psychopathology by attempting to develop sectors of misalliance in order to defend against and gratify his or her underlying Neurosis. Efforts of this kind are to be expected from the patient, although much will depend on the therapist's response. Should the therapist unconsciously collude with the patient, a pathological mode of relatedness and cure, including noninsightful symptom relief through framework deviation and misalliance cures, will result. If the therapist does not collude, the patient has an opportunity to experience this implicit nonparticipation and to communicate about the underlying factors in his or her own pathological needs for misalliance. The therapist may then interpret the implications of the patient's efforts toward misalliance in the adaptive context of the offer of a secure frame and a healthy mode of symbiotic relatedness.

Contributions by the therapist to sectors of misalliance require both rectification and interpretation at the behest of the patient's derivative material; while unilateral efforts to effect misalliance on the part of the patient will require interpretation in light of prior adaptation-evoking contexts. At times, these involve deviations by the therapist that have produced other sectors of therapeutic misalliance; while under other conditions, some patients will react to the therapist's offer of a sound alliance and healthy symbiosis by attempting to generate a misalliance in their place. As always, framework rectification and interpretive work is carried out in light of prevailing adaptive contexts.

Clearly, basic problems within a patient in regard to trust, object relatedness, pathological symbiotic and parasitic needs, cognitive understanding, capacity to communicate manifestly and through meaningful derivative expressions, frustration tolerance and ability to delay, instinctual drive management, ego defenses, superego pathology, and the like, may all create difficulties in both the manifest and latent alliance sectors. It is to be stressed, however, that many patients with basic impairments in these spheres are capable of establishing an important measure of alliance with the therapist, and that further, all such dysfunctions are necessary reflections of the patient's psychopathology and are based on unconscious mechanisms, processes, fantasies, introjects, and perceptions. They are also, once contact with the therapist is initiated, in constant interplay with inputs from the therapist, and therefore interactional creations to which both participants contribute.

The resolution of the pathological elements of these basic dysfunctions must rely on the therapist's basic framework management and interpretive approach. Direct efforts at reassurance, at the manipulation of the dysfunction, and any other noninterpretive measures tend to support and reinforce the dysfunction on an unconscious level, rather than undermine or modify it. As fundamental contributions to the alliance sector, these areas of disturbance within the patient, and within the therapeutic interaction, are first-order therapeutic contexts for the therapist's interventional efforts.

Realities of the Therapeutic Relationship

The realities of both participants as they are expressed directly and indirectly, and perceived and experienced on both sides, consciously and unconsciously, are basic to the therapeutic interaction and to the therapist's management and interpretive efforts. The patient exists as a real person, very much in need of help as a rule, in his or her relationship with the therapist, bringing to that relationship a variety of actual personality attributes and other assets and liabilities. The patient has a style and mode of relating to the therapist, and of communicating with him or her as well. The expressions of the patient's Neurosis are real and fluctuate in the course of treatment.

The therapist too is a real person, with a personality, a set of attitudes, a method of working with the patient, and a wide range of capacities—assets and liabilities. The therapist should be a professional with expertise in the technique of psychotherapy and capable in reality of helping the patient to resolve his or her Neurosis through insight and inevitable positive introjective identifications.

The actualities of the patient impinge upon the therapist as adaptive contexts that serve as one determinant of the therapist's silences and interventions. It must be recognized that these actualities—filled with manifest and latent meanings and functions—are perceived both consciously and unconsciously by the therapist, and that he or she must strive to be aware of as much of their impact and implications as possible. If any of these actualities evoke a countertransference-based response within the therapist, they must be subjected to self-analysis and resolution. An inability to do this work will considerably disturb the therapeutic effort.

The actualities of the therapist are also considered in terms of their manifest and extensive unconscious implications. The patient's Neurotic (and healthy) responses and communications are mobilized by these adaptation-evoking realities, which serve as the critical intervention contexts for the patient's derivative communications. While the stress throughout has been on the therapist's immediate interventions, his or her personality traits and attitudes may also serve as critical intervention contexts to which patients respond. All formulations of the material from patients are organized around the conscious and unconscious implications of these actualities.

The here and now, the realities of the therapeutic situation and of both participants, are at the heart of the therapeutic interaction and of the therapist's understanding and techniques. There is therefore no need whatsoever to separate out a so-called real relationship between the patient and therapist—every aspect of this relationship is real, just as every aspect is under unconscious and fantasy influence. The concept of a real relationship erroneously implies a distinction from another type of relatedness that is based primarily on the patient's pathological fantasies—the so-called transference relationship. Clearly, the patient's relationship with the therapist is founded on various gradations of intermixture of the actual traits and behaviors of the therapist (with their conscious and unconscious implications), and the perceptiveness and fantasy influences that derive from within the patient. It is here that the terms *nontransference* (essentially validly perceived and in keeping with reality) and *transference* (essentially distorted and not in keeping with reality) can be invoked. Similar considerations would apply to the therapist's noncountertransference and countertransference-based responses to the patient, which are always effected in terms of both actualities and inner experience.

The "real relationship" concept has led to many noninterpretive interventions, direct appeals to and manipulations of the patient, and to an essential failure to appreciate the unconscious influence on the patient's perceptions of and reactions to these actualities. Similarly, the concept of a transference relationship has led to a failure to appreciate the realities of the therapist and therapeutic interaction that serve to stimulate transference-based responses in the patient, and to a tendency to confine the conceptualization of these reactions to the sphere of the patient's intrapsychic fantasies. A balanced appreciation that takes into account the effects of both reality and fantasy, of valid perceptiveness and of distortion, in all situations, enables the therapist to maintain an essentially sound approach to the material from the patient, founded on the pursuit of the interpretive understanding of the patient's derivative communications as they pertain to the reality stimuli that have evoked them.

Chapter 32

Relatedness and Interactional Mechanisms

The level and type of object relatedness between the patient and therapist is a complex dimension that involves the nature of expressed and implied needs and the means by which they will be satisfied, the internal representations of the self and other person, the actual responses of both individuals, and the manifest and latent means of interacting. It is influenced by the nature of the major intrapsychic and interactional mechanisms used by the two participants to therapy, but the concept of object relatedness is far more broad than that of interactional mechanisms. The sphere of object relatedness includes the actual and fantasied roles of each participant, their self-images, and their manner of functioning within the therapeutic dyad—in particular the extent to which they operate consciously and unconsciously as patient or therapist.

Forms of Relatedness

There are three communicative modes of relatedness between a patient and therapist: Type A, Type B, and Type C. At times, the communicative mode will be shared by the two participants, while in other interludes, the patient will be attempting to effect one type of relatedness while the therapist will be engaged in attempting to relate through a different mode.

THE TYPE A MODE OF RELATEDNESS:
THE COMMENSAL OR HEALTHY
SYMBIOTIC RELATIONSHIP

The Type A mode can also be termed the Type Two derivative form of relatedness. It implies that the patient is prepared to relate to the therapist by clearly representing activated intervention contexts and supplying a meaningful reactive derivative complex.

An acceptance of the established ground rules and boundaries of the therapeutic relationship, and a preparedness to lie fallow and to engage in self-interpretive efforts in the absence of traumatic intervention contexts, is implicit to this type of relatedness.

The Type A mode of relatedness requires of the therapist a capacity to establish and maintain the basic framework of the therapeutic relationship, and to respond with appropriate efforts at framework management and interpretation-reconstruction when called for by the material from the patient. It also requires sound holding and containing capacities, and a judicious use of silence in the absence of material suitable for active intervention.

The implicit and explicit wish of the patient to be afforded insightful understanding into the nature of his or her Neurosis, and to be properly held and contained when necessary, is basic to the Type A mode of relatedness. It is therefore a mode of relatedness that is essentially symbolic; although in addition, it is founded upon selected measures of appropriate *relationship satisfactions*. For the patient, these include the establishment of a safe and secure setting, the reliability and consistency of the therapist, the therapist's capacity to understand and interpret, and the satisfaction of being sensitively understood and held. For the therapist, it implies working with a patient who is prepared to establish a manifest and communicative alliance, and to comply with the procedures and ground rules of therapy, to analyze infractions in this regard, and to cooperate by explicating the fundamental rule of free association. The therapist also has the limited satisfactions of a patient whom he or she can rely in a special sense of the term, someone with whom the therapist can experience some small measure of satisfaction in observing eventual therapeutic progress, and through whom the therapist obtains a part of his or her necessary income.

It is a matter of definition as to whether the Type A mode is termed *commensal* or *healthy symbiotic*. The former involves a relationship that provides reasonable and relatively equal satisfactions for both participants at the expense of neither one. Yet, while there are clearly gains for both participants, it would appear that in the treatment situation, the more extensive satisfactions should accrue to the patient. The treatment process is designed primarily to help him or her to resolve his or her Neurosis, and for expanded growth and understanding. The satisfactions of the therapist are placed in a secondary role. Thus the Type A or Type Two derivative therapeutic relationship seems best conceptualized as a form of healthy or therapeutic symbiosis. In this type of relationship, the gratifications are geared toward insight, maturation, and individuation. The relationship is designed, however, for the primary benefit of the patient (the *symbiotic recipient*), and less so for the therapist (the *symbiotic provider*). In this mode of relatedness, neither participant is notably harmed or damaged.

The mature or healthy symbiotic mode of therapeutic relationship implies relatively realistic internal representations of the patient within the therapist and a secure sector of similar representations of the therapist within the patient. Each participant treats the other as a whole object in keeping with the therapeutic needs of the patient and the need to be therapeutically helpful within the therapist. In particular, the healthy symbiotic relationship requires the renunciation of all needs other than those defined above, including wishes within the patient for direct forms of pathological gratification beyond those available through the silent holding-containing and interpretive or framework-management responses of the therapist.

The patient must therefore set aside wishes for the direct satisfaction of a wide range of inappropriate instinctual drive, object relationship, and superego needs that range from wishes for physical contact, direct battle, and other direct satisfactions, to advice and manipulation, the offer of inappropriate sanctions, and even the direct answers to questions and other immediate means of satisfying needs that might arise. Similarly, the therapist must set aside all personal therapeutic needs, and all other instinctual drive, object relational, superego, and other needs that extend beyond the reasonable satisfactions obtained in being paid to be an effective therapist. The direct satisfaction of aggressive and sexual needs, of advice and support from the patient, and of other types of ministrations from the patient are precluded from the commensal or therapeutic symbiotic relationship.

In essence, then, the healthy therapeutic symbiotic relationship involves the sacrifice by both patient and therapist of a wide range of highly personal and human, though pathological, internal and object-related needs. This proves essential for an insightful therapeutic experience, in that the pursuit of understanding will be set to the side when these other, more pathological and immediate needs, are directly satisfied. The symbolic search for truth and understanding is an arduous task, and relief from suffering is readily sought through other means. The healthy therapeutic symbiosis requires considerable renunciation and effort on the part of both patient and therapist for its achievement.

THE TYPE B MODE OF RELATEDNESS: PARASITIC AND PATHOLOGICAL SYMBIOTIC RELATIONSHIPS

The Type B mode of relatedness may have a number of different attributes and implications. Action-discharge, direct and immediate gratification, evacuation of disturbing inner affects and contents, and dumping and projective identification are characteristic. Although some patients initially express themselves in this manner and subsequently recover to the point where they attempt to understand the implications of their behaviors (The Type B-A patient), all patients who use this mode of expression, communication, and relatedness are using the relationship with the therapist during that particular interlude for direct and immediate noninterpretive, nonholding satisfactions. On both the conscious and unconscious levels, the patient is attempting to find pathological satisfaction and discharge; *there is no essential interest in comprehension and understanding.*

As a rule, patients of this type attempt to effect a manifest content form of relatedness with the therapist, expressing themselves through associations with little in the way of derivative implications. They make many manifest demands on the therapist for noninterpretive satisfactions that involve both alterations in the basic ground rules of the therapeutic relationship and the direct answer to questions. They engage in manifest attacks or attempts at seduction of the therapist, and tend to refute most, if not all, efforts toward framework management and interpretation. At times, these patients engage in Type One derivative interpretations of the therapist's behaviors and of their own associations, doing so however primarily to achieve deviant parasitic and pathologically symbiotic satisfactions.

The therapist who is interested in this type of action-discharge and inappropriate satisfaction (i.e., gratifications that extend beyond those accrued from responding interpretively and with holding, accepting the fee and such) tends to engage in manifest content interchanges with the patient, and makes use of Type One derivative interventions.

The underlying purpose of these maneuvers is to effect one of two types of pathological relatedness: *symbiosis or parasitism.* In the actual clinical situation, some small degree of pathological symbiosis is inevitable, though this realization cannot be used to justify more deliberate efforts along these lines.

THE TYPE C MODE OF RELATEDNESS: PATHOLOGICAL OR NONPATHOLOGICAL SYMBIOSIS AND AUTISM

The Type C mode of relatedness may involve either a manifest content or Type One derivative interaction. The former usually involves the inhibited and constricted, empty and boring, Type C communicator. The latter usually involves a Type C narrator who engages in extensive Type One derivative self-interpretations and manifest comments regarding the therapist. None of this material is a meaningful response to an activated intervention context, however, and interpretation is not feasable.

The Type C patient disrupts meaningful relatedness, and his or her basic mode of relatedness involves some sort of autism or symbiosis. Classification here may be difficult. To the extent that the patient is not conveying a meaningful communicative network, relatedness to the therapist is autistic. When this occurs in the presence of an activated intervention context, the mode of relatedness is a pathological form of autism. In contrast, when it takes place in the absence of activated adaptation-evoking contexts, as in the lying-fallow phase of therapy, the mode of relatedness is a healthy form of autism. However, since patients in the lying-fallow phase are also benefiting from the therapist's holding and containing capacities, there is a background sense of relatedness to the therapist that would lead to a classification of the mode of relatedness as involving a healthy symbiosis.

Strictly speaking, in the absence of communicated meaning—the K link (Bion 1962)—the relationship should be considered autistic rather than symbiotic. Thus the autistic mode of relatedness includes a healthy form that takes place in the presence of another person, who becomes part of the unobtrusive backdrop and who is prepared to relate meaningfully to the patient if need be, and toward whom, for the moment, the patient breaks meaningful relationship links. This type of autistic phase is clearly growth-promoting.

For the therapist, any intervention that does not center upon the implications of his or her own intervention contexts for the patient has strong autistic qualities. During periods of appropriate silence, the therapist's relationship is that of the healthy autism. On the other hand, inappropriate silence and erroneous interventions imply some measure of withdrawal from the patient in terms of meaningful relatedness. Thus erroneous interventions may serve two simultaneous or different functions: the use of words by a Type B therapist for evacuation and discharge, and the use of words by a Type C therapist as lie- or Type C barriers directed against meaningful relatedness. Clearly, the offer of an interpretation does not guarantee a Type A and healthy symbiotic mode of relatedness by the therapist toward the patient. The mode of relatedness can be determined only upon an analysis of the actual structure of the intervention, including its unconscious implications and validity.

In the pathological modes of relatedness—autism, symbiosis, and parasiticism—the patient's actual object relationship with the therapist, his or her self- and object-representations, and the unconscious fantasies and introjects that are of influence in this regard, tend to be infused with psychopathology. The other person is often treated as a part object, manipulated as a thing or tool, and used as a means of obtaining inappropriate instinctual drive and other forms of satisfaction. There is a tendency to disregard the needs of the other person. To some extent the autistic mode of relatedness implies some measure of obliteration in respect to the internal representation of the other person and in regard to the actual recognition of his or her meaningful existence.

CLINICAL EXAMPLE

The pathological parasitic and symbiotic modes of relatedness in a therapist's well meaning alteration of the ground rules are illustrated in this case of a depressed woman in her 50s being seen once-weekly in a clinic. A period of regression had set in after the therapist had initiated a change in the patient's hour. Depressive symptoms were prominent, and the patient had taken a leave of absence from her job. The therapist had been unable to adequately interpret the material from the patient, which reflected an enormous sense of rage and disillusionment because of the therapist's failings, and because of the great hurt involved in the shift in hour. The therapist soon became concerned about the patient's suicidal potential, and he gave her his home telephone number. There were many telephone calls, and on several occasions, the therapist's daughter and wife answered the telephone. In the midst of this chaos, the following exchange took place during a scheduled session:

Patient: I don't feel well. I felt especially bad after the last telephone call. I feel guilty calling you. I keep confusing the past with the present. I prostituted myself in my job by showing people how well the doctor did my feet [*he was a podiatrist*]. His wife stole from him. When I separated from my husband, they got me a lawyer. But then they sat in on the conference when I talked to him, and now I feel I shouldn't have depended on them or have let them get involved. The lawyer kept trying to seduce me, and kept saying my husband must be a latent homosexual, I'm so attractive. I kept waiting for my husband to come back, but he never did. My gynecologist removed my IUD and suggested I have my tubes tied. My friend told me the operation was unnecessary. Another doctor wanted to remove a cyst in his office, and my friend said it had to be done in the hospital.

Therapist: You are speaking of doctors and lawyers who became involved with you and seductive. This must connect to my letting you call me, which you experienced as seductive.

Patient: That's true, I feel terrible after I call. It keeps me from doing anything the whole day. I began to wonder why you did it. I had the thought that you want to keep me using the clinic. A friend who didn't know I was coming here saw me in the waiting room today.

Therapist: Our time is up.

Patient: I keep thinking of how the attorney said my husband must be a homosexual. If he's a homosexual, what am I? Sometimes I feel that I am not a complete woman. There are lots of things I have had trouble telling you about, things about sex.

This patient had been involved in efforts to establish a form of pathological symbiosis with the therapist, doing so through direct demands for reassurence, support, directives, alterations in the ground rules, and a variety of noninterpretive interventions. It is striking, however, that the patient responds with constructively-toned Type Two derivative communications to the therapist's establishment of a pathological symbiosis (which satisfied his own needs to be inappropriately in contact with the patient and to offer a form of noninterpretive repair rather than an interpretive response within a secure framework)—an effort that undoubtedly satisfied a variety of additional unconscious countertransference needs and fantasies. The patient offers clear models of rectification, proposes through derivatives a more commensal or healthy symbiotic form of relatedness, and appears to respond by attempting to effect a relatively healthy symbiosis with the therapist. The designated therapist has become the functional patient, and the designated patient the functional therapist.

The patient characterizes the pathological symbiotic needs of the therapist as a form of prostitution, and as an effort to gratify himself through the patient in a manner comparable to that obtained from a prostitute (this along the me/not-me interface)—expressions that suggest part object representations. The exploitative qualities of the pathological parasitic aspects of the therapist's deviant interventions are reflected in the podiatrist's wife stealing from her husband. The patient's lack of autonomy is seen in her permitting the podiatrist to arrange an attorney for her and to participate in what should have been a private discussion. This aspect touches upon other alterations in the basic framework that exist in this clinic therapy, with third parties to treatment a major factor (cf. the reference to being seen in the clinic by a friend).

The patient also characterizes the therapist's pathological relationship needs as creating an inappropriate form of treatment, one that is effected in the wrong locale. The allusions to the IUD and to having her tubes tied may well be derivative communications related to the qualities of the pathological therapeutic symbiosis and parasitism that derived from and related to early mother-child (fetus) interactions.

Following the therapist's intervention, which moved in the right direction while being rather incomplete, the patient indicates that engagement with the therapist in the therapeutic modes of relatedness renders her nonfunctional, mistrustful, feeling used (kept captive at the clinic), and incomplete as a person (i.e., unable to individuate). The allusion to homosexuality may well reflect an unconscious perception of, and interpretation to, the therapist, to the effect that he is attempting to merge with this patient in an effort to gratify latent homosexual wishes, and on another level, to defend against their influence. Pathological symbioses and parasitic modes of relatedness typically gratify and defend against sexual and aggressive instructual-drive needs.

The Roles and Images of Patient and Therapist

Many of the efforts by either participant to press the other member of the therapeutic dyad into adopting a particular role or experiencing a particular kind of self-image are quite unconscious, and they may be placed into two broad categories that exist on a continuum: (1) those that are healthy, constructive, positively-toned, and essentially nonpathological; and (2) those that are essentially destructive, disruptive, anxiety-provoking or depressing, and pathological. Thus the patient may attempt consciously, and especially unconsciously, to have the therapist intervene not only in an inappropriate manner, but also in keeping with valid techniques. This last is the offer of models of rectification (or models of positive identification) that usually arises in response to a technical error by the therapist.

In the above vignette, for example, the patient implies, through a mixture of correct comment and derivative communication, that the therapist's offer of his home telephone number is an inappropriate form of prostitution, a form of seduction and defense, an invasion of privacy (on both sides), an infantilization, and a form of merger that prevents individuation. She then indicates in encoded expressions that it is a form of poor therapeutic practice, and that a more appropriate therapeutic procedure should be instituted in its place (the cyst should be removed in a hospital rather than the office). Through these communications, the patient is attempting to evoke a series of destructive, self-images within the therapist—images that are, however, appropriate to his poor techniques. It could well be that on the basis of such inner experiences, the therapist could recognize and become motivated to change his techniques and his pathological mode of relatedness with the patient. In addition, there may well be efforts here to have the therapist experience appropriate guilt, partly to harm him and partly to motivate him to change.

This material is also designed unconsciously to make the therapist rectify and secure the ground rules and boundaries of this therapeutic reltionship. Nowhere in this material does the patient acknowledge the well-meaning, life-saving intentions of the therapist. This suggests that the patient is experiencing far more of the destructive implications of these deviations than their (however misguided) constructive intentions. It may well be that deviant efforts of this kind, used to deal with a therapeutic crisis of such proportions, serve mainly to further intensify the patient's symptoms and suicidal potential. The material in this hour suggests such a thesis, and even in the absence of its validation, it can serve as a strong reminder of the detrimental consequences of well-meaning noninterpretive interventions. The main point here, however, is how the patient is attempting to direct the therapist toward assuming his appropriate role in the therapeutic dyad.

DESIGNATED AND FUNCTIONAL ROLES

A particular aspect of role and image evocation, and of the relationship between the patient and therapist, involves two continuums: (1) the extent to which either participant is expressing therapeutic ministrations, and (2) the extent to which either participant is expressing therapeutic needs.

It must be recognized that the usual usage of the terms *patient* and *therapist* refers to the *designated patient* and *designated therapist*. One must then establish through an examination of the spiraling interaction which participant is *functioning* at a given moment as patient or therapist. The *functional patient* may in any given interlude be either the designated patient and/or the designated therapist. The *functional therapist* similarly may either be the designated patient and/or the designated therapist. These determinations can be made only in the light of a full analysis of a therapist's interventions and the patient's manifest and derivative responses.

In the above vignette, the intervention context of offering the patient the therapist's telephone number expressed a therapeutic need within the therapist, so that he could be labeled at that moment the functional patient. This is borne out in the patient's material in the allusion to the homosexuality within her husband. The corrective measures described by the patient, as well as her derivative unconscious interpretations, suggest that, in response, she had momentarily served as the functional therapist, albeit on a derivative level.

Unconscious interpretations are disguised and *derivative communications* from either patient or therapist that have the following encoded (nonmanifest) attributes: (1) they deal with an indicator or therapeutic context, a disturbance within the person toward whom the intervention is directed; (2) they are organized around an activated intervention or adaptation-evoking context; and (3) they include an understanding of some aspect of the responsive derivative complex. When all of this takes place without the direct awareness of the person who is commenting or intervening, and is carried out on a latent level of expression, it can be characterized as an unconscious interpretation. When it is done within awareness and deliberately, it is of course, an interpretive intervention.

Of course, in the therapeutic situation, the therapist is asked *not* to express his or her own therapeutic needs to the patient. Because of the presence of inevitable countertransferences, however, this ideal is never fully met. As a result, small degrees of pathological inputs and brief moments during which the designated therapist becomes the functional patient occur in the course of every theraputic experience. More compelling moments, based on preponderant countertransferences in which the assigned therapist becomes in some dramatic manner the functional patient, are likely to occur from time to time in the work of any therapist. The goal is to keep such interludes to a minimum, and to recognize their presence and influence so that the therapist may rectify and self-analyze his or her own disturbance, interpret the full interlude to the patient based on the latter's derivative associations, and benefit in passing from the patient's unconscious therapeutic ministrations. Clearly, if the therapist shifts too often, or engages in too many major thrusts toward adopting the role of the functional patient, the therapeutic experience will be disfigured and the pathology of the therapist will be too dominant for a sound therapeutic outcome for the patient. While therapeutic gain for the therapist is inevitable in the course of work with patients, especially if he or she attends to the therapeutic interaction in light of these considerations, the therapist has the responsibility to consistently strive against the expressions of his or her own psychopathology in treatment endeavors, and to keep such experiences to a realistic minimum.

In sum, then, the designated therapist is expected to operate as the functional therapist as much as possible, and to do so manifestly and directly. The therapist will inevitably express himself or herself as a functional patient from time to time, although this should always occur through inadvertent, countertransference-based derivative communications contained in well-meaning, but erroneous interventions. Such needs should never be expressed manifestly to the patient through self-revelation and direct appeal for aid.

In contrast, the designated patient is expected to express manifest therapuetic needs, backed up by derivative communications that reflect in part an appeal for therapeutic help. The patient's most valid therapeutic efforts will take place on an unconscious and derivative level, and seldom unfold directly and manifestly. It is self-evident that the therapeutic situation is designed for expressions of therapeutic need from the patient, though the patient may of course prove resistant in this area. Nonetheless, his or her expression of both therapeutic wishes and resistances against them are important reflections of his or her psychopathology, and are therefore to be expected and analyzed by the therapist. On the other hand, the patient is not expected to function manifestly as therapist, nor should this role be forced on the patient beyond the inevitable brief interlude.

On rare occasion, in face of a blatant error or transgression by the therapist, a patient may respond with manifest therapeutic ministrations. In most other situations, oddly enough, manifest therapeutic efforts by the patient prove, upon analysis for their derivative meanings, to have little in the way of sound therapeutic value for the therapist, and to serve mainly as encoded communications related to an activated intervention context. Thus most conscious efforts to be therapeutic by patients prove to serve some other function, and their more genuine therapeutic endeavors tend to be conveyed through derivative expressions. This last implies, of course, that the therapist can recognize these therapeutic ministrations only when he or she understands the manifest and latent implications of his or her interventions and attends to the patient's manifest and latent associations in light of their implications.

The extent to which a patient obtains some measure of therapeutic gain through unconscious therapeutic efforts on behalf of the therapist is difficult to determine. There is no doubt that when a therapist is able to recognize such an interlude, and to interpret its implications to the patient based on the latter's derivative material, considerable insight and growth will take place for both participants. Often, however, an intervention of this kind does not prove feasible; instead, the therapist must silently benefit from the patient's therapeutic ministrations and quietly adjust his or her errant techniques accordingly. It seems likely that the patient is in some way strengthened through such means. It is also quite clear, however, that the patient's Neurosis cannot be insightfully resolved on such a basis. Nonetheless, on an unconscious level, patients almost universally respond to consciously and especially unconsciously expressed therapeutic needs in the therapist with a shift on an unconscious level through which they become the functional therapist.

CLINICAL EXAMPLE

A middle-aged woman came into therapy for arthritis and a multiplicity of somatic complaints, though in addition, it was evident she had some problems relating to men (she had married rather late in life). The therapy had not gone well, and the therapist had difficulty in intervening in valid fashion. After seven months of once-weekly treatment, the patient announced her decision to terminate near the end of a session. During the earlier part of the session, the patient had been unconsciously working over several erroneous interventions by the therapist, though the therapist had failed to interpret the material in proper fashion. She simply advised the

patient to return for one more hour. The following is an excerpt
from the final session, which took place the next week:

> Patient: I dropped my purse and bumped my head in the car.
> There is a lever there, but it's a bad place for it to be. I also
> nearly knocked over your lamp in the waiting room. I have
> nothing to say. What does one say in the last session?
> *(Silence.)*
> Therapist: You're talking about getting in your own way and
> having nothing to say in this last session. This may have to
> do with your not wanting to talk about leaving and about
> this actually being your last hour.
> Patient: I don't want to start things that would have to be
> dropped. All I can think of is that my mother apologized to
> me. It's not all me. She really has a problem. She never says
> the right thing. Maybe it has to do with her relationship with
> her own mother, but that should be her problem, not mine.
> I'm feeling tense and overburdened on the job. I have to do
> everybody else's work and I don't get paid more for it. I'd like
> to file a grievance. I'm going to change things, and from now
> on just do my own job and no one else's work. My supervisor
> is a jerk. I've been married two years, and the accountant
> figured out that I would be better off single when it comes to
> my tax return. The people at work confide their problems in
> me. I wish I were they so I could talk to myself and give
> myself advice. There's something wrong with the whole
> situation.

In the adaptive context of the therapist's manipulative intervention through which she insisted that the patient return for one
last session, and in light of the background intervention context of
her poor therapeutic efforts, the material from this patient can be
organized as a response to the unconscious implications of the
therapist's mistaken efforts. Through erroneous interventions, the
therapist had expressed herself as a functional patient. Her interventions had distinctly quarrelsome and hostile qualities, and often
reflected a profound sense of confusion and a need for assistance.
The patient quickly represents these hurtful and aggressive attributes, which she has unconsciously perceived in the therapist's
efforts, by bumping her own head and nearly knocking over the
therapist's lamp. She comments too at the outset of the session that

something is in the wrong place, a derivative that represents her unconscious realization that she should not be present for this final session, but should have been allowed to carry out her autonomous decision to leave therapy.

It would appear that the therapist's early intervention in this hour, which was not developed in terms of an activated intervention context and was somewhat speculative, may have served as a reminder to the patient of the therapist's erroneous efforts. In any case, the patient went on to indicate through derivatives that the therapist was in actuality behaving in some way comparable to the patient's own quarrelsome mother who, in turn, had a problem with her own mother. Here, then, the patient, as an unconscious functional therapist, offers an unconscious interpretation to the therapist that her manipulative and aggressive interventions may be based on some unresolved problems with her own mother. In supervision, the therapist was able in a general manner to confirm this unconscious interpretive effort.

In this particular hour, the patient seems quite mindful of the extent to which this therapist pressed her into the role of functional therapist. She speaks of being overburdened, of having to do someone else's job, and of not being paid for it. She speaks of now deciding to do a job for herself and how she would be better off single. Finally, she alludes to how other people at work confide in her, and how she is pressed into a therapeutic role that she wishes she herself could avail herself of and benefit from. These are all powerful representations of valid unconscious perceptions of the extent to which, quite unconsciously, this patient was asked to serve as therapist to her therapist. It seems evident from this material that failing to obtain insightful therapeutic work for herself, this patient grew wary of serving as the unconscious functional therapist in this treatment situation. Since these were the main derivative communications in this final session, it seems quite likely that the patient's sense of being pressed into the role of functional therapist again and again in the course of this psychotherapy, and her realization that the therapist was unable to rectify the situation, were major factors in this patient's decision to terminate her treatment and to attempt to effect her own cure. This is a strong reminder that skewed therapeutic interactions of this kind do not ultimately benefit the patient and may lead to premature termination of the psychotherapy.

Interactional Mechanisms

Clearly, the nature of the defenses within the patient and therapist influence their interchanges. This applies as well to interactional mechanisms, of which projective identification and introjective identification are the most notable. These mechanisms may be distinguished from essentially intrapsychic defenses and processes in that they involve actual, though unconscious, attempts to influence the other person (the object), an effect that is absent or secondary with intrapsychic mechanisms. On the other hand, interactional mechanisms by no means constitute the totality of object relationships, which embrace many other dimensions, mechanisms, and processes, and involve both intrapsychic and interactional phenomena.

Projective identification may be defined as a form of *interactional projection* in which the subject (patient or therapist) attempts to interactionally place or dump into the object (therapist or patient) some inner fantasy, defense, or any other aspect of his or her inner mental world. It is a form of projection, in that the inner content or process is being extruded and stirred up and placed into the other person, though the stress here is on actual interactional efforts. It is a form of *identification* in a sense unusual for this term, in that it implies that the subject is still *identified with* the contents or processes being placed into and evoked in the object, and that in addition, the effort here is to *stimulate an identification* in the object with the subject. This interactional mechanism is essential to the Type B mode of communication and stresses action-discharge, riddance, and evacuation.

Introjective identification is the complementary process that takes place in objects open to the reception of projective identifications. The term implies an incorporation of the projectively identified contents and processes, as well as a subsequent working over. The recipient of a projective identification is termed the *container,* and the contents or processes that are projectively identified are the *contained* (Bion 1962). The working over of a projective identification is its *metabolism* or its metabolic processing, and when properly carried out, is sometimes referred to as a process of *detoxification*—in response to a toxic or pathological projective identification. The object may be refractory to the subject's projective identifications and refuse to contain. In general, however, containing does take place, and the processing of a projective identification is based on factors within the subject, the nature of that which is to be contained, and the containing and other capacities of the object.

In psychotherapy, projective identifications may be initiated by either participant. Those that stem from the therapist, usually in the form of modifications in the ground rules and through noninterpretive interventions, have not as yet received sufficient attention in the literature. However, they may be an important initiator (though always, under the influence of the patient) of a series of exchanges of pathological projective identifications without insight. There are situations in which a patient initiates a pathological projective identification and the therapist fails to metabolize the incorporated contents and processes toward interpretation. Instead, he or she responds with a pathological projective identification of his or her own. In these reactions the therapist is engaging in a *projective counteridentification* (Grinberg 1962).

The therapist's role is to contain and metabolize the patient's pathological projective identification toward understanding and interpretation (though not all such mechanisms are pathological). These are experienced as interactional pressures, often toward deviation and noninterpretive intervention, and as difficulties the patient is creating for the therapist. The appropriate response is containing (tolerating and mastering) until these efforts are represented in the patient's (cognitive) free associations, and interpretation is feasible.

Patients will usually respond to pathological projective identifications in the therapist by containing the contents and processes, and by unconsciously metabolizing them toward *unconscious* interpretation. Efforts to exploit the pathological projective identification from the therapist as a means of supporting the patient's own psychopathology will be mixed in with therapeutic responses. This leads to responsive pathological projective identifications back into the therapist. The original pathological projective identification from the therapist tends to mix with the pathology of the patient.

CLINICAL EXAMPLE

In the following session, a therapist experienced pathological projective identifications from his patient. These were part of a circular interaction that developed when the patient was unable to pay his bill for therapy for several months. At first the therapist continued to see the patient without comment, although for a few weeks prior to the session presented here, he had begun to respond both interpretively and noninterpretively to the problem, largely because the sum involved had become quite large. The matter came to a climax when the therapist, based on little derivative material from the patient, suddenly suggested that the patient would either have to begin to significantly reduce his indebtedness or temporarily terminate the treatment. The patient's responsive associations revealed derivatives that showed that the suddenness of the pronouncement, and the therapist's failure to base it on the patient's derivative associations, had had a major impact. It led the patient to experience this intervention as a pathological projective identification that constituted some type of assault, reflected difficulties within the therapist in managing his aggression, and dumped onto the patient the therapist's inability to cope with the situation.

> Patient: *(While standing:)* I'm very upset. Therapy is going nowhere. I don't want to pay the bill, but I don't want to terminate.
>
> Therapist: Perhaps you should be on the couch.
>
> Patient: *(Sitting on the couch:)* I've been throwing my money away. I don't know what I'll do. Maybe I'll leave now and return in the fall after I pay the bill. I've got a lot of projects in the fire. I just don't want to continue for now. That's it. I'm going to leave. *(Stands up to go.)* If I'm here next Tuesday, I'm continuing. If I'm not, I'm terminating.
>
> Therapist: You appear to be quite upset and to want to terminate, but you spoke about the money, and actually last session began to pay a small part of your fee.
>
> Patient: I'm leaving. *(Leaves.)*

The patient did appear for his next session and continued to reduce his indebtedness to the therapist. In the session described, the therapist felt under enormous pressure. He was in conflict and did not want to lose the patient, and yet wanted to resecure the frame. He found himself without derivatives to interpret, though the intervention context was clear: it was his own threat to terminate the patient. A manifest content, Type B mode of relatedness had been effected, and it had strong parasitic qualities: on both sides, there was a sense of destructiveness without effort to understand or to adaptively resolve the fee issue.

In terms of interactional mechanisms, the therapist experienced himself as being forced to contain the patient's sense of agitation, of blind destructiveness, of action and flight, and of uncertainty. Many of these qualities were confirmed in the patient's manifest and derivative associations in the following hour, although they could not be validated in the previous abbreviated session. Still, it was possible for the therapist to realize that the patient had interactionally projected into him, quite without detoxification, pathological pressures and mechanisms he himself had placed into the patient the previous hour. The patient's mode of communication was Type B-C, as had been the therapist's. The interlude here involved an exchange of pathological projective and introjective identifications, without sound containing and without processing toward interpretation—consciously by the therapist or unconsciously by the patient. It eventually proved possible for the therapist to interpret the patient's efforts at pathological projective identification in light of his own erroneous intervention (the adaptive context).

Summary and Conclusions

The ground rules and boundaries of the therapeutic relationship constitute the basic means through which both the mode of cure and primary mode of relatedness is established between the patient and therapist. When the therapeutic environment is securely established and maintained, the patient has an opportunity for a commensal relationship or therapeutic symbiosis. When altered through deviations, pathological autism, symbiosis, or parasitism prevails. All noninterpretive interventions reinforce these latter qualities.

Psychotherapy should be constituted in actuality through a basic relationship that has the attributes of a healthy symbiosis with appropriate boundaries between the patient and therapist, including the necessary frustration of merger and fusion wishes. This type of relationship motivates the patient to express his or her Neurosis through derivative communications, perceptions, and fantasies, which permits both interpretive and framework-management responses by the therapist. All departures from the patient's basic responsibilities to the therapist and therapeutic interaction, and by the therapist to the therapeutic needs of the patient as explicated through a fundamental interpretive and framework-management approach, will create basic modes of relatedness that are either pathologically autistic, parasitic, or symbiotic.

Both the patient's and therapist's intrapsychic defenses influence their mode of relatedness and the therapeutic experience. Similarly, the use of interactional mechanisms such as projective identification has an important bearing on the therapeutic transactions. All such mechanisms constitute but one dimension of the therapeutic relationship and interaction, however, and can be understood in part as a way of characterizing an aspect of the basic mode of relatedness between the two participants to therapy.

Two critical dimensions of the therapeutic relationship involve expressions of therapeutic need and of curative endeavors. It is necessary to analyze each therapeutic interlude in light of the implications of activated intervention contexts and the patient's manifest and derivative reactions in order to determine which member of the therapeutic dyad is *functioning* as patient and/or therapist. For each, the hallmarks of the therapeutic and patient roles are somewhat different. The recognition of shifts in unconscious role functions by both patient and therapist should involve a perspective in which it is recognized that the therapist will on occasion unconsciously express therapeutic needs; however, he or she must consciously strive to control or minimize all such occurrences and safeguard against their more open and blatant expressions.

In principle, since the mode of relatedness influences the meanings and functions of all communications to and from both the patient and therapist, it is essential that a healthy symbiosis be constituted between the patient and therapist as a foundation for framework management and interpretive responses. While the therapist's interventions influence this mode of relatedness, the basic qualities of the relationship itself in turn influence the implications of the therapist's interventions. The mode of relatedness and the meanings and functions of the therapist's interventions must be consonant for the patient to have an effective therapeutic experience. Similarly, the patient's professed wish to relate to the therapist in a healthy manner must find support and reinforcements in his or her actual conscious and unconscious communications to, and demands on, the therapist. Resistances and pathology in regard to mode of relatedness are first-order therapeutic contexts for the therapist's interpretive and framework-management responses. They are interactional products whose sources must be traced in both the patient and therapist.

Part V

Resistances and Interventions

Chapter 33

Resistances

Resistances are all efforts by the patient to oppose the appropriate procedures of psychotherapy and to therefore interfere with its insightful outcome. Resistance in essence implies opposition to the therapy and therapist. As such, the emergence of resistances disturb the progress of treatment, often disrupt the alliance sector, and constitute first-order *indicators (therapeutic contexts)* for framework management and interpretive interventions. Such work is carried out with the understanding that (1) the *evaluation* that the patient is resisting is a *subjective* one within the therapist, and requires validation; (2) resistances are unconsciously determined and meaningful phenomena; (3) resistances must be conceptualized in light of the communicative interaction and the interventions of the therapist; and (4) the analysis of resistances meaningfully touches upon important aspects of the patient's Neurosis. Intervention in terms of the patient's resistances and defenses must precede intervention related to nonresistant communications.

Gross Behavioral Resistances

The simplest class of resistances involves the gross behaviors of the patient and all evident forms of opposition to treatment. Included here are such behaviors as silence (a model of resistance: the failure to free associate), lateness to sessions, missed hours, infractions in regard to the other ground rules of therapy, and a direct refusal to cooperate with a therapist by becoming refractory to listening and to endeavoring to integrate the therapist's interventions.

Some therapists believe that patients ideally should fluctuate in associations between the past and the present, and there is some evidence that at the very least, long periods of failure to allude to important genetic figures may be seen as some type of resistance. Gross rumination and repetitiveness, and failures to produce fresh material (a criterion difficult to define on the surface), have also been included. Some therapists have proposed that long periods of stalemate suggest resistances that have been missed by the therapist.

In addition to these rather evident forms of resistance, any effort by the patient to unilaterally, or with the cooperation of the therapist, alter the basic ground rules and boundaries of the therapeutic relationship constitutes a form of resistance. These efforts would be included in a broad categorization termed *acting in,* which would involve all behaviors by the patient in the session designed to bypass the usual avenues of therapeutic work. There is also a final broad category of resistance that has been termed *acting out,* the reenactment by the patient, with the therapist or with others, of unconscious fantasy-memory and perception constellations in a manner designed for pathological gratification rather than for insight and understanding.

While the resistance qualities of certain behaviors are self-evident, the evaluation of such matters as acting out (i.e., the distinction between adaptive sequences of actions and those that are maladaptive) is fraught with subjective elements. Much must depend on the extent to which the patient communicates the particular incident in a manner that eventually permits interpretation, or in contrast, simply resorts to actions in a context that does not permit suitable interventions from the therapist. All patients in therapy will attempt to unconsciously reenact the pathogenic past and past pathogenic relationships in the interaction with their therapists. While these behaviors undoubtedly have a resistance dimension, this need not necessarily be the case. They also serve as rich sources of potentially interpretable material. Ultimately, it is the presence or absence of communicative resistances that proves crucial to the distinction between resistant and nonresistant acting out.

Communicative Resistances

The patient cooperates with or opposes the therapist not only on the surface, but unconsciously as well. The latter is most noticeable in the area of communication, and *communicative resistances* are quite readily identified with the adaptive context approach.

In the presence of an activated intervention context, the ideal resistance-free communicative network would include a direct allusion to an indicator (either the adaptive context itself, or some other therapeutic context, such as the patient's defensiveness), a reference to the intervention context made manifestly but in passing (i.e., the patient then changes the subject), and a series of coalescible derivative elements contained in the balance of the patient's manifest association. This is the criterion of absent or low-level resistance (the patient is probably never entirely resistance free), and it implies three possible forms of communicative resistance: (1) *the patient's failure to allude to a known indicator* (e.g., a break in the frame by either participant, such as when a therapist or patient is late for an hour and the patient fails to mention it directly in the course of his free associations); (2) *a failure to refer directly to the adaptive context, or to represent it with minimal disguise* (e.g., a failure to mention the therapist's lateness or a blatantly erroneous intervention, or to represent the former by referring to someone else who was late or the latter by mentioning how the comments made by a particular person outside of therapy never seem to be helpful); or (3) *a failure to produce a coalescible derivative complex* that can be meaningfully organized around the activated intervention context.

Communicative resistances imply, then, that the patient is opposing the therapeutic process by failing to provide the therapist with the material needed for interpretation or management of the frame. They indicate both resistance and intrapsychic defense, and may also receive critical contributions from the therapist. They are difficult to interpret because, by definition, the patient's material does not permit such an intervention. However, they do respond well to the rectification of the therapist's contributions to the communicative resistance, to silent holding and containing until the patient is able to resolve the resistance (as often happens under such conditions), and to occasional interpretations, which are feasible when the patient *represents the resistance* (the indicator) itself with minimal disguise and shifts to the momentary production of an interpretable communicative network (adaptive context and derivatives). On the whole, silent holding and containing, and the rectification of the therapist's contributions, lead to the resolution of most communicative resistances.

In the middle phase of most psychotherapies, the patient will not create pressures on the therapist to intervene, and will accept a holding-containing mode of relatedness for some time. With the framework intact, the patient is in a state of *lying fallow*, during which he or she tends to adaptively modify his or her own pathological defences and pathological lie-barrier systems. During these pathological periods, there is often no active intervention context, and because of this, the patient should not be considered to be in a state of resistance because he or she does not provide the therapist with an interpretable communicative network. Instead, this should be seen as an adaptive, necessary period of noncommunication without resistance and pathological implications. Most, if not all, patients will need a period of *adaptive* communicative "resistance," and the determination of the presence of pathological resistance depends upon the identification of an activated intervention context.

CLINICAL EXAMPLE

A young man with both alcoholic and homosexual problems was being seen in once-weekly psychotherapy by a woman therapist who had engaged in many alterations in the ground rules and boundaries of their relationship and of the treatment situation. Most recently, he had been given a session on a different day from usual in order to permit a trip for a week out of the country. In brief, the patient had spent the entire time of the makeup session pledging himself to give up drinking and detailing ways in which he would avoid the temptation of liquor. He had not had a drink for two weeks, and detailed the thoughts he had about the plane trip to Europe and how he would get his friends in London to protect him from the temptation of drink. The therapist had intervened noninterpretively with so-called supportive interventions designed to encourage the patient in his resolve and determination to avoid liquor.

In the hour excerpted here, the patient had been highly ruminative, and there had been long periods of silence. The rumination and silence could be viewed as gross behavioral resistance. In addition, it is quite likely that the patient's decision to be out of the country at this time (only weeks before the therapist's own vacation) was actually a form of acting out designed to deal maladaptively with the therapist's vacation and other issues in this treatment situation. As such, it may be postulated that this was a form of resistance designed to preclude the presence of, and therapeutic work with, the patient's separation anxieties and fantasied and perceptive responses to the pending absence of the therapist. As such, these resistances obtain considerable interactional support from the therapist's policy of offering makeup sessions, from her actual offer of a makeup session for this particular missed session, and from her failure to intervene interpretively and to maintain the framework itself in light of the patient's evident resistances.

In respect to communicative resistances, the patient in this hour never once alluded to the fact that the session was being held at a time different from his usual appointment with the therapist. He therefore failed to meaningfully represent an important indicator and intervention context (the therapist's deviation). The derivative complex also appeared to be highly resistant, in that the patient engaged in ruminative associations with little derivative implication, and there was a distinct lack of a set of coalescing derivatives.

Part of the session (excerpted in part earlier in this book), which took place upon the patient's return and at his usual time, is presented here:

Patient: I shouldn't be here. I took a bunch of downers. *(Silence.)* I had no drinks in Europe *(described in detail).* I kept thinking of calling to cancel my session. There was plenty of liquor around in London, but everybody kept me away from it. I felt like a baby. *(More details.)* Then I drank on the plane home. *(Silence.)* I was so indulged, I felt like a baby.

Therapist: You've taken some drugs and wanted to cancel your appointment. You've been drinking since you left London, but didn't drink there. Your friends helped to prevent it. That made you feel like a baby.

Patient: Yes, I felt so lonely. I and Daniella [*his boyfriend*] had the best sex we ever had, but it didn't satisfy me. I felt terribly alone. He kept telling me things about himself, and I pretended I was you, trying to help him. *(Silence.)* I remember asking one of my previous therapists how I could stop being gay. He told me I shouldn't stop, I should be what I am, and that I am gay.

Therapist: Feeling gay made you feel lonely.

Patient: It's not that I want sexual relations with a woman. It's just that I'd like a family and children. *(Silence.)* The psychiatrist said gay people are being treated with insulin comas, and that I'd better just accept it. It does make me feel lonely. Anyhow, I'm going home now. *(Patient stands up to leave.)*

Therapist: You're talking about feeling lonely and upset, and then rather than continuing to think, you act. It's reflected in your taking alcohol and downers, and then leaving the session.

Patient: *(Sitting for a moment.)* Whatever you say. I'm going home now to be alone. Can I have another session this week?

Therapist: I have no other time.

Patient: I'm leaving now. *(Leaves the session about 15 minutes early.)*

Several *gross behavioral resistances* are presented: some surface rumination, periods of silence, coming to a session under the influence of drugs, and leaving the hour early. On the *communicative* level, it may be proposed that the patient represents the therapist's decision to change his previous hour—a key adaptive context—through the allusion to how his friends had indulged and protected him. This is a highly disguised representation and speaks for relatively strong communicative resistances in this regard. A clearer representation is offered toward the end of the session in the request for an additional hour, though it is made just prior to the patient's departure and is itself somewhat disguised.

Next, the patient directly represents several significant indicators—his alcoholism, drug-taking, and homosexuality, among others—though he does not include the indicators derived from the therapist's breaks in the frame. There are therefore important sectors of moderate and high resistance in regard to the patient's representations of the therapeutic contexts for this hour.

A similarly mixed picture applies to the derivative complex. It is possible to identify a coalescing derivative complex around the therapist's break in the frame and her noninterpretive interventions. The material yields derivatives that reflect the patient's unconscious preceptions of these interventions as inappropriately protective, infantilizing, and as conveying the therapist's inability to help the patient to resolve his alcoholism. They are gratifying to both the patient and the therapist in a manner that has sexual overtones for both of them, and they constitute assaultive and destructive modes of treatment that serve to reinforce rather than resolve the homosexualty he wishes to give up. In all, then, there is a lower level of resistance in regard to this particular derivative complex than in respect to the representations of the activated intervention contexts.

These impressions also apply to the therapist's pending vacation, which is represented here by the patient's own vacation, his decision to leave the session early, and his sense of loneliness. While there appears to be a somewhat meaningful responsive derivative complex, it emerges in a form that does not readily lend itself to interpretation. On a communicative level, the specific criterion of resistance that is most important is *the extent to which the patient's material lends itself to specific framework management and interpretive responses by the therapist.*

In this excerpt, the patient's mode of relatedness is largely pathologically symbiotic and parasitic, modes that to some extent are comparable to those reflected in the therapist's frequently erroneous interventions. Efforts to establish a pathological mode of relatedness are, of course, forms of latent resistance that tend to correlate with communicative resistances. There is a mixed quality to the patient's material, in that it is conveyed in part in the Type B communicative mode designed for action and discharge rather than understanding, but on the other hand, it contains a sufficiently meaningful communicative network to permit the interpretation of the indicators of the patient's wish to leave the hour and his need to take drugs before the session (in light of the adaptation-evoking context of the therapist's change in the hour and secondarily, her noninterpretive interventions and pending vacation). Overall, then, the patient appears to be expressing himself in a Type B-A mode, while the therapist's communicative style has mixed qualities: Types B and C. Because most of her interventions did not involve an activated intervention context, there was a strong sense of the therapist's need to destroy any possibility of a meaningful mode of relatedness between herself and the patient, and it is likely that there are strong qualities of a pathological autism in her manner of relating to the patient. Pathological symbiotic qualities are also in evidence.

As noted, communicative resistances are measured in terms of the extent to which the patient's material lends itself to interpretation and to framework-rectification responses. In this hour, both might have been feasible, in that the patient is clearly suggesting that the techniques of the therapist are destructive and inappropriate, and need to be changed. Thus, it seems that overall, there is a relatively low level of communicative resistance in the patient in this session. It is also clear that the therapist has contributed significantly to those resistances that do exist.

There is usually an interplay between gross behavioral and communicative resistances. In situations in which both are significantly high, a patient is usually engaged in the Type B-C mode of communication and a pathological mode of relatedness. The therapist will be hard pressed to make an interpretive intervention. Silent rectification of the framework, of any contribution the therapist has made to the resistance, and efforts at containing are usually necessary under these most difficult circumstances. On the other hand, in the presence of strong gross behavioral, but low communicative, resistances, it is usually posssible to meaningfully interpret the unconscious basis for the overt resistance in light of an activated inervention context.

The major role of alterations in the ground rules and boundaries of the therapeutic relationship as a means of expressing both resistances and counterresistances is demonstrated here through the way in which deviations played a significant role in the resistances observed within both the patient and therapist. The vast majority of resistances involve some issue related to the framework—a postulate that highlights from a fresh vantage point the finding that much of all effective psychotherapy unfolds from issues related to the ground rules and boundaries of therapy.

Transference and Nontransference (Interactional) Resistances

Although resistances, by definition, take place within, or are expressed by, the patient, their impetus may derive from primarily within the patient, or may receive their major stimulus from the therapist's interventions or failures to intervene. The latter constitute *interactional or nontransference resistances,* and are quite common in psychotherapy. They are based on need systems developed within the patient as a consequence of his or her object relationship with the therapist (with minor contributions from the patient). In contrast, those resistances that stem primarily from factors within the patient, though never entirely devoid of inputs from the therapist, have as their most important source the patient's own unconscious fantasy and perception constellations, virtually always as they pertain to the therapist. They are therefore termed *transference resistances.*

Resistances are prompted by anxiety, depression, and other disturbing affects, and by intrapsychic and interpersonal conflicts, which create needs for defense and then lead to the invocation of protective measures within the therapy—resistances. They arise as a means of defending against and yet representing (through compromise formations) an essentially unconscious disturbance *(Type A communicative resistances),* or of sealing off, obliterating, and erecting lie-barrier systems against underlying chaos *(Type C or lie-barrier resistances).*

While some superficial resistances will arise at a point where a patient begins to explore a disturbing aspect of his or her conscious or unconscious feelings, fantasies, and perceptions as they pertain to outside relationships, virtually all important unconsciously founded resistances involve the therapeutic relationship itself. The first group, transference-based resistances, involve *unconscious* feelings, fantasies, and reactions toward the therapist, derived from anxieties and conflicts generated because of distortions and misperceptions that the patient has toward the therapist. The genetically derived pathological unconscious fantasy constellation may prompt both gross behavioral and communicative resistances. They can be effectively resolved only through framework-management responses and interpretations offered in light of meaningful intervention contexts. In general, the therapist's prior valid interpretations and efforts to secure the framework lead to transference-based resistances in the patient (while errors in intervention tend to prompt non-transference or interactional resistances). Interpretations of these resistances must be made in light of the adaptive stimuli to which the patient is responding within the treatment relationship.

The second major source of resistance, which tends to be far more common than transference-based resistances, is based on valid unconscious perceptions of the therapist who behaves in some way that threatens the patient, or who intervenes inappropriately or in error, leading the patient, as a consequence, to oppose the therapist and his or her procedures. Nontransference resistances may also arise when the therapist unconsciously encourages the patient into an oppositional position, or when a therapist conveys anxieties to the patient about certain types of material—often involving sound unconscious perception of his or her errors, or highly charged instinctual drive transference or nontransference percep-tions and/or fantasies—and unconsciously encourages avoidance and defensiveness.

Virtually all resistances are interactional or mixtures of trans-ference and nontransference. In those situations where the therapist has intervened erroneously and mismanaged the framework, the patient's opposition is *not* to ideal therapeutic procedures, but to the therapist's errant ways. While therapists tend to experience all opposition to their techniques and interventions as pathological forms of resistance, it is clear that a full perspective on the patient's oppositional attitudes and behaviors will reveal that at times they are quite sound and adaptive, and entirely appropriate to the underlying truths of the therapeutic interaction (i.e., forms of *nonpathological resistance*). It is here that the therapist's judgment is most vulnerable to countertransference-based influences. The major safeguard against such errors is a careful and in-depth evaluation of the implications of each of the therapist's interven-tions to which the patient is presently responding.

Within the therapeutic interaction, inappropriate resistances by the patient are, to some extent, efforts to *thwart or harm* the therapist, and to frustrate his or her therapeutic ambitions and wishes to help the patient. However, there are many interactional resistances that are designed to *protect* the therapist and to spare him or her communications of hurtful unconscious perceptions and types of material that threaten the therapist (as signalled by him or her to the patient through the derivative implications of erroneous interventions). This is most readily seen when a patient begins to express derivatives of unconscious transference and nontransference perceptions and fantasies regarding the therapist, and the therapist intervenes in a manner designed to cut off the flow of these associations and to shift the patient's conscious and unconscious attention into other areas. The patient then falls silent or becomes ruminative, not only to oppose the therapist on the surface, but actually to cooperate with him or her unconsciously in a sector of misalliance, thereby protecting the therapist through resistances.

In the preceding clinical example, most of the patient's resistances were interactional and nontransference-based. This therapist, through Type C barrier interventions, had repeatedly set aside the derivative implications of the patient's associations, especially as they involved unconscious perceptions of her seductiveness, infantalization of the patient, and her own needs for a pathological form of symbiotic relatedness. The therapist's failures to maintain the framework and to respond to the patient's material with interpretations fostered both acting out and acting in by the patient, in that her own interventions emphasized noninsightful actions geared toward pathological symbiotic gratifications and action-discharge and evacuation. Through her noninterpretive interventions and deviations, the therapist had unconsciously encouraged comparable actions in the patient, and by shifting the hour, she had unconsciously encouraged the patient to modify the framework.

In this light, the need for the therapist to rectify her contributions to these resistances, to secure the framework of the therapy, to listen more openly, and to interpret the derivative implications of this patient's material, can be seen as the first level of intervening necessary for the resolution of these obstacles to therapy. These efforts could then be supplemented with interpretations of the basis for the patient's gross behavioral and communicative resistances, much of it couched in terms of valid unconscious perceptions, introjections, and nontransference-based mechanisms. On that basis, many of these resistances could be resolved, and the remainder could then be subjected to analysis in terms of the patient's pathology and transferences, rather than disturbances in the therapist. With counterresistances quite prevalent, the designated patient became the functional therapist—a shift represented in the patient's allusions to the way in which he adopted the therapist's functions with a friend.

CLINICAL EXAMPLE

A young man entered twice-weekly psychotherapy because of multiple somatic symptoms. Soon after beginning this therapy, he also began a program of biofeedback desensitization. The therapist had accepted this supplementary treatment without comment or interpretation. Several sessions later, the following material emerged:

Patient: I've been thinking about stopping this therapy. I'm harried coming here, and it takes away from my work. My friends say I should understand why I'm sick, but the answers I'm getting here are simplistic. I want to run away from upsetting things. One of my friends upset me on the job and I walked away from him. I sweep things under the carpet. I'd like you to give me some answers here. Sometimes I wonder if I'm giving you the right stuff. You don't say very much, and I don't think it's worth coming here anymore. I need help, but I'm not getting it. I need encouragement and support. I don't want to hurt anyone, but maybe I'm malicious. I might have to miss a session and want to know if you will charge me. It's something we have to agree on. If you do it my way, I won't pay when I'm out. If I took a vacation, I wouldn't want to have to pay you for it. Maybe I'm not talking about the right things. I need you to put me on the right path.

Therapist: You recognize that you need help and press me to do something quickly in the way of support and encouragement. But you even say that my doing that will keep things hidden, under the carpet, and on the surface. You're concerned about my policy which has you paying for missed sessions and feel malice and want to hurt me. As to your thoughts about taking a vacation, you emphasize the issue of money, but perhaps that's just on the surface and is a way of avoiding the real issue.

Patient: The money is the real issue for me. I do avoid things. For me objects count, not people. The picture has two sides and you can turn it over, but all I see is the money. Maybe I'm being defensive, but I don't mind as long as I keep the money.

More briefly, in the session that followed, the patient described several efforts to become involved with women. He also reported being uncomfortable alone with an older man he knew. He spoke of being more comfortable with men when someone else is around. He also mentioned the biofeedback training program.

The patient shows gross behavioral resistances by wanting to prematurely terminate his treatment, by pressing the therapist to modify the ground rules so that he would not be charged for missed sessions, and by engaging in highly ruminative sessions that were difficult to understand on the surface. On a communicative level, in the hour extracted here, he represents one intervention context—the therapist's ground rule regarding fees—while failing to represent the more critical intervention context of the therapist's silent acceptance of a second therapist for the patient's emotional problems. There are therefore major resistances in respect to the patient's representation of this indicator and adaptive context, although there is a somewhat meaningful derivative complex. Thus the patient is indicating that the deviation interferes with his communicative relationship with the therapist, but maintains it on a manifest content and pathological symbiotic level. This enables him to conceal expressions that pertain to the unconscious basis for his somatic symptoms. The patient's effort to have the therapist modify his ground rule regarding fees may be postulated to be a derivative representation of the break in the frame involving the additional therapy and therapist, and a means by which the patient is encouraging the therapist to secure that aspect of the frame as well.

The resistances within this patient are primarily non-transference-based or interactional, in that they derive in a significant way from the therapist's silent acceptance of the second therapy. In the second hour alluded to briefly above, the patient's material on a derivative level suggests that both he and the therapist accepted the third party to treatment as an expression of and defense against underlying homosexual anxieties. In the context of this unconscious interpretation by the patient, which undoubtedly applies to both participants to treatment, the patient then represents the critical adaptive context of his biofeedback treatment. This could have provided the therapist with an opportunity to interpret the patient's thoughts of termination, his tendency to be ruminative and to conceal, and his need for an additional therapist as being based on anxieties he perceives in the therapist regarding being

632 / Psychotherapy: A Basic Text

alone with the patient in treatment, anxieties with which he himself is also struggling. This type of *transversal* interpretation would deal with several critical resistance-indicators and the key adaptive context, using the patient's responsive derivative complex in terms first, of unconscious perceptions and then, of unconscious fantasies.

In this clinical situation, the sources and motives for the patient's resistances lay within both himself and the therapist, some of it in the form of unconscious homosexual perceptions, fantasies, and anxieties—on both their parts. Once these are represented in the patient's material, they should be interpreted as a means of modifying the patient's gross behavioral and communicative obstacles to therapeutic progress. This patient clearly represented his gross behavioral and communicative resistances, although he certainly did not consciously understand the existence and functions of the latter.

The protective aspect of the patient's resistances for the therapist can be seen here in the way in which the patient's use of a second therapist and of massive communicative defenses helped to protect the therapist from his own homosexual anxieties and unresolved fantasy-perception constellations. Similar protection is, of course, afforded the patient himself. On another level, these resistances are ultimately interfering and hurtful to the patient, although they are also hurtful to the therapist, who felt quite thwarted and frustrated in their presence, and found it difficult to understand the communications from his patient. This type of intermixture for both participants is quite common, and virtually all resistances do indeed serve to both harm and protect the therapist.

In addition to the interpretation and self-corrective efforts proposed here, the therapist would have to rectify any other contribution he was making to the patient's resistances before expecting to resolve them entirely. This could be accomplished by intervening, when material permitted, with interpretations regarding the unconscious meanings and functions of the second therapy, and by permitting full derivative communication of the patient's homosexual conflicts and anxieties. In addition, maintaining a secure frame in regard to fee and responsibility for sessions would also unconsciously convey the therapist's preparedness to be alone with the patient in some consistent way, and to deal with the consequent homosexual fantasy-perceptions and anxieties. Such efforts would have to be supported by self-analytic work by the therapist, carried out privately.

The patient's thoughts of termination—a gross behavioral resistance—occurring at a time when the therapist has been unable to secure the frame, to resolve homosexual countertransferences, and to offer sound interpretations to the patient, can from one vantage point be seen as more adaptive than maladaptive. While one would certainly expect the patient to make every effort to resolve this impasse with the therapist, the decision to terminate with a therapist who is unable to offer a healthy symbiotic relationship and an interpretive frame-securing approach cannot be viewed as an essentially pathological form of resistance. Thus, while resistance may be defined in a practical sense as any obstacle or opposition to therapy within the patient, one must carefully determine its sources in light of activated intervention contexts, fully recognizing contributions from both patient and therapist, and be prepared to evaluate their adaptive and maladaptive dimensions. Resistances are always efforts by the patient to cope with inner disturbances and disturbances with the therapist, but they may be inappropriately defensive or soundly adaptive.

Resistances and Defenses

In principle, gross behavioral resistances are overt actions based only in part on intrapsychic defenses. They are also founded on many other conscious and unconscious processes and mechanisms, such as unconscious perceptions, introjective identifications, projective identifications, and such. They are more comparable to *grossly defensive behaviors* in other situations than to intrapsychic defenses. Similarly, communicative resistances reflect both intrapsychic and interactional defensive operations and a number of additional supplementary mechanisms.

The key distinction between resistances and defenses lies in the finding that patients express themselves through disguised derivatives that reflect the continued operation of intrapsychic defenses even when they show a relatively low level of gross behavioral and communicative resistance. Communicative resistances are therefore intermittent, while intrapsychic and interactional defenses are ever-present (though, of course, they too tend to fluctuate). The latter are, however, far more pervasive than resistances and continue to operate in the relative absence of obstacles to therapy.

Silence as a Model of Resistance: A Clinical Example

The patient was a middle-aged, depressed woman in psychotherapy whose internist had felt an abdominal mass. Although there was reason to believe the lesion was benign, the patient was quite concerned about a pending gastrointestinal x-ray series.

In the session prior to the one excerpted here, the patient spoke of her anxieties that she might have a serious illness and that surgery might be recommended. She felt she was handling the situation well, and spoke of certain securities she had locked in a safety box at home that would protect her children's future. There was some concern about how her two children were doing in high school, but her son had shown considerable improvement with help. There had been a young woman in the therapist's waiting room (while he had rectified many deviations, he still maintained an office with a shared waiting room), and the patient didn't want to talk to her, even though the young girl had tried to engage in conversation. The patient had to visit a friend in a distant area, but was proud that she had found her way on her own. She was having thoughts of calling other therapists for help.

The therapist intervened and commented on the patient's anxiety about the pending x-rays and her own future, as well as the future of her children. He pointed to the patient's strong wishes for autonomy, and then commented upon her not wanting to talk to the girl in the waiting room. He linked this decision to the fact that he shared the waiting room with another therapist, and suggested that this arrangement interfered with her own sense of security and generated a sense of anger that he, the therapist, had someone else to rely on at a time when the patient wanted to be more independent. The patient responded that she had been thinking about her children. If she wasn't going to be around too long, she didn't want to give them too much, otherwise the separation would be difficult for them. She wanted really to help them with their autonomy.

The therapist had attempted to respond with sympathy to the patient's concern about the mass in her abdomen and her pending x-rays, and to link up in some way the patient's reaction to that particular situation with her response to the lack of privacy in the waiting room. In supervision, it was felt that the patient was in actuality attempting, in response to a life crisis, to maintain some communicative distance from the therapist and to deal with her problems in a relatively independent manner. Thus, while she did indeed represent an unresolved and unrectified intervention context in respect to the shared waiting room, she provided her own model of rectification and an actual sense of separateness by not talking to the other person who was present.

While interesting, her derivative communications do not coalesce around that particular intervention context, except perhaps by alluding to the therapist's own failure to achieve relative autonomy as reflected in his continued need to share the waiting room space. In the absence of meaningful and coalescible derivatives, it was felt that the intervention offered to the patient was unnecessary at the time, and that it would have been better to allow the patient to continue to lie fallow, to make use of some Type C barrier defenses, and to await further developments.

This assessment is strikingly borne out in the patient's derivative responses to the therapist's actual intervention. The patient reflects her unconscious perception of the therapist as having a need to give her too much, based on his own separation anxieties and difficulties with autonomy. At the same time, these associations reveal the unconscious basis for the patient's communicative resistances: she wishes to maintain some distance from the therapist in order not to experience his loss too deeply if she is, indeed, seriously ill. She indicates that she is doing this for both herself and the therapist, whom she has experienced unconsciously as overly dependent on her.

It might well have been possible to have offered an intervention along these lines to the patient, using the intervention context of the therapist's unneeded comment toward the end of the hour. The patient's derivative reaction is a reminder that despite the well-meaning claim of some therapists that conscious sympathy is essential when patients are in a state of crisis, patients who might accept such comments from their therapists on a manifest level would also on a derivative level, as seen with this patient, unconsciously experience such interventions as infantilizing, interfering with autonomy, and reflecting unresolved separation anxieties. The rules of communication and intervention in psychotherapy are in many important ways distinct from those that prevail in social contacts.

The subsequent hour included the following material:

> Patient: I had the x-rays today, and the technician didn't talk to me. I should get a report tomorrow. My son is having rectal bleeding again, and our physician wants to check it out. It's probably hemorrhoids, but we're concerned. There are so many things that we can't control in our lives. It's just an illusion that we control our own fate. I visited a friend and saw people on the GI ward, and some of them were very sick. I'm not even sure I would accept surgery if it is recommended. It taught me to accept delay, and I have learned that. But you can make it easier for me and you don't. When I was in school I would be an outsider even though I tried to participate. I thought of calling Dr. B. [*the therapist who shares the office with this therapist*] because he'd be kinder. Doctors don't tell the truth, and I want to know the truth so I can decide what to do once I have the x-ray report. *(Here, the patient fell silent for 15 minutes.)*

The therapist eventually responded to the patient's silence with a lengthy intervention about the patient's wish for reassurance and yet contradictory wish to not have it, since thoughts of reassurance led her to become silent. He also spoke of her wish to make her own decision as it seemed in conflict with her wish to be dependent upon himself, and of her resentment that he relied on Dr. B. In response, the patient spoke again of wanting to be independent and of how hurt she feels that if she needs surgery, the therapist will replace her with another patient.

In the intervention context of the therapist's previous unneeded intervention, the first level of meaning of the patient's silence in this hour is that of a maladaptive model of rectification. The patient offers silence to the therapist as a model of what she needs. In addition, the therapist's intervention reflects some sense of helplessness on his part, since he did not in that hour know how he could help the patient. In this light, the patient's silence reflects an introjective identification of the therapist's sense of difficulty.

The patient's associations regarding ways in which the therapist has not met her conscious wishes for direct reassurance suggests an additional adaptive context that takes the form of the therapist maintaining much of the frame and a basic interpretive stance. In the light of that particular context, the patient's silence may be viewed as a projective identification through which the patient is creating interactional pressures to have the therapist, who seems capable of maintaining most of the frame, experience some disruption in his functioning.

The patient began the hour by alluding to her own sense of helplessness in response to secondary contexts related to illness in both herself and her son. This is a cognitive representation of the patient's subsequent efforts at interactional projection through which she attempts to place into the therapist her own sense of inadequacy and difficulty. Quite often, silence is used in this way by patients, though frequently the intervention context, instead of being efforts by the therapist to secure the frame, is actually constituted by breaks in the frame. Such deviations tend to express pathological projective identifications by the therapist into the patient, so that the patient's silence must be understood in light of such an intervention context as a responsive pathological interactional projection. Under these hypothesized conditions, the therapist must, of course, rectify his or her contribution to the silence, which is always an *interactional resistance*.

In the present case, while one element of the silence derives as a response to the continued situation of the shared waiting room, most of it appears to be a reaction to the therapist's recent signs of integration and autonomy as reflected in his ability to secure this previously highly damaged therapeutic environment. Thus this particular silence represents in part a transference-based effort to destroy the therapist's competence at a time when the patient is experiencing a deep sense of inadequacy within herself. An interpretation could have been offered to the patient along such lines, and might well have received Type Two derivative validation. The therapist's own efforts failed to appreciate the implications of the activated adaptive contexts and the patient's derivative communications, and did little to modify this particular resistance.

In dealing with silences, one must adhere to the basic principle of working interpretively and with framework-management responses in light of the patient's derivative communications as organized by activated intervention contexts. In sessions where the patient begins the hour by being silent and maintains this stance for a long period of time, the therapist should be guided by what he or she can recall of the previous session. If the session seems to reflect a need for patient holding, the therapist might continue with his or her own silence. If there are indications of pathological projective identification and Type C barrier formations, the therapist might simply reflect upon the silence as a derivative communication. Thus the therapist might state that the patient seems to need to be silent and to cut off positive communication with the therapist. It is well to shape such comments in light of what is already known about the patient from previous sessions, but the therapist must maintain the principle of permitting each session to be its own creation; because of this, the therapist should not allude directly to previous material. A simple descriptive response is usually best, and will often help the patient to begin more active verbal-affective communication.

Since silence is both a gross behavioral and communicative resistance, it is especially difficult to deal with interpretively and through framework-management responses. Its very nature lends itself to interactional projection antithetical to insight and under-standing. As a basic principle, however, the therapist should always begin his or her investigation of a period of silence by the patient—and of all resistances—with efforts to identify his or her own contribution to the obtacle to treatment. Following that, the thera-pist's approach is essentially rectifying and interpretive. Silences that occur after the patient has already offered a verbal expression may often be understood in light of prior intervention contexts with the full aid of the understanding imparted by the patient's earlier derivative material.

Summary and Conclusions

Resistances may be of a gross behavioral or communicative nature. The former entails overt obstacles to therapy, while the latter involves disturbances in one or more of the elements of the communicative network.

The therapist's evaluation that the patient is in a state of resistance is a subjective one, and in need of validation through the patient's ongoing associations and further subjective considerations within the therapist. Essential to this determination is a sound grasp of the listening-experiencing process.

All resistances have inputs from both the patient and therapist, and are therefore constituted as interactional resistances. However, primarily nontransference-based resistances may be distinguished from those that are mainly transference-based. These relationship resistances are the major sources of disturbances in treatment. Nontransference resistances derive from unconscious perceptions of the therapist that either encourage resistant behaviors in the patient or prompt them as adaptive, or more rarely maladaptive, responses. Transference resistances occur in response to sound interventions by the therapist, and stem from genetically founded unconscious transference constellations.

There are many possible ways in which the therapist may influence the level of the patient's gross behavioral and communicative resistance. A correct intervention, once validated, may be followed by a diminution or intensification of resistances, just as an erroneous intervention may have a comparable effect. Because of this, fluctuations in resistance must be analyzed in light of prevailing intervention contexts. When the therapist unconsciously supports or seeks out resistances in the patient, the latter will tend to intensify his or her defensive position. On occasion, however, in the face of unconscious efforts by the therapist to reinforce or establish resistances within the patient, the patient will respond with a diminution of resistances on the communicative level, and sometimes on a gross behavioral level as well. (This in an effort to call the therapist's attention to the presence of the resistance and its underlying nature, including the therapist's contributions.) By rectifying his or her contribution to the patient's resistances, the therapist will usually effect a diminution in this area. By interpreting the unconscious basis for a resistance, the therapist will tend to generate a lessening of resistances, after which a new group of resistances may sometimes develop, either nontransference-based in response to a new countertransference-based error of the therapist, or transference-based in response to the therapist's sound intervening.

Patients tend to represent the presence of communicative resistances through derivatives. They are more likely to allude directly to gross behavioral resistance-indicators. In principle, resistances are a first-order indicator, and require interpretation in light of activated intervention contexts and the patient's derivative material. They are to be subjected to the interpretation of the unconscious meanings and functions of the resistance as revealed by the nature of adaptive stimuli and derivative material. They may also require framework-management responses in light of the patient's derivative directives. Rectification of the therapist's countertransference-based contributions to resistances, expressed through either erroneous interventions or mismanagements of the frame, is an essential step in dealing with all nontransference resistances. Transference-based communicative resistances are often best handled through sound holding and containing, which creates a mode of relatedness and setting in which the patient tends to spontaneously modify the resistances at hand.

Resistances are adaptive responses to the conscious and unconscious implications of the therapist's interventions. They may therefore be pathological or nonpathological, maladaptive or adaptive. Their underlying structure and function can be revealed only in light of the manifest and latent implications of the adaptation-evoking stimuli. These aspects of resistance tend to be illuminated in the patient's derivative material. However, resistances are *not* themselves adaptive contexts, but are instead *therapeutic contexts* created in response to the interventions by the therapist.

An understanding of the basic structure of resistances, behavioral and communicative, is essential to their therapeutic management. Type A resistances are meaningful derivative formations with unconscious implications that can be identified through the discovery of the intervention context that has evoked the resistance and the derivative complex that reveals their unconscious nature and function. Type C, lie-barrier resistances tend to destroy meaning and meaningful relatedness with the therapist, and to function as opaque barriers to underlying chaos and fantasy-perception constellations. Unconsciously, resistances are designed to harm and thwart the therapist, but also to protect him or her. The latter function arises on the basis of unconscious communications contained in the therapist's interventions that direct the patient away from painful material, toward therapeutic work unconsciously undertaken on behalf of the therapist, and toward other kinds of obstacles that provide an aura of safety for the therapist. Resistances also serve similar functions for the patient, in that they interfere with his or her insightful recovery and yet have protective value.

Resistances should be distinguished from intrapsychic defenses, in that the latter are ever-present, while the former may at times be quite low, such as when the patient communicates through meaningful (nonresistant) derivatives that reflect the continued operation of his or her intrapsychic and interpersonal defenses.

Chapter 34

Interventions: Basic Principles

Psychotherapy unfolds and leads to the essential resolution of the patient's Neurosis on the basis of three fundamental interventions by the therapist: (1) the establishment and maintenance of the ground rules and boundaries of the therapeutic relationship and situation; (2) silence; and (3) interpretations-reconstructions. Even in emergencies, it is best for the therapist to adhere to these three interventions, and to apply them entirely at the behest and in terms of the patient's material, since all other interventions involve notable detrimental consequences. For the delineation and management of the ground rules of the therapeutic relationship see Part III. This chapter will focus on the two additional basic tools: silences and interpretations-reconstructions.

The Therapist's Use of Silence

There are, on a continuum, two basic forms of silence: (1) that which conveys patient and necessary listening, while engaged in holding and containing, and maintaining a sound therapeutic symbiosis, and (2) that which represents a failure to intervene in light of the patient's expressed need for framework-management response or interpretation. The two extremes can be distinguished by attending to the patient's material using the intervention context of the silence and organizing the derivative expressions as commentaries on its use. When appropriate, the derivatives indicate the patient's acceptance of nonintervention and his or her recognition of the lack of an expressed need for an active response from the therapist.

When silence is in error and the therapist has missed a necessary intervention, the patient's derivative communications will touch upon themes of failures to understand, failures to be helpful, mistakes, missed opportunities, and other representations of the therapist's lapse. In the course of all extended periods during which the therapist remains silent because of the apparent absence of major therapeutic contexts, and especially because of the lack of interpretable material, the therapist must monitor the patient's associations for such commentaries. Continual subjective reevaluation is also of help. The decision regarding the validity of silence by the therapist depends in part on an understanding of the indications for, and nature of, interpretations.

Interpretation-Reconstruction

Aside from management of the ground rules, the sole act of intervention needed by therapists (with very rare exception) is that of interpretation and reconstruction. These two modes of intervening tend to merge together. The former is an effort to clarify an active therapeutic context in light of an activated intervention context and the patient's derivative responses, which include important potential or actual genetic elements. Reconstruction is that variation of interpretation, developed with the same fundamental elements, through which the therapist proposes, based on the patient's material in light of an activated intervention context, the existence of an unmentioned or unremembered significant event or fantasy in the patient's childhood (or later life).

An interpretation is an attempt at a propitious moment in therapy to enable the patient to become aware of some content or function of which he or she had previously been unaware. This definition, however, is too oversimplified to provide a basic tool for intervention that will obtain Type Two derivative validation.

All interpretations should be derived from the patient's material in a given hour. Each session should be its own creation, and the therapist should not use material from previous hours since (1) it is not active and meaningful for the moment, and (2) such selectivity is usually based on countertransference difficulties rather than on the patient's therapeutic needs. It is important to have faith in the patient and in his or her need to express and ultimately resolve his or her Neurosis, and to place into the therapist communicatively and interactionally all of those elements that the therapist will need in a particular hour where the patient requires an interpretive response. It is therefore critical to make use of the patient's representations and derivative complex, and to respond with a *synthesis* of these manifest (pertaining to the adaptive context) and disguised (pertaining to the derivative complex) elements—thereby making use of the material, manifest and latent, made available by the patient. In this way, the therapist carefully avoids the introduction of idiosyncratic associations and other unilateral contributions. As a rule, patients will, when necessary, provide the therapist with all of the components of the communicative network necessary for an interpretation. In the main, the patient's defenses and mode of self-communication tend to create problems that lie primarily in his or her not being able on his or her own to integrate and understand consciously the implications of his or her derivative associations as they illuminate indicators in light of an activated intervention context. The patient is capable, then, of representing, but not consciously integrating. This becomes the task of the therapist, who fulfills its requisites through an interpretation.

In principle, the patient's therapeutic need for an interpretation arises in the presence of an uninsightful reaction to an activated intervention context. Should the patient be stirred up by an outside figure or by an outside experience, he or she will, as a rule, create a framework (or other) issue with the therapist in order to obtain an intervention. Technically, the therapist will respond by maintaining the frame to the greatest extent possible, and the patient will then be in a position to react with meaningful derivatives to these efforts. This in turn permits interpretive comment through which the therapist makes conscious for the patient the unfolding derivative reaction to his or her framework-management response, doing so in a way that will usually link this reaction to the patient's outside difficulty and the pertinent aspects of his or her Neurosis that have been mobilized. Thus understanding the ways in which the patient or therapist can create interpretive interludes is basic to an understanding of the nature of interpretation.

The key element needed for an interpretation is the patient's direct (in passing) representation of the intervention context that is mobilizing his or her adaptive and maladaptive responses. The indicator or therapeutic context must also be present, usually in the form of a direct representation of the source of the patient's inner disturbance as it expresses some dimension of the patient's Neurosis. The therapeutic context is often a response to the main adaptive context, though not necessarily so. It is, however, to be understood in light of that context and in terms of the patient's derivative responses. This, in turn, leads to the derivative complex, with its conscious and unconscious perceptions and fantasies, its genetic and dynamic components, and its reflection of the patient's adaptive and maladaptive reactions to the intervention context.

Thus an interpretation is an effort to explain the unconscious basis of a therapeutic context (a manifestation of the patient's Neurosis) by identifying the intervention context to which it is related and the derivative complex of which it is a part, and that clarifies its unconscious dynamic and genetic basis. In this way, each session in which the therapist is able to offer an interpretive response constitutes a kind of minianalysis, in that it deals with some represented and activated aspect of the patient's illness in light of its unconscious determinants.

Each of these three elements must be included in an interpretation, and especially in reconstructions made on a comparable basis. Therapists tend to reconstruct in isolation and without consideration of the manner in which the ongoing communicative interaction between patient and therapist has stirred up expressions within the patient that permit reconstructions of the past. Such recreations may actually exist within the therapeutic relationship because of the therapist's errors and deviations (nontransference), and must be distinguished from those interludes in which the reexperiencing is primarily a matter of the patient's distorted fantasies (transference).

THE PLAYBACK OF SELECTED DERIVATIVES

A variation on interpretation can be utilized when the patient does not clearly represent the activated intervention context, especially in situations where there are strong indicators and a highly meaningful and coalescible derivative complex that organizes clearly and meaningfully around the *unmentioned* adaptive context. This type of communicative situation is quite common when there is a major break in the fixed frame, as is seen when the therapist is late for a session, changes an hour, or happens to extend a session.

Because of the power of the indicators and the richness of the derivative complex, the patient appears to require an intervention, although it cannot take the form of a complete interpretation since the patient has not directly represented the intervention context. Under these conditions, the therapist may resort to a playback of selected derivatives organized around the unmentioned intervention context. In doing so, the therapist must be extremely selective, must clearly choose those manifest representations that contain derivative implications pertinent to the unmentioned context, and must organize them in a manner that creates a state of tension (an unsaturated preconception) that can be resolved only through the identification of the unmentioned adaptive context (resulting in a saturated conception). When properly applied, the patient will typically respond by referring to the missing context and by suddenly seeing in an integrated fashion the ways in which he or she has been responding to it. A less powerful form of validation takes the form of fresh but still disguised representations of the unmentioned intervention context and the emergence of still clearer, closer, derivative responses. As a safeguard, a playback should always begin with the clearest encoded representation in the patient's material of the unmentioned adaptive context.

It is quite easy to misuse the playback of derivatives by not organizing them properly, by not coalescing them around a critical and unmentioned intervention context, and by turning to random allusions or manifest elements that are supposed to contain some derivative meaning as a kind of fishing about for a response from the patient. Such efforts become confronting and clarifying interventions that prove detrimental to therapeutic progress.

Interpretations and Communicative Style

Interpretive interventions must be carried out with a keen sense of timing and with due tact and concern. Interpretations should be clearly stated and as brief as possible, although by their very structure (through which they cover the interplay between indicators, adaptive contexts, and derivative complex) they are seldom terse. They should be offered in a direct and organized fashion, shaped by a recognition of the unconscious implications of the stimulus (the adaptive context) and the nature of the patient's response (indicators and derivative complex). As such, many interpretations begin with a statement of the patient's unconscious perceptions of a particular intervention by the therapist and clarify the patient's responses in terms of indicators (symptoms, resistances and such) and derivative responses (further perceptions and fantasies).

No interpretive intervention can be considered to be helpful and correct without Type Two derivative validation in both the cognitive and interpersonal spheres. Absence of validation must be taken as an indication of a technical error and should call for reformulation (see Chapter 12). In general, an interpretation should not be repeated or elaborated upon, nor should it be extended without clear derivative confirmation from the patient and the development of quite unique new material.

This type of validating methodology must be maintained throughout psychotherapy. The therapist must not overinvest in interpretations to the point where he or she fails to examine the patient's material for both validation and derivative commentary responses on the nature of his or her efforts. It is therefore vital that the therapist attempt to analyze, both before an intervention is made to the patient and afterwards, the unconscious implication of each proposed or actual comment. Such an analysis will include a study of the material alluded to in the effort, as well as a sense of what has been omitted, the structure of the interpretation itself, the mode of communication within which it was phrased, and other conscious and unconscious implications. Interpretations are complex offerings on the surface and in terms of their latent implications. Careful periods of anticipatory and subsequent analysis are an essential part of the interpretive process.

With patients who use the Type A mode, interpretations that are actually correct tend to obtain both cognitive and interpersonal Type Two derivative validation. Unique realizations that further the therapist's interpretation are common, and selected facts are in evidence. Gross behavioral resistances, which are themselves important indicators for interpretation, tend to be accompanied by meaningful communicative networks that lend themselves to this type of response by the therapist. In general, the patient tends to be involved in efforts to communicate meaningfully, and the substance of the interpretive effort will fall into the affective-cognitive sphere.

In the Type B field, interpretations will center upon the

patient's interactional pressures and on his or her efforts to effect pathological symbioses or parasitic modes of relatedness. Such interventions represent the metabolism toward interpretation of pathological interactional and object relationship pressures. In the Type C field, interpretations will tend to illuminate the patient's use of Type C barriers, his or her quiet adherence to a pathological symbiosis, and efforts to destroy meaningful relatedness and to establish a pathological state of autism. All such work by the therapist must meet the criteria of interpretation, however, and especially must await the meaningful representation of an intervention context or a strong opportunity for the playback of derivatives.

The Recipe for Intervening

The listening process embodies the analysis of sessions in terms of the direct representations of adaptive contexts and indicators, and in respect to a search for coalescible derivatives. In developing interventions, the therapist reverses this process and prepares a series of silent interventions while listening to the patient. These efforts are enlarged as the patient's material supports the therapist's basic formulation, and proposed interventions are revised when such support is lacking.

The *recipe for intervening* is a set of ingredients that the patient must provide the therapist if he or she is to offer an interpretation (or manage the frame). As a rule, the patient who is in need of an interpretation will place these ingredients or disparate elements into the therapist, who then proposes a meaningful synthesis in adaptive terms. Attention to this recipe is an aid to the intervening process, in that the therapist, in the course of a session, quickly learns which components of a potential interpretation are available and which are lacking. Often, with an intervention that the therapist has been developing silently and for which he or she has received silent validation and an accumulation of meaning, the therapist will intervene at the moment when the patient provides the missing element to the recipe.

The basic recipe simply turns around the essential factors identified in the listening process. It includes a manifestly or thinly disguised representation of the intervention context, the presence of manifest indicators, and the communication of a meaningful derivative complex.

Inappropriate Interventions

A number of interventions in common use by psychotherapists today cannot be validated and are, in fact, consistently detrimental.

QUESTIONS

Questions interrupt the flow of the patient's free associations and disturb the natural propensity to shift from one theme to another that provides a series of coalescible derivatives. They tend to focus the patient on the manifest contents of his or her associations, and to lead to intellectualization and rumination. By interfering with derivative communication, they disturb any tendency within the patient toward Type A expression. They serve unconsciously as directives for the patient to remain on a manifest level and as revelations of the therapist's failure to understand the *derivative implications* of material that pertains manifestly to relationships outside of treatment. They serve too as Type C barriers to underlying issues within the therapeutic interaction and often express pathological symbiotic (or parasitic) needs within the therapist. Questions tend to ask the patient to function manifestly as therapist to the therapist and to involve qualities of merger and fusion that are inappropriate to a healthy therapeutic symbiotic relationship.

Questions have been justified as a way of clarifying seemingly meaningful manifest elements in the patient's associations. This approach mistakenly views derivative communication as a form of expression in which a manifest element contains within itself, unconsciously or preconsciously, critical hidden meanings that the patient has repressed. The belief is to the effect that a deeper probing will reveal the previously covered over implications of the particular association. In this type of work, the revelation of a previously unreported manifest fantasy is taken as validation of the methodology involved. Such conscious fantasies are treated as having emerged whole-cloth from repression and as reflecting inappropriately displaced fantasies shifted from the past into the present with the therapist. There is a concentration, then, on seemingly meaningful single communicative elements and far less interest in scattered derivative communication.

The concept of derivative communication in this volume is somewhat different. It is based on the finding that encoded, unconscious fantasy-memory and perception constellations tend not to be concentrated into a single communicative element. Instead, they tend to be represented through a series of disparate and scattered elements that require both decoding and integration. The unconscious fantasy or perception image is not represented in a single expression, but is a composite that can be determined only by attendance to a variety of representations. Thus the listening process is geared toward the patient's free associations and to the expectation that, should the patient wish to express himself or herself in meaningful fashion, he or she will shift from theme to theme, each with a fresh derivative expression. The patient is therefore given freedom to wander and to thereby represent what will eventually be a coalescible derivative complex.

Any concentration on a single manifest element is an expression of counterresistance in the therapist and may promote both gross behavioral and communicative resistances in the patient. While such direct questioning may reveal unexpected derivative elements on occasion, this is by far the exception rather than the rule. Resistances are minimized by the judicious use of silence by the therapist and by carefully maintaining a basic therapeutic approach that does not promote resistances within the patient. The attitude is one of faith in the patient's wish to express and resolve communicative resistances on his or her own. The patient will tend to move from one expressive element to another, and these divergent elements can then be integrated and coalesced by the therapist. The resultant composite image is then viewed in terms of perception and fantasy according to the implications of activated intervention contexts. Genetic implications are then more properly formulated in terms of possible unconscious replications of the past by the therapist (nontransference), as well as possible sources of distortions from within the patient (transference).

CLARIFICATIONS

Clarifications, or efforts to clear up or illuminate some ambiguous aspect of the patient's material, fall somewhere between questions and confrontations and share with these efforts a focus on the patient's manifest material. They almost always lead to nonvalidating responses in patients because of considerations similar to those already defined for questions. This type of intervention often reflects countertransference-based confusions in the therapist and difficulties that the therapist is having in developing Type Two derivative formulations of the patient's material. They tend to concentrate the patient on the manifest content or Type One derivative levels of communicating and on single communicative elements. They seldom involve critical intervention contexts and have a naive, clichéd quality.

CONFRONTATIONS

Confrontations involve calling to the patient's attention aspects of his or her manifest associations and their evident implications that the patient has failed to recognize consciously. Some confrontations involve efforts to render general unconscious contents and processes conscious by identifying their evident manifestations in the patient's material. However, most confrontations address the surface of the patient's associations and secure the communicative interaction on the manifest content or Type One derivative level. In addition, the vast majority of confrontations express unconscious, countertransference-based hostility and aggression within the therapist, often with penetrating, controlling, and manipulating qualities.

Confrontations have been justified by therapists as a means of promoting derivative expression. Nevertheless, they tend to focus the patient on a particular set of communicative elements and to interfere with the free flow of the patient's associations, and with the emergence of coalescible derivative elements.

OTHER NONINTERPRETIVE INTERVENTIONS

Interventions ranging from bits of advice to the expression of personal biases and preferences modify the anonymity and neutrality of the therapist and are unconsciously perceived and incorporated by the patient in terms of the therapist's countertransference-based needs. They tend to involve pathological autistic, symbiotic, and parasitic modes of relatedness with the patient, and manifest content and Type One derivative listening and intervening. Patients will often, on the surface, be rather accepting of such comments and behaviors, but their derivative communications almost universally reflect the highly damaging unconscious communications, projective identifications, and introjects involved. The destructive qualities of such efforts have been overlooked by therapists primarily because of a failure to attend to the patient's responses to such work as *derivative commentaries* on their meanings and implications.

Two Integrating Schema for Intervening

A sound interpretive approach is essential to the healthy symbiotic form of relatedness. Conversely, the healthy symbiotic form of relatedness is the only basis on which interpretations can have their intended effects upon the patient without disturbance from contradictory unconscious communications conveyed in mismanagements of the ground rules and framework and in other unconscious thrusts toward pathologically symbiotic and parasitic modes of relatedness. The establishment of a relationship of this kind requires considerable mastery of intrapsychic and interpersonal anxieties on the part of both participants. For the patient, sources of these anxieties will emerge in his or her associations and behaviors, and will tend to be open to interpretation. For the therapist, mastery must be achieved through personal therapy and self-analysis as a basic condition for effective and insightful therapeutic work. While the demands are inordinant, the positive outcome for the patient, and secondarily the therapist, is commensurate with the sacrifice and level of mastery involved.

The two technical schemas developed in Part II of this book have proven to be extremely useful in shaping the intervention process with patients. The first schema involves the listening-intervening efforts of the therapist. The three elements in this schema have been alluded to repeatedly throughout this volume: (1) a manifest reference to an indicator; (2) a direct representation of an activated intervention context; and (3) a meaningful and coalescible derivative complex. They are restated here to indicate that the formulation of these three dimensions of the patient's material is sufficient to the development of all interpretation-reconstructions and framework-management responses. Thus, when it comes to that aspect of the listening-formulating process that leads to interventions, it is this particular schema that must be adopted.

THE SIX-PART OBSERVATIONAL SCHEMA

In the model of interpretation and framework-management response, both the indicators and adaptive context are sought after in terms of relatively direct and manifest representations. This proves, as a rule, to be a fairly straightforward effort by the therapist. Matters are somewhat different when it comes to the derivative complex, which touches first upon the unconscious implications of the therapist's interventions (unconscious perception-introjects), as well as upon evoked reactions and pathological fantasy-memory constellations (unconscious fantasies). It involves as well the genetic implications pertinent to these perceptions and fantasies, and includes considerations of instinctual drives, superego manifestations, and defensive-resistance formations. It is therefore in this area of the derivative complex that a second schema is necessary to organize the enormous range of informational inputs from both the patient and therapist. This is the *six-part observational schema:* (1) the frame, (2) the mode of relatedness, (3) the mode of cure, (4) the style of communication, (5) dynamics and genetics, and (6) the person to whom these formulations belong, including the issue of whether the dynamics and genetics organize most meaningfully around unconscious fantasy-memory constellations or those related to unconscious perception-introjects—i.e., the issue of whether the patient's or therapist's psychopathology is central to the therapeutic interaction for the moment. Each of these categories is studied directly in light of the actual transactions between patient and therapist, and through the manifest and latent expressions in the patient's material. Each is studied separately for patient and therapist, and then for their interaction.

THE STATUS OF THE FRAME

Is each participant attempting to adapt within the stated ground rules and boundaries of the therapeutic relationship as ideally defined, or endeavoring to do so through a modification of the frame? Working within the frame implies a quest for meaning and insight, while breaking the frame implies the search for action-discharge and riddance. In the presence of a frame break, language and words are used for evacuation and discharge, and are not used as an expression of meaning and as symbols. They serve as defensive lie-barrier formations.

In intervening, the therapist must know whether the material available from the patient contains meaning and permits meaningful interpretation or framework-management responses. In the presence of a break in the frame, meaning is destroyed except as it applies to the deviation itself. Two possibilities exist: (1) that the break in the frame has obliterated meaningful communication, and interpretation and sound framework-management responses cannot be carried out; or (2) the patient communicates with a meaningful communicative network in regard to the break in the frame in light of prior intervention contexts; here, the only area of true meaning and interpretation involves the deviation itself.

In a basically damaged therapeutic relationship and setting, meaningful therapeutic work is essentially undermined. Meaning can accrue only in light of acute deviations, or when the patient occasionally attempts to work over the long-standing alterations in the therapeutic environment. All other efforts at so-called interpretation actually constitute pathological projective identifications and lie-barrier formations.

As a means of preparing interventions in this area, the therapist attends to the patient's material with a constant search for allusions pertinent to the status of ground rules, boundaries of relationships, the adherence or nonadherence to laws and other regulations, and for other comparable images. In each of the observational spheres, the patient will from time to time provide the therapist with critical derivative imagery with which to monitor the particular area involved. Although there may also be manifest allusions to specific modifications in the ground rules, meaningful work with frame issues can unfold only in the presence of a coalescible derivative complex. As previously demonstrated, such material organizes primarily around valid unconscious perceptions of the therapist and of the implications of his or her deviations or other prior interventions.

MODE OF RELATEDNESS

The manner in which the patient and therapist create, adhere to, and violate the ground rules of psychotherapy is a basic determinant of their respective modes of relatedness. The mode of relatedness itself is constituted through these responses to the ground rules of therapy and in terms of the nature of the communications from each participant. Involved here are issues of object relationship satisfactions, problems of renunciation, and the search for truly appropriate gratifications within the treatment relationship. Since much of this has already been discussed in detail, it will not be pursued here.

The modes of relatedness in psychotherapy tend to be healthy or pathological autism, healthy or pathological symbiosis, and parasitic. (As a matter of definition, the healthy commensal form of relatedness is generally not given consideration.) Each of these modes of relatedness has a distinct set of attributes. Patients tend to characterize modes of relatedness through their derivative communications in describing their relationships with others and in alluding to relationships between outside figures. More rarely, the patient will offer a manifest characterization of his or her relationship with the therapist that contains manifest and derivative meaning. In preparing for an intervention, the therapist must continually monitor the material from the patient for valid representation, based on unconscious awareness, of the mode of relatedness of both participants to treatment.

MODE OF CURE

The basic issue in mode of relief or mode of cure involves the question as to whether it will be developed through a search for the truth of the underlying factors in the patient's Neurosis as influenced by the therapeutic interaction, or as an effort to find relief through some other uninsightful and action-discharge means. A third issue is whether cure or relief is actually being sought at all.

The mode of cure is determined by the responses of the patient and therapist to the framework, and by the mode of relatedness that they adopt, as well as by important communicative factors. In general, true insightful cure is feasible only within a secure frame or through the working over of an acute break in the frame. It is possible only in the presence of a healthy sumbiotic mode of relatedness on the part of the therapist and the presence of either a similar mode of relatedness in the patient or interpretable and framework-rectifying material that permits the analytic resolution of a pathological mode of relatedness on his or her part.

Noninsightful, action-discharge modes of cure stem from breaks in the frame, the development of sectors of unconscious misalliance and collusion, and the acceptance by the therapist of pathological modes of relatedness. The absence of the search for relief tends to involve the parasitic mode of relatedness and often framework deviations as well.

The therapist must monitor the patient's material for all allusions to means of relief, ways of solving problems, and manner of handling issues and difficulties. These representations are taken first as valid unconscious perceptions of the therapist's efforts to effect relief for the patient, and second, as expressing the means of relief sought after by the patient.

THE STATUS OF THE COMMUNICATIVE RELATIONSHIP AND THE COMMUNICATIVE STYLE OF EACH PARTICIPANT TO TREATMENT

Through methods with which we are now familiar, the therapist determines his or her own and the patient's communicative style—A, B-A, B-C, or C—with special interest in identifying communicative resistances and breaks in the frame that are disturbing the openness of the communicative relationship with the patient. Breaks in the frame and pathological modes of relatedness, as well as the search for deviant means of cure, are expressions of the Type B and Type C modes of communication. It is the responsibility of the therapist to respond to these disturbances with the Type A mode of communication as represented by a valid interpretation or framework-management response.

A patient will often respond to the expressed pathology of the therapist with a somewhat defended Type A mode replete with derivative efforts designed to rectify the situation and cure the therapist. Simultaneously, the patient will at times join the therapist in the effected Type B or Type C mode, and often will engage in exchanges of pathological projective identifications without insight and understanding.

The nature of the communicative interchanges between himself or herself and others, and between outside figures as well, will be represented in the patient's material. In particular, communicative resistances tend to be represented by allusions to fears of speaking, secrets, mistrust of others, and other ways in which open expression is threatened or inhibited. Monitoring on this level therefore prepares the therapist for his or her intervention responses.

DYNAMIC AND GENETIC CONSIDERATIONS

The therapist must attempt to formulate the anxieties, conflicts, dynamic interplay, and genetic implications reflected in the patient's material. The unconscious forces and resistances within the patient must be identified and specified as well.

Ultimately, all dynamic and genetic formulations must be developed in light of prevailing intervention contexts. There must be an openness to the full recognition of unconscious perceptions as well as unconscious fantasy-memory constellations. All of the therapist's understanding of psychodynamics, of problems in the area of self-psychology, of the dynamic implications of the maturational mode of object relatedness, and anything else that has a bearing on unconscious conflict and unconscious fantasy and memory formations, come into play.

The therapist continually monitors and formulates the patient's material along dynamic and genetic lines, remaining open to specifying the exact nature and function of the dynamics and genetics in light of activated interventions contexts, and to identifying to whom they most meaningfully pertain—patient or therapist.

THE CENTRAL PATHOLOGICAL FIGURE
FOR THE MOMENT

The therapist must identify whose psychopathology the patient is working over on an unconscious level. This can be done only in light of a full analysis of activated intervention contexts. While all of the patient's associations meaningfully reflect aspects of his or her own inner mental world, at a given interlude the greater meaning in his or her material may apply to the therapist.

In the presence of a communicated error and countertransferences, the main thrust of the patient's dynamic and genetic communications will pertain to the therapist. Such material is replete with valid unconscious perceptions and introjects of the therapist, with lesser extensions into reaction, distortion, and fantasy. It is here, of course, that nontransference formulations are generated. Genetic implications then involve the repetition by the therapist of past pathogenic interactions in the life of the patient. The therapist's interpretations are shaped accordingly.

In the presence of a secure frame and validated interventions by the therapist, the psychopathology of the patient becomes central.

The dynamics and genetics therefore involve the disturbances within the patient and pertain to his or her distortions of the therapeutic relationship. This is, of course, the realm of transference. Here, the genetic factor is inappropriately introduced by the patient in a way that distorts his or her perception of and reactions to the therapist, who is behaving quite differently from the earlier pathogenic figure. The therapist's interpretations are again shaped accordingly.

While each of these dimensions is complex in itself, it proves possible to continuously monitor the material from the patient in each of these spheres. The schema extends considerably beyond the usual focus on dynamics and genetics, with occasional consideration of the mode of relatedness between the patient and therapist. As such, the use of these categories greatly enhances the therapist's interventions and the patient's therapeutic experience.

Chapter 35

Interventions: Clinical Applications

Three clinical examples are presented in this chapter to demonstrate the interpretive process and its validation.

Clinical Example I

A married woman patient with some half-dozen prior therapeutic experiences was now involved in a rather successful course of treatment with her present therapist. In recent weeks, she had begun to consider termination and to work over this possibility. During the course of her therapy, the therapist had rectified several major framework deviations to the point where he now had his own office (previously he had shared his office with two other therapists, and with them a receptionist and secretary), although he still shared a waiting room. The patient had offered him models of rectification in this regard, doing so through her derivative communications. It had been possible to interpret a number of implications of this deviation to her, although, of course, rectification was not effected. These interpretive efforts were, however, rather incomplete.

In the hour previous to the one that is extracted here, the patient had been concerned about a possible abdominal mass that could prove cancerous, and had been quite depressed about the evident ways in which doctors were withholding the truth from her. There had been some allusion to the colleague with whom the therapist had shared his office, someone whom the patient had seen during an earlier interlude when the therapist had been away on vacation. An interpretation had been offered in respect to the

659

manner in which this particular deviation had created needs in the patient for direct reassurance under stress and the way in which the patient felt abandoned when the therapist was not available to her in some immediate fashion. The patient had responded by expressing her anger that the therapist seemed prepared now to terminate her therapy.

> Patient: I'm dressed up because we're going out tonight. My x-rays were normal, and part of me was disappointed, ready to die; but mostly I was against it. I'm angry with how you reacted, but then again I understood why I felt so badly about the possibility of an operation. With Dr. A. [*one of her previous therapists*] I felt better, but after a while therapy was awful again. With Dr. B. [*another prior therapist*], it was the same, and I'm afraid it will happen here again. But then again, what do you do for me? You tell me about one theme at the end of the hour. If I can do that, I don't need to see you. There was a father and his daughter in the waiting room, waiting to see Dr. C. [*the therapist's colleague with whom he shares the waiting room*]. She was on crutches, and the father said he wanted some records from Dr. C., but the daughter didn't want him to have them. There was some talk about his being an alcoholic and needing to go to a hypnotist to stop drinking. Imagine, the daughter's seeing a therapist and telling him to get a hypnotist. Dr. D. [*another therapist to whom the present therapist had referred the patient sometime earlier during one of his vacations*] has his office next to my internist. Doctors have too much money. The mother of a friend of mine committed suicide and the friend talks too much; she reveals too many family secrets. You're like a wall; if I overdose on Librium would you react? It would be all right with you if I left treatment. When I was a little girl, I tried to reach people and couldn't. Why do I come here?
>
> Therapist: You bring up why you're coming here, and your fear of leaving when our work is completed. You're afraid you'll feel worse after termination. You also spoke of a daughter telling her father to stop drinking, to give up a self-destructive addiction. The father wanted something from Dr. A., and there's a lot here about inappropriately releasing

information. You seem to be trying to let me know that my sharing a waiting room with Dr. A. and my proximity to him leads you to see me as addictive and as upset, and this seems related to your fear of separating from me and your own feelings of addiction to me and therapy. You want me to realize what is going on—to react—and you do it in a self-destructive way such as with threats of overdosing with drugs, which is similar to how you behaved as a child in order to get others to react to you.

Patient: *(Interrupting.)* You have never made more sense. The thought of terminating makes me dizzy. At home I always felt my brothers and sisters got more than me. My mother was depressed and withdrawn, and my father only gave us something when we competed for it. I would beat one of my brothers in competition and then be guilty because he was so much younger. Father would go into his bedroom on those rare occasions when he was home and always ask for things from us. I would try to make him react and did all I could, but he was aloof. I had this habit of becoming friendly with two people who were already friends, so I would be the third person. I didn't feel comfortable in a one-to-one relationship. Sometimes I would be friends with people who hated each other. My supervisor at the plant is leaving and everyone is frightened except me, because I've met the man who is replacing him and he is very nice and competent. I needed help at work yesterday; I saw I was having difficulty and I had to ask. Then he stepped in and helped me, but I kept wondering why I have to ask him first.

The discussion of this session will undertake the type of analysis a therapist should carry out with each hour in two related spheres: the listening-experiencing process and the intervening process. In the first area, one must identify the indicators and activated intervention contexts, as well as the attributes of the derivative complex. These listening-formulating efforts shade over into the development of a silent intervention: the therapist determines how clearly and manifestly the adaptive context and indicators have been represented by the patient, the intensity of the indicators themselves, and the extent to which he or she has available a meaningful and coalescible derivative complex that explains the unconscious basis for the therapeutic contexts. There is a balancing effort in which the therapist gauges the intensity of the indicators on a scale from one to ten and considers this determination in light of the clarity of meaning of the communicative network—this too measured on a scale of one to ten, inverse to the level of the patient's communicative resistances. In general, the more intense the indicators (i.e., the more clearly the patient requires an intervention) and the greater the information available to the therapist, the more likely it is that he or she will intervene. The clarity of the communicative network facilitates the intervening effort, while a high level of resistances interferes. In principle, with powerful indicators, the therapist will make the best possible interpretation or framework-management response available from the material. With less intense therapeutic contexts, the decision on intervening tends to depend upon the clarity of the communicative network.

In the example under consideration, the indicators include the continued alteration in the ideal therapeutic environment (the therapist is making use of a shared waiting room) and the residual effects of the therapist's use of consultants, including Dr. A., with whom he shares the office. These are, of course, object relationship pathology-related need systems within the patient. Other indicators belonging to this category include additional therapeutic contexts as derived from the therapist's prior interventions. His most recent efforts may be characterized as incomplete attempts to interpret the implications of the shared waiting room, of past deviations, and of the patient's reactions to these interventions; however, there was no effort made to rectify the remaining break in the frame.

In regard to indicators pertaining to the patient's own handling of the ground rules and boundaries, and to her resistances and symptoms, there is a major therapeutic context in the patient's manifest thoughts of contacting another therapist—a gross behavioral resistance that involves a break in the ideal therapeutic frame. There are also derivative indications of a positive nature in the patient's efforts to rectify the damaged frame and to have the therapist interpret the implications of this deviation. There is also a sense of gross behavioral resistance in the patient's wish that she had not come for her session that day, and her wondering why she is in treatment at all. There is also, of course, the indicator of the patient's realization that her therapeutic work is nearly completed and that there is a need to work through the termination process. A sense of depression is reflected in the patient's disappointment that she did not have a malignancy and in her feelings about terminating treatment.

As for the *intervention contexts*, there are, of course, the therapist's interventions in the previous session and, in addition, the continued use of a shared waiting room. The patient represents this most critical intervention context quite directly. She also manifestly alludes to several past breaks in the frame, mainly in the area of the therapist's use of consultants during past separations (violations of total confidentiality and the one-to-one relationship). It is not unusual for patients to bring up past deviations when dealing with one that is presently active.

As for the *derivative complex*, before the therapist's intervention, the material appears to coalesce quite meaningfully around unconscious perceptions of the therapist's need for pathological symbiotic ties of an addictive nature, as reflected in his use of a shared waiting room and a substitute therapist in his absence. Among the most meaningful manifest associations in respect to latent implications, the patient represents quite exquisitely the manner in which these deviations create violations in the total confidentiality of her therapy that are destructive to her best interests (and those of the therapist). In one sense, through the allusion to suicide, she appears to stress the self-destructive components and the way in which these deviations do damage to both the therapist and the therapy itself. Along the me/not-me interface, this also applies to the patient.

There is evidence too in this derivative complex of striking therapeutic efforts by this patient toward the therapist. This is best conveyed in the patient's associations regarding the young woman patient who finds it necessary to be therapeutic toward her caretaking father. The suggestion of the use of a hypnotist is another derivative related to the pathological symbiotic and addicting qualities of the therapist's deviations. The crutches may well reflect the impaired unconscious image that the patient has of the therapist on the basis of these alterations of the frame, and probably, in part, also on the basis of his split image: an ability to begin to understand some of the implications of these deviations and yet a concomitant failure to fully rectify the frame.

The patient also adds a rather general genetic connection to indicate that in some way she is experiencing the therapist in the present in a manner comparable to deprivations in the past. While this may well be a transference-based distortion, evaluation of the actual implications of the deviation in the ground rules reveals that the patient's derivative complex is highly perceptive and filled with valid commentaries, and that the material is largely non-transference-based, as is the patient's experience of the therapist. It is critical, however, to realize that the true source of the patient's complaints lies not in the therapist's relative silence and in the absence of manifest supportive comments from him, but in his failure to rectify an aspect of the damaged frame (his failure to completely understand the patient's efforts to reach him in this regard). It is the patient's unconscious perception of unresolved separation anxieties, and of a failure to achieve total individuation and reasonable autonomy, that constitutes the nontransference-based factors in the patient's fear of a regression after the termination of her treatment. In this hour it seems likely that the patient was making strong efforts to obtain both interpretation and rectification in this area, and to help the therapist resolve the inner difficulties that account for his failings in these respects.

Turning now to the recipe for intervening, the indicators in this session would be evaluated at a level of nine or ten on a scale of ten. The combination of an unresolved break in the fixed frame, which is causing considerable disturbance and therapeutic need within the patient, with the presence of depression and termination anxieties, creates a situation in which the therapist senses a need within the patient for an intervention if at all possible. Had the material been somewhat indefinite, and had the adaptive context not obtained direct representation, given the presence of any degree of meaning to the derivative complex, the therapist would have intervened with a playback of selected derivatives organized around the unrepresented intervention contexts. It seems likely that the powerful therapeutic needs within this patient prompted her to offer the therapist highly meaningful and interpretable material, and a strong basis for rectification as well.

The direct representation of the adaptive context gives the therapist the basic fulcrum for interpretive and framework-management responses. Further, the highly meaningful derivative complex hints strongly at genetic links and organizes powerfully around nontransference-based unconscious perceptions of the therapist, as well as curative and rectifying efforts by the patient. It would fail the patient considerably not to recognize these endeavors and not to respond with an interpretive intervention. Ideally, this would include a realistic announcement to the patient of plans to move to a private office if the therapist planned to do so; failing that, the need for rectification in the light of the patient's derivative communications must be acknowledged.

In analyzing the therapist's actual interpretation, one applies the same basic threefold criteria, and asks as well if anything has been added or deleted. There are many supplementary questions that can be raised as to timing, tact, clarity, the careful use of the patient's material, and especially of her derivative communications, but much of this will emerge from a study of the intervention in terms of its use of indicators, adaptive contexts, and derivative complex.

The intervention clearly attempts to deal with the indicator of the shared waiting room and to hint at the pertinence of involvement of the patient by the therapist with other therapists. In regard to the latter, it fails to allude specifically to the manifestly represented indicators of the therapist's prior use of consultants or substitute therapists, even though this context had been represented directly by the patient. There is also an effort to deal with the patient's sense of depression and her concerns about termination. Thus the intervention does indeed attempt to deal with the major indicators in this hour, though it omits a notable sector. It may well be that the therapist would have dealt with these indicators had the patient not interrupted him, although he did decide not to add to his intervention once the patient had done so.

The therapist makes use of the most important representation of the most critical adaptive context (the shared waiting room). Here too, he hints at the important issue of his proximity to, or involvement with, other therapists; however, he does not point to the reference to Dr. D. and the issue of his own use of substitute therapists in his absence—an important factor in the patient's fear that she herself will be unable to deal with ultimate termination. In this light, one may again note the extent to which patients will first work over nontransference-based anxieties and perceptions that pertain in important ways to their symptoms—here, the patient's unrealistic separation anxieties and fears of individuation—before expressing and working over the transference contribution to these problems. In many ways, this latter effort will be incomplete here. It cannot be fully explicated in respect to transference unless the therapist rectifies the frame, or at the very least acknowledges the need to do so.

Breaks in the frame are replete with unconscious implications that contribute to the patient's symptoms, and to object relationships, introjects, and unconscious perceptions that contribute to the psychopathology of the patient. From this it follows, of course, that interpretations and rectifications in this area are a substantial basis through which the patient could resolve these symptoms. Such efforts constitute a first step toward permitting the patient to communicate the unconscious transference fantasy constellations that also contribute to these difficulties.

The therapist's use of the derivative complex was valid. He did not appear to add anything significant from previous sessions or from his own associations to the patient's material. In keeping with a sound interpretive effort, he endeavored to synthesize the patient's manifest associations as derivative communications in response to a critical and activated intervention context. He accepted the patient's unconscious perception of his own sense of addiction, as *implicitly valid,* and had begun to deal with the patient's efforts to call this to his attention and with his failing her in some important way, when the patient interrupted. In supervision, the therapist indicated that he was indeed prepared to tie these feelings to his failure to rectify the frame, but did not do so in light of the highly meaningful material with which the patient had responded. Nonetheless, this addendum would be quite important to this particular intervention, and the entire interpretation should be directed as a means of identifying the adaptive context and derivative meanings that would account for the patient's concerns about completing her psychotherapy. In a supplementary way, her sense of depression and frustration, and her efforts to rectify the frame, would also then be clarified.

In all, then, this is a fairly sound interpretive effort, but incomplete in important ways—the most critical being the therapist's failure to rectify the frame. There are some shortcomings in the way the intervention was shaped, and in those aspects of the indicators, adaptive contexts, and derivatives that the therapist bypassed. Nonetheless, it was felt in supervision that this was an essentially valid interpretation, and that Type Two derivative validation would follow.

The final step in the listening-intervening-validating process is, of course, the search for Type Two derivative validation and for some sense of conscious insight and working through. In this case the patient's manifest initial confirmation is striking and suggests a potential for further conscious insight and working through. Although this is not true psychoanalytic validation, since it does not occur on the derivative level, it is an enormously encouraging pronouncement. And the material that follows does indeed provide the Type Two derivative validation that supports this initial manifest reaction. In this regard, the patient provides a number of meaningful genetic links to her present difficulties in the therapeutic interaction. She suggests that she feels guilty because she is more sensitive on an unconscious level to the problems in therapy than is the therapist and finds it necessary to help him. She connects the therapist's failure to respond to her therapeutic needs to the relative absence of her depressed mother and to the unavailability of her father—the latter in terms of details not previously described in the therapy. She then connects her own problems in one-to-one relationships with her unconsciously perceived image of the therapist who fears being alone. Her allusion to being friends with people who hate each other might well refer to her awareness from comments made to her by the other therapist (as she sat in the waiting room) and from other clues that there now had developed considerable tension between the two therapists who shared this waiting room.

Next there is a strong positive introject reflected in the patient's own sense of strength that she can now handle the loss of her supervisor at work, undoubtedly based on her realization that the therapist had become stronger in his capacity to deal with separation from the patient. Finally, the patient complains through an exquisite derivative that while she now realizes that the therapist has been quite helpful to her, why must she resort to so much in the way of distress and appeal before he does so?

The material that followed the intervention, then, provided both cognitive and interactional-interpersonal validation and a positive commentary on the therapist's efforts. The negative elements may well be linked to the therapist's failure to actually rectify the frame, and to the issues that would continue to unfold around this continued deviation. The therapist benefited considerably from the patient's unconscious efforts at interpretation, which are in evidence both before and after the intervention: in the former area, this revolved especially around the therapist's need for pathological symbiosis and his addictive difficulties, and following the intervention, around the sphere of fears of being alone with the patient. There may also be further unconscious interpretations here through which the patient is attempting to alert the therapist to earlier genetic factors in his own continued need for the deviation, a derivative suggestion that it involves his own depressive difficulties and problems with each of his parents.

This clinical example illustrates how an interpretation is structured around disturbing indicators, and how the adaptive context and derivative complex that account for the unconscious meanings and functions involved in these disturbances are identified. Had the therapist been able to rectify the break in the frame, this interlude would have provided a clear example of the interplay between interpretive efforts and framework-management responses.

Clinical Example II

A young man who appeared to be suffering from an ambulatory schizophrenic syndrome with paranoid ideation was in once-weekly psychotherapy. In addition to being seen by this therapist in a clinic, with the state paying his fee, the patient was in attendance at a day hospital where he had contact with two therapists, one of whom on occasion would prescribe medication. The therapist had been interpreting the patient's need for two therapies, and especially its defensive aspects in removing the patient from a threatening, though modified, one-to-one relationship with the present therapist. The patient had begun to give some thought to giving up the day hospital program, and then had missed a session. The following excerpt is from the subsequent hour.

> Patient: I was sick. I haven't gone to the day hospital for several days. I came in today so you wouldn't be annoyed. Things are actually a lot better at home between myself and my family. I've decided to accept termination of the day hospital program at the end of this month, and to then see if I can get a job and live by myself. I'm feeling divided, split, anxious. It could be because of all the drugs I used to take on my own.

It's like they damaged me. The doctor in the day hospital said I should have a spinal tap, that I'm not too damaged, and I can get better—have a normal life. I'll ask them there again about the needle—the tap; I don't like needles. Somehow I don't like being told that I can make it. Somehow, you're helping me. But my father's been pressing me to do more than I think I can handle. *(The patient cries.)* How would I manage if he died? Do you think I want to kill him? Sometimes sons don't grow up until their fathers are dead.

Therapist: You're upset and having thoughts of your father dying. You missed last session and talk about being split. You're feeling better, and you've been told you can put yourself together. You don't feel reassured and want another opinion. You mention leaving the day hospital, but now are talking about having two sets of therapists—mainly me and them. You talk about your father pressuring you, and seem to feel that from me. You have an opportunity to grow and be independent, but struggle against it. You seem afraid of giving up the day hospital, especially in light of the pressure you're experiencing from me to be independent.

Patient: Yes, I am afraid of you, just like I have been of my father. Will you help me or hurt me? I do think now I can get all better, but I've a long way to go. I was much sicker before. I'd give up my leg if someone would show me how to get out of the house. I'm afraid of my father's dying and of leaving the family. Now that I think of it, we've all had these terrible separation problems, including my brothers and sisters—even the one who got involved with the homosexuality. I'm thinking now of my married sister who calls our mother every single day, and how inappropriate it is. You know, this treatment is a lot different from the day hospital. They keep telling me what to do. It got me nowhere. I'm excited about trying to leave home, but afraid.

Although intervention contexts form the fulcrum for the listening process, one is well advised to first identify the therapeutic contexts in a particular session in the approach to intervening. Even though the indicators are second-order organizers of the patient's material, by being aware of the loci of the patient's therapeutic needs that one wishes to illuminate in a particular hour, the study of the adaptive context and derivative complex can be developed with a strong sense of utility.

The following *indicators* may be identified in this session: (1) the patient's absence (a gross behavioral resistance); (2) his physical illness; (3) his sense of anxiety and upset in this session and outside of the hour; (4) the anticipation of giving up the day hospital; (5) his plans to move out of his own home; (6) his concerns about his father's dying; and (7) the additional therapeutic needs derived from the therapist's erroneous interventions—those aspects of the ideal therapeutic environment that remain compromised and the specific interventions by the therapist in the previous hour (all adaptive contexts are also therapeutic contexts, while in contrast, not every therapeutic context is an intervention context).

The cumulative therapeutic need here might be rated at nine or ten on a scale of ten. The high rating is accounted for by the multiplicity of indicators, and especially by the presence of symptoms in the patient, and the existence of both efforts to rectify the frame and of continued alterations in the ideal therapeutic environment. Also, in light of a major gross behavioral resistance (the patient's prior absence), there is a sense that the patient would benefit considerably from an interpretation, and especially from framework-management efforts, if his material will at all permit. As with the previous patient, it might well be necessary to resort to a playback of derivatives if the essential intervention contexts were not manifestly represented by the patient in this hour. In particular, the therapist's efforts to rectify an aspect of the frame and his continued failure to secure the balance of the therapeutic environment are of special importance in this regard. Virtually all of these indicators are contained in the patient's manifest associations, with the notable exception of the deviations involved in the patient's being seen in the clinic without personal responsibility for his fee.

Several *adaptive contexts* may be identified: (1) the use of the day hospital and the presence of a second therapist; (2) the therapist's recent interventions regarding pathological aspects of this arrangement and his specific interventions in the previous hour; and (3) the clinic setting with the absence of a fee paid by the patient and the presence of a third-party payer—the state. The adaptive contexts that received the clearest manifest representations are those of the day-hospital-second-therapist arrangement and the therapist's interventional pressures to correct this particular alteration in the basic structure of the therapeutic relationship.

As noted in respect to indicators, the most notable adaptive context-indicator that the patient fails to represent manifestly is his continuation to see the therapist in a clinic setting with a third-party payer and without any responsibility for his fee. Since this is an important adaptive-context constellation, it is essential that the therapist identify its best representation in the patient's material from this hour. It is striking, however, that in the associations that preceded the therapist's intervention, it proves difficult to identify a reasonably meaningful derivative representation. Perhaps the best disguised allusions—and they are indeed remote derivative representations—are the reference to the day hospital and the comment regarding the patient's own use of drugs. It may well have been this relatively poor representation of this particular intervention context that led the therapist not to allude to this aspect of the patient's material and the therapeutic situation in his intervention. (As shall be seen, there was some lessening of defense in this regard within the patient after the therapist's intervention, probably because the area had been neglected.)

In formulating a strategy of intervening, the therapist can work best with those intervention contexts that are most clearly and manifestly represented. When the patient fails to represent a critical intervention context, or when he or she does so through relatively remote derivatives, the therapist can organize his or her intervention around the available intervention contexts and hint at additional issues with a brief allusion to derivatives related to that particular problem. When the more defended issue seems of lesser importance than those that are represented, the therapist should simply wait for another hour to deal with those areas being avoided by the patient.

The therapist must check his or her own subjective impressions against the representations in the patient's material. At times, these will coincide, in that the patient will represent manifestly those intervention contexts that the therapist feels are most critical for the moment. At other times, however, the patient will introduce an intervention context that has been overlooked by the therapist, or may poorly represent a therapeutic context that the therapist believes to be important. A useful rule of thumb involves the recognition that breaks in the frame are more critical to patients than efforts to rectify them, and that framework issues take precedence over all else.

The derivative complex may first be organized from the material prior to the therapist's intervention around the most clearly represented adaptive context: the efforts by the therapist to secure the frame through the elimination of the second therapeutic situation. In this light, the patient's derivative communications suggest an awareness on his part of a split within the therapist in this regard (for some time, the therapist had accepted this arrangement without intervening; in addition, note that the patient is consciously aware of his own split in this area). The rectification creates an air of optimism that frightens the patient. The day hospital is likened to drug taking and seen as damaging. Its loss is equated with the death of his father. The therapist is experienced as pressing the patient to effect this change (cf. the allusion to pressure from the patient's father). Finally, through the allusion related to the patient's fear of living by himself, there is a hint of anxiety (on both sides) of being in a one-to-one relationship.

The material points to a sense within the patient of some type of pathological symbiotic merger through which he has obtained noninterpretive gratifications and direct reassurance even though these are infantalizing and destructive. At this level it seems likely that the patient is indicating that the loss of this arrangement would be comparable to giving up some aspect of a pathological mode of relatedness he has with his own father. Nevertheless, in light of the patient's plans to stop going to the day hospital (the necessary rectification measure), the patient points out, in a final derivative before the therapist intervenes, that he must make this renunciation if he is ever to grow up (i.e., to achieve relative autonomy and individuation).

Before briefly considering other derivative implications of this material, it is well to pause here and integrate what has been developed silently through this discussion. A series of rather strong therapeutic contexts have been identified, and a critical adaptive context has been recognized that is in part a major stimulus for these therapeutic needs within the patient—the efforts at rectifying the frame through the elimination of the day hospital program. A coalescible derivative complex reveals a number of unconscious perceptions of difficulties in this regard within the therapist, and of constructive interventions and pressures from him as well. The complex also reveals a number of anxieties in this respect within the patient and an important genetic representation in the material related to his father.

There is a mixture here of both transference and non-transference. At this level the patient is dealing with an effort by the therapist at rectifying the frame. The material is therefore shifting from working over the split in the therapist, and his separation anxieties in respect to the loss of the second therapist (in dual treatment situations, each therapist often unconsciously has a deep need for the other), toward the patient's own separation-individuation anxieties, and possibly toward his own fears of being in a single treatment situation with the present therapist. Thus the father here is primarily a transference figure being imposed upon the present therapeutic situation, in that the patient dreads the loss of the day-hospital therapist because he will experience it as a loss of some aspect of the pathological mode of relatedness with his father. At this level the therapist is *not* behaving in keeping with the patient's pathology-evoking father and may be distinguished from that person by his efforts to help the patient to separate and individuate, and to gain insight into the related conflicts and anxieties, perceptions and fantasy constellations.

As long as the therapist accepts the two-treatment arrangement, he repeats on some level an aspect of the patient's pathogenic relationship with his father. At the point where the therapist proves capable of interpretation and rectification, he becomes different from this aspect of the father-introject and of the patient's relationship with the father. At this point, the introduction of the father into the patient's associations involves an unconscious transference constellation—the patient in some manner has a distorted image of the therapist in terms of earlier disruptive experiences with the father. The derivatives related to the patient's relationship with the therapist reveal a notable measure of distortion, in that the patient sees the therapist as pressuring him in a destructive manner as his father had done in the past, while the implied pressures involved at this level are actually quite constructive and meant to be helpful.

The *timing of interventions* must also be considered. There are several possible patterns. In those sessions in which indicators and a represented adaptive context emerge early in the hour, the therapist simply waits for a sufficiently meaningful, multiple-element derivative complex to unfold before intervening. As in the present example, the appearance of a particularly compelling derivative element after the build-up of a sufficient derivative complex will often dictate the immediate moment at which the therapist decides to intervene. When the derivative complex is highly charged with meaning, it is advisable for the therapist to intervene once a workable number of critical components have been obtained, since there will be much to say at that juncture. On the other hand, in the presence of a weak derivative complex, the therapist should await at least one or two important derivative elements before speaking.

In those sessions in which indicators emerge early in the hour, along with a growing and meaningful derivative complex, but in which the intervention context has not been directly represented, the therapist should wait for some time before intervening with a playback of selected derivatives. This provides the patient with time to either represent the activated adaptive context or to provide the therapist with additional derivative material. Under these conditions, it is well to intervene by beginning with the best disguised representation of the intervention context and the most meaningful derivative elements. This is done usually about two-thirds of the way through the session, thereby providing the patient with ample opportunity to respond. Under these conditions, the stronger the indicators, the more likely the therapist will make use of the playback, if at all possible.

Finally, even in the presence of moderate indicators, the relative absence of a represented intervention context and coalescible derivative complex calls for silence, holding, and containing by the therapist, and for the silent rectification of any contribution he or she may be making to the patient's communicative resistances, if present. It may well be that the patient is in a lying-fallow stage and requires no intervention of the therapist for the moment. Clearly, silence and silent rectification of countertransference-based inputs are the most important interventions available to the therapist to promote meaningful communication and relatedness between therapist and patient.

In the clinical example under study, the therapist chose to intervene at the point at which a genetic element became available within the derivative complex. In analyzing his intervention, one might first consider this material in light of known intervention contexts other than the efforts to rectify the framework in regard to the presence of the second treatment situation. Just one of these will be analyzed here for purposes of discussion: the presence of continued compromises in the framework in terms of the clinic setting and the third-party payer to whom information was released from time to time. This particular adaptive context received quite poor representation in the patient's material. However, the derivative complex, as related to this context, appears to be relatively meaningful (i.e., the patient's defenses have led him to develop communicative resistances directed toward the representation of the intervention context—the alterations in the fixed frame—though not against the communication of a meaningful derivative complex—a not uncommon response under this type of condition). Thus the allusion to illness in the patient may well represent an unconscious perception of the pathological countertransferences within the therapist that led him to participate in these conditions of treatment without interpretation and rectification.

If the therapist had at least offered sound interpretations in this area, and acknowledged the need for rectification and worked through with the patient the realization that he could not for the moment afford therapy under any other set of conditions, the patient would then continue to perceive some destructive qualities to the therapist's efforts, but they would be strongly counterbalanced by a realization of the realities of the situation and the therapist's sound efforts at interpretation. Further, there is a strong possibility that given such realizations and interpretations, this patient would have sought employment and entered a low-fee private psychotherapy. In this regard the particular alteration in this therapeutic environment gave unconscious support to the patient's own pathological parasitic and symbiotic adjustment and relative nonfunctioning.

The decision to terminate at the day hospital, organized around the intervention context of these deviations, is a clear model of rectification in respect to the clinic and fee arrangements. Here one may note the way in which a given manifest element contains a layer of meanings in encoded form, each detectable by identifying its implications in view of a series of specific intervention contexts. Such communications are adaptive responses to multiple adaptation-evoking stimuli, and therefore yield meaning on each pertinent level.

The patient's allusion to feeling divided, split, and anxious organizes along the me/not-me interface as conscious self-realizations and, in addition, as unconscious perceptions and introjects of the therapist who rectifies the frame in one sphere while failing to do so in another. The drug-taking is a type of addiction unconsciously perceived in therapists by their patients in settings in which there are such deviations as shared waiting rooms and third parties who receive information and pay the fee. The therapist himself benefits from the fee arrangement and from the presence of others, and this is viewed unconsciously as addicting and inherently destructive.

The need for a spinal tap may well be a questionable procedure under these conditions and a derivative representation of the questionable aspects of the deviant therapeutic conditions. The patient's own resistances against getting well are probably based in part on an unconscious introject of the therapist's attitude toward these other alterations in the frame. Then too, the patient's split image of himself as feeling damaged and yet hopeful is a reflection of the presence of both rectification and failures to rectify in the efforts of the therapist. The patient's concerns about leaving home, managing without his father, and his sense of rage, all have derivative meaning in response to an introjection of the therapist's anxieties regarding giving up the clinic setting and the third-party payer. In addition, destructive and murderous themes, as well as themes of death, are common in the presence of an alteration in the fixed frame—true treatment is to some degree destroyed. Finally, the patient's last associations before the therapist's intervention allude along the me/not-me interface to the growth-promoting potential for the therapist, and for the patient himself, if the therapist were capable of securing a private therapeutic space for his own therapeutic endeavors and for this patient in particular.

The *recipe for intervening* for this session includes relatively strong indicators, with one of the two crucial intervention contexts represented directly while the other is represented quite poorly, and a highly meaningful derivative complex with an important genetic element, which organizes well around the represented and unrepresented contexts—the elimination of the second therapy and the continued deviation through the clinic-fee arrangement. Under these conditions, some therapists might wait a bit longer in this hour to see whether the patient would represent the missing intervention context. Others would choose to organize the material around the represented context and then make a playback around the one that did not receive clear representation. Either of these two possibilities would be acceptable in light of the extent to which the patient has fulfilled the therapist's requirements in respect to the receipe for intervening.

The intervention actually offered by the therapist may be characterized as an attempt at interpretation, in that it is designed to comprehend the unconscious meanings and functions of a number of indicators, including the patient's absence, his symptoms, his concerns about his father and about leaving home, and the pending rectification of the framework. It does not, however, deal with the indicators related to the continued breaks in the frame. In addition, while accepting selected unconscious perceptions of the therapist, it also identifies most of the struggle regarding separation and individuation within the patient, rather than alluding to these difficulties in a transversal manner that would accept the patient's unconscious perceptions of comparable problems within the therapist while affording due recognition to their existence within the patient. Most of the erroneous qualities of this intervention involve the therapist's failure to take into consideration his own previously fixed response to the second therapy situation and the presence of other breaks in the framework of this treatment situation. Still, it is to the therapist's credit that he attempted to interpret the patient's unconscious perceptions of the pressures the therapist had been creating on him in regard to rectifying the frame, a prospect that the patient (and therapist) both welcomed and feared.

The therapist attempted to clarify the unconscious meanings and functions of several disturbances within the patient in light of the intervention context of the pending elimination of the second therapist. The stress on a derivative level was on the patient's responsive unconscious perceptions of the therapist, and on the patient's own anxieties and fantasies as evoked by this precipitant. The adaptive-context-derivative-complex integration constitutes a means of understanding the unconscious basis for the patient's symptoms and other disturbances.

In addition to analyzing whether an intervention has fulfilled the properties of an interpretation, one must consider its timing and whether the therapist has added or deleted anything of significance. This discussion leads to the impression that the intervention is well-timed and meets the criteria of an interpretation. It adds virtually nothing from previous sessions or from the therapist's own subjective responses and personal associations, and is in the main an attempt to integrate meaningfully a derivative complex in light of an adaptive context, as this constellation illuminates the patient's emotional difficulties.

The intervention is most at fault, however, in failing to hint at the presence of a second and more critical intervention context, the clinic-fee deviation. The therapist fails to make even a tentative playback of selected derivatives in light of this intervention context, and in keeping with this omission, fails to make use of a number of important derivative communications that actually touch upon both contexts: the patient's sense of damage (as a derivative in respect to both himself and the therapist), his fear of penetration, his rage against the father-therapist and the loss of the father, and the patient's more direct concerns about his father. The therapist neither clearly acknowledges the model of rectification offered by the patient nor interprets to the patient the striking derivative regarding the importance of giving up the second therapy as a basis for growth and maturation.

In supervision, it was suggested that this particular intervention was a moderately good interpretation that was, however, lacking in certain specific elements, especially the genetic material related to the father, and that it failed to attend to a major activated intervention context—the clinic-fee arrangement. It was predicted that there would be some measure of validation, and that possibly the patient would also attempt to deal more clearly with the therapist's omissions.

The material that followed this intervention must be examined for both validation or its lack and as a commentary on the therapist's effort. In regard to validation, on the interpersonal level there are mixed images: on the positive side, the patient's sense of optimism that he can get better and that he could leave home, and a sense that the therapist is using a more constructive approach in this therapy than that applied in the day hospital; on the negative side, there is a fear of the therapist, the image of losing a leg and of his father dying, and the allusion to the patient's overly-dependent sister. As the reader may have formulated, these negative derivatives probably stem more from the therapist's failure to deal with the deviant aspects of the framework than from the constructive parts of this interpretation.

On a cognitive level, this material appears to provide Type Two derivative validation of the therapist's intervention in several unanticipated ways. For example, there is the patient's willingness to give up a leg if he could be shown how to leave his house. This serves as a derivative expression that considerably clarifies the patient's separation anxieties as they pertain not only to his living at home, but also to his surrender of the second therapy. On one level the image suggests that the patient has indeed been involved in a pathological symbiotic merger with the second therapist and that he is experiencing the loss of the day hospital as the loss of a body part. It is now clear that he also fears that in leaving the day-hospital therapist he will do damage to the therapist, and he might not survive. Similarly, the patient himself fears for his existence in the absence of this type of pathological symbiosis.

Another previously unknown and important selected fact emerges in the allusion to separation problems in the patient's siblings. This is an important genetic element, in that it alludes to unconscious perceptions of both therapists, as well as to introjects and difficulties within the patient. This realization is followed by thoughts of renunciation and by a sense that there are highly constructive qualities to this treatment situation, and therefore to the therapist's interpretation. The patient seems to understand that this type of pathological symbiosis gratifies him, but also that it maintains him in an infantile, dependent, and merged state.

Another important derivative element is the allusion to the homosexual sibling. Here the patient unconsciously acknowledges the homosexual implications of the threesome: himself and the two therapists. This involves unconscious perceptions of homosexual needs and anxieties in both therapists, as well as comparable difficulties within the patient. At the same time, it is an important factor in the therapist's—and patient's—difficulty in establishing a private therapeutic situation for this patient.

In all there is strong Type Two derivative validation in this material in response to the therapist's interpretation. The patient's associations provide several selected facts that would become important avenues of subsequent therapeutic work. Simultaneously, it is evident that the patient is consciously working over the insights that he has gained into his own pathological symbiotic and dependency needs, his fear of separation, and his hostility toward his father. Less clear are conscious realizations regarding the disruptive and constructive inputs from the therapist, although there is some sense of working over in this area in the patient's initial remarks about the therapist. There are indications too that the patient is now prepared to deal with his unconscious homosexual anxieties, fantasies, and perceptions, and that he believes that the therapist is ready as well.

In the main, the commentary aspects of this responsive material involve the presentation by the patient of clearer derivatives of his unconscious perceptions of the therapist in light of the continued deviations of the clinic setting and third-party-fee therapy. Although the patient still does not directly represent these intervention contexts, he does make a manifest reference to the present therapeutic situation, thereby offering a less disguised representation than before.

The therapist's own avoidance is contributing to interactional resistances within the patient. There is some hint in the therapist's interpretation that he is now prepared to deal with these areas, although it may well be that the patient's lessening of communicative resistances is also based on his unconscious awareness that the therapist continues to avoid this critical issue. In general, resistances will diminish either as the therapist lessens his or her countertransference-based contributions to them or, on selected occasions, when the therapist continues his or her unconscious participation or intensifies it, producing a point at which the patient, as a model and in an unconscious effort to correct the situation, momentarily lessens his or her defenses. It seems likely that a study of the session after the present one would clarify the basis for the patient's more meaningful expressions after the therapist's interpretation. For the moment the most likely dynamic factor appears to be the therapist's capacity to offer a sound interpretation that may well have encouraged the patient to deal more meaningfully with the remaining issues that concerned him.

In terms of the deviant context, the patient now indicates that he is afraid of the therapist and that the therapist fears giving up the third-party payer and the clinic setting because of his own pathological symbiotic and merger needs. The fear of rectifying the frame involves fears of death, separation, and of homosexuality—a dread of being alone with the patient. The patient concludes this highly pertinent commentary with a model of rectification: try to leave home (the clinic and third-party payers) even though you are afraid.

In regard to technique, it might well then have been possible for the therapist to offer a playback of derivatives around the unmentioned deviant adaptive context. Because the issues involve the fixed frame, such a playback is likely to have produced additional meaningful and confirmatory material. As an alternative, the therapist could have remained silent and awaited the following hour, during which the patient was likely to deal with this issue once again. Still, because of the clarity of the derivative complex, a playback would have been preferred.

The Therapist's Use of Silence

As noted, there are two basic constellations in respect to the therapist's silences: (1) valid periods of silence in the absence of material that permits interpretation and framework-management response, and (2) the erroneous use of silence in a form that constitutes a missed intervention. These two types of silence form another continuum typical for psychotherapy, and there is a middle range in which the therapist tends to struggle with the question of whether there is sufficient material for an intervention or further associations are needed. Especially during such interludes, and in the presence of all extended periods of silence on the therapist's part, the patient's material must be evaluated in order to determine whether or not the silence appears to be facilitating the patient's communicative expressions. In addition, the therapist must monitor the patient's material for valid commentaries on his or her use of silence.

Patients consistently but unconsciously have a strong sense of just when they have provided their therapists with sufficient material for interpretation or framework-management response. On this basis, if the therapist fails to offer a needed intervention for a notable period of time, the patient will become engaged in reactions to the unconscious perception of the missed intervention. Themes of error, missed opportunities, exploitation, insensitivity, failed moments, and the like tend to emerge in the patient's associations. There are often direct complaints about some aspect of the therapist's technique, though it usually does not involve his or her silence. A therapist should reevaluate his or her failure to intervene when derivative themes of this kind emerge in the material from a patient after an extended interlude of silence on his or her part.

In supervision, it has been possible in a large number of presentations to formulate a patient's material as containing a sound communicative network, with a well-represented adaptive context, strong indicators, and a meaningful and coalescible derivative complex. When the therapist has not intervened under these conditions, the patient soon shifts to the negative and complaining themes noted above. Their emergence, as noted before, calls for a reappraisal of the patient's material and a questioning of the validity of the therapist's silence. With proper reformulation, the therapist can then offer the patient the missed interpretation or framework-management response. If the intervention context of the failure to intervene has also been represented clearly, the patient's reaction to this adptation-evoking context can also be interpreted.

It is clear, then, that silence by the therapist is appropriate only in the absence of interpretable material. There are definitive indications for intervening, and these can be consensually validated among observers and clinically validated by the patient's Type Two derivative responses to missed interventions. There is no substitute for a well-timed intervention, just as the judicious use of appropriate silence—with its holding and containing qualities, and the capacity for inner management, which it reflects within the therapist—is an equally vital part of the treatment experience for all patients. Careful monitoring of the patient's material during interludes with silence by the therapist is essential. It is necessary to seek both validation of the silence, through the emergence of increasingly meaningful material, and constructive commentaries that serve to reflect an introjection of its appropriate use.

Most of the difficulties in assessing the therapist's silence occur during the lying-fallow phase of psychotherapy, a time when the patient's material remains, sometimes for many sessions, in a relative state of nonmeaning. In these instances, the material does not appear to deepen and expand in respect to meaningful qualities, but at the same time there is no detectable activated intervention context, and negative commentary is absent. Instead, there often are occasional positive images that reflect a constructive introjective identification with a therapist capable of silent holding and containing, which meet the immediate therapeutic needs of the patient.

The two clinical examples presented in this chapter illustrate the sound use of silence with patients utilizing the Type A mode of communication. With each patient, the therapist's silence fostered the development of the communicative network to the point where sound intervention proved feasible. Both interventions were relatively well-timed and were met with Type Two derivative validation. A third example is presented in which a therapist's extended silence proved to be countertransference-based and to involve a missed intervention.

Clinical Example III

A young woman who worked as an anesthesiologist in a hospital entered treatment because of an episode of depression when Marvin, the young man with whom she was living, left her in order to marry someone else. The therapist, also a woman, had maintained a relatively loose set of ground rules with this patient, and often engaged in noninterpretive interventions. The session excerpted here took place a week before the Fourth of July holiday, which fell on the day of the patient's session:

Therapist: I don't work on legal holidays. If you want to, we can reschedule your next session since it falls on the Fourth of July. We can either do it now or sometime later.

Patient: Let's do it later.

Therapist: All right. I won't charge you a fee, and we can do it in the next few days or skip it altogether. You can call me.

Patient: It's all right with me if we don't reschedule it at all. I've been angry at Marvin for getting married on me. He abandoned me, but it's better that way. I can eat when I want, and I don't have to clean up for him. Some nursing students I was working with at the hospital gave me a present. I have nothing to say; my mind is a blank. I realize you're my link to people. I have no one else, that's why I come here. I avoid others because I feel they're going to control me. When I think about it, I feel like smashing into something or killing someone—I feel so furious. I'm afraid if I visited my sister and her husband I would say terrible things to their friends. I told them to go fuck themselves. At this wedding, this man said something about this woman's tits. I said, "Look at that cock." I guess I invite it in a way. In the hospital, this little child was coughing and they turned him upside-down, but the doctor was wrong—the child wasn't aspirating and didn't need that kind of treatment. I felt panicky and angry toward the doctor. I had this dream about how I turned on a football team and we beat the

administrators of the hospital to a pulp. When my parents
died, it was like getting rid of a cancer. After they died, I used
disinfectant to get rid of the cancer. My brother-in-law tells
me what to do and I resent it. I don't feel that way here, but I
did with my other two therapists.

The determination of the extent to which material from a
patient permits interpretation is based upon an analysis in terms of
indicators, activated adaptive contexts, and the presence of a derivative complex. The stronger the indicators and the clearer the communicative network, the more definitive the call for an intervention.
With other combinations of therapeutic context and degrees of
communicative resistance, the decision will be a little more difficult
to specify. Still, empirical studies indicate that it is possible to
generate a fair and specific appraisal of whether or not to intervene
in most situations.

In this particular session, the therapist, after her initial two
comments, remained entirely silent. As for the indicators, there are:
(1) the therapist's offer of a make-up session (a break in the fixed
frame); (2) the therapist's necessary cancellation of the following
session, carried out in a somewhat traumatic manner at the beginning of the session, without allowing the patient to free associate
and initiate the hour (which should always be the patient's prerogative), and without sufficient advance notice (cancelled hours should
be announced at least three or four weeks ahead of time); (3) the
patient's symptoms, which involve mainly depression, rage, and
feelings of panic; and (4) a possible characterological difficulty in
the patient's relationship with men and others, and in her
seemingly vulgar manner of expressing herself. Because the session
includes a current effort by the therapist to modify the framework of
treatment, and in light of the additional therapeutic contexts, the
intensity of these indicators rate at a level of nine or ten and speak
for a rather intense therapeutic need for intervention within this
patient.

To what extent does this communicative network provide the
therapist with the elements necessary for an interpretation or framework-management response? Most of the representations of indicators are manifest. Because of this, it would be possible, if the
balance of the communicative network proved to be meaningful, to
interpret directly the unconscious basis of many aspects of the

patient's characterological and symptomatic problems, and of the disturbances evoked in her by the therapist due to her breaks in the frame.

There are several adaptive contexts for this session, including the therapist's interventions in the previous hour (omitted from this discussion for purposes of exposition), the pending missed session and the manner in which it was introduced, and the therapist's offer of a make-up session. The most important of these intervention contexts is the therapist's offer of the make-up hour. One must ask first, of course, how well this particular adaptation-evoking context is represented. The patient alludes to it directly, initially commenting that she would like the make-up hour although she prefers to arrange the time for it in the future, and later commenting that it is all right with her if the missed session is not rescheduled. Thus a manifest representation of the adaptive context is alluded to in passing, after which the patient goes on manifestly to other matters. This constitutes an ideal representation of an intervention context and bodes well for the possibility of interpreting and managing the frame in this hour.

Finally, one must consider the derivative complex to determine how diverse, meaningful, and coalescible its elements appear to be. Since the derivative complex is actually quite rich, only the most compelling implications will be cited, each organized around the unconscious meanings and functions of the therapist's offer of a make-up session. In keeping with principles developed earlier, formulations are primarily shaped around valid unconscious perceptions of the therapist and of the implications of her proposed deviation. This principle must be adhered to in the presence of any break in the frame by the therapist, as well as in response to any other type of erroneous intervention (including misused silences). Were the therapist to intervene, the patient's own reactions, and any possible extensions into distorted fantasy, would either not be mentioned initially or would be placed in a secondary position as compared to the patient's unconscious perceptions of the therapist.

In the session, the patient immediately conveys an unconscious (derivative) perception that the therapist is angry with her and has deserted her (the allusion to Marvin), although she states a preference to have things this way. There is an allusion to a present, which implies that the therapist's offer of a make-up session is unconsciously viewed as a gift to the patient and as a request for a gift from the patient (in the form of an additional fee). Next, the patient's mind becomes blank, suggesting the manner in which the break in the frame interferes with her communicative relationship with the therapist.

The patient's reference to how the therapist is for her a link to people is on a derivative level an unconscious perception and introject of the therapist's undue attachment to the patient as reflected in her offer of the make-up hour. The unconscious implication is that the patient perceives the therapist's excessive need for her presence to be based on some sense of isolation. On one level, this derivative material contains an unconscious interpretation to the therapist.

Then there are allusions to being controlled and to crashing into or killing someone. (Deviations tend to do violence to the treatment situation and to the patient, and to evoke angry responses as well.) There is a reference to having said terrible things and to language with strong sexual-aggressive overtones. This latter may well allude to the unconsciously instinctualized qualities of the therapist's offer of the make-up hour, which is both seductive and destructive in quality.

Next there is the doctor's error and mistreatment of the child. There are allusions to a sense of panic and a further mention of hostility. There are references to competition and to defeating someone. There is then an allusion to a genetic experience in which the patient lost both of her parents, who had been quite cruel to her, and which she speaks of as getting rid of a cancer. It is here that the distinctly parasitic qualities of the therapist's offer of the make-up session is represented, though the earlier material also reflects perceived wishes in the therapist for a pathological symbiotic mode of relatedness. In this regard, one may identify the patient's divided response: repudiation of comparable needs for these modes of relatedness as reflected in her decision to forgo the make-up hour, and wishes to engage in these modes of relatedness and be both the symbiotic recipient and the parasitic victim.

As the hour closes, the patient again speaks of being told what to do. She then provides an interesting bridge to therapy and a final effort, it would seem, to help the therapist connect this material to her relationship with the patient: through negation, she denies that she feels manipulated in this therapy, though she did in her previous treatment experiences. This denial is an interactional defense that reflects not only the patient's use of this mechanism, but the therapist's use as well—this last reflected in her failure to intervene. In this way, the patient characterizes the therapist's silence as a failure to appreciate the implications of the communications from her patient.

It would be difficult, of course, to specify the exact point in this session where the therapist should have intervened. There is no doubt that within the total hour the patient provides her with clearly represented indicators, a manifestly represented adaptive context, and an extremely meaningful derivative complex. Since both the indicators and adaptive context are represented directly quite early in the session, the decision about intervening depends entirely on the point at which the therapist feels she has sufficient derivatives for interpretation. In this hour, meaning appears quite early, much of it in the patient's initial associations after the therapist's second intervention. The therapist might well have waited for the intense instinctual drive material that emerges toward the middle of the hour before interpreting and managing the frame. Perhaps the most propitious moment occurs after the allusion to the doctor who had mistreated his infant patient. At that point, the therapist has a clear model of rectification in the patient's decision not to reschedule the session. She also has a rich derivative complex with which to explain the patient's reactions to the make-up offer and many aspects of her symptomatic disturbance.

It is of interest then that beyond that point in the session, the patient's material involves the themes of beating the hospital administrators to a pulp, the death of her parents, the getting rid of cancer through disinfectant, being manipulated by the brother-in-law, and the final negating reference to treatment. For the moment it would be difficult to attribute all of these negative images to the therapist's seemingly erroneous use of silence—her failure to intervene—since many of these images also organize meaningfully around the unrectified and uninterpreted break in the frame. Nonetheless, the therapist's supervisor strongly favored the hypothesis that this was a session in which a definitive intervention—both framework-management and interpretive—was required, feasible, and missed. In light of this appraisal, it is useful to turn to the following hour, which took place two weeks later because of the session missed on the Fourth of July.

Patient: Marvin gets me so mad. He called and wanted to know where I was. He came barging into my house for his things. *He* has *my* number, but *I* can't reach *him*. I don't know why he's still hanging on. What could he want with me? He's married now. He has someone new. He's manipulating me and wants to use me in some kind of a deal he's putting together. I did so much for him, and I deserve some compensation. He gives me nothing. I thought it would be different because of his mother; she accepted me. I stop talking to people I lose—like when my father and mother were ill. I try to reach out to people but they don't respond. Oh, here's my insurance form. Please fill it out for the month.

Therapist: We'll talk about it next week.

Although some of this material continues to organize meaningfully around the adaptive context of the therapist's offer to make up the missed session, this discussion will now concentrate on the most recent proposed intervention context: the therapist's missed intervention, her erroneous use of silence. In general, this type of missed intervention is a strong indicator that creates a powerful therapeutic need within the patient. The patient's sense of depression is another therapeutic context for this second hour, although it is also an aspect of the derivative complex—part of the patient's unconscious perception of and reaction to the therapist, based on both the deviation and the erroneous use of silence.

The therapist's undue silence is best represented through displacements and derivatives in which the patient alludes to how Marvin gives her nothing, and refers to her own failure to talk to others and her sense of having been abandoned by them. Almost without exception, patients fail to represent this type of intervention context manifestly; were they able to do so, they could also work over its implications primarily on a conscious level and in truly adaptive form. Instead, the traumatic qualities of this type of adaptive context prompt derivative representations of the context itself, along with what is usually a highly meaningful derivative complex. At that juncture, the best intervention available to the therapist is a playback of selected derivatives organized around the unrepresented intervention context.

The derivative complex itself, organizing its meanings around the intervention context of the therapist's seemingly erroneous use of silence, again includes an unconscious image of the therapist as mad (perhaps both angry and crazy), which along the me/not-me interface also represents the patient's own reactive anger. Through derivatives, the patient indicates that she feels she is being exploited by the therapist, who gets something from her patient while giving nothing in return and being unreachable. The patient feels manipulated and unrewarded (i.e., she has not obtained the necessary intervention she requires). There seems to have been a promise of good mothering that failed. The therapist is then lost to the patient as a meaningful figure, and the patient now attempts to protect herself by creating distance of her own—here, communicatively, by failing to represent the activated intervention context and thereby engaging in some level of communicative resistance. The patient concludes this session by introducing a compensating deviation of her own—the insurance form.

Feelings of abandonment, depression, and exploitation are common after a missed intervention by the therapist. This material appears to lend Type Two derivative support to the formulation that the therapist had failed to intervene appropriately in the previous hour. Unfortunately, the therapist did not offer an interpretation on the basis of these hypotheses, so more definitive confirmation is not available.

The Six-Part Observational Schema

The first hour of the clinical example presented above will be analyzed in terms of the six basic areas of conceptualization (presented earlier in synthetic form) in order to systematically demonstrate how these six areas were represented in the material from the patient and in the therapist's silence. In actual practice, the yield from formulations in each of these categories is funneled into the therapist's thinking regarding the indicators, intervention context, and especially, the derivative complex.

The first area involves the *framework* of the treatment relationship. In this respect, it is interesting to observe that the therapist attempted to modify the frame and the patient initially intended to participate only to finally secure it from the deviation proposed by the therapist. This implies that the therapist wished to deal with her own anxieties and problems in her relationship with the patient through a framework-deviation cure, and that the patient had mixed feelings in this regard, though she ultimately expressed a preference to work within the defined frame. The therapist's effort to deviate may have been a factor in her failure to intervene, since her own adaptive efforts were in the direction of action-discharge and misalliance. At the same time, the offer to change the hour became the critical adaptation-evoking context for the patient's diverse responses.

The second area is the *mode of relatedness*. In this respect, as already noted, the material indicates a variety of tendencies within the patient. Her decision to maintain the frame suggsts a wish for a healthy symbiosis with the therapist. There may be a similar implication in the receipt of a present from her students, an interaction that may also represent a commensal relationship (one in which both sides obtained equal and healthy satisfaction). The need to use the therapist as a link to people suggests a pathological symbiosis, while the patient's violent feelings toward others suggests a need for pathological parasiticism.

As for the therapist, the offer of the make-up hour has both pathologically symbiotic and parasitic qualities. These are represented in derivative form in the material from the patient in ways already cited. The therapist's failure to intervene properly suggests an autistic mode of relatedness through which the meaning links between herself and the patient were severed. In this context, it may be noted again that while Bion (1962) proposed three relationship links between persons—love, hate, and knowledge—it appears that the knowledge link is the most critical determinant of the maturational mode of relatedness between patients and therapists. While there may, of course, be both loving and hateful links, psychotherapy is founded on a quest for understanding the nature of the patient's Neurosis. Because of this, it appears that the knowledge-meaning link has an especially great influence, both consciously and unconsciously, on the qualities of relatedness between the two participants to treatment.

The third area is the *mode of cure*. The patient alludes to eating when she has need, which speaks for healthy therapeutic wishes expressed within usual boundaries. However, the main image in this area during this hour involves the doctor's turning the little child upside down in error. While this image may reflect the patient's wish to be mistreated, its most powerful meaning seems to involve the therapist's errant effort at cure through a framework break and her failure to crystalize a moment of cure through a sound interpretation-rectification effort. Finally, there is the patient's use of disinfectant after the death of her parents from cancer. This image has mixed qualities, though it appears to reflect a strong sense of anxiety and an unhealthy effort to obtain relief.

The fourth area is *communicative style*. The patient here is expressing herself through a highly creative and symbolic use of the Type A mode. At the point in the session when she says that she has nothing to say, she leans momentarily toward the Type B or Type C mode, but does not extend herself in this direction. As for the therapist, her proposed deviation has qualities of the Type B and Type C modes, while her silence expresses a combination of these modes: it was a B-C form of expression. There is, then, on the part of the therapist a sense of pathological interactional projection and the invocation of lie-barrier systems.

The fifth area is *dynamics and genetics*. In this respect, the material involves issues of control, unmanaged hostility and rage, violent qualities of sexual impulses, depression and loss, and the defensive use of denial. There is in addition the genetic allusion to the death of the patient's parents.

The sixth area is the *central pathological figure*. Without attempting to sort out and formulate the specifics of the patient's unconscious conflicts and anxieties, it seems likely that, to the question of whose pathology is in focus (i.e., does unconscious perception or unconscious fantasy-memory predominate?), one must answer that the main thrust of this material involves the pathological dynamics and genetics of the therapist and the patient's valid unconscious perceptions of these difficulties. Whatever overflow there may be into problems within the patient, these could not be determined until the frame was clearly rectified and the therapist offered the necessary interpretations required by this patient.

Summary and Conclusions

The basic interventions of the therapist are those of silence (listening, holding, and containing), managing the ground rules and boundaries of therapy, and the offer of interpretation-recon-

692 / Psychotherapy: A Basic Text

structions. Active interventions are responses to expressed therapeutic needs in the patient—indicators or therapeutic contexts. Interventions involving the framework take precedence over those that are interpretive, although often the two supplement each other.

All interpretations and framework-management responses are based on the patient's *derivative* communications within the session in which they are offered. Efforts to rectify the frame and interpret to the patient are organized in terms of activated adaptive contexts and the patient's derivative responses—perceptions, fantasies, adaptive and maladaptive reactions, dynamic meanings, genetic connections, and the like. An interpretation is an effort by the therapist to afford the patient an understanding of his or her expressed therapeutic needs (indicators) in terms of their unconscious basis as revealed through an activated intervention context and a derivative complex that accounts for the disturbance at hand.

In deciding whether to intervene, the therapist should weigh the intensity of the indicators against the availability of meaningful communicative material (the clarity of the representation of the adaptive context and how the derivative complex coalesces).

In the presence of strong indicators, especially those that involve breaks in the fixed frame, the therapist is likely to intervene even in the presence of relatively thin derivative material. At times of emergency and acute deviations, the therapist will make the best possible intervention available from the material, doing so without fail. This last, of course, includes threats by the patient to terminate treatment, suicidal and homicidal crises, acute breaks in the frame, and major ruptures in the therapeutic alliance. In the presence of weak indicators, the therapist will intervene only in the presence of clear communicative material.

The specific timing of an intervention depends on the patient's fulfilling the recipe for intervening: the manifest communication of indicators, a direct or thinly disguised representation of the adaptive context, and a meaningful coalescible derivative complex. As these become available, the therapist often comments after an especially clear expression. In the absence of a directly represented intervention context, the therapist may offer a modified interpretation through the playback of selected derivative material organized carefully around the unmentioned adaptive context. This effort should always begin with the best available derivative representation of the unmentioned context, and should include the most meaningful derivatives available.

Interventions such as questions, clarifications, and confrontations have been discarded, since they interfere with the patient's communicative flow and tend to establish relatedness on a manifest content or Type One Derivative level. The entire gamut of so-called supportive and personally revealing interventions have also been rejected because they tend to parasitize the patient.

Once an intervention has been made, the therapist must attend to the patient's responsive material in two basic ways: (1) as a means of searching for validation or its lack (see Chapter 12); and (2) as a *commentary* on the therapist's efforts, filled with valid unconscious perceptions and possible distortion. The latter is a basis for corrective efforts by the therapist when necessary.

This chapter completes the study of the intervention process. The extensive and necessary stress has been on systematization. It deserves to be stated that, in addition to generating interventions that meet the formal properties of interpretations and rectifications of the framework at the behest of the patient's derivative material, the therapist must always carry out these endeavors with a sense of patience and concern. Interpretive work must be undertaken with a due sense of affect. There remains a need for human sensibilities, though these find their ultimate expression in the psychotherapeutic situation through the offer of a well-timed and well-stated interpretation or framework-management response. In this way, the therapist expresses the unique capacity to help his or her patients insightfully and meaningfully resolve their Neuroses and to individuate and grow.

Part VI

Perspectives

Chapter 36

The Phases of Psychotherapy

The familiar approach to psychotherapy envisions an opening, middle, and termination phase, along with a post-treatment period. The opening phase is seen as a period in which the patient reveals his or her pathology and tests out the therapist and the therapeutic relationship. The middle phase is seen as involving the therapeutic work with the unconscious factors in the patient's illness. The termination phase is seen as introduced by the resolution of the patient's symptoms, and separation from the therapist receives full analytic consideration. (Less has been said about the post-termination period, although it is certainly a time during which the patient completes the working through of his or her reactions to the loss of the therapy and the therapist and continues to pursue self-analytic efforts as necessary.) Empirical observation has led to a more precise delineation of these phases in terms of the spiraling interaction, enabling therapists to move beyond these all too general characterizations.

The Opening Phase

This volume has already presented the first session in some detail, and in many ways the first session characterizes the opening phase of therapy. In general, patients enter treatment wishing for some degree of pathological symbiotic or parasitic relatedness and express these needs through efforts to create a modified setting and an altered group of ground rules. The therapist's adherence to the framework provides a basic set of intervention contexts to which the

patient then responds in derivative form, revealing critical unconscious fantasy and perception constellations that illuminate the
nature of his or her Neurosis.

Some patients pressure the therapist to engage in manifest
content and Type One derivative (pathological) forms of relatedness. When the therapist does so erroneously, these become significant countertransference-based contexts to which the patient responds with powerful derivative communications. The error can be
subjected to rectification, and the material interpreted with considerable benefit.

A set of attributes specific to the opening phase of psychotherapy correlate with the patient's preferred communicative style.
Thus the Type A patient is one who wishes more for a healthy
symbiosis than for a pathologically symbiotic, autistic, or parasitic
relationship with the therapist. He or she tends to be a patient
experiencing acute symptoms and anxieties, and prepares to respond to the therapist's establishment and securing of the ground
rules and boundaries of the therapeutic relationship with highly
meaningful derivative expressions. Correct interpretations tend to
obtain Type Two derivative validation, and there is a continuing
(up to a point) unfolding of meaningful derivatives relevant to the
patient's emotional illness. At some juncture, usually within a few
months, this type of patient experiences a significant measure of
symptom relief, much of it founded upon the therapist's securing
and holding the frame, and upon his or her valid interpretations.
One or two possibilities are then most likely: (1) the patient decides
to terminate his or her treatment rather than probe deeper, or (2) the
patient enters the lying-fallow middle phase (see below).

The Type B-A patient enters therapy with powerful pathological symbiotic and sometimes parasitic needs. These are expressed
through intense efforts to modify the ground rules and boundaries
of the therapeutic relationship, and to force the therapist to respond
with intervention errors—i.e., to react on a manifest content and
Type One derivative level or with erroneous interpretations. These
patients, in addition, provide the therapist with meaningful representations of intervention contexts and coalescible derivative networks. It is therefore possible to interpret the unconscious basis of
these efforts, and the result is a rather stormy but highly insightful
opening phase.

Eventually—and this is often a matter of several to many

months—these patients will either terminate because of the symptom alleviation they experience, or shift into a basically lying-fallow middle phase, though with occasional disturbances. For therapists who can contain the pathological projective identification and pathological object relationship pressures created by these patients in the opening phase, the interpretive response to their derivative networks proves quite rewarding. These patients often show dramatic symptomatic and characterological changes, many of which are based on the insight and positive introjective identifications they are able to acquire unconsciously from such a therapist. They are often suffering from borderline and ambulatory schizophrenic syndromes, but they show a striking division in wanting a pathological symbiosis on the one hand and a healthy symbiosis on the other. They fluctuate intensely during the opening phase of treatment, although as a rule they move gradually toward a healthy symbiotic relationship and Type A communication.

The situation is somewhat different with Type B-C communicators. These patients enter therapy with powerful pathological symbiotic and parasitic needs, demanding a multitude of inappropriate satisfactions and a basically pathological mode of relatedness of the therapist. This is expressed through multiple efforts to modify the ground rules and boundaries, and to obtain noninterpretive interventions. These patients dread a nonpathological mode of relatedness, and the attendant emergence of direct and derivative expressions of disturbing instinctual drive-related material and of what are usually the expressions of a poorly defended psychotic core. They wish to establish a cure through pathological symbiosis or parasitism, and through the destruction of meaningful relatedness and meaning. They wish to use evacuation, action-discharge, and pathological projective identification to find symptom relief. They attempt to destroy understanding and meaningful derivative communication, all the while placing the therapist under enormous interactional and interpersonal pressures. The therapist who adheres to the framework and to an interpretive approach with these patients is experienced as persecutory and dangerous. It is a fundamental question whether these patients wish for or will accept psychotherapy along insightful lines. Many therapists have wondered whether they should respond with compromises in the ground rules and in their interventions as an effort to engage this type of patient in deviant therapy during the opening phase; they would then gradually modify the basic mode of relatedness, secure the frame, and shift to a more interpretive approach. Unfortunately, these efforts must be considered in light of the empirical finding that they are viewed unconsciously by the patient as a reflection of pathological, austistic, symbiotic and parasitic needs within the therapist, and efforts to destroy both meaning and meaningful relatedness. Negative introjects abound. This is rather striking, since on a conscious level the patient tends to welcome destructive interactions of this kind. Still, quite consistently on a derivative level, they are highly critical of therapists who participate in them.

It seems likely that some therapists will engage in compromises under these circumstances. They will modify their basic interpretive-framework management approach in order to engage the patient on his or her terms, and even to share sectors of misalliance and pathology in the belief that for many such patients, this is the only basis on which any semblance of therapy can be initiated. It may well be that therapists who can tolerate this type of lie-barrier therapy, and their patients' negative derivative responses, will then be in a position to interpret the patient's responsive unconscious perceptions and introjects. For some it might well prove feasible to gradually rectify the framework and thereby establish a truth therapy and a healthy symbiotic mode of relatedness. It can be expected, however, that there will be many disruptive repercussions to this approach, and that the subsequent course of therapy will be quite stormy. Still, it is essential to discover the means by which these highly resistant and destructive patients can be offered a helpful therapeutic experience. This is clearly one of the most critical areas in need of clinical research.

Some of these patients will, from time to time, provide an interpretable communicative network to the therapist. They will tend to validate the interventions offered to them on this basis, only to obliterate their implications and to destroy the insight that they have just gained. In this way, they are momentary Type B-A communicators on the expressive side, but remain Type C obliterators on the receptive end. These patients are difficult for all therapists, and generate highly destructive and parasitic projective identifications and modes of relatedness. They tax the therapist's containing, holding, and interpretive capacities, and sometimes appear to wish only to destroy these abilities in the therapist rather than benefit from them. They show an enormous envy of the therapist's constructive functioning and an overriding need to destroy these qualities in him or her.

A final group of patients enter therapy and quickly become Type C communicators, either Type C narrators or highly constricted in what they express. Often, they have been pressured to enter treatment by a third party and show an enormous fear of developing a relationship with the therapist based on meaningful derivative communication. They appear to prefer a pathological (and sometimes healthy) form of autism or symbiosis in which they are held and contained, with little in the way of meaningful interaction. Sometimes they are quickly disillusioned because the therapist is able to offer few interpretations and framework-management responses, and they terminate treatment quite early. Another subgroup of this kind quickly enters a middle phase of psychotherapy that is quiescent for a further extended period.

The Middle Phase

For the Type A patient, the middle phase of psychotherapy is characterized by a quiet acceptance of the therapist's holding and containing capacities, which establish the essential conditions for this period of therapy—*the lying-fallow phase.* At times, prompted by some disturbance within, with the therapist, or in outside relationships, the patient will create a framework or other issue. When the therapist maintains the frame, the patient then has an intervention context to which he or she can respond with meaningful derivatives—dynamic and genetic, perceptive and fantasied. The therapist's interpretations then help to resolve the anxieties and conflicts that have been aroused, and the patient tends to return to a relatively quiescent communicative state.

In this phase, this type of patient becomes either a Type C narrator or a constricted Type C communicator. Many of them, especially those inclined to narration, tend to become involved in conscious self-interpretations, and direct seemingly interpretive comments to the therapist, which are based on manifest content and Type One derivative considerations. Nonetheless, these efforts appear to modify their pathological derivative defenses and nonderivative lie-barrier systems to the point where they are more adaptively resourceful and open to growth and conflict resolution.

This period of *lying fallow* (Khan 1977) or of *quiescence*, during which the patient engages in self-curative efforts of this kind, appears to characterize the middle phase of treatment of many patients. This is true also of the Type B-A and Type B-C communicators who remain in treatment for an extended period of time, although it is characteristic of these patients to more often create framework and other treatment crises because of their more intense and frequent need for framework management and interpretive responses from the therapist. Virtually all Type C patients who remain in treatment enter into an extended phase of this kind as well.

The existence of the lying-fallow middle phase of psychotherapy requires a fresh perspective on the matter of communicative resistances. While gross behavioral resistances that may arise during this phase of therapy are a sign of therapeutic need in the patient and will require interpretive and framework-management responses in light of activated intervention contexts, the existence of relative noncommunication on a derivative level must be evaluated in terms of whether a disturbing adaptive context is in evidence. In the absence of such a context, lying fallow and derivative noncommunication is an appropriate and adaptive response, and cannot be viewed as a resistance in the sense of its being an obstacle to the progress of therapy. On the other hand, in the presence of such a context, communicative dysfunctions must be seen as a form of resistance, and their underlying basis formulated and eventually interpreted to the patient.

Patients prove surprisingly capable of considerable therapeutic gain during the lying-fallow phase with their efforts at direct self-interpretation, although they very seldom organize manifestly around activated intervention contexts. This suggests that therapists have been far too active in the past, and that much of extended psychotherapy has unfolded because of continual countertransference-based inputs by the therapist. It appears that far less needs to be accomplished in the way of definitive active interpretations to patients to help them to achieve structurally founded symptom alleviation.

The Termination Phase

The middle phase of therapy may extend from several months to a year or more, during which the therapist will only intermittently offer interpretations and framework-management responses. Nonetheless, during this time the patient, by working through the therapist's interventions and the patient's own self-interpretations, begins to show striking constructive characterological changes and consolidation, and the alleviation of symptoms and basic Neurosis. Many of these changes tend to follow interpretive framework-management interludes, and to be based on the insight and positive introjects that they provide to the patient. They follow the emergence of Type Two derivative validation and insightful selected facts that illuminate the patient's illness and its unconscious basis, and give sense and meaning to the symptomatic changes.

Once sufficient work of this kind has been accomplished, both on the surface and through derivatives, many of these patients will begin to express derivative allusions to the necessity of considering and effecting a termination of therapy. More rarely, they will bring up this prospect consciously. When expressed through derivatives, the patient will eventually generate some type of framework or interpretive issue in order to have an intervention context through which interpretations can be made of the patient's termination fantasies, perceptions, and anxieties. The termination phase, which may last from just a few weeks to several months, is then characterized by alternations between periods of Type C-barrier holding and containing and periods of Type A communication in response to an activated intervention context from the therapist. Of course, the anticipation of the therapist's acceptance of termination itself serves here as an important adaptive context, in addition to those that each individual patient and therapist help to generate.

The termination of psychotherapy should be effected at the behest of the patient's derivatives and through his or her own conscious decision to set a termination date and adhere to it. The therapist should silently accept the patient's decision and maintain an essentially holding and interpretive attitude. Under these conditions, the patient has the best opportunity to experience the relevant separation anxieties and fantasies-perceptions, and to work through the pending loss of the treatment situation and therapist.

Based largely on their own countertransference-based separation anxieties and conflicts, many therapists tend to modify the ground rules and boundaries of the therapeutic relationship in the termination phase. These erroneous interventions deprive the patient of a maximal opportunity for the adaptive and analytic resolution of the unique problems that emerge during this phase— and these are always related to important aspects of the patient's Neurosis. The deviations lead to introjects within the patient of the therapist's pathological separation anxieties and fears of individuation, as well as needs to remain merged with and to infantilize the patient. Adherence to a basic interpretive and secure framework approach maintains a healthy symbiotic relationship during this difficult period of psychotherapy, and enables the patient to end treatment on a note of optimal functioning.

The Post-terminantion Phase

In keeping with the principles described for the termination phase, the post-termination period is one in which the past boundaries and ground rules that pertain to the relationship between the patient and therapist should be *maintained* rather than modified. Thus social and other contact beteen patient and therapist is inadvisable, and efforts by either patient or therapist to effect such meetings or involvements must be viewed as a reflection of unresolved pathological symbiotic and parasitic needs. When initiated or accepted by the therapist, these contacts tend to undermine the constructive and healthy introject that the patient has derived from a sound treatment experience with the therapist, and to bring into question the interpretive work as well. While inadvertent or unexpected contacts can be handled politely and with reasonable distance, active efforts to meet socially or professionally, or to collaborate or make contact in any other way, are distinctly inappropriate.

The post-termination phase for the patient is characterized by a final working through of the loss of the therapist. While patients should not be deliberately taught how to engage in self-analysis, many patients are able to make use of the therapist's insightful and interpretive approach in their own self-analytic efforts. Empirically, however, it appears that much self-therapeutic work during and after psychotherapy takes place on a manifest content and Type

One derivative level rather than in terms of Type Two derivative responses. The main exception is seen in the termination and post-termination phases, where it is usually evident to the patient that the loss of the therapist is serving as a critical adaptive context. Nonetheless, all of these efforts at insight, however sound or unsound, when based on a past healthy symbiotic relationship with the therapist and an unconscious introjection of his or her effective interpretive functioning, tend to have positive consequences for the patient.

The individuation, autonomy, conflict-resolving, and self-care-taking functions of the patient are enhanced by the finality of the termination of psychotherapy. The success of this phase is predicated on the principle that the therapist *not* encourage or leave open the possibility that the patient return for sessions on occasion or with any other kind of regularity. It should remain *implicit* that the therapist's door remains open if necessary, while the explicit sense should be that treatment has ended and that the patient can now take over responsibility. Open-ended terminations tend to reinforce pathological symbiotic and parasitic needs in both participants.

Finally, the therapist may also expect to have some need to work through the loss of the patient; for the therapist, this is an important adaptive context. Such working through should be done privately and through self-analysis, and managed to the point where any need to deviate or to respond noninterpretively to the patient is brought under full control. Separation anxieties are a major source of difficulty for all human beings, patients and therapists alike. Every termination experience is an opportunity for the therapist to work out a segment of his or her own separation constellation, to serve as the interpreter of the patient's problems in this sphere, and as an implicit model of someone who can adequately contain and deal with this troublesome area. When this attitude and sense of mastery persists into the period after therapy, the therapist has done all that can be done to help the patient with this aspect of his or her Neurosis.

Chapter 37

Psychotherapy with Severely Disturbed Patients

Throughout this volume, questions have arisen regarding psychotherapeutic techniques with patients having relatively severe psychopathology, such as borderline and schizophrenic (or other psychotic) syndromes. The question is often asked whether this basic approach, its principles and techniques, can be applied to these patient populations. The suggestion is sometimes made that modifications in the basic approach are necessary because of the nature of these patients' object relationships and psychopathology. It should be remembered, however, that these evaluations are based on manifest content and Type One derivative listening and intervening, without substantial considerations to the patient's Type Two derivative expressions and to interventions offered on such a basis. Careful investigations point to rather different propositions, which will now be considered. Since the question is so broad, it will be possible here to touch only upon some of the more pertinent issues and clinical observations.

General Considerations

Initial clinical observations indicate that severely ill patients have suffered from internal malfunctions that are based on, and interact with, major failures in maternal and other caring functions, including those that are broadly subsumed under relating, holding, and containing (see Chapter 3). It follows, then (and this is amply borne out clinically), that they need from the therapist a sound, healthy symbiotic relationship and effective capacities for both holding and containing—both of which are conveyed not only through the therapist's silences, but also through sound interpretations. Failing these basic requirements, efforts at interpretive work are bound to be in error or undermined by the implications of the therapist's basic and pathological mode of relating to and interacting with the patient. As a result, in the presence of a pathological relationship, even seemingly sound interpretive comments will fail to help these patients to resolve their highly primitive intrapsychic and interpersonal conflicts, and to modify their extremely pathological inner mental worlds, psychic functions, and introjects.

On the other hand, the establishment of a seemingly sound mode of relatedness and holding by itself cannot lead to maximal resolution of the symptoms and characterological disturbances seen in these patients, unless it is also a means of providing the foundation for a sound interpretive approach. Both are essential: holding-relating soundly and interpretations, and each is a requisite for the effective use of the other. All to often, the relationship per se (and it is a deviant and pathologically symbiotic one at that) is stressed as the sole curative factor in the psychotherapy of these patients. The pathological symbiotic, and even parasitic qualities of the deviations that are proposed as part of this mode of relatedness are overlooked, and the constructive attributes of a relationship established by a therapist with sound listening and interpretive endeavors are *not* afforded the central role that they must have.

The therapist's basic interpretive approach is an essential component of the healthy symbiotic mode of relatedness. This holds especially true for relatively severely ill patients. Ego and superego dysfunctions are not merely organically based disturbances, but find significant contributions from pathological unconscious fantasy and perception constellations. These include fantasies and introjects based on the therapist's actual functioning with the patient, including his or her mode of relatedness and cure, and interpretive capacities—or their lack. Disturbances in these spheres, no matter how well-meaning on the surface, tend to enhance the patient's psychopathology rather than resolve it.

Therapists have too often overlooked the unconscious communications contained in the noninterpretive interventions used with these patients, implications that are consistently perceived unconsciously by the patient as highly hurtful and destructive despite their deceptively supportive manifest qualities. Only a therapeutic approach that understands the meanings and functions of the patient's communications on both the manifest and latent levels may be expected to be truly and consistently effective with this patient population. Even with their evident failings in object-relating and ego and superego dysfunctions, they require a soundly functioning therapist who properly uses interpretations and frame-work-management responses. This is the only possible means of providing a resolution of the underlying basis for the patient's severe symptoms, as well as constructive inner changes—the resolution of primitive conflicts, the modification of primitive introjects, and the easing of structural dysfunctions in the ego, id, and super-ego—as a basis for enhanced adaptation and growth.

Two Types of Severely Ill Patients

Generally speaking, severely ill patients fall into two groups in terms of their approach to psychotherapy and their efforts to relate to the therapist. One group deeply and unconsciously wishes for a healthy symbiotic mode of relatedness, and therefore readily accepts the basic conditions of treatment. They express themselves alternately as Type A and Type C communicators, depending on their inner needs and the presence of activated intervention contexts.

Therapeutic work with these patients is different from that seen with more neurotic individuals, in that their anxieties and conflicts are far more primitive and their behaviors and symptoms reflect their characteristic id, ego, and superego dysfunctions. As a result, these patients show varying degrees of impulsivity, poor judgment, disturbances in their contact and relationship with reality, and highly primitive fears of annihilation. Consequently, their associations and behaviors have a somewhat different cast from the neurotic patient. These differences influence the therapist primarily in regard to the specific nature and frequency of interventions. These patients benefit greatly from a secure holding environment and therapist, and from his or her occasional interpretations. There is little pressure on the therapist to deviate and no inherent reason to modify the *basic* holding-interpretive approach.

It is evident, however, that the actual nature of the therapeutic work will be different with this group of severely disturbed patients from that with the neurotic patient. The areas under exploration will tend to be more primitive, as will the underlying anxieties and responses. The healthy symbiosis effected between the patient and therapist may be tenuous, and the therapeutic alliance either impaired or vulnerable to disturbance. Resistances will tend to be more blatant on a gross behavioral level, although less so in the communicative sphere.

Sometimes these patients will require rather frequent intervening, and the therapist must have a full comprehension of the basic structure of the emotional illness with which these patients suffer in order to respond properly. Even with patients showing severe narcissistic pathology, the basic holding-interpretive approach described in this volume is the best means with which to offer a mode of relatedness that corrects *inherently*, permits the expression and analytic resolution of the patient's narcissistic pathology (including both grandiose and idealizing nontransference and transference contellations), and affords the patient the highest quality of conscious and unconscious emphatic and holding-containing responsiveness in the therapist.

The second group of severely ill patients tends to be Type B communicators and often uses the Type B-C mode. They therefore create incessant pressures on the therapist through demands for deviation, and through pathological projective identifications of a highly toxic and disturbing nature that are often difficult to contain and metabolize toward interpretation. Consequently, they hold the therapist very badly and make it very difficult for the therapist to hold them. They wish primarily to establish a pathological symbiotic or parasitic relationship with the therapist in order to dump into him or her much of their own highly primitive and threatening inner disturbance, and to seal off that which remains. They have little wish for understanding and attempt to destroy both meaning and meaningful relatedness. They appear to be involved in primitive attacks on the therapist based on envy and dread, and in massive efforts at riddance of psychic pain and tension. They dread the highly psychotic active inner mental world with which they are struggling, and appear to be convinced that even derivative contact with their own inner selves and fantasies and perceptions will annihilate them. They insist upon fusion or merger with the therapist, dreading what they believe will be the catastrophic consequences of any relative degree of separation and any possibility of individuation.

It is especially with this second group of patients that many therapists have advocated the use of a wide range of deviations and an essentially noninterpretive approach. These patients actually fall into two groups: (1) those with whom treatment may be structured in terms of an ideal therapeutic environment and hold, and with whom a basically interpretive approach may be adopted; and (2) those who will in the very first session raise powerful exceptions to this particular definition of the therapeutic relationship and experience.

With the first group, therapy unfolds in terms of a relatively healthy symbiosis and a relatively sound communicative alliance. Nonetheless, since these patients are both primitive and agitated, and have strong propensities toward projective identification, their course of therapy, and especially the opening phase, will be stormy and difficult. Most of these patients are Type B-A communicators, and sound framework management and interpretive responses prove feasible despite many intense pressures from the patient to have the therapist deviate and respond noninterpretively. There is a chaotic and primitive quality to the therapeutic experience, a need for far more frequent interventions than with the relatively neurotic patient, and a need to deal with frequent attacks on the therapist and his or her holding and containing capacities. Nonetheless, the basic interpretive-framework-management approach is maintained throughout, and there is no sound need or basis for deviation.

With those patients who insist upon an immediate pathological symbiosis or parasitic relationship with the therapist, the therapist has two choices: (1) to compromise his or her basic approach, or (2) to attempt to maintain it, to interpret the patient's objections and destructive responses, and to risk losing the patient almost immediately. These patients bring with them the need to destroy the ideal therapeutic-holding environment and therapist, and they have a deep and terrible dread of a meaningful therapeutic relationship and of being alone within a secure frame with the therapist. They show inordinate fears of annihilation, a paranoid-like sense of persecution, and phobic anxieties and fantasies in which the secure therapeutic situation is believed, on an unconscious level, to be a dangerous claustrum. Most of these convictions are transference-based, near-delusional in nature, and difficult if not impossible to modify interpretively. The very existence of meaning is experienced by them as devestatingly dangerous.

There is, then, a striking discordance between the therapist's use of the Type A mode of communication and a sound holding approach, and the patient's need for Type B-C expression and parasitism or autism. They attempt to effect a virtual destruction of meaning and of nonpathological relatedness. Because of this, the patient fails (dares not) to understand and integrate the therapist's efforts at interpretation and framework management. The patient is in a near-hopeless dilemma. In addition, based on unconscious transference constellations—highly traumatic and disturbing actual experiences with early parental figures and consequent introjects and fantasies—and on highly primitive persecutory fantasies and expectations, these patients experience interpretive-framework-management efforts by the therapist as a form of entrapment and as dangerous. It appears they lack almost entirely any capacity for basic trust, and any significant inner representations of positive introjects on whom hopeful expectations can be founded. Their inner persecutory mental world leads to difficulty in modifying persecutory images of others.

The therapist is faced with the difficult paradox of dealing with a patient who experiences most sound therapeutic efforts as a persecution and who will somehow experience unsound therapeutic endeavors as familiar and less threatening. When the therapist functions in a destructive manner, the patient's sense of envy is lessened, he or she is reassured that the therapist is now in important and pathological ways similar to him or her—and to his or her introjects and past relationship figures—and the patient is afforded an experience of an object relationship with both pathological symbiotic and parasitic (often masochistic) gratifications. Furthermore, the patient has the satisfaction of destroying the therapist's integrity, of parasitizing him or her, and of being in control of the therapeutic situation (whereby the patient feels less endangered). These pathological gains enable the patient to continue to see the therapist, secure in the knowledge that there is little likelihood for a constructive therapeutic experience.

In principle, the therapist should attempt to secure a sound mode of relatedness and an ideal therapeutic environment with patients who appear to fall into this category. Only when these efforts are met with attack and destruction by this type of patient and there is clear evidence that the patient will not tolerate a healthy form of symbiosis should compromise be considered. This should be kept to a minimum, proposed in terms of the patient's conscious insistence, and interpreted to the patient in light of activated intervention contexts and derivative material that reveals the destructive qualities of the compromise. Such efforts should be supplemented by similar interpretive work through which the negative introjects and the destruction of understanding that emerges are defined. Then, as the patient's derivative material permits, it may prove feasible eventually to introduce rectifications of these deviations and to establish a basically holding-interpretive, healthy mode of relatedness and treatment experience.

In this approach, the therapist makes clear the patient's unconscious preferences and his or her own conscious preferences—based on the patient's derivative material. The patient is allowed to realize that the therapist is compromising himself or herself at the behest of the patient's manifest insistence, even in the face of latent derivative contradictory messages. This affords the patient a sense of the struggle within the therapist, who must convey, through interpreting the patient's material, his or her own sense that the proposed deviations have destructive implications. This is essential in order for the patient to maintain a minimal degree of unconscious alliance and a sense of safety in his or her relationship with the therapist. If the therapist simply capitulated to the patient's recommendations without efforts at interpretation to identify the negative consequences, the therapist would then be perceived as highly destructive, and intensely negative introjects would be effected within the patient. Therapy can sometimes proceed on this basis, although what unfolds is the patient's unconscious therapeutic endeavors toward the countertransference-dominated therapist and the search for misalliance and framework-deviation cures.

The Therapist's Dilemmas

The therapist is faced with many dilemmas in regard to the question of compromised techniques. Knowledge that these efforts will produce negative introjects and restrict the possibility of cure to those based on misalliance and framework deviation will tend to lead the therapist to attempt to offer the patient something far more substantial, sound, and lasting in a constructive manner. The therapist will inevitably be uncomfortable with the negative introjects generated by compromises and reflected in the patient's subsequent associations and behaviors. The therapist will be distressed too when the patient acts out seductively and destructively based on such introjects and, when because of the therapist's own contributions, he or she finds himself or herself unable to offer sound interpretive responses or to rectify the necessary breaks in the framework that have contributed to the patient's active psychopathology. Thus the therapist will be all too intensely aware of the negative consequences of his or her deviations and their influence upon the patient, but mindful that in this small group of cases— and clearly, they must be carefully identified so that compromises are not utilized unnecessarily—there would be no other basis for the continuation of sessions. And yet, the therapist will also be haunted by the question of whether a more interpretive-securing approach might not afford the patient a few constructive introjects and insights, which would either prove quite helpful for the moment or provide a basis for therapeutic work in the future if the patient were to terminate.

The many difficult issues here cannot be explored fully in this volume. Part of the problem lies in the availability of therapists who are prepared to compromise with these patients at every turn, to gratify them pathologically, and to unknowingly risk the uncertain costs of the lie-barrier therapy upon which the patient insists. The direct and immediate gratifications, and the way in which regressions and other disturbances are written off to causes other than the therapist's erroneous interventions and failings in the therapeutic interaction, tend to place these patients in a position where they fail to realize consciously the destructive implications of the therapeutic modality they have chosen for themselves. It may well take the firm entrenchment of truth therapy and a sound interpretive-holding approach by a vast majority of psychotherapists before these patients will begin in large numbers to modify their destructive demands and become prepared for a modicum of insight and structural change.

The best technical precept is adherence to basic techniques to the greatest extent feasible. They should be modified only after they have been offered to the patient and a response has been obtained that indicates unmistakably that such efforts will lead to immediate flight. There should be a sense of struggle within the therapist as he or she succumbs reluctantly to the patient's demands for deviations. There should also be a consistent sense of vigilance in attending to the patient's subsequent material so that negative introjects and destructive consequences are identified in the direct and especially derivative material. These should then be interpreted to the patient, and models of rectification utilized as a way of proposing the gradual securement of the therapeutic relationship and environment.

With most severely disturbed patients, there is no reason to modify basic technical precepts and techniques. Instead, the specific nature, timing, content, and frequency of the therapist's interventions will be different from work with the more neurotic patient. A keen sensitivity to the basis for the patient's dread of a secure holding environment, and to the detrimental consequences of even necessary compromises, will help to guide the therapist through these difficult and treacherous treatment experiences.

Chapter 38

Truth Therapy, Lie Therapy

In one sense, all efforts at psychotherapy are on a continuum that can be established through the identification and correlation of the more critical elements of technique. *Truth therapy* is at one end, and *lie* or *lie-barrier therapy* is at the other. A characterization of these two treatment modalities serves as a way of integrating the various dimensions of psychotherapeutic technique developed in this book and provides a final synthesis.

It must be stressed that there are no moral implications involved in the terms *truth* and *lie,* and that the terms are being used entirely in their descriptive sense and as meaningful selected facts. Lie therapy is often carried out quite unconsciously by a well-meaning therapist who fails to realize the absence of Type Two derivative validation of his or her interventions and fails to understand the unconscious functions of his or her efforts as they are geared to avoid or falsify the true state of the most critical Neurosis-related factors within the patient, the therapist, and the therapeutic interaction.

Truth Therapy

The most critical truths in psychotherapy may be defined in terms of the activated elements of the patient's Neurosis as they are aroused by the therapeutic interaction. Thus truth in this sense alludes to those aspects of the patient's inner mental life that have been stirred up by adaptive contexts within the therapeutic interaction, and only secondarily through interchanges in the patient's outside life. This definition of truth centers on the unconscious communicative interaction between the patient and therapist. While it pertains primarily to the patient's maladaptive Neurotic responses, it refers secondarily both to the patient's adaptive, nonneurotic functioning and to the actual nature of the inputs—manifest and latent—from the therapist—nonpathological and pathological. A statement of the core truths in psychotherapy therefore encompasses the actualities, conscious and unconscious, within both patient and therapist and within their interaction. As a consequence, truth therapy is designed to approach, define, and interpret those truths that are pertinent and active as they pertain to the patient's Neurosis, consciously and unconsciously. Any effort to avoid these truths, or to falsify them, would be seen as a form of lie or lie-barrier therapy.

Truth therapy is based on the establishment of a healthy symbiotic therapeutic relationship, with clear and secure boundaries and ground rules, and the use of an essentially interpretive approach by the therapist. Alterations in the ground rules unconsciously express the therapist's wish to avoid the truth and to seek out cure for the patient on some other basis (i.e., through some form of lie-barrier, defense, and pathological mode of relatedness and gratification). Deviations also interfere with truth therapy, in that they lead the patient to be mistrustful of the therapist, unconsciously perceptive of his or her lie propensities, cognizant of his or her fear of the truth, and unworthy of the trust that is necessary for truthful derivative communication. In response to deviations, the only sector of truth in the bipersonal field (i.e., in the patient's derivative expressions) pertains to the implications of the deviation itself, consciously and unconsciously, within both therapist and patient. Thus extended truth therapy requires a secure therapeutic hold and a sound capacity within the therapist for the containment of the patient's pathological projective identifications, and a commitment by the therapist to respond interpretively (when indicated) to the patient's associations and behaviors.

As noted, truth therapy is founded upon the establishment of a healthy symbiotic therapeutic relationship. It requires reasonable interpersonal boundaries, an appropriate measure of both separation and intimacy, an overriding determination in the therapist to respond to the therapeutic needs of the patient, and a renunciation of pathological needs and relatedness on the part of the therapist. Austistic, pathological symbiotic, and parasitic interactions provide the patient with inappropriate satisfactions and *relief* that turn the patient away from the search for interactional, interpersonal, and intrapsychic truths. In one sense, these types of relatedness are false in and of themselves. Truth therapy requires a capacity for separateness and a sufficient renunciation of wishes for fusion and merger to permit the derivative expression of the truth, conveyed to a therapist who is reasonably separate, relatively autonomous, and individual enough to interpret their implications.

There is a correlation between truth therapy, a healthy symbiotic mode of relatedness, secure boundaries and ground rules to treatment, the expression (when activated) of Type Two derivative material from the patient, and the holding, containing, and interpretive capacities of the therapist. Under these conditions, the truth of the patient's inner mental world is revealed in terms of activated unconscious fantasy and perception constellations, and with interpretation, the patient develops conscious insight and adaptive structural change. There is a simultaneous experience of separateness, of sound relatedness, and of positive introjects that are supplementary avenues for the positive therapeutic effects of this treatment modality.

Truth is the sole condition under which sound growth and maturation, and relative autonomy and individuation, can develop. The truth is also the basis upon which the patient can derive the most flexible adaptive resources possible and the most lasting resolution of his or her Neurosis.

Nonetheless, one must be mindful of the extent to which the truths of the patient's unconscious fantasies, perceptions, and introjects can be intensely anxiety-provoking and even terrifying, and the great pain involved in the pursuit of these realizations. In addition, relative separateness and individuation is often experienced as persecutory, another stressful aspect of truth therapy. In all, then, while the analysis and conscious recognition of the truth within psychotherapy is an optimal means of cure, this work is carried through with considerable stress and distress for both participants.

Lie Therapy

Empirically, the hallmark of truth therapy is an interpretation or framework-management response that is developed around an activated adaptive context and the patient's derivative reactions. Lie therapy, then, departs from this fundamental approach, and is based on manifest content or Type One derivative listening, or on a failure to reasonably attend and respond to the material from the patient. While there is but one form of truth therapy, there are, of course, many lie therapy modalities.

Lie therapy is designed either to seal off the activated truths of the patient's Neurosis behind derivative or nonderivative defenses and barriers or to falsify the actualities involved. Lie therapy may involve the use of derivative defenses, such as those seen with an erroneous intervention that contains representations of the actual underlying truths in some disguised form. This type of therapy may also rely upon nonderivative defenses or Type C barriers, as illustrated by interventions that depart entirely from the truth of the moment and suggest instead some other purported truth that is in fact unrelated to the activated, usually chaotic and highly threatening truths that are being set to the side or obliterated through the intervention.

Among the common forms of lie therapies and lie therapists, first is the *use of psychoanalytic clichés*. In this type of intervention, the therapist makes use of aspects of psychoanalytic theory that he or she believes to be pertinent to the patient's material, doing so without attention to an activated intervention context. In this way the therapist introduces theoretical truths that serve *functionally* and *dynamically* within the therapeutic interaction as a means of departing from, substituting for, and creating barriers against the pertinent and activated meanings and truths contained within the derivative communications from the patient. There is also the *framework changer,* the therapist who promotes derivative and nonderivative defensiveness and pathological autistic, symbiotic, or parasitic modes of relatedness with the patient by modifying the ground rules of treatment in an effort to avoid the truths within the patient's associations and behaviors as they pertain to both the therapist and the patient. Then too, there is the *noninterpretive therapist,* who makes use of a variety of interventions unrelated to efforts at understanding and either ignores or falsifies the truth of the therapeutic interaction, while manipulating the patient and affording both participants pathological autistic, symbiotic, or parasitic satisfactions.

As it is presently constituted, most efforts at psychoanalytic psychotherapy (and psychoanalysis) are forms of lie therapy, in that the therapeutic work is *not* organized around activated intervention contexts and the patient's derivative reactions. Much of this work is founded upon psychoanalytic cliches and other forms of Type One derivative inference, and on manifest content statements that depart significantly from the active issues within the ongoing spiraling interaction. It is evident, then, that lie-barrier therapy can produce some measure of symptom alleviation, much of it through sealing off chaotic truths and by providing one or both participants with pathological gratifications. The relief gained, however, is essentially maladaptive and requires the repeated reinforcement of lie-barrier and derivative defenses and a maintenance of pathological modes of relatedness. All too often, both patients and therapists are accepting of such interludes of relief, and fail to examine their underlying basis. Nonetheless, it seems likely that there are powerful needs in both patients and therapists alike for this type of symptom relief.

Conclusion

Effective, truthful psychoanalytic psychotherapy is a remarkably arduous task, requiring of the therapist enormous degrees of renunciation, self-understanding, tolerance and patience, and particular empathic, intuitive, and cognitive skills. Nonetheless, the mastery of the art and science of psychotherapy and its unique techniques offers the patient and therapist alike a distinctive gratifying experience filled with constructive personality growth. It affords the patient—and secondarily the therapist—the kind of adaptive resources that are fundamental to the soundest form of symptom relief available, and provides both with coping capacities that enable them to steer the best possible course available to them through the arduous treatment experience and life itself.

Glossary

Abstracting-Particularizing Process. That aspect of the listening process in which first-order, manifest themes are used to derive more general or abstract themes, from which second-order specific themes are generated. The latter are often monitored in terms of the therapeutic relationship and the me/not-me interface.

Adaptional-Interactional Viewpoint. A clinical-metapsychological approach to the patient and therapeutic interaction that takes into account both intrapsychic and interactional processes, conscious and unconscious in both spheres.

Adaptation-Evoking Context. See *Adaptive Context*, a term with which it is synonymous.

Adaptive Context. The specific reality that evokes an intrapsychic response. *Direct* or *nonneurotic* adaptive contexts are those stimuli that evoke linear intrapsychic reactions and nonneurotic communicative responses; in essence, they are

720

unrelated to psychopathological reactions and mechanisms. *Indirect* or *neurotic* adaptive contexts are those precipitants that evoke convoluted, derivative intrapsychic responses that contain pathological unconscious fantasies, memories, and introjects; they are related to psychopathology and to Neurosis. Often an adaptive context ouside of the therapeutic relationship will have a direct context within its manifest content, and an indirect context in its latent content. The latter is, as a rule, a derivative of a significant adaptive context within the therapeutic situation itself, communicated in disguised form. On the whole, the major indirect and neurotic adaptive contexts derive from the therapeutic interaction. The term *primary adaptive task* is a synonym for adaptive context.

Adaptive Context, Form of Representation. The manner in which the patient portrays the manifest and latent contents of the adaptive context, and its links to the therapist, in the course of his or her behaviors and associations. A key factor in determining the possibility of interpretive and reconstructive interventions by the therapist, it is best conveyed via a passing manifest allusion to an intervention by the therapist.

Alliance Sector. Virtually synonymous with *therapeutic alliance*, it is intended to emphasize the alliance as an aspect of the total relationship between patient and therapist, rather than as an entity in itself. The attributes of this sector are identical to those of the therapeutic alliance and are defined under the latter term. See also *Therapeutic Alliance, Working Alliance.*

Associational Matrix. See *Communicative Network.*

Autism, Healthy. See *Mode of Relatedness, Healthy Autism.*

Autism, Pathological. See *Mode of Relatedness, Pathological Autism.*

Bastion. A split-off part of the bipersonal field which is under interactional repression and denial, so that the contents involved are avoided by both patient and therapist or analyst.

Bipersonal Field, the. A metaphor for the therapeutic situation that stresses the interactional qualities of the field and postulates that every experience and communication within the field receives vectors from both patient and therapist or analyst. The metaphor requires the concept of an *interface* along which communication occurs between the two members of the therapeutic dyad and points to the need to conceptualize the presence, role, and function of a framework for the field.

Bridge to the Therapist. A nonspecific manifest allusion to the therapist or therapy occurring in the patient's associations toward the latter part of a session. Its importance lies in facilitating both interpretive interventions and the playing back of selected derivatives that pertain to an unmentioned adaptive context related to the treatment situation.

Commensal Mode of Relatedness. See *Mode of Relatedness, Commensal.*

Commentary. An aspect of the patient's responses to interventions from the therapist (including managements of the framework). These associations and behaviors contain validating and nonvalidating communications, and they are to be viewed as a mixture of fantasy and reality, accurate perceptiveness and distortion. Commentaries often take the form of *transversal communications;* unconsciously, they convey the patient's evaluation of the intervention.

Communication, Convoluted. The presence of derivatives and the indirect expression of pathological unconscious fantasies, memories, introjects, and interactional contents and mechanisms. It is one of the hallmarks of Neurotic communication. See also *Neurotic Communication.*

Communication, Linear. A sequence evoked by an adaptive context in which the intrapsychic response is relatively logical, readily apparent or easily inferred, directly responsive, and relatively undisguised. It is a form of reaction that characterizes the direct adaptive context and non-Neurotic communication. See also *Nonneurotic Communication.*

Communicative Field. The amalgam from patient and therapist that characterizes the dominant mode of communicative interaction in a given bipersonal field. See also *Bipersonal Field, Type A Field, Type B Field, Type C Field.*

Communicative Interaction, Unconscious and Conscious, Spiraling. See *Spiraling Interaction, Unconscious and Conscious.*

Communicative Network. That aspect of the material from the patient that contains conscious and especially unconscious meaning. It comprises the adaptive context, the derivative complex, and the bridge back to the therapist or analyst. As a rule, analysis of the unconscious implications of the communicative network will reveal the implications of the therapeutic context or indicator. The term is synonymous with *associational matrix* and *network of communications.*

Communicative Space. A metaphor for the interior of the bipersonal field and for the realm in which communication occurs between patient and therapist or analyst. The image suggests that there are a number of possible communicative spaces, each with a set of defining attributes. It allows, too, for the recognition that patient and therapist may be in separate communicative spaces, rather than sharing the same mode.

Communicative Style or Mode. The form of expression that characterizes the interactional thrusts and form of relatedness of the patient and therapist or analyst. See also *Type A Field and Mode, Type B Field and Mode, Type C Field and Mode.*

Communicative Therapeutic Alliance. See *Therapeutic Alliance, Communicative.*

Confirmation, Secondary or Indirect. See *Validation via Type Two Derivatives.*

Contained. A metaphor first used by Bion (1962) to allude to the contents and psychic mechanisms that are projectively identified by an infant into his mother and by a patient into his analyst. More broadly, it alludes to the contents and functions of a projective identification emanating from a subject toward an object.

Container. A metaphor first used by Bion (1962) for the recipient of a projective identification. The container may be open to containing such projective identifications or may be refractory. The metaphor also implies the processing or metabolizing of the introjected contents and functions. An adequate container is seen as being in a state of *reverie.*

Containing and Containing Function. A metaphor used to describe the taking in and processing of projective identifications. An adequate containing function has been described by

Bion (1962) as a state of *reverie* in the mother or analyst, and may also apply to the therapist or patient. *Containing function* alludes to the receptiveness to projective identifications and to an ability to metabolize and detoxify pathological *interactional projections*, returning them to the subject in appropriately modified form. For the therapist or analyst, this process implies the metabolizing of a projective identification to conscious insight, imparted to the patient through a valid interpretation and the maintenance of a secure framework and hold.

Counterresistances. Applied to that aspect of the therapist's *countertransference* that creates obstacles to the progress of therapeutic work, counterresistances may appear in the therapist's gross behaviors—e.g., forgetting a session, lateness, touching the patient—or as part of his or her efforts to manage the framework and intervene verbally. Verbal interventions constitute communicative counterresistances and include interpretive errors, self-revelations, and mismangements of the framework, which reveal unconscious countertransference fantasies and pathological autistic, symbiotic, and parasitic needs. In principle, all countertransference expressions will contribute to disturbances in treatment and function as counterresistances. The term is best reserved for inappropriate silences and interventions that are most disruptive to the therapeutic process and significantly intensify the resistances within the patient.

Countertransference. All inappropriate and pathological responses of the therapist to his or her patient. These reactions are founded on pathological *unconscious* fantasies, memories, introjects, and interactional mechanisms.

Countertransference, Inevitable. Implies not only the inescapability of countertransference expressions in the therapist's work, but also its existence as some small element of every attitude, silence, and intervention. This minimal quota of countertransference is a reflection of the ever-present unresolved, though relatively controlled, psychopathology of the therapist.

Countertransference, Preponderant. Inappropriate silences, interventions, and mismanagements of the framework that constitute major errors and reflect significant and relatively uncontrolled psychopathology within the therapist. While these may sometimes be reflected in the therapist's personality and basic attitudes, they more often take the form of acute errors, which may be detected in the subsequent subjective reactions of the therapist, the absence of validation from the patient, and the patient's unconscious recognition and therapeutic work with the introjected conscious and unconscious qualities of the therapist's error.

Day Residue. A term first used by Freud (1900) to allude to the reality stimulus for the dream. More broadly, it may be seen as the external stimulus, filled with latent and unconscious meaning, that evokes any intrapsychic response. In that sense, it is virtually synonymous with the *adaptive context.*

Defense. All psychological efforts, conscious and unconscious, by an individual that are designed to protect him or her from danger situations, anxiety and other unpleasant affects, unbearable conflict, disruptive introjects, and disturbing conscious realizations. Defenses therefore constitute intrapsychically founded, protective, psychological mechanisms utilized by the ego in an effort to cope with disturbing external and internal realities, and conscious and unconscious fantasy and perception constellations that pose any degree of threat. Defenses may be pathological or nonpathological depending on their adaptive aspects and the extent to which they disturb the functioning of the user.

Delusion, Neurotic. A false belief, usually held unconsciously and expressed largely through derivative communication, which would be readily modified and corrected if called to the attention of the patient or therapist who has conveyed it. See also *Hallucination, Neurotic.*

Derivative Complex. The material from the patient as it is organized around a specific adaptive context in order to reveal unconscious implications, Type Two derivative meaning. This is one of the three elements involved in the basic formulations of each session.

Derivative Complex, Convoluted. See *Derivatives, Coalescing.*

Derivative Complex, Linear. A simplistic group of derivatives related to a particular adaptive context that tends to flatly repeat a single theme or function, without complexity or depth. See also *Communication, Linear.*

Derivative, Indirect Interactional. A manifest association that yields hidden and disguised meaning in light of an activated intervention context. The term is synonymous with *Type Two Derivative.*

Derivative, Inference. A manifest content element that is decoded for hidden meaning based on isolated implications derived from psychoanalytic theory or a general knowledge of the patient. These inferences tend to be highly intellectualized and general. Implications for the therapeutic interaction, and meanings organized by a particular adaptive context, are not included. The term is synonymous with *Translation Derivative.* Involved is a form of *Type One Derivative* formulation. It is to be contrasted with *Image Derivatives.*

Derivative, Translation. See *Derivative, Inference.*

Derivatives. Manifest communications, verbal and nonverbal, that contain expressions of unconscious fantasies, memories, introjects, and perceptions in some disguised form. These are, then, the communicative expressions of Neuroses and the basis on which they are maintained.

Derivatives, Close. Associations from the patient that contain disguised representations of unconscious processes and contents in a form that is readily detectable, minimally defensive, and easily understood as a manifestation of the underlying qualities.

Derivatives, Coalescing. A derivative complex that, when organized around a specific adaptive context, indirectly and quite unconsciously reveals a wide range of divergent, underlying meanings and functions in relationship to that context. Such a group of derivatives may include unconscious fantasies and unconscious perceptions, and reflect as well a variety of unconscious dynamics and genetics. They may also include the patient's unconscious interpretations and other speculations pertaining to both the therapist and himself or herself. Together, they form a divergent but organizable entity that reveals a multiplicity of meanings pertaining to the relevant adaptive context. See also *Communication, Convoluted.*

Derivatives, Distant. Those aspects of the patient's associations that represent unconscious processes and contents with considerable disguise, barely detectable meaning, and great defensiveness and resistance.

Derivatives, Embedded. A representation of an unconscious fantasy, memory, introject, or perception that is communicated as a seemingly irrelevant component of a sequence of manifest contents, in a form that seems peripheral to the main conscious intention and to the major first-order and general themes.

Derivatives, Image. A form of manifest expression that contains encoded fantasies and other contents and themes generated by the patient's imagination or perceptions. These formulations may be couched in Type One derivative terms without regard to the therapeutic interaction or may be formulated as Type Two derivatives in light of specific adaptation-evoking contexts. Image derivatives are rich in content and theme, affect-laden, and often developed through a composite made from a number of separate encoded elements. Image derivatives appear to be the unconscious basis for the patient's Neurosis and the means by which he or she communicates the unconscious perceptions and fantasies that pertain to this Neurosis. Their determination is the most meaningful form of decoding available to the psychotherapist.

Derivatives, Playing Back. An intervention offered in the presence of a strong indicator and a meaningful derivative complex, but in the absence of any clear representation of the adaptive context with an evident link to the therapist. It is designed to create a state of tension and need—a preconception—which can be transformed into a condition of fulfillment—a conception—only through the direct recall and clear representation of the adaptive context—a step that is essential to further interpretive work.

Designated Patient. The party to the therapeutic situation who is seeking help and likely to be paying the fee and free associating. He or she is usually symptomatic and the recipient of the manifest interventions of the designated therapist. See also *Functional Patient*.

Designated Therapist. The party to the therapeutic situation who represents himself or herself as capable of alleviating the emotional difficulties of those who seek his or her help— designated patients. He or she is likely to be the prerson who makes use of free-floating attention, shapes the conditions of treatment, receives the fee, and intervenes intermittently to the designated patient. See also *Functional Therapist*.

Detoxification. The metabolism of a projective identification so that its relatively primitive and destructive qualities are altered through some appropriate means, usually through cognitive understanding directed toward insight. This process is an essential quality of *reverie*.

Deviation Termination Therapy. See *Unrectifiable Framework Deviation Termination Therapy*, with which this term is synonymous.

Emotional Disturbance. Synonymous with *Neurosis* when it is used in its broadest sense to include all forms of psychologically and emotionally founded disorders. Emotional disturbances range from characterological pathology to psychoses and neuroses. They also include psychosomatic and other psychologically founded physical disorders.

Empathy. A form of emotional knowing and noncognitive sharing in, and comprehending, the psychological and affective state of another person. Empathy involves both affect and cognition, and is based on a relatively nonconflicted interplay of introjective and projective mechanisms, and a variety of forms of unconscious sharing. It is a temporary form of immediate engagement and understanding, which must then be processed and validated. It must include a sensing of the patient's derivative as well as manifest communications.

Faith. Used by Bion (1962) to describe a form of passive listening or intuiting by the therapist or analyst that is founded upon entering each session without desire, memory, or understanding. It implies a fundamental belief that the patient will put into the therapist or analyst in derivative form all that he or she needs for cure, and all that the latter requires for interventions. It also implies an appreciation of the principle that each session should be its own creation, and that, unconsciously, the patient will provide the therapeutic situation with all that is necessary for his or her cure, except for the therapist's or analyst's interpretive interventions and managements of the framework, which are themselves based on the ingredients provided by the patient.

First-Order Themes. See *Themes, First-Order*.

Frame. A metaphor for the implicit and explicit ground rules of psychotherapy or psychoanalysis. The image implies that the ground rules create a basic hold for the therapeutic interaction, and for both patient and therapist, and that they create a distinctive set of conditions within the frame that differentiate it in actuality and functionally from the conditions outside the frame. The metaphor requires, however, an appreciation of the human qualities of the frame and the therapist's role in its creation and management; it should not be used to develop an inanimate or overly rigid conception.

Frame, Fixed, Stable, or Steady. The relatively unchangeable or easily set ground rules such as the fee, time and length of sessions, the pshysical setting, and total confidentiality and privacy.

Frame, Variable or Fluid. Those aspects of the ground rules that will inevitably vary based on the presence of some degree of humanness and residual countertransference reflected in the ongoing work of the therapist. While the therapist strives to maintain these aspects of the framework at an optimal level, variations are bound to occur. Included here are the ground rules related to the therapist's relative anonymity and neutrality, the rule of abstinence, and for the patient, the fundamental rule of free association and the need to analyze all major decisions.

Framework. A term used synonymously with *frame*, usually as a means of referring to the ground rules of the bipersonal field.

Framework Cure. The maladaptive alleviation of symptoms through an inappropriate modification in the frame.

Framework-Deviation Cure. Previously termed *framework cure*, this concept covers the maladaptive alleviation of symptoms through inappropriate modification of the framework by either patient or therapist.

Framework-Rectification Cure. The adaptive symptom alleviation that occurs through the establishment, securing, and maintenance of the ground rules of psychotherapy or psychoanalysis. Although unaccompanied by immediate cognitive insight (supplementary interpretations are essential in that regard), such relief derives from unconscious positive introjects of the therapist in terms of his or her constructive management of the framework, and from the inherently supportive holding and containing functions that are expressed when the framework is rectified and then maintained in a stable manner.

Functional Capacity or Meaning. Indicates that associations never exist as isolated mental products, and that among their most essential dynamic implications are the unconscious communications contained within the patient's material as they pertain to the therapeutic relationship and interaction. In essence, it is a concept that stresses that all associations have some dynamic relevance to the prevailing primary adaptive context.

Functional Patient. The member of the therapeutic dyad who, in light of the prevailing adaptive contexts from either the designated patient or the designated therapist, is expressing himself or herself consciously or unconsciously as in need of help with emotional symptoms and conflicts.

This individual expresses himself or herself to the other member of the communicative dyad in a manner that reflects underlying psychopathology, doing so either through representations that state directly or imply in some relatively disguised manner a need for therapeutic help. Thus the *functional capacity* of such communications is to express illness. Within the treatment situation, the designated patient and/or the designated therapist may express himself or herself simultaneously or alternately as the functional patient. See also *Designated Patient.*

Functional Therapist. The member of the therapeutic dyad who expresses himself or herself directly and consciously, or indirectly and through derivatives, in a manner designed to cure the other participant and, at times, himself or herself. This individual, in light of the prevailing adaptive contexts contained in the patient's material and the therapist's interventions, responds with communications designed to be insightful and curative. It is crucial that when the designated therapist wishes to serve as the functional therapist he or she must do so on a conscious level, through direct valid interpretations and managements of the framework. On the other hand, it has frequently been observed that designated patients who shift to the role of functional therapist do so on an unconscious level, basing their therapeutic efforts largely upon valid unconscious perceptions of the therapist (and sometimes of themselves), as well as the consequent pathological

introjects. Such work therefore is expressed primarily through derivatives and entails unconscious interpretive, confronting, and framework-management types of interventions. See also *Designated Therapist.*

Ground Rules. The implicit and explicit components of the analytic or therapeutic situation that establish the conditions for treatment and the means through which it shall be undertaken.

Hallucination, Neurotic. A false image or perception, usually experienced in some unconscious and derivative way that would be readily modified and corrected if brought to the attention of the patient or therapist who has experienced it. See also *Delusion, Neurotic.*

Holding. Describes the therapist's or analyst's establishment and maintenance of a secure and safe therapeutic situation. The result is a holding environment that is created through the implicit and explicit delineation of the ground rules, explicated through their maintenance, and significantly elaborated through valid interpretive efforts. The holding capacity of the therapist or analyst may be likened to his or her containing capacity, although the former is a more general concept, while the latter specifically refers to the taking in of interactional projections.

Identification. An intrapsychic process through which the self-representations and other aspects of the subject's internal mental world and defenses are unconsciously modified in keeping with a model derived from an external object.

Image Derivative. See *Derivatives, Image.*

Indicators. Refers to all communications from the patient that point toward a need for an intervention from the therapist. See *Therapeutic Context.*

Informational Schema, Six-Part. See *Schema, Observational.*

Interactional Defenses. Intrapsychic protective mechanisms that are formed through vectors from both patient and therapist. This type of defense may exist in either participant to the therapeutic dyad, and has both intrapsychic and interpersonal (external) sources.

Interactional Projection. A synonym for projective identification.

Interactional Resistance. Any impediment to the progress of therapy that receives vectors, usually on an unconscious level, from both patient and therapist.

Interactional Symptom. An emotional disturbance in either participant to the therapeutic dyad with significant sources from both participants.

Interactional Syndrome. Clusters of interactional symptoms.

Interface, Me/Not-Me. See *Me/Not-Me Interface.*

Interpretation. An attempt through verbal communication by the therapist to render unconscious meanings

and functions conscious for the patient. Properly executed, this intervention alludes to an adaptive context and to the relevant derivative complex in terms of unconscious perceptions and fantasies to which genetic implications are appended. Proper execution requires also that the intervention be stated in terms of the prevailing unconscious communicative interaction between the patient and the therapist, and its extension into the present and past from that nodal point, and that it illuminate the prevailing therapeutic contexts.

Interpretation, Definitive. An intervention that identifies an activated adaptive context and a reactive derivative complex as a way of understanding the unconscious basis for an indicator or therapeutic context almost entirely in terms of a single dimension of the therapeutic relationship—transference or non-transference, reality or fantasy, patient or therapist. This type of intervention is to be contrasted with *transversal interpretations,* which tend to incorporate significant aspects of both extremes of these dualities. While all interpretations have minor transversal qualities, those that emphasize one dimension far more than its opposite are to be termed definitive interpretations. See also *Transversal Intervention.*

Intervention Context. See *Adaptive Context,* with which this term is synonymous.

Intervention, Manifest. An intervention, usually verbal, offered by the therapist to the patient, designed to meet the therapeutic needs of the latter. The major interventions include silence, establishment and management of the framework, and comments designed to impart cognitive understanding, either through interpretation or reconstruction, or through the playing back of selected derivatives around an unmentioned adaptive context.

Intervention, Silent. A tentatively formulated intervention constructed as the therapist listens to the patient, subjected to silent validation before being presented.

Introject. An intrapsychic precipitate that stems from the process of introjective identification. Its specific qualities are determined by the extent to which it is transient or becomes structuralized, the degree to which it is incorporated into the self-image and self-representations or maintained as separate from them, the extent to which it is pathological or nonpathological, and the degree to which it is constructive or benign rather than destructive or malignant. In addition, these internal representations of conscious and unconscious traits and interactions have a variety of specific qualities in keeping with the nature of the object, the subject, their relationship, and the qualities of their separate and shared experiences. See also *Unconscious Introject.*

Introjective Identification. The interactional process through which introjects are formed. As a rule, it is evoked by a projective identification from the object, although it may also entail active incorporative efforts by the subject. The process is influenced both by the nature of the object, the contents and processes that are being taken in, and the inner state of the subject.

Intuition. An immediate form of knowing, understanding, or learning developed without the conscious use of reasoning and knowledge.

Latent Content. The hidden dimension of the patient's associations contained in disguised form within the surface of that material. The term is usually used to refer to readily available inferences from the manifest content—disguised specific unconscious fantasies, memories, introjects, and perceptions.

Lie. Used nonmorally to refer to manifest, but more commonly latent and unconscious, falsifications as these arise in the free associations of the patient and the interventions of the therapist. By and large, such misrepresentations are designed to falsify the truth as it pertains to the patient's Neurosis, the therapist, and the therapeutic interaction. The effort here, which is largely unconscious, is to offer some substitute for the truth, to deny its presence, and to erect either derivative defenses or impervious barriers against its realization. Empirically, a therapist's unconscious lie is constituted by any intervention in which the framework is mismanaged or the therapist intervenes without organizing his or her response interpretively around the prevailing adaptive context and derivative complex. A patient's unconscious lie is expressed either by a failure to meaningfully represent the activated adaptive context or to generate a meaningful, coalescing derivative complex. See also *Truth*.

Lie, Derivative. A falsification or misrepresentation, conscious or unconscious, that contains expressions of the underlying and chaotic truths it is designed to cover in some disguised form.

Lie, Nonderivative. A falsification or misrepresentation that in no way reflects, and is therefore impervious to, the underlying chaotic truths it is designed to seal off.

Lie-Barrier, Derivative and Nonderivative. The type of defensive system seen in lie therapy, and in lie patients and lie therapists. Derivative lie barriers are seen in the Type A communicative field in which the patient's efforts at falsification reveal the underlying truths in disguised form. On the part of the therapist, derivative lie interventions, while erroneous, contain expressions of the truth of the therapeutic situation and of the patient's material in some disguised form. However, interventions of this kind are insufficient to generate conscious insight within the patient, although they may be part of an interchange in which such realizations are ultimately fulfilled. On the other hand, nonderivative lie-systems are relatively impervious barriers designed to seal off underlying chaotic truths without expressing the nature of the underlying disturbance in any disguised form. Lie patients and lie therapists tend to communicate in the Type C mode. The latter intervene erroneously in a manner unrelated to the true nature of the disturbance within the bipersonal field.

Lie Systems or Lie-Barrier Systems. Complex defensive formations generated by either patient or therapist that are designed to seal off underlying chaotic truths as they pertain to the activated pathology of the patient, and secondarily to that of the therapist and within the therapeutic interaction. There are many types of lie-barrier systems, and these include false genetic reconstructions, false statements of dynamics, and blatant misrepresentations. The patient and therapist may share and reinforce each other's lie-barrier systems, may make use of different lie-barrier systems, or may find themselves within an interaction in which one of the two participants utilizes a lie-barrier system while the other uses the single available truth system applicable to a particular segment of the therapeutic interaction. Lie systems may be derivative and reveal the nature of the underlying and chaotic truth, or nonderivative in disguised form, serving as impenetrable barriers against such truth.

Lie Therapy. Any form of therapy designed to bypass or falsify the true basis, conscious and unconscious, of the patient's Neurosis. In this type of therapy, even evident statements of fact are used *functionally* to deny and falsify the most active expressions of the patient's Neurosis within the ongoing communicative interaction. See also *Truth Therapy*.

Listening-Intervening Schema. See *Schema, Listening-Intervening.*

Listening Process. All conscious and unconscious intaking and organizing processes within both patient and therapist. For the therapist, the term includes all available cognitive and interactional sources of information about the patient, verbal and nonverbal, and his or her own use of sensory and nonsensory, conscious and unconscious, sensitivities. Included too are efforts at synthesizing and formulating cognitive material, the experience of role pressures and image evocations, and the metabolism of projective identifications. The process culminates in conscious understanding or insight, in proper holding and containing, and in the formulation of a valid intervention. Similar processes take place within the patient; although, as a rule, much of it is on an unconscious level.

Lying-Fallow Phase of Psychotherapy. The middle phase of many psychotherapies. During this period the patient is not faced with an acute intervention context arising either through his or her own provocation of the therapist or from some pathological need within the therapist himself or herself. In the absence of an activated intervention context issue, the patient tends to express himself or herself with a relative lack of derivative meaning. Manifestly, the patient often engages in manifest content and Type One derivative self-interpretations, thereby softening and rendering less pathological his or her derivative and nonderivative defenses. Eventually, this phase must yield to active therapeutic work which occurs in the termination phase. Failure to make this shift suggests the presence of pathological rather than healthy autism and major defenses against the ultimate termination of treatment.

Manifest Content. The surface of the patient's associations and the therapist's interventions. The term refers to the direct and explicit meanings so contained. See also *Relatedness, Manifest Content.*

Maturational Relationship Sphere. That dimension of the therapeutic relationship that involves the mode of relatedness between patient and therapist designed to effect instinctual drive and other satisfactions for one or both participants in a way that is geared toward (or against) growth, relatively autonomous functioning, and separateness and individuation. Maturational relationships may be autistic, healthy or pathologically symbiotic, parasitic, or commensal. The extent to which the therapeutic relationship is designed for the maturation and development of the patient (and secondarily, the therapist) is one of the basic dimensions of the object relationship between the two participants to therapy and of the therapeutic interaction itself. A synonym for this term is *developmental relationship sphere.*

Me/Not-Me Interface. An imaginary interface of the patients communications so designed that every aspect refers on one level to the patient, while on another level to the therapist or analyst. The me/not-me is stated from the patient's vantage point and indicates that every communication contains allusions to both the patient and the therapist or analyst.

Message, Raw. The threatening perception or fantasy that a patient, out of need for defense, disguises and encodes. The term is comparable to Freud's *latent dream thought,* which he postulated to be subjected to the primary process dream mechanisms in order to produce the manifest dream. *Raw message* is to be preferred to *latent dream thought* since it allows for both dangerous unconscious perceptions and disturbing unconscious fantasies.

Metabolism, or the Metabolism of Projective Identifications. Describes the processing by the therapist of temporary trial identifications with the patient. The concept is used more broadly to refer to all efforts to work over sensory and nonsensory inputs from the patient, and in another specific sense to refer to the introjective identification and containing of a projective identification from the patient, ultimately processed toward cognitive understanding and insight. This last sense of the term may also be applied to the patient's efforts to introjectively identify and contain projective identifications from the therapist, so long as efforts are made toward understanding.

Mini-psychotic Act. Actions by a patient or therapist, otherwise intact and in contact with reality, that indicate a (usually) brief, momentary break with reality and impairment in reality testing. This may be seen, for example, when a patient throws his keys away and tries to open the door to his apartment with a scrap of paper. These behaviors are on a par with neurotic hallucinations and neurotic delusions. See also *Delusion, Neurotic* and *Hallucination, Neurotic.*

Misalliance. A quality of the basic relationship between patient and therapist, or of a sector of that relationship, that is consciously or unconsciously designed to bypass adaptive insight in favor of either some other maladaptive form of symptom alleviation or the destruction of effective therapeutic work.

Mode of Relatedness, Commensal. A form of object relationship in which each participant satisfies the healthy needs of the other and receives in turn a full measure of appropriate satisfaction. While a symbiotic relationship is skewed toward the gratification of one of the members of the relationship dyad, a commensal relationship provides roughly equal satisfactions for both participants. By and large this is a healthy mode of relatedness and ideal for most dyads outside of therapy. However, within psychotherapy, because of the patient's Neurosis, the optimal therapeutic relationship is a *healthy symbiosis.*

Mode of Relatedness, Healthy Autism. A means of interacting with or responding to the other member of the therapeutic dyad in a fashion that nonpathologically momentarily severs the meaning link between the two participants. For the patient, this mode of relatedness occurs when there is no activated intervention context with which to deal. The patient then has no meaningful adaptive context to represent, nor a need to provide a meaningful and coalescible derivative complex. There is an absence of Type A communication and the prevelance of the Type C communicative mode. This type of defensiveness and withdrawal, which includes an absence of meaningful communicative expression, is considered to be nonpathological when the patient is in a lying-fallow state. His or her material may be quite sparse or involve Type C narrations. There is, however, no pressing need for meaningful expression, and the autistic quality permits the patient to engage in a self-healing process, with the therapist present as a silent background, holding figure. For the therapist, healthy autism is specifically constituted by his or her silence when the patient's material does not call for a framework management or interpretive-reconstructive response. There is a severing of the meaning link between himself or herself and the patient, although a meaningful intervention is not required. Such silences tend to represent sound holding and containing, and to permit the patient a period of self-exploration and self-cure.

Mode of Relatedness, Healthy Symbiotic. A relationship between two individuals (in this book, primarily patient and therapist) in which the needs of one (the object, or symbiotic receiver or recipient) are largely gratified, while the needs of the other (the subject, or the symbiotic donor or provider) are satisfied to a lesser degree. A healthy symbiosis is designed for the growth and ultimate separation and individuation of the object—as well as for the subject, though less so—and involves those gratifications appropriate to the therapeutic relationship and needed for its sustenance and eventual dissolution. For the patient, this implies being held and contained through the establishment and maintenance of clearly defined ground rules and boundaries in the therapeutic relationship and setting, as well as the patient listening and appropriate interpretations of the therapist. For the therapist, this entails the satisfaction of listening to and working interpretively with the patient, maintaining a sound therapeutic environment, receiving a fee, and seeing the patient eventually resolve his or her Neurosis. Contained within these manifest satisfactions are a number of growth-promoting instinctual drive gratifications, which are well modulated (sublimated) and essentially nonpathological.

Mode of Relatedness, Parasitic. A form of relationship in which the inputs of one or both participants exploit, misuse, and abuse the other person (the object) with essentially no concern for his or her appropriate needs. A parasitic mode of relatedness is essentially pathological and self-gratifying for the subject at the expense and destruction of the object.

Mode of Relatedness, Pathological Autism. A form of emotional withdrawal that involves a destruction of the meaning link between the patient and therapist. For the patient, pathological autism is reflected in the use of the Type C communicative mode in the presence of an activated intervention context. The patient fails either to represent this context with sufficient clarity or to provide a meaningful derivative complex. The autistic mode of relatedness may be expressed through his or her silence, relatively empty associations, or extended Type C narrations that fail to deal meaningfully with the adaptive context at hand. For the therapist, pathological autism takes two major forms: (1) the use of silence when a definitive framework managment or interpretive response is called for by the patient's material; and (2) the offer of an intervention that departs from a meaningful interpretation offered in light of the implications of prior intervention contexts. In the latter situation, the therapist engages in the use of the Type C communicative mode, offering the patient lie-barrier systems, psychoanalytic clichés, and other types of interventions that are the product of his or her own fantasies and pathological needs rather than a definitive, therapeutic response to the patient's own material and therapeutic needs. Critical here is the absence of a truly meaningful response to the patient's manifest and derivative communications.

Mode of Relatedness, Pathological Symbiotic. A form of relationship in which the object (or symbiotic recipient) obtains major satisfactions from the subject (or symbiotic provider) that are essentially pathological and are therefore designed to gratify inappropriate instinctual drive needs as well as to maintain a stultifying sense of fusion or merger between the two participants. A pathological symbiosis is designed for a variety of inappropriate immediate gratifications and does not serve as a basis for ultimate separation, individuation, and relative autonomy. For the patient, such satisfactions are derived from modifications in the ground rules and boundaries of the therapeutic relationship, and from the satisfactions of noninterpretive responses from the therapist. For the therapist, these arise from his or her own noninterpretive interventions, mismanagements of the framework, erroneous interpretations, and from any other inappropriate use of the patient beyond working with him or her toward insightful symptom alleviation. In a pathological symbiosis, both participants usually achieve inappropriate satisfactions, although they tend to accrue more to one member of the dyad, either patient or therapist.

Neurosis. Used at times in a special sense (with a capital "N") to allude to all forms of psychopathology, ranging from symptomatic disturbances to character disorders; from neurotic disturbances (in the narrow sense, using a small "n") to borderline syndromes and narcissistic disorders to psychoses; and from psychosomatic disorders to addictions, perversions, and other emotionally founded syndromes. In essence, then, the broad term refers to all types of syndromes based on intrapsychic and interactional emotional disturbances and dysfunctions. See also *Emotional Disturbance.*

Neurotic Communication. That form of behaving and conveying meanings that is related to the Neuroses and characterized by the use of derivative and convoluted sequences, related ultimately to pathological unconscious fantasies, memories, introjects, and perceptions.

Nonconfirmation. See *Nonvalidation.*

Noncountertransference. The essentially nonconflicted sphere of the therapist's or analyst's functioning expressed in his or her appropriate capacity to relate to the patient, listen, intervene, manage the framework, and the like.

Nonneurotic Communication. A means of conveying conscious and unconscious meaning that is essentially unrelated to Neuroses. It is characterized by manifest messages, readily available inferences, and linear causal sequences.

Nontransference. The essentially nonconflicted areas of the patient's valid functioning within the therapeutic relationship. It is exemplified by validatable conscious and unconscious perceptions and reactions to the therapist, and by other

spheres of adequate functioning and interaction. See also *Unconscious Nontransference Constellation.*

Nonvalidation. A response to an intervention by the therapist or analyst (management of the framework or verbal) that is flat, lacking in unique contents or a selected fact, repetitious, linear, and without surprise. It is an indication that the intervention has been erroneous, and falls largely into the sphere of secondary confirmation—here constituting secondary nonconfirmation.

Observational Schema. See *Schema, Observational.*

Parameter. Those alterations in standard psychoanalytic technique that are required quite specifically because of a patient's ego dysfunctions or impairments. The concept is based on the thesis that certain patients with severe psychopathology require a modified therapeutic situation. It properly includes the idea that these modifications should be kept to a minimum, should be rectified as quickly as possible, and that the entire experience—deviation and rectification—should be subjected to analysis. It was also noted that parameters can be utilized in the service of the therapist's countertransferences and as an inappropriate replacement for interpretive technique. In addition, the effects of parameters may not be resolvable through verbal analytic work and may result in unanalyzable restrictions in therapeutic outcome. The thesis that parameters are necessary in the psychotherapy and psychoanalysis of severely disturbed patients has been questioned by a number of analysts.

Parasitic Mode of Relatedness. See *Mode of Relatedness, Parasitic.*

Precipitant or Reality Precipitant. A synonym for *day residue;* and synonymous with *adaptive context* when used to refer to the evocation of an intrapsychic response.

Predictive Clinical Methodology. A mode of psychoanalytically oriented therapy founded on the validating process and especially on efforts at prediction so designed that validation takes the form of Type Two derivatives.

Primary Adaptive Task. A synonym for *Adaptive Context.*

Projective Counteridentification. A term coined by Grinberg (1962) to allude to all countertransference-based responses within the analyst to the patient's projective identifications. The term implies a failure to metabolize the relevant interactional projections and the reprojection into the patient of nondetoxified contents and mechanisms.

Projective Identification. An interactional effort by a subject to place into the object aspects of his or her own inner mental state, inner contents, and unconscious defenses. *Identification* is used here in the sense of remaining identified with the externalized contents and wishing to evoke in the object an identification with the subject.

Proxy, Evocation of. A form of projective identification described by Wangh (1962), which stresses an interactional effort to place areas of malfunctioning and disturbance into the object, largely as a means of evoking adequate responses that can then be introjected.

Psychoanalytically Oriented Psychotherapy or Insight Psychotherapy. A form of psychotherapy that takes place within a well-defined bipersonal field and is designed to provide the patient symptom relief based on cognitive insights and the inevitable positive introjective identifications that derive from the therapist's capacity to hold the patient, contain and metabolize his or her projective identifications, establish and manage the framework, and interpret the Neurotic communications and expressions from the patient.

Psychoanalytic Cliché. An intervention based on psychoanalytic therory and on the material from the patient at a point at which it is communicated in a non-Neurotic form. It is a statement of apparent psychoanalytic meaning or truth that is essentially and functionally false in light of the prevailing adaptive contexts— sources of inner anxiety and turmoil, conflict and disturbance within the patient and/or the therapist. It is therefore unconsciously designed to serve as a barrier to the underlying catastrophic truths and as a means of disrupting the meaningful relationship links between patient and therapist.

Raw Message. See *Message, Raw.*

Real Relationship Used by some analysts to refer to the reality-oriented, undistorted relationship between patient and therapist or analyst. More broadly, the term has sometimes been used to refer to the actualities of both patient and therapist, and of the therapeutic setting. However, in light of the usual use of the term in a sense that implies that the real relationship is one of several relationships between patient and therapist, of which the transference relationship is another, the term is of limited or questionable value. It seems preferable to speak of the realistic aspects of the therapeutic relationship and to include these qualities under the concept of nontransference and noncountertransference.

Reconstruction. An attempt by the therapist, through a verbal intervention, to indicate to the patient important events and fantasies from the past, most often in the patient's childhood, of which he or she has no conscious recall. Such an intervention would begin with the adaptive context and the derivative complex, would be linked to a therapeutic context, and would on this basis derive implications in regard to past actualities; it would always be rooted in the current communicative interaction and extend into the past from there.

Rectification. A basic intervention through which a therapist (often quite silently) corrects or modifies his or her errors at intervening and managing the frame. When needed, this measure is an essential prerequisite for effective interpretation.

Regression, Nontherapeutic. A shift toward more primitive communication and expression of derivatives of unconscious fantasies, memories, introjects, and perceptions that take place under conditions of unneeded modifications in the framework and in response to other errors in technique by the therapist or analyst. The impairments in the framework render such regressions difficult to analyze and resolve, and the restoration of the frame is essential to a shift from a nontherapeutic to a *therapeutic regression*.

Regression, Therapeutic. An adaptive form of regression that takes place within a secure bipersonal field and is a means of describing the constructive emergence of expressions of unconscious fantasies, memories, introjects, and perceptions related to the patient's Neurosis as mobilized by the therapeutic interaction and based on earlier genetic experiences and traumas. This emergence of relatively primitive material occurs in a form and under conditions that render the Neurotic components analyzable and modifiable through insight.

Relatedness, Manifest Content. A form of relationship and interaction initiated by either patient or therapist in which the communicative transactions take place in terms of the surface of both the patient's associations and the therapist's interventions. The therapist listens, formulates, intervenes, and "validates" in terms of the manifest content of the patient's material. The patient attempts to evoke direct comments and interventions from the therapist. Functionally, this type of relatedness is designed to exclude the *derivative* implications of the patient's material to the extent that they convey disguised expressions of his or her underlying unconscious fantasy and perception constellations. For the therapist, this mode of relateness constitutes an effort to exclude the unconscious implications of his or her attitudes and interventions, and to adhere only to their manifest meanings and functions. This mode or relatedness is a pathologically symbiotic, autistic, or parasitic, superficial, and often naive form of lie therapy in which non-derivative lie-barriers are common. See also *Manifest Content*.

Relatedness, Mode of. The nature of an object relationship, in this book applied primarily to the patient and therapist. The mode of relatedness includes, for both participants, self- and object representations, and efforts to obtain actual satisfactions or their renunciation. Among the important dimensions of the object relationship between the patient and therapist is the extent to which merger or fusion needs are satisfied, and these may be pathological or healthy and appropriate. There is also the extent to which the relationship satisfies healthy or pathological instinctual drive needs and superego pressures, as well as meeting the requirements of the ego-ideal in each participant. Also pertinent is relative autonomy and individuation. Another quality of this relatedness involves the extent to which the overall needs of each participant are given due consideration and satisfaction by the partner, as compared to exploitation, harm, or other misuse. Five

types of object relationships have been identified between patients and therapists; (see under *Mode of Relatedness*): healthy and pathological autism, healthy and pathological symbiosis, and parasitism.

Relatedness, Type One Derivative. A mode of relating and interacting that may be initiated by either patient or therapist, founded on speculations regarding the implications of the patient's material without any connection to an adaptive context. The therapist makes use of readily available inferences derived from the manifest content of the patient's associations, doing so based on his or her general knowledge of the patient, understanding of psychoanalytic theory, and broad sensitivity to implicit meanings and functions. The patient who participates in this mode of relatedness offers similar speculations. In general, this type of interaction is designed to exclude an understanding of the patient's derivative responses to specific adaptive contexts, and thereby to deny the pathological (and more rarely nonpathological) elements implicitly contained in the therapist's erroneous interventions— i.e., to deny the expressions and consequences of his or her countertransferences. This mode of relatedness is a form of pathological symbiosis, autism, or parasitism, as well as lie therapy, in that it excludes the most immediate expressions of the patient's psychopathology (and secondarily the therapist's) as these are mobilized within the interaction. Derivative lie-barriers, elaborate fictions, clichés, and false genetic reconstructions abound. Formulations in terms of transference and fantasy are characteristic, and, functionally, they often serve to exclude the patient's valid unconscious perceptions and introjects of the therapist. See also *Type One Derivatives.*

Relatedness, Type Two Derivative. A mode of relating and interacting that may be initiated by either patient or therapist in which the material from the patient is formulated and interpreted in terms of significant prevailing adaptive contexts derived from the therapist's interventions. These interventions are understood in terms of their manifest and latent contents and functions, and full attention is accorded the unconscious communicative interaction. The therapist maintains a secure therapeutic environment and framework, and confines himself or herself to interpretive-reconstructive interventions and sound managements of the ground rules and setting. All such interventions are created in light of adaptive contexts generated by the therapist. The patient's responses are in the Type A communicative mode: the adaptive context is clearly represented and there is a strong and meaningful derivative complex. It is this type of relatedness that characterizes truth therapy and permits access to the most meaningful derivative expressions of the patient's Neurosis— mobilized unconscious fantasy and perception constellations, and their dynamic and genetic components. Also implicit in this type of relatedness is a healthy symbiosis and the full recognition of the unconscious

ramifications of the therapist's interventions. See also *Type Two Derivatives.*

Relationship Sphere, Developmental. See *Maturational Relationship Sphere.*

Relationship Sphere, Maturational. See *Maturational Relationship Sphere.*

Resistance. Any impediment within the patient to the work of therapy or analysis. It is a conception based on a subjective evaluation by the therapist or analyst. In its narrow clinical sense, these obstacles are founded on defenses against intrapsychic conflict and anxiety as they are expressed within the therapeutic relationship. Within the therapeutic interaction itself, these impediments are often based on contributions from both patient and therapist. Resistance may be distinguished from defense in the finding that the former may be relatively absent on a communicative level in the presence of continued defensive operations within the patient that disguise his or her communications even at a point when they are easily understood and interpreted. See also *Interactional Resistance.*

Resistance, Communicative. Obstacles to the work of therapy or analysis that are discovered through an analysis of the communicative network. Most common among these are the failure to represent the adaptive context with the link to the therapist and the development of a fragmented or noncoalescing derivative complex. The evaluation of communicative resistances is subjective for the therapist and is open to countertransference-based influences. In addition, the presence of all such resistances may receive unconscious contributions from the inappropriate interventions of the therapist, including misinterpretations and mismangements of the framework. The analysis of all types of resistance requires the *rectification* of the therapist's contribution and *interpretations* in which both unconscious perceptions and/or introjections and distorted unconscious fantasies and/or projections are considered.

Resistances, Gross Behavioral. Impediments to the work of psychotherapy or psychoanalysis that appear in the direct behaviors and associations of the patient. While all such evaluations by the therapist are subjective and must be checked for possible countertransference contributions, these obstacles to therapeutic progress tend to be readily recognized. They include silences, gross disruptions of the session, thoughts about or efforts directed toward premature termination, absences, direct but inappropriate opposition to the therapist and repudiation of his or her interventions, and the like. As manifest phenomena their unconscious meanings and functions must be determined by an identification of the prevailing adaptive context and the relevant derivative complex—the associative network.

Resistances, Interactional. See *Interactional Resistance.*

Resistances, Nontransference. Those obstacles to treatment, reflected in the behaviors and communications from the patient to which the therapist has contributed more than the patient. These difficulties derive primarily from the patient's valid unconscious perceptions of countertransference-based interventions from the therapist. Technically, their recognition is especially important, in that they require not only an interpretation of the unconscious basis within the patient for the resistance, but also a recognition of the unconscious contribution from the therapist and the *rectification* of these inputs as well.

Resistances, Relationship. Alludes to all obstacles to treatment that are expressed behaviorally or communicatively by the patient and based on some aspect of his or her relationship with the therapist. Similar to *interactional resistance,* in that it implies the presence of inputs to the resistance from both the patient and therapist, relationship resistance is preferred to the terms *transference resistance* and *nontransference resistance* when obstructive behaviors and impaired communications of the patient have obtained significant contributions from both participants to treatment.

Resistances, Transference. Those obstacles to treatment reflected in the patient's behaviors and communications that are based on pathological unconscious fantasy constellations involving the therapist. The latter's input in respect to these resistances is minimal, while the patient's contribution is maximal. Transference resistances appear only when the therapist has secured the ground rules and framework of the therapeutic situation and is working with sound and validated interpretations.

Reverie. A term used by Bion (1962) to describe the state of the mother, therapist, or analyst who is capable of receiving the projective identifications from the infant or patient, appropriately metabolizing them, and returning them to the subject in a relatively detoxified form. In a psychotherapeutic situation, this implies a correct interpretation and appropriate management of the framework.

Schema, Informational. See *Schema, Observational.*

Schema, Observational. A six-part schema through which the therapist organizes the meanings and implications of the patient's behaviors and associations. Formulations in each sphere are arrived at through direct observation of the patient and through a study of the manifest and especially derivative implications of the patient's material. Formulations in each area are made first for the therapist and second for the patient. The six areas involved are: (1) the state of the frame; (2) the mode of relatedness; (3) the mode of cure; (4) the mode of communication; (5) dynamics and genetics; and (6) to whom the dynamics and genetics are most pertinent for the moment—patient or therapist (i.e., whether the patient is dealing primarily with unconscious perceptions or unconscious fantasies). The information so gathered

is funneled into the listening-intervening schema. See also *Schema, Listening-Intervening.*

Schema, Listening-Intervening. A tripartite means of organizing the patient's material as a way of listening and formulating its key implications, and as a basis for silent and then active interventions. The schema involves the identification of indicators or therapeutic contexts, the central and activated adaptation-evoking contexts, and the nature of the derivative complex. See also *Therapeutic Context, Adaptive Context,* and *Derivative Complex.*

Second-Order Themes. See *Themes, Second-Order.*

Selected Fact. A term used by Bion (1962), borrowed from Poincaré, to describe a newly discovered formulation, finding, or fact that introduces order and new meaning into, and unites into a whole, previously disparate elements. It is the realization that links together elements not previously seen to be connected.

Silent Hypothesis. A formulation derived from the various avenues of the intaking aspect of the listening process, developed, as a rule, around a specific adaptive context. Its development relies too on the abstracting-particularizing process, monitoring material around the therapeutic interaction, and utilizing the me/not-me interface, as well as all other means available to the therapist or analyst for generating dynamic, adaptive conceptions of the most pertinent unconscious meanings of the patient's material. In its most complete form, it will entail the identification of the most active unconscious fantasies, memories, introjects, and perceptions within the patient, and will include links to his or her psychopathology. While these hypotheses may be developed at any point in a session, they are especially common in the opening segments of each hour and are maintained by the therapist without intervening. In principle, they should be subjected to *silent validation* before the therapist or analyst intervenes, doing so most often at a point when there is a relevant bridge between the silent hypothesis itself and the communications from the patient.

Silent Intervention. See *Intervention, Silent.*

Silent Question. An issue that arises within the mind of the therapist as he or she listens to the patient, leading the therapist to raise it subjectively while not directing it to the patient. When pertinent, such queries will, as a rule, be answered in some derivative form by the patient's ongoing associations. In principle, silent questions are to be preferred to direct queries of the patient, which tend to serve a variety of defensive and countertransference needs within the therapist or analyst and to impair the patient's use of indirect, derivative communication.

Silent Validation. An aspect of the evaluation of the material from the patient that follows the development of a silent hypothesis. When subsequent material further coalesces with

the intitial hypothesis, and supports it through the communication of Type Two derivatives, the silent hypothesis is seen as confirmed. See also *Validation.*

Six-Part Informational Schema. See *Schema, Observational.*

Spiraling Interaction, Unconscious and Conscious. A term used to describe the central transactions between patient and therapist within the bipersonal field. It alludes to the conscious but, more especially, the unconscious exchanges between the two participants to therapy, as these exchanges take place as part of a to-and-fro interactional process.

Symbiosis, Healthy. See *Mode of Relatedness, Healthy Symbiosis.*

Symbiosis, Pathological. See *Mode of Relatedness, Pathological Symbiosis.*

Symbiotic Provider or Donor. That member of the symbiosis who offers to the other person the major share of gratification. The symbiotic provider therefore obtains a smaller measure of satisfaction than his or her partner, the *Symbiotic receiver or recipient.*

Symbiotic Receiver or Recipient. The member of a symbiotic dyad who obtains the larger measure of satisfaction or gratification.

Termination, Forced. The premature cessation of a therapeutic situation caused, as a rule, by some circumstance external to the direct therapeutic interaction. Among the most common causes are clinic policies, the move of therapist or patient, and a major change in life circumstance or health in either one. A termination of this kind modifies the standard tenet that psychotherapy should be undertaken until the point of insightful symptom resolution within the patient.

Themes, First-Order. The general contents and specific subject matter that can be derived from an examination of the manifest content of the patient's material.

Themes, Second-Order. Derivative contents developed through the use of the abstracting-particularizing process. First-order manifest themes are identified and general thematic trends are then formulated; inferences derived on that basis are considered second-order themes. As a rule, such themes are developed in terms of the ongoing therapeutic relationship and interaction, and take on specific form and meaning when related to pertinent adaptive contexts within that relationship.

Therapeutic Alliance. The conscious and unconscious conjoint efforts of patient and therapist to join forces in effecting symptom alleviation and characterological change for the former through development of cognitive and affective adaptive insight. This is the cooperative sphere of the relationship between patient and therapist, and requires of the patient trust and a variety of cognitive capacities and nonconflicted spheres of functioning, as well as an ability to communicate both consciously and through interpretable derivatives. Of the therapist, a sound therapeutic alliance requires a capacity to establish and maintain a secure therapeutic environment, and to offer well-timed and sensitive interpretations and reconstructions. The therapeutic alliance has a variety of surface attributes, which include the patient's free-associating, evident cooperation, and attention to the therapist's interventions, as well as the therapist's sensitive listening and sound therapeutic work. However, it also entails aspects of the therapeutic relationship that are part of the unconscious communicative interaction. On this level, it requires of the patient the Type A Communicative mode, and of the therapist sound management of the framework and interpretations consistently organized around the adaptive contexts of his or her interventions. There is thus a manifest and a latent alliance, each with conscious and unconscious attributes. See also *Alliance Sector* and *Working Alliance*.

Therapeutic Alliance, Communicative. An aspect of the unconscious communicative interaction between patient and therapist. A sound communicative alliance is one in which the patient is expressing himself or herself in the Type A communicative mode, and the therapist has secured the therapeutic environment and is responding interpretively to the patient's material—i.e., in terms of adaptive contexts and derivative complexes. Impairments in the communicative alliance are reflected in communicative resistances, primarily as failures to adequately represent the prevailing adaptive context and, at times, as failures by the patient to generate a meaningful derivative complex. Mismanagements of the framework, interpretive failures, and other types of errors form the basis for impairments in the communicative alliance stimulated by the therapist. These problems fall into the realm of countertransference responses and are based on failures to adequately comprehend and respond to the associations and behaviors of the patient. It is possible to have an impaired communicative alliance in the presence of a seemingly sound manifest alliance. See also *Therapeutic Alliance, Manifest; Therapeutic Alliance;* and *Working Alliance.*

Therapeutic Alliance, Manifest or Surface. Virtually synonymous with the working alliance, the direct and surface cooperation between patient and therapist. The state of the manifest alliance may correspond to, or differ from, the state of the communicative alliance. Thus there may be manifest cooperation but communicative dissidence, or there may be evident surface disruptions in the cooperative sphere at a point when the patient is expressing himself or herself meaningfully through derivative expressions. An additional dimension of the state of the communicative alliance is the extent to which the patient's derivative associations as organized around prevailing adaptive contexts serve to illuminate current indicators.

Therapeutic Context. Synonymous with *indicator,* and a component of the listening process. It refers to any communication from the patient that

suggests a need for understanding, resolution, and intervention from the therapist. Such communications serve as important second-order organizers of the patient's material. His or her associations and behaviors are first organized in terms of the communicative network—the adaptive context, its representation, the derivative complex, and the bridge back to the therapist—to provide Type Two derivative meaning in terms of unconscious processes, fantasies, perceptions, and introjects. Once these unconscious meanings and functions are identified, the material is then reorganized around the therapeutic context and the revealed derivative meanings as they pertain to the unconscious implications of the indicator. Therapeutic contexts may be divided into those involving life crises and symptoms within the patient (e.g., homicidal and suicidal concerns and impulses, acute regressions, acting out) and those involving disturbed aspects of the therapeutic interaction (e.g., alterations in the framework by therapist or patient, errors by the therapist, ruptures in the therapeutic alliance, and major and minor resistances).

Therapeutic Interaction. Describes the conscious and unconscious communicative interplays between the patient and therapist or analyst.

Therapeutic Misalliance. An attempt to achieve symptom alleviation through some means other than insight and the related positive introjective identifications with the therapist. See also *Misalliance,* an essentially synonymous term.

Therapeutic Relationship. Embraces all components, conscious and unconscious, pathological and nonpathological, of the interaction between patient and therapist. For the patient, the therapeutic relationship involves both transference and nontransference components, while for the therapist it involves countertransference and noncountertransference elements. The term is strongly preferred to "transference" when describing the patient's relationship with the therapist, and equally preferred to "countertransference" when describing the therapist's or analyst's relationship to the patient. See also *Transference, Nontransference, Countertransference,* and *Noncountertransference.*

Therapy, Lie. Any form of, or interlude in, psychotherapy or psychoanalysis in which the actual unconscious basis for the patient's symptoms, resistances, and the like are either not sought after or are sealed off. It entails both efforts at avoidance and attention to levels of meaning that in the therapeutic interaction serve primarily to create barriers and falsifications, to destroy more pertinent meaning, and thereby to seal off underlying chaotic truths.

Therapy, Truth. A form of therapy or analysis designed to foster the emergence and discovery, within the therapeutic interaction, of the unconscious processes, fantasies, memories, introjects, and transactions that are the basis for the patient's Neurosis.

Transference. The pathological component of the patient's relationship to the therapist. Based on pathological unconscious fantasies, memories, and introjects, transferenece includes all distorted and inappropriate responses to and perceptions of the therapist derived from these disruptive inner mental contents and the related mechanisms and defenses. These distortions may be based on displacements from past genetic figures, as well as on pathological interactional mechanisms. Unconscious transference fantasies and mechanisms are always communicated in some derivative form, while the manifest communication may allude to either the therapeutic relationship itself (disguised, however, in regard to the latent content) or to outside relationships. Transference responses are always maladaptive and can only be understood in terms of specific, indirect adaptive contexts. See also *Unconscious Transference Constellation.*

Transversal Communication. Associations from the patient that bridge, and therefore simultaneously express, both fantasy and reality, transference and nontransference, unconscious perception and distortion, truth and falsehood, self and object. Such communications are, on one level, entirely valid, while on another level, essentially distorted.

Transversal Intervention. A particular type of communication from the therapist or analyst to the patient that is shaped in keeping with the presence of a transversal communication. In essence, such interventions, usually in the form of interpretations, although sometimes developed through the playback of derivatives related to an unidentified adaptive context, take into account the dual qualities of transversal communications and are stated in a manner that is open to the contradictory elements contained in the patient's associations.

Trial Identification. An aspect of the listening process that is an important means of empathizing with and cognitively understanding the communications from the patient. It entails a temporary merger with, or incorporation of, the pateint and his or her material in the presence of distinct self-object boundaries in most other respects. It is a temporary form of being and feeling with the patient, and the cognitive-affective yield from such experiences must then be processed toward insightful understanding and subjected to the validating process.

Truth. The actualities, manifest and latent, conscious and unconscious, of the ongoing communicative interaction between patient and therapist, especially as it pertains to the Neurosis of the patient and, secondarily, of the therapist. Truth within the therapeutic experience pertains to the underlying basis of the patient's Neurosis as activated and mobilized by the adaptive contexts of the therapist's interventions and secondarily by intrapsychic factors within the patient. While such truths can be the subject of conscious realizations, they

are most commonly expressed in derivative form by the patient and therefore require interpretive realizations from the therapist. See also *Lie*.

Truth Therapy. That form of psychotherapy or psychoanalysis that is designed to arrive at the actual conscious and unconscious basis for the patient's Neurosis as mobilized by events within the ongoing, spiraling interaction. See also *Lie Therapy*.

Type A Field and Type A Communicative Mode. A bipersonal field and communicative style in which symbolism and illusion play a central role. Such a field is characterized by the development of a play space or transitional space within which the patient communicates analyzable derivatives of his or her unconscious fantasies, memories, introjects, and perceptions, ultimately in the form of Type Two derivatives. Such a field requires a secure framework and a therapist or analyst who is capable of processing the material from the patient toward cognitive insights that are then imparted through valid interpretations. Such endeavors represent the therapist's capacity for symbolic communication. The Type A communicative mode is essentially symbolic, transitional, illusory, and geared toward insight.

Type B Field and Type B Communicative Mode. A bipersonal field characterized by major efforts at projective identification and action-discharge. The mode is not essentially designed for insight, but instead facilitates the riddance of accretions of disturbing internal stimuli. It can, however, despite the interactional pressures it generates, be used in a manner open to interpretation.

Type C Field and Type C Communicative Mode. A field in which the essential meaning and relationship links between patient and therapist are broken and ruptured, and in which verbalization and apparent efforts at communication are actually designed to destroy meaning, generate falsifications, and create impenetrable barriers to underlying catastrophic truths. The Type C communicative mode is designed for falsification, the destruction of links between subject and object, and the erection of barriers designed to seal off inner and interactional chaos.

Type C Narrator. A patient who utilizes the Type C communicative mode through the report of extensive dream material or the detailed description of events and experiences within his or her life or in regard to the therapeutic interaction. Such material is characterized by the absence of a meaningful adaptive context, the lack of analyzable derivatives, and the use of these communications essentially for the generation of nonmeaning and the breaking of relationship links. It is not uncommon for the Type C narrator to interact with a therapist or analyst who makes extensive use of psychoanalytic clichés, generating a therapeutic interaction falsely identified as viable analytic work, while its primarily dynamic function falls within the Type C communicative mode.

Type One Derivatives. Readily available inferences derived from the manifest content of the patient's associations without he use of an adaptive context. These inferences constitute one level of the latent content, arrived at in isolation and without reference to the dynamic state of the therapeutic interaction and to the adaptive-dynamic function of the material at hand. See also *Relatedness, Type One Derivative.*

Type Two Derivatives. Inferences from the manifest content of the patient's material that are arrived at through the abstracting-particularizing process when it is organized around a specific adaptive context. These disguised contents accrue specific dynamic-adaptive meaning when so organized, and are the main medium for the therapist's or analyst's interpretations, primarily in terms of the therapeutic interaction. See also *Relatedness, Type Two Derivative.*

Unconscious Fantasy. The working over in displaced form of a particular adaptive context. The relative contents are outside the patient's awareness and expressed in derivative form in the manifest content of his or her associations. This is a type of daydreaming without direct awareness of the essential theme and may be either pathological or nonpathological. The derivatives of unconscious fantasies are an essential medium of interpretive work and have important genetic antecedents. Among the most crucial unconscious fantasies are those related to the therapist, and when they are distorted they fall into the realm of transference, while those that are nondistorted belong to nontransference. These daydreams include representations from the id, ego, superego, self, and every aspect of the patient's inner mental world, life, and psychic mechanisms.

Unconscious Fantasy Constellation. Intermixtures of unconscious fantasies (in the narrow sense), unconscious introjects, and unconscious memories. Together these constitute a major underlying basis for symptom formation and Neuroses. When the emphasis is on unconscious perceptions and valid introjects, the term *unconscious perception constellation* is to be preferred.

Unconscious Interpretation. A communication usually from patient to therapist, expressed in disguised and derivative form and unconsciously designed to help the therapist understand the underlying basis for a countertransference-based intervention. These interpretations can be recognized by taking the therapist's intervention as the adaptive context for the material from the patient that follows, hypothesizing the nature of the therapist's errors, and accepting the patient's material as reflecting an introjection of the error and an effort to heal the disturbing aspects of that introject. The patient's responses are viewed as a *commentary* on the therapist's intervention and are found to contain unconscious efforts to assist the therapist in gaining insight in regard to the sources of his or her errors.

Unconscious Introject. A network of intrapsychic precipitants derived from interactions between the subject and object in the past and present. It is derived from the process of introjective identification and depends on the nature of the contents and mechanisms involved, as well as qualities within both subject and object. Introjects may be short-lived or relatively stable, pathological or nonpathological, or incorporated into the self-image and self-representations or isolated from them, and may involve any of the structures of the mind, id, ego, and superego. In psychotherapy, an especially important form of introjection occurs in response to the therapist's projective identifications, either helpful or traumatic, nonpathological or pathological, which generate alterations in the inner mental world of the patient. Such a process is continuous with the therapeutic interaction and may, in addition, occur within the therapist as a result of projective identifications from the patient. See also *Introject*.

Unconscious Memory. Derivative precipitates of past experiences—mixtures of actuality and distortion—expressed through indirect communication and inner representations of which the subject is unaware. Such reminiscences without awareness may be pathological or nonpathological, and the former are an important aspect of the genetic basis of the patient's psychopathology.

Unconscious Nontransference Constellation. The unconscious basis for the patient's valid functioning in his or her relationship with the therapist or analyst. This constellation is constituted by the patient's valid unconscious perceptions and introjects of the therapist, and includes both earlier genetic counterparts and present dynamic implications. See also *Nontransference.*

Unconscious Perception. Evidence of valid perceptiveness of another person's (an object's) communications and cues of which the subject is unaware. These may be identified through a correct appraisal of the nature of an adaptive context, including an accurate understanding of the object's unconscious communications. While outside the subject's awareness, his or her derivative communications demonstrate an essentially veridical perception in terms of the prevailing underlying realities. When the adaptive context is known, unconscious perceptions are reflected in Type Two derivatives. They are the basis for nondistorted introjects.

Unconscious Perception Constellation. Both current unconscious perceptions and those derived from important genetic experiences with significant early figures. Such a constellation includes valid introjects and pertinent unconscious memories in which the veridical core is central.

Unconscious Transference Constellation. A core component of transference, constituting its underlying basis. The unconscious transference constellation includes all unconscious fantasy constellations that pertain to the therapist or analyst.

Within the therapeutic situation, it is these constellations that are actively mobilized by a valid therapeutic experience—sound interventions and a secure setting—and then form the focus of interpretive work. See also *Transference.*

Unrectifiable Framework Deviation Termination Therapy. A form of psychotherapy which takes place in the presence of a break in the fixed frame or another ground rule which cannot be corrected in actuality (e.g., a referral from a patient, or a personal relationship between a patient and a member of the therapist's family). Under these conditions, attention to the patient's derivative material will show his or her unconscious realization that the treatment must eventually and gradually be terminated because of the unmodifiable effects of the deviation on the patient and his or her introjection of the therapist.

Validated Hypothesis. A silent hypothesis that has been confirmed via Type Two derivatives, and especially an interpretation or management of the frame that has been communicated to the patient and is affirmed through the development of Type Two derivatives and the appearance of a *selected fact.*

Validating Process. Conscious and unconscious efforts within either patient or therapist to affirm, support, and substantiate conscious or unconscious formulations and hypotheses. It is a crucial component of the listening process, receives its ultimate test in the patient's responses to the therapist's interpretations and managements of the framework, and must take the form of confirmation via Type Two derivatives and the development of a *selected fact.*

Validation, Indirect. See *Validation via Type Two Derivatives,* with which it is essentially synonymous.

Validation via Type Two Derivatives. A form of confirmation that is synonymous with the development of a *selected fact* and the modification of repressive barriers. This type of indirect, derivative validation is the essential proof of the truth of a psychoanalytic clinical formulation and intervention. Every clinical psychoanalytic hypothesis can be accepted as a general truth only if it has been subjected to this type of validation.

Vested Interest Deviation. A modification in the standard framework regarding which the therapist has a special investment. Examples are having an office in his or her home and the signing of insurance forms in order to enable the therapist to receive his or her fee. The concept draws its importance from the finding that deviations in which the therapist has an inordinate investment tend to generate silent sectors of misalliance with the patient. The responses of the latter tend to be highly disguised and often appear in the form of embedded derivatives. As a result, the material related to such a deviation tends to be difficult to recognize and interpret. Often the therapist has a significant blind spot in this area, rendering the bastion and misalliance so generated difficult to identify and even more difficult to modify.

Working Alliance. That segment of therapeutic relatedness that is based on the patient's rational, nonneurotic wish to get well and on surface efforts in this direction, and on the analyst's rational, nonneurotic offer of assistance and his or her own capacity to cooperate with the patient in the therapeutic effort. The term stresses manifest cooperation as well as mutual respect and trust, mature object relatedness, and sound ego capacities. Because unconscious factors tend to be neglected, in respect both to the definition of this type of alliance and to the factors seen to influence its course, the term is of limited value. See also *Alliance Sector* and *Therapeutic Alliance.*

References

Balint, M. (1968). *The Basic Fault: Therapeutic Aspects of Regression.* London: Tavistock.

Beres, D., and Arlow, J. (1974). Fantasy and identification in empathy. *Psychoanalytic Quarterly* 43:26-50.

Bion, W. (1962). Learning from experience. In *Seven Servants.* New York: Jason Aronson, 1977.

———. (1967). Notes on memory and desire. *Psychoanalytic Forum* 2:271-280.

———. (1977). *Seven Servants.* New York: Jason Aronson.

Erikson, E. (1950). *Childhood and Society.* New York: W. W. Norton.

Fenichel, O. (1941). *Problems of Psychoanalytic Technique,* trans. Brunswick, D. New York: *Psychoanalytic Quarterly.*

Freud, S. (1899). Screen memories. *Standard Edition* 3:301-322.

———. (1900). The interpretation of dreams. *Standard Edition* 4-5: 1-627.

———. (1905). Fragment of an analysis of a case of hysteria. *Standard Edition* 7:3-122.

———. (1909). Notes upon a case of obsessional neurosis. *Standard Edition* 10:153-320.

———. (1912). The dynamics of transference. *Standard Edition* 12:97-108.

———. (1912a). Recommendations to physicians practicing psychoanalysis. *Standard Edition* 12:111-120.

———. (1913). On beginning the treatment (further recommendations on the technique of psycho-analysis, I). *Standard Edition* 12:121-144.

———. (1914). Remembering, repeating, and working through (further recommendations on the technique of psycho-analysis, II). *Standard Edition* 12:145-156.

———. (1915). Observations on transference-love (further recommendations on the technique of psycho-analysis, III). *Standard Edition* 12:157-171.

———. (1918). From the history of an infantile neurosis. *Standard Edition* 17:3-122.

————. (1919). Lines of advance in psychoanalytic therapy. *Standard Edition* 17:159-168.

————. (1937). Constructions in analysis. *Standard Edition* 23:255-269.

Gill, M. (1979). The analysis of the transference. *Journal of the American Psychoanalytic Association* 27 (Supplement): 263-288.

Grinberg, L. (1962). On a specific aspect of counter-transference due to the patient's projective identification. *International Journal of Psycho-Analysis* 43:436-440.

————. (1976). *Object Relations Theory and Clinical Psychoanalysis.* New York: Jason Aronson.

Khan, M. (1977). On lying fallow: an aspect of leisure. *International Journal of Psychoanalytic Psychotherapy* 6:397-402.

Kohut, H. (1959). Introspection, empathy and psychoanalysis. *Journal of the American Psychoanalytic Association* 7:459-483.

Kernberg, O. (1975). *Borderline Conditions and Pathological Narcissism.* New York: Jason Aronson.

————. (1971). *The Analysis of the Self.* New York: International Universities Press.

————. (1977). *The Restoration of the Self.* New York: International Universities Press.

Langs, R. (1973). *The Technique of Psychoanalytic Psychotherapy,* vol. 1. New York: Jason Aronson.

————. (1974). *The Technique of Psychoanalytic Psychotherapy,* vol. 2. New York: Jason Aronson.

————. (1976). *The Therapeutic Interaction,* 2 volumes. New York: Jason Aronson.

————. (1978). *The Listening Process.* New York: Jason Aronson.

————. (1979). *The Therapeutic Environment.* New York: Jason Aronson.

————. (1980). *Interactions: The Realm of Transference and Countertransference.* New York: Jason Aronson.

————. (1981). *Resistances and Interventions: The Nature of Therapeutic Work.* New York: Jason Aronson.

Leites, N. (1979). *Interpreting Transference.* New York: W. W. Norton.

Loewald, H. (1960). The therapeutic action of psycho-analysis. *International Journal of Psycho-Analysis* 41:16-33.

Mahler, M. (1979). *The Selected Papers of Margaret S. Mahler, M.D.,* vols. I and II. New York: Jason Aronson.

Sandler, J. (1960). The background of safety. *International Journal of Psycho-Analysis* 41:352-356.

Sandler, J. and Sandler, A. (1978). On the development of object relationships and affects. *International Journal of Psycho-Analysis* 49:285-296.

Searles, H. (1959). The effort to drive the other person crazy—an element in the aetiology and psychotherapy of schizophrenia. *British Journal of Medical Psychology* 32:1-18.

———. (1979). *Countertransference and Related Subjects: Selected Papers.* New York: International Universities Press.

Shapiro, T. (1974). The development and distortions of empathy. *Psychoanalytic Quarterly* 43:4-25.

Wangh, M. (1962). The "evocation of a proxy": a psychological maneuver, its use as a defense, its purpose and genesis. *Psychoanalytic Study of the Child* 17:451-469.

Index

contribution to listening-
formulating, 78
creations of, 68
depressive, 415
designated, *see* designated patient
destroying meaning, 70, 80, 281
direct observations of, 73
direct references to, 63
disturbances in life of, 141
establishing difficulties of,
404-405
establishing perceptions of
therapist, 152-161
evaluation of, 402-403, 433
functional, *see* functional patient
functioning and adaptation of,
6-9, 91
indicators of emotional
disturbance of, 128-129
life situation of, 84-85
material from, 57-70
active meaning of, 114
as commentary, 77
dynamic and genetic
implications of, 55-56
pathological autism in, 226
pathological symbiosis in,
228-229
perception of therapist, 43
as driving patient crazy, 45, 121,
123
position of, 459-461
projective identifications of,
246-247
relationships outside therapy,
83-84
role of, 222-223, 603-609
severely disturbed, 707-714
silence in, 456-459
suitability of, 383-396
symptoms of as indicators, 140
Type A, *see* Type A patient
Type B-C, *see* Type B-C patient

Type C, *see* Type C patient
unconscious efforts to cure or
harm therapist, 175-176
unconscious fantasies evoked in,
169-170
unconscious perceptions of, 510,
519, 527-528, 556
Payment, ideal form of, 118
Perception, unconscious, 40, 98-100
Personality
disorders of, 9-10
reflected in manifest contents, 83
Phallic phase, 21
Physical contact, 429
absence of, 307
Physical symptoms, 14
Position of patient and therapist,
459-461
Precipitant, 737
Predictive clinical methodology,
737
Preformed silent hypotheses, 193
Preponderant countertransference,
161, 548
Pressures from the patient, 71
subjective experience of, 75
Primary process mechanisms, 46-47
Primary symbiotic provider, 227
Privacy, 306, 475-481
in clinic office, 358-360
at first session, 403
Therapist's modification of,
477-478
Private office, 362-370
Private practice, first contact in,
381-382
Projection, 246
Projective counter-identification,
248-249, 611, 737
Projective identification, 205,
244-246
as interactional projection, 610
patient's, 246-247

Shapiro, T., 74
Signal experiences, 75
Signal images, 237
Silence
  as deceit, 156
  as model of resistance, 634-638
  noncountertransference, 548-549
  in patients, 456-459
  of therapist, 253-254, 642-643,
    681-683
Silent formulations
  self-analysis applied to, 76-77
  and silent efforts at validation,
    187-199
Silent hypothesis, 186, 742-743
  preformed, 193-194
Silent listening and formulating,
  189-192
Silent question, 743
Silent validation, 157, 743
  hallmarks of, 191-192
  importance of, 72
  silent formulations and, 187-199
  technical principles of, 198-199
Slips of the tongue, 69
Soundproofing, 363-364
  lack of, 358-359
Specific imagery, 103
Spiraling interaction, 248, 743
Splitting
  and confidentiality, 482
  ground rules and, 490
  in relationship with therapist,
    230
  in response to deviation, 322
  by therapist, 573
Structure
  of emotional disturbance, 17-25,
    36-43
  psychic, 19-24
Suicide, danger of, 381
Superego, 20
Supervision
  evaluation of intervention, 208

privacy and, 478
Supportive interventions, 203
Symbiosis
  healthy, 27, 51, 227
  pathological, 228-229, 599-602
    patient's demand for, 710-711
Symbiotic mode of relatedness, 10-11
Symbiotic provider and receiver,
  743
Symbolic representation, 46-47
Symptoms
  alleviation of, 464-465
  allusions to, 59
  of chronic and acute emotional
    disturbance, 14
  formation of, 41
  of neuroses, 7-9
  physical, 14
  of psychosis, 6-7
  reports of, 69

Technique
  for deviant contract, 333-336,
    340-341
  in first session, 401-407
  projective identification and,
    248-255
  with secure frame, 337-338
Termination, 703-704
  communicative modes during,
    432
  forced, 743-744
  and further contact with patient,
    396-397
  rectification of frame through,
    400
  as ultimatum to patient, 276-277
Themes, first and second order, 744
Therapeutic alliance, 576, 744
  and allusions to therapy, 86-87
Therapeutic context, 15, 38, 745
  break in frame as, 320-321
  recognition of, 53
  resistances as, 640

Therapeutic contracts, *see* contracts
Therapeutic environment,
    alterations in, 395-396
Therapeutic misalliance, 279,
    586-592, 745
Therapeutic relationship, 26-32, 51,
    530-531, 746
  anxieties aroused by, 495
  ground rules of, 54
  organizing dimensions of, 220-221
  realities of, 593-594
Therapist, 32
  in absence of validation, 216
  allusions to, 61-64, 86-88
  appropriate gratifications of, 224
  attention of, 306-307
  attitude of, 72
  cash accepted by, 117-118, 123
  constructive models for, 171-173
  containing capacity of, 28
  designated, *see* designated
    therapist
  deviation in frame as acting out
    by, 109
  dilemmas of, 712-714
  efforts to drive patient crazy, 45,
    121, 123
  errors by, 131-137
  establishing competency as,
    405-407
  establishing patient's perceptions
    of, 152-161
  fear of secure frame, 346-348
  as functional patient, 608-609
  goal of, 126-127
  indicators of disturbance within,
    127-128
  interactional pressures on, 71
    subjective experience of, 75
  interpretive function of, 29-31
  means for listening and
    formulating, 71-76
  modification of privacy by,
    477-478

  monitoring interactional pressure
    from patient, 249-251
  monitoring relatedness, 230
  obligation to treat patients
    entering office, 381-382
  pathological autism in, 226
  pathological symbiosis in,
    228-229
  patient's perception of, 43
    in home office arrangement,
    375
  patient's unconscious efforts to
    cure or harm, 175-176
  position of, 459-461
  as primary symbiotic provider,
    227
  projective identification by, 205
  role of, 223-225, 603-609
  silence of, 253-254
  splitting used by, 573
  stimulating derivative
    communication, 42
  subjective reactions of, 79
  suitability of patients for
    treatment by, 383-396
  tasks of, 15, 144, 574-575
  thinking of, 292
  threats to insecure contract,
    331-333
  Type A, *see* Type A therapist
  Type B, *see* Type B therapist
  Typce C, *see* Type C therapist
  Type One derivative, 115-117
  Type Two derivative, 115-117
  unconscious introjective
    identification with, 202-203
  uses of silence by, 642-643
  vacation of, 147-148
  well-functioning, 202
Therapy
  allusions to, 61-64, 86-88
  boundaries of, 309-319
  bridge to, 291
  insight, 129

NATIONAL UNIVERSITY LIBRARY

RC
480
L358
e.4

Langs, Robert,
1928-

Psychotherapy

050758

MAR 25 1996	DATE DUE		